Local Government Finance in a Unitary State

Local Government Finance in a Unitary State

by
C. D. FOSTER
R. A. JACKMAN
M. PERLMAN

with the assistance of B. Lynch

London
GEORGE ALLEN & UNWIN
Boston   Sydney

First published in 1980

GEORGE ALLEN & UNWIN LTD
40 Museum Street, London WC1A 1LU

© C. D. Foster, R. A. Jackman and M. Perlman

British Library Cataloguing in Publication Data

Foster, Christopher David
    Local government finance in a unitary state.
    1. Local finance – Great Britain
    I. Title   II. Jackman, Richard
    III. Perlman, Morris
    336.41   HJ9423   80-40155

    ISBN 0-04-336066-1

Set in 10 on 11 point Press Roman by Alden Press, Oxford
and printed and bound in Great Britain by
William Clowes (Beccles) Limited, Beccles and London

Contents

Acknowledgements

We would like to acknowledge the generous assistance we have received from many people during the preparation of this book. From local government, Mr W. Jolliffe, County Treasurer of Lancashire, Mr A. Morton, City Treasurer of Coventry, Mr R. Gandy, Treasurer, Greater London Council and Mr Hunt from the Treasurer's Department at Coventry gave their time and valuable advice. We were likewise assisted by Messrs A. Pelling, R. Gibson and D. Benson from the Department of the Environment. We are also very grateful for comments and advice from Sir Frank Layfield, Sir Harry Page, Professors George Jones, Wallace Oates, Alan Prest and Alan Williams and other academic colleagues.

The research work on which this book is based was financed jointly by the Chartered Institute of Public Finance and Accountancy, the Institute for Fiscal Studies and the Department of the Environment. The research was carried out at the London School of Economics and we are grateful to members of the administrative staff of the School, and of CIPFA and IFS, for their help with the project. We would also like to thank colleagues at the Centre for Environmental Studies for their help with the preparation of the final manuscript.

The research itself was carried out by the authors with the assistance of Michael Osborne, Dimitri Sophianopoulos, Helen Murphy, Brian Hayes and Phillipa Carling.

Finally, we are particularly grateful to Janet Barrett for typing innumerable drafts, and to Athleen Ellington, Sandra Miller and Annetta Burnett for administrative and secretarial assistance.

Introduction

British local government finance went through a crisis between 1973 and 1974 which had two stages. The first had much in common with a number of earlier crises started by widespread protest that particular, rapid, upward pressure of local expenditure on local taxation had become intolerable and therefore that new sources of revenue were needed. During 1975 the first stage passed into a second when the cry changed from a demand for more revenue to support more expenditure into one for expenditure cuts to prevent a rise in taxes. There has been only one, and not exact, parallel to this second stage. Local expenditure had been growing rapidly in the 1920s, creating a demand for a reform of local revenue sources which was met by the 1929 Local Government Act. But in that year, before the new system was fairly working, the stock market crashed and the Great Depression set in. By 1930, strong pressure was being exerted to make local authorities cut their expenditure.

A striking difference between the two periods is that local government finance was reformed in 1929, though not radically. No similar reform has come from the 1970s crisis, though there was almost unanimous demand for reform in 1974 of a kind which would have transformed the system. Instead, Anthony Crosland set up a Committee of Inquiry chaired by Sir Frank Layfield. When it reported in 1976, it presented a dilemma. Either, it argued, local government should be frankly recognised as subordinate and its finances arranged accordingly, or the encroachment of central control should be reversed and financial arrangements made which would enable local authorities to operate freely within defined limits. This conclusion was widely disliked within central government. With some injustice to the Committee who were not as unsophisticated, it was seen as posing two stark alternatives where there were, as always, infinite gradations of possibility. The alternatives were thought to be loaded in that increasing central control was an aim no one could openly admit to favouring, and the Committee did not disguise its preference for a policy aimed at reviving the liberty and spontaneity of local government. By the time the Committee reported, the second stage of the crisis was dominant, so that central government was being asked to increase local autonomy at a stage in the cycle when to all concerned in central government, political wisdom and macroeconomic policy demanded that local expenditure be cut as the economy took a plunge. Indeed, local authorities were blamed in part for the crisis in that their expenditure had risen especially rapidly in the 1960s and early 1970s. It was said to be 'out of the control' of central government. Thus the Layfield recipe arrived just at a time when central government and many others besides were persuaded more, not less, control was needed. The report gave the government little aid on attaining this, since its centralist solution though implying more government macroeconomic control was not specific enough on the means that might be used to exert it. Besides, the Committee's ideas on control generally were suspect as the crux of its argument was that the higher the proportion of local expenditure financed by central grant, the greater central control; the lower that proportion, the greater local accountability. We will argue later that the Committee's conclusion can be defended, though in our judgement its reasoning was defective. At the time the widespread central government reluctance to accept the Committee's views on the connection between size of grant and control was strengthened by Wynne Godley's and Francis Cripps's immediate, and apparently successful, demonstration that it had hinged its argument on a fallacy (see Part Two, Chapter 5 below).

As disquieting to those concerned in central government, and others who thought as they did, was the naïveté with which it was felt that the Committee, aside from Professors A. C. L. Day and G. C. Cameron who reserved their opinions on this point, asked for clarity in the financial arrangements between central and local government based on a clear definition and distinction of their functions and financial responsibility. In its reply to the Report, the government gave its stated view that such a distinction was both impossible and unwise, reducing its freedom for manoeuvre when it must be free to alter the direction and strength of its intervention as circumstances required. To an extraordinary degree, the power of central government — and therefore necessarily the liberty of other bodies, private as well as public, even of individuals — depends on ambiguities in the law which customarily are only seldom challenged in the courts. Never have these ambiguities — this flexibility in the law to use a favourite word — been as much used as in the 1970s to justify government action not explicitly and clearly recognised by statute. The most striking examples have been elsewhere — for example, in the enforcement of non-statutory incomes policy in 1977 and 1978 — but the same informal methods have been used in relations between central and local government. The advantage of this tradition is that great freedom can be allowed where central government is indifferent. In moments of crisis, or when an issue becomes important to it, central government can take over a responsibility and effect action it regards as vital. Of course, it means that local freedom in large measure is not grounded on legal rights but on the will — critics would sometimes say the caprice — of ministers and officials. Later we will want to examine the consequences for local government finance of the difference between a federal and a unitary state. To anticipate one element of that discussion, the crucial difference in a federal state is between powers and duties that have their basis in the law of the constitution and those powers and duties of local government which are based on statute law and therefore amenable to the ordinary processes of legislation. In Britain, this key difference is shifted a stage and is between powers and duties grounded in statute law and those that rest only upon the practices and conventions of central government, or upon regulations which in practice are very much determined by ministers without any, or any substantial, parliamentary discussion. It follows that it is central government's role to decide when to refrain from intervention or to intervene, and that therefore it has to be trusted to be wise in this matter. Moreover, the practical consequence of this flexibility of the system has been that it has been possible for central government over time broadly to increase its intervention more often than not through reinterpretation of existing legislation, rather than by new. While the Committee saw definition of the respective roles of central and local government as a means by which local freedom would be enhanced because clearly established within limits, it was possible to foresee the result of clearer definition of roles quite differently: as necessarily implying a rewriting of the law to give central government more powers at all times so that it possesses those it needs only occasionally. On this view, local authorities would have more practical freedom now when powers and duties are not explicit.

As this was the central recommendation from which others flowed, it was not surprising that replying in 1977, central government accepted virtually none of the Committee's proposals other than those it had itself submitted in evidence — all of which were useful rather than radical. Two years later in 1979 it would seem as if central government has dropped some of the changes it entertained in 1977. Indeed, the outcome of all the interest and work put into the subject is likely to be virtually nothing. The old arrangements will survive intact. The first explanation of this inertia is that interest in reform was a product of crisis. Reform was felt to be needed at the time to weather each stage of that crisis, but the crisis passed without it. The first stage was brought to an end by economic recession and anti-inflationary policy. Cuts in local expenditure were achieved in the second stage without new mechanisms. Persuasion, exhortation and indeed reliance on flexible interpretation of ambiguous legislation was used successfully to achieve very substantial reductions in expenditure. If the system achieved that, what need for change? The second explanation of inertia is very different. The one major innovation of 1975 was the creation of the Consultative Council, headed by the Secretary of State for the Environment, on which other ministers and the local authority associations are represented. It was a powerful engine through which central government persuaded local government to do what it wanted. But there was a price to be paid for such an arrangement. Just as in order to secure TUC and CBI co-operation on issues which central government regards as vital, those bodies have gained the right to be listened to on other matters and very often to blackball what they do not like, so corporatism in the relations between central and local government has reduced central government's freedom to introduce reforms. Whatever the balance of advantage for a reform, there is always someone who would lose. Closer co-operation between central and local government has made it more difficult for central government to proceed with the reforms it believed in, and this has nothing whatever to do with its chances of securing a majority in the House of Commons. Such stalemates become more common as the mutual interdependence of central government and the various representative bodies of pressure groups increases. If this were all there was to the matter, we would be entering on a period of further stagnation in reform and of making do. But the very interaction between central and local governments, which seems so unceasing for those engaged in it, is leading to a questioning of the mystery of mysteries, that is the method used for distributing central government grant, which is likely to lead to an insistence that the method should become rational — something that can only be achieved by simultaneous change in the balance of power between central departments and local authorities. All the signs are that the outcome is bound, in effect, to be more power for central government, which it does not entirely want. Local government finance is not inert, but its state of motion is at the mercy of short-run influences rather than of cool deliberations.

The research project on which this book is based was started in 1974, the year when the crisis started. The book is being published in 1980 when the crisis is not yet over and local expenditure is under attack. But there will eventually be pressures to increase local expenditure once again.

The first ambition of this book is to try to increase understanding of what is undoubtedly a complicated system. The Layfield Committee saw it as in a state of confusion. We would agree. There are two aspects to this. The purpose of the system, the roles of the principal agents, the functions of the different financial elements are confused, as the Committee found them to be. But they are also confusing. Local government finance has become an esoteric mystery with its own jargon, with which very few are really familiar. The mystery of mysteries, the Rate Support Grant, is an exceedingly complex mechanism by which central government distributes its contributions to local authorities. While a few in every Treasurer's department understand much of it, some is only understood by those few initiates who cluster round the throne of the Consultative Council and are on it or its working parties. Many of them would only claim they understood a part of what was going on. Yet in every local authority just how much it has to spend and what it must raise in rates depends on the mechanisms of the Rate Support Grant, varies annually and is not known until late in the year. Most councillors know that critical decisions depend on an algebra and the use of a statistical technique called multiple regression analysis whose purpose and workings are generally, and unsurprisingly, obscure to them.

In our judgement one cannot reach an understanding of the system by describing it as it is now. On a snapshot at a point of time much of it is frankly unintelligible. To understand why it is what it is, one needs to ask how it came about. Hence our use in Part One of the historical method. A historian would have gone into much greater detail to explain by what combination of intention and accident the system moved from stage to stage. We have been necessarily and deliberately selective in setting down what we believe relevant to answering the following questions. How did local government come to have its present form? How did the present relations between central and local government come to be what they are? How did local government come to provide the services it does and not others? What are the causes of the growth of local expenditure? Why is it that grant has increased so much as a source of local revenue? Why is the local tax an *ad valorem* property tax? And why has the grant system come to have its present complicated form? We believe the historical approach does illuminate now both what is confused and confusing. Over many centuries the system had a pattern to it, not always the same. During the last century and a half the growth of central influence over local authorities has been one force modifying the way in which the parts worked together. Even so, until after the Second World War the role of local government had a consistency within the British political system which it has since largely lost. The two main reasons why this happened, in our judgement, resulted from two peculiarities of the 1945–51 Labour government. It was the one and only British administration which started with very large economic resources it could easily divert to take very substantial new initiatives because, unlike other postwar administrations, it did not have to use the taxation released by the ending of the war effort to service an enormously increased National Debt (because of the way in which the war had been financed). But in taking new initiatives, its ideas on the respective roles of central and local government were confused, and contested within the Cabinet, so that different agencies were used in different cases without good reason. Moreover, central government became a provider of public goods and services for the first time on any scale. The lack of any clearly worked-out attitude towards the use of central and local government caused a confusion of roles which has persisted since and is partly responsible in our judgement for the weakening of the financial and political disciplines imposed by the old system of local government finance.

In Part Two, armed with the answers the historical method has given us, we try to answer the following analytical questions. Who ultimately bears the burden of rates and how does this differ from those who pay them? What would be the properties of an efficient rate system? What factors explain the expenditure of local authorities in the very recent past; in particular what has been the effect of increasing grant on expenditure? What are the properties of the grant system and of rates? How much spending freedom do local authorities appear to exercise? How does macroeconomic control operate and what instruments would seem sufficient for it?

With such a depressing recent history of initiatives for reform it may seem merely masochistic to advocate change. Nevertheless, it seems to us that without a limited number of changes the system as it now is must inevitably deteriorate. Unless capital valuation is introduced, the rating system will have no rational foundation. We still believe that the present geographical and personal inequities will be intensified to a point where the system will be swept away (as it has been in the Republic of Ireland) with a cry of injustice. And we do not believe that recent trends in the treatment of the non-domestic ratepayer can continue without serious cost nationally and to some areas particularly, especially centres of conurbations which are also the chief losers from the failure to adopt capital valuation. On the other hand, while the present grant system can be tidied up in a number of respects, we do not believe it can be altered, even in ways which are generally thought comparatively trivial, without changing quite radically the balance of power between central and local government. Thus in Part Three we consider the amelioration of the system.

More explanation is needed of the radical changes considered in Part Four. One excuse is that radical changes have happened in the past and could happen again; but they tend to happen without enough forethought and so have some consequences at least which were unpredicted. It is far from impossible that a government could come to power committed to replacing rates by a local income tax. As we argue, there is much merit in this proposal provided one is aware in advance of why one would want to do this, and what its consequences would be, particularly for the grant system. By contrast we find for example, that the Layfield Committee's proposals to superimpose income tax on rates would have made the grant system almost unworkable. We also believe there is a strong case for introducing charging, providing again it is introduced for appropriate services and provided also that due regard is given to coping with the redistributive consequences. While charging can mean charging what the market will bear, with suitable grant arrangements it is also consistent with providing services below cost when desired. Its introduction could be politically and distributionally neutral.

Perhaps the most likely cause of change is yet another local government re-organisation. Almost everyone agrees that that in 1974 was mistaken in many respects, yet the lessons need to be drawn before more changes are made. Many have argued that it is wrong to consider reorganisation without considering financing arrangements simultaneously. We would agree. But there is an even more egregious error. One cannot rationally consider either one or both without analysing the respective functions of central and local government, and deciding the division of labour between them. We see the analysis on which the 1974 reorganisation was based, and for that matter current proposals for regional devolution − themselves a kind of local government reorganisation − as essentially faulty. In our eyes almost the only good reason for the form of reorganisation adopted in 1974, and indeed for the forms of regional devolution advocated recently, is to increase the effective power of central government by reducing the number of authorities with which it has to deal. Most other arguments militate in favour of smaller local authorities except for those services where central government wishes to have a uniform service provided throughout the country. Even then we would argue greater efficiency could be achieved by devolution to smaller local authorities while making appropriate arrangements − probably through grant rather than through national taxes − to make sure that sufficient services are provided in all areas. Indeed we would argue that re-organisation can only hope to be satisfactory if the nation is prepared to make up its mind what are the purposes of central and local government in relation to various services, and so decide the size of local authorities, their scope and indeed whether there is not a case for reviving some elected special-purpose authorities which concentrate on one function, such as education or health.

In our final discussion we make no secret of our belief that it would be better it more power could be devolved from central government. The case for devolution is not the same as that for smallness in local government. It need not be joined to a belief in less government. Rather it follows from observation − we do not attempt any proof − that central government is over-congested. We see no special merit in devolving to regions: from central government to levels of government which in so far as they exist in Scotland and Wales, and in rudimentary form exist elsewhere, are agencies of central government. Real devolution would be more effective if based on the levels of government which exist and which, in more or less their present form, have a long tradition to be built upon.

PART ONE   DEVELOPMENT

1 What is Local Government?

There were local institutions of government in Britain long before any difference was perceived between central and local government; and today there are localised institutions of government not regarded as local government. The name is far younger than the fact. Beatrice and Sydney Webb — the greatest historians of English local government — did not find the phrase 'local government' used before the middle of the nineteenth century (Webbs, 1963, p. 8). Before that, local government existed but hid its identity. In Britain the power of local government is, and always has been, derived from that of national government. The earliest local government was whatever local presence the king was able to maintain and rely on to preserve his influence and protect his throne. The early Norman kings set up a network of sheriffs to extend their local influence (Jewell, 1972, pp. 9 and 36). When these became too independent and unsatisfactory, Edward III transferred their function as the local representatives of the crown to a new set of agents. They were the justices of the peace who have survived to this day. Almost from the beginning administrative functions were added to their judicial duties (ibid.; Redlich and Hirst, 1970, p. 14). In the shires and rural areas outside the chartered towns they became responsible for poor relief, prisons, law and order, and almost every other administrative duty. The crown developed no alternative sets of officials for domestic affairs until the nineteenth century. The justices of the peace remained the most important, and virtually the only, local agents of central government until they began to lose their administrative functions in that century, and became virtually magistrates alone.

From the beginning of the middle ages, or in embryo even earlier, there developed a parallel system of local government in the chartered or incorporated towns based on royal charters granted to them. The charters were widely different in the forms and duties of the town governments they established and so as a result was the development of urban government. Within the town boundaries the officials were usually elected, though under various and often heavily restricted franchises, and had both judicial and administrative duties. These forms of government, often modified in detail usually at the desire of the town itself, survived in their essentials until the 1835 Municipal Corporations Act. In both town and country there was a lower level of government, the parish, which many have argued was a civil unit before it became a religious one. Again the powers of the vestries and other bodies that controlled the parishes and the bases on which they were elected showed the greatest differences. In many areas tradition provided that the ultimate authority on parish affairs lay with the assembled parishioners, a tradition which survives today in the New England town meeting.

Late in the seventeenth century another kind of local authority became common; what Sidney Webb called the special-purpose authority whose geographical areas often overlapped the areas of other authorities. Each was set up by a separate Act of Parliament. Their purpose was to perform some function which could have been undertaken by an existing authority but was not because of inertia, internal conflict or other disinclination to act. As the old authorities ossified, these special authorities had to be created to take any new initiative required.

Local authorities multiplied in number as a multitude of authorities were created with overlapping territories and diverse constitutions for a diversity of purposes: water supply, sewers, highways and 'to improve' (Webbs, 1963, p. 27).

By the end of the eighteenth century the justices of the peace, the municipal corporations, the parishes and all the special-purpose authorities constituted local government, but as the Webbs said, it was not known as such. When Adam Smith discussed the functions of government he analysed many which we would now recognise as those of local government, but it did not occur to him to make this distinction (Smith, 1776, espec. bk 5, ch. 1). After the Napoleonic Wars, the old local authorities were under attack from opposing quarters, though as many writers have noted from Halévy (1972) to E. P. Thompson (1968) conflicting views often coincided in the same minds. The restrictive practices and physical environment of the old boroughs did not allow industrial development. The new areas outside the old boroughs where there were no obstacles to industrial development did not have a local government effective enough to mitigate the social consequences of development. Either way, what destroyed the old institutions at last was their inability to adapt to the changing conditions of the nineteenth century. The swarming of population to towns and cities, the growing filth and disease in those places, the terrible growth of pauperism and misery creating crime and disorder – all these undermined the old system and brought about its collapse. Its diversity became a source of weakness. The Royal Commission on the Municipal Corporations reported that Leeds, Doncaster, Bideford and Stratford, among others, were excellent. We are told Leicester and Coventry were infamous (Webbs, 1963, p. 39). The vestry of St George's, Hanover Square (in London) was widely extolled. The justices of Middlesex were portrayed as abominable. The adequacy of the old authorities depended largely on the absence of change. Since most of the population was swept up in change, most local authorities were inadequate and were pronounced so by the 1835 Royal Commission. The norm had become nearer a city guild of modern times – part social club, part charity – than what we would recognise as a local government.

However, it took another fifty years to alter the old forms of government in the counties. Though the greater need of the great towns for government was one reason why municipal reform came first, a far more important cause had nothing directly to do with local government. The main public function of the old municipal corporations had become that of returning Members of Parliament. Whatever balance one strikes between the various explanations that have been given for the interest in parliamentary reform which led up to the 1832 Reform Act, discrediting the corruption of the boroughs was inevitably part of that campaign. Their inadequacies, their narrowness, the fact that MPs varied greatly in the size of population they represented, and that very often it was the charter of the corporation that determined the franchise all made discussion of the condition of the municipal corporations a matter of national interest. When the

1832 Reform Act destroyed the parliamentary rationale of the corporations, little but their husk was left. Their reform by the 1835 Municipal Corporations Act seemed at the time mostly a tidying-up operation.

'In general', wrote the 1835 Royal Commission which prepared the ground for the Act, 'the corporate funds are but partially applied to the municipal purposes such as the preservation of the peace by an efficient police, or in watching or in lighting the town, but they are frequently expended in feasting and paying the salaries of incompetent officers' (quoted by Robson, 1954, p. 259). Thus without the excuse of being important in the election of MPs, they were revealed more often than not as sociable societies for a very few. Before the Act they had the power to do whatever the law did not expressly disallow. But because of their corruption the Act restricted their future activities to (1) the raising of local revenues, (2) police, (3) licensing, and (4) the passing of by-laws on a limited range of subjects (Redlich and Hirst, 1970, p. 130). What was meant to stop municipalities from wasting their substance in feasting and other forms of indulgence for the few, soon became a means by which local authorities were prevented from doing anything (except within very narrowly constrained financial limits — for many years the product of a penny rate) that was not expressly permitted by statute. Thus a major constitutional revolution was achieved without premeditation.

The 1835 Act was negative in that it was meant to check abuses. It did not galvanise the reformed corporations — there were only 178 — into activity. New corporations could only be established by a complicated and discouraging procedure and the ones that were founded in the new towns were often just as slow as the old ones to take on the new problems. 'Indeed anyone who wishes to understand why the legislation of the 1840s and '50s was so ineffective, and what the invincible resistance was that frustrated the energy of reformers will find the answer as clearly written in the proceeding of the Borough Council of Birmingham as in those of any corrupt and languid corporation left over from the reform of 1835' (Young, 1953, p. 125). During the period after that Act, the old and new special-purpose authorities were often still the most effective and conspicuous organs of local government. Even a year before the Act, the new Poor Law set up special authorities, the Boards of Guardians. In 1848 the Public Health Act created local boards of health, and the 1870 Education Act, school boards. To them were added gradually the municipalities where interests from within were able to capture them for reform. The most famous of these reinvigorated local governments was Birmingham under Joseph Chamberlain, but there were many others building up to a high point of spontaneously generated enthusiasm for municipal government in the 1880s and 1890s. (Briggs, 1963).

One lasting result of the 1832 and 1835 Acts was that it became broadly the practice for there to be some correspondence between the franchise for local and for national elections. Jeremy Bentham had argued in his *Constitutional Code* that if representative democracy were right for national government then it was logical it should be reflected in local government which he believed should be the mirror image of national government (Redlich and Hirst, 1970 pp. 95–102). John Stuart Mill maintained similarly that 'the principles which apply to it do not differ in any respect from those applicable to national governments'

(1910, p. 348). The elective principle in local government was, of course, ancient though much abused – in both municipal corporations and special-purpose authorities. As late as 1872, Goschen speaking on what he called the chaos that reigned in local government said that 'it is a curious fact that while we might expect to find not identical, but very similar principles governing the election of Guardians [of the Poor Law], the elections of local Boards [of Health], the election of highway surveyors and overseers, and the election of other local and parochial authorities, yet in all these cases a different form of election prevails' (1872, p. 190).

Yet in spite of this variety, there was after 1835 a general tendency towards a uniformity in which local franchise followed national franchise. Not that it always followed (Ensor, 1936, p. 214). The Liberals in 1882 allowed single, but not married, women the vote in local elections if otherwise qualified. In 1888 the Conservatives allowed this in county elections. In 1894 the Liberals allowed married women to vote and also let women stand for local election if they were qualified to vote. Women neither got the vote nor were allowed to stand for Parliament until after the First World War. On the other hand, multiple voting in municipal elections for those with commercial as well as residential property in more than one place survived until after the Second World War.

Another important development which followed from the 1832 and 1835 Acts was the gradual divorce of local authorities from Parliament. It was not simply that counties and boroughs had been the units which had returned members to Parliament, so that there was a sense in which the local authorities sent representatives to Parliament. There was also frequently the expectation that MPs would spend some of their time representing the interests from their locality to an extent which has not been seen since. In pocket boroughs where the franchise was such that one person or a small number disposed of the seat at will, local interests shaded uneasily into the interests of the patron or patrons of the seat. Some gave their nominees much discretion. Others did not. But where the franchise was broader, especially in the boroughs, Members of Parliament were not only expected to represent local interests in the promotion of local legislation but sometimes to be the mouthpiece more generally for local views (Dodd, 1956, pp. 139, 142, 166). The best-known reaction to such interference was Edmund Burke's to his electors at Bristol in 1777 where he laid down the doctrine, which later became accepted, that once elected, members were free to make their own minds up on how to vote in Parliament (Burke, 1780).

After 1832, there was a gradual separation between the geographical areas of the local authority and the parliamentary constituency that inevitably affected the way in which Members of Parliament related to local authorities. The changes in some constituencies came about slowly. For example, it was not until 1884 that the large cities began to be divided into single-member constituencies (Redlich and Hirst, 1970, p. 193).

It is interesting to speculate whether parliamentary representation could possibly have gone another way. The American constitution provided for popular representation in the lower house and representation of a different tier of government – that of the states – in the Senate. If in Britain before 1832 representation of the people was hard to distinguish from the representation of local authorities (excluding, of course, the special-purpose authorities) is it imaginable that the House of Commons might have continued as representative of (reformed) local authorities? One reason against such a development was the great influence of the democratic principle in pushing through even the relatively minor steps towards democracy achieved in 1832. Another was possibly the relative unimportance of local authorities by comparison with the sovereign states which came together to form the Union. But it is also not impossible that the extent of electoral corruption had its effect also. The idea that New York State and Rhode Island should both have two senators, given the great difference in their areas and populations, is not dissimilar from the idea that Birmingham and a mound outside Salisbury should both return two MPs.

> However, at the time the discrepancies between the sizes of the constituencies were so great, and in some cases the cause of endless wrangling in Parliament when it was debated which should lose or gain members, that any rationalisation of boundaries which might have been needed to make territorial representation a possible alternative, would seem to have been unthinkable (Brock, 1973, pp. 157–9)

Possibly if there had not already been a House of Lords, the result might have been something nearer the American model — one chamber based on popular representation and the other representing local governments. All this can be no more than speculation, of some interest perhaps for the future of local government.

1835 was a watershed. To recapitulate: it limited what local authorities could do, established some correspondence between the local and the parliamentary franchises, began the separation of local authorities and parliamentary constituencies. It established local government as a separate tier of government, and allowed vigorous towns to give themselves active local government. But county government remained appointed until the 1888 Local Government Act which extended democratic principles, as construed at the time, to the counties. The justices of the peace lost most of their administrative functions and were replaced by elected councillors; while at the same time some progress was made in reducing the number of special-purpose authorities by transferring functions to the counties. Some of the largest cities and towns became county boroughs — single-tier authorities with the powers and duties of both counties and boroughs for their areas.

The next stage was the rationalisation of the second-tier authorities. Urban and rural district councils were created in addition to the old municipal boroughs, while at the same time local self-government was introduced for the parishes as a third tier. Both innovations enabled more special-purpose authorities to be assimilated; while the geography of local government for the first time reflected the principle that the area of a local authority must fall entirely within the area of the next larger authority in the hierarchy above it. In 1902 the school boards set up by the Forster Education Act in 1870 were assimilated to the general-purpose authorities, leaving the boards of guardians of the Poor Law to be transferred to the counties and county boroughs in 1929. Thereafter, the basic structure did not alter until 1974. While called a major reorganisation and undoubtedly causing considerable administrative problems, the main innovation of the 1974 Act was the sweeping away of the county boroughs and the replacement of the old second-tier authorities by larger ones. Counties were divided into shire counties and metropolitan counties. In country areas the shire counties became the more important authorities. In cities most powers were given to the metropolitan districts. Thus now outside some authorities in Scotland, London and the Isles of Scilly there are only counties and districts.

Although these elected bodies are what is generally considered to be local government, appointed authorities also exist. In this century local government has lost functions to central government. Some, – such as the Poor Law (1934– 47), most civil airports (1945), electricity (1947), gas (1948) and more recently water (1974) – have been transferred to public corporations which are public bodies whose boards are appointed by ministers on behalf of the crown.[1] Others – such as trunk roads (1936 and 1946), hospitals (1947), and most remaining local health services (1974) – have been transferred to central government. It hardly needs saying that the administration of these last has not been transferred to centrally located Whitehall departments or to their inspectorates. New local agencies with some discretion have been appointed – in these cases the divisional road engineers, the road construction units and the regional hospital boards.

Moreover, numerous bodies have been appointed which it has recently become common to call QUANGOS, quasi-autonomous, non-governmental organisations. Many of them are also local – from some of the oldest, such as employment exchanges, through to consumers' committees and advisory committees of all kinds – and some such as the area health authorities have several members nominated by local authorities.

Therefore, there is both elective local government and non-elective localised central government operating directly or through the decentralised activities of other public bodies.

THE SIGNIFICANCE OF ELECTION IN LOCAL GOVERNMENT

What difference would one expect to find in the behaviour and policies of elective local government and localised central government which might help decide the most appropriate spheres of activity for each? One theory – it is the classic theory of democracy – gives plain, even startling, results. Elected local government will do what the majority of its electorate wants. Central government – and therefore localised central government – will do what the majority of its electorate wants. Therefore, the difference between the behaviour and policies of the two must be a reflection of the differences between the tastes and preferences of the two electorates. This view was implicit in the ideas of Bentham and John Stuart Mill on local government. A modern statement is that of Sir Ivor Jennings, the constitutional lawyer: 'Under this historic system of local self-government local authorities even now have a substantial amount of discretion.

They consist of persons responsible to the local electorate . . . within the limits laid down by Parliament and of central control, they adopt a policy which accords as they think with the views of the local electorate' (1947, p. 17) Many much more recent authorities can be found saying the same thing (Dearlove, 1973). Indeed, it has become the official view. Neither central nor local government can question the principle that the latter is responsive to the local electorate. Numerous White and Green Papers on local finance regard this as the foundation principle of local government. Most recently, Sir Frank Layfield's Committee on local government finance stated that 'accountability to the electorate is the essence of local democracy' (Layfield, 1976, p. 102, also p. 53). Many reforms are promoted on the grounds that they would further local democracy. In recommending local government reform in 1970 a Labour government said 'only if such a change occurs and local government is organised with strong units with power to make major decisions, will present trends towards centralisation be reversed, and local democracy resume its place as a major part of our democratic system' (Ministry of Housing and Local Government, 1970, Cmnd. 4276, p. 28). A Conservative government argued a year later that 'a vigorous local democracy means that authorities must be given real functions — with powers of decision and the ability to take action without being subjected to excessive regulation by central government through financial or other controls . . . above all else a genuine local democracy implies that decisions should be taken — and should be seen to be taken — as locally as possible' (DoE, 1971*a*, Cmnd. 4741, p. 1).

Some of the attempts to make local government more responsive to its electorate have to do with local government finance. That was certainly the view of the Layfield Committee. It argued that (1) there needed to be greater understanding between members and the general public, (2) that the financial implications of decisions in particular should be clearer and better publicised, (3) that there should be a clearer division of responsibility between central and local government, and (4) that central grant should be reduced and accountability increased by throwing more of the burden of financing local services on the electorate (Layfield, 1976, ch. 4).

The purpose of many of the suggested reforms, especially those in local government finance, is to create a closer link between decisions made by local government and the consequences of such decisions on the electorate. Whether the creation of such links is important depends on the discipline the electorate can impose on the elected. It may be true that as a norm one would like to see local authorities respond to the wishes of the majority of their electors, but do they actually do so?

As a description of reality, the assumption that government responds to the electorate has been strongly criticised by many political scientists. One criticism has been that it ignores the role of political parties with their own ideologies which they try to impose on the electorate. Political parties have a long history in local government, even though in some authorities they have formally only emerged quite recently (Bulpitt, 1967; Sharpe, 1960). However, the existence of political parties with their own ideologies and platforms is not a sufficient reason to question the responsiveness of government to its electorate. To get elected, a party has to choose a programme which it hopes will attract a majority of the electorate. If the majority changes its view, the party would have to change its platform if it is to remain in power or acquire power. Thus party platforms and party ideologies may themselves be a reflection of the views of the electorate and be responsive to such views (Downs, 1957). Professor Jones gave it as his view that in Wolverhampton, which he investigated in detail, parties had a major role in making local policymaking more responsive to the electorate (1969, pp. 348–9). Dearlove suggests that this view of the role of parties has been better researched and substantiated in national than in local politics (1973, pp. 31–8; see also McKenzie, 1955). It is not, however, inevitable and parties can be means by which the politically active can promote causes in which they believe, and which are contrary to the views of the majority (Downs, 1957).

One of the arguments put forward against the view that political platforms are constrained by the views of the majority of the electorate has been that electors do not have the information to make a rational choice between candidates or parties (Wallas, 1908). The meaning of this has often been debated. Even if in extreme cases people vote for parties which in some non-rational way they feel symbolise their aspirations and interests, this may still be some discipline upon politicians to undertake policies which do not conflict with their electors' image of the politicans or parties in question (Lipset, 1960). One has to accept some blurring of issues since even well-informed electors will have a problem not only in reaching a conclusion on each issue but of deciding their vote when different parties reflect their beliefs on different issues. It is the art of the politician to find the highest common factor which will enable their party either directly or within a coalition to command majority support.

More pertinent for our study are the criticisms which apply particularly to the assumption that local government is responsive to the majority of its electorate. Two related facts are cited as being inconsistent with such an assumption. First, that in local elections the turnout has on average been low and falling over the years. Second, the well-attested fact that in Britain and indeed in many countries, local elections are not decided by local but by national issues (Newton in Layfield, 1976, app. 6).

These facts may indicate that local electorates do not constrain local politicians, or that local government does not and cannot substantially affect the local electorate. Local elections may be decided by national issues because local government may be greatly constrained by the national government. Also the sheer size of the proportion of local expenditure financed by central government – nearly 61 per cent in 1977/8 – so reduces the impact of rate increases that they do not influence elections. (In 1975/6 domestic ratepayers provided only 40 per cent of the yield from rates in Great Britain) (Layfield, 1976, p. 149).[2] However, to try to decide how far elected local government has autonomy on this basis alone is to oversimplify a complicated question: one to which we will return, and one which is indeed perhaps the most important issue in local government finance, as it is in local government.

There are, of course, alternatives to the hypothesis that local politicians are influenced by what they believe the majority of the electorate will support. Their policies may be dictated by Whitehall, or by self-interest, or by pressure groups which may or may not be mediated through their party. Dearlove (1973) examined one local authority, Kensington and Chelsea, where there had always been a substantial Conservative majority. Wealthy enough to receive comparatively little grant, it can have great independence of both the electorate and central government. In such circumstances it responded to political influences and pressure groups. but in ways which reinforced its image of itself as a Conservative borough. Even so, it is difficult to argue that it did not reflect the opinions of the majority of its electors. Another indication that local authorities take some account of their electorate is that they regularly moderate their rate increases in the year of an election.

The difficulty is that in the end, while it is possible that local governments pursue their own self-interest or those of their bureaucracies or respond more to some pressure groups out of proportion to their electoral importance, it does not seem as if the political-science literature has provided enough convincing evidence on what motivates elected authorities and how this affects their behaviour. Thus even when modified to allow for parties, coalitions and defective information, one cannot know whether the classic doctrine is a description of how local authorities behave. One suspects pressure groups are important, though these have been more studied at national than local level; and also that some local actions, at least, are prompted by the interests of the bureaucracy. Yet it also seems likely that local politicians remain influenced by their sense of what the electorate would approve.

THE ECONOMIC SIGNIFICANCE OF LOCAL DEMOCRACY

The hypothesis that local government is responsive to its electorate has important implications for an analysis of the economic behaviour of local government. The economic significance of democratic local government is that election by those wholly or partly responsible for the financing of local government becomes a substitute for the economic discipline of the price mechanism. Moreover, in such a system there is a relationship between the economic constraints facing the electorate and the economic behaviour of the local authority.

Private-sector economics for the most part is concerned with the process by which supply and demand interact to clear the market so as to determine production, distribution and consumption. Prices are crucial in acting as signals which determine the outcome. While local government has engaged and still engages in trading services which could be priced as on an ordinary commercial market, most local goods are sold at non-market prices, or not sold at all. They are subsidised. Many local services could not be supplied by private enterprise for reasons to be discussed in Part One, Chapter 3. Thus the disciplines of the market do not directly influence local government; they do not expand production of a service when they make a profit, or contract or cease production when they make a loss. In Britain, it seems improbable that any local government would be allowed to go bankrupt even if it made a loss overall — though no one can be sure of this since it has never happened and no statute explicitly provides.[3] Moreover, because changes in demand for local services do not affect their price, such changes, to affect production, have to be signalled in some other way.

The voting mechanism can replace the price mechanism in co-ordinating the demand for the goods supplied by local authorities with the supply of such goods. A local authority which misspends, that is spends flagrantly at variance with the wishes of its electorate, will have to face the verdict of the polls. There is, moreover, a more precise implication of voting as a decision process. If the electorate had to choose among different amounts of spending in aggregate or on some particular item, the budget that would receive the majority vote would be that desired by the median voter, the voter whose desired budget is in between the extremes. An example of this proposition, which is called the 'median voter hypothesis', is the following. Assume there are three voters. A would most prefer a very small budget, B a medium-sized budget, and C a very large budget. If the alternatives are put to a vote the budget preferred by B, the median voter in our example, would be the only one to get a majority of votes. If we let the voters choose between the small and the medium budget, the medium budget will get two votes, those of voters B and C, while the small budget will get only one vote, that of voter A. If we let them choose between the medium and the large budget the medium budget will again get a majority of votes, those of voter B and voter A. (Black, 1948). Thus in a perfectly functioning local democracy the constraints facing the median voter are the ones that would determine the economic decisions of the local authority. Thus, for example, if the average income in a local authority is equal to the income of the median voter, and income affects his demand for local services, it can be used as a relevant variable affecting the spending decisions of the local authority.

Similarly, the hypothesis of local democracy allows us to develop the notion of a price to the electorate of the services provided for it by local government. If we take the electorate as a whole, then the price of all local government services is the cost of these services minus government grants and any other external sources of income. If one makes a further assumption and eliminates the non-domestic local ratepayer's contribution on the grounds that he may well not have a vote locally then the domestic effective price is broadly cost of service minus government grants, other external sources of income and non-domestic rates. In general, one would expect that the higher the price relative to the cost of services, the more voters would bother to vote so as to influence local expenditure and vice versa; though these will not be the only influences upon their voting behaviour. Also, the higher the price, the less of such services they would demand.

Of course, the above theories, both political and economic, of the behaviour of local government are based on the assumption that local government has power. If local government is a sham and central government requires local authorities to produce very similar packages of services, then the demands of the local electorate will have little effect on local expenditure. These various theories attempt to formalise the relationship between the decisions made by elected representatives and the desires of the electorate. Local democracy and autonomy are often lauded and the existence of local government justified on such grounds. Such justification is acceptable only if local decisions made by the elected represent or reflect the desires of the electorate. In this sense, the election process and the discipline of such a process may act as a substitute for prices for the purpose of linking the demands of the consumers (the electorate) with the services supplied by the decision makers (the elected).

CONCLUSIONS

(1)   The ancient institutions of local government in England and Wales were the municipal corporations and the justices of the peace outside the towns. The justices were crown appointees and remained the administrative agents of the crown until they lost these functions during the nineteenth century.

(2)   Before 1835, municipal corporations had been elected by a wide variety of franchises and principles of co-option. After 1835, the elective principle was more widely and uniformly introduced, generally becoming more democratic as the national franchise was extended.

(3)   In Britain, as in many other Anglo-Saxon countries, local government has now become synonymous with democratically elected local government. It is the sense in which the term will be used in this book.

(4)   The economic significance of this is that local democracy can provide a discipline which has affinities with the discipline of the market. One hypothesis is that local authorities will tend to act and to spend as in the interests of their 'typical' voter. This, the median voter hypothesis, is not the only economic hypothesis on the behaviour of local government. Moreover, we suspect that local government in Britain does not conform to the hypothesis, being much more influenced by national issues in its elections. But it is a useful touchstone when considering the practical autonomy of local government.

(5)   While the term 'local government' is normally restricted to elected governments, there remain many arms of central government and of public corporations which have a local presence, and are local government in a different sense. This distinction will be important later when we consider arguments for transferring goods and services between elected local government and local branches of central government.

(6)   The argument of most of the book can be conducted without distinguishing between sizes of local government or tiers of local government. The questions these distinctions raise are discussed in Part Four. It follows we make no distinction here between regional and local government, since the former are a type of the latter.

Thus we have elective local government and non-elective localised central government. Though the distinction is a useful one, we can exaggerate the difference in the power of central government in the two cases. Elected local government is far from autonomous. Indeed, some writers may have argued that elected local authorities now have comparatively little independence. Neither is localised central government the complete creature of Whitehall. As in any decentralised administration, local branches must have some discretion to act within policies laid down for them. Some of these decentralised agencies are more responsive to local views than others, and may indeed have elected local authority members co-opted on them. Therefore the differences between the two may be more apparent than real. In the United Kingdom, the name local government is now given virtually exclusively to elected bodies, but it would be wrong to suppose that these are the only 'local' government. In practice, as we shall see later in this book (Part One, Chapter 4), it is quite often unclear why some local functions of government are performed by elected local government and others by what we have called localised central government. Accident, that is the particular circumstances of the time when a policy decision has been taken, often seems to have been responsible. But the analogy with elected central government suggests that elected local government should be more responsive and autonomous than the local agents of central government. In this book we will deal almost entirely with elected government, though towards the end of our argument we shall return to ask if there is a more sensible dividing line between it and non-elected localised central government than now appears.

NOTES

1 Airports went to the Civil Aviation Board via the Ministry of Civil Aviation.
2 The balance was paid by non-domestic ratepayers, mainly businesses.
3 Until 1971 it was thought that the Mersey Docks and Harbour Board could not go bankrupt, but a Conservative government allowed it to, despite protests from mystified stock holders. The Board was in part a late survivor of the old type of special-purpose local authority, part a local public corporation. The terms on which local authorities borrow do not reflect their indebtedness relative to their prospective net income, because quite reasonably the market does not believe any local authority would be allowed to go bankrupt.

2 Relations between Central and Local Government

Britain is, and always has been, a unitary state: a state in which local government is formally subordinate to the central government. But British history shows how an unchanged constitution can accommodate great variations in the relative authority of central and local government. In the middle ages, as one would expect, the local influence of the crown varied with its military strength and the support it commanded in different parts of the country, as well as in the interest it had at any time in local matters beyond tax-gathering (Jewell, 1972, ch. 1). The Tudors had more power and a greater wish to influence local events. They set up offices and institutions to act as intermediaries between the crown and the local authorities (Elton, 1953, p. 346). Important Acts which the crown required local authorities to execute were passed through Parliament. The best known of these were the various Poor Laws from Henry VIII's reign, culminating in the great Elizabethan Poor Law of 1601.[1] Following the accession of William and Mary, the Bill of Rights forbade the crown interfering with the election of Members of Parliament (cf. Stubbs, 1896, p. 524). Though the immediate motive was to prevent a king forcing his religion on his subjects through altering local charters so as to return MPs favourable to the crown, it had the unintended consequence of giving those boroughs which were crown corporations unparalleled autonomy for a hundred years, and preventing the growth of a centralised autocratic regime as happened in many European countries. The Webbs (1963) called it a 'summary end' to arbitrary interference with local liberties.

The formal position had not changed. The power of the boroughs still rested on royal charters, but the Bill of Rights gave them more protection from royal intervention. Blackstone in his *Commentaries* (1773) on the English Constitution – the standard work of the day – described the justices of the peace, the county administrative and judicial authorities, as strictly subordinate (quoted by Redlich and Hirst, 1970, p. 77). But this was just the kind of fiction which brought down Bentham's anathema on Blackstone as a mythmaker (Bentham, 1948, esp. p. 50). The boroughs, and the justices administering the counties, had almost complete independence of the crown and its ministers. One constitutional historian described this situation as autonomy under the law: 'Their duty was to carry out the law and not obey the command of the central executive (Keir, 1948, pp. 312–16). It was as common for MPs to initiate legislation for local authorities in Parliament as it was for central government. More than half its Bills were private members' Bills and a very high proportion of these were local Bills meant to promote local interests. An MP was expected to do his duty and promote the legislation wanted in his locality, and to interest enough other MPs to get it through Parliament. For much of the time a few MPs sat in an almost empty chamber debating private Bills of limited local interest. It is doubtful whether the practical independence of the local authorities would have stayed intact if the crown had shown a strong interest in home affairs. But the inclination of the crown and its ministers during the eighteenth century was different. Neither crown, ministers nor Parliament were interested in formulating home policies that were uniform for the nation. They were interested, of course, in patronage, tax-gathering, and in criminal and civil law but otherwise the attention of the House of Commons was concentrated on foreign, colonial and military affairs. Crown, ministers and Parliament in any collective capacity were almost indifferent to what local government did.

Most of the laws local authorities administered, they themselves had promoted and that such legislation had been through Parliament did not imply any consistency in local policies or procedures. The judiciary had some effect in getting some uniformity in interpretation of similar statutes – for example in defining the tax base for rates as we shall see – but not in policy. Even the statement that local authorities depended on Parliament for their powers understates their practical independence. As Professor Plumb has pointed out, the decisions the justices of the peace gave in quarter sessions were often locally given the force of law. It was true of perhaps the best-remembered domestic 'Act' of the century:

> The famous Speenhamland Act of 1795 which altered fundamentally English poor relief by making the parish responsible for making the labourer's wage up to subsistence level was merely the decision of one of those local legislatures, in this case the Berkshire magistrates, which was thereafter copied by many other Quarter Sessions until it came to have the force of law in many, but not in all areas. (Plumb, 1950, p. 35)[2]

There were several reasons for the collapse of the old local independence. After the Napoleonic Wars, in the unrest that followed victory, Sidmouth and the government in London felt no longer able to leave questions of law and order entirely to the discretion of the local authorities. R. J. White (1957, pp. 115–18) and E. P. Thompson (1968, pp. 633–4, 708) have shown the contrivances they were driven to, attempting to impose order without any machinery when some magistrates were willing but others were lazy, lacked judgement or occasionally were bluntly uncooperative. Troops were almost the only resource central government had and were used frequently, with disastrous consequences as at the Battle of Peterloo which as a result became a working-class legend. Because of its concern for order during long periods of unemployment and unrest, central government began the slow task of persuading local authorities to have police, and where they had them, to improve their quality.[3] The first major central intervention was an 1823 Prisons Act requiring a common form of organisation and statistical reporting;[4] but other police measures followed. Later, central government became interested in other, arguably more radical, measures of reform – in poor relief, public health and sanitation, and eventually education. Central government developed a common pattern of intervention. The first stage was persuasion and exhortation. The second might be model enabling legislation which it hoped local authorities might follow. Third, there was legislation which enabled it to require laggard local authorities to catch up on the practice of the better local authorities. Nineteenth-century government made use of three techniques: first, the report by Royal Commission or the like which in scope, scale and statistical support was a powerful engine of persuasion; second, the inspector checking on the performance of local authorities; and third, the use of financial grants.[5]

In the nearly hundred years between the 1835 Municipal Corporations Act marking the end of the old independence and the 1929 Local Government Act, the essential characteristics of modern local government were evolved. A vast number of functions were spontaneously developed by local authorities or were imposed by central government. While many historians now stress the pragmatic and non-ideological foundations of government intervention, it was during this period that fundamental issues were debated by men with grand conceptions about the nature of society and government, of freedom and power. It was a period when it was still considered fashionable to deduce practical consequences from general principles: a period in which the ideas of Bentham and John Stuart Mill were applied to such practical problems as the administration and inspection of the Poor Laws and the newly created public-health services, and the distribution of money from central government. The present structure of local government with all its tension grew from the interactions of the ideas and events of this period.

The first half of the period, from about 1830 to 1880, was marked by the conflict between the Benthamites led by Edwin Chadwick, 'a fanatic for administrative uniformity and centralisation' (Halévy, 1972, p. 430), and the traditionalists represented by J. Toulmin Smith for whom centralisation was synonymous with 'irresponsible control; meddling interference and arbitrary taxation' (1851, p. 54). This conflict, though relatively short, was important. It established the essential conception of a unitary system of government with its concomitant structure of administrative control. Bentham's vision of ministers for interior communication, for public assistance, for education and for health did not take long before it became a reality. The function of these ministers 'consists in entering into relations with the local assemblies, so as to inspect and to advise them. To each sublegislature is attached "a set of administrative functionaries", . . . exerting within the local field the same functions as the ministers of the whole state' (Halévy, 1972, p. 430). One would guess that Bentham would view with a sigh of contentment the current structure with its Department of the Environment, Department of Health and Social Security, Department of Education and Science; with the immense quantity of various circulars sent to local authorities, and with the most recent creation of the Consultative Council.

Moreover, it was during this period that the conception of the good being imposed from above became established. The Benthamites were changing society, not just forms of government. They were reformers of social conditions, not just political structures. It was wrong that the introduction of such obvious goods as health, education and public assistance should be blocked by local interests. They considered that 'all increase in administrative power is favourable to the rights and the interest of the people.' (Halévy, 1972, p. 430). This irritation with the power of a subunit of government to block a reform considered necessary by the political part in central power is just as evident today, whether it has been the provision of free school milk, or the charging of 'fair rents' for council housing, or the introduction of comprehensive education. It represents the essentialism of a unitary system of government which claims that the central authority is the truly representative one and no minority within it can differ, except at its pleasure.

At the beginning of the period under discussion many were sceptical about the beauties of administrative control and more suspicious of the milk and honey flowing from the centre. Many agreed with *The Economist*'s (20 May 1848) comment on the 1848 Public Health Bill: 'The bill is but the beginning of an attempt, under the pretence of providing for the public health, to regulate by legislation, by boards and commissioners every business in every town of the empire . . . ' (p. 566). In 1851 J. Toulmin Smith wrote that

> . . . the exercise of that local self government must be entirely in the hands of the districts to all matters of general management, police, public works, taxation and every class of administrative arrangement whereon the common welfare of a local community depends . . . It can never be matter of surprise that men seeking to impose schemes of their own upon the public, should strive to shackle local self government and to impose control over this or that special matter. (p. 31)

About thirty years later such views were still heard, though they were less common. As T. H. Green, the Oxford political philosopher and city councillor, who was unusual among intellectuals in his enthusiasm for local government, put it in 1889:

> We are often warned nowadays against the danger of over-legislation; or, . . . of 'grandmotherly government'. There may be good ground for the warning, but at any rate we should be quite clear what we mean by it. The outcry against state interference is often raised by men whose real objection is not to state interference but to centralisation, to the constant aggression of the central executive upon local authorities. (p. 374).

Events had overtaken the debate. What were previously views to maintain the *status quo* became views whose implementation would have required major changes in laws and existing social arrangements. In 1850 few of the functions undertaken by local authorities were compulsory. In the next fifty years legislation imposed controls over police, public health matters, roads and education.

The spirit of inspectability — of Bentham and Chadwick — and the fears it conjures up are well set out by Edwin Cannon in a way which is quite as relevant today. This was in a preface to the 1927 revision of his great work on the *History of Local Rates in England*:

> It is true that the Government offices, with perhaps one or two exceptions, are sufficiently intelligent to distrust their own capacity to administer the whole of England in detail, and honest enough not to wish to do what they know they will do badly. But unsought powers may be thrust upon them by

politicians who despair of moving local councils in what they believe to be the proper direction either by their arguments or their votes. The unofficial bureaucrat is abroad in the land, bringing before men's eyes glowing pictures of a country governed by experts who will create efficiency in every branch of national life — regardless of expense. The New Chadwickianity which is being preached is not founded on a crude system of centralisation involving the disappearance of the organs of local self-government, nor on coercion enforced by reluctant law courts. It leaves all the old forms intact and proposes to lay no rude hands on the persons of recalcitrant councillors. It is founded on the ingenious expedient of inducing the nation to allow itself to be taxed to supply funds which are to be redistributed between the various localities according to general regulations laid down by Parliament, one of which is that the locality must satisfy the inspectors of some Government department that the service in respect of which the grant is made is 'efficient'. By this expedient the citizen delivers himself bound hand and foot into the custody of the official expert, who is able, by declining to regard the service as efficient, to compel him to raise more money in rates under penalty of 'losing the grant'. It is seldom that we meet an expert who does not think that more money ought to be spent in his own particular department: the local authority or the individual ratepayer who hopes for a reduction of rates from 'efficiency grants' is only to be likened to the proverbial donkey induced to proceed by a wisp of hay hung in front of his nose. (pp. viii, ix)

The rapid growth of the number of functions undertaken by local authorities at the behest of the central government made it clear that a new question had to be asked. Or, possibly more correctly, the same question had to be asked in a much more defensive manner. Was there any area in which the local authorities should have power? Was there any principle which could be used to allocate power between the central and local governments? In 1867 John Stuart Mill gave his famous exposition on this point.

It is obvious to begin with, that all business purely local, all which concerns only a single locality, should devolve upon the local authorities. The paving, lighting, and cleansing of the streets of a town, and in ordinary circumstances the draining of its houses, are of little consequence to any but its inhabitants. The nation at large is interested in them in no other way than that in which it is interested in the private well being of all its individual citizens. But among the duties classed as local or performed by local functionaries, there are many which might with equal propriety be termed national, being the share, belonging to the locality, of some branch of the public administration in the efficiency of which the whole nation is alike interested: the gaols, for instance; . . . the local police; . . . the local administration of justice . . .' (Mill, 1910*b*, p. 354)

There is, to say the least, quite a gap between the cleansing of the streets and the administration of justice. And all the interesting issues involve exactly those functions lying between these two extremes. How many of these functions would Mill classify as purely local? The answer must be, very few. Mill soon takes away with one hand even the little that he actually gave with the other:

'The administration of the poor laws, sanitary regulations, and others, which while really interesting to the whole country, cannot be managed otherwise than by the localities' because their administration requires local knowledge. And he concludes from his analysis of such functions: 'The principal business of the central authority should be to give instruction of the local authority to apply it' (ibid., p. 357). Mill leaves little scope for local power. If so little is given to local authorities by someone for whom 'the sole end for which mankind are warranted to interfere with the liberty of action of any of their number is self protection' (ibid., pp. 72–3), the supremacy of the centre, of Parliament, was surely established. Not only constitutionally, where the question was never at issue, but intellectually as a justification for such an arrangement. In 1897 G. L. Gomme could state that 'localities have never been allowed to develop their own system of government in a natural way and that everything is now governed not by the needs of the locality, but by the cast iron mould of legislation' (Gomme, 1897, quoted in Thornhill, 1971, p. 237). Thus by the end of the nineteenth century the pattern had been set. The Benthamites' fight for centralisation and administrative control had been won in principle and largely in practice as well. There were, of course, a few skirmishes still to come and a few pockets of resistance to be eliminated but the main battle was over.

Two important concepts were established during this period which are relevant to the development of local government since then. First, local government, which in Mill's terminology is the one 'most competent in details' and therefore 'should have details left to it' became the executive arm for the carrying out of social reforms in health, education, housing and many other areas. Second, administrative control had to stay in the hands of the central authority because it 'is the most conversant with principle' and therefore 'should be supreme over principles' (Mill, 1910, p. 357). If the principles laid down are applied in the desired manner by the local authorities all is well. If the principles are not carried out as desired, it is up to the specially created ministries to give the localities information and advice, to cajole them and to exhort them. If all this fails then it is up to the central government to use the power at its disposal to enforce the correct application of the principles it has laid down. And such power must be available to it.

The increasing activity of local government in health, education, police and roads, all by now compulsory functions imposed by the central government, led to a rapid rise in expenditure rates and grants. Between 1840 and 1870 local government expenditures rose from about £11½ million to £24 million; rates rose from about £8 million to £16 million and grants from about £½ million to £2½ million. The 1840 Rate Exemption Act had finally settled the long-standing issue of what kind of property was liable for rates. Liability for rates was to be confined to fixed property only. Moreover, local authorities' expenditures were mainly on urban services. The Committee established in 1870, with Goschen as chairman, reported that of the increase in rates between 1840 and 1870 more than 75 per cent was being spent in urban areas (Finer, 1950, p. 457).

The propertied rural interests, who in the 1859s were struggling for control of local government against central imposition and administration, were now struggling against the indirect imposition of payment for functions from which they did not derive any benefits. Both the ability-to-pay principle and the benefit principle of taxation had been evoked in much of the early discussion of local government financing (see Cannon, 1927). However, whatever may be the intellectual issues involved, when the discrepancy between those who are able and those who are willing becomes large, the sensibility of the pocket tends to overcome the niceties of the theory.

Another issue began to arise in this period, one which has been a problem ever since. Up to the Goschen reforms of 1888 all central government grants were given on a percentage basis on the expenditures of the local authorities. Initially in the 1830s, the purpose of the grant was to encourage the performance of certain functions, for example education, voluntarily undertaken by the local authorities. Later as many of these functions became compulsory the grant was naturally seen as part-payment by the central government for expenditures they had imposed. By the late nineteenth century expenditures and therefore grants had risen immensely. Between 1840 and 1890 grants as a percentage of the national tax revenue rose from just over 1 per cent to over 14 per cent. The first of many future rumblings began to be heard about the growing amount of revenue being siphoned off from the central government to local governments. Moreover, because of the percentage grant system this amount depended on the expenditure decisions of the local authorities. Percentage grants initially aimed at encouraging local authorities to spend became a means by which the local authorities, by increasing their spending, could 'encourage' the central government to contribute. Then as now, Chancellors of the Exchequer did not relish the idea. In the words of one such about thirty years later the problem was that 'The local authorities call the tune and it only remains to calculate the percentage upon which the exchequer pays the piper' (Winston Churchill in 1926, quoted in Chester, 1951, p. 192).

The 1888 Local Government Act, largely inspired by Goschen, introduced the assigned revenue system. This was meant to solve both the problem of the excessive burden, relative to benefits, of the rural interests and the automatic claims on the national tax revenue arising from increases in local authority expenditures. Briefly, the financial reforms involved the assignment to local authorities of certain excise taxes (mainly beer, wine and tobacco) and for England and Wales 40 per cent of probate duty. Because these taxes were not connected directly with the ownership of real property they would alleviate the relative burden on the agricultural interests. Because local authorities were to be confined to these sources their automatic claim on the national tax revenue would be limited. The exact details of how these assigned revenues were to be allocated among the local authorities will be discussed in Part One, Chapter 5. What is important now is that the whole question of grant distribution became a new issue. As long as all grants are distributed on a percentage basis the question of how to distribute grants among local authorities does not arise. Each authority gets the same proportion of what it spends. The whole reason for the assigned revenue system was to get away from the percentage grant system, from the link between expenditures and grants.

The major issues arising in the fifty years between about 1880 and 1930 were connected with the question of how subventions from the central government were to be distributed among local authorities – a question which is still at issue today. Two considerations were important and to some extent in conflict throughout the period. First, there was the question of equity in the bearing of the tax burden on different groups. Second, there was the problem of how to control the ability of local authorities to spend more than desired by the central government and then forcing the central government to contribute via the grant system. The discussions during this period are important because they clarified the connection between the financing of local expenditures and the reasons why the expenditures were or had to be undertaken.

What the nineteenth century showed was a very strong movement away from local autonomy to centralisation, in which new legislation, discussion of tax principles and the purpose of grants were all grounds for debate and even conflict between central and local government. Another profound change was at work. Before the nineteenth century, Parliament had been both the national and the local legislature. But in the nineteenth century the volume of national and imperial legislation crowded out all but the most important local legislation. The parliamentary timetable forced a change towards general Bills covering the interests of all local authorities simultaneously. The influence of central government on such legislation was almost certain to be greater, and was yet another factor making for the growth of central power.

These were not the only developments affecting relations between central and local government, and reducing local autonomy. The *ultra vires* principle, limiting local government freedom, appeared it would seem almost by stealth (Robson, 1954, pp. 261–6). Before the first quarter of the nineteenth century, corporations – both private and public, the latter including municipal corporations – had no limit set to what they might do, provided it was not prohibited by law. Like persons, they were judged to be able to turn their mind to any lawful activity. The 1835 Municipal Corporations Act was as much a protest at local authorities doing what they should not – feasting and wining at public expense – as it was a protest against their not providing the improvements and services required. But it did not explicitly introduce the *ultra vires* principle, the notion that a local authority could not do anything not expressly provided for in a statute. This revolutionary principle emerged in the early 1840s as a reaction against the excesses of the railway companies. When these came to Parliament to apply for corporate powers it became inevitable that there should be questions on the exact powers, rights and duties conferred upon them. So the doctrine developed that the money raised was to be used for the enacted purposes of the company or corporation. This was casemade law, and a key judgement was that of Chief Baron Pollock in 1859: 'There can be no doubt that a Parliamentary Corporation is a Corporation merely for the purposes for which it is established by Act of Parliament; and it has not existence for any other purpose. Whatever is done beyond that purpose is *ultra vires* and void' (*National Manure Co. v. Donald*, quoted in Robson, 1954, p. 262). A principle that, as it happened, was formulated in relation to the National Manure Company became a major constraint on local government, simply because by the 1850s it became recognised that they, too, were parliamentary corporations. As Professor Robson (1954, p. 262) – to whose account of *ultra vires* we are indebted – noted, there seems to have been no appreciation whatever of the consequences of failing to distinguish between an elected organ of government whose franchise was not markedly different from that used to elect MPs and a railway, or for that matter the National Manure Company. From the middle of the century there were a growing number of successful attempts to use the *ultra vires* principle to limit local government activity. So began the principle as it operates to this day, making the expenditure of funds by a local authority unlawful for any purpose not expressly or implicitly authorised by a charter, statute or other instrument by which such an authority can acquire power.

The *ultra vires* principle became the basis of another instrument to limit the freedom of local authorities. Before 1782, there was no question of any audit being required of local authorities. No satisfactory audit was required of a local authority until the 1834 Poor Law Amendment Act. In 1844, district auditors were appointed for the first time. The procedure of requiring audit grew until in 1888 all counties and in 1894 all district councils, but not boroughs, were required to have external auditors – auditors who had been appointed or approved by the then relevant department of central government, the Local Government Board, since 1879. That broadly established the present system. Until 1974 these auditors were all civil servants, but since then local authorities have been able to appoint professional auditors with the approval of the Secretary of State for the Environment.

The *ultra vires* rules have given these auditors greater powers than the ones exercised by those who audit company accounts. Included among their responsibilities is deciding whether expenditure is *ultra vires* and surcharging the councillors or officials responsible if it is. Up until the mid-1920s there were fluctuations in the courts' support of the auditors against the councils. But the Poplar wage case brought about a major increase in district auditors' power. Poplar Borough Council went on paying a minimum wage of £4 a week to its employees from 1920, but by 1923 the cost of living had fallen. The £4 had not, though it was by then above comparable wage levels. The Poplar Council was Labour and it wanted to pay high wages to be a model employer. The auditor argued that £4 was excessive and surcharged the councillors. The case went up to the House of Lords and was decided in favour of the auditor. The effect of this undoubtedly had been to give district auditors great power and indirectly to increase the power of central government for which they are watchdogs observing that the national laws are obeyed (Robson, 1954, pp. 380–3). In 1973 the district auditors were required by the Department of the Environment to check that:

(i)   expenditure is authorised by law;

(ii)   the accounts comply with statutory requirements relating to such matters as capital and renewal fund contributions and balances and proper provision for loan repayment;

(iii)   income is raised in accordance with the law and reasonable rents and charges are levied;

(iv)   proper accounting practices have been observed in the compilation of the accounts, for example in the apportionment of establishment expenses to trading activities and direct works departments;

(v)   systems of internal financial control are adequate to prevent serious loss;

(vi)   there have been no serious defalcations which could be reasonably discovered by audit tests undertaken for that purpose and frauds are disclosed to the proper authority;

(vii)   The accounts do not disclose any significant loss arising from waste, extravagance, inefficient financial administration, poor value for money, mistake or other cause. (Layfield, 1976, p. 94)

During this century one must also mention the rise of another source of power which has in effect reduced the autonomy of local authorities: the professional institutions, one of whose tasks has been to strive for uniformity in practice. While they have had no open or acknowledged connection with centralising tendencies, the National Union of Teachers and other professional associations have had a persistent interest in establishing similar standards in local authorities which has gone far beyond staffing ratios, common pay scales, qualifications and conditions of work. Mobility of staff between authorities has reinforced a tendency for uniformity of practice to develop as a result of the pervasive influence of professional journals, training and conferences.

Later — in Part Two — more will be said on the apparatus of control and influence now possessed by central government; but this is a continuation and development of the methods of the nineteenth century. As the most recent inquiry into local government finance concluded: 'What has become clearly visible over recent years has been a growing propensity for the government to determine in increasing detail the pace and direction in which local services should be developed, the resources which should be devoted to them and the priorities between them' (Layfield, 1976, p. 65). While there have been statements that both Conservative and Labour governments want more local independence, in practice the centralising tendency always seems to be reaffirmed.[6] The main change in the twentieth century has been that central government has tended to rely less for control purposes on financial means. Rather it has relied on a wide range of non-financial methods.

The answer to the question 'What is the relation between central and local government in Britain?' is that though, in appearance, local has always been subordinate to central government, in reality it could hardly have varied more. During some periods in the middle ages and between the Glorious Revolution of 1688 and the 1835 Municipal Corporations Act the practical independence of local government could hardly have been greater under a federal constitution. At other times in the middle ages, under the Tudors and at times under the early Stuarts, and again in a rising curve after 1835, the power of central government has been strongly asserted. Therefore in its relations between central and local governments there have been periods when despite the unitary form of the constitution, Britain's tiers of government have practised a separation of powers more typical of federalism, and others when local government has seemed more the agent of central government.

FISCAL FEDERALISM

The difficulty in most countries of deciding the allocation of power between central and local government, has led some writers to try to distinguish between two separate theories of local government finance. The first is held to apply in federal systems only, and has been given a special name: fiscal federalism. The second would be the theory of local government finance in unitary states – which by definition are those which are not federal.

There is no question that the theory and analysis of fiscal federalism has been far better developed than that of unitary states. This is partly because much of the analysis has been done in the USA; but also because the assumption of federalism makes it possible to give definite answers to the questions we have been discussing.[7] In his classic book on federal government, Wheare defined it as follows: 'By the federal principle I mean the method of dividing powers so that the general and regional governments are each, within a sphere, co-ordinate and independent' (1963, p. 10). In other words, the tasks of local government are precisely defined and central government does not interfere with local government's performance of these tasks. It is much easier to construct a model of local government finance on the basis of such a definite difference. But there is both a theoretical and several empirical problems in accepting the pure model of fiscal federalism.

The theoretical difficulty is that federal government, so defined, runs into one of the oldest problems in political philosophy. Innumerable writers have tried to assert that there is a law – either divine or of nature – which is in some sense binding and unalterable so that it limits the discretion the government has to alter human law. Unless there is such an over-riding law, a law defining co-ordinate powers and guaranteeing independence is itself mutable. But to believe that a sovereign legislature cannot legislate about itself is, as Bentham said, an 'abuse of language' (1948, p. 95). It is a fiction to suppose that a supreme authority can exceed its authority. Indeed, successful federal governments are not perfectly co-ordinate. They must have a procedure for change – which means that either one party is ultimately subordinate to another or both are subordinate to a supreme procedure for change. Wheare meets this difficulty by defining a federal government as one with a constitution distinguishing the powers of central and local government:

> If a government is to be federal its constitution, whether it be written or un-written, or partly written and partly unwritten, must be supreme . . . If the general and regional government are to be coordinate with each other, neither must be in a position to override the terms of their agreement about the power and status which each is to enjoy. (Wheare, 1963, p. 53)

This does not, of course, avoid the theoretical difficulty as the supreme procedure must be capable of being legislated about. If that is the point in principle, then one practical problem must be solved. There must actually be a constitution which makes it possible to change the sphere of local government; but this must be through machinery other than that of the normal legislative procedures central government must go through. The cost of this pragmatic answer to the problem of sovereignty is that so few states qualify as federal. Wheare said his definition was realised in the USA, Canada, Australia and Switzerland alone. In every other case what may appear to be a federal constitution resolves into one where central government is really dominant (or very occasionally the states are virtually autonomous – as for example in the very limited federation of the EEC). In the first case local government must have some autonomy. There is likely to be some distinction between legislation and execution which will mean that central government will not be able to impose its will in all matters instantaneously without some process of law. What this surely shows is that there is a continuum. All depends on what processes central government has to go through to change the sphere and powers of local government. At one extreme there is something as difficult as constitutional change; though as we have seen, eighteenth-century English government, fortified by its own indifference, found it as difficult to change local powers by centrally motivated Acts of Parliament. At the other extreme is a central government so instantaneously and effectively autocratic that local government is its creature. In between are all sorts of positions characterised by differences in what central government needs to do to change the division of powers and therefore in the length of time the governments are likely to remain co-ordinate and independent within their spheres without change.

It may reasonably be objected that Wheare's definition of federalism concentrates on the legal position, and ignores other relationships between levels of government. Wheare himself recognises that the actual relations may be very different from what the constitution specifies. Indeed, it is on these grounds that he excludes a large number of seemingly federal systems in Europe, South America and Africa and narrows his chosen number to four.

But financial relations affect the separation of powers. Wheare agrees with the *Federalist* (1788): 'It is therefore as necessary that state governments should be able to command the means of supplying their wants, as that the national government should possess the like faculty in respect of the wants of the union' (no. 31, quoted by Wheare, 1963, p. 93).[8] Wheare notes that in all his four remaining federations, separation of powers is not paralleled by separation of finance. The lower tiers 'have accepted in varying degrees, some measure of financial subordination to the general government' (Wheare, 1963, p. 109). They all receive central government grants. Wheare sees this as an important 'modification' of the federal principle.

Whether local government compromises its freedom when it receives grants is a hotly contested issue in local government finance and will be a major issue in chapters to come. All one need note at this point is:

(1)   That in the opinion of Wheare, the greatest authority on federalism, it strictly implies separate and independent sources of finance.

(2)   That over many years there has been strong feeling in local government and elsewhere that the growing dependence on grant, which has been such a feature of UK local government in this century, has seriously eroded its remaining autonomy. This opinion was endorsed by the Layfield Committee who argued that both the fast growth and amount of grant 'powerfully reinforced the political pressure for government intervention' (Layfield, 1976, p. 66).

(3)   But that directly contrary to this is a central government view that grants need not have any effect on local authority autonomy.

Finally, as if these arguments were insufficient, in three out of the four federations considered by Wheare, what is co-ordinated by the federal constitution is national, and state government not local government at all. Only in Switzerland can it be said that the lower tier in the federal constitution is local government. The US constitution does not define the place of local government. That depends upon the various constitutions and practices of the individual states, many of whom are not federal in the sense defined by Wheare. This surely is fatal to any belief that one can have a situation which can be analysed as purely federal.

If federation in any rigorous sense is not a good description of the relation between any central and its local government, then fiscal federalism which assumes that central and local government are co-ordinate and independent cannot be a complete basis for the theory of local government finance.

It would be utopian to expect such a radical transformation of local government and the British constitution that it would correspond with federalism defined as the separation of powers based on distinct functions with defined purposes. Yet the insights of fiscal federalism, and indeed of political federalism, are helpful in understanding local finance in all states. Framers of federal constitutions have attempted a separation of powers and duties which allows each level of government to get on with its tasks without interference from the other levels. But to survive, any constitution must have within it a procedure for change so that the responsibilities of the tiers may be altered as circumstances change. Nevertheless, to maintain stability the constitution must make revision difficult. One American writer on fiscal federalism defines its crucial characteristic as 'simply that different levels of decisionmaking do exist, each of which determines levels of provision of particular public services in response largely to the interests of the geographical constituency' (Oates, 1972, p. xvi). However, such a definition can be interpreted to cover almost any situation. Let us define quasi-federalism as a situation where at any one time there is clear division of powers and duties between central and local government. That is, when local government is free to take decisions where it has responsibility, even though there is no federal and distinct mechanism for change. In that weaker sense Britain was for a long time a quasi-federal state. Such a quasi-federalism may be based on the national legislature defining the co-ordinate responsibilities of both central and local government. The central government, in effect, can alter the powers of both, but between the necessary legislative changes the powers of the two are fixed and probably capable of policing by the judicature. Such a quasi-federalism would presumably be consistent with the behaviour of a highly autocratic state in which central government by a self-denying ordinance restricted its own powers over subordinate levels of government; though such devolution is unlikely in any but a democratic state. The essence of quasi-federalism is, therefore, that at any time the respective powers and duties of the respective tiers should be defined, and procedures for any changes in these definitions be themselves clearly defined. For quasi-federalism to have any interest, changes could not be too frequent.

Seen in this light, quasi-federalism was what the Layfield Committee of Inquiry wanted. Its avowed enemy in local finance was confusion. 'The present arrangements do not make clear where the real responsibility for spending lies . . . ' (Layfield, 1976, p. 41; also pp. 36, ch. 3 *passim*, pp. 64 ff., 238, 254). It asked central government to choose between such a federal solution in that weak sense and another in which local government was an agent, though it used the terms 'systems of central and local responsibility' to describe these policies.

> It is our view that a decision now needs to be taken to place responsibility firmly either with the government or with local authorities. This means either adopting a financial system which frankly recognises a need for strong central direction or taking positive steps to increase the ability of local authorities to manage local affairs. If this is not done we believe there is bound to be an increasing shift of power to the centre, but in circumstances in which responsibility for expenditure and local taxation will continue to be confused. (ibid, p. 74)

In its reply to the Layfield Report, the government avoided either alternative, selecting what it saw as a middle way, but which was really a deliberate decision to continue with confusion.

> The Government accepts that the dividing line between central and local responsibilities is not always clear. There are many reasons for this. The central/local relationship is changing all the time because national economic and social priorities can alter substantially even within quite short periods. Nevertheless the change in emphasis in the relative responsibilities of central and local government remains compatible with a well-understood and accepted constitutional relationship. Any formal definition of central and local responsibilities would lack the advantages of flexibility and rapidity of response to new circumstances. It would be likely to break down under the pressure of events. The Government's view is, therefore, that while clarification of responsibilities, wherever practicable, is desirable, redefinition is not necessary as a basis for solving the problems of local government finance . . . (DoE, 1977*b*, Cmnd. 6813, p. 34)

While refusing a quasi-federal solution, central government also rejects the idea that local government is its agent. In the same Green Paper it argued that it was central government's job 'to secure and promote an effective local democracy with genuine political choice' (p. 4).

THE AGENCY THEORY OF GOVERNMENT

At a polar extreme from federalism is what is often called the agency theory of local government. Given the rising curve of central intervention, it is not surprising that until recently it has been the dominant theory among political scientists and lawyers who have studied local government.[9] Its implications are not as well worked out. It would seem to see local authorities as carrying out central policies with little discretion. Two reasons for such central dominance adduced by many writers are as follows. First, the growing reliance of local authorities on central grants.[10] The oft-cited phrase which we have already seen used in an almost opposing sense has been that 'who pays the piper calls the tune'. The second reason is that there is a 'prevailing desire for uniformity of public services'. (Marshall, 1960, p. 15; see also Smellie, 1968, p. 108; Redlich and Hirst, 1970, Vol. 2, p. 155). Central government intervenes because public opinion does not want local discretion over standards provided.

These reasons for growing central intervention are of different status, incomplete and in part questionable. The first refers to a mechanism central government possesses: grants. But as Professor Griffith has shown there are many other weapons used to influence local authorities, statutory and non-statutory, formal and informal (1966, *passim*). Of these weapons, grants as such may now be among the least important. While it is true – we shall be analysing the development in Part One, Chapter 7 – that once many grants were specific enough to be described as enabling 'the Central Government to purchase many of the administrative powers it now possesses' (Chester, 1951, p. 84), this is not true of a block grant which local government is at least formally free to spend as it pleases; and which has been the predominant form of grant since 1958. We shall see that central government is surely right to argue that a high proportion of block grant as such does not give it such power over local expenditure though it is a major factor in making it harder for local governments to resist the influence exerted by central government in the numerous ways Professor Griffith has described.

The second reason for believing in the agency theory is that uniformity is what the nation wants and indeed, as we have seen, this was the presumption that was behind the Benthamite view which was so influential in the nineteenth century. But a desire for uniformity is only part of it. Mill puts it far more generally as a belief that central government should lay down policies, and inspect to see that local authorities carry them out wisely and honestly. Though no doubt important in explaining the influence of the agency theory, it again is incomplete as it leaves out other important aspects of central control – for example in the interests of macroeconomic policy.

But as Dearlove points out, the agency theory in any pure form runs into difficulties as an account of what exists (1973, pp. 11–20). If grant were so influential, then one would expect the influence of central government to vary with the proportion of the revenue local government receives in grant (which can vary from almost zero in the City of London to not far short of 100 per cent in a few rural authorities), but there is no evidence for this. More damagingly, if uniformity were central government's objective and it had the power to achieve this, how does one explain so much diversity of provision between local authorities in most services? It defeats reason to believe that the diversity that exists reflects the achieved ambition of central government.

Like federalism the agency theory has some value as a model; but in what consists the essence of the theory? To suppose that central government determines all local decisions absolutely is, of course, absurd.

THE AGENCY THEORY OF LOCAL GOVERNMENT

Economic theory provides an analogy by which it is possible to give more content to the notion of local government as the agent for central government. The arguments will not have to be detailed until near the end of the book, when it will become important to be more precise in discussing the problem of optimum size of government (Part Four, Chapter 6). Here a sketch is enough.

The analogy is with a firm. If government is regarded as the head office, then local government can be seen as analogous to its subsidiaries. As in 100 per cent-owned subsidiaries there is no question that ultimate control lies at the top: the board of directors in the one case, government in the other.

Such central sovereignty, however, is not inconsistent with considerable delegation of power. Neither a board of directors nor central government is wise if it tries to control everything. Lower levels will be given discretionary limits within which they can practise freedom. Very great delegation of practical freedom may be consistent with a central authority retaining all ultimate power. In an extreme, the agency theory could apply to a dictatorial state. Central government might allow its local authorities great latitude, but be able to impose its will whenever it so decides. While one must not be misled by words, the 1977 Green Paper on local government finance shows a central government using words that, not for the first time, seem to indicate that this is the relationship that they believe ultimately exists between central and local governments (DoE, 1977*b*, Cmnd. 6813).

In such a polar unitary state, the devolution of power becomes entirely a question of what is efficient. In favour of centralisation only are economies of scale. Against it are diseconomies of scale of which the most important tend to be administrative. Economists call these 'control-loss' diseconomies. If a management or a government centralises too many decisions (or is too arbitrary and quick in altering the limits of local decision) there will be congestion and inefficiency at the centres. Therefore, as government grows in its power and scope there is bound to be an increase in the practical freedom allowed lower echelons unless ever-growing congestion is to be tolerated. Even then unchecked congestion reduces the effective power of those at the top.

The difficulty confronting the student of local government finance is twofold. Even if he were to find a statement which was overtly and precisely claiming a state to be federal or unitary, such a statement of the constitution is not really to be believed. There are no pure federal states. In all states, central government seeks to influence local government. Even highly authoritarian states must, in practice, allow some freedom to their local authorities. But constitutions rarely are explicit. It is well known that Britain has no written constitution, but many other states that do have one are not explicit on the relations between central and local government, and on where the powers lie. Therefore, the second difficulty a student of local government finance has is to try to decide what government – both central and local – and indeed the law, think are the relations that obtain between the two tiers of government – a matter often no less obscure than the actual working relationships themselves.

However, in thinking about local government finance, whether in a federal or a unitary state, it is worth distinguishing between federalism or quasi-federalism, and devolved authority as in a firm, that is the agency concept of the relationship between central and local government. The former does suggest that the relationship should be explicit and plainly stated as the Layfield Committee recommended. The relevance of speculation on the nature of federalism, as in Wheare's analysis, is that it makes us wonder if even the state of clarity we have called quasi-federalism can be achieved without some institutional change. We do not take these matters up again until the end of the book, but it is at least arguable that some major changes in the power given to local authorities within the constitution might be helpful in dispelling the confusion to which the Layfield Committee objected.

CONCLUSIONS

(1) England, and after it the United Kingdom, has always been a unitary state in which any local government has been constitutionally subordinate to the crown in Parliament.

(2) Yet this unchanging constitutional position has been consistent with the widest variation in local autonomy.

(3) From the Glorious Revolution until the 1830s, the activities of local government were not only immune from central control and interest but domestic government was almost synonymous with local government.

(4) During the nineteenth century, central government influence revolutionised the position. The inability of local government to maintain law and order dramatically increased the interest of central government in local affairs. But all the tendencies during the nineteenth century were for central government to press reform on local government rather than for it to rely on local authorities developing their own momentum.

(5) Central government used a number of instruments to increase its influence – legislation, grants, the development of the *ultra vires* principle and that of the district auditor being among them.

(6) It has been common in the theory of local government finance for a distinction to be made between federal and unitary states in the belief that a different kind of theory was appropriate to each. Reflection suggests that while the essential federal notions that central and local government are co-ordinate and independent within their spheres would be helpful, both in theory and in practice it cannot be made operational. Thus, the clear-cut distinction between federal and unitary local finance breaks down.

Nevertheless, it is vital to decide whether one believes that local government should have a clear sphere of influence within which it is free to act even within a unitary constitution; or if central government must have such over-riding right to deal flexibly with local authorities when its own interests require this.

NOTES

1   The Webbs (1963, pp. 4, 5) instanced poor relief between 1590 and 1640, and the arbitrary regulation of the municipal corporations between 1638 and 1640 as the most intensive exercises of royal power towards local authorities in the sixteenth and seventeenth centuries.

2   Pitt tried to make Speenhamland into an Act of Parliament, but failed. See Halévy, 1972, p. 297.

3   Thompson (1968, pp. 89, 90) has shown how much Tory, Whig and Radical objection there was even to local police forces because they were seen as encroachment by the state.

4   Clark (1962, Ch. 4) has stressed the growth of interest in the collection of statistics as a means of extending central government knowledge and interest – of which this is among the earliest examples.

5   See Roberts (1960, Chs. 6 and 7) for the development of these techniques in the second quarter of the nineteenth century.

6   Contrast Ministry of Housing and Local Government, (1970, Cmnd. 4276) and Department of the Environment (1971a, Cmnd. 4741) which talk of more local independence, with Department of the Environment (1977b, Cmnd. 6813, pp. 3–4) which reaffirms the supremacy of central government and proposes increasing its power. But there are earlier forerunners of both.

7   Contrast Musgrave's (1959, pp. 179–82) treatment of pure federalism with the little he has to say that is precise about 'impure' federalism.

8   This is almost precisely the view taken by the Layfield Committee (1970, p. 78).

9   Robson (1933); Jennings (1947); Green (1959); Jackson (1965); Robson (1966).

10 Cole (1921, pp. 4–5); Finer (1950); Chester (1951); West Midland Study Group (1956, p. 2); Marshall (1960, p. 153); Jackson (1965, p. 267); Robson (1966, p. 149); Hepworth (1976, pp. 14–15).

3 The Division of Labour between Central and Local Government

The growth of local expenditure has been determined by the growth of total government expenditure and the allocation of this between central and local government. It is because these influences have varied between countries that the composition of local output varies and international statistical comparisons are perilous. Yet despite differences in what local governments provide, there are extraordinary similarities. In country after country one finds many of the same goods and services being provided by local government. This suggests there may be underlying reasons why some activities are generally held more suitable for local government. Several British authors before the First World War and American authors since the Second World War have been particularly interested in the problem. We shall begin the chapter by considering ideas on the goods and services that government in general is best fitted to provide, and follow this by distinguishing between what central and local government is the most appropriate for, before looking at the actual division of labour that has emerged in Britain.

THE FUNCTIONS OF GOVERNMENT

Before trying to distinguish between the functions of central and local government, we could list what government in general, or any particular government, does. However, the historical development of his subject inevitably inclines an economist to tackle the matter differently. He asks what it is that has to be done by government; or rather what it is that cannot be done by individuals or free associations of individuals, that is by private enterprise.

Most economists would agree that the economic functions of government would include at least the following (cf. Shoup, 1969, pp. 3, 5; Samuelson, 1955, pp. 355–6).

(1) To provide goods and services that cannot be provided by private enterprise, or if provided could only be provided inefficiently. These are called public goods.[1]
(2) To redistribute income (or wealth), or commodities.
    Each function needs some further explanation:

(1) PUBLIC GOODS

As used by economists 'public goods' has a precise meaning.[2] Private goods and services are those which can be supplied efficiently in a free market by private producers. Public goods are those which will not be provided by private producers even if it is efficient to provide such goods, or if provided privately they will be provided inefficiently. This does not mean that such goods must be physically produced by government or public enterprise, though they often are. If privately produced, they must be subsidised to achieve an efficient output.

If this is so, what determines whether a good is a public good? Economists have postulated two defining characteristics:

(a) *Non-excludability*
The first is called non-excludability. A good will not be produced efficiently if it is impossible to charge consumers for the output they consume. Lighthouses are a classic case of goods from whose consumption one cannot be excluded by charging. Similarly, it is impracticable or unprofitable or inefficient to charge the individual consumer for many services provided by government. Examples are the lighting and cleaning of streets, the administration of justice, the management of prisons and of the police. To take but one of these examples, it is possible to imagine some police services being charged for — for example the protection of property — but impossible to imagine the police stopping to ask which private person is going to pay them before making any arrest. Thus services which cannot be charged for may be provided more efficiently publicly.

(b) *Non-rivalness*
The second characteristic of public goods has been named non-rivalness. By this is meant that more of the good can be consumed without adding to the costs of the service. This is obviously true of lighthouses and television services. Their running costs are not affected by the number of passing ships or viewers. Once the cost of the overheads is incurred, the marginal cost of providing services to addititional consumers is zero. Among local services that have this characteristic (at least to the point of congestion) are museums and art galleries, the street system, parks and recreation centres. By a long-established economic argument, if a good has zero marginal cost, then it is economically efficient to charge nothing for it, and recoup overheads in some other way, usually through taxation. Dupuit, to whom we owe the argument, used a bridge as his main example (Dupuit, 1844, in Arrow and Scitovsky, 1969). Once built, he assumed it cost virtually nothing to maintain. Anyone crossing derived a clear benefit from doing so. Otherwise he would not cross. As the real cost of his crossing was nothing, zero charges conferred benefits without any losses. If a charge were made and anyone was priced off the facility, there would be a loss of benefit without any corresponding real gain.

It can be seen that these two characteristics provide very different arguments for public provision. One refers to the impracticality of charging, the other to an inefficiency in doing so. Virtually no government services have these two characteristics absolutely. Nevertheless, the concept is useful because upon analysis many goods that government provides are characterised by having beneficiaries — some or all — who cannot be charged and by high overheads and low marginal costs.

The characteristics of non-excludability and non-rivalness which define a public good are characteristics of the benefits provided by the good. Thus what is a public good depends both on technological characteristics and on a decision defining the benefits to which the characteristics are to be applied. Consider two not unimportant examples, one taken from health and one from education. Both curing an illness and preventing an illness are goods. Let us consider toothache and measles. Curing toothache and curing measles are both private goods. Charging is possible and those who do not pay will not acquire the benefits. Similarly, non-rivalness does not apply; there is a positive marginal cost of extra consumption. However, the good 'preventing an illness' is private for toothache but not for measles. Inoculation against measles will provide this benefit not only to the one inoculated but also to others. Because measles is infectious others cannot be excluded from the benefit (nor would it be efficient to do so) and this benefit can be provided to more consumers without any extra cost. However, a dental checkup might prevent future toothache to the individual getting the checkup, but it is still a private good. The benefits accrue only to him.

Is education a private or a public good? To answer this we have to ask what benefit is provided by education. If we say that education only increases the earning power of the individual educated, or it makes his life more pleasant because it increases his opportunities for enjoyment then education is a private good. If, however, we believe that a literate electorate improves the working of a democracy or improves the quality of life for all, then these benefits have the characteristics of a public good.[3] Thus even though non-excludability and non-rivalness do not apply to the actual teaching, i.e. the actual provision of education, they do apply to the benefits we consider are being provided.

The above discussion should make it clear that though the characteristics defining public goods are quite precise, the goods which possess these characteristics may not be clearly defined until some agreement is reached as to the benefits they provide. This makes the concept of public goods more difficult to apply. It nevertheless retains its usefulness. The decision about which goods are public goods may be dependent on a judgement about the value of the benefits to others; it thus may be a 'political decision'. However, the usefulness of the concept, and as we shall see, the way it has been applied in discussions of financing of local government, is that once such a decision is made it has certain implications about how the provision of such a good should be financed.

The provision of public goods follows from a concern for an efficient allocation of resources. If one considers a good like a lighthouse or a museum that cannot be efficiently provided privately because of non-excludability or non-rivalness, then government's role could be to provide lighthouses or museum services to the extent which maximised the surplus of social benefits over social costs.[4]

There is an old term, 'beneficial', which we will use to describe public goods where the motive behind the provision is of this kind. The costs of a beneficial public good could be recouped from those that benefit from it *if* a method of charging the individual consumer could be found so that each consumer was ready to pay a sum which collectively equalled the cost of provision and was equal or less than the value each consumer derived from it. However, because of non-excludability or non-rivalness or both, consumers cannot by assumption be charged as if it were a private good. This raises the question of how such goods should be financed.

(2) REDISTRIBUTION

Another way of defining a beneficial good is that its provision is not primarily motivated by redistributive considerations. Redistribution may be either in cash or kind. Local authorities do engage in cash redistribution i.e. income transfers. But the motive for the provision of some goods may also be redistributive. To this end their provision is subsidised. The old name for this in public finance was 'onerous'. Thus onerous public goods are characterised by some citizens paying to provide benefits for others. Thus poor relief from time immemorial has been a burden on the more affluent to help the indigent; and there are many other examples of public services which are onerous on groups of individuals who on redistributive grounds pay more than the value to them of what they receive.

The motive behind redistribution may be itself either redistributive or paternalistic. We need to distinguish the two. The former reflects an underlying judgement that what is desired is the transfer of income (or wealth) from some groups to others, notably the poor, to spend as they please. The provision of redistributive goods and services may be a means to this end, less direct but more practical, it is sometimes alleged, than cash transfers. Paternalism reflects a very different policy – the desire to impose on consumers more of a good or service than they would freely pay for if the same subsidy were transferred to them as cash. Sometimes this is in what is said to be their own 'real interest'. Private goods are also sometimes subsidised and thus provided redistributively or paternalistically.

The concepts used to allocate functions between the government and the private sectors have also been applied within a context of fiscal federalism to allocate functions between local and central government. The allocation function of local government is conceived of as providing local public goods. The distribution function of local government is much more problematic.

(a) *Allocation*

The case for local authorities providing local public goods is that it is more efficient for them to do so. We need to distinguish between central and local public goods. A public good which would obviously be more sensibly provided by central government is one whose benefits extend to the whole nation. Even here there is an element of judgement, but among those that most people would agree to be of this kind are defence, justice and the prison service. The argument for central provision in such cases is that if such services are provided by local authorities, there will normally be underprovision. Each local government in considering how much it will provide will take into account the benefits its citizens will derive and not those experienced by the citizens of other communities. For example, while public television or radio services could be provided by local authorities they would only be able to raise taxes from their own citizens, while they could not prevent others watching or listening to their programmes. This results in a 'free-rides' problem. As Olson and Zeckhauser put it:

Each gets only a fraction of the benefits of any collective good that is provided, but each pays the full cost of any additional amounts of the collective good. This means that the individual members have an incentive to stop providing the collective good long before the Pareto-optimal output for the group has been provided. This is particularly true of the smaller members, who get smaller shares of the total benefits accruing from the good, and who find that they have little incentive to provide additional amounts of the collective good once the larger members have provided the amounts they want for themselves, with the result that the burdens are shared in a disproportionate way. (1966, pp. 278–9; see also Oates, 1972)

By contrast, there are local public goods whose benefits do not need to extend beyond local boundaries. The parks, libraries, lighting and street-cleaning operations of local government are local goods. Some non-citizens may benefit, but these will be relatively small in number in relation to the benefits derived by citizens. The geography of benefits will not be such that the benefits of all local public goods come to an end at what are historically or artificially determined local boundaries. This does present problems for the drawing of such boundaries which we shall have to consider when we come to consider 'optimal size in local government' in Part Four, Chapter 6. At present we can make do with a commonsense distinction, of the kind Mill was striving after, between such goods and services that are of national or merely local interest.

The argument for local provision is also that the form of the goods or services provided can reflect local tastes and preferences. Non-excludability and non-rivalness mean that many public goods and services are provided in a fairly standard form. If their nature is determined locally, it will better reflect local preferences.[5] It is also likely that diversity in provision will mean more innovation and experiment (Ostrom, Tiebout and Warren, 1961; Tullock, 1969a; Oates, 1972); that local decision makers and citizens are likely to have a better understanding of the latters' needs in a small community (Tullock, 1969; Oates, 1972); that a closer relationship between expenditure and revenue-raising decisions will make local government more efficient than central government (Oates, 1972).

Moreover, the population of a local government will be more homogeneous in its tastes and preferences than that of central government, particularly if local governments are numerous and have small populations; but almost invariably so, relative to central government. Left to itself a poor area will want to provide a different package of goods and services from that of a rich area. An area with fewer children and more old people will again provide differently from another with many children – one with many working wives again differently from one with few. Such product differentiation is self-reinforcing, as it encourages citizens to move where they feel they gain most from the goods and services provided, net of rates and other local taxes or charges, that is, where their own negative fiscal wedge (the difference between benefits and taxes) is least. This last proposition is important in local government finance. Now known as the Tiebout hypothesis, the germ of it is to be found in Alfred Marshall and in Edwin Cannan, who believed they saw it at work in nineteenth-century and early twentieth-century Britain (Marshall, 1926; Cannan, 1927; Tiebout, 1956). It will be far from the only influence on migration, but because households will tend to gravitate towards areas providing the public goods and services they want at tax prices they want to pay, there will be a greater homogeneity of tastes and preferences in a local than in a central population.

(b) Redistribution

The larger a government jurisdiction, the more feasible is redistribution between its citizens (Rothenberg, 1970; Oates, 1972). One reason reversing the last argument is that the larger a jurisdiction, the more heterogeneous its population will be. Some difference in circumstances — for example, in income — is needed if redistribution is to be meaningful. For example, the relatively affluent South-East of England is better able to transfer income to the relatively poorer regions through a national system of redistribution, than any poorer region can pursuing its own internal policy of redistribution.[6]

Even if it is free, local government is limited in the redistribution it can engage in. This also follows from the Tiebout hypothesis. If any one jurisdiction acts so as to increase the fiscal wedge against some of its citizens, they will tend to move out. Hence the flight to the suburbs characteristic of American large cities as the affluent withdraw to areas where the amount of redistribution is less. While local governments may want to redistribute in either cash or kind, mobility will be a strong discouragement. A more equal distribution of income would be achieved, but through the emigration of the rich and possibly also the immigration of the poor, a fall in average real income per head will occur. In a nutshell that is the plight of New York.

To avoid some of these problems local authorities would have to have the power to control migration. Even in countries with a strong federalist tradition such power is not conceded to local authorities. Moreover, redistribution is based on some concept of equity which even in a federalist system is applied to all the members of the federality. Thus in the terminology of the last section it is considered a public good which is public over the whole country, not just a locality. It is for these reasons that redistribution is considered the province of the central government even in a federalist system.

The distinction between beneficial and onerous goods is mirrored by a traditional distinction in the types of taxation to be used to finance government expenditure. At least since Adam Smith two notions of taxation have been considered by economists, the benefit principle and the ability-to-pay principle. The first is essentially non-redistributive, though it may result in some net redistributions. The second is essentially redistributive in aim. According to the first principle, people should be taxed according to the benefits they receive from the expenditures on which the taxes are spent. If such benefits were known with certainty the difference between the tax levied on an individual and the benefits received by the individual would be zero. The services provided through taxation would be on a par with those acquired privately in the market. It would be as though the individual were buying these services from the government. Of course, if the government is providing public goods, charging is not possible because of non-excludability and not efficient because of non-rivalness. The tax would thus have to be based on some approximation of benefit received by the individual or group that is being taxed. Thus there would still be some redistribution. Some individuals would receive benefits whose value to them is greater than the tax they pay, some would by paying taxes which were greater than the value of the benefits they receive. There would be a fiscal wedge. It should be stressed, however, that such redistributions are unintended. They arise because of a lack of information about individual tastes for the goods provided and thus their evaluation of these goods. They arise not from any considerations of equity but from ignorance.

The ability-to-pay principle, on the other hand, is essentially redistributive. It is based on some equity judgement about the distribution of income or wealth. The underlying judgement would be as valid on direct redistributions of income even if the government did not provide any goods or services. If redistributions occur with a combination of provision of goods and taxation according to the ability-to-pay principle there may also be some unintended redistribution. It may be true, for example, that people with ability to pay also derive greater benefits from the goods provided by the government and, therefore, that the net redistribution is zero even though one is using the ability-to-pay principle on the tax side. But the aim is specifically redistributive.

These parallel notions of beneficial and onerous public goods and the associated principles of taxation, the benefit and ability-to-pay principles, dominated the debates about central and local government in the nineteenth and early part of the twentieth centuries. They were applied to resolve the problem of the allocation of responsibility between central and local government and, to an even greater extent, to the allocation of financial responsibility among the two tiers of government.

THE FUNCTIONS OF LOCAL GOVERNMENT

We can trace the discussion of this problem from the same passage of John Stuart Mill's (1910*b*, p. 354) we quoted in Part One, Chapter 2, p. 25. We cited it then to show that though Mill seemed to distinguish roles for both central and local government, the practical tendency of his argument was to leave small scope for local power. Despite that conclusion, Mill set down in that passage the principles which have governed both abstract theoretical discussion of these issues and practical attempts to resolve the problem. The ideas on public goods, redistribution and paternalism as an aid to distinguish the functions of central and local government can be seen developing in successive discussions of the problem.

Mill went on to classify those activities undertaken by local authorities in three groups (1910*b*, pp. 354–7):

(1)   Some — the paving, lighting and cleaning of streets — were of no national interest as one area could adopt a low or a high standard virtually without affecting the rest of the country.

(2)   There were others — justice, prisons and police — where it would be intolerable to the nation if any area fell short of the rest of the country, and which, therefore, it was illogical to provide as local services.

(3)   Finally, there were those —poor relief and the sanitation laws — whose administration had to be local because the detail varied so much from place to place, but where some uniformity in provision was a matter of national interest as it was with justice or the police.

In this were the germs of important ideas which Mill did not himself work out. First, on the demand side, whether or not a service should be local depends on whether the demand is only local and so what is provided is a matter of indifference to the rest of the nation. Second, on the supply side, the area of provision should be influenced by how far there are diseconomies of scale in attempting to manage at the national level services that are of more than local interest. Hence Mill's third group.[7]

Mill did not go far in probing the characteristics of a service which made its demand local or national. A few years later Goschen produced the seeds of a more fundamental analysis (1872, p. 10).[8] Local rates may be in 'discharge of burden'. By this he meant that ratepayers were paying to provide services for other citizens, generally poorer and non-ratepayers. Or they 'conferred direct and immediate benefits'. They provided services which were of direct value to the ratepayer. These ideas were developed by Cannan and Marshall into the more precise notions of onerous and beneficial local expenditures. Does the ratepayer get back at least the value of what he pays in the value of the services he receives? Thus far the expenditure is 'beneficial'. The rates he pays are 'beneficial' to him. Or does he pay more in rates than the value he, or his household, receives? To that extent his rates are 'onerous'. He is paying for services for others.

It was the Royal Commission on Local Taxation of 1901 (Cd. 638) and later the Kempe Committee in 1914 (Cd. 7315) who applied more clearly the distinction to the question of the financing of local expenditures.

Although both the Majority and the Minority Report of the 1901 Royal Commission made the distinction between national and local services, we shall concentrate on the Minority Report. It contains a much more coherent analysis of the principles of local government and a much more consistent application of these principles to the question of financing.

The chief characteristic of the class of services which we have described as national or quasi-national appear to be these:

(a) The locality is *required* by the State to undertake them, and uniform principles for their administration have been laid down by the Central Authority.

(b) Though undertaken by the locality for the purposes of administrative convenience, they are really services which, to a large extent, are performed *in the interest of the community at large* [italics in original] .

(c) Like the other national services which are administered by the Central Authority they do not as a rule confer any direct benefits upon the individual ratepayer or taxpayer.

The services which fall into the second category are, on the other hand, to a large extent:

(a) *Optional* — that is to say, the locality has a wide discretion as to the extent to which, and the manner in which, the services shall be performed: and

(b) *Directly Beneficial*, either to the individual ratepayer or to his immediate neighbourhood.

On the whole we are disposed to think that the best and simplest test which can be applied in order to determine the class to which any particular service belongs is the degree in which the ratepayer or the owner of rateable property derives direct or immediate benefit from it. (*Final Report*, Cd. 638, p. 123)

They label the first group of services as national and expenditure on them as 'onerous', and the second category of services as local and the expenditures on them as 'beneficial'. They then list the following services undertaken by local authorities as belonging to the 'onerous' class: poor relief and other services administered by Poor Law authorities; police and criminal prosecution; asylums for pauper lunatics; sanitary officers' salaries; main roads and county bridges, and education (technical and elementary). The implication they draw from their analysis for financing is that

the primary principles to be aimed at are (1) that persons should contribute as far as is reasonably practical, to 'onerous' expenditure *according to their ability to pay*. and (2) that they should contribute as far as is reasonably practical, to 'beneficial' expenditure *according to benefits received*. (ibid., p. 124)

The logical conclusion of the analysis should have been to transfer all the national services to the central government, or to finance them completely from the central revenues. Why did they not carry the logic of their argument to where it clearly led? The answer is of interest because it shows the conflict that is induced by, possibly necessary, compromise. This conflict has been the cause of much of the tension between the central and local governments over the last hundred years. The argument against the transfer of the services to the central government is based on the nature of the services:

the services in question are of such a nature as to make local management almost indispensible, because there must be investigation and minute supervision on the spot, and there ought to be personal knowledge of individuals and circumstances . . . Then again, the transfer of administrative duties from the Local Authorities to the State would be a reversal of the policy deliberately adopted for many years past . . . of extending and encouraging local government. More important still is the fact that . . . there is too great a tendency already toward centralisation — that the State has already, as things are, more than enough of duties to perform, more than enough of responsibility to bear, and more than enough of employees to manage; and that any additional strain on the official machinery might involve the risk of a breakdown. (ibid., p. 121)

If the services are such that they cannot be transferred to the central government, why should they not be financed completely by the central government? The answer to this is simple: 'It is obvious . . . that the responsibility for the raising of funds cannot be wholly divorced from those who administer the service . . . the Imperial subvention . . . cannot represent more than a proportion of the "onerous" expenditures' (ibid., p. 124). In fact they recommend that the subvention should never be greater than 50 per cent.

Here we have the source of the conflict. The services are national, but administrative efficiency requires that they be performed locally. The ability-to-pay principle which is supposed to apply to the national services would imply that they should be financed wholly from the national revenue, but administrative efficiency requires that they should be partly financed from local revenues, because the divorce of administration of expenditures and financing responsibility leads to inefficiency. If local taxes were not collected on the basis of ability to pay, as it was agreed they were not, the equity principle would have to succumb to the requirements of administrative efficiency. The Minority Report recognised the problem and tried to develop a scheme for the distribution of grants which would alleviate the inequity. In their grant distribution formula they incorporated a measure of a locality's ability to pay in terms of its rateable value.[9] Their suggestions for such a scheme and the powerful arguments they put forward for it lay dormant for nearly fifty years. Not until the Exchequer Equalisation Grant of 1948 did it come to fruition.

None of the changes recommended by the 1901 Royal Commission were introduced, but the problems which had inspired its deliberations continued to increase. Expenditures, especially on those services which the Commission had classified as national, continued to rise. Between 1890 and 1911 such expenditures had risen from about £18 million to £55 million. The assigned revenue system introduced in 1888 was slowly crumbling. New, specific grants were being introduced only a year after the beginning of the assigned revenue system. And these continued at an increasing rate over the next twenty years. There were also major changes made to the system. The most important of these were the 1910 Finance Act and the 1911 Revenue Act, whereby only fixed amounts of revenue from the various assigned taxes went into the local taxation account. The major premise underlying the Goschen system was that rising local expenditures would be met from the rising yield from the assigned taxes. By 1912, it was clear that this premise was based on an underestimation of the rise in local expenditures and an overestimation of the central government's willingness to give up its claim on a lucrative source of revenue.

The Departmental Committee on Local Taxation reporting in 1914 was set up to look once again at the relationship between central and local taxation. They based their analysis on the Minority Report of the 1901 Royal Commission. However, they did add a very crucial distinction to that analysis. The Minority Report had concluded that the national ('onerous') services carried out by local authorities ought in principle to be wholly financed from the national revenue. Only considerations of administrative efficiency prevented such an arrangement. The 1914 Committee disagreed.

Besides national and local services, they added another class of services which they called semi-national. The characteristic of these services was that the benefits they yielded did not accrue completely to the nation, nor completely to the locality but in some proportion to both. Thus even on the basis of the benefit principle of taxation the payment for these services should be divided between the national and the locality. Moreover, they argued that the services which had been grant-aided belonged to this semi-national category. On the basis of their distinction the Committee rejected the assigned revenue system and the suggested equalising element included in the Minority Report of 1901.[10]

The Committee does not examine the central–local relationship with respect to compulsion and uniformity of administration for these semi-national services. But their conception of this relationship is clear:

> We would point out that the claim which is sometimes put forward on behalf of local authorities for some check on the demands of the Central Government is based upon a misapprehension of their constitutional position. They are not, as appears to be thought, co-ordinate authorities and their revenues are not independent of Parliament. They and their revenues are, in fact, the creations of Parliament and subject to its control, direct and indirect. (Kempe, 1914, Cd. 7315, p. 22)

The Kempe Committee took the discussion as far as it has been taken in British public thinking. On this matter, subsequent White Papers and Green Papers and indeed the Report of the Layfield Committee have been reticent.

THE DIVISION OF LABOUR

As late as the first decade of this century, virtually all public (domestic) goods and services enjoyed by the citizen were supplied by local government. In 1905, out of the £114 million spent by central government,[11] 77 per cent was on defence, overseas services and the National Debt (which in those days was deferred payment for past wars). The remainder, £26 million, was about a fifth of local government expenditure in that year. Almost half was for the upkeep of Parliament, the civil service and the judiciary. Less than £14 million, or £0.30 per annum per head, was spent on a motley collection of social, economic and environmental services.

If we go back in time and consider local government's most ancient functions we find these to be both allocative and redistributive. From the middle ages local government was building bridges, local roads and various other public works which had 'public goods' characteristics, as we have defined them. It was either difficult to charge for their use — non-excludability — or inefficient to do so — non-rivalness. It appears as if the increased capital expenditure of the 1870s and 1890s was largely of this kind: Joseph Chamberlain described his mayoralty in Birmingham between 1873 and 1876 as the years in which that city was 'parked, assized, marketed, Gas-and-watered and improved' (Garvin, 1932, Vol. 1, p. 202).[12] All except the 'Gas-and-watering', of which more later, are activities which cannot be provided profitably by private enterprise without more ingenuity in pricing than seemed reasonable at the time. Redistributive motives were non-existent or secondary.

From the earliest times, local authorities had to distinguish their local from other national interests. While a local street is a public good whose benefits accrue locally, there are also national and regional roads which are partly used by through traffic. Until the eighteenth century, local parishoners were expected to meet all the costs of these roads. Not only did this lead to a running argument between long-distance travellers and local interest, but for the sake of higher speeds, the former wanted a higher-quality surface than the latter had any interest in providing. Thus long-distance travellers always grumbled at the state of local roads.[13] In the eighteenth century toll roads were a method of meeting this problem by removing such roads from the public to the private sector; though the inevitability of spatial monopoly caused constant problems as some toll keepers tried to make as much money as possible. In the nineteenth century the railways lessened the problem by making local roads less important for long-distance traffic; but in this century the rise of motor traffic has revived the old problem and, as we shall see, various grant systems have tried to deal with the division of costs to be borne by central and local government.

Police, prisons and the upkeep of local courts are also examples of local beneficial public goods whose intergovernmental externalities have become more important over time. They are public goods because one cannot identify the beneficiaries among the law–abiding and charge them. Until the nineteenth century, there were very substantial differences in the local provision of law and order. If an area wished to be comparatively lawless, this was almost a matter of local choice provided what was allowed was not too flagrant and did not affect other areas. In the early nineteenth century, there were many examples of local justices being reluctant to provide the police that central government began to feel were needed at a time when central government was becoming more conscious of the externalities from disorder. As we have seen, fear of local unrest expanding to national revolution – an externality – was at the root of that central interest in law and order which developed after the Napoleonic Wars. As a consequence, central government began to require more uniformity in local provision. Though still controlling local police in many vital respects of policy and provision, local authorities became agents of central government.

Before 1877 almost all prisons were locally owned and run, though under increasing regulation from the Home Office. That year, Disraeli transferred them to the Prison Commission, then as now an integral part of the Home Office.

The reasons for the transfer were the expression of a spirit very similar to that of the 1834 Poor Law (Howard, 1960, pp. 94–100). The Committee under Lord Carnarvon had recommended far harsher discipline in prisons and a complete overhaul of prison administration. They recommended that prisoners should be confined in separate cells, in isolation 'because it was terrible to criminals'. Hard labour, hard fare, and a hard bed 'should be the lot of all, whatever their age or sex'. The Report's principles were embodied in the 1865 Prisons Act. Many local authorities acted on it immediately, but many did not. They refused to provide single cells for all prisoners, or to provide the ghastly uniform diet insisted on for all prisoners, or in some cases to stop manufacturing goods for sale in prisons.

Wakefield Prison, for example, had an income of £40,000 a year from the sale of rush mats. This loss of income and the high cost of converting the prisons to the new standards meant that the objection to the Act was as much financial as humanitarian. In some cases local authorities closed down their prisons rather than convert.

The 1865 Act increased the difference between the more and the less harsh authorities, so there were complaints that news of where there was an 'easy nick' quickly spread among criminals. Thus to make all prisons of the standard of the harshest, it was decided to nationalise them. In Parliament the Bill was little opposed on the grounds of its inhumanity. There was much argument that as the first nationalising measure it was a 'gigantic and almost unparalleled centralisation' and a 'distinct slur upon local government'. What got it through Parliament, however, was the reduction in rates that would follow at a time when, as we shall see in Part One, Chapter 4, local expenditure and, therefore, local rates were rising substantially.

The different interest of central government was reflected in different grant arrangements. Those public goods which were most clearly local have always been the least grant-aided, as one would expect, until they eventually became absorbed in block grants. Roads, especially trunk roads, and police to this day are grant-aided to a higher level, reflecting their greater national interest. Indeed, this is what the hypothesis set out earlier in this chapter would suggest.

Not only was local government the supplier of nearly all public goods, it was also responsible for the redistribution function of government. Poor relief, which never could be anything but redistributive, was an ancient function of local authorities.

The principle we have advanced in this chapter would suggest that the Poor Law as an exercise in redistribution in cash and in kind was not a suitable local authority activity. That it was local from earliest times may be best explained by the practical inability of central government to administer a redistributive mechanism which necessarily had to have local outlets. The inevitable drawback of local administration was local discretion and this undoubtedly had a Tiebout kind of effect. The wandering of the poor in Tudor times from parish to parish to find charity was a major problem which the justices of the peace tried to deal with by every punishment from putting vagabonds in the stocks to hanging (Harrison, 1876, Chs. 10, 24). The preamble to the 1662 Settlement Act is far more explicit on the unrestrained poor who 'endeavour to settle' in a parish 'where there is the best stock, the largest commons and the most woods . . . and when they have consumed it then to another' (quoted in Clapham, 1949, p. 300). This Act, like earlier ones, allowed the local justices to move on the migrant poor.

Local management raised just the difficulties we would have expected from the arguments advanced earlier in this chapter:

(1) Vagrant poor wandering in search of more generous parishes and later unions.
(2) Parishes and unions doing their best to shift the poor on to other parishes and unions.

(3)   More affluent residents shunning areas where the burden of poor relief was heavy.
(4)   Central government from Elizabethan times interfering to try to get more uniform provision of poor relief.
(5)   Justices of the peace administering poor relief, getting together to try to standardise provisions. Such was the genesis of the Speenhamland system.

The 1834 Poor Law Act was in part an attempt to standardise the provision of poor relief, but it is also interesting that it created 'unions' of parishes to ease the problem of redistribution. We have argued that redistribution is more feasible the larger the area. Nevertheless, these unions did not overcome the objection that poor relief bore more heavily on some areas than others; nor did it avoid the tendency noted by Cannan for there to be a 'Tiebout' migration effect.

The 1870 Education Act gave local government a new redistributive task. Its aim was to provide central finance to establish schools in those areas inadequately served by voluntary schools. While some voluntary schools were charitable, that is redistributive, others were not. The 1870 Act aimed to provide a system of education which, though not free, would be available to most of the poor. Local school boards were appointed to provide schools where none existed. Just as much as poor relief, this was an onerous redistributive duty in so far as school boards levied rates upon the more affluent to provide subsidised, though not free, education for the less affluent. The 1902 Education Act was another major stimulus to local spending. It abolished the school boards and made the counties and county boroughs responsible for primary, secondary and technical education. They became the rating authorities for local education, contributing both to the old post-1870 secular 'board schools', as the school boards had done, and to voluntary, mostly religious schools in the same way.

A third type of locally provided good, the spatial monopoly good, was largely a creature of the 1870s and 1890s. Gas, water, sewerage and later electricity and buses were all examples of goods which could be, and indeed sometimes were, provided privately and profitably. But if many suppliers competed in the same place the overhead costs to be recouped were multiplied; and the disruption of the road surface by the various utilities digging their different holes was also criticised. It was more efficient to provide these as local spatial monopolies, but to avoid monopoly profits it became common for these to be provided for by municipal enterprise.

A characteristic of both improvement and education policy in the last quarter of the nineteenth century was the scope it gave to local initiative – in spite of the inspectorates, the cities that were most improved were bettered as the result of local enthusiasm. Again, it was local initiative which led some areas to take very great advantage of the 1870 Education Act while others lagged. All these led to a surge of civic pride and interest in local government which continued to the First World War. As the historian most sympathetic to local government has suggested, the increased vigour of local administration of these years – concern about education, health, sanitation and housing – may have been far more important for the welfare and prosperity of the nation than the preoccupation of Parliament with foreign and imperial affairs (Young, 1950, p. 198). Many took the hint from Mill and saw local government as a means of educating citizens in government and in acquiring a sense of responsibility. This was the feeling that led Beatrice Webb into her lifelong interest in local government, reinforced by a belief that she felt was widely shared, that Parliament in the 1880s in concentrating on foreign and imperial issues, on Ireland and religious questions was 'remote from the needs and thoughts of the British electorate' (Webb, 1948, pp. 144, 152). One finds the cautious Alfred Marshall telling a Royal Commission that 'the constructive work of government and especially of local government is life itself in one of its highest forms' (1926, p. 258). Several idealist political philosophers entered local government as the embodiment on earth of the Greek city-stage. One, Bosanquet, wrote 'The District as an ethical idea is the unity of the region with which we are in sensuous contact. . . . Local self-government acquires a peculiar character from the possibilities of ultimate knowledge of each other among those who carry it on. A man's whole way of living is in question when he sets up to be locally prominent . . .' (1919, pp. 286, 7). The prestige of local government and optimism for its future were probably at their height, and this was reflected in the 159 per cent increase in local expenditure shown between 1890 and 1905. Thus by 1905, local government as almost the sole provider of domestic goods and services was providing both beneficial and onerous or redistributive public goods. As well as providing redistributive services – education – it was engaged in cash redistribution – poor relief. It also supplied monopoly goods such as gas, electricity, water, sewerage and public transport.

A change came with the 1906 Liberal government, even more with the replacement of Campbell-Bannerman in 1908 by Asquith as leader of that government, and Lloyd George's promotion to the Treasury. This was the first government to introduce substantial and costly reforms which imposed a direct cost on the national exchequer. There was an Act to found labour exchanges in 1909, which increased central government expenditure on economic services and was a new kind of function for central government to perform, but was not in itself expensive. It had been inspired by Sir William Beveridge's book, *Unemployment*, which had argued that much employment was casual and would be remedied if it were easier to acquire information on the jobs and job-seekers available. But by 1910, the £12 million cost of the new old age pensions introduced by Lloyd George had doubled central government expenditure on the social services. The Conservatives' theory had been that if old age pensions were introduced they should be fully contributory, indeed an insurance scheme, so that no net cost should fall on the exchequer. The Liberals introduced a scheme that immediately introduced pensions for all over 70; and it was this that imposed the burden on the exchequer. Another costly measure was the 1911 Invalidity and Unemployment Insurance Act. This was in two parts, both much inspired by German legislation. One part established a contributory health insurance for practically all employees. This was the germ of the National Health Service – the 'panel' which first enabled poor people to get some medical assistance, though initially only for employed persons. This was contributory. The second part introduced an unemployment insurance scheme in shipbuilding, building and engineering. This again had a national contribution. It was a supplement to the traditional

poor relief administered and financed by the local authorities. The relation between the two was muddled from the start and inequitable. The reason for
choosing the three industries was that it was believed fluctuations in their employment were smaller and that therefore the scheme had a greater chance of
being self-financing; but in any case when the entitlement period expired,
employees were thrown back on to the poor relief. Neither part took effect
until the second half of 1912 and their financial effect was only just appearing
before the First World War.

By 1920, old age pensions, unemployment insurance and health insurance
(extended to more categories of employees) were mostly responsible for the
sixfold increase (in 1900 prices) that had occurred in central social-service
expenditure since 1905. The bulk of domestic central public expenditure in the
interwar period remained concentrated on these three. The cost of unemployment insurance had increased as it was extended to more groups until it became
almost universal in 1920 (Taylor, 1965, pp. 148–9). Unemployment insurance
had not, however, replaced the old locally administered Poor Law which remained
the source of relief for those not entitled to unemployment relief by their
contributions or whose entitlement had been exhausted. The Great Depression,
with the increase in the number unemployed, not only increased the overall cost,
but greatly increased the burden on local authorities for poor relief. Since their
resources and political sympathies varied, differences in the provision of poor
relief were intensified. There were widespread complaints that some local
authorities were providing more generous benefits than others. These were
chiefly Labour authorities asserting their local autonomy. But there was also
objection to the inequality of the burden. Ratepayers in areas of high unemployment had to pay more in rates to aid the unemployed and poor than in areas of
low unemployment which almost by definition were areas of greater prosperity.
This is an example of the difficulty with onerous redistributive public goods
mentioned previously. Since most of those who pay do not benefit, there is a
temptation for them to move out of areas where rates are high for this reason.

At the same time the orthodox public finance of the time argued that funds
for unemployment relief should be made to balance actuarially by a cut in the
rate of relief and by a means test. The orthodox economic instincts of Ramsay
MacDonald and the Chancellor, Snowden, warred with the more Keynesian or
humanitarian beliefs of other members of the Cabinet. Division of opinion on
this issue brought down the Labour Government in 1931 (Skidelsky, 1976,
passim, but esp. chs. 7, 8 and 13).

The incoming government considered the alternatives. They rejected the idea
of taking over the administration centrally, principally because of the burden
of Parliamentary Questions that would ensue, as the dissatisfied used MPs to
ventilate a host of grievances. Instead 100 per cent grants were paid to the local
authorities for them to administer a means-test scheme for the unemployed in
addition to the ordinary poor relief. The initial rates permitted meant a severe
reduction in benefits paid to most unemployed and the elimination of payments
to some. This produced enormous protest. While the rates and coverage were
made somewhat more generous, 100 per cent grants did not avoid local variations.
Where local authorities were well disposed to be generous, this was encouraged,

a sin in the Treasury's eyes. Local authorities varied greatly in how they applied means testing, even though they were fixed as to the rate of relief they could offer. A change was needed. Rather than central control in the normal manner, a QUANGO was created, the Unemployment Assistance Board, the forerunner of the present Supplementary Benefits Commission, to take the administration of discretionary, means-tested unemployment relief out of politics. Thereafter, the local authorities lost their poor-relief responsibilities in stages until the final abolition of the Poor Law in 1948.

This episode has probably had four main effects:

(1)   The Treasury has never forgotten what it then learnt of the disadvantages of 100 per cent grants.

(2)   It was a precedent for placing a redistributive activity under the administration of ministerial appointees distanced both from local and central politics.

(3)   As a corollary it has also been a precedent for those who handle welfare cases not being directly responsible to elected representatives, but being the comparatively lowly bureaucrats of a centralised but largely autonoumous and distant agency.

(4)   As a further corollary, since other services affecting the poor and the unemployed are run by central or by local government, it added to the fragmentation of these services as they affect the client.

If one makes an exception for this social-services expenditure, then in real terms there was practically no increase in central domestic public expenditure between the wars. Moreover, almost all the additional expenditure consisted of the redistribution of income from the more affluent members of the community to the various needy groups – of the poor, the aged, the sick and the unemployed. With the exception of a few financially relatively unimportant innovations such as the labour exchanges, this increase was in what national income statisticians have come to call 'cash transfers', not in the provision of goods and services. Until after the Second World War it was still true that central government was not providing goods and services –beneficial public goods in the terminology of this chapter – out of taxation. One has to say 'out of taxation' not to forget the Post Office which had been a centrally administered, self-financing service operating as a government department on a substantial scale since the middle of the nineteenth century.

By the end of the 1930s, the division of function between central and local government had become less clear than it had been in the nineteenth century, but some vestige of a rationale remained. To summarise, as was traditional, defence, foreign and commonwealth affairs remained the exclusive province of central government financed by central taxation, but the ancient practice of using local government as the main provider of domestic public goods and services was starting to alter. The most ancient function of local government, poor relief, a redistributive public good by the analysis of this chapter, expanded in scale and was gradually transferred to central government. As a consequence, central government had become engaged in making income transfers between classes for the first time.[14]

In domestic affairs, central government did not engage much in directly providing goods and services, but for the exception of the Post Office. Instead, it preferred the form of the public corporation. This was used to nationalise monopolistic goods when the Port of London Authority was set up in 1908, the Central Electricity Board (CEB) in 1926 and the London Passenger Transport Board in 1933. In each case, the main argument was that there had to be a monopoly if potential economies of scale were to be realised and a good public service provided.

Electricity was a particularly interesting case. In 1919 electricity commissioners had been set up to co-ordinate and standardise electricity provision. They could only use persuasion (Clegg and Chester, 1953, pp. 25–8). Consequently they largely failed and in 1926 the CEB was set up to establish an electricity grid, to concentrate generation in the most efficient stations and to standardise the industry. In 1936 the McGowan Committee on Distribution criticised the diversity and incoherence of the statutory rights and duties on the many different undertakings, and also the smallness of most of them. The Report concluded that central government ought to be able to impose coherence and standardisation as well as achieving enough amalgamation through persuasion to eliminate the smaller authorities. It did not recommend nationalisation though the technical arguments were later used by nationalisers. There seemed no doubt that the CEB worked a major change in rationalising electricity generation. The CEB was the ultimate progenitor of the present Central Electricity Generating Board (CEGB). National ownership was and can still be justified on the grounds that there are very substantial economies of scale, particularly in the provision of a national grid, and if realized such an undertaking would have enormous monopoly power. But nationalisation of operation and local distribution may not have been necessary. As at first envisaged the grid might have stayed a nationalised agency, buying electricity from a number of independent competing towns. If generation had been separated from distribution, it is likely that the technical and commercial objectives of the McGowan Report could have been realised by a strong Commission establishing the standardisation and coherence of policy required, without national public ownership. The advantage of the municipalisation of distribution – even municipalising the private undertakings – would have been to keep local monopolies under local political control. As Professor Robson wrote not long afterwards

there can be no doubt whatever that the transfer of the service from locally elected councils to centrally appointed boards signifies a loss of democratic control over that service. The citizen of Manchester or Birmingham formerly looked to the city council, elected by the voters who were both consumers and citizens, to the efficient running of the municipal gas or electricity undertakings . . . Today the citizen of Manchester or Birmingham must look to a public corporation whose governing board has been appointed by a remote administrator living in a distant town. We have moved from the principle of election to the principle of selection; from local control to remote control; from responsibility to the town hall to an uncertain accountability to Whitehall. (1952, p. 350)

Though attempts were made to replace the local councils as the consumers' watchdog by consumer councils, they have never proved very effective.

Almost the same arguments can be used about gas. In 1945 the Hayworth Report on the gas industry made a similar diagnosis to that of the McGowan Report. Standards were diverse. There were too many very small undertakings. But it advised nationalisation. Their main arguments were that they felt there was a need to amalgamate municipal undertakings and they had little confidence in local authorities being able to combine in joint boards to run large undertakings. Moreover, they felt higher salaries were needed than those normal in municipal undertakings. Before the Second World War it is probable that a Labour government would have made every effort to achieve standardisation and economies of scale through extending municipal control of the industry under the supervision of a Commission. After the war, the arguments for national public ownership prevailed. There was a much greater belief in national planning which suggested the need for overall planning of both electricity and gas. There were the trade unions keen to substitute one employer for a multitude, and the managers who saw more autonomy under national than under municipal ownership. The memory of problems that the Ramsay MacDonald government had in dealing with local authorities in the Great Depression in creating jobs, made many socialists less warm to local government. Just as with the National Health Service, it was said municipal government would have to be reformed – that is, its units enlarged – before it could take over electricity and gas.[15]

Central government was still distinctly uneasy when it came to providing goods and services itself where these could not be charged for on a self-financing basis – when in short they were non-excludable and beneficial. The BBC was set up in 1926 as a public corporation to handle a classic case of a beneficial public good. Roads presented far more of a problem. A special Roads Fund had been set up in 1910 to which fuel duty was to be paid. It was to use this to finance road-building. In 1926, Churchill had raided that Fund and, though its legal entity continued into the 1950s, thereafter central government financed roads from taxation. If there had been a major national road-building programme in the 1920s and 1930s, as there was notoriously in Italy and Germany, this would have engaged central government as a major producer of beneficial goods. But there was not. How far the form of administration influenced the spending rate it is hard to say. Central government was to spend very little on road-building until 1955.

It was only after the Second World War that central government moved into the substantial production of goods and services, and the division of function became still more blurred. Some of the most important functions taken away from local government – electricity, gas and, much later, water – were still entrusted to public corporations. But for the first time, central government became a major producer of domestic goods and services when it took over hospitals and other health services from local government and built upon these to found the NHS.

Most hospitals had been administered by local authorities and a natural way of realising the intention of both the wartime coalition government and the postwar Labour government to found a national health service would have been through the local authorities. Herbert Morrison, who was in both governments, supported this. He put pressure on Willink, the Conservative minister, to that end. As *de facto* deputy prime minister under Attlee, he used his influence to achieve this and it is clear that he made no secret of his views outside government (Abel-Smith, 1964, pp. 475 ff). This championing of local authorities was unsurprising as he had made his first political reputation and had started his political career in the London County Council.

Bevan, Minister of Health, and architect of the NHS, opposed Morrison and overcame the objections of most of his Cabinet colleagues who, unpersuaded by the precedent of the Unemployment Assistance Board, objected on democratic grounds to the NHS being set up similarly as a non-elected appointed body (Foot, 1962, p. 131).

Bevan explained to the House of Commons his reasons for taking the hospitals away from the local authorities and not using them as the basis of the NHS. He argued that they varied so much in size and wealth that there would be serious anomalies (Abel-Smith, 1964, p. 481). At this distance such arguments do not seem especially persuasive. After all, central government had had to meet an entirely similar problem in education and had succeeded in establishing, even by then, a fair degree of uniformity in educational provision. Neither does the evidence suggest that a centrally organised health service has indeed been successful in avoiding considerable anomalies in NHS provision between areas. It is arguable that its success in achieving uniformity is less than that of the Department of Education working through local authorities. As we have seen, the use of central legislation to bring the standard of the laggard up to that of the best was a time-honoured technique in British government.

Bevan also stressed the financial difficulty. One would have thought this could have been avoided in a system where health insurance money was paid to local authorities if not by more orthodox use of grants. Bevan also used the dubious argument, which was later to become so influential, that local authorities need to be much larger if they are to be entrusted with new, major responsibilities. Bevan suggested that he would have handed hospitals and medical services to local authorities if they had been enlarged by reform.

While these are the reasons Bevan gave to the House of Commons, they may not have been the most important. The doctors lobbied both Willink and Bevan against local authority administration. The overwhelming argument against the primacy of local authorities was simply that the medical profession would not wear it (Frazer, 1973, p. 216). Bevan also rejected the model of the Unemployment Assistance Board and made the NHS the direct responsibility of the Minister of Health, positively welcoming the increase in Parliamentary Questions that would result. Another argument against a QUANGO was that it would have been extremely difficult to prevent the doctors dominating it. Though powerful within the Ministry of Health, both the minister and civil servants provided a check to them.

The principle consequences of the founding of the NHS for local government were:

(1)   That for the first time central government became a major direct provider

of goods and services employing many thousands of staff, though some — doctors — were technically self-employed.

(2) There is the corollary that the practice of using local government to provide such services was departed from on a large scale for the first time.

(3) And that it was one of the first instances when it could be argued that the interests of the consumer, as mediated by the local authorities, lost out to worker and producer.

(4) It was also, however, a redistributive service in kind and its transfer to central government could have been justified on those grounds. But it did not provide much of a precedent. Other redistributive services stayed with local government. More have been added since.

After 1945, the division of labour between central and local government had become still more pragmatic and harder to rationalise. Central government had been acquiring functions which are not easily explicable in terms of any theory of government or public finance.

In 1946, the division of responsibility between central and local government was fairly logical, though it was a different logic from that which had distinguished them before the First World War. Central government had become the main agent for cash redistribution, administering national systems of pensions, poor and unemployment relief. While local government had got out of cash redistribution, it was still the provider of major redistributive goods and services where there were advantages in local administration. Education, housing, medical services could all have been provided privately if it had not been intended to provide them for the benefit of those who could not afford them, that is redistributively. These services tended to be in receipt of high rates of specific grant to reduce their impact on local finances. In education, in particular, there was considerable central control to ensure comparative uniformity of provision.

Of that category of mixed goods with both a high local and national interest, local government retained the police and roads, except for the provision of trunk roads. The extent of the national interest here was reflected again in high rates of specific grant. But the main argument for the retention of a local police force was a peculiar one: local control lessens the possibility of central forces using a united police force to introduce a police state.

Both the more purely local public and the spatial monopoly goods remained with local government.

Within a few years the division of labour had become far more confused. The reason for this confusion, from which local government has never recovered, was Labour Party disenchantment with local government. During the 1920s, Labour had been strongly identified with local government, practically and intellectually. Belief in local government and municipal enterprise had been a key tenet of the Fabians. Many politicians learnt their craft in local government and had been able to introduce socialist policies or attitudes there, before it was possible in national government.

There were four main reasons why the 1946 Labour government had lost earlier generations' enthusiasm for local enterprise. There was first the fact of becoming a majority government for the first time. Piecemeal reform from the bottom seemed less attractive and less necessary. Imposing it from the top was at last possible and more economical of effort.

Second, there were strong union and other forces demanding nationalisation with such slogans as co-ordination, planning, integration and rationalisation. National union leaders – and indeed those captains of industry who, for one reason or another, wanted national conglomerates – had no interest in working through local authorities.

Further, rates were less buoyant as a source of revenue than national taxation. While central grants were increased, too large an increase would have seemed imprudent by the criteria of the time, and the alternative of establishing a new source of local income – for example, by transferring part of income tax to local authorities – was not very seriously considered at the time, though in retrospect it is arguable that it was the period where there was the strongest case for it.

Lastly, there had been the experience of the MacDonald government and the influence of Keynes. Skidelsky has shown both the ambivalence and impotence of the Ramsay MacDonald governments, in their policies of public spending to counter unemployment (1976, pp. 104–9). Those who argued for counter-cyclical public spending were thwarted, first by those ministers who held as strongly as the Treasury did to the view that deficit spending was self-defeating. Philip Snowden as Chancellor had been utterly committed to more orthodox, balanced budget policies. But at a more fundamental level, they were frustrated by central government's lack of control over public spending as this had been almost entirely in the hands of the local authorities. Two agencies, the Unemployment Grants Committee and the Ministry of Transport, both administered grants with which they could influence local authorities to spend money on public works. But the amounts to be spent were small, the Ministry of Transport officials, particularly, reluctant to spend it, and neither could have much effect on the majority of authorities who were reluctant to match government money out of their own resources. Though transfer of services to central government was canvassed, there was a tendency for both Labour and Liberal manifestoes and pamphlets to go on promising public-works programmes which the machinery of government could not deliver (Skidelsky, 1976, pp. 41, 57–8). Sir Oswald Mosley, responsible in 1929 for unemployment policy, was among those who argued most strongly that counter-cyclical policies were only possible if they were set up as 'national schemes'.

By 1945, many of the new Labour administration had digested the lessons of the Ramsay MacDonald governments and all were 100 per cent convinced of the necessity of Keynesian economic measures. Protagonists of local government, like Herbert Morrison, fought a losing battle. All these four factors, but most especially the fourth, were important reasons for the transfer of gas and electricity undertakings to new public corporations and of local medical services to form the NHS (Chester, 1975).

Since then, we have learnt the limitations of public-spending programmes as instruments of counter-cyclical policy. Long gestation periods make it difficult to time the changes and more often than not the lags have been such as to make such programmes actually destabilising. Even before Keynesian policies began to yield to a combination of fiscal and monetary measures, taxation and cash transfers have been recognised as far more effective instruments of macro-economic policy than public-works programmes. Thus from the standpoint of economics, the transfer of local services was unnecessary. Financially, there would have been no difficulty if local government had kept municipal trading services such as gas and electricity, since these were chargeable and not met out of local taxation. The development of a comprehensive health service through local authorities would have imposed much additional financial burden, however, and either a very great increase in grant or some new source of local income would have had to be found and tolerated.

To return to the distinctions set out earlier in this chapter, there are arguments against the new division of labour effected by the Attlee government. If the division had borne in mind the principles of the 1901 Royal Commission or the Kempe Committee one might have expected a different result. In the light of the principles we have advanced, there would have been a case for both local public goods and monopoly goods staying with local government. There were economies-of-scale arguments for nationalising the electricity grid, as indeed was done in the 1920s, and possibly for extending its control over the production, as was done by the creation of the CEGB. But the distributive activities now undertaken by the Electricity Council and the CEGB could have stayed with local authorities. Arguably they would have been more responsive to local needs. Similar arguments might have led to gas, and later water, staying with local authorities. These questions are considered in more detail in Part Four, Chapter 7. An argument against the creation of a national health service has always been that it has led to too much power being given to doctors. Various ways have been attempted to make the NHS more responsive to local influence. With hindsight, there would have been an advantage in continuing a local system instead of the national one introduced by Aneurin Bevan. Far more difficult is the division of labour in redistribution. The transfer of cash redistribution to central government was what one would have expected given the principles advanced in this chapter. The argument for giving redistributive goods and services to local authorities is that for this local administration is particularly beneficial. Locally elected members are more likely to understand the needs of local beneficiaries of such services. This is plainly a strong argument. One difficulty is inconsistency in treating these services. While housing, education and more recently social services of various kinds are the prerogative of local government, very similar services are provided by the NHS, and a number of other national organisations. A corollary of this difficulty is that it is partly responsible for the lack of coherence in the net benefits received from the welfare state by individuals in apparently similar circumstances, but in different places. When allowance is made for rate rebates for poorer households, local authority services do have a substantial effect on the distribution of income, especially for poorer families. The division of responsibility has been partly responsible for inconsistency in treatment. One possibility would have been to separate redistribution from provision of local goods and services to a much greater extent by relying much more on income redistribution and less on redistribution in kind. In that case, some of these services might have been continued to be provided as local public goods, while arguably others, like housing, with few or no public-good characteristics, could have been returned to the private sector. Another possibility would have been to accept more explicitly an agency principle for redistributive goods and services and reflect this in grant provisions.

The 1945 to 1951 principles, or lack of them, have not been altered since. In recent years, the most important functional changes in local government services have been two. The first was the growth of social services in the 1960s, when local authorities took over responsibility for many redistributive activities to aid various disadvantaged groups. The second was the transfer of water and health to new public corporations in 1974.

The reasons given for the transfer of water were similar to those for the nationalisation of municipal electricity and gas. Water nationalisation had long been in the Labour Party programme (though eventually accomplished by a Conservative government) and there were, therefore, several investigations and reports whose main argument was that reorganisation was necessary to realise economies of scale and internalise conflict which existed between many authorities in the supply, distribution and treatment cycle. The difficulty of pricing water at all points in the cycle has made it difficult to set up an accounting framework for the various parts of the water industry. In 1969, the Central Advisory Water Committee reported that there were

> increasing conflicts of interest between the various authorities responsible for providing water services and inadequate mechanisms for solving them, apart from intervention by Central government. They identified as the most important areas and causes of conflict: (1) inflexibility in the use of existing resources, (2) the division of responsibility for new sources between River Authorities and water undertakers, (3) the promotion of joint or national schemes, and (4) the treatment of water after use. They concluded that in addition to detailed improvements in legislation and production in the number of operating units (which was generally agreed as desirable) the relationship between the various authorities must be changed so that a comprehensive water management plan can be drawn up for every river basin and so that the system of organisation and the financial arrangements will permit the implementation of such a plan. (DoE, 1971c, Circular no. 92/71).

When central government came to recommend the creation of regional water authorities they accepted these arguments, except that the Committee had differed on how far it was necessary to nationalise all constituent bodies (ibid. p. 9).

The chief argument for setting them up was to reduce the need for central government to act so as to avoid conflict. Arguably this has not happened. Conflicts are not necessarily reduced by being internalised. Though the intention was to create a public enterprise and to replace water and sewerage rates by charges, one does not make a tax into a charge by saying so. For the most part the charges remain unrelated to costs of provision. Regional water authorities are not easily made subject to pricing and investment criteria such as are intended to govern the operations of nationalised industries. In fact, they charge what they need to finance their operations as monopoly suppliers. They have been removed from local democratic control without being put under central democratic control or becoming subject to market disciplines.[16]

CONCLUSIONS

(1) Before analysing the division of labour between central and local government, it is useful to classify functions of government. A convenient classification is;
(a)   the provision of public goods;
(b)   redistribution of income or wealth.
(2) By definition, public goods have two characteristics, non-excludability and non-rivalness. Non-excludability means that consumers cannot be 'excluded' by charging, because the price mechanism does not work. Non-rivalness means that additional consumers do not impose additional costs and that therefore charging is inefficient.
(3) Another way of classifying government activity is between those that have to do with allocation – the provision of goods which cannot be provided profitably because of imperfection in the price mechanism, and redistribution.
(4) From these distinctions we derive various principles on the division of labour between central and local government. There is a long literature, starting with John Stuart Mill on the most efficient division of labour between local and central government in which are to be found the seeds of ideas which were developed later by Goschen, the 1901 Royal Commission, the Kempe Committee and later by others, mainly in the USA.
(5) Various reasons were given for it to be more efficient for local government to engage in allocative rather than redistributive activity. In particular, if local authorities differ in their redistributive policies, this is likely to have effects on the migration of population but this will not happen in so far as local authorities are agents of central government.
(6) The history of provision of local goods and services is examined to show how it has been affected by the principles advanced. One pattern obtained before the First World War, another until the end of the Second, but thereafter there seems to be greater confusion of purpose.

NOTES

1 Samuelson (1954). Other terms less frequently used are social wants and social goods, Musgrave (1959) and (1969), and group consumption goods, Shoup (1969). The definition used here leaves out one type of goods which in economic theory will not be private provided because unprofitable – increasing return goods under perfect competition – but they have no practical importance and can in fact be reconciled with the definition of a public good. See appendix 1.3.A1.
2 See Appendix 1.3.A1 for a more formal and detailed discussion.
3 For G. E. Moore (1903), 'the pleasure of human intercourse and the enjoyment of beautiful objects' were intrinsically good and were 'the sole criterion of human progress' (quoted in Barrett and Aiken, 1962, p. 474). If education provides these goods it would be considered as a public good.

4   A more exact but technical definition is in terms of economic efficiency. Provision is said to be efficient if it maximises the sum of individual net gains. An economist will note that any such action will be a potential Pareto improvement satisfying the Hicks–Kaldor criterion. They will be Pareto improvements if government also decides, and is able, to compensate any losses.

5   Tiebout, 1956; Ostrom, Tiebout and Warren, 1961; Tullock, 1969*a*; Rothenberg, 1970; Oates, 1972, ch. 1. It is often argued that economies of scale and the internalisation of intergovernmental externalities may favour central provision. Later we shall argue this is not so.

6   Whether politically the nation is as willing to redistribute as the region is another question, far more important in more federal countries like the USA or Canada than in Britain (Rothenberg, 1970).

7   Given the technology of the time, it did not occur to Mill to define a fourth group of services for which the demand was purely local but which could be produced most efficiently at national level because of economies of scale. This argument was to be used later to justify taxing gas, electricity and water from local government. We shall question its validity in Part Four, Chapter 6.

8   He also defined a third group of 'reproductive' services that benefited the ratepayer indirectly through betterment. For the moment this can be regarded as a special case of his second category, though we will want to return to it.

9   For a more detailed discussion of their suggested grant system, see Part One, Chapter 7.

10   For more details of their grant proposals see Part One, Chapter 7.

11   At 1900 prices. All the figures exclude central grant to local authorities.

12   Other cities were at work at the same time as Birmingham or followed its example.

13   This is a perfect example of the proposition that the presence of intergovernmental externalities will mean the underprovision of a public good. Exceptions to this are unlikely in practice, but see Williams (1966); Brainard and Dolbear (1967).

14   When proportional and later, towards the end of the nineteenth century, progressive taxation became accepted as the basis for contributions, government was engaged in redistribution on the income side through altering relative incomes. The measure of the 1908 government was the first that deliberately set out on a major scale to use government expenditure to redistribute income.

15   This was heard again when it was proposed to set up passenger transport executives in the 1968 Transport Act. It was then decided to set them up in advance of the creation of new and larger local authorities. They were run by, in effect, joint boards until after local government reorganisation.

16   Layfield (1976, p. 8, annex 7) reports complaints against the rating practices of the new water authorities.

Appendix 1.3.A1   The Definition of Government Output

INTRODUCTION

According to the criteria of conventional welfare economics, government provision of goods and services can be justified by reference to three main criteria:

(1)   non-appropriability of benefits,[1]
(2)   redistribution,
(3)   'paternalism'.[2]

The first criterion, the non-appropriability of benefits, covers cases of 'market failure', that is cases where the market mechanism will fail to provide a socially efficient (or Pareto optimal) output of the good. As is well known, the attainment of Pareto optimality requires that two conditions be satisifed. First, that the marginal social benefit of additional output of any good be equal to the marginal social cost, which may be termed the 'marginal condition'. Second, that the total social benefit of any activity be greater than or equal to the total cost, which we may call the 'total condition'.

The marginal condition will be satisfied under competitive market conditions, if firms are able to appropriate the full marginal social benefit of an additional unit of output (through prices received from consumers), and pay the full marginal social cost of production (through payments to factor inputs). This condition will clearly be violated if it is impossible, or prohibitively expensive, to charge consumers for the output they consume. This possibility is known as 'non-excludability'.[3] A classic example of non-excludability is the lighthouse, when, given free access to the sea, it is impossible (or at any rate very expensive) to exclude ships from perceiving the lighthouse's signal, and hence (given free access to the sea) no means of charging them. We consider the issues raised by non-excludability in more detail below.

A second circumstance in which the marginal condition may be violated is where there are benefits (or costs) to third parties associated with the production and consumption of an additional unit of output, and such third parties cannot be charged for such benefits (or extract compensation for costs imposed on them). These cases are known as 'externalities'. Clearly, externalities can arise only if the third party beneficiaries are 'non-excludable'. The production of additional mutton may involve the production of additional wool also, but there is no externality because the consumers of the wool can be made to pay for it. The only difference between activity-generating externalities and a pure (non-excludable) public good is that the former has some excludable (and hence chargeable) benefits, while the latter has none, and hence private production may occur in the case of goods with external benefits but could not in the case of pure public goods.

The marginal condition is violated if firms are unable to appropriate the full marginal social benefits of additional units of output. The total condition is violated if firms can, and do, charge prices to appropriate full marginal social benefits, but the total revenue raised fails to cover the total costs of production. The problem is essentially that firms are unable to appropriate part of the consumers' surplus on intra-marginal units.

The problem is well known in the context of goods whose production is subject to increasing returns to scale. In such circumstances, marginal costs are lower than average costs and, if prices are set equal to marginal costs (as required for Pareto optimality), revenues will not cover total costs of production. For some goods the marginal cost may fall to zero; such goods are said to display 'non-rivalness' in consumption.[4] The best-known example of non-rivalness is that of the television programme, in that the cost of producing the television programme does not vary with the number who watch it. Non-rivalness is, however, no more than an interesting special case of increasing returns; it need not be regarded as a separate category.

Goods produced under conditions of increasing returns to scale may be produced by private firms, but they will be obliged to charge prices at least equal to the average costs of production, and hence violate the conditions for Pareto optimality. Since, where there are increasing returns, there is likely to be a tendency towards monopoly there is the further difficulty that private producers may be able to set prices in excess of average costs, thus reducing production even further below the optimal level.

Even in such a case there are possibilities of profitable private production without violation of the Pareto principle. The use of a two-part tariff which is a pricing system involving a fixed charge plus a per unit charge allows profitable marginal cost pricing. Such a system is not dissimilar to a tax on all consumers of a commodity accompanied by a charge per unit, which might be zero, equal to the marginal cost of production. This kind of pricing, however, still raises all the issues of optimality raised by public goods (see Buchanan, 1966).

It should be stressed that the problem with increasing returns to scale in the present context is that of appropriating revenue from the consumers' surplus. The 'perfect' discriminating monopolist will produce at an efficient level of output, but he needs to know his customers' preferences, and to be able to prevent the formation of resale markets. Given that these conditions are not normally met, the producer may be obliged to charge the same price to all consumers, perhaps well in excess of marginal cost, resulting in an inefficient level of output.

We may then group instances of non-appropriability, or market failure, under two main headings: non-excludability and increasing returns. If goods with these characteristics are provided, or subsidised, by governments, their costs can be financed from taxation. Ideally, it would be desirable if the tax could be borne by those enjoying the non-appropriable benefits of the good. In practice, it may be no easier for government than for the market to identify beneficiaries, and tax burdens may bear little relationship to benefits received. The provision of such goods may then involve income redistributionary effects. Their provision then no longer presents an unambiguous Pareto improvement in economic welfare (in the sense of making some people better off, and no one any worse off), but a potential Pareto improvement (in that the gainers could compensate the losers, and still be better off, but will not in fact do so).[5]

In contrast to the unintended (and possibly capricious) redistributionary effects associated with the provision of goods, whose benefits are non-appropriable, are those goods whose provision serves an explicit redistributionary purpose.

The specific objective of redistribution of income can, of course, best be served by redistributing income and does not involve the provision of goods. However, there may be constraints on the extent of income redistribution in cash (for example, local governments may not be empowered to make cash transfers based on income levels), obliging governments, as a second-best measure, to pursue redistributionary objectives through the provision of goods. Second, the objective of redistribution may not be confined to income. If, for example, the objective is to redistribute from the healthy to the sick (rather than from the rich to the poor), it may make more sense to provide medical goods and services free of charge, rather than to attempt to assess the financial costs of each ailment, and to provide appropriate cash payments.[6]

Analytically, redistribution objectives may be envisaged in either a 'democratic' or an 'autocratic' form. In the democratic form, the argument is that people, in general, care about the welfare of the poor, or the sick, or other people generally. In this case, assisting the poor, or whoever, contributes to the well-being of others in society also. There is a 'psychic' externality, which is non-excludable,[7] and redistribution becomes analytically equivalent to other public goods.

In its autocratic form, the redistribution argument is based on the preferences of some authority (normally described as 'the social planner'). The authority is assumed to have some means (sometimes described as a 'social-welfare function') of evaluating the relative well-being of different individuals, and will redistribute when, according to this criterion, the gain to the recipient exceeds the loss to the individual making the payment.

In the context of local government, this distinction is particularly helpful. Redistributionary expenditure which is supported by the majority of the local electorate ('democratic redistribution') has different implications from redistributive expenditures imposed on local government by central government. In Marshall's terminology, the former may be beneficial, and the latter an onerous, expenditure.

The third motive for public provision has been termed 'paternalism'. The underlying motive is to induce individuals to consume more of a particular good or service than they would otherwise choose (given their income), and one means of attempting to do this is for the government to provide the good free of charge or at a subsidised price.[8] The principle of paternalism is that the donor is concerned about the well-being of the recipient, and defines that well-being in terms of specific goods and services (education, housing etc.) consumed by the recipient. Redistribution in terms of money will be wasteful because recipients may spend the money on goods which do not contribute to their well-being as defined by the donor.

The paternalistic approach assumes that the recipients are not the best judges of their own interests (for example, they may be regarded as myopic, inexperienced or otherwise incapable of pursuing their own best interests). Paternalistic arguments have been used, in particular, to justify the public provision of education, with arguments going back to John Stuart Mill concerned with the protection of children (from their parents), but similar arguments might well be applied, for example, to the social services.

As with redistribution, paternalism may take a democratic or an autocratic form, according to whether it is public opinion or the 'social planner' that wishes to influence the recipients' consumption of particular goods and services.

The next section examines these cases more formally, in terms of economic theory.

FORMAL ANALYSIS

In the introduction we suggested three citeria for government provision of goods and services: non-appropriability, which we argued could be attributable to non-excludability or to increasing returns, redistribution and paternalism. We now examine these different arguments more formally.

NON-EXCLUDABILITY

Traditionally, non-excludability has been held to depend on the impossibility of excluding consumers from the benefit of some particular good or service, and the consequent impossibility of charging them for the use of it. Impossibility is a strong criterion, and Shoup (1969) has usefully extended the concept to cover cases where exclusion is not impossible, but simply expensive. Indeed, it could be suggested in this context that 'impossible' means no more than 'extremely expensive' and that the cost of exclusion is the only relevant criterion. Such a generalisation is not strictly correct: there are some goods for which exclusion is possible, at a price, and others in which exclusion is impossible.[9]

There are two cases of non-excludable goods to consider. The first is where exclusion is impossible, or prohibitively expensive, in the sense that it is impossible, whatever the price charged, to cover the cost both of providing the good and of excluding those who do not wish to pay for it. Goods in this category cannot be provided by normal commercial methods. The second case is where exclusion is costly, but revenues may none the less cover both production costs and exclusion costs. Such goods may be produced by private firms, but the level of output will be sub-optimal.

Goods in the first category will not be provided at all by private firms. If they are to be provided it must be by collective action, where the community of individuals involved contract to provide the good for their benefit, and to share the costs between them. The difficulty is that there is no obvious mechanism to enable the collective decision maker to decide what public goods should be produced, and in what quantities, consistent with the criteria of economic efficiency. We consider this problem in three stages:

(1)   the definition of efficient output,
(2)   allocation under the benefit principle, and
(3)   allocation with pre-assigned tax shares.

To define efficient output, it may be helpful to consider an example: how many policemen should be hired in some community? Assuming more policemen will increase law enforcement and reduce crime, all individuals in the community will be affected. But the benefits derived by each will be different, for although all receive the same degree of additional protection they each value this additional protection differently. Some may value the additional protection greatly, others may be indifferent (because, for example, they find alsatians more effective), and others (for example, habitual offenders) may derive negative benefits from the extra police. In principle, the correct approach would be to add up the net benefits to each member of the community of one additional policeman and, if the sum of the net benefits exceeds the cost, to hire that additional policeman. Diagrammatically, this is achieved by the vertical summation of the individual demand curves for the good or service. Optimal provision can be defined as the level of output, where the sum of the marginal utilities of an additional unit of output to all of the consumers of the good is equal to the marginal cost of producing an additional unit.[10]

The fact that individuals value the benefits of a non-excludable public good differently (though, of course, the good is equally available to all) suggests that it might be appropriate to charge individuals for the public good according to the benefits each received from it. Each individual might, for example, be charged his marginal valuation of the good, multiplied by the number of units supplied. This pricing policy would be equivalent to the pricing of private goods and exactly cover the cost of provision of the good. If this pricing rule were adopted, the socially optimal level of output would also be individually optimum for each consumer (see Figure 1.3.A1).

The trouble with this procedure is that the incentives for individual consumers to reveal their true preferences are missing. Each individual will in fact have an incentive to understate his preference, arguing that, in a large group, understating his demand will not affect the total demand curve at all significantly while he can thereby reduce his contribution to the total cost. In consequence, it will not be possible to achieve an efficient output by asking individuals to reveal their preferences for the good and charging them accordingly.

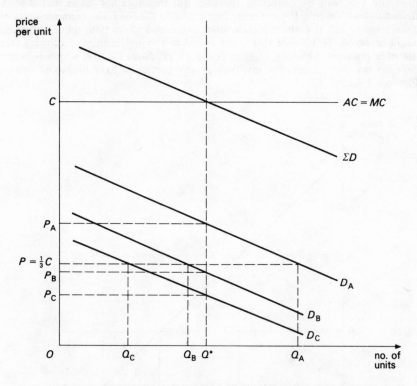

At Q^*, $OC = OP_A + OP_B + OP_C$ (benefit pricing). If all are charged one-third of the cost ($P = \frac{1}{3}C$), they will each want to consume a different level of output.

Figure 1.3.A1   *Optimal pricing for a public good*

As an alternative, tax shares may be pre-assigned. If the costs of public goods are to be borne, say, equally amongst the individuals of the community, each can then judge the benefit of an expansion in some public service as against the costs (in terms of higher taxes) to him. Tax shares being given, individuals will differ in the types and quantities of public goods which yield net benefits (i.e. net of tax payments) to them. Since there will no longer be unanimity, collective decisions will have to be based on some other criterion, for example, majority voting.

In any case, with pre-assigned tax shares some individuals are likely to be worse off as a result of the provision of public goods, even if the level of output is efficient in terms of the Hicks–Kaldor criterion. As a result, it will be impossible to make judgements as to the desirability of the provision of, or changes in the level of output of, public goods without explicit redistributive criteria. We ignore this problem at this stage only because it is analytically convenient to investigate non-excludability separately from redistribution.

The second category of non-excludable goods covered those for which exclusion, though costly, was not prohibitively costly, and private production was therefore feasible. A good example would be a road. It may well be possible to raise through a toll enough revenue to cover both the costs of maintaining the road and the costs of collecting the toll. But this does not mean that it is efficient to levy the toll. If there were free access to the road, the resource costs of collecting the toll (i.e. the toll collectors, toll gates and the time spent queueing) could be saved. To balance this, there would be the inefficiency of allowing free use of a resource which is socially costly to produce. Clearly, which is better depends on the magnitudes involved in any particular example, as shown in Figure 1.3.A2.

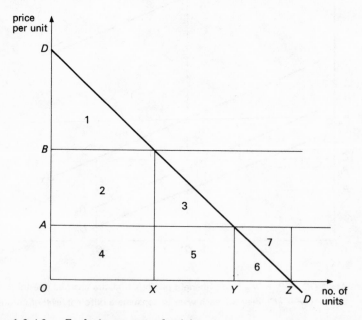

Figure 1.3.A2   *Exclusion costs and pricing*

In Figure 1.3.A2 OA is the production cost of the good, AB the exclusion cost per unit and DD the market demand curve. In private production the price will be OB and output OX. The total gross consumer benefit will be measured by area $(1 + 2 + 4)$, the social cost of production by area 4 and exclusion costs by area 2. The net social benefit, or consumer surplus, will then be area 1. If, however, the good is provided free of charge by government, output will be OZ, gross consumer $(1 + 2 + 3 + 4 + 5 + 6)$, and total social production cost area $(4 + 5 + 6 + 7)$. Exclusion costs are zero because no one is excluded. Net social benefit is therefore area $(1 + 2 + 3 - 7)$. Social benefit will be greater than with private production, therefore, if area $(2 + 3)$ is greater than area 7.

It is obvious from this result that, as might be expected, the higher are the exclusion costs relative to production, the more likely it is that government provision will be more efficient than private provision. Perhaps slightly less obviously, the more inelastic is the demand for the good, the more likely is public provision to be the more efficient. This is shown in Figure 1.3.A3.

It follows that the existence of exclusion costs does not as such provide a sufficient case for government intervention, nor does the fact that a good may be produced profitably in the private sector provide a sufficient case for leaving it there. Equally, the fact that a good cannot be produced profitably in the private sector does not necessarily imply that it should be produced by government. Figure 1.3.A4 illustrates the case of a good for which there is demand but that will not be produced in the private sector and should not be produced in the public sector. If this good is supplied by government, gross benefit to consumers will be area $(1 + 2 + 3)$ and the production costs area $(2 + 3 + 4)$. Production will be justified only if area 1 is greater than area 4.

Where the benefits provided by a good are non-excludable, the case for public provision depends not on whether or not private provision is profitable, but on the magnitude of exclusion costs relative to production costs and on demand conditions.

The second type of non-appropriability is the case of increasing returns, where marginal costs of production are below average costs. We may take the case of non-rivalness (marginal costs zero) as an example. In Figure 1.3.A5 curve AC measures the average cost of provision of the service per unit consumed. As marginal costs are zero, it measures the fixed costs divided by the number of units consumed. DD is the demand curve. If the producer is to cover costs, production must be at most OX units, and the benefit to consumers area $(1 + 2 + 3)$. If the good is now taken over by government and provided free of charge, demand will increase to OY and gross consumer benefit to area $(1 + 2 + 3 + 4)$. Since the costs of provision will be unaffected, there will be an increase in consumer benefit equal to area 4. Moreover, if the firm were a local monopoly, it could charge a price in excess of P_0, say P_1 (where marginal revenue was zero), reducing output to OX' and thus generating a lower gross consumer benefit under private production (area $(1 + 2 + 3)$ is reduced) and consequently greater benefit to be derived from public production (area 4 is increased).

This argument is in a way too powerful. There are a host of local trading enterprises operating under conditions of increasing returns to scale. A good example is a local cinema, where the marginal cost of an extra customer is zero when the cinema is not full. It is inefficient to exclude people who would like to see the film but are not willing to pay the admission price. Provided there are seats available, their seeing the film imposes no costs on others and, if they benefit, there is an overall gain from admitting them.

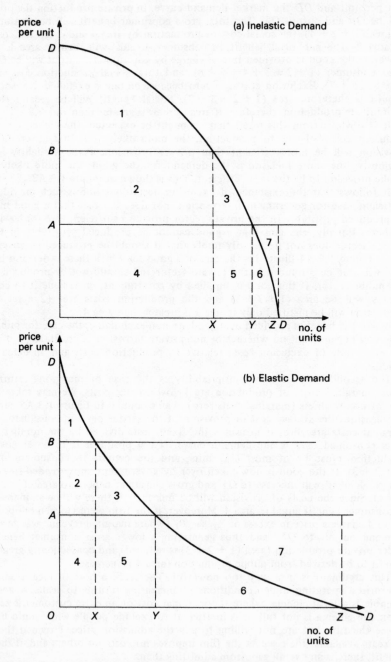

Figure 1.3.A3   *Elasticity of demand and public provision*

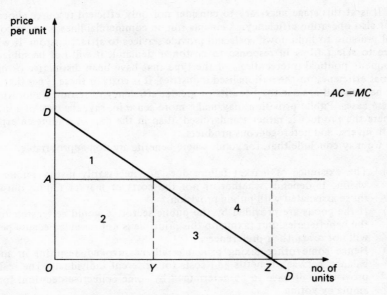

Figure 1.3.A4   *Exclusion costs and public production*

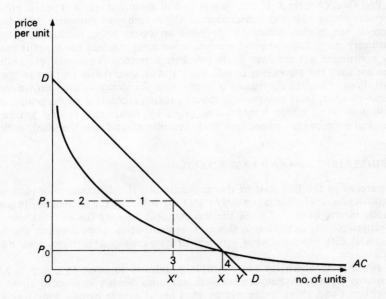

Figure 1.3.A5   *Increasing returns and public production*

It is at this stage necessary to consider not only efficient resource allocation but also operating efficiency. A cinema run on commercial lines is under continual pressure to hold down costs and provide services to attract custom. It will be free to select films in response to customer demand. It will not be subject to frequent political interventions of the type that have been distinctive of managerial efficiency in the nationalised industries. It is costs of these types that have to be weighed against the benefits of greater efficiency of resource allocation in these cases. Public provision may make more sense in, say, the case of a bridge, where the product is rather standardised, than in the case of trading enterprises with diverse and heterogeneous products.

We may conclude that, for goods where benefits are non-appropriable:

(1)   The existence of market failure does not necessarily justify public provision. It depends whether or not the costs of market failure outweigh those associated with public provision.
(2)   If the goods are provided by the public sector, it would be sensible to tax the beneficiaries. But taxing on this principle is not feasible because people will not reveal their preferences.
(3)   Hence some other taxing principle will be invoked, resulting in an imbalance between benefits and costs for different individuals. The scale of provision will have to be determined by some collective decision, for example by voting.

And, although the justification for providing the good is that of greater efficiency, public provision will entail some redistribution of income. In some cases, the efficient (or beneficial) and the redistributive motives for public provision may become blurred.

We discuss criteria for local as against central government provision of services in Part One, Chapter 3. It is sufficient to note here that efficient public provision requires either that the jurisdiction of the government authority be at least as large as the market served by the good or service being produced, or that an authority providing the good receives some compensation for benefits received by consumers not resident in its jurisdiction (intergovernmental externalities). Against this, the arguments of efficiency and accountability that are reviewed in Part Four, Chapter 6, suggest a strong case for decentralising provisions. On these grounds, local government should provide secondary roads, police, refuse collection etc., where benefits are primarily local, and central government national defence etc., where benefits necessarily extend over the whole nation.

REDISTRIBUTION AND PATERNALISM

We argued in the first part of this appendix that if redistribution or paternalism were 'democratic', that is consistent with the wishes of the community in general, public intervention was none the less required because the benefits were non-appropriable. Analytically, in this case, redistribution or paternalism are simply a special case of the general problem of non-appropriability and raise no new difficulties.

However, concern for other people is unlikely to come to a stop at a local authority boundary. People may well feel more directly concerned about their neighbours and those living nearby than about people living a long way away, but there can be little doubt that, at least in the UK, this concern is more

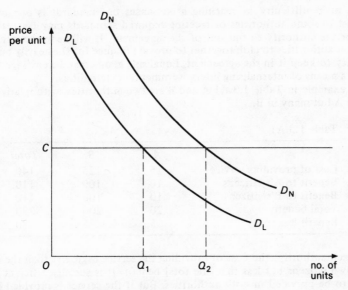

Figure 1.3.A6   *Redistributive spillovers*

national than local in nature.[11] It follows that redistribution cannot efficiently be undertaken by local government, for the citizens in each locality will be concerned about redistribution nationally, but argue that redistribution in their own authority will make little difference to the national picture while being costly to them. Everyone may be in favour of redistribution except at their own expense (in their own locality).

Figure 1.3.A6 depicts this argument. Along the horizontal axis is measured the scale of provision of some redistributive service. The vertical axis measures costs and benefits per unit provided. We may assume the cost per unit to be constant, measured by OC. Curve $D_L D_L$ represents the local demand for the service, that is, the benefits as perceived by citizens of the locality providing the service. Curve $D_N D_N$ represents the national demand, that is, in addition, the benefits accruing to people living outside the locality. If the local authority were concerned only with its own citizens, it would provide OQ_1 units of the service. Further provision would be onerous, in the sense that costs would exceed benefits to the local citizens. But, taking account of national benefits, the optimal scale of provision is OQ_2.

The effect is reciprocal. Just as inhabitants of other localities benefit from redistributive services provided in this local authority, so citizens of this locality benefit from redistributive services provided outside its boundaries. Because of this reciprocal effect, it is in the interests of local authorities to get together and agree each to provide more of the service, on the understanding that others will too. (This process is known as 'internalising the externality'.) This may explain why local authorities often seem keen to reach agreement on the scale of services to be provided, and opt for conformity rather than to reflect the diversity of local preferences and conditions. Alternatively, central government may be the agent of conformity, but there need be no conflict of interest between central government and local authorities collectively on this matter.

The main difficulty in reaching a consensus on standards is one of costs. The cost to some authorities of meeting required standards may be sufficiently high for the authority to opt out of the agreement. It will be in the interests of the other authorities to club together to provide finance for the heavily burdened authority to keep it in the agreement. Equalising grants may be envisaged in this way as a means of internalising intergovernmental externalities.

For example in Table 1.3.A1 A and B are two authorities, with relatively few poor in A but many in B.

Table 1.3.A1

	A	*B*	*Total*
Cost of providing service	15	125	140
Benefit to A's citizens	10	100	110
Benefit to B's citizens	10	100	110
Total benefit	20	200	220
Benefit less cost	5	75	80

In each authority, the cost of providing the service is greater than the benefit to its own citizens but less than the total benefit. It is socially efficient for the service to be provided in both authorities. But if the service is provided in both authorities, the citizens of each will derive 110 benefit, but while the citizens of A will pay only 15, those of B will pay 125. Clearly, the citizens of B will not be party to the agreement. But a transfer payment from A to B could enable the citizens of both authorities to benefit. A transfer which equalised the cost (net of transfer) of providing the service would equalise benefits and maximise agreement on service provision.

NOTES

1 The term is due to Head (1974).
2 Sometimes known as 'merit wants'. See, for example, Musgrave, (1959, p. 13).
3 The concept is from Musgrave (1959, p. 86).
4 This term is also due to Musgrave (1959). The basic analysis goes back to Dupuit (1844).
5 This potential Pareto improvement, or 'Hicks–Kaldor', or 'compensation' criterion, forms the basis of conventional welfare economics.
6 This is intended only as an illustrative example. Clearly, there are many cogent arguments for charges and cash transfers for medical services.
7 If A, B and C will each feel better if some individual, X, receives an additional £1, there is no means, if the payment is made, of excluding any of them from that benefit and, in consequence, no means of charging them privately to finance it.
8 The government has other means at its disposal for this purpose, in particular legal obligations. It is sometimes suggested that where the consumption of a good is a legal obligation (as with education) it should be provided free of charge. The logic underlying this suggestion is not clear, however.
9 For example, an individual who chose not to contribute to the costs of the war against Hitler cannot be excluded from the benefits of victory. Likewise, with the arrest of IRA terrorists at the present time.
10 For some of the problems involved even in this case see Samuelson (1954).
11 As evidence by the national, rather than local, interest excited by, say, the Maria Caldwell case, or the William Tyndale School Inquiry.

4 The Growth of Local Expenditure

In money terms the growth of local expenditure has been almost continuous; but money comparisons are virtually meaningless over long periods where there have been huge changes in price levels. In real terms, however, the growth in local expenditure has also been very great. Unreliable though the figures are there was a 700 per cent increase between 1790 and 1870. The rate of growth in the next quarter century was 420 per cent. Between 1900 and 1975 it increased 900 per cent while gross national product (GNP), also in real terms, rose by 600 per cent.

More interesting is the growth in real local expenditure per head (Table 1.4.1) which gives some indication of the growth in the amount of local services consumed by the average citizen, though since there is no price index specific to expenditure, there will be distortions because of changes in local prices relative to the gross domestic product (GDP) index we have used. Between 1890 and 1975 real current expenditures per capita increased by about 850 per cent and capital expenditure by about 2,100 per cent.

Table 1.4.1   *Real total, current and capital expenditure per head (1975 prices) (1790–1890 – England and Wales; after 1890 – Great Britain)*

| Year | Expenditure per head (£) | | |
	Total	Current	Capital
1790	6	–	–
1840	11	–	–
1870	19	–	–
1880	34	–	–
1890	33	29	4
1900	55	41	14
1910	74	57	17
1921	74	58	16
1930	119	95	24
1950	114	82	32
1960	152	116	36
1970	289	217	72
1975	334	250	84

Notes: Detailed information on each year and functional head is shown in Appendix 1.4.A1 to this chapter. Sources are explained there and they are for all tables and figures presented in this chapter. As one expects over such a long historical period it has not always been possible to measure the same items in every year.

Most of our analysis will be in terms of aggregate local expenditure for Great Britain. Over the whole period the average growth rate of current expenditure has been 3.4 per cent per annum and of capital expenditure, 3.9 per cent. These averages hide large variations in growth rates in different sub-periods. During both world wars local expenditure fell drastically. If we ignore the postwar catching up to prewar levels of expenditure, the largest average growth rates occurred between 1870 and 1900 and between 1955 and 1975. In both these periods the annual rate of growth exceeded 5 per cent. The longest peacetime period undisturbed by previous wartime falls in expenditure for which we have continuous data is 1870–1914. Over this period the average growth rate was 4.5 per cent per annum. However, most of this growth occurred between 1870 and 1900. Between 1900 and 1914 the growth rate only averaged about 2.5 per cent per annum. In 1921, expenditure again reached its prewar level. Between then and 1938 the growth rate was 4.2 per cent per annum. The average annual growth rate of local expenditure in the three peacetime periods has been just under $4\frac{1}{2}$ per cent per annum, with the highest growth rate occurring after the Second World War.

Local expenditures increased from about 3 per cent of GNP in 1870 to about 18 per cent in 1975. Figure 1.4.1 shows the ratio of local current and capital expenditure to GNP over the whole period. Between 1870 and 1880 the ratio of total local expenditure to GNP increased from just under 3 per cent to about 5 per cent. This was a period of rapid growth in local expenditure at a time of low growth in GNP. Between 1880 and 1900 the ratio of both current and capital expenditure to GNP remained nearly constant. Though this was a period in which local expenditure grew at an extremely high rate, so did GNP. Between 1900 and the First World War current and capital expenditure behaved differently. Current expenditure rose slowly but persistently as a proportion of GNP while with the exception of the first three or four years of this century, capital expenditure started falling as a fraction of GNP and reached its lowest point by the beginning of the war. After the war both current and capital expenditure rose as a proportion of GNP with current expenditure reaching a peak of just under 13 per cent of GNP in 1932, a fraction not reached again until over thirty years later in 1969. Between the wars capital expenditure fluctuated around 3 or 4 per cent of GNP and did not start rising above this level until 1965. Between 1965 and 1975 current expenditure has been rising quite rapidly as a proportion of GNP, while capital expenditure has been reasonably constant at around 5 per cent.

What mainly distinguishes the history of local expenditure in Britain in the 1960s and early 1970s is the combination of a high, but not unprecedented rate of growth in local expenditure, with an unprecedented increase in local expenditure as a proportion of GNP. As we shall see in the next chapter, however, the direct impact on the ratepayer in the 1960s and 1970s was cushioned by increases in grant which kept the proportion of local expenditure financed out of rates an almost constant proportion of GNP.

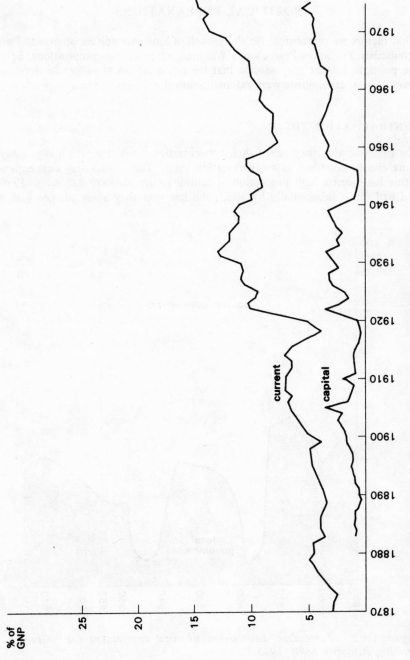

Figure 1.4.1 *Local current and capital expenditure as a proportion of GNP*

POLITICAL EXPLANATIONS

What factors are responsible for the growth of local expenditure observed? Two economists, Professors Peacock and Wiseman, advanced two propositions. Both are political, in that they assume that the prime factors affecting the development of local expenditure were external political attitudes or events.

CENTRALISATION THESIS

The first was what they called their concentration thesis, but which is possibly more clearly described as a centralisation thesis. They noted that local expenditure had been a high proportion of central government expenditure in 1890 and had fallen substantially by 1955, the last year they analysed. (As Figure

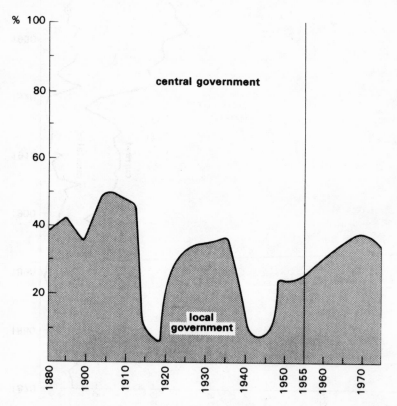

Figure 1.4.2. *Percentage distribution of total government expenditure by spending authority 1890–1975*
Sources: Peacock and Wiseman (1961, p. 109); *National Income and Expenditure* (Blue Books).

1.4.2 shows it was 38 per cent in 1890, 24 per cent in 1955.) Their proposition was that over time there is a persistent tendency for the scope of local government to decline relative to that of central government, so that there is a progressive 'restriction to the central level of the important growth in government activities and responsibilities as a whole' (Peacock and Wiseman, 1961, p. 10). They predicted this concentration or centralisation would continue and that, therefore, there would be a relative decline in local government. Experience has falsified this prediction. By 1975, local government expenditure had risen to become more than 35 per cent of total government expenditure.

Investigation of Figure. 1.4.2 suggests that rather than centralisation of expenditure what has happened in Britain is more complex. In peacetime, local expenditure has tended to rise as a proportion of total government expenditure. It rose from 1840 to 1895 (though Figure 1.4.2 does not show this); from 1900 to 1905; from 1921 to 1937; and from 1946 to 1970. Not surprisingly, both wars and preparations for war have the opposite effect. We do not have data to show the effect of the Napoleonic or Crimean Wars, but both the Boer War and the two world wars increased central government's share. This increase began a few years earlier with the preparation for war. The Boer War did not lead to a reduction in real local government expenditure, but both the two world wars did. This is most probably a reflection of the effect of their greater length and scale in discouraging local expenditure. The reasons for these opposite consequences of major wars and of peace are not surprising, and are a reflection of the pattern we discovered in the eighteenth century where local government tends to provide the government goods and services wanted in peace; while central government's expenditure has been more concentrated on expenditure for war, and on imperial and foreign affairs. One might formulate a peacetime decentralisation hypothesis: the longer peace lasts, the higher will be local public expenditure as a proportion of total public expenditure.

Yet even this peacetime decentralisation thesis is too facile a basis for prediction for two reasons. First, the First and Second World Wars had some lasting effect in lowering the local proportion of total government expenditure. In spite of the recurrent peacetime trends, there is a sense in which Peacock and Wiseman are right. The local government proportion has never been as high again as it was in 1905 before preparation for the First World War increased central expenditure. Thirty years after the Second World War that proportion has not reached the level achieved after the First World War by 1925. There has been a secular shift of activities and responsibilities from central to local government.

Second, there has been more variability in the local proportion in peacetime than is consistent with relying much on a peacetime decentralisation thesis. In the depths of the 1930s slump there was an increase in absolute central expenditure per head relative to local expenditure. (A parallel can be drawn between this and the increase in central expenditure relative to local expenditure in the economic crisis of the mid-1970s.) Even in the early 1930s when local government bore much more of the burden of unemployment relief, there was a tendency for the slump to impose a greater burden of expenditure on central government. This is *a fortiori* true in the mid-1970s when central government shoulders almost all the burden of unemployment relief.

Thus neither the centralisation thesis, nor its partial antithesis the peacetime decentralisation thesis, would seem to be true in any pure form.

DISPLACEMENT THESIS

Peacock and Wiseman called their second proposition the displacement effect (1961). Each war has meant a very large increase in central government expenditure and consequently in some mixture of national taxation and borrowing to pay for it. After the war is over, war-related expenditure falls, but the fall in national taxation in this century has not been as great. As Lady Hicks once put it, 'the high level of taxation which can be established in war-time, almost without protest, conditions tax-payers to permanently higher taxation' (1938, p. 13). Thus it is argued that the nation becomes used to higher taxation in war — and that postwar governments take advantage of this to raise peacetime public expenditure, central and local, to a new level.

There are difficulties with this thesis also. Veverka (1963, pp. 111–27) has argued that there is no sign of such a displacement effect after the Napoleonic Wars when the need to maintain a higher level of national taxation to pay interest on the National Debt created by the war has been allowed for. As we have seen, central government was indeed almost immediately anxious that more should be spent on police and prisons, and later on sanitation and health, but central government did not have the apparatus, and local authorities mostly had neither the will nor the competence, to take on these responsibilities. Therefore total government expenditure fell after 1815. There was no effective or politically acceptable way of using the higher levels of taxation accepted during the wars for peaceful purposes.

Figure 1.4.1 shows no displacement effect on local expenditures after the Boer War. On the contrary, the rise in local expenditures occurred before and during the war. Between 1902 and 1907, local expenditures remained constant. As can be seen from Figure 1.4.2 central government expenditure must have been falling at least until 1905.

After the First World War, a large part of the surplus taxation was used to pay interest on the National Debt created to pay for the war. However, there was an increase in public expenditure, though as we shall argue later this was mostly used to finance the consequences of legislation passed before that war.

The only occasion when there has been a clear displacement effect was after the Second World War when a Labour government was returned with a very different attitude to public expenditure and plainly intended to use wartime tax levels to finance new expenditure; but one true example does not prove a hypothesis.[1] While there may be some general assent to the proposition that war familiarises society into higher tax levels which it might otherwise have not wished to experience, the causes of the increasing expenditure, both central and local, are scarcely illuminated by such a generalisation as the displacement effect. Moreover, to use such a hypothesis to argue that one must wait for a war to prepare public opinion for a major increase in public expenditure would be seriously misleading. During most of the 1960s central expenditure rose relative to GNP at the same time as local expenditure was also rising relative to GNP;

though central expenditure growth started a few years later. Though not on the scale of the expenditure required to finance a war, it amounts to a not inconsiderable increase in total government expenditure relative to GNP for peaceful purposes.

However, we are most interested in any implications the displacement effect might have for local expenditure and its financing. The effect of a war on the division of financing between central and local government itself requires some explaining. After the Boer War it turned almost on accident. Balfour had intended that the very important 1902 Education Act which established rate-borne primary education as a duty of all local authorities should be financed from central taxation; but the tenacity and commando tactics of the Boers which unexpectedly prolonged the war into 1902 made him change his mind. Since expenditure had not fallen, he would have had to increase national taxation which he would not do. He decided that a high proportion of the expenditure must be borne by the rates. The example shows how accidental the division of financing between local and central government has sometimes been. Even so, one may argue that there was a covert displacement effect. The expectation that the war would end and revenues be released may have been one reason why Balfour was able to pass education legislation of a kind which had failed to get through Parliament before the Boer War.

Between 1921 and 1925, the annual growth of local expenditure was 5 per cent per annum. Between 1946 and 1950 it was 4.6 per cent. It is plausible that the aftermath of war is a period of dislocation when a country is trying to get back to normal, when there is a demand for public expenditure to help achieve this — to smooth the transition from war to peace. This demand may not be met, as after the Napoleonic Wars, because the machinery is not available to effect it, and central government is generally averse from such expenditures. The dislocation after the Boer War was comparatively trivial but there was nevertheless some pressure to spend more. After the First World War, the pressures were far greater and Lloyd George, as Prime Minister, was personally keen on social public expenditure; but he faced three difficulties. The first, as we have seen, that established public opinion was hostile to such expenditure, and as a leader of a coalition dependent on Conservative support, he was vulnerable to this. Second, the overhang of a huge National Debt limited his freedom to spend from national taxation. Third, most of the goods and services which he was under pressure to provide to help the returning servicemen were, in fact, traditionally provided by local government who could not benefit directly from any surplus national taxation. After the Second World War, the Attlee government was less prevented from increasing public expenditure than Lloyd George had been. Because of the influence of Keynes and because the Labour government had a clear majority, it was freer to spend. Because under Keynes's influence, the Second World War had been financed by taxation rather than primarily by borrowing, much more of the surplus taxation released by the end of the war was available to finance increased public expenditure. Third, while local expenditure increased at an even more rapid rate than after 1918, there was also a large increase in central expenditure. For the first time the provision of goods by government was less exclusively effected through local government.

Thus in each case there was a displacement effect, though much modified by the circumstances of the times. In each case this century, one effect of the ending of a major war has been an increase in local expenditure, but it would be a mistake to see this as mainly a consequence of the coming into being of surplus taxation. The ending of a war creates social problems and a political climate more receptive to increases in public expenditure. Before 1946 most of this demand was for the kinds of goods and services local government traditionally provides.

Yet in spite of these plausible reasons for a displacement effect, taking a longer time period puts these postwar rises into a quite different perspective. If, instead, one calculates a growth rate from the last prewar year substantially unaffected by war — 1913 and 1938 — even if one assumes that this year immediately preceded the peacetime years unaffected by war — 1920 and 1946 — so that one is in effect assuming that the war counts for nothing, then the rapid growth disappears. (This is *a fortiori* if one plots the average annual rate of growth over all the years between 1913 and 1925, and 1938 and 1946). Thus the postwar rapidity of growth in local expenditure is an illusion. It is little more than a process of returning to immediately prewar levels of local expenditure. When this is allowed for, local expenditure grew little in real terms immediately after either the First or Second World War.

Thus it would seem that the displacement effect also does not have much to contribute to our understanding of the growth of local expenditure.

THE EFFECT OF GOVERNMENTS

Let us see whether there is any relation between the government in power and the rate of growth of local expenditure. Table 1.4.2 shows the annual growth of local expenditure during each term in office. It is inevitably crude. Governments do not finish at the end of financial years. Some governments have been combined in the table. The effect of lagging by one year has been explored. While substantial in a few instances, it does not affect the conclusions we come to in this section.

Tables 1.4.2 and 1.4.3 appear robust enough to cast doubt on some of the more obvious political hypotheses. Table 1.4.3 ranks administrations in order from the highest to the lowest growth rates, for total, current and capital expenditures separately.

If we take growth in total local expenditure first, and use the lower figures for postwar governments which are adjusted to allow for catching up to prewar levels of expenditure:

(1) One Labour administration is among the six with the highest expenditure growth rates.

(2) Some Conservative administrations show low increases, but others — Disraeli (1874—80), Salisbury (1895—1902), Macmillan and Home (1957— 64) and Baldwin (1924—9) show high increases in local expenditure.

(3) There is as much variability in Liberal administrations. One cannot easily distinguish between nineteenth-century administrations which one might

Table 1.4.2. *The relationship between change of government and the rate of growth of local expenditure*

	Total	Current	Capital
Gladstone (Dec. 1868–Feb. 1874)	1.7	–	–
Disraeli (Feb. 1874–April 1880)	7.3	–	–
Gladstone (April 1880–June 1885)	2.3	–	–
Salisbury (June 1885–Aug. 1892)	3.0	3.2	1.7
Gladstone (Aug. 1892–June 1895)	4.9	3.9	10.4
Salisbury (June 1895–July 1902)	5.5	3.9	10.8
Balfour (July 1902–Dec. 1905)	2.1	4.5	−5.9
Campbell-Bannerman (Dec. 1905–April 1908)	−0.6	0.9	−8.2
Asquith (peacetime) (April 1908–Dec. 1914)	1.8	2.1	−0.3
Lloyd George (peacetime)(Dec. 1920–Oct. 1922)	4.8(18.9)[a]	2.9(15.3)[a]	13.7(31.5)[a]
Law and Baldwin (Oct. 1922–Jan. 1924)	−5.4	−0.2	−24.8
MacDonald (Jan. 1924–Nov. 1924)	3.3	1.2	16.2
Baldwin (Nov. 1924–June 1929)	4.5	4.2	6.3
MacDonald (June 1929–Aug. 1931)	3.7	2.5	9.0
National government (Aug. 1931–June 1935)	1.6	2.6	−2.9
Baldwin and Chamberlain (peacetime)(June 1935–March 1938)[b]	2.8	0.7	12.7
Attlee (peacetime) (May 1945–Oct. 1951)	−1.2 (3.6)[a]	−1.9(−1.3)[a]	0.9(35.5)[a]
Churchill and Eden (Oct. 1951–June 1957)	3.6	4.1	2.3
Macmillan and Home (Jan. 1957–Oct. 1964)	5.2	4.7	6.3
Wilson (Oct. 1964–June 1970)	5.7	6.9	2.5
Heath (June 1970–Feb. 1974)	4.2	3.3	6.6
Wilson (Feb. 1974–March 1975)	−2.5	−0.7	−7.3

[a] First figure is adjusted for war.
[b] It has only been possible to calculate growth rates up to date shown rather than over the whole period of office.

Table 1.4.3. *Governments and their expenditures ranked by growth rates*

(1) Total	%
Disraeli 1874–80	7.3
Wilson 1964–70	5.7
Salisbury 1895–1902	5.5
Macmillan and Home 1957–64	5.2
Gladstone 1892–5	4.9
Lloyd George 1920–2	4.8
Baldwin 1924–9	4.5
Heath 1970–4	4.2
MacDonald 1929–31	3.7
Churchill and Eden 1951–7	3.6
MacDonald 1924	3.3
Salisbury 1885–92	3.0
Baldwin and Chamberlain 1935–8	2.8
Gladstone 1880–5	2.3
Balfour 1902–5	2.1
Asquith 1908–14	1.8
Gladstone 1868–74	1.7
Campbell-Bannerman 1905–8	−0.6
Attlee 1946–51	−1.2
Wilson 1974–5	−2.5
Law and Baldwin 1922–4	−5.4

(2) Current	
Wilson 1964–70	6.9
Macmillan and Home 1957–64	4.7
Balfour 1902–5	4.5
Baldwin 1924–9	4.2
Churchill and Eden 1951–7	4.1
Salisbury 1895–1902	3.9
Gladstone 1892–5	3.9
Heath 1970–4	3.3
Salisbury 1885–92	3.2
Lloyd George 1920–2	2.9
National government 1931–5	2.6
MacDonald 1929–31	2.5
Asquith 1908–14	2.1
MacDonald 1924	1.2
Campbell-Bannerman 1905–8	0.9
Baldwin and Chamberlain 1935–8	0.7
Law and Baldwin 1922–4	−0.2
Wilson 1974–5	−0.7
Attlee 1946–51	−1.9

(3) Capital	
MacDonald 1924	16.2
Lloyd George 1920–2	13.7
Baldwin and Chamberlain 1935–8	12.7
Salisbury 1895–1902	10.8

Table 1.4.3   *(continued)*

	%
Gladstone 1892—5	10.4
MacDonald 1929—31	9.0
Heath 1970—4	6.6
Baldwin 1924—9	6.3
Macmillan and Home 1957—64	6.3
Wilson 1964—70	2.5
Churchill 1951—7	2.3
Salisbury 1885—92	1.7
Attlee 1946—51	0.9
Asquith 1908—14	−0.3
National government 1931—5	*−2.9
Balfour 1902—5	−5.9
Wilson 1974—5	−7.3
Campbell-Bannerman 1905—8	−8.2
Law and Baldwin 1922—4	−24.8

expect to be most influenced by *laissez-faire* attitudes and least keen on government intervention, on the one hand, and twentieth-century Liberal administrations which one might think more of as forerunners of Labour government on the other.

(4)   Neither do the administrations which have a historical reputation as reforming ministries appear to be high spenders. Neither Gladstone (1868—74), Asquith in peacetime nor Attlee were high spenders.

(5)   Those eight governments associated with the highest rates of growth in local expenditure have surprisingly little in common which is obvious. Five were Conservative, one Liberal, and a Liberal/Conservative coalition and one was Labour.

In each case, it is not difficult to find plausible reasons why administrations have the rank order shown in the table. Some will emerge later in this chapter. It is also worth noting that until after the Second World War it is plausible that national politics had much less effect on local expenditure than it has had since. What does seem clear, however, is that there is no simple connection between the politics of a government or its reputation as a reforming administration, and the growth of total local expenditure.

If we now look at current expenditure growth rates in Table 1.4.3 there is a similar variety of politics and reforming reputation in those governments with high and low growth rates. What does emerge, however, is the high growth of current local expenditure that has taken place in every administration since Sir Winston Churchill's in 1951, except during 1974 and 1975. Interestingly, this higher growth rate does not begin with Attlee over whose period of office (adjusted to allow for catching up) there was a fall in local current expenditure.

The implication of the third part of Table 1.4.3 — 'capital expenditure' — is again not political. There is much greater variability in capital expenditure between administrations than there is in current though there is a tendency for earlier administrations to have higher growth rates.

ECONOMIC EXPLANATIONS

CYCLICAL INFLUENCES

Let us now turn to economic factors affecting local expenditure and first see how far it has been affected by cyclical influences.

(1) While trade cycles obviously cannot explain the upward trend in local expenditure since 1870, they might be expected to have caused fluctuations in it. Local government might react to a fall in the income of its ratepayers by reducing its expenditure and the rates it raises from them. In this case, local expenditure would be cyclical, falling in a slump and rising in a boom. We might expect that if ratepayers experience a fall in income in a recession, they will wish to cut down their expenditure on local goods and services via the rates, as they do their private consumption and saving. Otherwise all the cuts would have to be taken by the last two. Similarly, when local output and incomes rise, local expenditure would be expected to rise so that consumption of its products would rise with private expenditure. The ultimate sanction for this behaviour on local politicians might be fear of losing an election if they behaved unpopularly. But more immediately one would expect them to be responsive to current public opinion. The cyclical theory of local expenditure postulates that local authorities behave like private citizens, cutting their expenditure with a fall in output, employment and income. Since British local authorities have severe restrictions on their ability to save so that they are less able to maintain consumption out of reduced income, cyclical pressures might be expected to lead to greater fluctuations in their expenditure than in that of private consumers. On this theory also local government would be acting like a pre-Keynesian central government which cut its expenditures to achieve a balanced budget.

(2) The alternative is that local expenditure is counter-cyclical. Local government might react to offset fluctuations in local output, employment and income. Thus it would increase its expenditure in recession and possibly rein it back in cyclical upswings. For this to be true on the expenditure side, one does not have to postulate that local authorities knowingly behave in a Keynesian manner. Local authority responsibility for poor relief up until 1934 was a built-in stabilising mechanism which raised local expenditure automatically when there was local poverty and unemployment. For this reason, poor relief rose from 10 per cent of local current expenditure in 1920 to 15 per cent in 1927. This could not be a Keynesian mechanism in the full sense, since the additional poor relief had to be financed from increasing the rates so that aggregate local incomes were unchanged. In a more limited sense, there could be a stimulating effect on the local economy in so far as the local ratepayer was richer and had a higher propensity to save than those on poor relief. The statutory inability of local authorities to run a budget deficit, however, limits severely the ability of a local authority to act in a Keynesian manner to offset cyclical fluctuations. Even if they had this ability, it is questionable whether it would benefit any individual local authority so to act since experience suggests that a high proportion of local spending is on goods and services produced elsewhere (see Oates, 1972, app. to ch. 2). Therefore, the multiplier effect on any local stimulus on local employ-

ment is likely to be low. But what is pointless for a single authority would not be so for the collectivity of local authorities. It is possible to imagine them acting together in a Keynesian manner.

The data we have before the First World War is both incomplete and in many respects suspect. Our knowledge of economic conditions in any year is worse than of local government finance. Even so there is evidence of cyclical influences. From 1870 to 1883 the data do not make it possible to distinguish between the growth of capital and current expenditure. Yet is is fairly clear from the growth of local authority loan charges that the most rapid growth under Disraeli's 1874 to 1880 government was in local capital spending, as it was also in the second period of rapid growth between 1892 and 1902. This is one reason for thinking it plausible that economics were more important than national political considerations in prompting these growth spurts. They were periods when we know from other evidence that many of the major British cities were investing in civic improvement, sanitation, gas, water and sewerage. What is interesting is that the main spurts were counter-cyclical. Both the late 1870s and the early 1890s were periods of relative depression as economic activity fell from peaks in 1874 and 1891 to troughs in 1879 and 1893. As Rostow notes of the late 1870s, 'The building industry was still finding a fair amount of work although the full activity of 1873–6 had gone. In some districts local government contracts for municipal building and schools constituted a substantial part of new construction' (1948, p. 209). Goschen also observed that low interest rates made borrowing very attractive to local authorities at this time (1905, pp. 198–200). While it would need more detailed inquiry than we can give, it seems far from unlikely that the wish of builders to mitigate the effects of a slackening in their orders from the private sector and the influence they exerted on local authorities in pursuit of this, were as important reasons for the local authority expenditure booms of the 1870s and 1890s as was civic pride.

Just before the end of the century, capital expenditure started growing rapidly and continued until 1903. From then until the First World War it declined steadily. Throughout this period changes in GNP are not clearly associated with movements in local capital expenditure. The fall in capital expenditure during the first decade of the twentieth century was, however, at a time of substantial capital migration overseas.

Figure 1.4.1 shows that in the 1920s current total local expenditure tended to be cyclical. If we ignore the spurt in local expenditure between 1921–2 unaccompanied by any major change in GNP, and the spurt in GNP between 1924–5 (reversed a year later) unaccompanied by a major change in current expenditure growth, the pattern of the two series is very similar. However, in the 1930s current expenditure showed countercyclical tendencies. Excluding the very great increase in capital expenditure after the First World War, it was generally counter-cyclical during the 1920s and 1930s except for the large fall in the middle of the Great Depression from 1933 to 1935. After the Second World War, from about 1949 to 1961, and again from about 1971 to 1975 current expenditure was cyclical, as was capital expenditure except for the years between 1955 and 1959. The big spurt of expenditure between 1946 and 1949 was mainly capital expenditure and can be attributed to postwar catching up and recovery.

But between 1961 and 1971 the two series do not mirror each other. In this period, current expenditure and its rate of growth seemed impervious to movements in GNP. The same held for capital expenditure until 1966. This was a decade of unprecedented growth of local expenditure. Over this period both current and capital expenditure more than doubled.

There is clearly a very close relationship between movements in local expenditure and in GNP. A measure of this relationship is income elasticity, defined in this case as the proportionate change in real local expenditure associated with a proportionate change in GNP.[2] The income elasticity has been amazingly stable between 1870 and 1975 (see Table 1.4.4). For current expenditure it has, with a few exceptions, been between 2.3 and 3.7 — a 1 per cent change in GNP was associated with between 2 per cent and 4 per cent change in local expenditure. Between 1883 and 1900 it was 3.3. Between 1900 and 1914 it was 2.5. Between 1921 and 1938 it was 2.3. Between 1953, when local expenditure returned to previous levels, and 1975 it was 3.1. The elasticity for capital expenditure has been much more volatile.

Table 1.4.4.   *Elasticities of expenditure*

	Total expenditure			Expenditure per head		
	Total	Current	Capital	Total	Current	Capital
1870–83	2.8	–	–	5.8	–	–
1883–1914	3.4	3.7	2.0	3.6	4.0	1.7
1883–1900	3.8	3.3	6.2	4.0	3.2	7.2
1900–14	1.6	2.5	−1.1	2.0	3.8	−3.0
1921–38	2.3	2.3	2.4	2.6	2.5	2.7
1953–75	2.7	3.1	1.8	3.0	3.5	1.9
1953–60	1.4	2.3	−0.4	1.4	2.5	−0.8
1960–75	3.0	2.9	3.4	3.3	3.2	3.7

Arguably a more meaningful measure is in terms of elasticities of expenditure per head. The effect is to increase the elasticity in the nineteenth century. Since then, declining population growth shows that local authorities' willingness to spend for a given increase in real income per head was comparatively steady from 1921 to 1960 (current expenditure) but has increased since. The fluctuation in capital expenditure elasticities still exists.

A major outcome of this analysis is its relevance for the prediction of current expenditure. The long-run stability of the relationship suggests that for purposes of prediction a 1 per cent increase in real income per head is likely to be associated with a 3 per cent increase in local current expenditure per head.

Table 1.4.5. Current and capital expenditure by major services as a percentage of total current, and total capital expenditure respectively (Selected years) – England and Wales. (Figures do not sum to 100 because of missing data.)

	1880	1890	1900	1910	1920	1930	1940	1950	1960	1970	1975
Current Expenditure											
Education	6.6	8.5	11.6	21.9	21.2	19.8	17.0	30.3	37.3	35.1	35.9
Poor Relief	13.9	13.7	11.1	9.9	7.2	8.0	6.1	–	–	–	–
Welfare	–	–	–	–	–	–	–	2.9	3.1	3.0	6.1
Housing	–	–	0.1	0.5	0.5	8.3	8.2	9.5	15.0	14.7	16.6
Highways	–	13.1	12.0	11.2	9.9	12.0	7.7	7.4	6.0	4.7	3.6
Hospitals	–	0.4	1.3	1.5	3.3	2.7	5.7	–	–	–	–
Health	–	–	–	–	–	–	–	3.8	3.7	3.1	–
Sewerage	–	2.1	2.4	3.7	2.7	2.4	2.2	2.1	2.1	2.4	–
Refuse	–	–	2.2	1.7	2.4	1.7	1.5	2.4	2.0	1.8	1.9
Parks	–	0.5	0.8	1.1	0.9	1.2	1.2	1.6	1.5	1.2	1.3
Fire	–	0.4	0.5	0.5	0.5	0.5	0.6	1.6	1.5	1.2	1.3
Police	6.2	8.1	6.7	5.3	6.6	5.1	5.4	5.7	5.8	5.6	5.4
Trading Services											
Water	–	1.9	2.0	6.7	4.9	4.5	4.2	4.2	3.4	2.9	–
Gas	–	5.8	6.1	5.5	6.5	4.0	3.2	0.4	–	–	–
Electricity	–	–	0.8	2.8	5.0	6.8	10.3	–	–	–	–
Transport	–	–	1.4	5.9	7.7	6.3	4.3	5.9	4.1	2.1	0.6
Harbours	1.8	2.5	2.2	5.4	5.6	3.1	2.5	3.0	2.4	1.3	0.2
Capital Expenditure											
Education	–	11.3	8.4	7.1	2.9	5.5	12.3	8.5	5.1	12.9	10.2
Work-houses	–	5.6	4.8	1.0	0.4	0.8	0.9	–	–	–	–
Welfare	–	–	–	–	–	–	–	0.9	0.9	1.2	1.8
Housing	–	1.4	3.2	1.0	20.1	39.3	24.9	70.6	56.9	48.4	65.9
Highways	–	15.5	12.9	4.7	5.0	14.9	8.4	1.5	4.6	9.7	7.5
Hospitals	–	0.4	1.3	1.5	3.3	2.7	5.7	–	–	–	–

Table 1.4.5. (continued)

Health	—	—	—	—	—	—	—	3.8	3.7	3.1	—
Sewerage	—	12.7	8.0	5.2	2.9	4.1	4.9	2.9	6.2	6.7	0.5
Refuse	—	—	—	—	—	0.3	0.3	0.2	0.2	0.7	1.8
Parks	—	5.6	2.0	0.7	0.8	1.6	1.2	0.4	0.5	0.7	0.2
Fire	—	—	—	—	—	0.2	0.6	0.1	0.4	0.3	0.2
Police	—	—	—	—	—	0.4	0.1	0.7	0.6	1.0	0.9
Trading Services											
Water	—	18.6	16.9	6.4	7.9	4.7	5.4	4.6	4.9	4.1	—
Gas	—	2.8	4.0	1.0	3.8	1.4	1.5	0.2	—	—	—
Electricity	—	—	11.2	2.7	15.1	14.0	12.7	—	—	—	—
Transport	—	—	5.6	5.7	5.9	2.2	1.8	2.7	0.4	0.6	0.1
Harbours	—	8.5	6.4	56.9	8.8	1.6	1.3	1.0	1.3	0.7	0.3

GROWTH OF SERVICES

Though arguably the most interesting conclusions to this chapter have already been reached, let us see how far we can increase our understanding of the growth of local expenditure by looking at what happened to different services. Unfortunately statistical difficulties – changes of definition and incompleteness of the data – make it difficult to trace the growth of services through from beginning to end.

Over the long run, however, one can form an impression of changes in each service both as a percentage of total expenditure and in absolute terms (see Figure 1.4.3 and Appendix 1.4.A1). Education current expenditure increased as a percentage until the 1960s, but has been more stable since then. Poor relief used to be important, but was taken away from local authorities in the 1930s and 1940s. From 1960 the increase in personal social services has been rapid. Current and capital expenditure on roads have declined as a proportion over time. The huge drop in gas and electricity is reflected in the figures from the late 1940s when these services were taken away from local government.

Of particular interest to us are the periods of greatest growth, and also decline, in the earlier years. Since the late 1950s we are interested in all the period up to the present as a prelude to our later analysis.

(1) 1875–80

The breakdown of figures for this period is incomplete. We know that local authority borrowing was running at £200 million per annum in real terms by 1879/80 (see Part One, Appendix 1.5.A1). Thus the impression is one of a period dominated by an increase in capital expenditure. We also have data on total educational expenditure which rose by 68 per cent over the period. We do not know how much of this was itself school-building; and though a large increase, education was still a small proportion of total local expenditure rising from 5.4 per cent to 6.6 per cent in these years. Moreover, it would be unwise to attribute too much of this increase to W. E. Forster's Education Act passed by Gladstone's administration in 1870. As Cannan (1927, p. 136) observed, while many schools were built and staffed because of that Act, one of its main effects was that many schools which would have been built anyway were now grant-aided.

(2) 1880–1900

Total real expenditure on sewerage rose by 161 per cent during the decade; on highways by about 159 per cent; water and gas by 164 per cent and harbours by 331 per cent. Education also increased very rapidly by 286 per cent, though again much of this will also have been capital expenditure.

(3) 1920–25

Examination of data for 1920–25 confirms this as a period in which the displacement effect created by the surplus of national taxation carrying over from

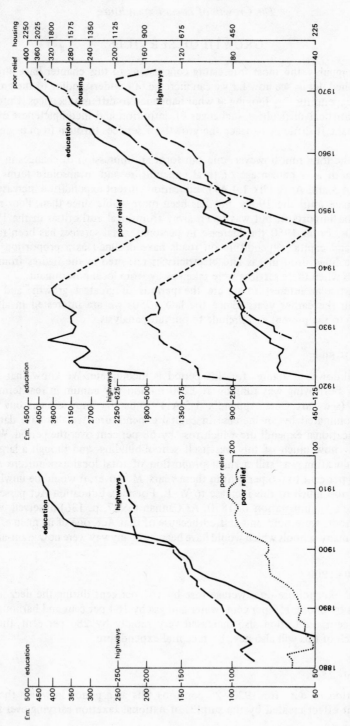

Figure 1.4.3. *Local authority current expenditure: selected services – England and Wales*

the war was simply not enough to finance the strong demands for public expenditure that were themselves a product of the ending of the war. Lloyd George induced a huge increase in local capital expenditure, which rose by £400 million in real terms, or 70 per cent in one year. £300 million of this was expenditure by local authorities on housing. As A. J. P. Taylor has written when Lloyd George talked of making 'a fit country for heroes to live in' his record in social legislation seemed to justify the promise (1965, ch. 4). On this basis, he won the 1919 election and then had to deliver what he had promised. He had promised 'homes for heroes'. One estimate was that 600,000 were needed. Without central machinery he turned to the local authorities to build the houses and because few had any inclination to do so, gave them exceptionally generous grants as an inducement. In 1921, Addison was paying £910 for houses which a year later could be built for £385 each. There were rapid but less dramatic increases in other local expenditures. The most severe and unexpected was in poor relief. Many of those returning from the war could not find jobs. Unemployment doubled between December 1920 and March 1921, and most of the burden fell on local poor relief. In June 1921, more than 2 million were out of work. The combination of the burden of the National Debt, inflation, rapidly rising public expenditure, most of it concentrated on local authorities, and yet the inevitable disappointment of those who had hoped that he would bring about sweeping social reforms helped to destroy Lloyd George. Bonar Law and Baldwin then brought to an end the most rapid increase in local expenditure Britain has experienced.

(4) 1930–35

The years of the world slump were riven by a schizophrenia in central government, which was reflected in local expenditure (Skidelsky, 1976). One wing of the Labour Party was anxious to increase public expenditure to create employment. The party was defeated by a number of forces. It found that most of the public expenditure which would create jobs was in the control of local, not central government. Without paying very high grant percentages, even 100 per cent as was urged on a number of occasions, most local authorities were extremely reluctant to raise expenditure at a time of pressure on incomes. Cuts were initially concentrated in capital expenditure, particularly in expenditure on roads.

If one looks at Figure 1.4.3, one can see the cut-backs in local current expenditure on such items as highways, education and housing that occurred between 1932 and 1935. It is difficult to determine how far these were spontaneous reactions of local authorities to high interest rates and low local incomes, and how far they were caused by central government's exhortation, following the report of the May Committee which urged cuts in all public expenditure. The effect of the rapid increase in unemployment in 1931 and 1932 is visible. But the growing importance of central government provision of unemployment relief, as well as a sustained high level of unemployment, can be seen having its effect in reducing fluctuations in this item thereafter.

(5) 1946–51

The very rapid increase in local expenditure during the Attlee administration was all recovery to prewar levels of expansion. Indeed, local expenditure in real terms had not recovered to its 1938 level even by 1951. This was especially true of current expenditure. While about 60 per cent of the lower level of local current expenditure in 1946 by comparison with 1938 can be explained by the transference of health expenditure to the NHS and its residual poor-relief functions to central government, the rest was the result of the tight rein kept on current expenditure on roads, sewerage, refuse disposal and, oddly, current expenditure on housing which were all kept well below prewar level. Despite the displacement made possible by high wartime levels of taxation, prolonged high levels of defence expenditure and capital reinvestment to replace what was damaged during the war made the central government keep a check on what it saw as less necessary public expenditure. Priority was given to local capital expenditure rather than current. The whole net increase in capital expenditure between 1938 and 1951 (£180 million in 1975 prices) is accounted for by the increase in capital expenditure on housing (£500 million). Rises in other service capital expenditure – by comparison with 1938 – were absolutely small, while the failure of capital expenditure on roads and sewerage to recover to the 1938 level was large enough to find room for the extra housing capital expenditure. Just as after the First World War, political priority was given to housing. Aneurin Bevin was given the task of achieving a far larger housing programme than Lloyd George had attempted. Until 1948 the growth was astonishing, more than 180 per cent in two years (Foot, 1962, Vol. 2, ch. 2). In 1947 it was realised that both the state of the economy and competing demands for capital expenditure should not be allowed to permit such a rapid growth to continue. Thus the rapid growth in housing expenditure was a casualty of the 1947 sterling crisis. Housing capital expenditure continued at roughly the 1947 level through into 1951.

Thus in so far as there was a local expenditure boom between 1946 and 1951, more than 60 per cent of it was accounted for by housing capital expenditure, but over the longer run not even the extraordinary growth of housing capital expenditure was able to prevent overall real decline in local expenditure by comparison with 1938.

(6) THE CHURCHILL AND EDEN ADMINISTRATIONS (1951–6)

In January 1951, the Korean War led the Labour government to a massive re-armament programme which was the principal influence constraining civil public expenditure for the following three years. Nevertheless, Conservatives have been particularly critical of the inadequacies of the Labour housing programme almost throughout the Attlee administration, and it was a main plank in the programme that returned them to power in 1951. By comparison with Bevan's achievement of 200,000 new homes a year, the Conservative target was 300,000 houses a year. As a result, there was an immediate surge in housing capital expenditure of 23 per cent in two years; thereafter it had climbed, but in 1956 it was again well above the level of 1948. Harold Macmillan was then Housing Minister and had achieved his target of 300,000 houses in 1953, but without a proportional increase in capital expenditure. Thus real expenditure per house fell. Part of this achievement may have been an improvement in efficiency, but there was also a decline in the size of houses and in other housing standards.[3]

However, the decline in public capital expenditure on housing (partly matched by a rise in private investment in housing) by the end of the period to a level below that of 1951, and the very moderate increase in other capital programmes with the partial exception of education, sewerage and roads, meant that overall these years were characterised by little growth in capital expenditure.

By contrast, current expenditure grew at the secularly high rate of $6\frac{1}{2}$ per cent per annum on average, continuing postwar trends. Current expenditure on roads − principally maintenance − stayed low. By far the biggest absolute increase was in education which accounted for nearly half of all the increase in both current and capital expenditure over this period. Part of this was attributable to the increase in school population, but not all, since real expenditure per child increased.

(7) MACMILLAN AND HOME ADMINISTRATIONS (1957−64)

These years were marked by the slackening in the rate of growth of current local expenditure and an increase in the rate of growth of local capital expenditure, particularly after 1960. Current expenditure on most services grew at a fairly even rate, though police expenditure rose especially rapidly.

Capital expenditure fell until 1960 when there were large increases in investment in roads and police. A year later, education and housing capital expenditure started to increase more rapidly, especially the last which rose by 50 per cent between 1960 and 1964. Over the whole period, about 22 per cent of the total increase in capital expenditure was accounted for by housing, 17 per cent by roads, and 11 per cent by education.

Many reasons can be adduced for this upturn in capital expenditure. In an influential article, Redfern showed how little investment had taken place in many sectors to offset the depreciation of the war years.[4] Road expenditure was not even keeping pace with the deterioration of existing roads, let alone allowing for rapidly increasing volume of road traffic. It was argued similarly that there had been underinvestment in railways and in social services, for example health. At the same time several commentators pointed out that public investment, even in housing, was low by European standards.[5] There was also a period during which public expenditure was progressively exempted from cyclical influences. In 1957 capital expenditure on roads was excluded from the investment cuts made that year. By 1960, government was beginning to rely more on monetary measures than on changes in public expenditure to control cyclical influences. During this period also the Treasury relaxed its control over public expenditure. The Treasury began to delegate some of its control over spending. As late as 1957 individual building projects by the Ministry of Works had to be sanctioned by the Treasury if they exceeded £1,000 (Brittan, 1964, pp. 83, 84). In 1959, Lord Plowden, an ex-senior civil servant, was asked to review expenditure control.

The main effect of his Report published in 1961, besides recommending greater delegation of spending authority, also initiated the five-year forward plans for public expenditure which have developed into the current PESC system. This had the effect of replacing a system in which individual projects were scrutinised with the Treasury playing a traditional role and tending to oppose any demands for increased expenditure by one where there was expectation that each department's public expenditure would continue as a given proportion of the total unless there were strong positive reasons for lowering or raising.

(8) FIRST WILSON ADMINISTRATION (1964–70)

Both current and capital expenditure increased quite fast in this period. Capital expenditure increased at a lower rate than in the previous period, current expenditure at a higher. The net effect was a slightly lower overall rate of growth, substantially less than between 1961 and 1964. Housing capital expenditure rose relatively slowly, but began at such a high level that it contributed more than 30 per cent of the whole net increase in these years. Capital expenditure on roads rose at a particularly fast rate and contributed 32 per cent of the total increase. Education growth was slower, and sewerage faster; each contributed 18 per cent of the net increase.

By far the largest part of the increase in current expenditure was in education (38 per cent), mostly because of its large size. Indeed, its share of current local expenditure actually fell from 38 to 35 per cent. During this period social services grew very fast, increasing by more than 150 per cent between 1964 and 1970. Nevertheless, it was still a relatively small part of expenditure in 1970 – less than 5 per cent.

(9) HEATH ADMINISTRATION (1970–4)

During the third consecutive period of rapid growth, the expansion of current expenditure slowed down and actually fell in housing as a consequence of the 1972 Housing Finance Act which reduced housing subsidies. The largest increases in current expenditure were in education, local social services and administration. The biggest increase in capital expenditure was education, housing and sewerage.

(10) SECOND WILSON ADMINISTRATION (1974–5)

Table 1.4.6 is from the 1977 Public Expenditure White Paper (HM Treasury, 1977, Cmnd. 6721, Part II). 1973/4 figures show how rapidly public expenditure was increasing in the last year of the Heath administration. Exceptionally, expenditure on law and order increased its growth rate but this was after a cutback in the preceding year. Overall increase in both current and capital expenditure in 1973/4 was accounted for by housing which rose by almost 35 per cent in 1973/4 over 1972/3.

In 1974/5 the pattern was repeated. The growth of the other programmes was either falling or almost steady. Again, there was a large leap of 38 per cent

Table 1.4.6.   Local authority expenditure in England and Wales: percentage changes in expenditure from previous year

	1972/3[a]	1973/4[a]	1974/5[a]	1975/6[a]	1976/7[a]	1976/7[b]	1977/8[a]	1977/8[b]	1978/9[a]	1978/9[b]
roads and transport	+8.1	+2.8	+3.9	−0.8	−2.1	−5.6	−12.8	−10.9	−6.1	−10.2
housing	+5.2	+34.2	+32.9	−12.9	−15.0	−13.7	−15.1	−1.1	+0.1	+1.8
environmental services	+8.2	+4.8	+7.8	+1.6	−4.3	−9.9	−11.3	+1.1	−3.1	−3.8
law and order	−2.9	+4.5	+6.2	+7.3	+4.3	+0.3	−1.4	−0.1	−1.1	−0.8
education	+6.7	+4.5	+1.6	+1.9	+0.6	+1.7	−1.1	−1.0	−1.5	−1.2
health	+15.5	+16.2	+9.3	+7.2	−1.0	−3.7	−1.4	+1.0	+2.1	+1.8
current expenditure	+7.0	+8.8	+10.0	+3.8	+3.3	+0.2	+0.2	−0.2	−0.6	−0.6
capital expenditure	+4.4	+12.6	+9.4	−11.4	−18.8	−13.9	−25.1	−5.3	−5.3	−3.6
total expenditure	+6.2	+10.9	+9.8	−1.2	−3.2	−4.1	−6.1	−1.6	−1.5	−1.4

[a] this year's White Paper   [b] last year's White Paper
Source: a) Public Expenditure (HM Treasury, 1977), Part II.
         b) Public Expenditure (HM Treasury, 1976).

in total local authority housing expenditure. The dominance of housing can be shown in a number of ways. One is to suppose that housing had stayed in real terms at its 1971/2 level until 1974/5. Then local authority capital expenditure would actually have fallen on aggregate during those years and there would have been such a reduction in current expenditure that the growth of all local expenditure would have been halved to 14 per cent over that period from 28 per cent. Indeed, local expenditure would have grown less than central government expenditure.

Housing capital expenditure rose because the government was exhorting local authorities to build more houses in 1974/5. The rise on current account was partly due to enormous increases in rent rebates and was also due to the unintended effects of the 1972 Housing Finance Act. This was meant to raise rents by 50p. But inflation accelerated, and interest rates rose to the point that real rents rose relatively little in 1972/2 and 1973/4, so that there was an unintended and remarkable increase in housing subsidies.

The squeeze on total local authority expenditure began in 1975/6 when the total fell by 1.2 per cent. In the same year, total central expenditure excluding nationalised industries and state interest was still rising by about 3 per cent. In 1976/7 local expenditure fell by just over 3 per cent while central expenditure fell by $\frac{1}{2}$ per cent. The total also shows the predicted rates of growth up until 1978/9. Thus the intention (1977/8) is that local expenditure should fall by about 9 per cent between 1975/6 and 1978/9. In detail, housing is intended to bear the heaviest cost relatively and absolutely. As real current expenditure on housing is planned to rise throughout this will represent a cut-back in housing investment. Others heavily affected by changed plans of investment are education and roads and transport.

1978/9 is the first year in which an actual downturn in local current expenditure is planned, by no more than $\frac{1}{2}$ per cent. By comparison, a large reduction in local capital expenditure has been planned for 19 per cent in 1976/7. Between 1974/5 and 1978/9 the position intended (in 1977/8) is that local capital expenditure will have fallen by as much as 48 per cent.

However, it is far from unlikely that such expenditure plans will be revised upwards before they are implemented.

CONCLUSIONS

There has been a steady growth in both local current and capital expenditures. There have been cycles, of course, but the trend has been inexorably upwards. No simple thesis, either political or economic, explains both the cycles and the trend. A rapid growth rate has occurred under all kinds of political administrations. Historically, the political manifestoes of the party in power would not have been a good predictor of the growth rate of local expenditure.

We have found that most of the rapid growth of local expenditures after wars can best be explained by a catching-up effect; a return to the growth path after the cessation of growth or even decline that occurred during the wars. There has been one remarkably stable element in the relationship between the growth of local expenditure and the growth of GNP. The elasticity has been amazingly constant at about 3 — a 1 per cent increase in GNP has resulted in a 3 per cent increase in local expenditure.

NOTES

1 Even this must be modified in so far as increased local expenditure was compensating for very substantial wartime cuts which did not occur in the First World War.
2 The income elasticity is defined as:

$$e_i = \frac{\text{the proportionate change in purchases of good } X}{\text{proportionate change in income}}$$

It it is high, say 10, this means that a 1 per cent increase in income is associated with a 10 per cent increase in expenditure on X. If low, say 0.25, a 10 per cent increase is associated with only a 2.5 per cent rise in expenditure on X.
3 Foot (1962, Vol. 2, p. 87) quotes D. Barton, author of *A Hope for Housing*? as saying that a Macmillan council house required nine-tenths of the materials used in the Bevan house.
4 Redfern (1955) shows, for example, that real net fixed capital formation in roads in the postwar period up to 1953 has been negative ranging from —£700 million in 1949 to —£1,100 million in 1953 (at 1948 prices).
5 See, for example, Political and Economic Planning (1960, pp. 17–8, 151–9), influential at the time, which argued very strongly for increased public expenditure, particularly in the social services. The same point was made as late as 1968 by Shephered in Caves (1968, p. 444).

Appendix 1.4.A1　Expenditure - Statistical Series: Revenue and Capital Expenditure in Current and 1975 prices – England and Wales; and Scotland

SOURCES

The real expenditure tables are derived from the expenditure figures in current prices deflated by a GNP deflator based on the deflator used by Peacock and Wiseman (1961).

ENGLAND AND WALES

1790 and 1840 –	Veverka, 'The Growth of Government Expenditure in the United Kingdom 1790' (1963). Figures refer to total UK expenditure for the calendar years 1790 and 1840.
1868 to 1929 –	Mitchell and Deane (1962), table 9: 'Public Finance' pp. 414–5.
1930 to 1975 –	Ministry of Health, later Ministry of Housing, later Department of the Environment, *Local Government Financial Statistics* (formerly *Local Taxation Returns*), annual series since 1934/5.

SCOTLAND

1880 to 1939 –	Mitchell and Deane (1962), p. 423.
1940 to 1958 –	Mitchell and Jones (1971), p. 167.
1950 to 1975 –	*Local Financial Returns – Scotland*, annual series. The Scottish Office.

Revenue Account (in current prices) – England and Wales (£m.)

Year ended 31 March	Total	Rate fund services							Housing							Trading services				
	Total	Ed.	Lib. and Mus.	Hospitals	Poor Relief	Sewer	Refuse	Parks	HRA	Other	Highways	Lighting	Fire	Police	Total	Water	Gas	Elec.	Trans.	Harbours[a]
1790	4.0	—	—	—	—	—	—	—	—	—	—	—	—	—	—	—	—	—	—	—
1840	15.0	—	—	—	—	—	—	—	—	—	—	—	—	—	—	—	—	—	—	—
1868	30.2	—	—	—	7.4	—	—	—	—	—	—	—	—	—	—	—	—	—	—	—
1870	27.3	—	—	—	—	—	—	—	—	—	—	—	—	—	—	—	—	—	—	—
1871	29.9	—	—	—	—	—	—	—	—	—	—	—	—	—	—	—	—	—	—	—
1872	31.2	—	—	—	—	—	—	—	—	—	—	—	—	—	—	—	—	—	—	—
1873	32.7	—	—	—	—	—	—	—	—	—	—	—	—	—	—	—	—	—	—	—
1874	36.4	—	—	—	—	—	—	—	—	—	—	—	—	—	—	—	—	—	—	—
1875	40.7	2.2	—	—	6.7	—	—	—	—	—	—	—	—	—	—	—	—	—	—	—
1876	43.3	—	—	—	—	—	—	—	—	—	—	—	—	—	—	—	—	—	—	—
1877	48.4	—	—	—	—	—	—	—	—	—	—	—	—	—	—	—	—	—	—	—
1878	49.3	—	—	—	—	—	—	—	—	—	—	—	—	—	—	—	—	—	—	—
1879	52.2	—	—	—	—	—	—	—	—	—	—	—	—	—	—	—	—	—	—	—
1880	50.3	3.3	—	—	7.0	—	—	—	—	—	5.7	—	—	3.1	—	—	—	—	—	0.9
1881	52.6	3.2	—	—	7.1	—	—	—	—	—	6.1	—	—	3.1	—	—	—	—	—	1.4
1882	55.5	3.4	—	—	7.2	—	—	—	—	—	6.3	—	—	3.2	—	—	—	—	—	3.8
1883[b]	43.5	2.7	—	—	6.8	0.6	—	—	—	—	5.7	—	—	3.3	—	0.8	2.6	—	—	1.1
1884	43.4	2.8	0.13	0.1	6.8	0.8	—	0.14	—	0.10	5.7	0.9	0.2	3.4	—	0.9	2.4	—	—	1.2
1885	44.1	3.2	0.14	0.1	6.8	0.9	—	0.15	—	0.11	5.6	0.9	0.2	3.5	—	0.8	2.4	—	—	1.2
1886	44.5	3.5	0.14	0.1	6.6	0.8	—	0.22	—	0.11	5.8	0.9	0.2	3.5	—	0.8	2.4	—	—	1.2
1887	45.1	3.6	0.14	0.1	6.5	1.0	—	0.17	—	0.05	5.7	0.9	0.2	3.8	—	0.8	2.5	—	—	1.1
1888	45.8	3.8	0.17	0.1	6.7	1.0	—	0.19	—	0.02	5.8	0.9	0.2	3.8	—	0.9	2.5	—	—	1.1
1889	47.1	3.9	0.18	0.2	6.6	0.9	—	0.21	—	0.02	6.1	0.9	0.2	3.9	—	0.9	2.6	—	—	1.1
1890	48.2	4.1	0.19	0.2	6.6	1.0	—	0.23	—	0.02	6.3	0.9	0.2	3.9	—	0.9	2.8	—	—	1.2
1891	50.7	4.3	0.22	0.2	6.7	1.1	—	0.27	—	0.02	6.4	1.0	0.2	4.1	—	1.0	3.3	—	—	1.4
1892	53.1	4.8	0.27	0.2	6.9	1.1	—	0.33	—	0.02	6.9	1.0	0.2	4.5	—	1.0	3.5	—	—	1.3
1893	56.2	5.4	0.29	0.3	7.2	1.2	—	0.35	—	0.04	7.4	1.0	0.3	4.7	—	1.0	3.5	—	0.1	1.4
1894	57.8	5.7	0.31	0.5	7.5	1.4	—	0.37	—	0.03	7.7	1.1	0.3	4.8	—	1.1	3.7	—	0.1	1.4
1895	59.7	6.4	0.32	0.4	7.7	1.3	—	0.40	—	0.04	7.4	1.1	0.3	4.6	—	1.1	3.6	—	0.1	1.4
1896	62.2	6.9	0.34	0.4	7.9	1.4	—	0.41	—	0.04	7.7	1.2	0.3	4.7	—	1.2	3.6	—	0.1	1.5
1897	64.7	7.5	0.37	0.4	8.0	1.4	1.1	0.44	—	0.03	7.9	1.2	0.3	4.8	—	1.2	3.8	0.2	0.2	1.6
1898	67.8	7.8	0.38	0.4	8.3	1.6	—	0.52	—	0.04	8.2	1.3	0.3	4.9	—	1.3	4.0	0.2	0.3	1.6
1899	71.2	8.2	0.39	0.5	8.6	1.7	1.4	0.51	—	0.05	8.7	1.3	0.4	5.0	—	1.4	4.1	0.3	0.7	1.6
1900	76.0	8.8	0.40	1.0	8.4	1.8	1.7	0.57	—	0.05	9.1	1.5	0.4	5.1	—	1.5	4.6	0.6	1.1	1.7
1901	82.4	9.5	0.42	1.0	8.8	1.9	1.8	0.58	—	0.09	9.6	1.8	0.4	5.2	—	1.6	5.7	0.8	1.4	1.9
1902	87.4	10.1	0.46	1.3	9.3	1.9	1.9	0.63	—	0.09	12.4	1.9	0.5	5.5	—	1.7	5.7	1.0	1.8	1.8
1903	92.9[d]	12.9[c]	0.53[c]	2.0	10.7[c]	3.9[c]	2.0	1.1[c]	—	0.10	12.7[c]	2.0[c]	0.5	5.8[c]	—	4.6[c]	6.7[c]	1.9[c]	3.3[c]	3.3[c]
1904	98.5[d]	15.6[d]	0.52	1.8	11.1	4.1	2.1	1.1	—	0.12	13.1	2.0	0.5	6.0	—	4.7	6.7	2.2	4.2	3.5
1905	107.7[d]	21.9[d]	0.63	1.7	11.5	4.2	2.1	1.1	—	0.12	13.5	2.0	0.5	6.1	—	7.4	6.6	2.5	4.9	3.6

Revenue Account (in current prices) – England and Wales (£m.) (continued)

Rate fund services comprise the columns Total, Ed., Lib. and Mus., Hospitals, Poor Relief, Sewer, Refuse, Parks, Housing (HRA and Other), Highways, Lighting, Fire, Police. *Trading services* comprise the columns Total, Water, Gas, Elec., Trans.

Year ended 31 March	Total	Total (rate fund)	Ed.	Lib. and Mus.	Hospitals	Poor Relief	Sewer	Refuse	Parks	Housing HRA	Housing Other	Highways	Lighting	Fire	Police	Total (trading)	Water	Gas	Elec.	Trans.	Harbours[a]
1906	113.3		23.5	0.72	1.7	11.7	4.4	2.0	1.2		0.18	13.6	2.1	0.5	6.2		8.5	6.5	2.7	5.4	3.7
1907	114.1		24.7	0.75	1.9	11.6	4.5	2.1	1.2		0.20	13.5	2.2	0.5	6.5		8.0	6.5	3.0	6.5	3.9
1908	118.7		25.7	0.73	2.0	12.0	4.6	2.1	1.2		0.56[c]	13.5	2.2	0.6	6.6		8.1	7.1	3.3	7.0	4.2
1909	121.9		26.8	0.70	1.9	12.3	4.7	2.1	1.3		0.55	13.9	2.2	0.6	6.6		8.3	7.2	3.3	7.3	4.3
1910	125.8		27.5	0.71	1.9	12.4	4.7	2.2	1.4		0.58	14.1	2.2	0.6	6.7		8.4	6.9	3.5	7.4	6.8
1911	129.4		28.3	0.72	1.8	12.5	4.8	2.2	1.4		0.58	14.6	2.3	0.6	6.9		8.6	7.2	3.7	8.0	7.0
1912	134.1[e]		29.7[f]	0.68	1.9	11.9	4.9	2.3	1.5		0.61	15.0	2.3	0.7	7.2		8.7	7.3	4.2	8.6	7.3
1913	140.3		30.6	0.69	2.0	12.3	5.1	2.4	1.5		0.64	15.6	2.3	0.7	7.5		9.0	7.8	4.7	9.2[‡]	8.4
1914	148.3		31.8	0.70	2.4	12.3	5.2	2.5	1.6		0.62[†]	16.5	2.3	0.7	7.7		9.1	8.5	5.2	10.0	7.8
1915	153.3		32.8	0.68	2.9	12.9	5.8[f]	2.6[e]	1.7[f]		0.90[†]	17.6[†]	2.3	0.9	8.2		9.4	8.6	5.5	10.5	8.2
1916	154.0		32.6	0.68	3.8[h]	13.0	8.6		1.6		1.0	15.8	1.7	0.9[e]	8.1		9.8	9.8	6.6	10.7	8.8
1917	156.1		32.4	0.64	3.8	13.0	8.9		1.5		1.1	14.7	1.1	0.9	8.0		10.2	10.8	8.0	11.5	8.9
1918	170.0		37.2	0.69	4.4	13.7	9.6		1.5		1.0	15.1	1.1	1.0	8.6		10.4	12.2	9.3	12.9	9.6
1919	193.5		42.6	0.76	5.4	14.9	4.2	4.6	1.7		1.1	15.8	1.3	1.1	10.3		11.3	13.8	10.7	15.6	11.0
1920	265.5		56.4	1.0	8.8	19.2	7.3	6.5	2.5		1.4	26.4	2.4	1.4	17.4		13.1	17.2	13.4	20.5	15.3
1921	343.2		73.9	1.4	13.6[h]	25.3	8.7	8.3	3.5		4.3	39.1	3.5	1.9	20.8		15.6	21.7	17.9	25.2	17.7
1922	365.0		77.8	1.5	13.6	34.8	8.9	7.9	3.9		10.2	42.1	3.7	2.0	21.3		16.4	20.8	17.4	24.4	16.4
1923	346.7		74.8	1.5	11.9	35.7	8.1	6.9	3.5		14.6	40.2[i]	3.7	1.9	18.9		15.1	16.8	16.0	22.5	15.3
1924	343.3		72.3	1.5	11.3	32.5	8.3	6.5	3.8		16.3	41.4	3.6	1.9	18.8		15.4	16.8	17.6	21.7	14.3
1925	354.9		73.9	1.6	11.6	31.4	8.7	6.6	4.2		18.1	45.8	3.7	2.0	19.1		15.8	17.0	19.1	22.5	14.2
1926	373.1		75.5	1.7	12.2	34.6	9.0	6.8	4.4		21.3	48.8	3.9	2.1	20.0		17.0	16.7	20.4	23.7	14.2
1927	402.2		76.0	1.8	13.1	43.7	9.3	6.9	4.5		26.2	49.5	3.9	2.1	21.0		17.3	21.4	25.2	24.1	13.8
1928	402.6		77.0	1.8	13.2	34.7	9.6	6.9	4.7		32.2	52.1	4.1	2.2	21.1		17.6	17.4	24.1	25.1	15.0
1929	414.7		81.7	1.9	13.8	33.4	9.8	6.9	5.0		36.6	51.4	4.2	2.2	21.4		18.2	16.8	25.5	26.1	14.5
1930	423.7	311.8	83.7	2.0	11.5	33.9	10.1	7.1	5.2		35.1	50.9	4.3	2.3	21.7	108.6	19.0	16.9	28.6	26.7	13.9
1931	432.7	322.9	86.6	2.2	16.1	32.0	10.5	7.2	5.4		38.0	52.4	4.5	2.4	22.3	110.7	19.3	16.7	30.4	27.0	13.4
1932	435.0	324.9	85.1	2.2	19.3	30.4	10.7	7.3	5.5		40.1	51.9	4.6	2.5	22.3	111.7	19.3	16.3	32.2	26.9	13.2
1933	430.3	320.8	82.6	2.2	20.2	32.7	11.1	7.1	5.3		41.8	46.8	4.6	2.4	21.5	112.3	19.6	16.0	34.2	26.2	12.2
1934	433.2	326.5	83.4	2.3	21.3	33.9	11.4	7.1	5.5		42.8	46.3	4.7	2.5	21.5	111.9	20.2	16.1	36.6	21.8	12.5
1935	454.8	340.3	86.9	2.5	22.6	36.2	11.6	7.2	5.7		44.4		47.5	4.9	2.6	22.3	116.2	20.5	16.1	40.3	22.2	12.7
1936	470.9	348.5	92.2	2.6	24.4	37.8	11.8	7.5	6.0	33.5	6.0	48.6	5.1	2.7	23.9	122.9	20.9	16.4	43.3	23.0	13.0
1937	484.6	359.5	95.0	2.8	26.6	37.2	12.0	7.8	6.3	34.6	5.7	50.1	5.4	2.9	24.7	130.2	21.7	17.1	47.9	24.2	13.2
1938	505.6	372.0	98.0	3.0	30.2	34.2	12.5	8.3	6.9	36.4	5.7	49.6	5.6	3.0	25.3	139.1	22.5	17.9	52.5	25.0	14.1
1939	532.8	390.8	100.4	3.2	33.3	35.3	12.7	8.5	7.1	39.0	5.6	50.4	5.8	3.1	26.1	145.2	23.4	18.1	56.9	25.1	13.9
1940	578.8	436.4	98.6	3.2	32.8	35.3	12.8	8.7	6.7	41.6	5.6	44.7	3.1	3.4	31.0	149.7	24.4	18.8	59.6	25.1	14.3
1941	631.1	478.7	99.5	3.2	31.7	31.2	13.0	10.0	6.2	42.2	5.5	39.3	1.6	3.7	34.0	157.1	25.4	20.8	64.7	26.9	13.1
1942	707.4	535.1	105.4	3.5	33.0	28.3	13.3	11.2	6.1	42.2	5.6	38.9	1.5	29.4	37.4	177.3	27.0	23.9	74.0	30.5	14.2
1943	694.3	514.0	113.4	3.6	35.4	27.6	13.4	12.5	6.3	41.9	5.5	39.8	1.5	14.0	37.4	189.6	27.4	26.1	76.3	33.1	15.0
1944	698.1	505.9	120.5	3.9	39.6	28.4	13.7	12.8	6.6	41.8	5.3	38.9	1.5	6.9	36.1	205.0	27.2	28.1	81.4	35.0	18.3

Year					Health[1] (24.5)	Welfare (16.3)															
1945	729.1	519.6	128.1	4.1	42.9	30.0	13.8	13.1	7.0	42.2	5.7	39.8	2.4	5.0	34.1	220.0	28.6	30.6	87.6	36.4	21.2
1946	779.9	538.5	156.3	4.4	49.4	32.5	13.8	14.0	7.8	42.5	5.9	43.4	4.8	3.5	35.1	229.7	29.2	32.9	94.2	37.7	19.4
1947	873.7	607.1	183.2	5.5	60.4	37.3	14.9	16.1	9.6	46.8	5.9	56.6	5.5	3.4	36.1	257.5	30.4	37.2	108.3	40.7	20.5
1948[m]	959.9	678.5	209.4	6.5	72.7[j]	42.5	15.6	18.3	11.3	54.5	5.0	61.2	5.7	3.5	41.1	276.7	32.1	40.6[j]	119.0[j]	44.4	22.8
1949[m]	866.2	672.5	236.4	7.6	24.4[k]	11.7	16.6	19.8	12.5	66.0	4.2	58.6	7.2	12.2	44.1	171.5	33.3	46.9	—	48.3	23.7
(1949)																					
1950	849.1	703.5	257.1	8.3	32.1	25.0[m]	17.7	20.6	13.8	76.9	3.9	62.8	8.5	13.8	48.6	134.2	35.5	3.8	—	49.9	25.4
1951	887.4	740.8	268.7	8.8	36.0	27.1	18.0	21.7	14.6	87.1	4.1	62.8	9.1	14.9	54.4	132.9	36.6	—	—	51.9	26.1
1952	987.7	840.9	318.2	10.0	38.5	31.7	19.2	24.3	15.8	99.2	4.9	70.0	10.0	16.5	61.5	142.6	38.4	—	—	56.7	29.8
1953	1,062.3	914.2	345.4	10.7	42.9	35.5	20.8	26.2	16.9	116.5	5.8	74.4	11.0	17.9	66.3	149.1	41.0	—	—	60.3	29.5
1954	1,127.5	977.8	364.5	11.2	43.0	37.9	22.2	26.9	17.6	136.5	6.9	77.8	11.7	18.6	69.1	156.9	44.0	—	—	61.2	32.9
1955	1,225.3	1,057.3	409.1	12.1	45.1	39.9	23.7	28.0	18.5	154.9	8.8	84.6	12.2	19.1	71.8	162.4	45.8	—	—	62.9	33.5
1956	1,330.8	1,159.3	451.3	13.2	49.1	42.6	25.8	30.8	20.4	173.0	25.0[o]	90.3	13.4	20.4	78.8	174.5	49.9	—	—	66.2	37.2
1957	1,497.1	1,313.3	527.1	15.1	54.1	46.6	29.8	33.6	22.3	196.0	25.9[o]	96.4	14.7	22.2	91.6	184.6	53.7	—	—	70.5	38.3
1958	1,630.2	1,435.4	587.0	16.5	57.8	50.4	33.4	35.3	24.1	217.7	27.1	103.8	15.7	24.1	95.2	196.2	58.7	—	—	73.6	40.3
1959	1,731.3	1,537.7	633.9	17.7	61.7	53.9	36.7	36.9	26.3	234.6	28.1	105.7	16.8	25.5	102.6	201.8	60.4	—	—	75.0	41.2
1960	1,865.7	1,657.7	696.8	19.6	68.1	57.3	40.0	38.1	27.1	249.7	29.5	112.8	17.6	27.1	108.2	210.8	63.8	—	—	76.1	43.8
1961	2,018.5	1,791.8	752.4	21.8	72.5	62.1	43.9	41.0	28.9	271.1	30.1	119.9	18.6	29.2	122.2	221.0	67.7	—	—	78.7	45.8
1962	2,232.3	1,977.5	830.7	24.1	81.3	68.9	49.2	45.2	30.7	297.4	35.2	133.7	19.9	32.0	136.8	233.9	72.0	—	—	82.8	48.2
1963	2,446.9	2,174.5	929.7	26.3	87.3	75.9	53.8	47.9	32.5	316.9	38.9	149.3	21.2	36.2	146.5	245.3	77.3	—	—	83.9	51.4
1964	2,667.5	2,383.9	1,019.3	28.8	95.7	84.6	58.3	50.9	36.1	343.2	43.4	165.8	22.1	38.7	162.4	260.1	80.8	—	—	89.1	53.9
1965	2,902.8	2,605.7	1,101.1	32.0	104.5	91.8	66.0	54.8	38.7	381.7	53.6	178.0	23.7	42.7	176.1	275.3	87.8	—	—	90.9	57.7
1966	3,306.4	2,966.1	1,262.4	37.0	118.0	105.6	75.0	62.3	43.3	432.2	67.8	197.1	25.6	46.7	196.9	292.7	94.8	—	—	95.4	60.6
1967	3,621.4	3,266.6	1,386.2	41.1	128.8	119.0	85.0	68.6	46.9	480.8	77.2	210.6	27.2	51.1	220.0	301.6	103.8	—	—	98.3	56.0[r]
1968	3,988.4	3,617.7	1,525.6	46.2	140.6	133.5	94.5	75.5	50.8	532.9	86.1	247.2		55.5	245.6	311.8	110.4	—	—	99.1	58.4
1969	4,322.3	3,918.1	1,644.2	50.0	152.1	147.5	106.7	82.1	55.9	605.9	93.8	240.3	29.4	59.5	263.9	344.4	120.1	—	—	102.5	72.6
1970[t]	5,405.3	4,693.4	1,894.7	58.3	167.6	164.1	131.9	95.8	66.5	701.1[p]	96.1	256.1	31.8	67.0	303.2	387.2	154.6	—	—	111.0	70.5
1971	6,185.5	5,403.0	2,145.5	66.8	199.2	194.0	150.8	109.0	74.2	783.9	112.9	287.5	35.5	75.1	367.5	414.1	160.8	—	—	68.8[q]	78.4
1972	7,080.7	6,270.6	2,492.1	78.2	141.9	314.4	169.9	124.7	89.0	856.0	125.1	347.4	40.2	90.4	425.6	431.1	175.7	—	—	75.9	63.2[r]
1973	8,004.2	7,366.8	2,902.8	91.0	165.0	390.5	196.3	143.5	107.0	1,019.0	157.7	399.4	44.2	106.0	466.7	407.5	185.5	—	—	82.0	13.3[r]
1974	9,732.6	8,948.9	3,356.7	105.8	193.6[s]	522.4	242.1[s]	166.9	134.0	1,231.1	282.7	471.2	48.4	122.8	534.8	470.9	208.2[s]	—	—	90.3	14.3
1975	12,253.9	11,441.6	4,404.4	139.4	—	753.1	—	229.7	157.6	1,621.2	412.1	439.8	48.4	165.2	660.9	292.7	—	—	—	74.2	23.5

Revenue Account (in 1975 prices) – England and Wales (£m.)

Year ended 31 March	Total	Rate fund services: Total	Ed.	Lib. and Mus.	Hospitals	Poor Relief	Sewer	Refuse	Parks	Housing HRA	Housing Other	Highways	Lighting	Fire	Police	Trading services: Total	Water	Gas	Elec.	Trans.	Harbours[a]
1868	404.5	—	—	—	—	111.1	—	—	—	—	—	—	—	—	—	—	—	—	—	—	—
1870	423.2	—	—	—	—	—	—	—	—	—	—	—	—	—	—	—	—	—	—	—	—
1871	411.6	—	—	—	—	—	—	—	—	—	—	—	—	—	—	—	—	—	—	—	—
1872	414.6	—	—	—	—	—	—	—	—	—	—	—	—	—	—	—	—	—	—	—	—
1873	413.8	—	—	—	—	—	—	—	—	—	—	—	—	—	—	—	—	—	—	—	—
1874	460.7	—	—	—	—	—	—	—	—	—	—	—	—	—	—	—	—	—	—	—	—
1875	544.3	—	29.3	—	—	109.6	—	—	—	—	—	—	—	—	—	—	—	—	—	—	—
1876	596.1	—	—	—	—	—	—	—	—	—	—	—	—	—	—	—	—	—	—	—	—
1877	670.9	—	—	—	—	—	—	—	—	—	—	—	—	—	—	—	—	—	—	—	—
1878	692.9	—	—	—	—	—	—	—	—	—	—	—	—	—	—	—	—	—	—	—	—
1879	771.4	—	—	—	—	—	—	—	—	—	—	—	—	—	—	—	—	—	—	—	—
1880	752.0	—	49.3	—	—	125.5	—	—	—	—	—	—	—	—	46.2	—	—	—	—	—	13.4
1881	767.7	—	46.6	—	—	124.0	—	—	—	—	—	83.1	—	—	45.2	—	—	—	—	—	20.3
1882	823.7	—	50.4	—	—	129.0	—	—	—	—	—	90.5	—	—	47.4	—	—	—	—	—	56.3
1883[b]	650.3	—	40.4	—	—	101.7	9.0	—	—	—	—	54.2	—	—	49.3	—	12.0	—	—	—	16.4
1884	657.5	—	42.4	—	1.5	103.0	12.1	—	2.1	—	—	86.4	13.6	3.0	51.5	—	13.6	38.9	—	—	18.2
1885	704.5	—	51.1	2.0	1.6	108.6	14.4	—	2.4	—	1.5	89.5	14.4	3.2	55.9	—	12.8	36.4	—	—	19.2
1886	750.2	—	59.0	2.2	1.7	111.3	13.5	—	3.7	—	1.8	97.8	15.2	3.4	64.1	—	13.5	38.3	—	—	18.5
1887	775.0	—	61.9	2.4	1.7	111.7	17.2	—	2.9	—	1.9	98.0	15.5	3.4	65.3	—	13.7	42.1	—	—	18.9
1888	793.8	—	65.9	2.9	1.7	116.1	17.3	—	3.3	—	0.9	100.5	15.6	3.5	65.9	—	15.6	43.3	—	—	19.1
1889	813.6	—	67.4	3.1	3.5	114.0	15.5	—	3.6	—	0.3	105.4	15.5	3.5	67.4	—	15.5	44.9	—	—	19.0
1890	825.9	—	70.3	3.3	3.4	113.1	17.1	—	3.9	—	0.3	108.0	15.4	3.4	66.8	—	15.4	48.0	—	—	20.6
1891	868.7	—	73.7	3.8	3.4	114.8	18.8	—	4.6	—	0.3	109.7	17.1	3.4	70.3	—	17.1	56.5	—	—	24.0
1892	907.1	—	82.0	4.6	3.4	117.9	18.8	—	5.6	—	0.3	117.9	17.1	3.4	76.9	—	17.1	59.8	—	—	22.2
1893	955.1	—	91.8	4.9	5.1	122.4	20.4	—	5.9	—	0.7	125.8	17.0	5.1	79.9	—	17.0	59.5	—	1.7	23.8
1894	1,001.6	—	98.8	5.4	8.7	130.0	24.3	—	6.4	—	0.5	133.4	19.1	5.2	83.2	—	19.1	64.1	—	1.7	24.3
1895	1,078.2	—	115.6	5.8	7.2	139.1	23.5	—	7.2	—	0.7	133.6	19.9	5.4	83.1	—	19.9	65.0	—	1.8	25.3
1896	1,143.0	—	126.8	6.2	7.4	145.2	25.7	—	7.5	—	0.7	141.4	22.1	5.5	86.4	—	22.1	66.2	—	1.8	27.6
1897	1,182.4	—	137.1	6.8	7.3	146.2	25.6	—	8.0	—	0.5	144.4	21.9	5.5	87.7	—	21.9	69.4	3.7	3.7	29.2
1898	1,206.2	—	138.8	6.8	7.1	147.7	28.5	19.6	9.3	—	0.7	145.9	23.1	5.3	87.2	—	23.1	71.2	3.6	5.3	28.5
1899	1,241.7	—	143.0	6.8	8.7	150.0	29.6	24.4	8.9	—	0.9	151.7	22.7	7.0	87.2	—	24.4	71.5	5.2	12.2	27.9
1900	1,328.0	—	153.8	7.0	17.5	146.8	31.5	29.7	10.0	—	0.9	159.0	26.2	7.0	89.1	—	26.2	80.4	10.5	19.2	29.7
1901	1,385.1	—	159.7	7.1	16.8	147.9	31.9	30.3	9.7	—	1.5	161.4	30.3	6.7	87.4	—	26.9	95.8	13.4	23.5	31.9
1902	1,481.1	—	171.2	7.8[c]	22.0	157.6	32.2	32.2	10.7	—	1.5	210.1	32.2	8.5	93.2	—	28.8	96.6	16.9	30.5	30.5
1903	1,569.3	—	217.9[c]	9.0[c]	33.8	180.7[c]	65.9[c]	33.8	18.6[c]	—	1.7	214.5[c]	33.8[c]	8.4	98.0[c]	—	77.7[c]	113.2[c]	32.1[c]	55.7[c]	55.7[c]
1904	1,645.8[d]	—	260.7[d]	8.7	30.1	185.5	68.5	35.1	18.4	—	2.0	218.9	33.4	8.4	100.3	—	78.5	111.9	36.8	70.2	58.5
1905	1,785.2[d]	—	363.0[d]	10.4	28.2	190.6	69.6	34.8	18.2	—	2.0	223.8	33.2	8.3	101.1	—	122.7	109.4	41.4	81.2	59.7
1906	1,872.4	—	388.4	11.9	28.1	193.4	72.7	33.1	19.8	—	3.0	224.8	34.7	8.3	102.5	—	140.5	107.4	44.6	89.2	61.1
1907	1,861.9	—	403.1	12.2	31.0	189.3	73.4	34.3	19.6	—	3.3	220.3	35.9	8.2	106.1	—	130.5	106.1	49.0	106.1	63.6
1908	1,916.4	—	414.9	11.8	32.3	193.7	74.3	33.9	19.4	—	9.0[c]	218.0	35.5	9.7	106.6	—	130.8	114.6	53.3	113.0	67.8
1909	1,995.1	—	438.6	11.5	31.1	201.3	76.9	34.4	21.3	—	9.0	227.5	36.0	9.8	108.0	—	135.8	117.8	54.0	119.5	70.4

Year																					
1910	2,031.0	—	444.0	11.5	30.7	200.2	75.9	35.5	22.6	9.4	—	227.6	35.5	9.7	108.2	—	135.6	111.4	56.5	119.5	109.8
1911	2,049.7	—	448.3	11.4	28.5	198.0	76.0	34.8	22.2	9.2	—	231.3	36.4	9.5	109.3	—	136.2	114.1	58.6	126.7	110.9
1912	2,092.4[e]	—	463.4[f]	10.6	29.6	185.7	76.5	35.9	23.4	9.5	—	234.0	35.9	10.9	112.3	—	135.7	113.9	65.5	143.5	131.1
1913	2,130.0	—	464.5	10.5	30.4	186.7	77.4	36.4	22.8	9.7	—	236.8	34.9	10.6	113.8	—	136.6	118.4	71.3	139.6[g]	127.5
1914	2,229.1	—	478.0	10.5	36.1	184.9	78.2	37.6	24.0	9.3	—	248.0	34.6	10.5	115.7	—	136.8	127.8	78.2	150.3	117.2
1915	—	—	—	—	—	—	—	—	—	—	—	—	—	—	—	—	—	—	—	—	—
1916	—	—	—	—	—	—	—	—	—	—	—	—	—	—	—	—	—	—	—	—	—
1917	—	—	—	—	—	—	—	—	—	—	—	—	—	—	—	—	—	—	—	—	—
1918	—	—	—	—	—	—	—	—	—	—	—	—	—	—	—	—	—	—	—	—	—
1919	—	—	—	—	—	—	—	—	—	—	—	—	—	—	—	—	—	—	—	—	—
1920	2,161.5	—	465.4	8.8	85.7[h]	159.3	54.8	52.3	22.0	27.1	—	246.3	22.0	12.0	131.0	—	98.2	136.7	112.7	158.7	111.5
1921	2,878.5	—	613.6	11.8	107.3	274.4	70.2	62.3	30.8	80.4	—	332.0	29.2	15.8	168.0	—	129.3	164.0	137.2	192.4	129.3
1922	2,883.4	—	622.1	12.5	99.0	296.9	67.4	57.4	29.1	121.4	—	334.3[i]	30.8	15.8	157.2	—	125.6	139.7	133.1	187.1	127.2
1923	2,844.0	—	599.0	12.4	93.6	269.2	68.8	53.8	31.5	135.0	—	343.0	29.8	15.7	155.7	—	127.6	139.2	145.8	179.8	118.5
1924	2,910.9	—	606.1	13.1	95.1	257.5	71.4	54.1	34.4	148.5	—	375.7	30.3	16.4	156.7	—	129.6	139.4	156.7	184.5	116.5
1925	2,900.1	—	586.9	13.2	94.8	268.9	70.0	52.9	34.2	165.6	—	379.3	30.3	16.3	155.5	—	132.1	129.8	158.6	184.2	110.4
1926	3,475.3	—	656.7	15.6	113.2	377.6	80.4	59.6	38.9	226.3	—	427.7	33.7	18.1	181.5	—	149.5	184.9	217.7	208.2	119.2
1927	3,440.7	—	658.1	15.4	112.8	296.6	82.0	59.0	40.2	275.2	—	445.3	35.0	18.8	180.3	—	150.4	148.7	206.0	214.5	128.2
1928	3,584.9	—	706.3	16.4	119.3	288.7	84.7	59.6	43.2	313.8	—	444.3	36.3	19.0	185.0	—	157.3	145.2	220.4	225.6	125.3
1929	—	—	—	—	—	—	—	—	—	—	—	—	—	—	—	—	—	—	—	—	—
1930	3,758.2	2,765.7	742.4	17.7	102.0	300.7	89.6	63.0	46.1	311.3	—	451.5	38.1	20.4	192.5	963.3	168.5	149.9	253.7	236.8	123.3
1931	4,034.9	3,011.0	807.5	20.5	150.1	298.4	97.9	67.1	50.4	354.3	—	488.6	42.0	22.4	207.9	1,032.3	180.0	155.7	283.5	251.8	125.0
1932	4,143.3	3,094.6	810.6	21.0	183.8	289.6	101.9	69.5	52.4	381.9	—	494.3	43.8	23.8	212.4	1,063.9	183.8	155.3	306.7	256.2	125.7
1933	4,201.7	3,132.5	806.6	21.5	197.2	319.3	108.4	69.3	51.8	408.2	—	457.0	44.9	23.4	209.9	1,096.6	191.4	156.2	334.0	255.8	119.1
1934	4,212.4	3,174.8	811.0	22.4	207.1	329.6	110.9	69.0	53.5	416.2	—	450.2	45.7	24.3	209.1	1,088.1	196.4	156.6	355.9	216.8	118.6
1935	4,396.8	3,289.8	840.1	24.2	218.5	350.0	112.1	69.6	55.1	429.2	—	459.2	47.4	25.1	215.6	1,123.4	198.2	155.6	389.6	210.8	122.8
1936	4,460.1	3,300.8	873.3	24.6	231.1	358.0	111.8	71.0	56.8	317.3	56.8	460.3	48.3	25.6	226.4	1,164.0	198.0	155.3	410.1	210.3	123.1
1937	4,405.5	3,268.2	863.6	25.5	241.8	338.2	109.1	70.9	57.3	314.5	51.8	455.5	49.1	26.4	224.5	1,183.6	197.3	155.5	435.5	209.1	120.0
1938	4,519.9	3,325.6	876.1	26.8	270.0	306.6	111.7	74.2	61.7	325.4	50.4	443.4	50.1	26.8	226.2	1,243.5	201.1	160.0	469.3	216.3	126.1
1939	—	—	—	—	—	—	—	—	—	—	—	—	—	—	—	—	—	—	—	—	—
1940	—	—	—	—	—	—	—	—	—	—	—	—	—	—	—	—	—	—	—	—	—
1941	—	—	—	—	—	—	—	—	—	—	—	—	—	—	—	—	—	—	—	—	—
1942	—	—	—	—	—	—	—	—	—	—	—	—	—	—	—	—	—	—	—	—	—
1943	—	—	—	—	—	—	—	—	—	—	—	—	—	—	—	—	—	—	—	—	—
1944	—	—	—	—	—	—	—	—	—	—	—	—	—	—	—	—	—	—	—	—	—
1945	—	—	—	—	—	—	—	—	—	—	—	—	—	—	—	—	—	—	—	—	—
1946	3,762.7	2,598.1	754.1	21.2	238.3	156.8	66.6	67.5	37.6	205.0	28.5	209.4	23.2	16.9	169.3	1,108.2	140.9	158.7	454.5	181.9	95.6
1947	3,669.6	2,549.9	769.5	23.1	253.7	156.7	62.6	67.6	40.3	196.6	24.8	237.7	23.1	14.3	151.6	1,081.5	127.7	156.2	454.9	170.9	86.1
1948	4,173.3	2,949.9	910.4	28.3	316.1[j]	184.8	67.8	79.6	49.1	236.9	21.7	266.1	24.8	15.2	178.1	1,203.0	129.6	176.5[j]	517.4[j]	193.0	99.1
1949[n]	3,673.9	2,852.4	1,002.7	32.2	103.5[k]	49.6	70.4	84.0	53.0	279.9	17.8	248.5	30.5	51.7	187.0	727.4	141.2	198.9	—	204.9	100.5
(1949)[n]	3,592.4	2,976.4	1,087.7	35.1	Health[l] (103.9)	Welfare (69.1)	74.9	87.2	58.4	325.4	16.5	265.7	36.0	58.4	205.6	567.8	150.2	16.1	—	211.1	107.5
1950[n]	3,492.2	2,915.3	1,057.4	34.6	135.8	105.8[m]	70.8	85.4	57.5	390.4	19.3	275.5	39.4	64.9	242.0	561.2	151.1	—	—	223.1	117.3
1951	3,415.0	2,907.5	1,100.2	34.6	141.7	106.6	66.4	84.0	54.6	343.0	16.9	242.0	34.6	57.0	212.6	493.1	132.8	—	—	196.0	103.0
1952	—	—	—	—	133.1	109.6	—	—	—	—	—	—	—	—	—	—	—	—	—	—	—

Revenue Account (in 1975 prices) – England and Wales (£m.) (continued)

Year ended 31 March	Total	Rate fund services								Housing						Trading services					
		Total	Ed.	Lib. and Mus.	Health	Welfare (Personal Social Services from 1972)	Sewer	Refuse	Parks	HRA	Other	Highways	Lighting	Fire	Police	Total	Water	Gas	Elec.	Trans.	Harbours[a]
1953	3,724.6	3,205.4	1,211.0	37.5	150.4	124.5	72.9	91.9	59.3	408.5	20.3	260.9	38.6	62.8	232.5	522.8	143.8	–	–	211.4	103.4
1954	3,878.7	3,363.7	1,253.9	38.5	147.9	130.4	76.4	92.5	60.5	469.6	23.7	267.6	40.2	64.0	237.7	539.8	151.4	–	–	210.5	113.2
1955	4,146.7	3,578.1	1,384.5	40.9	152.6	135.0	80.2	94.8	62.6	524.2	29.8	286.3	41.3	64.6	243.0	549.6	155.0	–	–	212.9	113.4
1956	4,240.5	3,694.0	1,438.0	42.1	156.5	135.7	82.2	98.1	65.0	551.3	79.7	287.7	42.7	65.0	251.1	556.0	159.0	–	–	210.9	118.5
1957	4,584.6	4,021.7	1,614.1	46.2	165.7	142.7	91.3	102.9	68.3	600.2	79.3[o]	295.2	45.0	68.0	280.5	565.3	164.4	–	–	215.9	117.2
1958	4,696.6	4,135.4	1,691.2	47.5	166.5	145.2	96.2	101.7	69.4	627.2	78.1	299.0	45.2	69.4	274.3	565.3	169.1	–	–	212.0	116.1
1959	4,833.6	4,293.1	1,769.8	49.4	172.3[1]	150.5	102.5	103.0	73.4	655.0	78.5	295.1	46.9	71.2	286.4	563.4	168.6	–	–	209.4	115.0
1960	5,276.9	4,688.6	1,970.8	55.4	192.6	162.1	113.1	107.8	76.6	706.2	83.4	319.0	49.8	76.6	306.0	596.2	190.5	–	–	215.2	123.9
1961	5,526.0	4,905.4	2,059.8	59.7	198.5	170.0	120.2	112.2	79.1	742.2	82.4	328.3	50.9	79.9	334.5	605.0	185.3	–	–	215.4	125.4
1962	5,913.2	5,238.5	2,200.5	63.8	215.4	182.5	130.3	119.7	81.3	787.8	93.2	354.2	52.7	84.8	362.4	619.6	190.7	–	–	219.3	127.7
1963	6,344.9	5,638.6	2,410.7	68.2	226.4	196.8	139.5	124.2	84.3	821.7	100.9	387.1	55.0	93.9	379.9	636.1	200.4	–	–	217.6	133.3
1964	6,747.5	6,030.2	2,578.4	72.9	242.1	214.0	147.5	128.8	91.3	868.1	109.8	419.4	55.9	97.9	410.8	657.9	204.4	–	–	225.4	136.3
1965	7,043.1	6,322.2	2,671.6	77.6	253.5	222.7	160.1	133.0	93.9	926.1	130.0	432.9	57.5	103.6	427.3	668.0	213.0	–	–	220.6	140.0
1966	7,717.3	6,923.0	2,946.5	86.4	275.4	246.5	175.1	145.4	101.1	1,008.8	158.2	460.0	59.8	109.0	459.6	683.2	221.3	–	–	222.7	141.4
1967	8,227.5	7,421.4	3,149.3	93.4	292.6	270.4	193.1	155.9	106.6	1,092.3	175.4	478.5	61.8	116.1	500.0	685.2	235.8	–	–	223.3	127.2[x]
1968	8,757.2	7,943.3	3,349.7	101.4	308.7	293.1	207.5	165.8	111.5	1,170.1	189.0	542.8		121.9	539.3	684.6	242.4	–	–	217.6	128.2
1969	9,152.4	8,296.5	3,481.6	105.9	322.1	312.3	225.9	173.8	118.4	1,283.0	198.6	508.8	62.3	126.0	558.8	729.3	254.3	–	–	217.0	153.7
1970[1]	10,610.5	9,213.0	3,719.3	114.4	329.0	322.1	258.9	188.1	130.5	1,376.2[D]	188.6	502.7	62.4	131.5	595.2	760.1	303.5	–	–	217.9	138.4
1971	11,007.8	9,615.2	3,818.2	118.9	354.5	345.2	268.4	194.0	132.0	1,395.0	200.9	511.6	63.2	133.6	654.0	736.9	286.2	–	–	122.4[q]	139.5
1972	11,439.3	10,130.5	4,026.1	126.3	229.2	507.9	274.5	201.5	143.8	1,382.9	202.1	561.2	64.9	146.0	687.6	696.5	283.9	–	–	122.6	102.1[x]
1973	11,857.9	10,913.6	4,300.4	134.8	244.4	578.5	290.8	212.6	158.5	1,509.6	233.6	591.7	65.5	157.0	691.4	603.7	274.8	–	–	121.5	19.7[x]
1974	12,495.8	11,489.6	4,309.7	135.8	248.6[a]	670.7	242.1[a]	214.3	172.0	1,580.6	363.0	605.0	62.1	157.7	686.6	604.6	267.3[a]	–	–	115.9	18.4
1975	12,253.9	11,441.6	4,404.4	139.4	–	753.1	–	229.7	157.6	1,621.2	412.1	439.8	48.4	165.2	660.9	292.7	–	–	–	74.2	23.5

a This covers docks, piers and similar services.

b Prior to 1883 all figures include expenditure out of loans, which was not at that time separately distinguished.

c Loan charges attributable to these items are not included with them until these dates.

d These figures are incomplete, since the total spent in 1904, and the amounts spent on maintenance in 1905, by school boards outside London and the county boroughs were never ascertained.

e There is a break in these series as a result of the London County Council substituting actual repayments of debt for payments into their sinking fund in reckoning their loan charges.

f Some small, previously unascertainable portion of loan charges is included from these dates.

g Prior to 1914 this heading covered tramways and light railways only, but from that year expenditure on motor bus and trolley undertakings is included.

h Maternity and child welfare and other public health expenditure was included under this heading in two stages in 1916 and 1921.

i From 1923, expenditure on ferries is no longer included, making a difference of a little over 1 per cent.

j Owing to legislative changes these items disappear or emerge under other headings between 1948 and 1950.

k Prior to 1949 this column was an aggregate of 'Maternity and Child Welfare', 'Hospitals, Sanatoria, Dispensaries, etc.', and 'Other items' under the general heading 'Public Health'. Following the establishment of the NHS on 5 July 1948 the first two elements disappear or emerge under other headings.

l This column is an aggregate of 'Care of Aged, Handicapped and Homeless' and 'Protection of Children'. In the earlier years these were called 'National Assistance – Accommodation and Welfare', and 'Child Welfare and Child Life Protection'.

m That is, Local Authority Health Services (e.g. care of mothers and young children, ambulances, health visiting).

n These breaks result from the transfer of various items from local authorities to nationalised industry boards and the National Health Service.

o After 1956 this column includes expenditure in respect of requisitioned houses.

p HRA becomes a separate account. In this table it is included in Rate-Fund Services.

q Refers to municipally owned transport services only.

r In 1966 a number of docks and harbour authorities adopted the recommendation of the National Ports Council that their accounts be kept on a calendar year basis. Consequently entries against this item do not reflect a full year's transaction in 1967 and 1968. In 1972 Mersey Docks and Harbour Board is excluded and in 1973 the Port of London and similar bodies are excluded.

s Transfer of services from local authorities after 1973/4.

t Data collected by a revised system of returns. The figures do not necessarily bear a direct comparison with those of previous years.

Capital Account (in current prices) – England and Wales (£m.)

Year ended 31 March	Total	Rate fund services								Housing							Trading services				
		Total	Ed.	Lib. and Mus.	Hospitals[a]	Work-houses	Sewer	Refuse	Parks	HRA	Other	Highways	Lighting	Fire	Police	Total	Water	Gas	Elec.	Trans.	Harbours[b]
1883	9.4	—	—	—	—	0.4	1.1	—	—	—	—	—	—	—	—	—	1.2	0.4	—	—	1.1
1884	8.8	—	1.2	—	—	0.5	0.9	—	0.1	—	0.1	1.8	—	—	—	—	1.2	0.5	—	0.1	0.7
1885	9.9	—	1.4	—	—	0.6	1.0	—	0.1	—	—	2.6	—	—	—	—	1.2	0.6	—	0.1	0.8
1886	9.4	—	1.4	—	—	0.6	1.1	—	0.1	—	0.1	2.2	—	—	—	—	1.1	0.7	—	0.1	0.6
1887	8.6	—	1.0	—	0.1	0.4	1.0	—	0.2	—	0.1	1.9	—	—	—	—	1.1	0.3	—	—	0.7
1888	9.3	—	0.7	—	0.1	0.3	0.9	—	0.2	—	0.2	1.4	—	—	—	—	3.3	0.2	—	—	0.6
1889	7.0	—	0.7	—	0.1	0.3	0.9	—	0.3	—	0.1	0.9	—	—	—	—	1.5	0.2	—	—	0.5
1890	7.1	—	0.8	—	0.1	0.4	0.9	—	0.4	0.1	—	1.1	—	—	—	—	1.3	0.2	—	—	0.6
1891	7.2	—	0.8	—	0.1	0.3	1.1	—	0.3	—	—	1.2	—	—	—	—	1.3	0.3	—	—	0.4
1892	10.6	—	1.0	—	0.1	0.3	1.2	—	0.2	—	0.1	1.2	—	—	—	—	1.3	0.5	0.1	—	0.5
1893	10.6	—	1.2	—	0.1	0.4	1.2	—	0.5	—	0.3	1.3	—	—	—	—	1.4	0.5	0.2	0.1	0.5
1894	14.0	—	1.6	—	0.2	0.7	1.5	—	0.5	—	0.2	1.4	—	—	—	—	1.7	0.8	0.4	0.1	0.6
1895	13.4	—	2.0	—	0.2	0.8	1.8	—	0.3	—	0.2	1.4	—	—	—	—	1.8	0.6	0.7	0.2	0.6
1896	13.4	—	2.3	—	0.2	0.8	2.2	—	0.2	—	0.2	1.6	—	—	—	—	1.6	0.5	0.6	0.1	0.7
1897	13.8	—	2.4	—	0.2	0.8	1.9	—	0.2	—	0.3	1.4	—	—	—	—	1.4	0.6	1.1	0.2	0.6
1898	17.1	—	2.0	—	0.2	1.2	2.0	—	0.3	—	0.3	2.1	—	—	—	—	1.9	0.8	0.8	0.1	0.6
1899	21.5	—	2.0	—	0.3	1.4	2.1	—	0.3	—	0.5	2.3	—	—	—	—	2.6	1.3	2.1	1.6	0.9
1900	24.9	—	2.1	—	0.4	1.2	2.0	—	0.5	—	0.8	3.2	—	—	—	—	4.2	1.0	2.8	1.4	1.6
1901	27.9	—	2.2	—	0.5	1.4	2.4	—	0.6	—	0.5	4.8	—	—	—	—	2.8	1.3	3.3	2.9	1.1
1902	33.9	—	2.6	—	0.9	1.6	2.6	—	0.6	—	0.8	5.4	—	—	—	—	3.2	1.9	3.9	4.7	1.3
1903	36.1	—	2.5	—	0.9	1.8	2.5	—	0.8	—	—	6.4	—	—	—	—	4.3	1.0	4.2	4.8	1.5
1904	30.7[c]	—	2.1[c]	—	0.6	1.3	2.4	—	0.5	—	1.0	4.9	—	—	—	—	3.8	0.7	3.4	4.3	1.8
1905	65.5[c]	—	2.4[c]	—	0.7	1.1	2.9	—	0.4	—	0.7	4.4	—	—	—	—	37.6[d]	0.8	4.2	4.3	2.0
1906	25.4	—	2.4	—	0.5	1.0	2.8	—	0.3	—	0.6	3.1	—	—	—	—	3.2	0.5	2.4	3.1	1.8
1907	23.4	—	2.8	—	0.3	0.8	2.6	—	0.3	—	0.5	2.1	—	—	—	—	2.8	0.4	1.8	4.2	1.5
1908	19.4	—	2.6	—	0.1	0.5	2.0	—	0.3	—	0.3	1.9	—	—	—	—	2.7	0.5	1.5	2.8	1.5
1909	18.4	—	3.0	—	0.1	0.5	2.0	—	0.3	—	0.3	1.9	—	—	—	—	2.9	0.5	1.3	2.0	1.4
1910	40.6	—	2.9	—	0.1	0.4	2.1	—	0.3	—	0.4	1.9	—	—	—	—	2.6	0.4	1.1	2.3	23.1[e]
1911	18.2	—	3.2	—	0.1	0.4	1.9	—	0.3	—	0.2	1.8	—	—	—	—	2.7	0.4	1.2	1.4	1.9
1912	17.1	—	2.7	—	0.1	0.4	1.8	—	0.4	—	0.2	1.7	—	—	—	—	2.3	0.4	1.4	1.3	1.4
1913	18.3	—	3.0	—	0.1	0.6	1.7	—	0.4	—	0.4	1.9	—	—	—	—	2.0	0.5	1.6	1.3	1.3
1914	21.1	—	2.9	—	0.2	0.6	1.9	—	0.5	—	0.7	3.2	—	—	—	—	2.0	0.9	1.9	1.4	1.6
1915	21.8	—	2.7	—	0.3	0.6	1.8	—	0.5	—	0.9	3.0	—	—	—	—	1.8	0.7	2.4	0.7	1.5
1916	11.6	—	1.3	—	0.3	0.3	—	—	0.2	—	0.6	1.2	—	—	—	—	1.2	0.4	1.6	0.2	1.4
1917	5.8	—	0.3	—	0.1	0.1	—	—	—	—	0.5	0.4	—	—	—	—	0.6	0.3	1.7	0.1	0.7
1918	3.6	—	0.1	—	0.1	—	—	—	—	—	0.1	0.2	—	—	—	—	0.4	0.1	1.7	—	0.4
1919	4.6	—	0.1	—	0.1	—	0.1	—	—	—	0.1	0.1	—	—	—	—	0.3	0.2	2.1	—	1.0
1920	23.9	—	0.7	—	0.3	0.1	0.7	—	0.2	4.8	—	1.2	—	—	—	—	1.9	0.9	3.6	1.4	2.1
1921	94.5	—	1.9	—	1.2[g]	0.2	2.3	—	0.5	52.2	—	3.7[f]	—	—	—	—	4.0	1.9	8.4	2.8	3.6

Year																				
1922	128.7	—	1.8	1.1	0.3	3.5	—	0.9	81.7	—	6.2	—	—	—	—	5.5	2.9	11.5	3.5	2.6
1923	71.6	—	0.9	0.7	0.4	4.6	—	1.1	29.6	—	9.0	—	—	—	—	5.4	2.0	9.3	2.5	1.9
1924	50.0	—	0.9	0.6	0.5	4.8	—	1.3	11.3	—	8.4	—	—	—	—	5.2	1.2	8.5	2.1	2.0
1925	70.3	—	1.4	0.9	0.7	5.0	—	1.4	24.0	—	9.9	—	—	—	—	6.7	1.4	9.7	2.6	2.4
1926	100.7	—	3.1	1.0	0.9	5.6	—	1.8	47.0	—	10.0	—	—	—	—	6.5	1.9	11.8	2.6	2.2
1927	117.4	—	4.4	1.2	1.1	4.5	—	1.3	65.3	—	9.5	—	—	—	—	5.3	2.8	12.1	2.7	2.0
1928	120.0	—	5.7	0.9	1.3	4.2	—	1.2	66.2	—	8.4	—	—	—	—	4.9	2.3	13.1	2.6	3.7
1929	90.5	—	6.0	0.9	1.2	3.9	—	1.2	38.1	—	8.0	—	—	—	—	4.6	1.5	14.4	2.4	2.4
1930	108.9	80.9	6.0	1.2	0.9	4.5	0.3	1.7	42.8	—	16.2	0.1	0.2	0.4	28.0	5.1	1.5	15.3	2.4	1.7
1931	110.9	84.1	7.8	1.7	0.8	6.5	0.3	2.2	37.4	—	18.9	0.1	0.3	0.2	26.6	4.9	1.7	14.3	2.6	1.5
1932	116.8	90.2	9.8	1.5	0.6	9.0	0.3	1.7	39.6	—	19.0	0.1	0.3	0.2	26.6	5.5	1.4	13.6	2.7	2.0
1933	84.8	64.1	5.7	1.0	1.1	8.3	0.2	0.8	28.2	—	10.2	0.1	0.2	0.2	20.6	4.2	1.2	10.9	1.6	1.4
1934	89.3	59.3	3.9	0.9	0.6	5.7	0.3	0.8	30.6	—	8.7	0.1	0.2	0.1	30.0	3.7	1.2	11.4	11.1	1.3
1935	80.7	58.5	4.3	1.2	0.8	5.5	0.2	1.4	29.3	—	7.2	0.1	0.2	0.2	22.2	4.0	1.4	12.7	1.8	1.0
1936	96.9	71.2	5.8	1.7	0.7	5.3	0.3	1.9	24.9	12.8	8.3	0.2	0.4	0.2	25.6	4.7	1.4	15.3	2.3	0.9
1937	116.8	86.4	7.9	2.4	1.0	5.5	0.3	2.5	32.3	12.2	9.7	0.3	0.4	0.9	30.3	5.8	1.8	17.4	4.0	1.2
1938	142.1	105.8	11.1	2.6	1.2	6.3	0.3	3.5	40.7	13.0	12.2	0.2	0.5	1.1	36.3	6.2	2.2	19.5	5.0	2.2
1939	150.8	116.4	14.8	3.6	1.5	7.5	0.5	3.0	46.4	8.8	13.5	0.2	0.6	1.3	34.3	7.2	1.8	18.3	8.1	1.4
1940	117.0	87.7	14.4	3.5	1.0	5.7	0.3	1.4	23.8	—	9.8	0.2	0.7	0.3	29.3	6.3	1.8	14.9	2.1	1.5
1941	62.0	44.2	6.8	1.5	0.3	2.4	0.2	0.4	6.1	—	3.1	—	0.4	0.1	17.9	3.8	1.0	11.1	0.3	0.8
1942	47.3	29.9	1.9	0.9	0.2	1.3	0.1	0.1	2.7	—	1.5	—	0.4	—	17.4	2.8	0.9	11.8	0.1	0.9
1943	38.2	20.1	0.8	0.5	0.1	1.2	0.1	0.1	3.2	—	1.8	—	0.2	—	18.1	2.1	1.3	12.1	0.4	1.1
1944	25.4	13.2	0.6	0.3	0.1	0.7	—	0.1	4.1	—	0.6	—	—	—	12.1	1.6	1.0	8.0	0.5	0.5
1945	23.8	13.2	0.4	0.2	0.1	0.4	0.1	0.1	4.9	—	1.4	0.1	0.4	—	10.5	1.2	0.9	6.7	0.7	0.6
1946	46.5	30.2	0.8	0.5	0.1	0.6	0.1	0.2	21.6	—	0.5	0.1	0.3	0.1	16.2	1.6	1.3	11.2	1.1	0.6
1947	162.4	126.2	0.2	0.9	0.4	1.9	0.2	0.8	106.2	—	1.7	0.2	0.4	0.3	36.2	5.0	3.0	22.8[h]	1.9	1.8
1948	303.5	252.0	8.3	1.6	0.7[h]	4.5	0.4	1.0	209.3	—	3.4	0.2	0.5	0.7	51.5	6.3	4.2[h]	31.4[h]	5.0	1.8
1949	329.5	298.8	18.4	1.0[i]	0.3	7.3	0.5	1.0	243.3	—	3.3	0.2	0.2	1.5	30.7	11.2	6.0	—	8.1	3.5
(1949)				Health (0.7)	Welfare (1.2)[j]															
1950	331.1	300.3	28.0	1.6	2.9	9.5	0.5	1.3	220.4	13.4	5.1	0.3	0.4	2.4	30.8	15.3	0.7	—	8.9	3.3
1951	368.8	336.2	39.8	1.4	3.5	11.0	0.6	1.5	227.8	21.0	5.8	0.6	0.9	3.3	32.6	17.5	—	—	7.3	4.4
1952	426.5	392.5	53.5	1.8	4.3	15.3	0.8	2.1	251.2	30.4	5.8	0.9	1.3	4.6	34.0	20.8	—	—	4.8	4.6
1953	497.8	462.5	58.0	1.5	4.2	17.6	0.7	2.0	313.0	29.9	6.3	1.2	1.5	6.1	35.3	23.5	—	—	3.7	4.6
1954	543.6	506.0	58.7	1.4	3.7	18.9	0.8	1.4	334.6	39.2	6.5	1.6	1.7	6.3	37.7	24.8	—	—	4.8	5.2
1955	525.7	489.6	60.1	1.5	3.3	19.5	0.7	2.1	296.6	63.6	8.1	2.3	1.7	6.1	36.1	23.8	—	—	3.0	5.0
1956	541.1	501.4	68.8	1.5	3.9	23.7	1.0	2.6	260.1	89.1[k]	10.8	3.3	1.9	6.3	39.6	24.4	—	—	3.7	5.7
1957	555.0	510.1	86.0	1.3	3.3	26.5	1.3	2.2	250.0	88.3	13.5	3.7	1.7	5.5	45.0	28.3	—	—	4.4	6.7
1958	528.6	488.1	96.3	1.2	3.1	27.3	1.4	1.3	233.0	76.9	15.1	3.1	1.2	4.3	40.5	25.8	—	—	3.2	5.4
1959	511.9	467.9	92.0	1.4	3.4	28.3	1.0	1.6	205.8	80.2	21.0	2.8	1.7	4.0	44.0	26.1	—	—	3.0	7.5
1960	571.5	525.5	89.2	2.3	4.9	35.2	1.2	2.6	226.5	94.7	26.5	4.4	2.3	3.7	46.0	28.1	—	—	2.3	7.4
1961	620.8	569.7	88.2	3.3	5.6	37.0	1.2	3.8	220.0	125.6	31.7	5.1	2.1	3.6	51.0	31.7	—	—	1.7	6.2
1962	741.2	680.6	111.0	4.5	7.3	46.4	2.4	5.7	247.4	152.0	35.7	5.8	2.6	5.0	60.6	34.4	—	—	1.7	7.8
1963	793.7	729.9	122.3	6.2	9.4	53.2	2.3	5.6	269.0	145.0	43.9	4.6	3.8	6.0	63.8	36.9	—	—	3.0	6.8
1964	979.4	911.2	123.9	7.2	10.2	58.4	2.0	6.8	350.3	203.3	59.7	4.7	4.6	7.8	68.2	39.0	—	—	3.6	6.0

Capital Account (in current prices) – England and Wales (£m.)   (continued)

Year ended 31 March	Total	Rate fund services														Trading services				
		Ed.	Lib. and Mus.	Health	Welfare (Personal Social Services from 1972)	Sewer	Refuse	Parks	Housing HRA	Housing Other	Highways	Lighting	Fire	Police	Total	Water	Gas	Elec.	Trans	Harbours[b]
1965	1,223.8	134.6	4.0	8.6	15.7	62.8	2.6	9.2	436.4	287.0	72.6	5.4	4.2	9.1	79.9	42.1	–	–	2.9	10.1
1966	1,289.3	129.3	4.5	8.4	15.5	62.0	2.7	9.5	492.0	287.9	69.4	3.9	3.8	10.5	92.3	43.8	–	–	3.8	14.2
1967	1,411.9	143.6	3.9	7.4	15.6	73.6	3.0	7.0	596.5	252.4	77.2	3.3	3.3	20.0	106.9	48.9	–	–	4.1	21.4[n]
1968	1,563.3	187.6	5.5	9.4	17.0	91.8	5.7	6.4	651.3	243.3	114.4		4.5	17.3	103.8	51.1	–	–	4.9	18.6
1969	1,597.2	195.4	5.6	10.4	18.6	101.6	9.1	8.3	663.0	210.9	130.2	2.1	5.0	15.4	101.0	48.5	–	–	7.5	17.3
1970[p]	1,715.4	222.1	6.3	13.9	20.7	115.0	11.6	11.5	660.8[l]	170.5	166.1	3.5	5.7	16.6	152.5	71.0	–	–	10.6	29.6
1971	2,050.2	264.1	8.2	19.1	24.6	142.7	16.6	18.6	655.1	298.4	190.7	5.5	7.3	19.6	180.0	83.5	–	–	6.9[m]	31.8
1972	2,231.5	315.3	9.9	13.6	37.7	163.6	21.3	22.6	655.9	350.9	213.6	5.7	9.1	26.1	184.0	95.0	–	–	6.6	25.7[n]
1973	2,794.8	385.3	13.5	16.2	50.8	211.7	18.9	37.5	837.6	455.1	234.4	6.1	9.7	36.8	205.2	113.5	–	–	7.9	8.6[n]
1974	3,739.3	457.4	17.6	21.5[o]	74.3	283.8[o]	18.4	52.6	1,106.7	773.8	272.2	5.6	9.1	45.6	290.4	153.1[o]	–	–	18.5	10.3
1975	4,075.7	415.0	20.9	–	72.3	–	21.5	73.2	1,620.5	1,066.3	305.9	3.4	8.1	35.0	119.2	–	–	–	6.1	10.2

Capital Account (in 1975 prices) — England and Wales (£m.)

Year ended 31 March	Total	Rate fund services														Trading services					
		Total	Ed.	Lib and Mus.	Hospitals[a]	Work-houses	Sewer	Refuse	Parks	Housing HRA	Housing Other	Highways	Lighting	Fire	Police	Total	Water	Gas	Elec.	Trans.	Harbours[b]
1883	140.5	—	—	—	—	6.0	16.4	—	—	—	—	—	—	—	—	—	17.9	6.0	—	—	16.4
1884	133.3	—	18.2	—	—	7.6	13.6	—	—	—	1.5	27.3	—	—	—	—	18.2	7.6	—	—	10.6
1885	158.1	—	22.4	—	—	9.6	16.0	—	—	—	—	41.5	—	—	—	—	19.2	9.6	—	—	12.8
1886	158.5	—	23.6	—	—	10.1	18.5	—	—	—	1.7	37.1	—	—	—	—	18.5	11.8	—	1.6	10.1
1887	147.8	—	17.2	—	1.7	6.9	17.2	—	3.4	—	1.7	32.7	—	—	—	—	18.9	5.2	—	1.7	12.0
1888	161.2	—	12.1	—	1.7	5.2	15.6	—	3.5	—	3.5	24.3	—	—	—	—	57.2	3.5	—	—	10.4
1889	120.9	—	12.1	—	1.7	5.2	15.5	—	5.2	—	1.7	15.5	—	—	—	—	25.9	3.5	—	—	8.6
1890	121.7	—	13.7	—	1.7	6.9	15.4	—	6.9	—	1.7	18.8	—	—	—	—	22.3	3.4	—	—	10.3
1891	123.4	—	13.7	—	1.7	5.1	18.8	—	5.1	—	—	20.6	—	—	—	—	22.3	5.1	—	—	6.9
1892	181.1	—	17.1	—	1.7	5.1	20.5	—	3.4	—	1.7	20.5	—	—	—	—	22.2	8.5	1.7	—	8.5
1893	180.1	—	20.4	—	1.7	6.8	20.4	—	8.5	—	5.1	22.1	—	—	—	—	23.8	8.5	3.4	1.7	8.5
1894	242.6	—	27.7	—	3.5	12.1	26.0	—	8.7	—	3.5	24.3	—	—	—	—	29.5	13.9	6.9	3.5	10.4
1895	242.0	—	36.1	—	3.6	14.4	32.5	—	5.4	—	3.6	25.3	—	—	—	—	32.5	10.8	12.6	1.8	10.8
1896	246.2	—	42.3	—	3.7	14.7	40.4	—	3.7	—	3.7	29.4	—	—	—	—	29.4	9.2	11.0	3.7	12.9
1897	252.2	—	43.9	—	3.7	14.6	34.7	—	3.7	—	5.5	25.6	—	—	—	—	25.6	11.0	20.1	1.8	11.0
1898	304.2	—	35.6	—	3.6	21.3	35.6	—	5.3	—	5.3	37.4	—	—	—	—	33.8	14.2	14.2	30.2	16.0
1899	375.0	—	34.9	—	5.2	24.4	36.6	—	5.2	—	8.7	40.1	—	—	—	—	45.3	22.7	36.6	27.9	26.2
1900	435.1	—	36.7	—	7.0	21.0	34.9	—	8.7	—	14.0	55.9	—	—	—	—	73.4	17.5	48.9	24.5	28.0
1901	469.0	—	37.0	—	8.4	23.5	40.3	—	10.1	—	8.4	80.7	—	—	—	—	47.1	21.9	55.5	48.7	18.5
1902	574.5	—	44.1	—	15.3	27.1	44.1	—	10.2	—	13.6	91.5	—	—	—	—	54.2	32.2	66.1	79.6	22.0
1903	609.8	—	42.2	—	15.2	30.4	42.2	—	13.5	—	—	108.1	—	—	—	—	72.6	16.9	70.9	81.1	25.3
1904	512.9[c]	—	35.1[c]	—	10.0	21.7	40.1	—	8.4	—	16.7	81.9	—	—	—	—	63.5	11.7	56.8	71.8	30.1
1905	1,085.7[c]	—	39.8[c]	—	11.6	18.2	48.1	—	6.6	—	11.6	72.9	—	—	—	—	623.2[d]	13.3	69.6	71.3	33.2
1906	419.8	—	39.7	—	8.3	16.5	46.3	—	5.0	—	9.9	51.2	—	—	—	—	52.9	8.3	39.7	51.2	29.7
1907	381.9	—	45.7	—	4.9	13.1	42.4	—	4.9	—	8.2	34.3	—	—	—	—	45.7	6.5	29.4	68.5	24.5
1908	313.2	—	42.0	—	1.6	8.1	32.3	—	4.8	—	4.8	30.7	—	—	—	—	43.6	8.1	24.2	45.2	24.2
1909	301.1	—	49.1	—	1.6	8.2	32.7	—	4.9	—	4.9	31.1	—	—	—	—	47.5	8.2	21.3	32.7	22.9
1910	655.5	—	46.8	—	1.6	6.5	33.9	—	4.8	—	6.5	30.7	—	—	—	—	42.0	6.5	17.8	37.1	372.9[e]
1911	288.3	—	50.7	—	1.6	6.3	30.1	—	4.8	—	3.2	28.5	—	—	—	—	42.8	6.3	19.0	22.2	30.1
1912	266.8	—	42.1	—	1.6	6.2	28.1	—	6.2	—	3.1	26.5	—	—	—	—	35.9	6.2	21.8	20.3	21.8
1913	277.8	—	45.5	—	1.5	9.1	25.8	—	6.1	—	6.1	28.8	—	—	—	—	30.4	7.6	24.3	19.7	19.7
1914	317.2	—	43.6	—	3.0	9.0	28.6	—	7.5	—	10.5	48.1	—	—	—	—	30.1	13.5	28.6	19.5	24.0
1915	—	—	—	—	—	—	—	—	—	—	—	—	—	—	—	—	—	—	—	—	—
1916	—	—	—	—	—	—	—	—	—	—	—	—	—	—	—	—	—	—	—	—	—
1917	—	—	—	—	—	—	—	—	—	—	—	—	—	—	—	—	—	—	—	—	—
1918	—	—	—	—	—	—	—	—	—	—	—	—	—	—	—	—	—	—	—	—	—
1919	—	—	—	—	—	—	—	—	—	—	—	—	—	—	—	—	—	—	—	—	—
1920	—	—	—	—	—	—	—	—	—	—	—	—	—	—	—	—	—	—	—	—	—
1921	595.2	—	12.0	—	7.6	1.3	14.5	—	3.1	328.8	—	23.3	—	—	—	—	25.2	12.0	52.9	17.6	22.7
1922	1,015.0	—	14.2	—	8.7[g]	2.4	27.6	—	7.1	644.3	—	48.9[f]	—	—	—	—	43.4	22.9	90.7	27.6	20.5

Capital Account (in 1975 prices) – England and Wales (£m.) (continued)

Year ended 31 March	Total	Rate fund services															Trading services				
	Total	Total	Ed.	Lib. and Mus.	Hospitals[a]	Work-houses	Sewer	Refuse	Parks	Housing HRA	Other	Highways	Lighting	Fire	Police	Total	Water	Gas	Elec.	Trans.	Harbours[b]
1923	595.5	—	7.5	—	5.8	3.3	38.3	—	9.1	246.2		74.9	—	—	—	—	44.9	16.6	77.3	20.8	15.8
1924	414.2	—	7.5	—	5.0	4.1	39.8	—	10.8	93.6		69.6	—	—	—	—	43.1	9.9	70.4	17.4	16.6
1925	576.6	—	11.5	—	7.4	5.7	41.0	—	11.5	196.9		81.2	—	—	—	—	55.0	11.5	79.6	21.3	19.7
1926	782.7	—	24.1	—	7.8	7.0	43.5	—	14.0	365.3		77.7	—	—	—	—	50.5	14.8	91.7	20.2	17.1
1927	1,014.4	—	38.0	—	10.4	9.5	38.9	—	11.2	564.2		82.1	—	—	—	—	45.8	24.2	104.6	23.3	17.3
1928	1,025.6	—	48.7	—	7.7	11.1	35.9	—	10.3	565.8		71.8	—	—	—	—	41.9	19.7	112.0	22.2	31.6
1929	782.3	—	51.9	—	7.8	10.4	33.7	—	10.4	329.4		69.2	—	—	—	—	39.8	13.0	124.5	20.7	20.7
1930	965.9	717.6	53.2	1.8	10.6	8.0	39.9	2.7	15.1	379.6		143.7	0.9	1.8	3.5	248.4	45.2	13.3	135.7	21.3	15.1
1931	1,034.1	784.2	72.7	2.8	15.9	7.5	60.6	2.8	20.5	348.8		176.2	0.9	2.8	1.9	249.9	45.7	15.9	133.3	24.2	14.0
1932	1,112.5	859.1	93.3	3.8	14.3	5.7	85.7	2.9	16.2	377.2		181.0	1.0	2.9	1.9	253.4	52.4	13.3	129.5	25.7	19.0
1933	828.0	625.9	55.7	2.0	9.8	10.7	81.0	2.0	7.8	275.4		99.6	1.0	2.0	2.0	201.2	41.0	11.7	106.4	15.6	13.7
1934	868.3	576.6	37.9	1.9	8.8	5.8	55.4	2.9	7.8	297.5		84.6	1.0	1.9	1.0	291.7	36.0	11.7	110.9	107.9	12.6
1935	780.2	565.5	41.6	2.9	11.6	7.7	53.2	1.9	13.5	283.3		69.6	1.0	3.9	1.9	214.6	38.7	11.6	122.8	17.4	9.7
1936	917.8	674.4	54.9	1.9	16.1	6.6	50.2	1.9	18.0	235.8	121.2	78.6	0.9	2.8	3.8	242.5	44.5	13.3	144.9	15.2	8.5
1937	1,061.8	785.5	71.8	3.6	21.8	9.1	50.0	2.7	22.7	293.6	110.9	88.2	1.8	3.6	8.2	275.5	52.7	16.4	158.2	20.9	10.9
1938	1,270.3	945.8	99.2	3.6	23.2	10.7	56.3	2.7	31.3	363.8	116.2	109.1	2.7	4.5	9.8	324.5	55.4	19.7	174.3	35.8	19.7
1939	—	—	—	—	—	—	—	—	—	—		—	—	—	—	—	—	—	—	—	—
1940	—	—	—	—	—	—	—	—	—	—		—	—	—	—	—	—	—	—	—	—
1941	—	—	—	—	—	—	—	—	—	—		—	—	—	—	—	—	—	—	—	—
1942	—	—	—	—	—	—	—	—	—	—		—	—	—	—	—	—	—	—	—	—
1943	—	—	—	—	—	—	—	—	—	—		—	—	—	—	—	—	—	—	—	—
1944	—	—	—	—	—	—	—	—	—	—		—	—	—	—	—	—	—	—	—	—
1945	—	—	—	—	—	—	—	—	—	—		—	—	—	—	—	—	—	—	—	—
1946	224.3	145.7	3.9	0.5	2.4	0.5	2.9	0.5	1.0	104.2	15.9	2.4	—	—	0.5	78.2	7.7	6.3	54.0	5.3	2.9
1947	682.1	530.1	0.8	0.4	3.8	1.7	8.0	0.8	3.4	446.0	34.0	7.1	0.4	—	1.3	152.0	21.0	12.6	95.8	8.0	7.6
1948	1,319.5	1,095.6	36.1	0.4	7.0	3.0[h]	19.6	1.7	4.3	910.0	50.9	14.8	0.9	—	3.0	223.9	27.4	18.3[h]	136.5[h]	21.7	7.8
1949	1,397.5	1,267.3	78.0	0.4	4.2[i]	1.3	31.0	2.1	4.2	1,031.9	38.2	14.0	0.8	0.8	6.4	130.2	47.5	25.4	—	34.4	14.8
(1949)	—	—	—	—	Health (3.0)	Welfare (5.1)[j]	—	—	—	—		—	—	—	—	—	—	—	—	—	—
1950	1,400.8	1,270.5	118.5	0.8	6.8	12.3	40.2	2.1	5.5	932.5	56.7	21.6	1.3	1.7	10.2	130.3	64.7	3.0	—	37.7	14.0
1951	1,451.3	1,323.0	156.6	1.6	5.5	13.8	43.3	2.4	5.9	896.5	82.6	22.8	2.4	3.5	13.0	128.3	68.9	—	—	28.7	17.3
1952	1,474.7	1,357.1	185.0	1.0	6.2	14.9	52.9	2.8	7.3	868.5	105.1	20.1	3.1	4.5	15.9	117.6	71.9	—	—	16.6	15.9
1953	1,745.4	1,621.6	203.4	1.1	5.3	14.7	61.7	2.5	7.0	1,097.4	104.8	22.1	4.2	5.3	21.4	123.8	82.4	—	—	13.0	16.1
1954	1,870.0	1,740.7	201.9	1.0	4.8	12.7	65.0	2.8	4.8	1,151.1	134.9	22.4	4.5	5.8	21.7	129.7	85.3	—	—	16.5	17.9
1955	1,779.1	1,656.9	203.4	1.4	5.1	11.2	66.0	2.4	7.1	1,003.8	215.2	27.4	5.5	5.8	20.6	122.2	80.5	—	—	10.2	16.9
1956	1,724.2	1,597.2	219.2	2.2	4.8	12.4	75.5	3.2	8.3	828.8	283.9[k]	34.4	10.5	6.1	20.1	126.2	77.7	—	—	11.8	18.2
1957	1,699.6	1,562.1	263.4	2.1	4.0	10.1	81.2	4.0	6.7	765.6	270.4	41.3	11.3	5.2	16.8	137.8	86.7	—	—	13.5	20.5
1958	1,522.9	1,406.2	277.4	1.7	3.5	8.9	78.7	4.0	3.7	671.3	221.5	43.5	8.9	3.5	12.3	116.7	74.3	—	—	9.2	15.6
1959	1,429.2	1,306.3	256.9	2.2	3.9	9.5	79.0	2.8	4.5	574.6	223.9	58.6	7.8	4.7	11.2	122.8	72.9	—	—	8.4	20.9
1960	1,616.4	1,486.3	252.3	4.2	6.5	13.9	99.6	3.4	7.4	640.6	267.8	75.0	12.4	6.5	10.5	130.1	79.5	—	—	6.5	20.9

Year																					
1961	1,699.6	1,559.7	241.5	5.7	9.0	15.3	101.3	3.3	10.4	602.3	343.9	86.8	14.0	5.7	9.9	139.6	86.8	—	—	4.7	17.0
1962	1,963.4	1,802.9	294.0	6.4	11.9	19.3	122.9	6.4	15.1	655.3	402.6	94.6	15.4	6.9	13.2	160.5	91.1	—	—	4.5	20.7
1963	2,058.1	1,892.6	317.1	8.6	16.1	24.4	137.9	6.0	14.5	697.5	376.0	113.8	11.9	9.9	15.6	165.4	95.7	—	:	7.8	17.6
1964	2,477.4	2,304.9	313.4	8.6	18.2	25.8	147.7	5.1	17.2	886.1	514.3	151.0	11.9	11.6	19.7	172.5	98.7	—	—	9.1	15.2
1965	2,974.2	2,780.3	326.6	9.7	20.9	38.1	152.4	6.3	22.3	1,058.8	696.3	176.1	13.1	10.2	22.1	193.9	102.1	—	—	7.0	24.5
1966	3,009.3	2,793.9	301.8	10.5	19.6	36.2	144.7	6.3	22.2	1,148.4	672.0	162.0	9.1	8.9	24.5	215.4	102.2	—	—	8.9	33.1
1967	3,207.7	2,964.8	326.2	8.9	16.8	35.4	167.2	6.8	15.9	1,355.2	575.4	175.4	7.5	7.5	45.4	242.9	111.1	—	—	9.3	48.6n
1968	3,432.5	3,204.8	411.9	12.1	20.6	37.3	201.6	12.5	14.1	1,430.0	534.2	251.2		9.9	38.0	227.9	112.2	—	—	10.8	40.8
1969	3,382.0	3,168.2	413.8	11.9	22.0	39.4	215.1	19.3	17.6	1,403.9	446.6	275.7	4.4	10.6	32.6	213.9	102.7	—	—	15.9	36.6
1970p	3,367.3	3,067.9	436.0	12.4	27.3	40.6	225.7	22.8	22.6	1,297.1[1]	334.7	326.1	6.9	11.2	32.6	299.4	139.4	—	—	20.8	58.1
1971	3,648.6	3,328.4	470.0	14.6	34.0	43.8	254.0	29.5	33.1	1,165.8	531.0	339.4	9.8	13.0	34.9	320.3	148.6	⊢	—	12.3m	56.6
1972	3,605.1	3,308.0	509.4	16.0	22.0	60.9	264.3	34.4	36.5	1,059.6	566.9	345.1	9.2	14.7	42.2	297.3	153.5	—	—	10.7	41.5n
1973	4,140.4	3,836.4	570.8	20.0	24.0	75.3	313.6	28.0	55.6	1,240.9	674.2	347.3	9.0	14.4	54.5	304.0	168.1	—	—	11.7	12.7n
1974	4,800.9	4,428.2	587.3	22.6	27.6o	95.4	364.4o	23.6	67.5	1,420.9	993.5	349.5	7.2	11.7	58.5	372.8	196.6o	—	—	23.8	13.2
1975	4,075.7	3,956.4	415.0	20.9	—	72.3	—	21.5	73.2	1,620.5	1,066.3	305.9	3.4	8.1	35.0	119.2	—	—	—	6.1	10.2

NOTES TO p.p. 110–115

a Includes public-health clinics.

b This covers docks, piers and similar services.

c These figures are incomplete, since the total spent in 1904, and the amounts spent on maintenance in 1905, by school boards outside London and the county boroughs were never ascertained.

d This exceptionally large sum results from the formation of the Metropolitan Water Board.

e This exceptionally large sum results from the formation of the Port of London Authority.

f From 1921 ferries were no longer included under this heading. The difference was very slight.

g From 1921 certain public-health items were newly included under this heading. They accounted for 0.3 in 1921.

h Owing to legislative changes these items disappear or emerge under other headings between 1948 and 1950.

i Until the establishment of the NHS this column is an aggregate of 'Maternity and Child Welfare', 'Hospitals, Sanatoria and Dispensaries', and 'Other items', all of which came under the general heading of 'Public Health'. After 1949 the first two of these constituents disappear from local authority accounts or are included in 'Welfare'.

j This column is an aggregate of welfare services provided by local authorities since the legislative changes of the postwar years. It consists of 'Care of Aged, Handicapped and Homeless' and 'Protection of Children'.

k From 1955/6 expenditure in respect of requisitioned houses is included in this column.

m HRA becomes a separate account. In this table it is included in Rate Fund Services.

n Refers to municipally owned transport services only.

o In 1966 a number of docks and harbour authorities adopted the recommendation of the National Ports Council that their accounts be kept on a calendar year basis. Consequently entries against this item do not reflect a full year's transaction in 1967 and 1968. In 1972 Mersey Docks and Harbour Board is excluded and in 1973, Port of London and similar bodies are excluded.

o Transfer of services from local authorities after 1973/4.

p Data collected by a revised system of returns. The figures do not necessarily bear a direct comparison with those of previous years.

Revenue Account (in current prices) – Scotland (£m.)

Year ended 15 May	Total	Rate fund services								Housing							Trading services				
		Total	Ed.	Lib. and Mus.	Hospitals	Poor Relief	Sewer	Refuse	Parks	HRA	Other	Highways	Lighting	Fire	Police	Total	Water	Gas	Elec.	Trans.	Harbours
1893[a]	9.0	—	1.6	—	0.1	0.9	—	—	—	—	—	0.7	—	—	0.4	—	—	—	—	—	0.7
1894	8.1	—	1.4	—	—	0.9	—	—	—	—	—	0.7	0.1	—	0.5	—	—	0.9	—	—	0.4
1895	9.2	—	1.5	—[b]	—	1.0	—	—	0.1	—	—	0.7	0.2[b]	—	0.5	—	—	1.1	—	0.2	0.4
1896	9.3	—	1.8[b]	—	0.1	1.0	0.2	—	0.1[b]	—	—	0.8	0.2	—	0.5[b]	—	0.7	1.3	—	0.3	0.9
1897	9.5	—	1.9	—	0.1	1.1	0.2	—	0.1	—	—	0.8	0.2	—	0.5	—	0.6	1.3	0.1	0.4	0.9
1898	10.2	—	2.0	—	0.2	1.1	0.2	—	0.1	—	—	0.9	0.2	—	0.5	—	0.7	1.3	0.1	0.4	0.9
1899	10.5	—	2.0	—	0.2	1.1	0.2	—	0.1	—	—	0.8	0.2	—	0.5	—	0.7	1.4	0.1	0.5	1.0
1900	11.1	—	2.1	—	0.2	1.1	0.2	—	0.1	—	—	0.9	0.2	—	0.5	—	0.7	1.6	0.2	0.5	0.9
1901	12.1	—	2.3	—	0.2	1.2	0.2	—	0.1	—	—	0.9	0.2	—	0.5	—	0.8	1.9	0.2	0.6	1.0
1902	12.5	—	2.4	—	0.3	1.2	0.2	—	0.1	—	—	1.0	0.3	—	0.6	—	0.8	1.8	0.3	0.7	1.0
1903	13.0	—	2.6	—	0.2	1.2	0.2	—	0.1	—	—	1.0	0.3	—	0.6	—	0.8	1.8	0.3	0.8	1.1
1904	13.6	—	2.7	—	0.3	1.3	0.3	—	0.1	—	—	1.0	0.3	—	0.6	—	0.9	1.8	0.4	0.9	1.1
1905	14.0	—	2.8	—	0.3	1.4	0.3	—	0.2	—	—	1.1	0.3	—	0.6	—	0.9	1.7	0.4	0.9	1.0
1906	14.5	—	2.9	0.1	0.3	1.4	0.3	—	0.2	—	—	1.1	0.3	—	0.6	—	1.0	1.8	0.5	1.1	1.1
1907	15.1	—	3.0	0.1	0.3	1.4	0.3	0.4	0.2	—	0.1	1.1	0.3	—	0.7	—	1.0	1.8	0.5	1.1	1.2
1908	15.8	—	3.2	0.1	0.3	1.5	0.3	0.5	0.2	—	0.1	1.1	0.3	—	0.7	—	1.0	2.1	0.6	1.2	1.1
1909	16.1	—	3.4	0.1	0.3	1.5	0.4	0.5	0.2	—	0.1	1.2	0.3	—	0.7	—	1.0	1.9	0.6	1.2	1.2
1910	16.5	—	3.7	0.1	0.4	1.6	0.4	0.5	0.2	—	0.1	1.2	0.3	—	0.7	—	1.0	1.9	0.6	1.2	1.2
1911	16.9	—	3.8	0.1	0.4	1.6	0.4	0.5	0.2	—	0.1	1.2	0.3	—	0.7	—	1.1	2.0	0.6	1.2	1.2
1912	17.4	—	3.9	0.1	0.4	1.5	0.4	0.5	0.2	—	0.1	1.3	0.3	—	0.7	—	1.1	2.3	0.7	1.3	1.2
1913	18.3	—	4.0	0.1	0.4	1.6	0.4	0.5	0.2	—	0.1	1.3	0.3	—	0.7	—	1.1	2.5	0.7	1.4	1.3
1914	19.1	—	4.2	0.1	0.4	1.6	0.5	0.5	0.2	—	0.1	1.4	0.3	—	0.8	—	1.2	2.4	0.8	1.5	1.3
1915	19.5	—	4.2	0.1	0.6	1.4	0.5	0.6	0.2	—	0.2	1.5	0.3	—	0.8	—	1.2	2.9	0.8	1.5	1.3
1916	20.3	—	4.3	0.1	0.6	1.4	0.5	0.6	0.2	—	0.2	1.4	0.3	—	0.8	—	1.2	3.1	1.0	1.6	1.3
1917	21.0	—	4.4	0.1	0.6	1.5	0.5	0.6	0.2	—	0.2	1.3	0.2	—	0.8	—	1.3	3.6	1.1	1.6	1.3
1918	23.0	—	4.9	0.1	0.7	1.5	0.5	0.7	0.2	—	0.2	1.4	0.2	—	0.8	—	1.4	4.1	1.5	1.7	1.4
1919	26.6	—	5.7	0.1	0.8	1.7	0.6	0.8	0.2	—	0.2	1.5	0.3	—	1.1	—	1.5	—	1.6	2.1	1.6
1920	36.7	—	9.5	0.1	1.0	2.1	0.6	1.1	0.3	0.3	—	2.6	0.5	—	1.9	—	1.7	4.7	1.9	2.9	2.0
1921	45.2	—	11.3	0.2	1.3	2.8	0.7	1.3	0.4	0.5	—	3.5	0.6	—	2.1	—	1.9	6.2	2.6	3.6	2.1
1922	47.3	—	11.5	0.2	1.3	3.8	0.7	1.3	0.5	1.0	—	3.9	0.6	—	2.3	—	2.0	6.0	2.4	3.5	2.0
1923	45.4	—	10.6	0.2	1.2	4.5	0.7	1.1	0.5	1.6	—	4.2	0.7	—	2.1	—	1.9	4.5	2.2	3.6	2.0
1924	46.7	—	10.6	0.2	1.2	4.4	0.7	1.1	0.6	1.9	—	4.7	0.7	—	2.1	—	2.0	4.8	2.4	3.5	1.9
1925	48.5	—	11.0	0.2	1.1	4.0	0.7	1.1	0.6	2.1	—	5.3	0.7	—	2.2	—	2.1	4.9	2.5	3.9	2.1
1926	50.2	—	11.4	0.2	1.1	4.4	0.7	1.2	0.7	2.4	—	5.7	0.7	—	2.3	—	2.1	4.8	2.5	4.0	1.9
1927	56.2	—	11.9	0.2	1.2	5.6	0.8	1.2	0.7	2.9	—	5.9	0.7	—	2.4	—	2.3	6.8	3.1	4.0	1.9
1928	54.0	—	11.9	0.2	1.2	4.9	0.8	1.2	0.7	3.5	—	6.1	0.7	—	2.4	—	2.2	4.6	2.8	4.0	2.0
1929	54.7	—	12.1	0.2	1.2	4.6	0.8	1.2	0.7	4.1	—	5.9	0.8	—	2.4	—	2.3	4.4	3.1	4.2	2.1
1930	56.8	—	12.6	0.2	1.3	4.7	0.8	1.2	0.7	4.7	—	6.3	0.8	—	2.4	—	2.2	4.5	3.3	4.4	2.0
1931	57.3	—	12.9	0.2	1.3	3.9	0.8	1.2	0.8	5.0	—	6.6	0.8	—	2.4	—	2.3	4.4	3.1	4.5	1.8

Year					Health (2.0)[e]	Welfare (2.2)[f]														
1932	58.0	—	12.4	0.2	1.3	4.3	0.9	1.2	0.8	5.3	2.4	—	0.8	7.2	—	2.2	4.4	3.0	4.5	1.8
1933	56.5	—	12.1	0.2	1.3	5.1	0.9	1.2	0.7	5.5	2.3	—	0.8	6.0	—	2.3	4.1	3.1	4.4	1.7
1934	57.7	—	12.0	0.2	1.4	5.9	0.9	1.2	0.7	5.0	2.3	—	0.8	5.5	—	2.3	4.1	3.2	4.4	1.7
1935	60.0	—	12.6	0.2	1.4	6.9	0.9	1.2	0.7	6.1	2.5	—	0.8	5.3	—	2.3	4.1	3.5	4.4	1.7
1936	62.6	—	13.2	0.2	1.4	7.4	1.0	1.3	0.8	6.4	2.6	—	0.9	5.3	—	2.3	4.5	3.6	4.6	1.8
1937	64.8	—	13.6	0.3	1.4	7.1	1.1	1.3	0.8	6.8	2.6	—	0.9	5.6	—	2.4	4.4	4.1	4.8	1.8
1938	66.3	—	13.9	0.3	1.6	5.7	1.1	1.4	0.9	7.2	2.7	—	1.0	6.1	—	2.4	4.7	4.4	5.1	2.0
1939	69.0	—	14.1	0.3	2.0	5.4	1.2	1.4	0.9	7.9	2.8	—	1.0	6.3	—	2.5	4.8	4.6	5.4	1.9
1940	74.5	—	13.9	0.3	2.0	5.4	1.4	1.6	0.9	8.7	3.0	—	0.6	5.2	—	2.6	4.9	4.8	5.4	1.9
1941	78.6	—	14.0	0.3	2.4	4.4	1.3	1.8	0.9	9.1	3.4	—	0.6	4.6	—	2.7	5.8	5.4	5.9	2.2
1942	85.3	—	14.9	0.3	2.6	4.0	1.2	2.0	0.6	9.5	3.8	—	0.6	4.7	—	2.8	6.4	5.9	6.1	2.5
1943	84.4	—	15.7	0.3	2.7	3.9	1.3	2.0	0.8	9.4	3.9	—	0.6	4.6	—	2.8	7.0	6.0	6.4	2.5
1944	87.0	—	16.9	0.3	3.0	4.0	1.3	2.2	0.9	9.5	3.8	—	0.6	4.5	—	2.9	7.6	6.5	7.1	2.9
1945	89.0	—	18.1	0.3	3.5	4.4	1.3	2.2	0.9	9.8	3.8	—	0.7	4.4	—	2.8	8.4	6.6	7.5	2.7
1946	95.9	—	23.1	0.4	3.6	4.7	1.3	2.3	1.1	9.9	3.9	—	1.0	5.0	—	2.9	9.1	7.0	7.6	2.6
1947	105.2	—	25.0	0.4	4.1	4.9	1.4	2.7	1.2	10.9	4.2	—	1.1	6.6	—	3.0	10.0	7.6	7.9	2.4
1948	115.7	—	28.5	0.5	4.7	5.3	1.7	2.9	1.5	12.5	4.6	—	1.2	6.9	—	3.3	10.9	7.6	8.5	2.8
1949	105.8	—	30.9	0.6	0.7[d]	0.7[d]	1.7	3.2	1.5	13.8	4.9	—	1.5	6.5	—	3.7	11.4[d]	7.0[d]	9.1	2.9
(1949)																				
1950	100.3	—	32.8	0.6	2.6	2.7	1.7	3.3	1.7	15.2	5.4	—	1.8	7.0	—	3.6	—	—	9.5	3.1
1951	108.4	—	34.6	0.6	3.3	2.9	2.2	3.6	1.8	16.7	5.8	—	1.9	7.2	—	3.7	—	—	10.2	3.2
1952	122.8	—	40.4	0.7	3.5	3.2	2.1	4.1	2.0	19.1	6.5	—	2.0	8.1	—	4.1	—	—	11.3	3.3
1953	133.5	—	43.7	0.8	4.0	3.5	2.4	4.3	2.2	23.1	6.8	—	2.4	8.6	—	4.7	—	—	12.1	3.5
1954	142.0	—	45.5	0.8	4.1	4.0	2.6	4.5	2.2	26.9	7.1	—	2.5	8.7	—	5.2	—	—	12.9	3.7
1955	156.5	—	51.2	0.9	4.4	4.2	2.8	4.8	2.4	30.0	7.9	—	2.7	9.3	—	5.4	—	—	13.1	3.9
1956	170.8	—	55.9	1.0	4.7	4.5	3.2	5.3	2.8	33.7	8.5	—	2.9	10.2	—	6.4	—	—	14.1	4.3
1957	195.0	—	67.8	1.1	5.3	4.9	3.7	5.7	2.9	39.1	9.9	—	3.3	11.2	—	7.1	—	—	15.3	4.7
1958	202.3	—	71.7	1.2	6.0	5.3	3.4	6.2	3.1	36.9	10.6	1.2	3.4	12.2	—	7.5	—	—	15.9	5.0
1959	213.1	186.0	75.2	1.2	6.1	5.7	3.6	6.5	3.4	37.6	11.4	2.5	3.6	12.3	25.9	8.2	—	—	15.8	5.0
1960	221.2	196.3	79.7	1.3	6.5	5.9	3.7	6.8	3.7	39.8	12.0	2.6	3.7	12.9	25.9	8.4	—	—	15.8	5.0
1961	241.6	212.7	86.5	1.3	6.7	6.2	4.0	7.0	3.8	43.0	13.8	2.8	3.8	14.7	28.1	8.9	—	—	16.9	5.7
1962	264.4	235.4	96.7	1.5	7.0	7.0	4.6	7.8	4.3	47.3	15.2	3.2	4.0	15.9	28.4	9.6	—	—	16.8	6.1
1963	281.9	251.1	103.2	1.6	7.7	7.3	4.7	8.2	4.4	50.4	16.2	3.6	4.3	17.0	29.3	10.5	—	—	17.1	6.2
1964	307.7	275.6	113.8	1.6	8.2	8.3	5.2	9.4	4.6	54.1	17.9	4.1	4.6	20.1	30.6	11.2	—	—	17.9	6.1
1965	333.3	299.4	122.6	1.8	9.0	9.1	5.7	9.6	5.0	61.8	19.6	4.4	4.9	19.6	32.0	11.8	—	—	18.5	6.4
1966	365.8	331.0	134.0	2.0	10.1	10.2	6.5	10.7	5.5	69.1	21.6	4.8	5.2	21.6	33.6	12.9	—	—	19.3	6.7
1967	407.4	370.2	152.0	2.2	10.8	11.1	7.5	11.5	5.9	78.2	23.6	5.0	5.6	23.4	36.6	14.3	—	—	19.4	6.9
1968	445.1	405.0	158.9	2.4	11.6	12.5	8.2	12.8	6.7	87.7	25.8	5.5	5.4	27.4	37.1	14.8	—	—	19.9	6.7
1969	490.9	446.2	173.7	2.6	12.6	14.0	9.5	14.1	7.7	101.8	27.8	6.0	5.7	26.3	41.3	17.3	—	—	20.5	9.3
1970	554.4	501.7	191.6	2.9	7.3	23.0	10.5	16.0	8.3	120.4	30.2	7.0	6.9	28.6	47.3	21.2	—	—	21.5	8.9
1971	640.7	579.0	227.1	3.5	9.2	26.1	12.9	18.4	10.0	134.6	36.4	8.0	7.7	33.7	58.2	23.0	—	—	23.9	9.7
1972	721.6	653.4	254.8	6.8	11.2	33.3	14.3	20.7	11.6	142.0	41.5	9.6	9.0	39.1	65.0	27.2	—	—	26.2	10.7
1973	841.6	765.9	299.6	8.0	12.0	43.1	17.3	23.4	14.6	156.3	48.2	11.4	10.0	45.2	72.2	29.6	—	—	28.3	11.9
1974	1,001.4	937.6	353.0	9.6	12.7	56.3	22.5	28.1	18.2	197.5	55.7	13.4	10.9	53.6	60.5	33.5	—	—	12.2	12.8
1975	1,344.1	1,254.4	488.7	12.8	—	77.3	30.0	36.6	26.3	255.7	70.7	18.1	13.2	70.2	72.5	41.5	—	—	14.8	15.8

Revenue Account (in 1975 prices) – Scotland (£m.)

Year ended 15 May	Total	Rate fund services — Total	Ed.	Lib. and Mus.	Hospitals	Poor Relief	Sewer	Refuse	Parks	Housing HRA	Housing Other	Highways	Lighting	Fire	Police[c]	Trading services — Total	Water	Gas	Elec.	Trans.	Harbours
1893[a]	153.0	—	27.2	—	1.7	15.3	—	—	—	—	—	11.9	—	—	6.8	—	—	—	—	—	11.9
1894	140.4	—	24.3	—	—	15.6	—	—	—	—	—	12.1	1.7	—	8.7	—	—	15.6	—	—	6.9
1895	166.2	—	27.1	b	—	18.1	—	—	1.8	—	—	12.6	3.6	—	9.0	—	—	19.9	—	3.6	7.2
1896	170.9	—	33.1[b]	—	1.8	18.4	3.7	—	1.8[b]	—	—	14.7	3.7[b]	—	9.2[b]	—	12.9	23.9	1.8	5.5	16.5
1897	173.6	—	34.7	—	1.8	20.1	3.7	—	1.8	—	—	14.6	3.7	—	9.1	—	11.0	23.8	1.8	7.3	16.4
1898	181.5	—	35.6	—	3.6	19.6	3.6	—	1.8	—	—	16.0	3.6	—	8.9	—	12.4	23.1	1.8	7.1	16.0
1899	183.1	—	34.9	—	3.5	19.2	3.5	—	1.7	—	—	14.0	3.5	—	8.7	—	12.2	24.4	1.7	8.7	17.4
1900	194.0	—	36.7	—	3.5	19.2	3.5	—	1.7	—	—	15.7	3.5	—	8.7	—	12.2	28.0	3.5	8.7	15.7
1901	203.4	—	38.7	—	3.4	20.2	3.4	—	1.7	—	—	15.1	3.4	—	8.4	—	13.4	31.9	3.4	10.1	16.8
1902	211.8	—	40.7	—	5.1	20.3	3.4	—	1.7	—	—	16.9	5.1	—	10.2	—	13.6	30.5	5.1	11.9	16.9
1903	219.6	—	43.9	—	3.4	20.3	3.4	—	1.7	—	—	16.9	5.1	—	10.1	—	13.5	30.4	5.1	13.5	18.6
1904	227.2	—	45.1	—	5.0	21.7	5.0	—	1.7	—	—	16.7	5.0	—	10.0	—	15.0	30.1	6.7	15.0	18.4
1905	232.1	—	46.4	—	5.0	23.2	5.0	—	3.3	—	—	18.2	5.0	—	9.9	—	14.9	28.2	6.6	14.9	16.6
1906	239.6	—	47.9	1.7	5.0	23.1	5.0	—	3.3	—	—	18.2	5.0	—	9.9	—	16.5	29.7	8.3	18.2	18.2
1907	246.4	—	49.0	1.6	4.9	22.8	4.9	6.5	3.3	1.6	—	18.0	4.9	—	11.4	—	16.3	29.4	8.2	19.6	19.6
1908	255.1	—	51.7	1.6	4.8	24.2	4.8	8.1	3.2	1.6	—	17.8	4.8	—	11.3	—	16.1	33.9	9.7	19.4	17.8
1909	263.5	—	55.6	1.6	4.9	24.5	6.5	8.2	3.3	1.6	—	19.6	4.9	—	11.5	—	16.4	31.1	9.8	19.6	18.0
1910	266.4	—	59.7	1.6	6.5	25.8	6.5	8.1	3.2	1.6	—	19.4	4.8	—	11.3	—	16.1	30.7	9.7	19.4	19.4
1911	267.7	—	60.2	1.6	6.3	25.3	6.3	7.9	3.2	1.6	—	19.0	4.8	—	11.1	—	17.4	31.7	9.5	19.0	19.0
1912	271.5	—	60.9	1.6	6.2	23.4	6.2	7.8	3.1	1.6	—	20.3	4.7	—	10.9	—	17.2	31.2	10.9	20.3	18.7
1913	277.8	—	60.7	1.5	6.1	24.3	6.1	7.6	3.0	1.5	—	19.7	4.6	—	10.6	—	16.7	34.9	10.6	21.3	19.7
1914	287.1	—	63.1	1.5	6.0	24.0	7.5	7.5	3.0	1.5	—	21.0	4.5	—	12.0	—	18.0	37.6	12.0	22.5	19.5
1915	—	—	—	—	—	—	—	—	—	—	—	—	—	—	—	—	—	—	—	—	—
1916	—	—	—	—	—	—	—	—	—	—	—	—	—	—	—	—	—	—	—	—	—
1917	—	—	—	—	—	—	—	—	—	—	—	—	—	—	—	—	—	—	—	—	—
1918	—	—	—	—	—	—	—	—	—	—	—	—	—	—	—	—	—	—	—	—	—
1919	—	—	—	—	—	—	—	—	—	—	—	—	—	—	—	—	—	—	—	—	—
1920	—	—	—	—	—	—	—	—	—	—	—	—	—	—	—	—	—	—	—	—	—
1921	284.7	—	71.2	1.3	8.2	17.6	4.4	8.2	2.5	3.1	—	22.0	3.8	—	13.2	—	12.0	39.0	16.4	22.7	13.2
1922	373.0	—	90.7	1.6	10.3	30.0	5.5	10.3	3.9	7.9	—	30.8	4.7	—	18.1	—	15.8	47.3	18.9	27.6	15.8
1923	377.6	—	88.2	1.7	10.0	37.4	5.8	9.1	4.2	13.3	—	34.9	5.8	—	17.5	—	15.8	37.4	18.3	29.9	16.6
1924	386.9	—	87.8	1.7	9.9	36.5	5.8	9.1	5.0	15.7	—	38.9	5.8	—	17.4	—	16.6	39.8	19.9	29.0	15.7
1925	397.8	—	90.2	1.6	9.0	32.8	5.7	9.0	4.9	17.2	—	43.5	5.7	—	18.0	—	17.2	40.2	20.5	32.0	17.2
1926	390.2	—	88.6	1.6	8.6	34.2	5.4	9.3	5.4	18.7	—	44.3	5.4	—	17.9	—	16.3	37.3	19.4	31.1	14.8
1927	485.6	—	102.8	1.7	10.4	48.4	6.9	10.4	6.0	25.1	—	51.0	6.0	—	20.7	—	19.9	58.8	26.8	34.6	16.4
1928	461.5	—	101.7	1.7	10.3	41.9	6.8	10.3	6.0	29.9	—	52.1	6.0	—	20.5	—	18.8	39.3	23.9	34.2	17.1
1929	472.9	—	104.6	1.7	10.4	39.8	6.9	10.4	6.1	35.4	—	51.0	6.9	—	20.7	—	19.9	38.0	26.8	36.3	18.2

Year																			
1930	503.8		111.8	1.8	11.5	41.7	7.1	10.6	6.2	41.7	55.9	7.1	21.3		19.5	39.9	29.3	39.0	17.7
1931	534.3		120.3	1.9	12.1	36.4	7.5	11.2	7.5	46.6	61.5	7.5	22.4		21.4	41.0	28.9	42.0	16.8
1932	552.4		118.1	1.9	12.4	41.0	8.6	11.4	7.6	50.5	68.6	7.6	22.9		21.0	41.9	28.6	42.9	17.1
1933	551.7		118.2	2.0	12.7	49.8	8.8	11.7	6.8	53.7	58.6	7.8	22.5		22.5	40.0	30.3	43.0	16.6
1934	561.1		116.7	1.9	13.6	57.4	8.8	11.7	6.8	58.3	53.5	7.8	22.4		22.4	39.9	31.1	42.8	16.5
1935	580.0		121.8	1.9	13.5	66.7	8.7	11.6	6.8	59.0	51.2	7.7	24.2		22.2	39.6	33.8	42.5	16.4
1936	592.9		125.0	1.9	13.3	70.1	9.5	12.3	7.6	60.6	50.2	8.5	24.6		21.8	42.6	34.1	43.6	17.0
1937	589.1		123.6	2.7	12.7	64.5	10.0	11.8	7.3	61.8	50.9	8.2	23.6		21.8	40.0	37.3	43.6	16.4
1938	592.7		124.3	2.7	14.3	51.0	9.8	12.5	8.0	64.4	54.5	8.9	24.1		24.5	42.0	39.3	45.6	17.9
1939	—		—	—	—	—	—	—	—	—	—	—	—		—	—	—	—	—
1940	—		—	—	—	—	—	—	—	—	—	—	—		—	—	—	—	—
1941	—		—	—	—	—	—	—	—	—	—	—	—		—	—	—	—	—
1942	—		—	—	—	—	—	—	—	—	—	—	—		—	—	—	—	—
1943	—		—	—	—	—	—	—	—	—	—	—	—		—	—	—	—	—
1944	—		—	—	—	—	—	—	—	—	—	—	—		—	—	—	—	—
1945	—		—	—	—	—	—	—	—	—	—	—	—		—	—	—	—	—
1946	462.7		111.4	1.9	17.4	22.7	6.3	11.1	5.3	47.8	24.1	4.8	18.8		14.0	43.9	—	36.7	12.5
1947	441.8		105.0	1.7	17.2	20.6	5.9	11.3	5.0	45.8	27.7	4.6	17.6		12.6	42.0	33.8	33.2	10.1
1948	503.0		123.9	2.2	20.4	23.0	7.4	12.6	6.5	54.3	30.0	5.2	20.0		14.3	47.4	31.9	37.0	12.2
1949	448.7		131.1	2.5	3.0[d]	3.0[d]	7.2	13.6	6.4	58.5	27.6	6.4	20.8		15.7	48.4[d]	30.4[d]	38.6	12.3
(1949)		519.3	138.8		Health (8.4)[e]	Welfare (9.3)[f]													
1950	424.3		136.2	2.5	11.0	11.4	7.2	14.0	7.2	64.3	29.6	7.6	22.8		15.2			40.2	13.1
1951	426.6		139.7	2.4	13.0	11.4	8.7	14.2	7.1	65.7	28.3	7.5	22.8		14.6			40.1	12.6
1952	424.6		153.2	2.4	12.1	11.1	7.3	14.2	6.9	66.0	28.0	6.9	22.5		14.2			39.1	11.4
1953	468.1		156.5	2.8	14.0	12.3	8.4	15.1	7.7	81.0	30.2	8.4	23.8		16.5			42.4	12.3
1954	488.5		173.3	2.8	14.1	13.8	8.9	15.5	7.6	92.5	29.9	8.6	24.4		17.9			44.4	12.7
1955	529.6		178.1	3.0	14.9	14.2	9.5	16.2	8.1	101.5	31.5	9.1	26.7		18.3			44.3	13.2
1956	544.2		207.6	3.2	15.0	14.3	10.2	16.9	8.9	107.4	32.5	9.2	27.1		20.4			44.9	13.7
1957	597.2		206.6	3.4	16.2	15.0	11.3	17.5	8.9	119.7	34.3	10.1	30.3		21.7			46.9	14.4
1958	582.8		210.0	3.5	17.3	15.3	9.8	17.9	8.9	106.3	35.1	9.8	30.5		21.6			45.8	14.4
1959	595.0			3.4	17.0	15.9	10.1	18.1	9.5	105.0 / 3.4	34.3	10.1	31.8	72.3	22.9			44.1	14.0
1960	625.6	555.2	225.4	3.7	18.4	16.7	10.5	19.2	10.5	112.6	36.5	10.5	33.9	73.3	23.8			44.7	14.1
1961	661.4	582.3	236.8	3.6	18.3	17.0	11.0	19.2	10.4	117.7	40.2	10.4	37.8	76.9	24.4			46.3	15.6
1962	700.4	623.6	256.2	4.0	18.5	18.5	12.2	20.7	11.4	125.3	42.1	10.6	40.3	75.2	25.4			44.5	16.2
1963	731.0	651.1	267.6	4.1	20.0	18.9	12.2	21.3	11.4	130.7	44.1	11.2	42.0	76.0	27.2			44.3	16.1
1964	778.3	697.1	287.9	4.0	20.7	21.0	13.2	23.8	11.6	136.8	50.8	11.6	45.3	77.4	28.3			45.3	15.4
1965	808.7	726.4	297.5	4.4	21.8	22.1	13.8	23.3	12.1	149.9	47.6	11.9	47.6	77.6	28.6			44.9	15.5
1966	853.8	772.6	312.8	4.7	23.6	23.8	15.2	25.0	12.8	161.3	50.4	12.1	50.4	78.4	30.1			45.0	15.6
1967	925.6	841.1	345.3	5.0	24.5	25.2	17.0	26.1	13.4	177.7	53.2	12.7	53.6	83.2	32.5			44.1	15.7
1968	977.3	889.2	348.9	5.3	25.5	27.4	18.0	28.1	14.7	192.6	60.2	11.9	56.6	81.5	32.5			43.7	14.7
1969	1,039.5	944.8	367.8	5.5	26.7	29.6	20.1	29.9	16.3	215.6	55.7	12.1	58.9	87.5	36.6			43.4	19.7

Revenue Account (in 1975 prices) – Scotland (£m.)

| Year ended 15 May | Total | Rate fund services | | | | | | | Housing | | | | | | Trading services | | | | | |
		Ed.	Lib. and Mus.	Health	Welfare	Sewer	Refuse	Parks	HRA	Other	Highways	Lighting	Fire	Police[c]	Total	Water	Gas	Elec.	Trans.	Harbours
1970	1,088.3	376.1	5.7	14.3	45.1	20.6	31.4	16.3	236.3	8.0	56.1	13.5	13.7	59.3	92.8	41.6	–	–	42.2	17.5
1971	1,140.2	404.2	6.2	16.4	46.4	23.0	32.7	17.8	239.5	8.2	60.0	13.7	14.2	64.8	103.6	40.9	–	–	42.5	17.3
1972	1,165.8	411.6	11.0	18.1	53.8	23.1	33.4	18.7	229.4	7.8	63.2	14.5	15.5	67.0	105.0	43.9	–	–	42.3	17.3
1973	1,246.8	443.8	11.9	17.8	63.9	25.6	34.7	21.6	231.6	21.2	67.0	14.8	16.9	71.4	107.0	43.9	–	–	41.9	17.6
1974	1,285.7	453.2	12.3	16.3	72.3	28.9	36.1	23.4	253.6	37.9	68.8	14.0	17.2	71.5	77.7	43.0	–	–	15.7	16.4
1975	1,344.1	627.4	12.8	–	77.3	30.0	36.6	26.3	255.7	40.5	70.2	13.2	18.1	70.7	72.5	41.5	–	–	14.8	15.8

NOTES TO p.p. 116–120

a The figures for 1893 include expenditure out of loans, which cannot be distinguished separately.
b Loan charges attributable to the various items are not included with those items until 1896.
c 'Administration of Justice' included.
d Owing to legislative changes these items disappear or emerge under other headings between 1948 and 1950.
e That is, Local Authority Health Services under the NHS since 5 July 1948.
f This comprises 'National Assistance', 'Child Welfare' and 'Child Life Protection', etc.

Capital Account (in current prices) – Scotland (£m.)

Year ended 15 May	Total	Rate fund services Total	Ed.	Lib. and Mus.	Hospitals[d]	Work-houses	Sewer	Refuse	Parks	Housing HRA	Housing Other	Highways	Lighting	Fire	Police	Total	Water	Gas	Elec.	Trans.	Harbours[a]
1894	2.1	–	0.3	–	–	–	–	–	0.1	–	–	0.1	–	–	–	–	–	0.1	0.1	0.2	0.3
1895	2.3	–	0.3	–	–	–	–	–	0.1	–	–	0.1	–	–	–	–	–	0.1	0.1	0.4	0.2
1896	2.1	–	0.4	–	0.1	–	0.1	–	0.1	–	–	0.1	–	–	–	–	0.4	0.1	0.1	–	0.3
1897	2.8	–	0.4	–	0.1	–	0.1	–	0.1	–	–	0.2	–	–	–	–	0.4	0.3	0.1	0.2	0.3
1898	2.6	–	0.3	–	0.1	–	0.1	–	0.1	–	–	0.1	–	–	–	–	0.4	0.1	0.1	0.3	0.4
1899	3.1	–	0.3	–	0.1	–	0.1	–	0.1	–	–	0.1	–	–	–	–	0.5	0.3	0.3	0.3	0.4
1900	3.7	–	0.3	–	0.1	–	0.2	–	–	–	–	0.1	–	–	–	–	0.5	0.3	0.6	0.5	0.4
1901	4.5	–	0.4	–	0.2	–	0.2	–	0.2	–	–	0.1	–	–	–	–	0.5	0.4	0.5	1.1	0.3
1902	4.2	–	0.4	–	0.1	0.1	0.3	–	–	–	–	0.1	–	–	–	–	0.5	0.5	0.5	0.5	0.3
1903	4.1	–	0.4	–	0.1	0.3	0.5	–	–	–	–	0.2	–	–	–	–	0.6	0.5	0.4	0.2	0.2
1904	4.5	–	0.5	–	0.1	0.3	0.4	–	0.1	–	–	0.2	–	–	–	–	1.1	0.4	0.4	0.1	0.2
1905	3.7	–	0.4	–	0.1	0.2	0.3	–	0.1	–	–	0.2	–	–	–	–	0.6	0.3	0.4	0.2	0.3
1906	3.5	–	0.4	–	0.1	0.2	0.3	–	–	–	–	0.2	–	–	–	–	0.5	0.3	0.3	0.1	0.6
1907	3.3	–	0.4	–	0.1	0.1	0.3	–	–	–	–	0.1	–	–	–	–	0.4	0.2	0.3	0.1	0.4
1908	3.5	–	0.4	–	0.1	0.1	0.4	–	–	–	–	0.1	–	–	–	–	0.4	0.1	0.3	0.9[b]	0.3
1909	2.8	–	0.5	–	0.1	–	0.3	–	0.1	–	–	0.1	–	–	–	–	0.4	0.1	0.3	0.2	0.3
1910	2.4	–	0.4	–	0.1	–	0.3	–	–	–	–	0.2	–	–	–	–	0.4	0.1	0.2	0.1	0.3
1911	2.2	–	0.5	–	0.1	–	0.2	–	–	–	–	0.1	–	–	–	–	0.4	0.1	0.1	0.1	0.2
1912	2.4	–	0.5	–	–	–	0.1	–	0.1	–	–	0.1	–	–	–	–	0.5	0.3	0.1	–	0.3
1913	2.3	–	0.4	–	–	–	0.1	–	0.1	–	–	0.1	–	–	–	–	0.4	0.1	0.2	0.1	0.2
1914	3.0	–	0.5	–	0.1	–	0.1	–	–	–	0.1	0.2	–	–	–	–	0.3	0.3	0.3	0.1	0.3
1915	3.3	–	0.4	–	0.2	–	0.1	–	0.1	–	0.1	0.2	–	–	–	–	0.4	0.5	0.3	0.1	0.3
1916	1.9	–	0.2	–	0.1	–	0.1	–	–	–	0.1	0.1	–	–	–	–	0.2	0.2	0.2	–	0.1
1917	1.3	–	0.1	–	0.1	–	–	–	–	–	0.1	–	–	–	–	–	0.2	0.1	0.4	–	0.1
1918	1.1	–	0.1	–	0.1	–	–	–	–	–	–	–	–	–	–	–	0.2	0.1	0.4	–	0.1
1919	1.5	–	0.1	–	0.1	–	–	–	0.1	–	–	0.1	–	–	–	–	0.2	0.1	0.7	–	0.1
1920	4.4	–	0.1	–	0.1	–	–	–	0.1	–	0.8	0.2	–	–	–	–	0.4	0.4	1.4	0.3	0.2
1921	10.8	–	0.4	–	0.1	–	0.2	–	0.1	–	3.9	0.4	–	–	–	–	0.7	1.5	2.2	0.3	0.3
1922	16.7	–	0.4	–	0.3	–	0.3	–	0.2	–	8.9	0.8	–	–	–	–	0.9	1.4	1.7	0.8	0.3
1923	13.0	–	0.3	–	0.1	–	0.3	–	0.3	–	6.0	0.8	–	–	–	–	1.0	0.7	1.7	1.2	0.2
1924	8.9	–	0.3	–	0.1	–	0.2	–	0.3	–	2.8	1.0	–	–	–	–	0.8	0.4	1.0	1.1	0.3
1925	10.0	–	0.3	–	0.1	–	0.3	–	0.3	–	3.8	1.0	–	–	–	–	0.9	0.5	1.1	0.7	0.4
1926	11.8	–	0.5	–	0.2	–	0.3	–	0.2	–	5.2	1.1	–	–	–	–	0.9	0.5	1.2	0.4	0.6
1927	13.3	–	0.5	–	0.2	–	0.4	–	0.2	–	7.5	1.0	–	–	–	–	0.6	0.3	1.2	0.2	0.5
1928	13.5	–	0.5	–	0.2	–	0.3	–	0.1	–	8.1	0.7	–	–	–	–	0.6	0.3	0.9	0.3	0.6
1929	13.1	–	0.8	–	0.2	–	0.3	–	0.1	–	7.5	0.8	–	–	–	–	0.5	0.3	1.0	0.5	0.4
1930	11.1	–	1.0	–	0.2	–	0.3	–	0.1	–	5.2	1.3	–	–	–	–	0.5	0.3	0.7	0.4	0.3
1931	11.3	–	1.7	–	0.1	–	0.6	–	0.2	–	4.3	1.0	–	–	–	–	0.7	0.3	0.6	0.7	0.5
1932	11.8	–	1.1	–	0.1	–	0.8	–	0.1	–	5.3	1.2	–	–	–	–	0.9	0.2	0.5	0.2	0.4

Capital Account (in current prices) – Scotland (£m.) (continued)

Year ended 15 May	Total	Rate fund services								Housing		Highways	Lighting	Fire	Police		Trading services				
		Total	Ed.	Lib. and Mus.	Hospitals[d]	Work-houses	Sewer	Refuse	Parks	HRA	Other	Highways	Lighting	Fire	Police	Total	Water	Gas	Elec.	Trans.	Harbours[a]
1933	11.5	–	0.7	–	0.1	0.1	0.6	–	–		6.3	0.7	–	–	–	–	0.7	0.2	0.5	0.1	0.2
1934	11.8	–	0.6	–	0.1	–	0.4	–	0.1		7.7	0.5	–	–	–	–	0.5	0.2	0.6	0.1	0.2
1935	11.5	–	0.7	–	0.1	0.1	0.3	–	0.1		7.4	0.5	–	–	–	–	0.4	0.2	0.7	0.2	0.1
1936	12.2	–	0.8	–	0.1	0.1	0.5	–	0.2		7.1	0.4	–	–	–	–	0.5	0.3	0.8	0.4	0.1
1937	15.0	–	1.1	–	0.2	0.1	0.8	–	0.2		7.9	0.6	–	–	–	–	0.8	0.4	1.5	0.3	0.1
1938	18.7	–	1.2	–	0.2	0.1	1.1	–	0.2		10.3	0.8	–	–	–	–	0.8	0.4	1.7	0.7	0.1
1939	20.4	–	1.2	–	0.3	0.1	1.2	–	0.1		12.0	0.8	–	–	–	–	0.8	0.6	1.5	0.4	0.3
1940	15.9	–	1.3	–	0.3	0.1	0.9	–	0.1		8.1	0.6	–	–	–	–	0.9	0.7	1.3	0.3	0.3
1941	7.2	–	0.7	–	0.2	–	0.3	–	–		3.3	0.2	–	–	–	–	0.5	0.4	0.6	0.1	0.1
1942	4.5	–	0.3	–	0.1	–	0.1	–	–		1.9	0.1	–	–	–	–	0.4	0.3	0.4	0.1	0.4
1943	4.0	–	0.1	–	0.1	–	0.2	–	–		1.7	–	–	–	–	–	0.5	0.3	0.6	0.1	0.2
1944	3.0	–	0.2	–	0.1	–	–	–	–		1.6	–	–	–	–	–	0.2	0.4	0.4	0.1	–
1945	3.7	–	0.1	–	–	–	0.1	–	–		2.3	–	–	–	–	–	0.1	0.6	0.3	0.1	–
1946	8.3	–	0.2	–	–	–	0.3	–	–		5.7	–	–	–	–	–	0.4	0.6	0.7	0.1	–
1947	21.7	–	0.2	–	0.1	–	1.0	–	–		16.4	0.4	–	–	–	–	0.8	1.0	1.2	0.2	–
1948	34.5[f]	–	0.9	–	0.1	0.1	1.5	–	0.1		26.7	0.3	–	–	–	–	1.4	1.0	1.6[e]	0.1	0.1
1949	42.4[f]	–	1.7	–	0.1	–	1.6	–	0.1		32.5	0.7	–	–	–	–	2.0	0.9[e]	–	1.3	0.5
(1949)					*Health*	*Welfare* (0.1)[e]															
1950	44.9[f]	–	2.5	–	–	0.2	2.3	–	0.2		32.4	0.7	–	–	–	–	3.1	–	–	1.6	0.6
1951	47.4	–	3.4	–	–	0.3	1.9	–	0.2		33.7	0.8	–	–	–	–	3.8	–	–	0.9	0.8

Year	(1)	(2)	(3)	(4)	(5)	(6)	(7)	(8)	(9)	(10)	(11)	(12)	(13)	(14)	(15)	(16)	(17)	(18)	(19)	(20)	(21)
1952	58.3	—	4.3	—	—	0.4	2.1	—	0.1	41.1	—	0.6	—	—	—	—	6.7	—	—	0.2	0.9
1953	69.2	—	5.5	—	—	0.3	3.1	—	0.2	49.4	—	0.8	—	—	—	—	6.1	—	—	0.3	1.0
1954	74.2	—	5.3	—	—	0.4	3.0	—	0.2	53.4	—	1.0	—	—	—	—	6.1	—	—	0.4	1.2
1955	73.2	—	6.7	—	—	0.3	3.5	—	0.2	49.0	—	1.2	—	—	—	—	5.2	—	—	3.1	1.0
1956	72.3	—	8.8	—	—	0.3	3.1	—	0.3	45.6	—	1.9	—	—	—	—	6.1	—	—	2.1	0.6
1957	70.7	—	10.4	—	—	0.4	2.4	—	0.3	44.0	—	2.1	—	—	—	—	4.7	—	—	1.8	1.2
1958	71.3	—	12.1	—	—	0.4	2.3	—	0.3	42.3	—	2.6	—	—	—	—	3.8	—	—	1.7	1.7
1959	71.3	63.3	12.8	—	0.2	0.2	2.1	0.6	0.2	38.5	1.5	4.3	0.6	0.3	0.8	8.0	3.7	—	—	1.8	2.1
1960	72.2	64.1	13.8	—	0.2	0.2	2.5	0.4	0.4	34.2	1.7	6.7	0.8	0.4	0.9	8.1	5.0	—	—	1.6	1.2
1961	78.4	70.3	14.1	0.2	0.2	0.3	2.7	0.6	0.5	34.8	2.6	9.0	0.8	0.2	0.8	8.1	6.0	—	—	1.0	0.7
1962	91.0	81.7	15.7	—	0.3	0.4	4.0	0.5	0.4	37.3	5.2	11.5	0.8	0.4	0.8	9.3	5.4	—	—	1.3	2.1
1963	99.6	90.2	18.7	N/A	0.2	0.4	4.3	1.0	0.5	42.6	5.1	9.8	0.8	0.4	0.9	9.4	5.2	—	—	1.5	2.3
1964	130.1	119.9	21.0	0.1	N/A	0.5	4.1	1.4	0.5	66.7	5.4	10.4	0.8	0.5	1.1	10.3	6.2	—	—	1.0	2.3
1965	146.9	133.4	22.3	0.2	0.5	0.6	5.8	0.6	0.8	72.0	6.3	11.8	0.8	0.5	1.0	13.5	9.7	—	—	0.9	2.0
1966	154.8	140.3	20.5	0.2	0.6	0.8	5.8	0.7	0.7	74.7	6.6	11.4	1.0	0.7	1.1	14.6	9.5	—	—	0.5	3.6
1967	187.5	170.1	21.1	0.3	0.6	1.2	7.0	0.9	0.9	95.3	8.4	15.9	0.6	0.8	1.2	17.4	10.6	—	—	1.3	4.7
1968	228.0	205.6	29.7	0.3	0.7	1.9	7.8	1.3	1.0	111.9	7.4	21.2	0.9	1.1	1.8	22.4	11.0	—	—	1.4	7.2
1969	257.8	232.7	38.1	0.3	0.9	1.9	10.5	2.8	2.0	122.2	9.0	20.2	—	0.9	1.6	25.1	13.2	—	—	0.9	8.3
1970	250.2	223.5	41.1	0.6	0.4	1.8	9.7	2.6	2.3	118.3	7.5	16.7	1.2	0.7	1.4	26.7	14.6	—	—	1.0	8.8
1971	251.3	229.2	40.1	0.3	0.5	2.2	11.6	2.2	1.9	112.0	10.0	22.4	1.5	0.5	1.7	22.1	14.1	—	—	1.7	4.1
1972	260.8	239.1	40.3	0.5	0.7	2.4	14.9	1.6	2.7	108.9	13.4	26.1	1.7	0.5	2.2	21.7	11.9	—	—	1.6	4.8
1973	303.7	280.1	51.2	1.1	0.8	4.5	22.1	2.2	4.2	101.9	25.5	32.9	1.5	0.5	3.1	23.6	13.4	—	—	2.7	5.6
1974	397.2	374.2	55.9	1.9	0.7	6.2	28.4	2.0	5.2	147.2	37.8	41.1	2.1	0.4	3.2	23.0	13.9	—	—	0.8	6.3
1975	493.4	462.7	62.7	2.4	—	7.4	29.8	2.8	6.0	193.6	50.4	49.0	2.0	0.4	5.2	30.7	14.0	—	—	1.7	12.5

Capital Account (in 1975 prices) – Scotland (£m.)

Year ended 15 May	Total	Rate fund services Total	Ed.	Lib. and Mus.	Hospitals[d]	Work-houses	Sewer	Refuse	Parks	Housing HRA	Housing Other	Highways	Lighting	Fire	Police	Total	Trading services Water	Gas	Elec.	Trans.	Harbours[a]
1894	36.4	–	5.2	–	–	–	–	–	1.7	–	–	1.7	–	–	–	–	–	1.7	1.7	3.5	5.2
1895	41.5	–	5.4	–	–	–	–	–	1.8	–	–	1.8	–	–	–	–	–	1.8	1.8	7.2	3.6
1896	38.6	–	7.4	–	1.8	–	1.8	–	1.8	–	–	1.8	–	–	–	–	7.4	1.8	1.8	–	5.5
1897	51.2	–	7.3	–	1.8	–	1.8	–	1.8	–	–	3.7	–	–	–	–	7.3	5.5	1.8	3.7	5.5
1898	46.3	–	5.3	–	1.8	–	1.8	–	1.8	–	–	1.8	–	–	–	–	7.1	1.8	1.8	5.3	7.1
1899	54.1	–	5.2	–	1.7	–	1.7	–	1.7	–	–	1.7	–	–	–	–	8.7	5.2	5.2	5.2	7.0
1900	64.7	–	5.2	–	1.7	–	3.5	–	–	–	–	1.7	–	–	–	–	8.7	5.2	10.5	8.7	7.0
1901	75.6	–	6.7	–	3.4	1.7	3.4	–	3.4	–	–	1.7	–	–	–	–	8.4	6.7	8.4	18.5	5.0
1902	71.2	–	6.8	–	1.7	5.1	5.1	–	–	–	–	1.7	–	–	–	–	8.5	8.5	8.5	8.5	5.1
1903	69.3	–	6.8	–	1.7	5.0	8.4	–	–	–	–	3.4	–	–	–	–	10.1	8.4	6.8	3.4	3.4
1904	75.2	–	8.4	–	1.7	3.3	6.7	–	1.7	–	–	3.3	–	–	–	–	18.4	6.7	5.0	1.7	3.3
1905	61.3	–	6.6	–	1.7	3.3	5.0	–	1.7	–	–	3.3	–	–	–	–	9.9	6.6	6.6	3.3	5.0
1906	57.8	–	6.6	–	1.7	3.3	5.0	–	–	–	–	3.3	–	–	–	–	8.3	5.0	5.0	1.7	9.9
1907	53.9	–	6.5	–	1.6	1.6	4.9	–	–	–	–	1.6	–	–	–	–	6.5	3.3	4.9	3.3	6.5
1908	56.5	–	6.5	–	1.6	1.6	6.5	–	–	–	–	1.6	–	–	–	–	6.5	1.6	4.8	14.5[b]	4.8
1909	45.8	–	8.2	–	1.6	–	4.9	–	1.6	–	–	1.6	–	–	–	–	6.5	1.6	4.9	3.3	4.9
1910	38.7	–	6.5	–	1.6	–	4.8	–	–	–	–	3.2	–	–	–	–	6.5	1.6	3.2	1.6	4.8
1911	34.8	–	7.9	–	1.6	–	3.2	–	1.6	–	–	1.6	–	–	–	–	6.3	1.6	1.6	1.6	3.2
1912	37.4	–	7.8	–	–	–	1.6	–	1.5	–	–	1.6	–	–	–	–	7.8	4.7	1.6	–	4.7
1913	34.9	–	6.1	–	–	–	1.5	–	–	–	–	1.5	–	–	–	–	6.1	1.5	3.0	1.5	3.0
1914	45.1	–	7.5	–	1.5	–	1.5	–	–	–	1.5	3.0	–	–	–	–	4.5	4.5	4.5	1.5	4.5
1915	–	–	–	–	–	–	–	–	–	–	–	–	–	–	–	–	–	–	–	–	–
1916	–	–	–	–	–	–	–	–	–	–	–	–	–	–	–	–	–	–	–	–	–
1917	–	–	–	–	–	–	–	–	–	–	–	–	–	–	–	–	–	–	–	–	–
1918	–	–	–	–	–	–	–	–	–	–	–	–	–	–	–	–	–	–	–	–	–
1919	–	–	–	–	–	–	–	–	–	–	–	–	–	–	–	–	–	–	–	–	–
1920	–	–	–	–	–	–	–	–	–	–	–	–	–	–	–	–	–	–	–	–	–
1921	68.0	–	2.5	–	0.6	–	1.3	–	0.6	24.6	–	2.5	–	–	–	–	4.4	9.4	13.9	1.9	1.9
1922	131.7	–	3.2	–	2.4	–	2.4	–	1.6	70.2	–	6.3	–	–	–	–	7.1	11.0	13.4	6.3	2.4
1923	108.1	–	2.5	–	0.8	–	2.5	–	2.5	49.9	–	6.7	–	–	–	–	8.3	5.8	14.1	10.0	1.7
1924	73.7	–	2.5	–	0.8	–	1.7	–	2.5	23.2	–	8.3	–	–	–	–	6.6	3.3	8.3	9.1	2.5
1925	82.0	–	2.5	–	0.8	–	2.5	–	2.5	31.2	–	8.2	–	–	–	–	7.4	4.1	9.0	5.7	3.3
1926	91.7	–	3.9	–	1.6	–	2.3	–	1.6	40.4	–	8.6	–	–	–	–	7.0	3.9	9.3	3.1	4.7

															Health	Welfare (0.4)[e]				
1927	4.3	1.7	10.4	2.6	5.2				8.6	64.8	1.7		3.5		1.7		4.3		114.9	
1928	5.1	2.6	7.7	2.6	5.1				6.0	69.2	0.9		2.6		1.7		4.3		115.4	
1929	3.5	4.3	8.6	2.6	4.3				6.9	64.8	0.9		2.6		1.7		6.9		113.2	
1930	2.7	3.5	6.2	2.7	4.4				11.5	46.1	0.9		2.7		1.8		8.7		98.5	
1931	4.7	6.5	5.6	2.8	6.5				9.3	40.1	1.9		5.6		0.9		15.9		105.4	
1932	3.8	1.9	4.8	1.9	8.6				11.4	50.5	1.0		7.6		1.0		10.5		112.4	
1933	2.0	1.0	4.9	2.0	6.8				6.8	61.5	—		5.9	1.0	1.0		6.8		112.3	
1934	1.9	1.0	5.8	1.9	4.9				4.9	74.9	1.0		3.9		1.0		5.8		114.7	
1935	1.0	1.9	6.8	1.9	3.9				4.8	71.5	1.0		2.9	1.0	1.0		6.8		111.2	
1936	0.9	3.8	7.6	2.8	4.7				3.8	67.2	1.9		4.7	0.9	0.9		7.6		115.6	
1937	0.9	2.7	13.6	3.6	7.3				5.5	71.8	1.8		7.3	0.9	1.8		10.0		136.4	
1938	0.9	6.3	15.2	3.6	7.2				7.2	92.1	1.8		9.8	0.9	1.8		10.7		167.2	
1939	—	—	—	—	—				—	—	—		—	—	—		—		—	
1940	—	—	—	—	—				—	—	—		—	—	—		—		—	
1941	—	—	—	—	—				—	—	—		—	—	—		—		—	
1942	—	—	—	—	—				—	—	—		—	—	—		—		—	
1943	—	—	—	—	—				—	—	—		—	—	—		—		—	
1944	—	—	—	—	—				—	—	—		—	—	—		—		—	
1945	—	—	—	—	—				—	—	—		—	—	—		—		—	
1946	—	1.4	3.4	2.9	1.9				1.7	27.5	—		1.4	—	—		0.5		40.0	
1947	—	0.8	5.0	4.2	3.4				1.3	68.9	—		0.4	—	0.4		0.8		91.1	
1948	0.4	0.4	7.0[e]	4.3	6.1				3.0	116.1	0.4		6.5	0.4	0.4		3.9		150.0[f]	
1949	2.1	5.5	—	3.8[c]	8.5				—	137.8	0.4	1.7	6.8		0.4		7.2		179.8[g]	
(1949)																				
1950	2.5	6.8	—		13.1				3.0	137.1	0.8		9.7	0.8	—		10.6		190.0[f]	
1951	3.1	3.5	—		15.0				3.1	132.6	0.8		7.5	1.2	—		13.4		186.5	
1952	3.1	0.7	—		23.2				2.1	142.1	0.3		7.3	1.4	—		14.9		201.6	
1953	3.5	1.1	—		21.4				2.8	173.2	0.7		10.9	1.1	—		19.3		242.6	
1954	4.1	1.4	—		21.0				3.4	183.7	0.7		10.3	1.4	—		18.2		255.3	
1955	3.4	10.5	—		17.6				4.1	165.8	0.7		11.8	1.0	—		22.7		247.7	
1956	1.9	6.7	—		19.4				6.1	145.3	1.0		9.9	1.0	—		28.0		230.4	
1957	3.7	5.5	—		14.4				6.4	134.7	0.9		7.3	1.2	—		31.8		216.5	
1958	4.9	4.9	—		10.9	22.3	2.2	0.8	7.5	121.9	0.6		6.6	1.2	—		34.9		205.4	
1959	5.9	5.0	—		10.3				12.0	107.5 {4.2}	0.6	1.7	5.9	0.6	0.6		35.7	176.7	199.1	
1960	3.4	4.5	—		14.1	22.9	3.2	1.1	19.0	96.7 {4.8}	1.1	1.1	7.1	0.6	0.6		39.0	181.3	204.2	
1961	1.9	2.7	—		16.4	22.2	2.2	0.5	24.6	95.3 {7.1}	1.4	1.6	7.4	0.8	0.5		38.6	192.5	214.6	

Capital Account (in 1975 prices) – Scotland (£m.)

Year ended 15 May	Total	Rate fund services Total	Ed.	Lib. and Mus.	Health	Welfare	Sewer	Refuse	Parks	Housing HRA	Housing Other	Highways	Lighting	Fire	Police	Trading services Total	Water	Gas	Elec.	Trans.	Harbours
1962	241.1	216.4	41.6	0.5	0.8	1.1	10.6	1.3	1.1	98.8	13.8	30.5	2.1	1.1	2.1	24.6	14.3	—	—	3.4	5.6
1963	258.3	233.9	48.5	—	0.5	1.0	11.2	2.6	1.3	110.5	13.2	25.4	2.1	1.0	2.3	24.4	13.5	—	—	3.9	6.0
1964	329.1	303.3	53.1	N/A	N/A	1.3	10.4	3.5	1.3	168.7	13.7	26.3	2.0	1.3	2.8	26.1	15.7	—	—	2.5	5.8
1965	356.4	323.7	54.1	0.2	1.2	1.5	14.1	1.5	1.9	174.7	15.3	28.6	1.9	1.2	2.4	32.8	23.5	—	—	2.2	4.9
1966	361.3	327.5	47.8	0.5	1.4	1.9	13.5	1.6	1.6	174.4	15.4	26.6	1.9	1.6	2.6	34.1	22.2	—	—	1.2	8.4
1967	426.0	386.5	47.9	0.5	1.4	2.7	15.9	2.0	2.0	216.5	19.1	36.1	2.3	1.8	2.7	39.5	24.1	—	—	3.0	10.7
1968	500.6	451.4	65.2	0.7	1.5	4.2	17.1	2.9	2.2	245.7	16.2	46.5	1.3	2.4	4.0	49.2	24.2	—	—	3.1	15.8
1969	545.9	492.7	80.7	0.6	1.9	4.0	22.2	5.9	4.2	258.8	19.1	42.8	1.9	1.9	3.4	53.1	28.0	—	—	1.9	17.6
1970	491.1	438.7	80.7	1.2	0.8	3.5	19.0	5.1	4.5	232.2	14.7	32.8	2.4	1.4	2.7	52.4	28.7	—	—	2.0	17.3
1971	447.2	407.9	71.4	0.5	0.9	3.9	20.6	3.9	3.4	199.3	17.8	39.9	2.7	0.9	3.0	39.3	25.1	—	—	3.0	7.3
1972	421.3	386.3	65.1	0.8	1.1	3.9	24.1	2.6	4.4	175.9	21.6	42.2	2.7	0.8	3.6	35.1	19.2	—	—	2.6	7.8
1973	449.9	415.0	75.9	1.6	1.2	6.7	32.7	3.3	6.2	151.0	37.8	48.7	2.2	0.7	4.6	35.0	19.9	—	—	4.0	8.3
1974	510.0	480.4	71.8	2.4	0.9	8.0	36.5	2.6	6.7	189.0	48.5	52.8	2.7	0.5	4.1	29.5	17.8	—	—	1.0	8.1
1975	493.4	462.7	62.7	2.4	—	7.4	29.8	2.8	6.0	193.6	50.4	49.0	2.0	0.4	5.2	30.7	14.0	—	—	1.7	12.5

NOTES TO p.p. 121–126

a   This covers docks, piers and similar services.
b   Of this figure, 734 was expenditure incurred in previous years and met out of contingency funds, etc.
c   Owing to legislative changes these services disappear or emerge under other headings between 1948 and 1950.
d   Formerly called, 'Hospitals, clinics, etc.' this consists of expenditure on general hospitals, hospitals for infectious diseases, and hospitals for the treatment of tuberculosis until 1949.
e   This column is an aggregate of expenditure on capital works for those welfare services provided by local authorities since the legislative changes of the post war years. It consists of 'Care of the Aged, Handicapped, and Homeless', and 'Protection of Children'.
f   Nationalisation of municipal services affects comparability before and after these years.

Appendix 1.4.A2   International Comparisons of Government Expenditure

While not dwelling on their significance, international comparisons suggest that in most other countries, too, central government expenditure has fallen as a proportion of total government expenditure over the period since the Second World War. This appendix shows this for a number of nations for which data are available. Again one must point to the difference in definitions, yet the overall trend seems clear (IBRD, *World Tables*, 1976. The UK figures are based on different definitions from those we have used.) Only Burma, Ireland, Jamaica, Mauritius, Nigeria, Peru, Norway, Switzerland and, more uncertainly, South Africa, show an opposite trend.

Central Government Share in General Government Current Expenditure

Country	1950	1960	1965	1970	1973
Argentina	–	89.0	81.9	78.0	84.6
Australia	79.9	70.8	57.9	56.6	55.6
Austria	73.0	48.8	45.5	43.1	37.1
Belgium	66.9	55.1	51.1	49.8	49.0
Bolivia	–	57.9	68.2	64.4	65.0
Botswana	–	92.3	82.7	82.7[d]	84.8[f]
Brazil	–	47.6	44.3	–	–
Burma	–	–	61.9	65.0	77.5
Canada	54.7	58.0	50.0	42.2	41.9
Chile	–	69.4	63.5	40.6	–
Finland	61.7[a]	54.5	53.5	48.3	46.9
France	–	53.7	49.2	47.1	45.6
Germany, Federal Republic of	35.2	24.4	26.7	22.9	20.9
Greece	77.8	61.3	55.8	59.4	66.1
Iceland	67.1	61.9	55.0	–	–
Ireland	66.8	74.3	65.2	77.6	76.4
Israel	–	82.7	80.2	82.0[f]	–
Italy	58.0	48.2	43.7	40.6	39.9
Jamaica	–	95.5	99.6	103.0[B]	103.0[B]
Japan	56.0[b]	31.7	29.5	30.2	35.4
Libyan Arab Republic	–	–	94.5	93.0	91.1[e]
Luxembourg	86.2[c]	47.0	44.3	39.6	40.0[f]
Malaysia	–	–	82.1	82.1	81.3
Mauritius	–	94.3	95.2	90.0	97.3
Netherlands	48.3[b]	35.3	28.8	30.9	28.2
New Zealand	87.0	85.5	82.2	82.8	81.5
Nigeria	–	36.6	42.5	63.3	62.8
Norway	65.8[a]	69.5	69.3	75.6	74.0
Pakistan	–	–	–	76.5	76.1
Peru	94.6	94.6	96.2	96.0	96.3

Portugal	79.1	75.9	75.0	77.7	70.1[f]
Rhodesia	91.7[b]	–	90.0	91.0	–
South Africa [A]	55.9	57.1	66.1	64.6	65.4[f]
Sweden	54.3	45.1	42.6	33.2	32.0
Switzerland	28.1	42.7	51.6	46.1[d]	–
Thailand	–	93.5	94.5	94.5	–
UK	72.5	64.6	57.4	55.1	56.3
USA	54.4	53.3	50.2	42.8	38.3
Venezuela	–	99.9	97.4	88.5	87.3
Zambia	96.9	85.1	90.4	93.7	93.5[f]

[A] Includes SW Africa
[B] Due to large central government transfers to local government
[a] 1953 figure
[b] 1955 figure
[c] This estimate is not strictly comparable with those from 1961 on
[d] 1969 figure
[e] 1971 figure
[f] 1972 figure

5 Sources of Local Income

Local authorities have three main sources of revenue: the taxes they levy, charges made for goods and services they provide and grants from central government. Their expenditure must be financed by these or by receipts from loans.

Later chapters discuss the development of rates and grants. Here our interest is in different types of local taxes and how the contribution made by each source of income has varied over time.

LOCAL TAXES

Rates on property have always been the major source of local tax revenue. Until 1840, rates were levied on both immovable and some types of movable property, for example stock in trade (see Part One, Chapter 6). However, in 1849 the Poor Rate Exemption Act was passed excluding movable property from rates (see Finer, 1950, p. 411). The local tax became a tax on only one kind of property. The rapid rise of local expenditure and rates in the latter half of the nineteenth century was accompanied by increasing complaints about the equity of rates as the sole source of local tax income. These complaints were also probably fuelled by the increasing amount of personal income which was being derived from sources other than fixed property. The major complaint was that the burden on owners of rateable property was excessive relative to that on owners of other property, or earners of income from sources other than fixed property. This was a complaint about the narrowness of the tax base for the purpose of financing local expenditures. Another aspect of the complaint was that the amount of fixed property on which rates were levied was not necessarily related to individuals' ability to pay taxes. Those in agriculture and in the industries which used a relatively large amount of fixed property argued that they were excessively burdened by what was essentially a tax on one factor of production and, therefore, it discriminated against heavy users of that factor.

These complaints about the equity of the rating system were not confined to the nineteenth century. They reappeared periodically and are still with us today. Every major inquiry into local government finance considered alternative sources of local tax revenue. However, with the exception of the assigned revenue system introduced in the Goschen reforms of 1888 and lasting for about twelve years, rates on fixed property have remained the only local tax source.

Under the assigned revenue system introduced in 1888 the bulk of the revenues from excise licence duties, which were henceforth called local taxation licence duties, was assigned to local authorities. They also received 40 per cent of probate duty, and when this was abolished in 1894 they received 40 per cent of the estate duty. In 1890, two additional sources of revenue were assigned to local authorities. They received 80 per cent of the surtax introduced on beer and spirits.

These assigned revenues went into the local taxation account from which they were redistributed to local authorities. Two methods of distributing the monies from the local taxation account were used. The local licence duties were distributed to counties and county boroughs on the basis of the source of collection. These thus represented a local tax, though the collection of the tax and the setting of the rate of tax was in the hands of the central government. Initially, it had been proposed that local authorities should collect these duties and in some cases to set their own rates of tax (Royal Commission on Local Taxation, 1901, Cd. 638, p. 69). If this proposal had been carried through — it never was — these would have been truly new local taxes. As it was, they were local taxes in so far as the amount received by each authority depended on the amount paid in such taxes by its residents, but without the local power to set the rates of tax.

The other monies in the local taxation account were distributed among local authorities in the same proportion as their receipt of grants in the period 1887/8. These were thus a different form of grant, rather than a new form of local tax income.

By 1911, even the licence duties could no longer be considered as a local tax. The 1910 Finance Act and the 1911 Revenue Act introduced a system in which the amounts of the duties flowing into the local taxation account were to be fixed independently of the amount of duties collected. Of the duties assigned in 1888 those of beer and spirits, carriage (including motor car) licences and liquor licences were all fixed at the level they were in 1908–9. Thus the most profitable duties and the ones with the greatest growth potential were taken away from local authorities. The central government could not, or rather would not, give up such a profitable tax source.

Goschen's assigned revenue system was the last attempt to introduce a new source of revenue for local authorities. Suggestions for new sources did not, however, stop.

The Royal Commission on Local Taxation of 1901 considered two major alternative sources of revenue, especially to finance what they considered onerous expenditure. After commenting that the Elizabethan Poor Rate was 'perhaps originally intended to be something like a local income tax' they continue that

> It is clear on reflection that a local income tax . . . tends more and more to be incompatible with modern social and political arrangements. The very conception is indeed obscure, for to what locality does an income belong? To the place or places from which it is derived? or to the place or places where it is enjoyed? i.e. where the recipient more or less permanently resides? (Cd. 638, p. 13)

The Majority found these problems insoluble. Not only did they consider the administrative problems of introducing an income tax too difficult, they believed that the problems of principle could not be solved. If the tax was levied on the basis of the place of residence they thought that it would not meet the objections to the current system because

circumstances not unnaturally often lead wealthy people to congregate in districts far from those in which the source of the wealth lies. In such districts the present system of local taxation is not oppressive and relief is little needed. But many purely agricultural and industrial districts number very few wealthy residents, and a tax on the income of the residents would be more burdensome and less productive than the present rates. (ibid., p. 13)

With this argument they eliminated an income tax based on place of residence. They considered it to be too difficult to tax income at its source, because many people had income from various sources, and many organisations carry on business in many areas 'in a way that it is almost impossible to say what proportion of their profit is derived from any of those districts. In what districts are the incomes of the thousands of shareholders in these concerns to be taxed? Instances of the chaos that would ensue might be indefinitely multiplied' (ibid., p. 13).

As a possible proxy for an income tax the Majority also considered a special local levy on inhabited houses. This suggestion was rejected on the same grounds as that used to reject a local income tax on the basis of residence.

The Majority Report favoured the continuation of the assigned revenue system with some extensions of the licences to be given to local authorities, and possibly more scope for the initial suggestion of Goschen that local authorities might collect the duties and set the rates themselves.

The Kempe Committee in 1914 also considered alternative sources for local taxes. Their arguments against the introduction of local income taxes were essentially the same as those of the 1901 Royal Commission (Kempe, 1914, Cd. 7315). Moreover, they were in general not very favourably disposed to transfer more taxes to local authorities. When discussing the possibility of extending the licence duties to be assigned to local authorities and possibly introducing other local duties — as, for example, an amusement tax — the major objection was 'that the continued assignment of these revenues to local authorities would deprive the Imperial Exchequer of a potential source of revenue' (ibid., p. 65). It was clear by this time that the government was not willing to give up a major potential source of revenue to local authorities and in fact it had already taken back from them the licence duties which were the biggest revenue yielders.

The assigned revenue system was slowly being replaced by specific grants. By 1928, of the total amount being transferred from the central government to local authorities only 18 per cent came through the local taxation account, that is, via the assigned revenues.

The 1929 Local Government Act scrapped all the assigned revenues and reverted to direct grants. The only local taxation duties that were retained were licences to deal in game, to kill game, for dogs, guns, armorial bearings and male servants. (Ministry of Housing and Local Government, 1928, Cmnd. 3134, p. 13). Obviously the government did not see in these duties a major potential source of revenue.

There was no further serious discussion of alternative tax sources for local authorities until the 1973 Green Paper on local government finance, and then the Layfield Report and the subsequent Green Paper (DoE, 1977b, Cmnd. 6813). We leave a discussion of these to Part Four. In the White Paper of 1957 the possibility of alternative tax sources was briefly dismissed:

> The government does not think it practicable to devise a satisfactory new
> source of local revenue by authorising the collection of local income tax or
> other such imposts on top of the national system of taxes, nor do they think
> it appropriate . . . to hand over to local authorities the motor duties or any
> other of the taxes now levied nationally. (Ministry of Housing and Local
> Government, 1956–7, Cmnd. 209, p. 3)

The 1966 White Paper recognised the same criticism of the rating system that
was raised seventy years earlier: 'Under modern conditions the value of a man's
fixed property is no measure of his capacity to pay' (Ministry of Housing and
Local Government, 1965–6, Cmnd. 2923, p. 3). But the criticism did not result
in any suggestion for alternative tax sources because 'consideration of other
sources of revenue, be they taxes on income or consumption or an activity such
as gambling continually runs up against the fact that present local authority
areas do not make satisfactory taxation units' (ibid., p. 4). Why this is so is not
explained.

For over a hundred years it has been recognised that the financing of an ever-
growing amount of local expenditure with a tax on fixed property only might
be inequitable, especially as these expenditures were more and more imposed
on local authorities. There has also been a great reluctance by the central government to give up any of its profitable tax sources. To overcome the problem without giving up any tax sources, the government has become more and more a tax
collector for local authorities. It collects the taxes and transfers income to local
authorities via grants.

The conflict between the equity of the single local authority tax source and
the government's reluctance to give to the local authorities any other tax source,
combined with the rising expenditures undertaken by local authorities, has been
the major reason for the rising proportion of grant financing of local expenditures.

RATES AND GRANTS

Until about a hundred years ago central government grants were comparatively
unimportant. There were no regular annual grants before 1835. Before then
central government had sometimes made specific contributions where it had an
interest in doing so. For example, it had contributed to Thomas Telford's rebuilding of the London–Holyhead road in the eighteenth century because
improvement of our communications with Ireland was held to be of strategic
and military importance. In 1868/9, the first year for which we have reasonable
data, grants were only 4½ per cent of rates and grants taken together.[1] As Figure
1.5.1 shows, the increase in the grant proportion has been huge, from 9.4 per
cent in 1879/80 to 65.3 per cent in 1974/5. The grant proportion has not increased continuously. There have been several periods in which it increased
noticeably; while there are long periods in which it has remained relatively
constant.

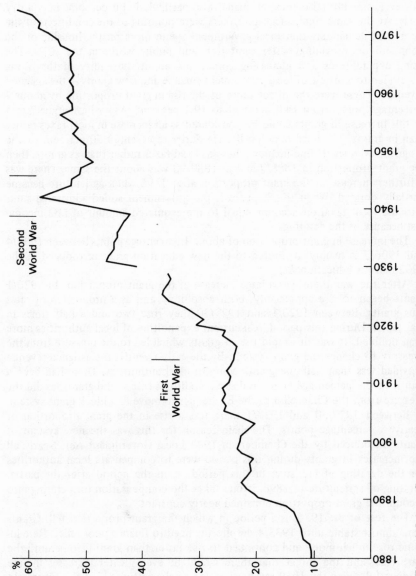

Figure 1.5.1. *Grants as a proportion of grant and rate income*

It is interesting to consider the reasons for the increase in the grant proportion at various times. We do not have detailed information for the 1870s, when the grant proportion more than doubled from 4.5 per cent to 9.4 per cent. The main reason for the increase was almost certainly the new grants from the 1870 Forster Education Act, though these did not begin to flow until the middle of the period.

The 1880s, as we have seen, was a time of slow growth in local expenditure. However, agricultural depression made rates particularly burdensome in country areas. At the same time, social reformers were pointing to the conditions of the slums and demanding that local government spend more on the housing of the poor and on providing better sanitation and public works in the cities. The rising expenditures and increasing complaints about the equity of the rating system led to a review of local government finance and new grants – the assigned revenues. These were the direct cause of the rise in grant proportion by about 4 percentage points from 14.9 per cent to 19.1 per cent. As we have argued, part of this increase in grants could be considered as an increase in local taxes rather than in grants. The local taxation licence duties represented 50 per cent of the assigned revenues. If one includes these as local taxes rather than as grants, then the grant proportion in 1888/9 and in 1889/90 was about the same. There was a further increase in the grant proportion after 1896 when agriculture became partially derated. When this happened, the government added additional sums into the local taxation account equal to the estimated amount of rate income lost because of the derating.

The increase in grant proportion of about 4 percentage points between 1903/4 and 1906/7 is mainly attributed to the new education grant introduced in the 1902 Balfour Education Act.

After the war there was a large increase in the grant proportion. In 1920/1 grants began to rise appreciably, both absolutely and as a proportion of rates plus grants. Between 1920/1 and 1929/30 they rose two and a half times in real terms. During this period, real current expenditure of local authorities more than doubled. It was this rapid rise in grants which led to the pressure from the Treasury to change the grant system. By the early twenties the assigned revenue provided less than half the grants going to local authorities. There had been a return to the percentage grant, and as expenditures rose so did grants, as did the pressure from the Chancellor of the Exchequer to move to a block grant system.

Between 1929/30 and 1930/1 there was a rise in the grant proportion of nearly 6 percentage points. The main reason for this was the new system of grants introduced by the Chamberlain 1929 Local Government Act. Nearly all the increases in grants during this period were to compensate local authorities for the derating of industry. In this period, as in the period after the partial derating of agriculture in 1896, if one takes the compensation for derating into account the grant proportion remained nearly constant.

The rest of the 1930s is a period in which the grant proportion fell. Grants were almost stable until 1933/4 despite the need to finance poor relief. Rate income rose much more; and continued to rise faster than grant income until the war. This, and the threat that there would be even greater increases in rate burdens following the 1939 revaluation, led to the setting up of the Fitzgerald

Committee, the first to look into the hardship rates caused the poor (Ministry of Health, 1939, published 1944).

During the Second World War rate income and non-specific grants remained mainly unchanged. There was, however, a large increase in specific grants connected with the war. This increase caused the large rise in the proportion of grant income during these years.

Though there was some drop in the grant proportion to 1947/8, it rose again to 50 per cent in 1948/9. Immediately this can be attributed to the new grant system of the Bevan 1948 Local Government Act, but at a deeper level one may suggest some influence of the displacement effect mentioned in the preceding chapter which led central government to act to retain the grant proportion around 50 per cent.

The 1948 system, with its element of matching grants, worked so as to keep the proportion of grant very stable during the early 1950s. A new grant system came into effect in 1958/9 and did not disturb that proportion. However, beneath that surface the behaviour of education grant was particularly interesting. We have noted that education expenditure was both absolutely high and growing particularly rapidly in the 1950s. Education was the one major specific grant to survive from the pre-1929 system until it was absorbed into block grant from 1958/9. Of the increase in grant of £644 million from 1948/9 to 1957/8, £459 million was in education grant, that is 71 per cent of the increase; though the increase in education expenditure as a proportion of the increase in total local expenditure over the period was only 42 per cent. (Non-specific grant rose by very little – in real terms only from £252 million to £274 million in the same period.)

During the last period of exceptionally rapid increase in grant proportion – between 1966/7 and 1974/5 – it rose by about 13 percentage points to a high point of 65.3 per cent in 1974/5. Some of the increase is accounted for by a new grant payable in respect of domestic ratepayers only – the domestic element in Rate Support Grant. In money terms, the domestic element grew from zero in 1966/7 to £446 million in 1974/5 (Layfield, 1976, p. 387); but during that period total government grant increased by £4,259 million.

RATES AND GROSS DOMESTIC PRODUCT

While viewing the movement of grants and rates against historical events and economic trends gives an impression of the forces that have combined to increase the grant proportion over time, an economist would expect the relationship of both with movements in gross domestic product also to be significant. When GDP moves up does rate income also seem more buoyant? Figure 1.5.2 should provide the answers.

The period immediately after the First World War was one in which rate income rose in real terms. It rose faster relative to GDP until 1922 or 1923. This must have contributed to the reaction against Lloyd George's postwar spending which led to his downfall. Aside from a fall in GDP in 1926, movement in rate income and GDP are fairly similar until 1930 when GDP falls, rate income much less so. What this illustrates is the pressure that poor and unemployment relief nevertheless put on local authorities to maintain rate demands, despite the large increases in grant after 1929.

Towards the end of the 1930s, GDP was rising faster than rate income which first rises slowly and then actually falls in real terms. One would expect this to lessen protests against rate increase. That the Fitzgerald Committee was set up suggests this was not so. A possible explanation is that the high unemployment existing in some areas prevented local rises in real income and that it was from these areas that most of the protest originated.[2]

By contrast, after the Second World War the relationship between rates and GDP was far less volatile than it had been in the 1920s and 1930s, and to a greater extent than is easily explained by the economy being less volatile.

From 1947/8, rate income fell relative to GDP. The start of the local expenditure boom of the Macmillan—Home era can be seen pushing rates up between 1955/6 and 1956/7.

THE COMPARATIVE CONSTANCY OF DOMESTIC RATE BILLS AS A PROPORTION OF PERSONAL DISPOSABLE INCOME

In an economy where local expenditure was not insulated from government protection, one would expect it to fluctuate in some relation to the trade cycle. In the preceding chapter we saw how such cyclical fluctuations seemed no longer present after the Second World War. The relative stability of local expenditure appears even more remarkable when one observes the postwar relationship between personal disposable income (PDI), that is income after taxes, and domestic rate payments. Data are not available on this before 1938 but Figure 1.5.2 makes it clear that it cannot have been stable through the interwar years. Indeed, the proportion must have fallen during the 1930s to the 1938 level which none the less is the highest point in Table 1.5.1.

By contrast, postwar stability in the relationship is remarkable. It has risen very slowly from about 2 per cent in the late 1940s to about $2\frac{1}{2}$ per cent more recently. But it has increased by about 25 per cent over a period when local expenditure as a proportion of PDI has risen by about 223 per cent.

It would be tempting to think that the central government has acted consciously so as to increase government grant to maintain this relationship. But there is no evidence at all that the relationship was even noticed until it was pointed out quite recently (Foster, 1975, para. 18). Neither can one point to any economic factors likely to result in such a stable relationship. The most rational explanation of this is that there is some tendency for increase in rates paid relative to GDP to cause protest that stimulates central government to provide more grant, which has the effect of maintaining more or less the constant proportion observed. As we shall see in the next chapter, Richard Crossman's account of the introduction of rate rebates and the domestic element in 1966 can be interpreted as suggesting something of this kind. To this we may add a more conscious intention of central government since 1946 to maintain steady

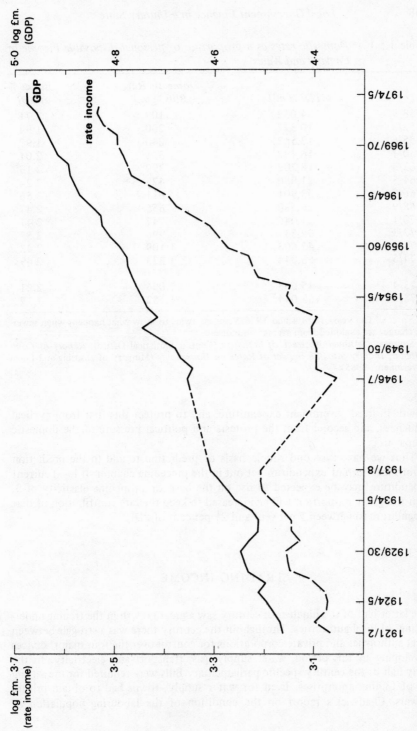

Figure 1.5.2. *Local authority rate income and gross domestic product at 1975 prices*

Table 1.5.1.   *Domestic rates as a proportion of personal disposable income in England and Wales*

Year	PDI (£m.)	Domestic Rate Bills (£m.)	Bill as % of PDI
1938/9	4,032	109	2.71
1952/3	10,327	200	1.94
1955/6	12,552	240	1.92
1960/1	16,452	331	2.01
1962/3	18,702	399	2.13
1964/5	21,080	473	2.24
1966/7	23,901	611	2.56
1968/9	26,530	655	2.47
1970/1	31,046	747	2.41
1972/3	39,531	996	2.52
1973/4	45,603	1,109	2.43
1974/5	53,044	1,323	2.49
1973/4	45,603	1,006	2.21
1974/5	53,044	1,152	2.17

Note: The years 1973/4 and 1974/5 appear twice to show what happens when sewerage charges are excluded from average poundages.

Sources: *Annual Abstract of Statistics* (Central Statistical Office); *Report of Committee of Inquiry into the Impact of Rates on Households* (Ministry of Housing and Local Government, 1965).

growth in local government expenditure; and to protect this first from cyclical influences, and second from the protests and political pressure of the domestic ratepayer.

Thus we have a second simple basis of prediction to add to the prediction about local current expenditure set out in the preceding chapter. If local current expenditure may be expected to rise on the basis of an income elasticity of 3, then the grant proportion will be increased to keep the rate contribution of that expenditure to between 2 per cent and $2\frac{1}{2}$ per cent of PDI.

TRADING INCOME

The latter half of the nineteenth century saw a great growth in the trading undertakings of local authorities. Throughout the century there was a struggle between local authorities and private corporations for control over the four major services developing in this period, water supply, gas, transport and electricity. In the early half of the century specific parliamentary Bills were required for the setting up of trading enterprises. Even for water supply, towns had to obtain private powers. Chadwick's report on the condition of the labouring population of

Great Britain strongly criticised the general sanitary conditions and was highly critical of the water supply in most towns. The report favoured a transfer of existing and future water companies to local authorities. Though the 1848 Public Health Act empowered the transfer of waterworks to town councils, it was not until the 1870 Gas and Water Facilities Act that such transfers and the setting up of municipal waterworks became much easier. Under this Act it became unnecessary to get a private Bill to set up waterworks. The Board of Trade was empowered to grant authority for such undertakings. The 1875 Public Health Act gave urban authorities the general powers to provide adequate water supply either directly or from private companies.[3]

More and more authorities started providing water. In 1904, current expenditures on water were eight times as large as they were twenty years earlier in 1884.

The Act of 1875 was also an enabling legislation for the provision of gas. Though in Manchester the police and improvement commissioners started manufacturing gas for lighting their office building in 1807 and in 1817 made gas available for public consumption, few authorities undertook their own supply of gas. In 1860, only 27 authorities were providing their own gas. By 1880 nearly 100 more had their own provision.

Local transport undertakings developed slowly in the last two decades of the nineteenth century, and then grew rapidly in the beginning of the twentieth. Current expenditure on transport was just over £1 million in 1899, rose to just under £5 million in 1904, to £10 million by 1913 and to over £20 million by 1918.

What was to become the largest and most profitable of the trading services was, however, electricity. In this field, local authorities were involved at a very early stage, and from the beginning did not have to go through private Bills to establish the service. By the 1882 Electric Lighting Act, moreover, private companies needed the approval of the local authority to establish supply. From an initial current expenditure of £$\frac{1}{2}$ million in 1900, expenditure rose to about £3 million in 1905 and £13 million by 1918.

From the beginning of the twentieth century, revenues from the major trading services started rising rapidly; so, however, did expenditure on the services. In 1910, the trading receipts on the four services were about £25 million. By 1936 they had risen to £100 million. In column 1 of Table 1.5.3 we show the proportion of total local authority income arising from the trading services. In the 1920s and 1930s trading income represented more than a quarter of total income. With the transfer of electricity and gas from local authorities after the Second World War there was a sharp fall in trading income. There was a further fall when water was transferred in the early 1970s. Now trading services represent only about 2 per cent of local authority income.

Income from trading services, especially those voluntarily undertaken by local authorities, is slightly different from income from rates and grants. To receive such income, local authorities have to provide the services and, therefore, it is an income which is dependent on expenditure undertaken. Possibly more relevant from the point of view of an authority is whether the income from trading

Table 1.5.2. *Trading Services in England and Wales*

	1930	1935	1940	1945	1950	1955	1960	1965	1970	1975
water	+1,071.6	+1,012.7	+1,237.0	+1,524.1	+1,625	+3,420	+4,785	+5,366	+10,702	—
	5.6	4.9	5.0	5.3	4.5	7.4	7.5	6.1	7.0	—
gas	−166.7	−92.5	−6.8	−5.6	−41	—	—	—	—	—
	1.0	0.6	—	—	0.8	—	—	—	—	—
electricity	−458.5	−615.6	+197.0	−106.6	—	—	—	—	—	—
	1.6	1.5	0.8	0.1	—	—	—	—	—	—
transport	+8.0	+2.5	−223.8	−305.9	−204	+49	−31	+173	+1,382	+7,975
	—	—	0.9	0.8	0.4	0.1	—	0.2	1.2	10.8

Note: Net transfers to (−) or from (+) rate accounts for certain years − % of total trading receipts for that expenditure heading on revenue account.

services has to be supplemented from the rate fund to reduce charges. In Table 1.5.2 we show the amounts and percentage of expenditures transferred from the rates to the four trading services. A negative number means that the amount is what has been transferred to the rate fund from the servcie.

We can see that the transfers between the trading services and the rate fund have generally been small either way. Except for water, which has always been a subsidised trading service (see Finer, 1950, pp. 122–7) the transfers have never represented much more than 1 per cent of the total expenditure on the service. Even the most profitable of the services – electricity – only contributed $1\frac{1}{2}$ per cent of expenditure to the rate fund. These figures should, however, be treated with some caution. Many authorities could not use any surplus from the trading services to reduce rates. Some of the early Acts establishing the trading services compelled the authorities to use any surpluses to reduce charges. What the figures do imply, however, is that on average the trading services and trading income do not constitute any major source of revenue for local authorities to finance any expenditures other than those on the trading services.

RENTS

Though housing expenditure became an important item of local expenditure immediately after the First World War, housing rents were a comparatively small part of income throughout the interwar period. Thereafter, they grew steadily until they overtook trading income at the beginning of the 1960s, so reflecting the growing importance of public housing.

Table 1.5.3, column 2 shows housing rents as a proportion of total local authority income. The major expenditure on housing in the early 1920s raised this proportion to just under 5 per cent where it remained until the later 1940s. It then started rising, and in the ten years between 1949/50 and 1959/60 it rose by about 5 percentage points. Since then it has remained at around 11 per cent. Though expenditure on housing increased very greatly between 1960 and 1975, this growth was not reflected by a high growth in rent income. For example, between 1970 and 1975 expenditure on housing at current prices rose by nearly 300 per cent while rent income rose by only about 120 per cent. During this period, the various government policies to reduce or maintain rents at a low level have stifled the growth of this source of income. These constraints on rent income have resulted in increasing contributions from the rate fund to housing expenditures. In 1973/4 such contributions represented 8 per cent of housing expenditure. In 1974/5 this rose to over 12 per cent.

FEES AND CHARGES

Fees and charges now represent about 13 per cent of total income and over 50 per cent of rate income. Table 1.5.3 column 3 shows fees and charges as a proportion of total income for selected years. By the beginning of this decade, fees and charges outstripped both rents and income from trading services.

Table 1.5.3. *Receipts from trading services, housing rents and rate fund services: fees as a proportion of total income*[a] *(Selected years – England and Wales*

	Trading Services	Housing rents	Rate fund services
1879/80	6.0	–	–
1889/90	11.3	–	–
1899/1900	12.1	–	–
1901/10	16.1	–	–
1919/20	27.8	0.3	–
1929/30	25.7	4.5	6.2
1939/40	24.6	4.4	5.7
1947/8	28.6	3.5	8.4
1948/9	19.6	4.8	8.5
1949/50	15.5	5.8	8.5
1959/60	10.9	10.3	6.7
1969/70	7.5	11.2	11.5
1973/4	4.7	11.6	14.2
1974/5	2.3	11.1	12.8
1976/7	1.2	5.9	4.1

[a] Prior to 1929/30 receipts from trading services refer only to water and gas, electricity, transport and harbours. Beginning 1929/30 all receipts from trading services are included. Prior to 1929/30 total income includes receipts on capital account. Starting 1929/30 they are omitted.

CONCLUSIONS

The most striking fact about local governments' sources of revenue is the enormous increase in their dependence on central grant over a century. It has not happened smoothly, but in a number of jumps. Most often the reason for the increase in grant has been a wish to reduce the burden of local rates on some group of ratepayers – agriculture in the 1890s, industry in 1921, and the domestic ratepayer in 1966. Since the Second World War an unconscious principle seems to have emerged which has had the effect of increasing grant to maintain an average domestic rate increase as an acceptable proportion of PDI. Now that this is recognised, it is difficult to predict whether it will continue as a conscious principle or not. If the experience were to be repeated, this would be a basis for predicting the likely future course of grant increase as local expenditure rises.

Trading services have been slowly taken away from local authorities, but their net contribution to revenue has never been substantial. Over the past decade, housing has imposed a net burden and an increasing one on the rate fund. A change in policy towards rents could raise this source of income substantially. Fees and charges have slowly become a major source of revenue, now representing more than 50 per cent of rate income. In Part Four we shall consider the case for an expansion in this source of revenue.

NOTES

1 The advantage of calculating grant percentages in this way is that it separates ordinary revenue expenditure from both capital and trading expenditure. Except for housing, capital expenditure is generally but not invariably financed through loans, though local authorities may at times meet some capital expenditure out of revenue. Trading expenditure is generally self-financing – the necessary revenue coming almost 100 per cent from charges. Housing is best regarded as a form of trading service, its revenue coming mostly from rents and central government grants, until very recently. In concentrating on grants as a percent of rates plus grants, attention is being drawn to the financing of that expenditure which is most sensitive to changes in rates and grants. For the data see Appendix 1.5.A1.
2 This would seem to be implied by Rhodes in Layfield (1976, App. 6, p. 117ff).
3 For a fascinating account of this period see Finer (1941, ch. 3).

Appendix 1.5.A1   Receipts of Local Authorities – England and Wales; Scotland

SOURCES AND NOTES

ENGLAND AND WALES

1868 to 1929 – Mitchell and Deane (1962), table 9: 'Public Finance', pp. 414–5.
The itemised receipts are principal constituent items only and do not sum to the total.
All receipts designated for expenditure on capital works are included under the individual headings.
From 1888, loans advanced out of the London County Council Consolidated Loans Fund are included. The break is very small.
The main trading services include water and gas, beginning in 1880, transport (1884), electricity (1895), and harbours, docks and piers (1911).

1930 to 1975 – Ministry of Health, later Ministry of Housing, later Department of the Environment, *Local Government Financial Statistics* (formerly *Local Taxation Returns*), annual series since 1934/5.
Revenue account – all receipts itemised except for Special Funds which are included in the total for the revenue account.

Fees include fees and recoupments.

Housing fees pertain to non-grant specific income for 'Housing' (Housing Revenue Account, Requisitioned Houses, Other) and Small Dwellings acquisition.

Capital Account — all receipts itemised except for 'Other' in both the Rate Fund and Trading Services accounts which are included in their respective totals. 'Other' includes 'Sales' and 'Other'.

Rates: from 1935 rates on local authority houses were excluded from 'Housing Fees' and included under 'Rates'; from 1949, payments in lieu of rates made by the British Transport Commission and the Central Electricity Authority are included.

Grants: Specific grants — from 1939 this includes local taxation duties and grants and reimbursement for services arising solely from the Second World War. Non-specific grants — 1941—45 — includes advances to certain local authorities where the income from rates in their areas had been so reduced by war conditions as to endanger the maintenance of essential public services.

Trading Services: All revenue included owing to legislative changes — gas (1950), electricity (1949), and water (1975) disappear or emerge under different headings.

Housing: Beginning in 1970 the housing revenue account became a separate account. Here, it is included with the rate fund services.

SCOTLAND

1880 to 1939 — Mitchell and Dean (1962), p. 422.

1940 to 1958 — Mitchell and Jones (1971), p. 167.

The itemised receipts are principal constituent items only and do not sum to the total.

All receipts designated for expenditure on capital works are included under the individual headings.

The main trading services include water and gas, transport, electricity and harbours, docks and piers.

1959 to 1975 — The Scottish Office, *Local Financial Returns — Scotland*, annual series.

Revenue account — all receipts itemised except for Special Funds which are included in the total for the revenue account.

Fees include fees and recoupments.

Housing fees pertain to non-grant specific income for 'Housing' (Housing Revenue Account, Requisitioned Houses, Other) and Small Dwellings acquisition.

Receipts of Local Authorities – England and Wales (£m.)

Year ended 31 March	Total	Principal constituent items				
		Loans	Rates	Total Govt. grant	House Rents (Fees)	Main Trading services
1868	30.4	5.5	16.5	0.8	–	–
1871	30.2	–	–	–	–	–
1872	31.7	–	17.6	–	–	–
1873	32.8	–	18.1	–	–	–
1874	37.4	–	18.9	–	–	–
1875	43.6	–	19.3	–	–	–
1876	43.4	–	19.5	–	–	–
1877	48.1	–	20.1	–	–	–
1878	51.8	–	21.1	–	–	–
1879	54.4	–	21.8	–	–	–
1880[a]	53.0	13.7	22.5	2.7	–	3.2
1881	53.9	12.9	22.8	2.7	–	3.5
1882	57.5	15.0	23.9	2.9	–	3.6
1883	53.8	10.7	24.5	3.3	–	5.1
1884	51.2	7.2	24.9	3.5	–	5.5
1885	55.5	10.9	25.7	3.6	–	5.5
1886	56.0	11.0	26.2	3.8	–	5.5
1887	54.7	8.7	26.6	4.0	–	5.7
1888	55.0[b]	8.6	27.2	4.3	–	5.9
1889	55.0	7.0	27.4	4.8	–	6.2
1890	57.3	7.1	27.7	6.5	–	6.5
1891	57.6	6.2	27.8	7.1	–	6.9
1892	63.3	10.0	28.5	8.0	–	7.1
1893	67.6	12.1	30.2	8.9	–	7.1
1894	72.6	14.3	32.2	8.8	–	7.5
1895	75.9	15.5	33.9	9.0	–	8.0
1896	75.5	12.2	35.9	9.2	–	8.2
1897	79.9	13.3	37.5	9.6	–	8.7
1898	83.9	14.5	37.6	11.0	–	9.4
1899	91.9	19.7	38.6	11.8	–	10.4
1900	100.6	23.4	40.7	12.2	–	12.2
1901	111.9	29.9	43.0	12.7	–	14.0
1902	121.6	34.4	46.4	12.5	–	15.4
1903	129.2	35.3	50.3	12.8	–	17.1
1904	133.6[c]	31.3[c]	52.9	15.6	–	18.8

Receipts of Local Authorities – England and Wales (£m.) (continued)

Year ended 31 March	Total	Loans	Rates	Principal constituent items		
				Total Govt. grant	House Rents (Fees)	Main Trading services
1905	180.6^d	67.5^e	56.0	19.5	—	22.6^d
1906	141.2	24.5	58.3	19.9	—	23.4
1907	141.2	20.4	59.6	21.0	—	24.9
1908	143.7	21.4	59.6	20.6	—	26.5
1909	145.5	20.6	61.3	21.4	—	26.8
1910	171.9^e	42.0^e	63.3	20.9	—	27.7
1911	152.2	18.2	65.2	21.2	0.5	35.8
1912	157.0	17.8	66.4	22.3	0.5	37.9
1913	160.8	17.5	68.2	21.9	0.5	39.7
1914	169.3	20.0	71.3	22.6	0.6	41.5
1915	175.7	22.4	73.7	23.2	0.6	42.4
1916	168.5	9.0	75.9	23.4	0.7	46.3
1917	165.6	5.4	72.9	22.9	0.7	49.8
1918	176.6	4.1	75.4	26.3	0.8	55.2
1919	199.2	4.3	84.7	28.9	0.8	63.5
1920	282.2	24.3	105.6	48.3	0.9	78.4
1921	457.2	116.1	151.8	63.0	2.3	93.1
1922	501.8	127.4	170.9	76.7	4.4	90.4
1923	422.2	61.1	157.3	75.8	6.7	89.8
1924	396.0	46.5	143.3	78.3	8.0	87.4
1925	424.4	69.6	142.0	81.7	9.3	89.2
1926	471.4	99.2	148.6	84.6	11.7	91.7
1927	515.1	119.4	159.0	87.0	15.3	98.2
1928	544.0	128.0	166.7	90.1	20.0	101.2
1929	516.5	92.9	166.5	92.3	23.5	101.9

Receipts of Local Authorities – England and Wales (£m.) (continued)

Year ended 31 March	Total	Revenue Account Total	Rate Fund Services Total	Rates	Grants Specific	Grants Non-spec.	Fees Housing	Fees Excl. Hous.	Trading Services Total	Trading Services Grants	Trading Services General Fees Other	Capital Account Total	Rate fund services Total	Rate fund services Loans	Rate fund services Grants	Trading services Total	Trading services Loans	Trading services Grants
1930	530.3	428.7	311.3	156.3	87.1	20.4	21.1	26.4	110.3	0.4	109.9	101.6	75.0	62.1	5.1	26.6	25.3	0.1
1931	566.1	449.2	329.0	149.9	81.6	48.2	22.9	26.4	112.3	0.4	111.9	116.9	87.5	71.9	7.0	29.4	28.1	0.1
1932	556.6	446.9	326.0	148.3	79.5	46.6	24.7	26.9	113.6	0.5	113.1	109.7	83.4	67.3	7.6	26.3	25.3	0.1
1933	537.2	441.7	319.3	146.3	73.5	46.4	26.0	27.1	114.5	0.6	113.9	95.5	72.6	59.1	4.8	22.9	21.7	0.0
1934	533.3	446.6	323.6	148.6	73.7	47.2	26.8	27.3	115.0	0.7	114.3	86.7	57.6	44.7	3.6	29.1	18.1	0.0
1935	539.6	461.4	335.1	154.8	77.1	47.2	20.2	35.8	117.9	0.7	117.2	78.2	55.7	43.8	2.1	22.5	21.1	0.0
1936	577.2	481.3	348.5	164.9	85.4	46.8	22.1	29.3	124.1	0.7	123.3	95.8	70.9	58.6	2.4	25.0	23.7	0.1
1937	621.1	503.1	361.4	172.8	87.7	47.2	22.5	31.2	131.1	0.7	130.4	118.0	88.2	73.1	3.9	29.9	28.0	0.3
1938	659.2	517.7	370.2	177.3	85.8	49.5	23.4	34.1	139.2	0.8	138.4	141.6	106.8	89.8	5.0	34.8	32.9	0.4
1939	692.3	543.9	390.3	191.4	89.7	49.7	24.9	34.6	144.3	0.8	143.5	148.4	112.8	96.5	6.3	35.5	33.3	0.3
1940	711.8	601.9	443.1	201.3	131.9	49.2	26.7	34.1	148.1	0.8	147.3	109.9	81.3	62.6	12.0	28.6	26.7	0.5
1941	734.9	662.9	494.7	203.9	176.1	49.1	27.5	38.1	157.0	0.9	156.1	72.0	49.2	30.4	14.0	22.8	21.2	0.4
1942	787.8	740.1	548.4	198.9	224.7	52.3	27.3	45.2	179.3	1.3	178.0	47.6	31.9	12.1	15.3	15.7	13.3	1.3
1943	769.0	731.1	526.4	200.4	195.8	50.9	27.5	51.8	190.6	1.4	189.2	37.9	20.7	6.9	9.2	17.2	14.9	1.1
1944	766.8	739.0	515.5	204.1	177.0	50.4	27.6	56.0	209.1	1.0	208.0	27.8	14.9	6.5	3.8	12.9	11.3	0.8
1945	786.3	762.3	524.0	206.7	178.9	50.4	27.5	60.9	221.3	1.1	220.3	24.0	13.9	5.9	2.6	10.2	8.8	0.5
1946	835.7	795.9	549.7	222.6	171.0	63.9	27.8	64.5	228.4	1.0	227.5	39.7	24.2	16.8	2.0	15.6	14.3	0.3
1947	1,034.8	872.3	595.8	243.2	187.8	63.4	30.1	71.2	255.9	0.9	255.0	162.5	128.5	118.1	3.3	34.0	31.8	0.2
1948	1,253.7	963.1	666.8	283.3	205.7	63.2	34.0	80.5	275.0	0.7	274.3	290.6	238.7	218.4	10.0	51.9	48.6	1.0
1949	1,196.1	878.1	686.1	284.4	226.2[f]	58.2[f]	42.3	75.0	171.8	0.5	171.3	318.0	290.4	262.3	20.4	27.6	24.9	0.7
1950	1,204.5	866.1	712.1	294.3	246.2	47.8	50.1	73.7	134.4	0.4	134.0	338.3	300.2	281.0	10.8	38.1	26.5	1.2
1951	1,261.3	899.2	747.3	304.9	255.0	49.2	58.2	75.4	131.4	0.4	131.0	362.1	332.0	313.6	7.4	30.1	26.7	1.5
1952	1,421.8	1,002.4	837.4	311.9	293.6	55.9	67.7	88.3	142.7	0.3	142.4	419.4	389.3	372.0	6.5	30.1	25.9	2.2
1953	1,579.1	1,077.0	903.8	350.9	324.3	60.2	77.9	90.5	149.3	0.3	149.0	502.1	465.0	442.1	7.9	37.2	31.8	2.5
1954	1,709.2	1,176.2	992.4	392.5	350.6	63.2	91.9	94.3	157.7	0.4	157.3	533.0	498.1	464.4	16.2	34.9	30.3	3.2
1955	1,784.8	1,256.7	1,064.9	410.5	384.8	67.6	105.3	96.7	163.2	0.4	162.8	528.1	494.0	463.1	9.4	34.1	28.4	3.9
1956	1,901.3	1,352.4	1,147.0	421.1	426.5	73.6	125.6	100.3	174.4	0.4	174.1	549.0	509.9	477.8	6.8	39.1	34.1	1.2
1957	2,097.4	1,555.8	1,334.8	513.5	484.5	83.2	148.1	105.5	186.6	0.3	186.2	541.6	499.0	461.6	8.9	42.6	39.3	0.9
1958	2,205.1	1,685.5	1,450.3	552.1	525.9	89.6	168.5	114.3	196.3	0.5	195.8	519.6	483.1	437.6	10.8	36.5	33.1	1.2
1959	2,311.0	1,788.5	1,543.6	579.3	562.6	95.7	185.3	120.7	203.1	0.6	202.5	522.5	469.9	416.5	15.0	52.6	47.1	1.1
1960	2,530.9	1,949.0	1,685.9	649.9	212.6[g]	492.3[g]	200.8	130.3	212.5	0.8	211.7	581.8	528.4	464.0	16.5	53.5	49.5	0.9
1961	2,701.2	2,090.9	1,807.7	696.7	227.9	527.2	216.3	139.7	221.5	0.8	220.6	610.3	565.4	490.9	18.2	44.9	39.5	1.0
1962	3,000.2	2,268.1	1,968.5	747.4	248.5	581.1	240.2	151.4	231.7	1.0	230.7	732.0	678.3	599.8	18.1	53.8	48.3	1.0
1963	3,303.7	2,491.8	2,164.4	831.3	265.6	640.3	268.2	159.0	245.6	1.0	244.5	811.9	740.6	640.9	22.7	71.3	63.8	0.4
1964	3,730.7	2,772.2	2,419.8	923.1	286.7	734.6	297.7	177.8	263.0	1.1	261.8	958.5	893.4	771.7	28.3	65.1	57.5	0.7
1965	4,214.2	2,994.2	2,617.9	991.2	311.5	790.2	325.6	199.5	278.0	1.3	276.7	1,220.0	1,145.6	1,001.6	35.4	74.4	67.9	0.5
1966	4,690.4	3,394.2	2,973.7	1,131.5	339.6	919.0	370.4	213.2	293.5	1.4	292.2	1,296.3	1,193.8	1,056.3	33.3	102.4	95.4	1.2
1967	5,151.3	3,742.9	3,307.5	1,266.1	380.6	1,007.0	418.5	235.4	302.5	1.5	301.0	1,408.3	1,305.8	1,139.6	33.4	102.5	91.3	1.5
1968	5,637.9	4,100.5	3,643.2	1,323.4	295.5[h]	1,293.8[h]	472.1	258.4	312.4	1.7	310.7	1,537.4	1,449.3	1,231.7	73.6	88.1	74.9	5.1
1969	6,029.1	4,440.3	3,935.3	1,398.0	302.4	1,405.9	525.7	303.3	342.9	4.6	338.3	1,588.9	1,482.0	1,250.4	80.8	106.8	91.3	4.9

Receipts of Local Authorities – England and Wales (£m.) (continued)

Year ended 31 March	Total	Revenue Account											Capital Account						
		Total	Rate Fund Services					Trading Services					Total	Rate fund services			Trading services		
			Total	Rates	Grants		Fees		Total	Grants	General				Total	Loans	Grants	Total	Loans	Grants
					Specific	Non-spec.	Housing	Excl. Hous.	Total	Grants	Fees	Other								
1970[i]	7,391.0	5,666.0	4,747.1	1,515.2	334.2	1,612.4	632.4	652.9	423.3	9.1	261.3	152.9	1,725.0	1,572.9	1,232.9	88.3	152.1	117.5	5.6
1971	8,336.9	6,258.5	5,430.3	1,640.5	400.0	1,878.6	712.0	799.2	412.0	5.5	233.6	172.8	2,078.4	1,892.0	1,454.6	107.0	186.4	142.8	4.2
1972	9,561.7	7,292.6	6,342.5	1,911.7	471.3	2,176.7	760.3	1,022.5	435.5	6.0	255.3	174.3	2,269.1	2,072.7	1,564.4	116.4	196.4	137.3	5.7
1973	11,058.8	8,214.8	7,395.1	2,179.6	571.4	2,557.8	904.8	1,181.5	410.1	5.8	220.5	183.8	2,844.0	2,631.6	1,986.7	124.3	212.4	163.1	5.9
1974	13,601.9	9,830.2	8,846.2	2,414.6	786.3	3,105.0	1,144.2	1,396.1	457.9	6.0	232.5	165.2	3,771.7	3,466.2	2,724.0	148.5	305.5	236.5	6.7
1975	16,557.3	12,478.4	11,554.3	2,927.2	1,256.7	4,390.0	1,381.5	1,598.9	287.4	5.0	149.3	133.0	4,078.9	3,957.7	3,325.6	136.2	121.2	82.0	3.5

a   Slight break resulting from a change in sources.
b   The inclusion of receipts from pilotage and light dues was discontinued, resulting in a fall of about 2 per cent.
c   These figures do not include loans raised by school boards outside London and the county boroughs, the amount of which was never ascertained but was probably a little over £1.0 million.
d   These unusually large figures result from the formation of the Metropolitan Water Board.
e   These unusually large figures result from the formation of the Port of London Authority.
f   Introduction of 1948 Equalisation Grant.
g   Introduction of the General and Exchequer Equalisation Grants.
h   Introduction of the Rate Support Grant.
i   Duplicate reckonings – transfers between accounts – are no longer deleted. Although this does not affect net expenditure the incomes figures are not strictly comparable to previous years.

Receipts of Local Authorities – Scotland (£m.)

Year ended 15 May	Total	Principal constituent items				
		Loans	Rates	Total Govt. grants	House rents (Fees)	Main trading services
1880	6.1	1.1	2.6	0.6	–	–
1881	6.1	1.0	2.9	0.5	–	–
1882	6.3	1.1	3.1	0.6	–	–
1883	6.2	0.9	3.1	0.6	–	–
1884	7.3	1.7	3.3	0.6	–	–
1885	7.7	2.1	3.3	0.7	–	–
1886	8.1	2.5	3.4	0.7	–	–
1887	7.5	1.8	3.4	0.7	–	–
1888	7.6ᵃ	1.8	3.5	0.8	–	–
1889	7.5	1.5	3.5	0.8	–	–
1890	7.5	1.4	3.6	1.0	–	–ᵇ
1891	8.0	1.8	3.2	1.1	–	0.5
1892	8.5	2.0	3.3ᵇ	1.3	–	0.5
1893	9.8	1.9	3.3	1.4	–	1.7
1894	10.4	2.1	3.4	1.7	–	1.7
1895	11.0	2.0	3.4	1.6	–	2.0
1896	11.1	1.9	3.7	1.6	–	2.2
1897	12.7	3.1	3.8	1.7	–	2.4
1898	12.5	2.3	3.8	1.8	–	2.6
1899	13.6	3.1	4.0	1.9	–	2.8
1900	15.2	4.1	4.2	2.0	–	3.0
1901	16.5	4.7	4.5	2.0	–	3.3
1902	16.8	4.1	4.9	2.1	–	3.7
1903	16.7	3.5	5.0	2.1	–	3.7
1904	18.2	4.4	5.3	2.3	–	3.9
1905	17.9	3.6	5.5	2.4	–	4.0
1906	18.0	3.3	5.7	2.4	–	4.4
1907	18.4	3.1	5.9	2.6	0.1	4.5
1908	19.5	3.7	6.1	2.6	0.1	4.9
1909	18.5	2.5	6.4	2.6	0.1	4.7
1910	18.8	2.2	6.6	2.8	0.1	4.9
1911	19.5	2.2	6.8	2.9	0.1	5.0
1912	20.0	2.4	7.0	3.0	0.1	5.3
1913	20.7	2.2	7.4	2.9	0.1	5.5
1914	22.3	3.0	7.7	3.0	0.1	5.9
1915	23.1	3.3	8.2	3.1	0.1	5.9
1916	22.2	1.5	8.2	3.0	0.1	6.9
1917	22.4	1.2	8.1	3.2	0.1	7.2
1918	24.3	1.1	8.5	3.5	0.1	8.1
1919	27.1	1.3	9.3	3.9	0.2	9.2

Receipts of Local Authorities – Scotland (£m.) (continued)

Year ended 15 May	Total	Principal constituent items				
		Loans	Rates	Total Govt. grants	House rents (Fees)	Main trading services
1920	40.6	4.0	13.0	8.0	0.2	11.1
1921	55.0	9.8	18.1	8.3	0.2	14.2
1922	67.0	19.2	18.4	11.0	0.3	13.6
1923	55.6	10.2	17.3	10.3	0.6	12.9
1924	54.5	7.7	17.7	10.9	0.8	13.0
1925	57.5	9.4	18.1	11.4	0.9	13.0
1926	60.9	11.6	18.6	12.1	1.0	12.9
1927	66.4	12.3	20.5	12.8	1.3	14.6
1928	71.0	14.3	21.7	13.4	1.7	14.6
1929	68.1	11.5	21.9	13.3	2.0	14.2
1930	67.8	10.5	19.4	16.1	2.4	14.4
1931	70.3	10.9	19.6[c]	19.7	2.6	12.8[c]
1932	69.3	11.8	18.1	19.7	2.8	12.4
1933	68.4	10.8	18.6	18.8	3.0	12.4
1934	69.8	10.3	19.6	18.3	3.2	12.6
1935	70.1	9.3	20.1	18.9	3.6	13.3
1936	75.0	11.3	20.5	21.0	3.6	13.3
1937	81.2	15.4	21.6	21.3	3.8	14.4
1938	84.4	17.0	21.8	21.4	4.1	15.0
1939	89.0	19.2	22.4	22.0	4.4	15.5
1940	87.4	13.1	23.5	25.1	4.7	15.8
1941	88.4	8.3	23.7[d]	27.3[d]	5.0	18.3
1942	50.9	4.7	23.9	30.6	5.1	19.8
1943	89.5	2.9	24.0	28.5	5.3	21.0
1944	90.4	3.1	24.2	27.0	5.4	22.3
1945	91.4	3.6	25.8	25.3	5.5	23.4
1946	102.8	6.7	27.8	29.5	5.4	24.3
1947	127.1	22.7	29.7	32.6	5.8	26.7
1948	148.5	32.7	32.8	38.3	6.6	27.4[e]
1949	146.9	37.0	31.2[f]	36.6	7.3	21.5[e]
1950	143.3	39.3	31.7	38.2	8.0	10.4
1951	152.2	42.5	33.3	39.9	8.7	11.0
1952	177.9	54.0	38.2	44.9	9.5	12.4
1953	210.2	70.1	46.0	48.8	10.4	14.0
1954	225.1	71.7	50.7	54.6	11.6	15.2
1955	226.6	63.9	51.2	60.6	12.8	15.4
1956	247.1	70.2	55.6	66.8	13.5	18.0
1957	261.8	63.1	64.9	74.3	14.8	18.3
1958	270.1	60.7	68.8	84.1	10.9	18.5

Receipts of Local Authorities – Scotland (£m.) (continued)

Year ended 31 March	Total	Revenue Account									Capital Account						
		Total	Rates	Rate Fund Services				Trading Services			Total	Rate fund services			Trading services		
				Grants Specific	Grants Non-spec.	Housing	Fees Excl. Hous.	Total	Grants	General Fees Other		Total	Loans	Grants	Total	Loans	Grants
1959	293.2	217.8	187.7	73.1	75.6	15.7	11.3	11.3	25.7	0.3	25.4	75.3	65.9	60.9	2.5	9.5	8.6	0.3
1960	304.4	230.5	198.2	76.9	30.3	65.7	13.7	11.6	26.4	0.5	25.8	73.9	65.9	59.5	4.3	8.0	7.5	0.2
1961	320.5	245.8	210.3	79.7	32.4	70.6	14.8	12.8	29.3	0.6	28.6	74.7	67.3	59.4	5.6	7.4	6.6	0.6
1962	360.2	270.9	236.4	94.6	34.6	77.3	16.4	13.4	28.2	0.6	27.5	89.2	78.9	72.9	3.0	10.4	8.7	0.6
1963	387.3	287.7	252.2	99.4	36.7	81.6	21.3	13.2	29.8	0.7	29.0	99.6	89.7	82.5	4.1	9.9	9.2	0.4
1964	444.4	317.8	280.0	107.9	40.8	93.4	23.4	14.5	30.2	0.9	29.2	126.7	115.5	108.6	3.8	11.1	10.6	0.4
1965	483.2	339.9	300.3	116.1	41.8	100.0	25.9	16.4	31.8	1.1	30.7	143.3	131.2	122.1	5.3	12.1	11.3	0.6
1966	530.8	373.7	330.9	126.5	45.4	110.9	29.7	18.4	34.0	1.2	32.8	157.0	143.2	132.6	5.6	13.8	12.5	0.6
1967	604.0	423.0	376.4	148.6	48.9	124.8	33.3	20.8	36.7	3.0	33.7	181.1	165.2	150.1	9.5	15.8	13.6	0.3
1968	668.9	454.7	406.0	150.9	40.5	155.5	37.1	22.0	37.1	1.3	35.8	214.2	193.1	173.3	13.3	21.0	17.9	1.6
1969	747.0	497.2	440.7	163.0	41.0	168.8	43.3	24.6	41.7	1.4	40.4	249.8	225.7	202.2	15.4	24.1	21.1	1.5
1970	809.7	561.4	500.6	177.1	48.3	194.7	52.1	28.5	44.8	1.4	43.4	248.3	221.5	203.2	10.5	26.8	24.7	1.3
1971	899.1	656.4	583.8	198.3	57.9	234.4	61.6	31.7	56.7	1.7	55.0	242.7	221.0	196.0	13.9	21.8	19.9	1.3
1972	1,013.2	756.3	669.3	227.4	65.1	273.0	68.8	35.0	63.8	1.8	62.1	256.9	233.4	201.9	14.3	23.5	20.2	1.8
1973	1,163.5	867.1	770.1	240.0	86.1	318.7	84.4	40.8	72.4	1.9	70.5	296.4	274.7	232.3	20.4	21.6	18.3	2.5
1974	1,429.0	1,039.9	949.8	267.4	116.0	406.5	114.5	45.4	61.2	2.1	59.1	389.0	366.8	324.7	22.9	22.2	17.1	1.9
1975	1,802.3	1,323.0	1,215.5	304.5	160.5	564.4	129.2	56.8	74.1	2.5	71.5	479.3	456.3	406.6	28.8	23.0	12.0	2.8

a Prior to 1888, receipts from pilotage and light dues are included under this heading. Since these were not recorded separately for the different parts of the United Kingdom it is impossible to indicate the extent of the difference made by their exclusion, but it cannot have been large.

b Prior to 1891, receipts from water and gas services were included under the heading Rates.

c From 1931, water rates, which formed the bulk of the receipts of water services, were included with 'Rates' generally.

d Up to 1941, 'Government Grants etc.' includes Exchequer grants under Local Government (Scotland) Acts and compensation for loss of rates due to the derating provisions of the Acts of 1929. After 1941 these amounts are included under 'Rates'.

e Owing to legislative changes, gas and electricity disappear in the years 1949–50.

f From 1949, this heading includes payments in lieu of rates made by the British Transport Commission, British Electricity Authority (later South of Scotland Electricity Board), and the North of Scotland Hydro-Electric Board.

6 History of Rates

The UK locally determined property tax has its own name. It is not called a tax, but the rates. So accepted is this usage that most of us can be forgiven for supposing that rates are and always were synonymous with this local property tax. There is more than one rate as every household is rated by more than one body. Not all spending authorities have the power to levy rates. Those that do not have such powers receive their income by precepting – requiring some other authority to collect rates for them. In England and Wales higher-tier authorities (shire counties and metropolitan counties) precept on lower-tier authorities (shire districts and metropolitan districts), except that parishes – a lower tier – precept on the districts – a higher tier. Water authorities can rate directly, and in some places there are peculiar survivals, such as commons rates. (In Scotland, the actual arrangements differ, but there is similar precepting.) But almost without exception all the rates have the same property tax base – called rateable value, which is an assessment of the value of the property, and are all levied by assessing a rate poundage which is a proportion of such rateable value (quantified as so many pence in the £). Thus they are virtually all what the rest of the world would call local property taxes – on land and buildings.

This has not always been so. Cannan, writing at the end of the last century was even then able to say that popularly rates were another name for local taxes (1927, p. 4). But then and in the not so distant past there were many more kinds of rates. There had been highway rates, improvement rates, poor rates, school rates, bridge rates, indeed an almost limitless variety, even – it is illuminating to recall – households paid for their gas and electricity through what were called gas rates and electricity rates. Some of these were rates on the same property base. Others, as we shall see, were not.

Though there was a multitude of different rates when Cannan wrote, he pointed out that there was a pattern. Two principles of payment had warred from the earliest times in determining the form of rates in Britain.

There was one ancient tradition which had become especially enshrined in the poor rate which based payment on 'ability to pay'. During the nineteenth century, most other rates were assimilated to this form so that it has become normal to base rates on this principle. It is its triumph that explains the uniformity of the rate base today.

But there was another tradition which by the end of the nineteenth century had become limited in its application to the water and sewerage rate and to some rating for improvement, though it had applied earlier to many other rates – for example, those for the upkeep of streets, highways, and bridges, and of the police. This second principle related payment to benefit received by the household or other entity – hereditament is the legal term – rated. It has now virtually died out except for industrial users of water who are partly charged *pro rata* for consumption, and for certain improvements to property or infrastructure provided by authorities where there remains an attempt to preserve beneficial rating.

Thus historically, there were two basic rating principles – the ability to pay and the beneficial – just as we have seen there were two kinds of expenditures – the redistributive and the beneficial. Neither is this an accident. Beneficial rating and expenditure relate to the same idea: that there is expenditure incurred by a local authority which could reasonably be charged to those who derive the benefit. The connection between ability-to-pay rating and redistributive expenditure is in equity. Redistributive expenditure is expenditure deliberately incurred to benefit certain sections of the community, usually the poor. By assumption it is a cost that has to be borne by others to whom it is inevitably a burden, except in so far as they derive satisfaction from the well-being of the poor. The required revenue is therefore raised from those 'able to pay'.

Since this chapter is historical, most of it will deal with the triumphant principle; but it will be a theme of this book that there is a case for restoring the beneficial principle in local government finance. Two matters are worth some attention. How did it operate when it existed? Why did it die out? We may be able to learn something from the history of both.

The second issue to be explored in this chapter is the fluctuation that has taken place in the interpretation of what was meant by ability-to-pay taxation. A clear notion of an income tax is a comparatively recent development in public finances. Therefore, it is anachronistic to call rating on the ability-to-pay principle, as it existed at the end of the eighteenth century, an income tax. Yet, as we shall see, it is plausible to see it as an attempt to levy what was then the most desirable approximation to what we would now call an income tax.

Under the influence of Ricardo, however, there were attempts to turn rates into a pure land tax. These persisted through the nineteenth century and were nearly successful early in this. The echoes of this interpretation are still heard in the arguments for site value rating.

Finally, a third conception emerged during the nineteenth century, of rates as a tax on a limited class of capital, that is on buildings and land. Also during the nineteenth century, the number of taxes multiplied and it became relevant to ask what was the place of rates in the whole tax structure rather than to justify them on their own.

Going back over old discussions of the scope and meaning of rates is not just an historical indulgence. One can still believe it is desirable to introduce the beneficial, or charging, principle into local finance. There is still a case for local services to be financed by an income tax. There remain respectable and interesting arguments for site value rating. The growth of other capital taxation has complicated the role that rates play in the tax structure. Moreover, among the lessons of the past is the extent to which political conflict and class interest shape the development of local government finance as we know it.

BENEFICIAL RATING

The use of the benefit principle in rating means an intention to divide expenditure incurred on a service between ratepayers in relation to cost of provision for each, or the benefits received by each.

One must never forget that all the old rates were rooted in separate Acts of Parliament. In many of the earlier statutes the assessment procedures to be used are only lightly indicated. Someone was given the duty — whether the rates were "for sea defence, the rebuilding of Scarborough pier, re-edification in the northern counties, or the improvement of the Lea and the Thames" — of assessing the benefit derived by each ratepayer (Cannan, 1927, p. 50). It is hardly surprising that faced by such a time-consuming and delicate task, the assessors fell back on rules of thumb. The customary method was to assume that the benefit was proportional to the value of fixed property.

Some of the earliest discussion of local taxation was concerned with how the benefit principle should be applied. In 1250 there was a dispute in Romney Marsh over the repairs of the seawalls and watercourses protecting the lands. The decision in the case was very clear. After the walls had been measured by a group of 'twelve lawful men', they should measure all the lands and tenements subject to danger. The seawalls and watercourses were then assigned to each owner of land in proportion to the land they possessed, and it was their duty to keep that portion of the seawall in good repair. This represented a straightforward use of the benefit principle of taxation. Though in the case of Romney Marsh the quantity of land was the proxy used to determine benefits, this was soon modified. In a case in 1287 extending the judgement laid down in Romney Marsh, repairs were apportioned in proportion to the quantity and value of the lands (ibid., p. 11).

In the years to come, the benefit principle was followed in those cases where benefits could be reasonably attributed to particular ratepayers. Rates for sea defence followed the principle set down in Romney Marsh. An Act in 1566 'for preservation of grain' enacted that the money to be paid as a reward for the destruction of birds and vermin was to be raised in proportion to lands possessed in the area. In 1605 an Act for 'clearing the passage by water from London to and beyond the city of Oxford' clearly specified that it was only those who benefited who should contribute to the costs in proportion to the benefits received. The charges were initially allocated among all the counties en route, and the city of Oxford. Eighteen years later the Act was repealed and replaced by one which made the inhabitants of Oxford fully liable for the costs on the grounds that 'the principle benefit thereof will rebound immediately to the university and the city of Oxford' (ibid., p. 48).

But there were other practices to achieve this principle. For example, an Act of 1690 was typical in requiring that the cost of repairing paved streets should be recouped at the expense of, or undertaken by, each 'householders' inhabitants' in respect of the part of the street in front of his house 'as far as the middle of the channel' — the sewer or drain then commonly being in the middle of the street where it existed (ibid., pp. 126–7).

Another application of the benefit principle is exemplified by an Act of 1662 for London and Westminster which allowed commissioners to pull all the houses down on one side of a street:

> Whereas the houses that shall remain standing on the other side of the said street or streets, or behind the said houses that shall be so pulled down as

aforesaid, will receive much advantage in the value of their rents by the liberty of air and free recourse for trade and other conveniences by such enlargement, it is also enacted . . . that in case of refusal or incapacity . . . of the owners and occupiers of the said houses to agree and compound with the commissioners for the same, thereupon a jury shall and may be empannelled . . . to judge and assess upon the owners and occupiers of such houses such competent sum or sums of money or annual rent in consideration of such improvement and renovation, as in reason and good conscience they shall judge and think fit. (ibid., p. 125)

As Cannan points out, this was a form of betterment levy and can again be paralleled in other legislation. Such connections between expenditure and changes in property values were often the justification for using fixed property as the tax base. Many of the benefits — particularly those from capital expenditure on water supply, sewerage, highways, bridges and on electricity and gas mains — will be reflected in rising land values and could, therefore, be taxed on investment principles. It was, therefore, felt that the benefit principle in such circumstances could best be approximated by rating changes in property values.

The benefit principle decayed for a number of reasons. One already mentioned was the practical difficulty of making exact and not-too-contentious estimates of benefits received at a period when the techniques for doing so were rudimentary, especially when most of the officers required to do this were unpaid, undertaking the duty by rote and themselves ratepayers. It is not difficult to see how such hazardous assessment as required, for example, by the Act of 1662, mentioned earlier, was fruitful of conflict and shaded into using a fixed property rate as a rule of thumb. Such assessment becomes especially difficult for expenditures which have public-goods characteristics.

Recognition that much local beneficial expenditures have characteristics of what we now call non-excludability and non-rivalness became explicit towards the end of the nineteenth century.

A second reason for the decay of the benefit principle was more understandable than defensible, since it was founded in administrative convenience. A multiplicity of types of assessments was both confusing to the ratepayer and more liable to local manipulation, often of a corrupt nature. Hence there was a growing tendency to assimilate one rate to another during the eighteenth and nineteenth centuries. As early as 1633, the Lord Chief Justice directed that where there was doubt and the statute gave no clear direction — as was often the case in early statutes — 'it is good discretion to go according to the rate of taxation for the poor' (ibid., p. 109). Gradually this example was copied and eventually made the Poor Law method of assessment triumphant.

But though administrative tidiness was useful, and the other reasons we have mentioned helpful, assimilation would have been less likely if it had not been possible to argue, as Cannan did as late as 1927, that 'it happens in practice that the nearest approximation to ability and to benefit are one and the same thing, namely the rating of person in respect of fixed property in the district' (p. 159). He upheld this by stating that the cost of providing services was 'roughly proportional to the value of the property'. This was of doubtful validity when he wrote, but there are almost no services, even those most ordinarily considered as beneficial, of which this can be said now. The value of property, even in so far as it is related to size, is an utterly inadequate guide to the amount of refuse a building will produce, to the cleansing of streets and pavements it will induce, or to its use of recreation facilities, let alone libraries or schools. Cannan's equation, if we may call it so, is a most convenient fiction but it simply is not true.

This was recognised by the Allen Committee who treated the lack of relation of rates paid to benefits received as so obvious that it did not need to be demonstrated (Ministry of Housing, 1965, Cmnd. 2582, ch. 3)[1]. But instead of pursuing the matter, the Allen Committee accepted a proposition put by the Association of Municipal Corporations which while it saved argument, defeated reason. The Association told the Committee that 'the justification for any form of local tax is that the residents of an area derive benefits from the spending of money. These benefits do not have to be direct' (ibid., p. 17). Against the specific objection of why people without children should pay for the education of other people's children, it observed that 'no man is an island'. The Association maintained that a modern community could not exist unless children were adequately educated and the general population was maintained in adequate health. The Allen Committee itself went somewhat further in defining and accepting this notion:

> The essence of local government is that it provides services, such as law and order, the benefits of which are indivisible by their very nature. Any charge for these services must be arbitrary and also compulsory, that is, a tax. Although the benefits of many present-day services, particularly the social services which have been developed so notably since the First World War, can be ascribed in a rough and ready way to particular groups and individuals it is widely accepted that such services should be heavily subsidised. (ibid., p. 17)

What, of course, this is saying is that local government finance has or even should abandon the benefit principle altogether. To give still more precision to the notion, it appears that while it is admitted that not all local services have the characteristic of a pure local public good, it is being suggested that the package put forward by a local authority should be regarded as a pure local distributive public good, its redistributive implications being sanctioned by consensus. Now, as a matter of fact, it is not possible to argue that all local services are non-rival and non-excludable. Neither can we be sure that it is the intention of Parliament that all services should be redistributive and that therefore the ability-to-pay principle is appropriate. However, both genuine and emotive non-excludability were reasons why in many cases benefit rating was replaced by ability-to-pay rates.

The elimination of the benefit principle from the rating system was slow and gradual. It was long common to levy street rates at a lower rate on houses in courts than on those fronting a street, while, contrary to recent practice which has caused such outcry, places that were not supplied with water or whose roads were not lit were exempt from lighting and water rates as deriving no benefit

(Cannan, 1927, p. 130). The 1833 Lighting and Watching Act modified the principle of the property tax by providing that houses and buildings should pay a rate three times greater than land because the benefits were greater (Goschen, 1872, pp. 101–2). Water rates were once levied on a percentage that declined with rateable value, on the argument that the consumption of water did not normally rise proportional to rateable value but at a lower rate (Cannan, 1927, p. 166). For many years, woods and forests were not rated for poor relief, though they were for highways on the grounds that their existence did give rise to extra highway costs but did not create paupers. Until very recently, the derating of empty property could be rationalised for the reason that no services are provided to them and no benefit accrues to owner or occupier. The rating of empty property is a very recent and clear triumph of the ability-to-pay over the benefit principle. Empty land is still not rated and this is a rare survivor of the principle. Agricultural derating was argued for, and may still be justified on the basis that agricultural land as such (as distinct from buildings) occasions no costs and derives no benefits. As the 1901 Royal Commission on Local Taxation put it:

> We consider it to be well established that in view of the character of agricultural property, the amount of the produce and profits derivable therefrom and the relative extent to which benefits accrue to the property and its occupier by reason of the expenditure incurred by the Local Authorities, it would be inequitable that rates should be paid in respect of it on the basis of its full annual value. (Cd. 638, p. 37)

If the benefit principle is to be reintroduced into local government finance it cannot be done through *ad hoc* adjustments of the rating system nor through the fiction of the Cannan equation. We cannot pretend that a property tax reflects both the benefit and ability-to-pay principles. If the principle is to be reintroduced successfully it will be through specific charges, rather than through adaptation of the rating system.

THE ABILITY-TO-PAY PRINCIPLE

RATES AS A TAX ON INCOME

Rates existed long before there were income taxes as we now know them. While we must avoid reading the precise concepts of the present into the past, the idea that some expenditures should be paid for according to financial circumstances, rather than benefits received, was well established in the fourteenth and fifteenth centuries. What most needs explaining is why the ideal of rating households according to their ability to pay comes to be reflected in a property tax.

Among the earliest rates based on ability to pay was the church rate. Until it was abolished in the nineteenth century, this had a somewhat special status. Though obligatory on all, it was paid to the Church, and to the established Church at that, a fact that proved embarrassing with the growth of dissent and eventually brought about its end. The ability-to-pay principle can be found in an Act of 1340 where it was stated that every parishioner was to contribute to the repairs of the parish church in proportion to 'the land he possesses in the parish and in proportion to the number of animals he keeps and feeds there'. In 1370 a rate to repair the roof of a parish church was raised by an assessment of 6d per carucate of land (the amount of land that could be tilled with one plough and eight oxen in a year), 1d in respect to each head of cattle, and 1d in respect to every ten sheep (Cannan, 1927, pp. 15–16).

Christian charity also dictated that poor relief should be paid for by greater contributions by the rich than the poor. Cannan (ibid., p. 50) refers as well to other rates being based on this principle from early times – those for building jails, paying Members of Parliament, reimbursing persons robbed on the highway, relieving persons suffering from the plague and conveying malefactors to jail. Again one must not forget that innumerable statutes meant almost limitless variation in local practice. For example, in a royal letter of 1387 ordering that the wall of Chichester be repaired, people are ordered to contribute to the costs 'according to their ability and possessions, privileged persons, the sick and mendicant poor excepted' (ibid., p. 17).

The earliest assessment methods were informal and personal. Some parishioners would be given the task of estimating the income and wealth of their fellow parishioners. One can see the process at work in the regulations of the Common Council of the City of London in 1587 which directed that

> the lord mayor and such as be thereunto authorised by the statutes will sit again and peruse the books of taxation for the poor, that by the assessing of such as be come in place since the last assessment and were not assessed before, and by advancing such as God hath further blessed with ability, and with reasonable consideration of such as be less able, the book may be renewed and made as beneficial as reasonably may be for the poor. (Quoted by Cannan, 1927, p. 79)

Often enough expenses, as well as income and wealth, were taken into account when assessments were made. Remarkably, in a few places this kind of interrogation survived into the nineteenth century. In Whitechapel in 1823 it was stated categorically that assessment was 'without respect to [property] value but according to the ability of the party charged, such ability being estimated with reference to property whether in the parish or out of it' (quoted by Cannan, 1927, p. 79).

Ironically, rating became a property tax in order to become a fairer and more effective income tax.[2] Local initiative brought this about in many parishes. It is hardly surprising that informal and personal assessments were unpopular and contentious with both the assessed and the unpaid assessors who were also ratepayers and rotated in office. Central government began to intervene in the sixteenth century when troops of sturdy poor, beggars and vagabonds evicted from one parish tried descending on more generous ones leading to repeated attempts to 'nationalise' the Poor Law, that is to ensure sufficiently similar obligation to help the poor in each parish to discourage movements of poor from one place to another. A succession of statutes refined and unified the basis of assessment, culminating in the great Elizabethan Poor Law of 1601, which however left the question of assessment still unclear. It took over two centuries to establish the principle that rates should no longer be assessed by neighbours acquainted with the ratepayers' ability but should be based on the annual value of land and buildings occupied.

Quite early some parishes rated stock in trade. During the eighteenth century Acts were passed which enlarged the number of items on which rates should be levied. In 1711 an Act for the establishment of a workhouse for the parishes of Norwich proposed a rate on 'all persons having and using stocks and personal estates or having money out at interest in equal proportion as near as may be according to their several and respective values and estates' (Cannan, 1927, p. 89). However, by the end of the eighteenth century after various cases and litigations it was more or less established that salaries, money in coin and in real securities were not rateable but that ships and stock in trade were. The rating of stock in trade posed so many problems and raised so much opposition that an Act in 1840 explicitly excluded it from rating. Thus by the end of the nineteenth century a tax which was to be levied according to the ability-to-pay principle became a tax on immovable property only.

Throughout there were two underlying tendencies. The first was to assimilate other rates to the Poor Law ability-to-pay model. We have seen the various reasons why this overtook beneficial rates. The justices were requiring assimilation in the early seventeenth century for various minor rates. Both local complaints and the practice of the courts gradually brought about the assimilation of other ability-to-pay rates to the model of the Poor Law — recorded in detail by Cannan — so that by the mid-nineteenth century it was virtually complete except for a residue of beneficial rates or charges. Thus it was natural that the new rates of the nineteenth century — the police rates and the school rate — should also conform to the model of the poor rate.

The second tendency was for the poor rate itself to progress from a locally and informally assessed 'income' tax to the property tax we know today. The changes that took place were to make it easier for the courts to cope with litigation by establishing some tentative uniformity of assessment principle and the elimination of subjective judgement. The first change was from personal assessment of financial circumstances in the large to assessment of the rental value of property. This was followed by the derating of machinery, stock in trade and movables. Though these measures simplified the system, they were open to obvious criticisms if rates were to be used as a proxy for ability to pay. Thus when Ricardo in 1817 cast his eye over the rating system as it then existed he was critical of it as a hybrid and a muddle: 'The farmer being rated according to the actual productions he obtained, the manufacturer only according to the value of the building in which he works, without any regard to the value of the machinery, labour or stock which he may employ' (Ricardo, 1962, p. 260). Not only was this unfair, but it would lead to a distortion in the allocation of capital from agriculture to manufacturing because the heavier burden of rates in the former depressed the return on capital there, relative to that obtainable in manufacturing and commerce.

There were, however, other defects of rates as an income tax. While it taxed income from property and land, even in this it was not entirely satisfactory; whether a ratepayer owns or rents his house can make a substantial difference to his effective income but not his rate burden. English law remained very confused as to whether the owner or the occupier was being rated and what were the implications of the distinction. The earnings of labour as such were never taxed through the rates which was early thought to give an unfair advantage to professional men. It did not seem too important until the nineteenth century — when their numbers were no longer small. The earnings of the poor except in so far as they were householders were, of course, exempt.

Quite another kind of problem has still not been solved satisfactorily even by the more recent proposals for a local income tax put to, and by, the Layfield Committee. It was an endless source of discord until the end of the eighteenth century and the law changed its mind. Should someone who had property in more than one place be rated in both places according to his total financial circumstances or only his local property? If the latter, how should the exclusion be made? If the answer seems obvious in a rating system, it is not so long as rates are seen as a local income tax. A parish with one wealthy squire will feel aggrieved if they see him living very richly, but are only able to rate him on the property he possesses in the one parish — which may in some cases be relatively small. Or take the case of a wealthy man who lives in a comparatively small house in a small town but has abundant property elsewhere. He may pay lower rates than a shopkeeper or a farmer unless, as was often the case, a parish tried to rate him on all his property, wherever it was, which itself was not only contentious but raised difficult problems of assessment at a distance. In the context of a local income tax, the question of whether income should be taxed at source or where spent is insoluble except as an act of political judgement.

During the nineteenth century the drawbacks of rates as an income or wealth tax increased. Its very improvement as a property tax made it more inequitable as an income tax. As the numbers in the professional and middle classes increased, the land-owning classes, in particular, were not slow to point out how they suffered by comparison because of the higher ratio of rated property values to their incomes. Yet even so, it is worth noting that as late as 1901 the Royal Commission on Local Taxation recalled that 'The theory which underlay the Act of Elizabeth, upon which the whole system of local rating was founded, seems to have been that the rates were to be a kind of local income tax, toward which every member of the community should contribute according to his means' (Cd. 638, p. 33). Whatever the inadequacies of rates as an income tax, the notion that it should be one persisted. One must remember that rates remained the main form of income taxation through the nineteenth century. A national income tax had been introduced by the younger William Pitt in 1799. It had only affected a tiny minority and was dropped in 1816. Sir Robert Peel reintroduced it in 1842. Successive chancellors hoped to get rid of it. It was a long time before in fact it became a permanent feature of the tax structure and longer before it was accepted as such. It remained a tax on a small proportion of the population. Perhaps the best indication of its relative unimportance, and therefore of rates as the main effective income tax, is that as late as 1913/14

£82 million was raised by rates, almost twice the yield of income tax (£44 million) (Prest, 1958, pp. 158, 182). It was not until after the First World War that the revenue from income tax exceeded that from rates. Even by 1938/9 rates yielded £215 million and income tax £336 million. By the beginning of the 1960s the yield from income tax was five times that of rates. By 1975 it has risen to seven times.

It is this relative importance of rates as an income tax which is the most important reason why there was so much political controversy over rates in the nineteenth and early twentieth centuries. This is worth some attention because of the effect it had on the rating system. During the nineteenth century there was frequent dispute between the agricultural and manufacturing interests which often turned explicitly on the various economic arguments produced by Ricardo and his successors and which underlay not only many of the overt economic issues of political controversy but also battles over parliamentary reform and other political issues of importance. The inequity of the rating system caused persistent argument about distributive justice, itself complicated by the survival of the sentiment that rates were or should be beneficial and the growth, as we shall see, of the post-Ricardian argument that rates should be converted into a land tax.

The immediate riposte to Ricardo was to point out that the heavier incidence of rates on agriculture — especially the poor rate — was some rough justice for the protection afforded the agricultural interests by the Corn Laws. Time and again the campaign that led to the repeal of the Corn Laws returned to the monopoly advantage they have conferred on landowners. Since the Corn Laws kept the price of bread high to the advantage of the landowner, it was only reasonable for the landowner to contribute most to the poor rate to relieve the poverty caused by these laws. Both manufacturing and workers' interests were able to make some common cause in the political campaign that aimed at shaking the power of the landowners which resulted in the 1832 Reform Act as well as the campaign for the repeal of the Corn Laws.

After repeal, the landowners not unnaturally turned round to demand their price.[3] From 1846 to 1849 deep agricultural depression reinforced their clamour (Rostow, 1948, ch. 2). To which, ever resourceful, those who represented the manufacturing interests replied by finding yet other privileges landowners enjoyed for which the burden of poor rates might be held to be some compensation:

the land had been granted originally for military service, commuted afterwards for the convenience of all parties into the payment of certain taxes, that the lands had changed hands with the burden of these taxes, and under proportionate deductions for the same and therefore that the landowners had no right to be asked to be relieved of this burden now become hereditary.[4]

Particularly in times of agricultural distress, the landowners returned to the attack periodically throughout the rest of the century — and the manufacturing classes found new privileges which justified the weight of rates upon the land. It died down by about 1850 to rise again in the 1860s (Perkin, 1969, p. 263), so that in his last speech in 1860, the victor of the Corn Laws said that if he had his life again he 'would take Adam Smith in hand, and I would have a league for free trade in land just as we had a league for free trade in corn' (Morley, 1903, p. 920). But, as his biographer says, Richard Cobden did not say what he meant by free trade in land. Yet others built up a campaign against entail, primogeniture, tenants' rights, on the general proposition that English tenants had fewer rights in the land than those of any European country. At the same time, landowners went on complaining of their burdens. This was the background to the first major report on the rating system by Goschen in 1870. The burden of his Report was that when one looked at the figures, landowners had comparatively little to complain about since:

(1)   the proportion of rates that were raised on land had apparently fallen from 70 per cent in 1814 to only 33 per cent in 1868;
(2)   rateable values had actually risen more than rates everywhere except in Cornwall, Monmouth and Lincoln so that rate poundages had actually fallen — and
(3)   land was taxed at a heavier rate in most European countries.

As a Liberal and a representative of the manufacturing interests, Goschen's conclusion that the burden on land should not be reduced was bitterly contested. The political battle-lines on land had been draw for the rest of the century. As agriculture declined from the 1870s under the pressure of cheap wheat from across the Atlantic, so the Conservatives returned to try to relieve the burden of rates upon the agricultural interests. But in 1874, an American, Henry George, popularised another argument of Ricardo's to justify a land tax and incidentally rates as a land tax. Inspired by this, the Liberals in the 1880s under Joseph Chamberlain renewed the efforts for land reform and argued for a land tax. It was, however the Conservatives and the landed interests that won. The Liberals' enthusiasm became channelled into a campaign for the land tax or site value rating. After a particularly severe agricultural depression, the landed interests achieved their objective with the partial derating of agriculture (by one half) in 1896 and finally by its complete derating at Churchill's insistence in 1929. In the long run it has to be said that the derating was not due to political pressure groups as much as to the economic decline of the industry. Yet repeatedly the landed interest did rely on two arguments of interest to a student of the rating system:

(1)   The beneficial argument that because relatively few services are provided for land as land, its owners derive no benefits and therefore that it should be derated. This argument was considered by the Layfield Committee (1976) but set aside as outside its terms of reference.[5]
(2)   The argument that landlords were unfairly rated in relation to ability to pay by comparison with manufacturers and those that dwelt in cities.

Against this another two arguments were offered which were as interesting for the development of the rating system.

(1) The first, as we have seen expressed by John Stuart Mill and Goschen, was that even if there were an excess burden it had become capitalised in the price the landowner or his ancestors had paid for his land so that there was no case for compensation.

(2) The second was the dawning of arguments that it was possibly more appropriate not to regard rates as an approximation to an income tax at all.

Ricardo clearly saw the poor rate as a mixed tax on property and incomes. So did Mill writing in the middle of the century, who seems to have seen rates as a form of direct taxation (except in so far as they were beneficial rates) (Mill, 1848, Bk V, Ch. 2). Like Ricardo, he did not appear to connect local rates with a land tax, though both wrote copiously on its characteristics. When the idea that rates were a form of income taxation died away is for the historian to decide. All one can conjecture is that there were two main influences. The first was the extension of the income tax to many more income classes, so that it took over the foreground as the principal form of direct-income taxation. The second was the growth of other taxes, especially during this century, which has made it possible to think of rates as performing a different function within the structure of a more complex taxation system.

Yet the idea that local government should depend on an income tax or some other tax approximating ability to pay dies hard. Where the benefit principle has no application because the services provided are redistributive or paternalistic, a prime consideration is the equity with which the tax is raised. These considerations reappeared in the various attempts that have been made to influence the rating system, so that the poor should be protected against its full force. The earliest protection of the poor was that the very poor lived in work-houses and those that were less poor lived in overcrowded property of low value. While there were a few nineteenth century Acts which exempted the poor from particular rates there was little direct manipulation in their interest until after the First World War. The earliest instrument was the manipulation of the repair allowances used to proceed from gross to net rateable values which were made relatively large on the poorest property in ways which could not easily be justified by comparative repair costs. Some statutes made the remission of rates possible where very poor households were unable to pay; but the worries persisted and were the subject of the Report of the Fitzgerald Committee completed in 1939 but not published until 1944 (Ministry of Health, 1939, pt 4).

The only action taken after the war was of a different kind – the introduction of a resources grant to help the poorest authorities. But the slow growth of local expenditure from 1938 until the 1950s, and the fact that rates remained a lower proportion of personal disposable income per head than in 1938 cushioned the effect on the poor. It was only after local expenditure began increasing rapidly from 1969 that the argument for some rate relief to the poor again became urgent. But it was not only the poor that complained. The growth of local expenditure led to the more general relief of the domestic ratepayer. In October 1965 Richard Crossman, the minister responsible, records how and why he pushed rate rebates.

I went to Cabinet this morning at 10.30 for my rate-rebate item much too free-and-easy in my mind . . . This was the first occasion on which I definitely misjudged Cabinet and did very badly. I mistakenly started by bluntly saying that politically we had lost five hundred seats in the municipal elections last March and that we should lose another five hundred if we didn't give some relief to the ratepayer and fulfil our election pledge to shift the balance of the burden from rates on to taxation. To do that on a large scale we shall first have to carry out our major reorganisation of the system of central grants to local authorities . . . The moment I finished, James Callaghan weighed in. He said he didn't agree with my political argument; there were no votes to be got out of rate rebates since the people who got the rebates wouldn't be grateful to us . . .

When Callaghan had finished, the Lord Chancellor said that the proposal was unjust, unhappy, unpopular. I realised that by talking about the elections I had upset a number of my colleagues. The Prime Minister came in quickly to put me right. He said that if it was a question merely of votes next March in the municipal elections he wouldn't consider the proposal at all, but what mattered was its social justice. So than I switched quickly into reverse and used the arguments one needs to win the support of Douglas Houghton and Willie Ross. Then Barbara [Castle] waded in and said, 'Aren't we supposed to be in favour of helping the poor and the weak? Isn't it time we did something solid for them? The rates went up last year by 10 per cent and they will be up another 10 per cent this year. How can we leave the old-age pensioner in a high-rated house to suffer in this way?' Then things began to swing my way. James Callaghan was supported by the Lord Chancellor, by Arthur Bottomley, and by virtually nobody else. Finally, George Brown said, 'Well, if we are all declaring ourselves, I must admit that I came to this meeting thinking the proposal was too complicated and not worth doing. But I fancy I have now been convinced of its social justice.' (Crossman, 1975, Vol. 1, pp. 348–9)

Crossman had two instruments in mind to effect his proposal: rate rebates and what developed into domestic rate relief. Crossman went to Wilson in December to persuade him of the advantages of the second, which had become more practical because less expensive than the first.

The first item on my list was rating and how to shift the burden to taxes. I told him I had got into a dead-end [over rate rebates] because the Chancellor just hadn't the money. I therefore proposed to de-rate the domestic ratepayer. This is my own bright idea which Crocker, my Accountant-General, has accepted as a practical proposition at last. The idea is beautifully simple. If the Chancellor can only spare me £30 million a year of rate relief I am going to make sure that every penny of that £30 million relieves the domestic rate-payer, and that is going to be done by making him a special government grant which the shopkeepers and industry don't share. I got the PM into thoroughly good humour by telling him about this idea, which he immediately liked and regards as the sort of thing a Minister is there to invent. (ibid., p. 419, see also p. 463)

While discursive, these extracts surely show that both the political and equity issues of the rating system are as much alive in the middle of the twentieth century as they were in the nineteenth. Thus while rates had become far less important as an income tax, their incidence on persons — as distinct from industry and commerce — and on poor persons in particular — has attracted greater attention as interest in the distribution of income has itself increased.

There are however, problems in considering the equity of the rating system in isolation. When rates were almost the only tax paid by a large proportion of the population, such a concern may have been justified. But as rates have fallen as a proportion of all taxes (see Part One, Appendix 1.6.1), it is arguable that the equity of rates taken on its own has no longer any special significance. What matters is the equity of the whole tax system as it falls on the individual. One of the criticisms made by opponents of Goschen in the late nineteenth century was that he failed to take into account other taxes and other sources of income (Goldschmid in Goschen 1872, pp. 141–4). Goschen had to admit that he did not have the data to attempt a complete analysis of the incidence of taxes on all classes against which to judge the fairness of rates. The Royal Commission on Local Taxation was set up in 1897 at the depth of the agricultural depression, which had already led to the first partial derating of agriculture, to see if this wider question could be answered.[6] The Commission was to establish what was the incidence of all taxes, central and local, on all the various forms of property and income; to establish whether, taken overall, the incidence of rates was no longer considered in isolation; and the transition was complete from thinking of rates as *the* income tax to seeing it as part of a complicated tax structure.

With the general spread of income and other forms of taxes, such an overall view of equity might seem even more appropriate. To say of an individual, for example, that he is taxed progressively in total but regressively in respect of rates might not seem to be a proposition of great interest. Though such a view would be convincing for any other tax, it is less so for a local tax. One of the criteria for a good tax to finance local expenditure is that it should be a local tax and that there should be a close link between the expenditure undertaken locally and the tax collected locally. The purpose of a local tax, the expenditure it is to finance, is much more specific than that of any particular national tax. For centuries, rates have been the local tax financing local expenditure. It is not surprising, therefore, that the equity of the rating system in conjunction with the expenditure they financed has been judged separately from the total national tax and expenditure system.

What does emerge from this discussion of the history of rating as a proxy for income taxation, are some of the difficulties of using rates in this way so as not to create inequities and cause conflict. As we have seen, rates were only conceived of as a proxy for local income tax because administrative procedures did not allow for the development of accurate and fair direct income-tax assessment, nationally or locally. That is no longer true. There are many examples of local income taxes in existence in the world now and the Layfield Committee has demonstrated its feasibility in Britain. Thus if what is required is a local income tax, it is arguable that one should be designed rather than any reliance placed on rating for this purpose. Rates were only conceived as a proxy for local income tax because the administrative procedures of the time did not allow for the development of an accurate and fair direct form of income-tax assessment. That is no longer true.

RATES AS A TAX ON LAND

A tax on land rent has had distinguished and influential advocates. Malthus acquired the notion from Ricardo, and transmitted the arguments to generations of Britons whom, as professor at the Imperial Staff College at Haileybury, he taught on their way to govern India. By the 1830s, his teaching had already inspired a land tax in Bengal. At home in Britain, the Ricardian tradition continued to exert some influence, but it was an inspired populariser who made a burning political issue out of the land tax. The American economist, Henry George, picked up the idea and broadcast it in his best-seller *Progress and Poverty*. It was to be the 'single tax' which would abolish poverty, return power to the people and make it possible to simplify government.[7] The enthusiasm he generated caused legislation to establish site value rating (SVR) in many cities and other units of government in Australia, New Zealand, South and other parts of British Africa, Canada, the USA, Germany and Denmark. Much more than Ricardo or any British economist, George's book was the mainspring of the vigorous campaigning for a land tax that started in Britain in the 1880s.

In 1885, the Royal Commission on the Housing of the Working Class advocated such a tax.[8] In 1889, the LCC almost promoted a private Bill to establish it in London. After several years of fiery discussion, Glasgow promoted such a Bill for Glasgow in 1896, but it did not get a second reading. A similar LCC Bill did not get its second reading in 1901; but in that year the chairman and four members of the Royal Commission on Local Taxation signed a minority report advocating site value rating.

After the Liberal Party came to office in 1906, the stage was set for the liveliest period in the history of this idea (see Jenkins, 1954, *passim*; Ensor, 1936, pp. 414, 430; and Gretton, 1922, ch. 15). In 1907, a Bill for Scotland passed the Commons, but was thrown out by the Lords. Lloyd George was himself a long-standing believer in land reform. When he became Chancellor of the Exchequer he hit upon an ingenious but perilous expedient to bypass the opposition of the landed interests in the Lords. He included it in the 1909 Budget. By tradition, finance is a Commons prerogative and the Lords pass Finance Bills automatically. They threw this one out and brought about a constitutional crisis. After two elections the Liberals worked upon George V to be ready to create enough peers to get a Liberal majority in the Upper House. But this proved unnecessary. A parliamentary Act was passed limiting the House of Lords' right to veto any Bill. At last the site value provisions of the Finance Bill were enacted. But the difficulties were not over. The landed interests were actively hostile. There were genuine problems in valuing every parcel of land to establish its liability to the new tax. Implementation of the measure was postponed by the 1911 Finance Act. Site value rating was overtaken by the war. The postwar coalition government killed it in 1920 by repealing the SVR provisions. But this was not the end. Manchester tried to get a local Bill in 1920. There was a last major chance of national legislation when the Labour Chancellor, Snowden, got SVR on to the statute book once again in 1931.[9] As in 1910, implementation had to be delayed while a committee tackled the problem of valuation, and again it was a casualty of coalition. In 1932, the Conservative partners in the National government insisted that it be dropped. The last attempt to get SVR was another London Bill in 1936, but this was also unsuccessful.

After the Second World War interest had diminished. It remains preserved in the Liberal Party manifesto. Otherwise, support has dwindled to that of a few well-organised bands of enthusiasts who keep alive some of Henry George's fervour. Generally, support for SVR has disappeared. The Report of the Sime Committee, set up by the government to look into SVR, was adverse (Ministry of Housing and Local Government, 1952). Site value rating was possible but administratively difficult. Litigation would be stimulated by the teething problems of a new system, and in the form in which they considered it – the 1936 LCC Act – it was additional to ordinary rates and not, they felt, likely to generate much extra revenue. They were also impressed by the arguments over valuation that had impeded the undertaking of the 1910 and 1931 Finance Acts commitments to SVR. The Committee was also puzzled as to how to define the land value to be taxed, given the new statutory control of planning brought about by the 1947 Town and Country Planning Act. They chose the 'restricted value' – the value conferred by the planning permission obtaining and not any additional 'hope value' which anticipated planning permission. A similar conclusion was reached by a Royal Institution of Chartered Surveyors Working Party in 1964 (RICS, 1964), and by central government in its Green Paper on local government finance in 1971 (DoE, 1971*a*, Cmnd. 4741). Finally, the Layfield Committee decided that the 'passing of the Community Land Act [in 1975] providing for development values to be realised by local authorities has now effectively removed site value rating from consideration' (Layfield, 1976, p. 171).[10]

We shall argue that this is the wrong reason for reaching what may well be a reasonable conclusion. Later, we will go more deeply into questions of the relative efficiency of different local taxes. For the moment, a much briefer treatment will do. The essence of the Ricardian case, and the economic case for a land tax, is that because land is fixed in supply, the price of land will be determined by demand which will mean that land rent will normally reflect a scarcity factor – 'unearned increment'. This may be taxed away without affecting the use to which land is put or the efficiency with which it is used. Since it has no disincentive effect, it is the perfect tax.

This economic argument has often been reinforced with a moral one. If rent is unearned increment, what right do landowners have to it? They have neither worked nor invested to gain this unearned increment. It came to them merely by virtue of possession. Many turned Ricardo's argument round on the landowner – 'lazy, luxurious, good-for-nothing man, monopolising to his own use the profit of twenty thousand acres of land' (in *Blackwood's* 1830, Vol. 28, p. 692, quoted by Perkin, 1969, p. 263). As might be expected, the argument – against Ricardo's intentions for he was a landowner as well as a stockbroker – was used in the conflict between the manufacturers and the landed interests to which we have already referred (Halévy, 1972, pp. 368–9). Later it was taken up by Henry George and by socialists. To this day, it has been a powerful element in the argument for the taxation or even the nationalisation of what are often held to be exorbitant profits or rent on land, especially those made in the process of development.

The Ricardian argument had important consequences for local government finance.

(1)   It provided the rationale of the argument which through Henry George led to the campaign for SVR. This would in its purest form replace, and in its less pure form supplement, rates as a form of taxation. Indeed, local authorities outside Britain do rely on a land tax for their revenue, and this because of Ricardo's arguments, working through Henry George, whose influence was profound.

(2)   It also gives a rationale within the rating system to that part of rates which falls on land (but not buildings). Towards the end of the nineteenth century, this became increasingly important in discussions of local finance and provides an alternative rationale to that of the ability-to-pay criterion in its income-tax form. In so far as it is a land tax, it does not matter whether rates are progressive or regressive in relation to income. Instead, they are seen as a tax on unearned increment, an increment not created by the effort of the owner – who can perfectly well be an absentee – but by society, as it became common to say. The exclusive taxation of unearned increment as it appeared in land values can be justified by its infrequency or impermanence elsewhere. To find other commodities of similar scarcity to earn long-standing rent, the textbooks have to resort to Rembrandts and other works of art which are similarly non-reproducible and whose value equally depends on demand; or to rare minerals similarly limited in supply and whose economic rent may also be taxed.

RATES AS A TAX ON BUILDING

In the next part we will go deeply into the analysis of rates as a tax on building, as indeed on land. While economists have long recognised that rates are a tax on building, since they discourage it by raising its price, this has always seemed a side-effect of property taxation, not its intention.

Nevertheless some analysts have not unreasonably seen rates primarily as a tax on building (notably Netzer, 1966, ch. 3).

Seen purely as a tax on buildings, rates are at a high rate compared with the generality of excise (though not by comparison with taxes on drink, tobacco or vehicle fuel). On rather arbitrary assumptions (which include assuming that the imputed net income stream from a dwelling is 5 per cent of its sales value, and that any difference between real and money interest rates will be reflected in money capital appreciation) it is far from unlikely that rates will be a 100 per cent excise tax on annual housing costs (net of maintenance and depreciation). This is far higher than VAT rates on other commodities.

But if we regard rates as a tax on building, subsidies must not be forgotten. Local authority tenants benefit from housing subsidies, the mortgagee from interest relief, the tenant from rent control. The advantage of the last we cannot quantify, but we can compare rate payments with average subsidy value for two years, as the Layfield Committee commissioned a special extract from the *Family Expenditure Survey*. Thus it would appear that viewed in this light alone, subsidy can be seen as a substantial offset against rates for those who receive subsidy. But there is no planned relation between the two.

Table 1.6.1. *Rates and Subsidies paid and received*

Range of gross household income	Rate payments	Average subsidy or tax relief
(£)	(£)	(£)
Under 1,000	162	59
1,000–1,999	416	84
2,000–2,999	736	102
3,000–3,999	815	129
4,000 or over	882	205

Note: Rate payments relate to head of household and wife's income. Average subsidy and tax relief to gross household income. As a result the income bands for the two columns are only approximately equal.

Source: Local Government Finance (Layfield, 1976), p. 431, table 37; *Housing Policy Review Report* (DoE, 1977a), pt I, p. 221, table IV. 34.

Where does this analysis leave us? We have different ways of regarding rates — as an approximation to

(1)   benefit charging;
(2)   an income tax;
(3)   a land tax;
(4)   a tax on buildings.

In the history of ideas we can see how these notions succeeded and overlapped each other, many being important in defining political controversies in their day. But it is reasonable to ask how one can decide which of these rates are. Is it merely a matter of opinion or political choice? No politician, no statute, has said what kind of a tax rates are meant to be, and only analysis can tell us what kind of tax they really are. There is an element of choice in deciding how local expenditure should be financed from taxation. Respectable appeals to intuition can be made for financing local expenditure on the benefit principle, from a tax (progressive) related to income and from one on unearned increment. Given their imperfection and other taxes that exist, there is less immediate rational appeal in a tax on buildings. History will not, however, tell us which of these taxes rates really are. This is a question we shall pursue in Part Two.

CONCLUSIONS

(1)   The distinction between the beneficial and the ability-to-pay principle is very old, and reflects two approaches. The first would raise rates from households

as far as possible proportionally and not exceeding the benefits received. The second broadly seeks an acceptable way for the rich to contribute proportionally more for the benefit of the poor. The beneficial tradition had largely died by the end of the last century, mostly because given the administrative techniques of the seventeenth to eighteenth centuries it was difficult to relate costs to benefits, because of some of the dawning implications of what later became public-goods theory, and because a tax related to value of property became widely accepted as a measure of benefit, as well as of ability to pay. Even so, the beneficial principle is an important one and re-examination of its application will be a major thrust of this book. There is a logical correspondence between beneficial expenditure and beneficial rating on the one hand, and between redistributive expenditure and ability-to-pay rating.

(2) The ability-to-pay principle triumphed. From earliest times until late in the nineteenth century, rates were regarded as a tax on the financial circumstances of the ratepayer. Again, given the administrative techniques available, rates developed into a tax on property in the eighteenth century as the fairest method of achieving an income tax. But by the end of the eighteenth century, the properties of rates as an income tax, as it had then developed, were becoming strongly criticised — for example by Ricardo. Throughout the nineteenth century, there were conflicts between the landed and the manufacturing interests — the former seeing it as an income tax bearing particularly heavily on land, the latter finding reasons for disbelieving this. The contribution of the 1901 Royal Commission is that it tried and failed to establish the equity of rates in the context of the whole tax structure. The tradition of judging local taxes as they approximate to an income tax survives and was a major theme of the Layfield Report. In the past, and currently, it has been responsible for most of the worry about the regressiveness of rates.

(3) Another rationale of rates developed from Ricardo's argument on the economic case for taxing the pure economic rent component of land values. Logically this built up into the case for a pure land tax — SVR. But that it was, in part, a tax on unearned increment became a partial justification of rates in so far as it was a land tax. This was important for discussions of the incidence of rates. Now that there are other land taxes these complicate the place given to rates in the tax structure.

(4) If rates are not to be seen as a proxy for an income tax and only part is a land tax, the remainder is either an excise tax on buildings and improvements or conceivably beneficial payments. In Britain, there has certainly never been any political intention to put on a tax to discourage building and improvements. This is an inadvertent result of the ancient form of rates. It is now less likely to have an effect on the efficient allocation of resources because of the growth of indirect taxes, especially VAT, on other commodities — though as far as can be judged regarded purely as an excise tax, rates on buildings are at a substantially higher rate than VAT is currently on other goods and commodities.

(5)   However, the incidence of rates like that of other taxes is not a matter of opinion – whatever legislatures may say – but in principle of fact.

NOTES

1   Similar arguments are to be found in Ilersic (1965, pp. 9, 10) and Hepworth (1976, pp. 79–80).
2   This was the start of a long process to make assessment fairer by making it more uniform. Once a property base replaced subjective judgement, it was the assessment that came under progressive scrutiny, culminating in the transfer of assessment to the Inland Revenue, which, as will appear, has still not made assessment fair.
3   Disraeli in 1849 tried to argue for the transfer of some of the burden to national taxation, coupled with the suggestion that there might be a grant system to achieve what he called 'equalisation' of rates. However, he was firmly put in his place by his Tory leader, Stanley, who observed that though it might be popular in Buckinghamshire, Disraeli's home, where rates were high, it would not be in Lancashire – Stanley's – where rates were low. Blake (1966, p. 290).
4   Hume in the debate on Disraeli's motion of 1 March 1849 (8 March 1849. *Hansard*, Vol. 103, 3rd series, p. 454). The argument that landlords deserve no compensation was used by Mill in 1848 (Mill, 1852 edn, Vol. 2, p. 384). Mill was quoted by Goschen (1872, p. 148).
5   It argued that beneficial rating was not rating but charging (Layfield, 1976, pp. 164–5).
6   The Royal Commission's questions to this end are printed in Marshall (1926, pp. 329–31) and are followed by Marshall's answers.
7   Whether the revenue should be local or central was for him a matter of detail (George, 1886, p. 621). George himself was not interested in detail or problems of implementation. He was a preacher and, he hoped, a prophet.
8   On the history of SVR see Long (1939).
9   'The main feature of the 1931 Budget was to set up a valuation committee to plan a SVR on land at 1d in the £' (Skidelsky, 1976, p. 307).
10   It was also dismissed rather summarily in the DoE Green Paper on local government finance (1971a, Cmnd. 4741).

Appendix 1.6.A1   Yield of Income Tax and Rates

Year	(A) Net Income Tax yield (£m.)	(B) Rate Income (£m.)	A/B	(C) Total domestic Rate bill (£m.)	A/C
1880	9.2	25.1	0.37	—	—
1890	12.8	31.3	0.41	—	—
1900	18.8	44.9	0.42	—	—
1910	37.7	69.9	0.54	—	—
1920	336.6	118.6	2.84	—	—
1930	234.0	175.7	1.33	—	—
1939	330.8	213.8	1.55	—	—
1946	1,361.3	248.7	5.47	—	—
1950	1,438.4	310.8	4.63	—	—
1955	1,873.5	440.6	4.25	—	—
1960	2,215.5	721.2	3.07	—	—
1964	2,750.4	1,024.7	2.68	—	—
1966	3,682.5	1,250.9	2.94	473	7.79
1968	3,819.1	1,502.0	2.54	655	5.83
1970	4,907.3	1,772.4	2.77	747	6.57
1972	6,432.3	2,274.6	2.83	996	6.46
1973	6,477.0	2,572.5	2.52	1,109	5.84
1974	7,136.6	2,930.0	2.44	1,323	5.39
1975	10,270.9	3,223.0	3.19	*	*
1976	15,040.8	4,073.0	3.69	*	*

Notes: (A) Relates to the United Kingdom. (B) and (C) Relate to Great Britain.
Years relate to financial years (1970 = 1969/70).

Sources: (A) and (B): 1880 to 1939 – Mitchell and Deane (1962), tables 9, 12 and 16: 'Public Finance'.

(A): 1946 to 1976 – Central Statistical Office, *Financial Statistics* and *Monthly Digest of Statistics*, monthly series.

(B and C): 1946 to 1976 – Ministry of Housing and Local Government, later the Department of the Environment, *Rates and Rateable Values for England and Wales*; and Scottish Office, *Rates and Rateable Values for Scotland*.

*   Data not available.

7 Grants

1835 to 1929

The first grant to a whole class of local authorities was introduced in 1835. It covered the cost of removal of prisoners to their place of trial, and 50 per cent of the cost of prosecutions at assizes and quarter sessions. For the next thirty years, police and the administration of justice were the main grant-aided services. By the end of the century, all major local government services, including health, education, welfare and highways, were grant-aided. Within each major category of grants, there were minor ones for particular services. To take one of the more bizarre examples: in 1888 the following grants were available in schools: a fixed grant based on average attendance, a special-merit grant in three categories of merit (fair, good and excellent), a grant for singing by ear, and one for singing by note (the latter worth twice as much per head as the former). There was a special grant for needlework (only for girls), and one for cookery (worth four times that for needlework) (Chester, 1951, p. 170). The grants multiplied and acquired a life of their own. In 1842, grants amounted to just under £½ million, by the end of the century the figure had risen to just under £20 million.

The variety and complexity of grants continued to increase. By 1918, there were some 57 separate grants in education alone (17 in elementary and 40 in higher education). They were calculated on ten different bases or combinations of bases and related to seven different periods (ibid., p. 170). An attempt to describe the system of grant distribution in 1901 concluded that 'It is not easy to explain the anomalies of the present system, or rather systems of allocation. Perhaps it is not too much to say that it may not have lasted so long as it has if its obscurity and complexity had not made it almost impossible for the public to follow' (Royal Commission on Local Government, 1901, Cd. 638, p. 115). It was not just the public who were confused. In 1912, Sidney Webb, whose outstanding ability to unearth the most esoteric information is surely attested by his work on local government, tried to analyse the methods of grant distribution. His conclusion was: 'How exactly the grants are allocated among the different local authorities seems past all finding out' (1920 edn., p. 7) and after making a brave effort to examine the method of distribution of the education grant he ends candidly, 'I hope that I have got all these complications right, but it is impossible to be sure' (ibid., p. 77).

By 1928 there existed an immense variety of grants distributed on the basis of many different rules. The whole field of grants, described by Webb in 1912 as 'a chaos which practically no one understands' had if anything become even more chaotic. Moreover, the total grant paid out had become very large. In 1928 it amounted to £110 million, nearly 16 per cent of total central government tax revenue.

Though the century or so between the first grant and the 1929 Reform Act had ended in a chaotic grant structure this was not due to any lack of understanding of the issues involved. On the contrary, it was during this period that some of the best analyses of grant structures were developed, applied by Royal Commissions, and recommended by them. Moreover, the issues were not specific to that century. Many were not resolved until the major reforms of 1948 and 1958, some are still with us today, and in some areas there is a regression to the chaos of the earlier period.

Three themes dominated the discussions of grants during this first hundred years. The first theme was that of control. In the first forty years, up to about 1870, grants were considered as a means by which the central government could encourage the voluntary services provided by local authorities. As these services became compulsory, grants could be used to control how they were performed. Robert Peel's justification for the amendments to the financing of Poor Law authorities was that:

> there have been frequently, just grounds of complaint in respect of the administration of medical relief, and for the purpose of meeting the view of those who object to the present system and for the purpose of giving the Executive government *a greater degree of control over it* and gradually introducing an amended system we propose to take one half of the charge of the payment of Medical Officers upon the Treasury.

Similarly, with regard to the education provided by the Poor Law authorities he said 'We require qualifications, we require a right of dismissal and the right of inspection' (quoted in Finer, 1950, pp. 454–5, our italics). This concern with control led naturally to a proliferation of detailed grants.

The second theme was that of how the growing burden of local government spending should be shared between ratepayers and central government grant. Property owners were not the only ones becoming worried by the growth of local government spending in this period. Chancellors of the Exchequer and others concerned with central government finance became equally worried about the increasing proportion of national tax revenues absorbed by local government grants. The idea of assigned revenues (see Part One, Chapter 5) gave a brief illusion that the problem could be solved by placing part of the burden directly on to the general taxpayer. But the introduction of assigned revenues raised the question of how they should be distributed between local authorities, which raises the third theme of our discussion. What is the equitable distribution of grants between local authorities?

By 1887, just before the Goschen reforms, nearly all the grants paid to local authorities were on a percentage basis. There were, however, some exceptions. One was the education grant, which had two interesting features. First, it was a unit grant, based on average daily attendance. Second, it had a provision toward equalisation; where the yield of a 3d rate was less than £20 or less than 7s 6d per child an additional deficiency grant was given. Although the rate deficiency part of the grant was of very minor importance in the early period, accounting for only about $\frac{1}{2}$ per cent of the education grant in 1891, it was the first expression of the concept of equalisation. By 1911 it accounted for nearly 25 per cent of the elementary school grant. Thus the education grant which by 1903 represented over 50 per cent of total grants given to local authorities, was a unit grant with a rateable value deficiency provision.

The Goschen reforms of 1887 scrapped all the specific grants except the education grant, which at that time accounted for about a quarter ot the grants received by local authorities. In their place was substituted the assigned revenue system. The grant to be distributed came from the collection of certain excise taxes and probate duties. In the initial discussions on how to distribute the assigned revenues the government considered three possibilities: rateable value, population and indoor pauperism. Rateable value was rejected because the largest amount would go to the richest districts, population was rejected on similar grounds, because the larger population might also be the most prosperous, so indoor pauperism was the method chosen for submission to the House of Commons. The initial proposal was thus to distribute the grant according to some measure of need. However, this proposal was subsequently withdrawn. The reason was that indoor pauperism was not judged a good measure of needs, because there were many authorities which gave relief to the poor outside the work-house. These authorities would be penalised if the measure of need took account only of indoor paupers. This problem of finding the correct or acceptable indicator of needs has bedevilled block grant distribution ever since. Sooner or later all the needs formulae evoked a tension which led to their demise. Even the most successful one, the 1958 formula slightly modified in 1966, only lasted for about fifteen years.

Going back to 1888, the rejection of an acceptable-needs criterion led to the adoption of a system of distribution (see below) which, in the words of Mr Ritchie introducing the Bill in Parliament, would be to 'stereotype a condition of things which had never been regarded as embodying any principle of abstract justice' (Royal Commission on Local Government, 1901, Cd. 638, p. 116).

Two different methods of distributing the assigned revenues were adopted. The licence duties were distributed among the authorities in the same proportion in which they were collected. They thus became a local tax with the central government setting a uniform rate of tax and acting as tax collector. The probate duties, and later the surtaxes on beer and spirits, were distributed in the same proportion as the total grants in aid received by the authorities in the period preceding the Goschen reforms, namely 1887–8.

Both these methods of distributing the assigned revenues were strongly criticised by the Minority Report[1] of the 1901 Royal Commission. The distribution of the probate duties was criticised on the obvious grounds that it froze a particular distribution at a point of time. Even if the distribution at that point of time, 1887, was in some sense equitable, it would hardly remain so for ever more.

The criticism of the distribution of the licence duties is more interesting. The Minority Report argued that

the districts in which licences are numerous are (roughly speaking) those which happened to be prosperous and well to do in the days when licences were freely granted. Generally speaking also, though this is not invariably true, a prosperous district is likely to have a larger yield from licence duties than a very poor district. In any case, the product of licences is fortuitous and quite independent of the real needs of a locality and its ability to meet them. (Cd. 638, p. 117)

The Minority Report was making two points. First, that there was generally a relationship between the new tax base, namely the licence duties, and the existing tax base, rateable value. Second, that there might not be a relationship between the size of the new tax base and the needs of the authority. If the assigned revenues did not effectively compensate authorities for differences in their spending needs or in their taxable resources, the resultant burden on the rate-payer could vary greatly between different authorities. From their analysis of onerous expenditures the authors of the Minority Report had concluded that individuals with the same ability to pay living in different localities should pay the same taxes (see Part One, Chapter 3). Hence the concept of equalisation. They developed a scheme of distributing the grant among local authorities which took account of the needs of the authorities and their resources. This is obviously consistent with the principles they had laid down for the financing of onerous expenditures.

Inevitably, a thorough discussion of grants entails an examination of the different grant formulae that have been proposed or used.

Lord Balfour's formula was as follows.[2] We take a particular service, say the Poor Law services, and find what is the lowest expenditure per head of population on that service in any local authority. Call this the standard expenditure for that service (he did not use this terminology) and label it e_s. Choose some rate poundage, such that in the authority with the highest rateable value per head, levying that rate poundage would just yield the standard expenditure times their population. Call this r_s, the standard rate poundage. The actual grant to any authority consists of two parts. The first part would enable every authority to finance its standard expenditure at the standard rate poundage. With this grant, rate poundages would be equalised across all authorities spending the standard amount per head of their population. This grant is equal to

$$Pe_s - r_s V$$

where V is the rateable value in the authority and P its population. The above, is a formula for a unitary grant which allows all authorities to finance their standard expenditures at the standard rate poundage, where standard expenditures are defined as the minimum expenditure per capita to finance a particular service. Of course, different definitions of standard expenditures can be devised and used in the above formula without changing the general conception of the function of the grant. However, Lord Balfour argued that expenditure above his choice of standard expenditure 'may be and probably is necessary in many places' (Cd. 638, p. 76). He thus proposed an additional grant for such expenditures. The additional grant was to be given as a percentage grant for the expenditures above standard. If x is the percentage for this the grant would be

$xP(e-e_s)$ where e is the actual expenditure per head of population in the authority. The total grant would be, call it G,

$$G = Pe_s - r_s V + xP(e-e_s)$$
$$= xPe + Pe_s(1-x) - r_s V$$

The actual rate poundage resulting from this grant distribution would be

$$r = \frac{Pe-G}{V} = \frac{(1-x)(e-e_s)}{v} + r_s$$

where v is the rateable value per head of population in the authority. From the above we can see the equalising provision. If $e = e_s$, i.e. an authority only spends the standard amount per head of population, then its rate poundage will be equal to r_s which is the standard rate poundage.

The final formula for the grant proposed by Lord Balfour is thus a unitary grant with a proviso for mistakes in the measure used for necessary expenditures. Though devised in 1901, it was not until seventy-five years later that this kind of grant was rediscovered and taken up seriously. An essentially similar grant system was proposed in the 1977 government Green Paper on local government finance (DoE, 1977b, Cmnd. 6813, p. 7).

The effects of the distribution formula suggested by Lord Balfour as compared to a percentage grant system are shown in the example below.

From the example we can see some of the strengths and weaknesses of the Balfour formula. First, compare authorities B and C. Both spend the same amount per head, but under the percentage grant system the rate poundage in authority C would be six times that in authority B. The reason for this is that authority C has a rateable value per head of only one-sixth that of authority B. Under the formula suggested by Lord Balfour B and C end up with the same rate poundage. Here is an extreme example of the equalising effect of the formula. For those authorities whose expenditures per head are equal to the minimum, the rate poundage is the same. The limitation of the formula and the criticisms it received can be seen by comparing authorities A and B. A spends twice as much per capita as B. If we accept that the expenditures undertaken are onerous and imposed by the central government then according to the ability-to-pay principle the rate poundages should be the same in both. Under the percentage grant system A's rate poundage is higher than B's and this differential remains under the Balfour formula. This problem was one of the major criticisms of the formula made in the next twenty years or so, though it had not been overlooked by the proposers initially. They had a problem which has been there with every need formula since: how does one compensate authorities for differences in their spending per head of population when those spending differences result from obligations imposed on them? How does one define a measure of 'spending need'?

When proposing the formula, Lord Balfour himself used population as the measure of need as a second-best solution. He was aware that for certain services, population would not be a good criterion of needs. Thus when discussing

Table 1.7.1. *Percentage grants and the 'Balfour formula'*

Authority	Total expenditure (£)	Population P	Expenditure per head e (£/head)	Rateable value V (£)	Percentage formula		'Balfour formula'	
					Grant received (£)	Rate poundage (p)	Grant received (£)	Rate poundage (p)
A	20,000	100,000	0.20	200,000	10,000	5.00	5,000	7.50
B	10,000	100,000	0.10	200,000	5,000	2.50	0	5.00
C	30,000	300,000	0.10	100,000	15,000	15.00	25,000	5.00
Total	60,000	500,000			30,000		30,000	

Note: Under the percentage grant system, each authority receives a grant of 50 per cent of its expenditure. Under the 'Balfour formula', the standard expenditure (e_s) is 10p per head, the standard rate poundage is 5p and the percentage grant on spending in excess of the standard (x) is 30 per cent.

education he does say that the number of students would be a better guide to needs than size of population (Royal Commission on Local Government, 1901, Cd. 638, p. 81). As we shall see in our examination of the history of grant distribution, education was always an exception. It is the one local authority service for which a measure of need is reasonably obvious.

Nothing came of the Balfour scheme. The grant system continued its chaotic way with the assigned revenue system slowly breaking down. There was a slow reversal to percentage grants. By 1913 only about 14 per cent of total grants were general. The problems of grant distribution had not however disappeared. In 1914 the Kempe Committee reported (Kempe, 1914, Cd. 7315). Before looking at their proposals it may be useful to recall the difference between their view of the function of grants and that of the Minority Report of the 1901 Commission. The Kempe Committee introduced the concept of semi-national goods. This distinction may seem a matter of semantics but it does have important implications for a grant system. The Minority of the 1901 Commission was led by its analysis of the type of services performed by local authorities to conclude that all onerous expenditures should be financed by the central government. Only the problem of administrative efficiency stood in the way of a 100 per cent grant. The function of the grant system was to eliminate discrepancy in tax payments across local authorities. They were essentially working with an agency model of local government in respect of the grant-aided functions.

The Kempe Committee, on the other hand, rejected the agency model in its extreme form. It argued that the services performed by local authorities yielded benefits to them, though they also yielded benefits to the rest of the nation. The reason for the nation's contribution was not so much the need of the local authorities but the 'need' of the nation at large. The nation was buying the service from the local authorities and it should pay for it. This view led them to reject the equalising provision of the Balfour formula.

In their view one of the major functions of a grant system was to provide the nation's share of the cost of the semi-national services. Their rejection of the equalisation scheme of Lord Balfour is of interest. The reason for it is 'the adoption of a scheme like Lord Balfour's which will give a rich district less than the normal contribution was deprecated as inconsistent with the ideas on which their claim to contributions was·based' (ibid., p. 12). If the reason for the claim on the central contribution is that the local authority is providing some services which also benefit the central government, then the fact that the local authority is rich or poor is irrelevant. As long as it provides these services to the nation it has a right to claim payment for them.

They then go into the problem of unit versus percentage grants. They had two arguments against a unit grant. First, it is difficult to specify the relevant units in all cases. Second, expenditure per unit might depend on many factors and can vary from locality to locality. They therefore opted for a mixed system of unit and percentage grants. As far as education was concerned, they accepted the general formula of Lord Balfour except that expenditure per child was used rather than expenditure per capita. They also in this case continued with the equalising provision in the grant. Though why this should be so is not clear, given the criticism of the equalising element they had. For poor relief they rejected Balfour's proposal on the ground that population was not a good measure of need and that rateable value per head was not a good measure of the wealth of the district. They looked at the problem straight in the face and moved on: 'the best course in the present unsettled state of affairs as regards this service is to be content with the removal of some of the more serious faults of the existing system and leave its thorough reform to a more suitable occasion' (ibid., p. 38). As for the public health services, which at this time represented about 14 per cent of local authority expenditures, they believed that 'in matters which concern public health population affords some indication of need' (ibid., p. 49) and wanted to distribute the grant for these services on the basis of 6d per head. For most of the other services, they recommended a percentage grant system. One interesting innovation was their recommendation for the roads grant. They divided roads into main, county and district and wanted a grant for the former two classes. The grant was to be paid on the mileage of the main roads at the average cost per mile of the urban areas of the adjacent administrative county or counties. This idea, which has not been much explored, is of some interest as a method of checking efficiency.

Before examining the theoretical issues raised by the proposals of the Kempe Committee we shall examine another critical work of this period — Sidney Webb's *Grants in Aid*. Webb rejected two propositions that were the basis of much of the previous discussions of grants. First, he rejected the idea that the function, or one of the functions, of grants was to reduce the burden on owners of fixed property, that is that the function of the grant system was to equalise the burden as between one form of taxpayer and another. The second, and possibly related, proposition is his rejection of the whole distinction between national and local services.

There were two strands in the rejection of the assumed inequity between ratepayers and taxpayers. The first was a very general one. To judge the equity of the tax system one has to consider the system as a whole. Webb cites evidence of the Royal Commission that 'the owners and occupiers of real estate furnish as such the greater part of the revenue of Local Authorities, these particular persons contribute as such much less to the revenue of the Central Government' (Webb, 1920, p. 14). The second general argument, which had been more fully developed by Cannan, was that one could not look at the level of rates on property to judge the burden of the tax. Given the long history of rates, and the expectation that such rates would continue, the value of the property takes into account the rates and expected rates.

> If the rates were reduced the owners would be able to charge more for their properties. Consequently these high rates are at bottom an owners' grievance, and to any complaint against them on the ground of equity it may be answered, as before, that property has been bequeathed and inherited, bought and sold, and made the subject of innumerable contracts on the assumption that the inequalities of rates existed and would remain in existence'. (Cannan, 1927, p. 171)

Webb rejects the distinction between national and local goods on two grounds.

His first reason is 'that it is impossible to make out, with any clearness of principle or consensus of opinion what are the services of national and of local benefit respectively' (1920, p. 87). His second reason is most curious, given his own views. He argues that

> if it were really accepted by the Government and the Legislature that certain services were so essentially of national concern that the locality ought not, as such, to be made to bear any part of its cost, the end of local autonomy, as regards these services is surely at hand ... [and] ... in the interest of genuine local self-government which they and I have alike at heart I abjure them to abandon so suicidal a contention. (ibid., p. 90)

From all his arguments, he concludes that 'Grants must be made not for services arbitrarily styled as national but in aid of certain definitely selected services in which the real object of Grants in Aid can be most conveniently attained, and in the efficacy of which the community as a whole has a considerable interest.' And from his view of grants, he concludes that the grants should be dependent on local efficiency, that they should be administered by departments of the national government

> charged with the supervision of those services ... and that no grant should be payable unless a certificate is given by the department concerned that the local authority is administering the service to be aided in general accordance with the law and with the authoritative regulations of the department; that the service, alike in adequacy of supply and degree of efficiency ... reaches at least what may be considered the national minimum. (ibid., pp. 91–2)

Webb rejects the jargon while embracing the idea it expresses with great ardour.

The concept of a national minimum plays a major role in Webb's suggested grant system. The aim of the grant system is twofold. First it is to 'prevent an extreme inequality of burden between one district and another' (ibid., p. 16). Here he is referring to the inequalities in burdens arising from differences in those variables which affect necessary expenditures, for example the different number of children, different amounts of sickness, premature invalidity etc. The second major function of the grant system is control: 'The second reason for a system of Grants in Aid is of even greater moment than the equalisation of burden. They are needed to give weight to the suggestions, criticisms and authoritative instructions by which the central authority seeks to secure greater efficiency and economy of administration. This indeed is the most important aspect of the grants in aid' (ibid., p. 18).

Webb's argument against a unit grant system is the usual one, that it is difficult to define the units on which to base the grant and to take account of the special circumstances which may make it more costly to provide the service in some authorities. He believes that adequate provision can be better guaranteed by administrative control. He also recommends an equalising provision. Here there is a certain confusion in his analysis. He suggests the setting of a national minimum rate of expenditure per head of population taking something like the minimum which experience shows to be anywhere necessary for efficiency, and a standard rate in the pound taking, it may be suggested, something like the average of the rates in the country as a whole. If the product of the standard rate does not produce in the area of a local authority the amount of its national minimum of expenditures for its population the deficiency might be made wholly good by what has been called the Primary Grant. (ibid., p. 104)

There would also be another grant for the difference between standard expenditures and actual expenditures. This would be a proportional grant. This scheme is very similar to that of Lord Balfour's examined above.

There is one major difference, however, between the Balfour scheme and Webb's. Balfour defines minimum expenditures per capita as the actual minimum which can be found in some authority. Webb's minimum standard is more difficult to define. How does 'experience' help to find the minimum which is anywhere necessary for efficiency? Webb himself, in his argument against unit grants, was concerned with the variety of factors which make it difficult or impossible to define either the unit or the amount necessary to spend on it. Some authorities may have a large number of children but a small number of pauper lunatics; some may have a large number of sick but a small number of some other expenditure-determining element. If the minimum is determined by the average, or an actual minimum as in Balfour's scheme, all the same objections as were made against Balfour's scheme by the Kempe Committee would apply against Webb's proposal also.

Webb's approach to the determination of the minimum standard seems to be closely related to his view of strong central control. To show how his scheme might be implemented he quotes from the 1910 Prevention of Destitution Bill. The grants to be given to the local health authorities under this Bill were to be determined by the local government board in accordance with the following principles:

> a) There shall be determined for each year by the Local Government Board a rate of expenditure per head of population (to be termed the National Minimum of Health Expenditure), which in the opinion of the Local Government Board will amount to the least sum at which under the most favourable circumstances the Council of any County or County Borough can possibly discharge efficiently the duties laid upon them by Parliament . . .
> b) There shall be determined for each year . . . a rate in the pound assessable value (to be termed the Standard Average Health Rate), which . . . represents as nearly as can be ascertained the average rate in the pound required . . . to defray the aggregate expenditure . . . of all the Counties and County Boroughs in the discharge of their duties as aforesaid. (ibid., p. 105).

The grant to be given would then be such that all authorities can finance their minimum expenditure at the standard rate. A secondary grant was also to be given. This was to be a proportional grant for all expenditure above standard.

The actual proportion would depend on the amount of money left, from the total that had been allocated for the health grant, after the primary grant had been paid.

The above scheme is, of course, the Balfour scheme described earlier except that the standard expenditure for each authority was to be determined by the government. The problem still remains as to how the local government board is to determine the minimum sum necessary to discharge the duties imposed by Parliament on local authorities. If one accepts Webb's own criticism of the use of units to determine needs what should the local government board use as its criterion for determining minimum standards? Moreover, even to attempt such an exercise, the duties laid on local authorities by Parliament would have to be specified much more precisely than they have been. Sixty odd years after the above scheme was suggested, the Layfield Committee concluded

> Better accountability would be achieved if expenditure which local authorities incurred because of government requirements could be distinguished from expenditure incurred at their own discretion. At present it is impossible to distinguish the respective responsibilities for expenditure, but it might be possible in future. Any specification of responsibilities in this way would involve a major change in the statutes governing local services. (Layfield, 1976, Cmd. 6453, p. 63)

Had the grant schemes proposed seventy years earlier been taken seriously, Layfield's conclusions about the possibility of allocating responsibility between central and local government might have been more optimistic.

Nothing much came of the schemes to make the grant system more equitable and base it on some more coherent conception of the function of local government and the role of grants within such a framework. Nearly all the grants continued on a percentage basis. There was, however, another force working for the unit system which had little to do with the question of equity in grant distribution, and which in the early and mid-1920s started coming to the forefront. The aggregate percentage grant, and even more so the distribution of the grant on a percentage basis, was making the Treasury very nervous. There seemed to be no limitation that they could impose on the revenues being claimed by local authorities. The arguments against the percentage system were usually phrased in terms of the extravagance encouraged by the percentage grants, and the detailed control they require. Throughout the 1920s Committees were set up to examine the grant system and to look at possible alternatives. The Chancellor of the Exchequer was pushing for a block grant system and for the abolition of the percentage system. There seemed to be a unanimous view by both committees and outside bodies against the abolition of the percentage grant system. There was no evidence to suggest that percentage grants encouraged extravagance by local authorities. The block grant was not considered very favourably. It was seen as ' . . . crude and empirical, difficult (if not impossible) to establish on any equitable basis and most troublesome to adjust on periodic revision' (the IMTA, quoted in Lees *et al.*, 1956, p. 164). The arguments for the block grant system were very simple. It would limit the Exchequer's liability.[3] These arguments, with the backing of the Chancellor of the Exchequer, won through. And the Act of 1929 was introduced.

1929 to 1948

The 1929 Local Government Act introduced a new concept into the grant system. This was the block grant, and the first actual attempt to distribute grant according to a formula incorporating some criteria of needs and resources. Not all the grants were to be distributed by the formula. In fact, the education grant, the police grant and the housing grant remained on the old basis. These grants accounted for between 80 per cent and 90 per cent of the revenues distributed by central government. The formula grant system replaced the small number of discontinued grants and compensated for the lost revenues due to the derating of industry. In the first grant period, even these were not completely distributed on the formula basis. However, the formula is important. It is the first of many attempts to devise a formula so that grant distribution would be based on 'objective' factors. The main argument given for the block grant system was simple.

> No scheme for providing an alternative source of revenue for the local authorities can take the form of a grant varying from year to year with the expenditure of individual authorities. Under such a scheme, the Government would be committed to finding a material proportion of every local authority's general expenditure without any possibility of effective control, and the financial interest of local authorities in their administration would be surely impaired. (Ministry of Housing and Local Government, 1928, Cmnd. 3134, p. 5)

This was the straight Treasury line.

We next turn to the formula for the distribution of the grant. This was a mixture of needs and resources factors. But the actual way the mixing was done was not particularly understandable. The factors going into it were individually probably quite defensible but their combination was not. The fundamental concept used was that of weighted population. The grant was then distributed on the basis of so much per head of weighted population. The weighted population was the actual population weighted by the following factors: children under 5, rateable value, unemployment, and a measure of sparsity (For details of the formula see Part One, Appendix 1.7.A1.) The first two factors worked very simply. If the number of children under 5 per 1,000 population was greater than 50, the population was increased by the percentage by which the number exceeded 50. Population was also increased by the percentage by which rateable value per capita fell short of £10. The base numbers, 50 for the children weighting and £10 for the rateable value weighting, were so chosen that nearly every authority would receive something from each. In the first grant period only the City of London, seven county boroughs and a few metropolitan boroughs did not receive the weighting for rateable value. The unemployment and, for counties, the sparsity weightings were then applied to the weighted population resulting from the first two weightings. In 1937, an additional unemployment and sparsity weighting were applied to the weighted population resulting from all the previous weightings. By this time the formula was completely incomprehensible.

The justification for the formula given was that 'In deciding what characteristics should be adopted and what weights should be given to each, the aim has been so to adjust the distribution of this new revenue so as to make the assistance vary with the need for local government services in any area in relation to the ability of the area to meet the cost (Ministry of Housing and Local Government, 1928, Cmnd. 3134, p. 14). This is, of course, a very commendable goal. But it is far from explaining why the weightings should have been as they were. According to Mabel Newcomer, 'One of the officials who assisted in the investigations preliminary to the recommendation of the formula explained to the writer that cumulative weighting was carried this far and no further because they knew what results they wanted and this gave just those results' (1937, p. 192).

When Chamberlain introduced the Bill in Parliament he stated that population was the main basis of the formula as it is the principal factor which governs need, but that the formula also takes into account rateable value and children under 5. Applied together to weight the population, they would indicate a general index both of need and relative wealth. The formula was not well understood. Very few members were, however, quite as frank about it as Lady Astor who admitted that 'I do not understand one quarter of it, but neither does anyone else. I do not understand electricity but I derive a benefit from it' (*Hansard*, 5th series, Vol. 223, p. 345). The benefits of electricity were much more obvious though, than those of the complicated weightings in the formula. In the debate over the Bill Chamberlain made light of the mathematical complexities: 'Of course it is very easy to present any mathematical formula in such a way as to seem ridiculous to those who have never had the opportunity of learning algebra' (ibid., p. 97). But the problem was much deeper than that. It is true that mathematical formulae can be presented in various ways. They can cover up as much as they reveal, and the 1929 formula managed to cover up a great deal. Even the simple claim when the Bill was introduced that population was the main factor because it is the principal factor which governs need was not quite correct. In the first grant period, population accounted for only 39 per cent of the grant with the children and rateable value weightings accounting for another 39 per cent. In the second grant period population accounted for only 37 per cent of the grant.

There was also much criticism of the weight given to children in the formula. The reply given by the government was that children did not represent just a need factor: We have not only to have regard to the actual needs created by children but we find that we can safely take that as a measure of the relative wealth and poverty of a population' (ibid., p. 98). This assertion was disputed. (*The Economist*, 8 December 1928). There was also much criticism of the low weight given to unemployment.

As far as the equalisation of rate poundages was concerned, the new grant system was a failure. According to one study, the differences in rate poundages were greater under this system than they would have been under the old system

(Newcomer, 1937, p. 280). The examination of the grant formula in Appendix 1.7.A2 shows why. Essentially the formula gives a very low weight to deficiencies in rateable value, relative to differences in the proportion of children under 5. Going back to Table 1.7.1 (p. 178), the 1929 grant would be very unhelpful to an authority like C whose high rate poundage is a result of low rateable value per head. It might, however, be helpful to an authority like A whose high rate poundage is due to high expenditure per head – provided, of course, that higher expenditure is associated with a high proportion of children under 5.

Before leaving the 1929 formula it is useful to compare its equalisation provision with that contained in the suggested formula of Lord Balfour. The latter formula had a very clear concept of the aim of an equalising provision. It was to allow every authority, whatever its rateable value, to finance some minimum amount of expenditure per head at a standard rate poundage. The equalisation provision in the 1929 Act is much more difficult to disinter. Poorer authorities would have a higher rate poundage than richer authorities for any level of expenditures. Moreover, if the needs factor included was not a good indication of needs – as was persuasively claimed with the major one of these, children under 5 – the net effect of the grant would be to reduce equalisation as compared to the previous percentage grant system. The criticisms of the Balfour formula made in the beginning of the century were that the expenditures he chose might not be a good measure of need. One of the main criticisms of the 1929 Act became that the chosen measures of need were not a good measure of needed expenditures.

1948 to 1958

The 1948 Local Government Act revolutionised the concept of equalisation. All the previous ideas were concerned with helping the 'poor' authorities. The aim of the 1948 Act was to eliminate them. The idea was brilliant in its simplicity. A poor authority is one which has low rateable value per capita. Why not provide it with more rateable value? As soon as this idea is considered seriously it is not difficult to devise a method to achieve it. The method chosen was to consider the central government as a fictitious ratepayer possessing whatever rateable value was required to bring an authority's rateable value up to the desired level. Initially the level chosen was the average rateable value per head in the country. Thus for all relevant purposes every authority could consider itself as having at least the same rateable value per capita as the national average. Some would belong to its own ratepayers, the rest to the fictitious but beneficent ratepayers, the Treasury.

Ignoring some complications (to which we return below) the amount of rateable value 'owned' by the Treasury on which it was to be charged rates could easily be calculated. This amount, called credited rateable value (CV) was

$$CV = P_j v - V_j \tag{1}$$

where P_j is the population in the j'th authority, v is the national average rateable value per capita, and V_j is the authority's rateable value. Thus each grant-receiving authority could, for rate purposes, consider its rateable value as being equal to $P_j v$; of this amount V_j belonged to its residents and the rest credited to it by the Treasury. The amount of grant received by the authority would then depend on its rate poundage.

If we write an authority's expenditure net of all other grants as $\bar{E}_j$ and its rate poundage as r_j, its budget equation takes the form

$$\bar{E}_j = r_j V_j + r_j CV_j \tag{2}$$

$r_j V_j$ being the amount it collects from its own ratepayers, and $r_j CV_j$ the amount it collects from the Treasury in grant. From the definition of credited rateable value in equation (1) this can be simplified to

$$\bar{E}_j = r_j P_j v$$

or

$$r_j = \bar{e}_j / v \tag{3}$$

so that an authority's rate poundage is equal to its expenditure per head $(\bar{e}_j)$ divided by the standard rateable value per head. Thus, for all authorities in receipt of grant, their rate poundage is independent of their own rateable value and depends only on their expenditure per head.

The grant received by each authority is given by:

$$G_j = r_j CV_j$$

$$= \frac{\bar{E}_j}{P_j v} [P_j v - V_j] \text{ from (1) and (3)} \tag{4}$$

$$= \bar{E}_j (1 - v_j / v)$$

where v_j is the authority's 'own' rateable value per head (V_j / P_j).

The grant can thus be seen as a percentage grant, the percentage depending on the authority's deficiency of rateable value.

At one stroke the poor authorities were eliminated. Provided, of course, rateable value per capita was a good measure of poverty. This troublesome problem had been raised briefly by the Kempe Committee in its criticism of Lord Balfour's formula, and it was to be seriously raised again twenty-five years later by the Layfield Committee, but at this time it was not an issue, though there was some discussion of the problem (see Lees *et al.*, 1956).

The Exchequer Equalistion Grant, as it was called, solved the problem of differences in the resources of an authority. What about differences in 'needs'? Here the 1948 Act went back to a percentage grant system. For nearly all services except education, which continued to maintain its imperviousness to all changes, a percentage grant was introduced. With this grant system the actual rate poundage in an authority receiving the equalisation grant was

$$r_j = e_j (1 - x) 1 / v \tag{5}$$

where x is the percentage grant received, and e_j is its per capita expenditure, so that $\bar{e}_j = (1 - x) e_j$, and the above equation can be derived directly from equation

(3). It is interesting to compare this grant and the resulting rate poundage with the formula suggested by Lord Balfour fifty years earlier. With the formula suggested by Lord Balfour the rate poundage[4] would be

$$r_j = \frac{(1-x)(e_j - e_s)}{v_j} + r_s$$

Here we can clearly see the main difference in the concepts of equalisation in these two approaches. In both, rate poundages are equalised for authorities who spend the standard amount per capita. However, the added rate poundage for those expenditures above standard depends on rateable value in Lord Balfour's formula but not in the formula of the 1948 Act.

There was one complication which we have so far ignored to which we now turn. New grant systems nearly always contain vestigial remains of old ones. The 1948 grant was no exception. The calculations we described above to determine an authority's credited rateable value, and thus its grant, were based on rateable value per head of population. The actual measure used for the grant was rateable value per head of weighted population. The concept of weighted population introduced in the 1929 formula was retained though how it was measured was changed. Actual population was weighted by children under 15 and by a sparsity measure. The weighting was done very simply. The actual population was increased by the number of children under 15 and by the number of people required to bring the population per mile of roads to 70 (see Appendix 1.7.A1).

For an authority whose children and sparsity measures are equal to the national average the credited rateable value, which is the amount of rateable value for which the Treasury is a ratepayer, is the same whether population or weighted population is used. However, if the number of children per head of population or the sparsity measure per head of population in the authority is not equal to the national average its credited rateable value is adjusted accordingly (see Appendix 1.7.A2).

In 1952/3, for example, the average rateable value per head of weighted population was £6.33. Thus with respect to credited rateable value one child under 15 was worth £6.33 in reateable value (see Appendix 1.7.A2).

In the 1929 formula the trade off was one child for £200 in rateable value as far as grants were concerned.

The equalisation of rate poundages achieved by the 1948 formula was quite dramatic. In Figure 1.7.1 we show the variation of rate poundages around the average from 1933 to 1973. The fall in the variation with the introduction of the 1948 grant is apparent.

The 1948 grant system achieved one of its major aims which was to eliminate discrepancies in rate poundages arising from variations in the rateable value of authorities. It, however, retained the percentage grant system. This soon came under pressure, similar to that which had occurred twenty-five years earlier and which ultimately led to the block grant of 1929. The open-endedness of a percentage grant system was worrying to the Exchequer. Throughout the early 1950s, the whole debate between a percentage grant system and a unit grant system continued. The arguments against a unit system were the same as they had been in the early part of the century, namely that it was impossible to find

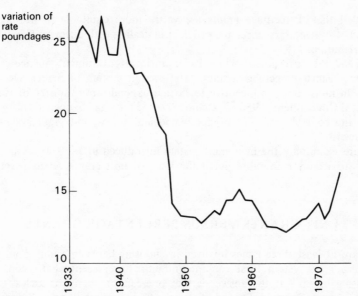

Figure 1.7.1.   *Coefficient of variation of rate poundages of county boroughs:*
1933–73

the right units on which to base the distribution of grants. This time, however, the arguments were accompanied by more solid evidence.

In the early 1950s many government departments made attempts to devise units and determine variations in costs of providing certain services. The results were not optimistic. The difficulties were brought out by the Public Accounts Committee:

> Departments are making and will continue to make further efforts to ascertain and examine the unit costs of services provided by Local Health Authorities. The problem is, however, not one that lends itself to rapid progress . . . Owing to variations in local conditions the authorities concerned were faced with widely different problems . . . and it was difficult to distinguish accurately between the effect of factors which were or were not within the authorities' control. (Quoted in Lees *et al.*, 1956, p. 174)

Similar problems were encountered by the Ministry of Education: 'The circumstances which determine the cost per pupil differ widely from one area to another, and no experienced reader will be likely to fall into the error of supposing that it is possible to . . . deduce a standard figure of cost above which any expenditure should be regarded as excessive and below which it should be regarded as inadequate' (ibid., p. 175). Lees *et al.* after analysing a large amount of data on cost statistics concluded 'that nothing in our researches or in the more fundamental researches of government departments points to the conclusion that unit costs, derived from present data, would provide the basis for an equitable and efficient distribution of specific Exchequer grants' (ibid., p. 179). They thus concluded that 'Percentage grants are vastly more equitable in dealing with differences in necessary costs and efficient in dealing with different standards of service' (ibid., p. 179).

In 1957 the government White Paper on local government finance gave its argument against percentage grants: 'The present system of percentage grants acts as an indiscriminate incentive to further expenditure (Ministry of Housing and Local Government, 1956–7, Cmnd 209, p. 3). As had happened thirty years earlier, the control argument predominated and a new unit grant system was introduced.[5]

Before examining the new grant system introduced in 1959 we shall digress slightly to examine in more detail the issue of unit grants versus percentage grants.

UNIT GRANTS VERSUS PERCENTAGE GRANTS

There are at least three issues involved in choosing between a unit grant and a percentage grant system. First, can one find units to represent what is considered as creating 'needs'? If the answer is that one cannot, then it is useless to talk about a unit grant system. Second, if one can find some relationship between the chosen units and expenditures, what is the nature of this relationship and therefore what differences will exist if one uses units as compared with expenditure, to distribute the grant? Third, is one worried about the deviations from any relationship between units and expenditures and what do the deviations represent? On a more basic level, why this search for units to represent needs of the authority and with whose needs are we concerned?

Consider Figure 1.7.2. On the vertical axis we measure expenditure per head of population, and on the horizontal axis we measure some units of 'need' per head of population, for example, the number of children under 5 or the number of pupils. Assume first that there exists a relationship between the number of units of need per head and expenditures per head across local authorities. This relationship is shown by line $E = a + bN$. If there is a percentage grant system based on expenditures, the percentage grant will be shown by line gE. Let line uN represent the grant per head that would be received by any authority with the specified number of units with a unit grant system. For a given number of units, the expected expenditure of such an authority is shown by line E. This is expected in the sense that, on average, authorities with that number of units will be spending the amount shown. Of course, not all will be spending this amount; some may be spending more and others less.

We have drawn line uN parallel to line E. This means that we have assumed that the grant given for each additional unit is exactly equal to the expected expenditure incurred because of the additional unit. For example, if an increase in one unit leads to an increase in expenditure (on average) of £5, the unit payment in the grant will be £5.

From the figure, we can read off the following for any authority with some given number of units: the grant that it gets under the unit system, the grant under a percentage system, the amount that it has to finance under the two

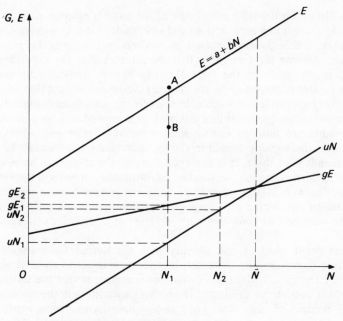

Figure 1.7.2. *Percentage and unit grants*

systems from rates, and, with a bit of imagination, the difference in rate payments of different authorities assuming that their rateable value is the same. Consider first the grants that an authority expects to receive under the two systems. It is clear from the figure that whether an authority receives a higher or lower grant under the unit system depends on the number of units that it has relative to the average number of units in the country. For all values of N below $\bar{N}$, the expected grant is higher under the percentage system than under the unit system. For all values of N greater than $\bar{N}$, the expected grant is lower under the percentage grant system.

Consider now the differentials in rate payments across local authorities under the two systems. For this purpose let us assume that all the authorities have the same rateable value, allowing us to concentrate on the differentials in rate payments arising solely from differences in expenditure, which in turn, on our present assumption, arise because of the different number of units per head across authorities. Consider the two authorities with units N_1 and N_2 in Figure 1.7.2. The grants received by the two authorities can be read off in the figure. The differences in the grants received under the two systems can also be seen. It is clear that, with the relationships shown in Figure 1.7.2, the difference in grant received is always greater under the unit grant system than under the percentage system (line uN is always steeper than line gE). In terms of the rate differential, this means that the expected rate differential is smaller under the unit grant system. In fact, with our assumption that the unit grant exactly compensates for the expenditure arising from the unit the expected rate differential is zero. The amount that has to be raised with rates is the distance between line E and line *uN*. This distance is the same irrespective of the number of units in the authority. Are the differences in grants received and rates under the two systems equitable? The answer to this question depends on the reasons for giving the grant in the first place. Assume for a moment that we consider that the expenditures are onerous, in the sense of the 1901 Minority Report. They should, therefore, really be financed completely by the central government, except that for administrative purposes this is not feasible. In this case, the unit grant is more equitable than the percentage grant. Authorities with large expenditure because they have a large number of units to finance should receive a larger grant. They do not benefit from the higher expenditures, they undertake them because the government demands it of them. It is also equitable that the amount to be raised from rates should in this case be independent of the number of units in the authority. An authority with a large number of units has greater 'needs' because it has greater obligations. With a percentage grant system residents in such an authority would be penalised as compared with residents of authorities with fewer units of need.

On the other hand, if one assumes with the Kempe Committee that the expenditure undertaken by the authorities yields benefits to them as well as to the rest of the nation, the justification for the grant is that the services yield some benefit outside the authority. The higher expenditure in the authority with a greater number of units does yield greater benefits to people living in that authority. In this case, it is not inequitable that residents of such an authority should pay higher rates, and a percentage grant system rather than a unit grant system is justified. It should be stressed again that in both cases we have assumed that the units chosen are a good measure of expenditures.

So far we have looked at the two grant systems on the basis of the expected grant under the percentage system. The actual grant received by any authority will not be equal to the expected grant unless it is actually spending as much as expected. Consider two authorities, A and B, both of which have the same number of units of 'need', N_1 in Figure 1.7.2. A's expenditures are below average; B's expenditures are above average for that number of units. Thus their grants under the percentage system will differ but under a unit system will be the same. Whether this is a cause of worry clearly depends on why there is the discrepancy. Consider the following possibilities. First, assume that the discrepancy is truly an error term in the sense that in the following year and the years after, A and B have an equal likelihood of being above or below the line. Then the discrepancy between actual and expected expenditures is due to some random factors that may affect any authority in some period. In this case, the grants received on average by an authority over a period of years will be related to its needs, and discrepancies in its spending will tend to cancel out.

However, the errors may be due to some omitted factors in the relationship between units and expenditures. In such a case, the authorities whose expenditures are higher than expected in one period on the basis of the particular relationship shown in Figure 1.7.2 will also have higher expenditures in other periods. In this case, these authorities will continue to receive small grants relative to their spending. This is one interpretation of the criticism of unit grants, that they do not measure all the relevant need-determining factors.

Whether one should worry about this also depends on what these factors are. If A is inefficient and B is efficient, there is presumably no argument for compensating A with higher grants. If there are actually factors that are relevant, a percentage grant will reduce the rate differential among the authorities like A and B, but, as we saw above, it will increase the rate differential among those authorities which have different quantities of need factors. The net effect on rate differential will depend on the relative importance of the two factors.

In summary, even if there is a measure of need which on average is closely related to expenditures there is still a problem in choosing between unit and percentage grants. One cannot jump from the existence of such a needs measure to a conclusion about the desirability of a particular grant system.

1958 to 1974

The 1958 grant system contained two parts: a resource element and a needs element. The resource grant was essentially the Exchequer Equalisation Grant of 1948 now relabelled the Rate Deficiency Grant. The major change in this grant was that the children weighting for weighted population was abolished. There were also a few minor changes in the exact specification of the grant (see Appendix 1.7.A1). The major change, however, was the needs element which replaced nearly all the percentage grants with a unit grant system.

The formula used to distribute the grant in 1958 and the units chosen were much more sophisticated than those used in 1929. Also, for the first time, education was incorporated into the general grant. The basic grant consisted of a certain payment per head of population and per child under 15. A supplementary grant was given on the basis of the following units: children under 5, old people (over 65), high density, low density, declining population, high cost in metropolitan districts. From these grants a deduction of a certain rate poundage was made (in the first year it was the product of a 9d rate). (For details see Appendix 1.7.A1.) The reason for the rate poundage deductions was not clear. It was presumably a vestigial remainder of the education grant which always had a rate poundage deduction. Its inclusion was also probably necessary to give the results which were wanted, namely not to change the distribution too greatly (see Boyle, 1966, p. 77).

We show in Appendix 1.7.A2 that the 1958 needs element formula means that the grant given to any authority is equal to the average per capita grant with deductions or additions to this if the per capita need factor in the authority is greater or less than the national average of these factors (Appendix 1.7.A2, section C, equation 4). The coefficients on these factors are those specified in the grant orders. If these coefficients represent the actual cost of providing the needs represented by the specified factor, the grant would fully compensate an authority for any discrepancy in its needs relative to the national average. (It could then be represented by the unit grant line used in Figure 1.7.2.) If we compare the 1958 system with the 1929 system, the similarity is apparent. Both provide for higher grant for authorities in relation to their units of need per head of population. In the 1929 formula the units of need were children under 5, unemployment and population sparsity, whilst as we have seen the units of need were different in the 1958 formula. The important difference is, however, less obvious. In the 1958 formula the coefficients on the need factors were specified in the grant orders and could be chosen to represent the cost of providing for the units specified. They could also be changed without changing the units incorporated in the formula or the authorities eligible for grants. In the 1929 formula the coefficients were set by the specification of the criteria making an authority eligible for grant and the total grant available for distribution.

For those authorities receiving only the children and rateable value weightings the coefficient for children, in the 1929 formula, was 20 times the grant per head of weighted population (see Appendix 1.7.A2). This number was so, because the weighting for children was specified in terms of the number of children per 1,000 population in excess of 50. To change it, the criterion for this weighting would have to be changed.

In 1929, one of the criticisms of the unitary grant was that it was 'most troublesome to adjust on periodic revisions' (IMTA, quoted in Lees *et al.*, 1956, p. 164). This criticism was valid with the 1929 formulation, but it is not valid for the 1958 formulation in which the coefficients can be changed without changing the structure of the grant.

In 1966 a Royal Commission on Local Government was set up to look into the whole structure of local government organisation. The grant system introduced in 1967 was essentially a stop-gap operation not attempting to introduce radical changes before the report of the Royal Commission on reorganisation. The grant formula for distributing grants consisted of the 1958 formula with some minor amendments. Instead of basing the education-element calculation on the number of pupils, it used education units which gave weights to different types of education. It also incorporated the roads grant into the general grant (see Appendix 1.7.A1). A new element, however, was introduced into the rate support grant. Besides the needs element and the resource element, a domestic element was introduced. This was essentially a special subsidy via grants to domestic ratepayers as compared with commercial and industrial ratepayers. The rate product deduction of the 1958 formula was eliminated.

The unit grant system introduced in 1959 continued with minor modifications until 1974. Fourteen years is a long time for a grant system to survive in a recognisable form, but ultimately the straightjacket of a fixed unit system in a world in which the determinants of local expenditures keep changing will introduce enough pressure to break the system. A new grant system is always constrained by the past. Existing claims will always exert an influence on the formulation of a new system. When a change is made from a percentage system to a unit system, the units chosen have to leave the distribution of the grant reasonably similar to what it was before. Thus, at that point in time, the units do reflect expenditures. Over time, however, the determinants of expenditures change. There is some scope for avoiding drastic changes in the distribution of the grant relative to actual expenditures by changing the coefficients attached to the units. Sooner or later, however, the relationship between the units and expenditures becomes tenuous. It is at that point that the pressure to change the system starts to build up. It is reasonably clear that by the late 1960s and

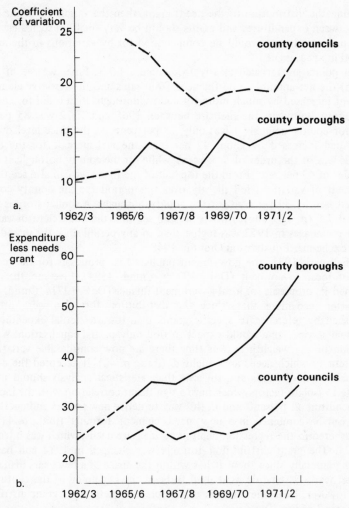

Figure 1.7.3 (a) *Coefficient of variation of rate poundages* (b) *Expenditure less needs grant − averages*

early 1970s the relationship between expenditures and the units determining the grant distribution began to diverge, especially for county boroughs. The large increase in expenditure during this period was not accompanied by an increase in the number of units that determined the grant distribution. In Figure 1.7.3(a) we show a measure of dispersion − the coefficient of variation − of expenditures minus the needs grant from 1965 to 1973 for counties and county boroughs. In Figure 1.7.3(b) we show the means for counties and county boroughs of the per capita difference between expenditure and needs grant. This is the amount that has to be financed from rates and the resource element of the grant. If the variables which determine expenditures were the same as those that determine the distribution of the needs grant, then the variations in the difference between expenditures and grants should be very small. In such a case, variations in expenditures would be compensated for by variations in the amount received in needs grant.

Two points are revealed clearly from Figure 1.7.3. First, we see in Figure 1.7.3(b) the net amount to be financed from rates and the resource element of the grant increased by much more for county boroughs than it did for counties. For county boroughs, the increase between 1965 and 1972 was 85 per cent while for county councils it was only 46 per cent. As the price level over this period had increased by about 42 per cent, the real increase for the county councils was of the order of 5 per cent, while for the county boroughs it was of the order of 43 per cent. From the top half of the figure we can also see that the coefficient of variations fell slightly over this period for the county councils, but increased by 34 per cent for the county boroughs. A similar story is told in Figure 1.7.1 (p. 189 above) where we can see that the coefficient of variation of rate poundages in 1973 was higher than in any period since the introduction of the Exchequer Equalisation Grant in 1948.

In February 1971, the government published its proposals for the reoganisation of local government (DoE, 1971*b*, Cmnd. 4584). Five months later it published its proposals for local government finance (DoE, 1971*a*, Cmnd. 4741). The latter recognised that 'since the distribution formulae were originally established by reference to specific grants paid towards actual expenditure on individual services, one would expect to find only partial equalisation. With the evolution of the weightings over time there are now considerable variations in the extent to which needs are equalised' (ibid., p. 40). It accepted the concept of equalisation of needs and suggests that 'statistical analysis should make it possible to isolate factors which have a significant correlation with the incidence of expenditure at present, and in this way to derive new factors and coefficients which can be combined in a new 'needs element' formula' (ibid., p. 41). This hope ushered in the regression analysis to measure needs, which was introduced in 1974. The grant distribution formula was changed in 1974 and has been changing annually since then. It has within the space of a few years managed to become nearly as chaotic as it used to be at the beginning of the century. We shall, however, leave the analysis of the present method of grant distribution to Chapter 3 of Part Two.

CONCLUSION

Our excursion into the history of grants was not motivated just by curiosity. Three points are strikingly obvious. The first is that bad grant systems are not due to a lack of insight into the objectives of grants, or a lack of understanding of how grants can be devised to achieve those objectives. The idea of equalising rate poundages for the finance of at least some of the expenditures of local authorities was brilliantly analysed, and a grant to achieve it proposed, by the Minority Report of 1901. The idea was not introduced, even partially, until the Exchequer Equalisation Grant fifty years later, and its full realisation has yet to be achieved.

The second point is that changes in grant system are often prompted by considerations of control of local expenditures, rather than by considerations of the purpose of such expenditures, and the role of grants within a coherent framework for the allocation of functions between central and local governments. As we saw, both the block grant of 1928 and that of 1958 were strongly motivated by fears of excessive commitments on the Treasury. A grant system which might be good at achieving the objective of control might be extremely bad at achieving the other important objectives of grants.

The third point is that new grant systems are always constrained by the existing grant distributions. Existing distributions create politically powerful pressures resisting change. If such pressures are recognised explicitly and accepted, it may be possible to deal with them explictly, for example by generous transitional arrangements. Such a solution is better than contorting new grant systems so as to avoid the conflict.

NOTES

1 There were in fact a number of Minority Reports of the 1901 Royal Commission. Their authors were in agreement on the major issues, however, and their viewpoint will be referred to collectively as that of 'the' Minority Report.
2 Lord Balfour was one of the Minority Report authors (see Royal Commission on Local Government 1901, Cd. 638, pp. 74 ff.).
3 The Exchequer's liability under a percentage grant system could be controlled by adjusting the percentage grant paid. It is the combination of percentage grants and political resistance to changes in the percentages that leaves the Treasury with no control over the grant total.
4 This is the same formula as that on p. 177 except for the addition of the subscript *j* to facilitate comparison with equation (5).
5 Although now the concern was more with control over local government spending as such than with control over grant disbursements (see Part Two, Chapter 8).

Appendix 1.7.A1   Original Grant Formulae

(I)   THE 1929 FORMULA

The 1929 formula distributed the grant according to the weighted population of a local authority (P_w). The weighted population was calculated by first adjusting the actual population (P) by the following two factors

(a)   the number f children under 5 (C)
(b)   the rateable value per head $\bar{V}$.

(a) and (b) determined the intermediate weighted population (P_w^1) in the following way:

Let
$$w_c = 20\frac{C}{P} - 1 \geqslant 0$$

$$w_v = 1 - \frac{\bar{V}}{£10} \geqslant 0 \tag{1}$$

Then
$$P_w^1 = P(1 + w_c + w_v)$$

To get the weighted population for grant purposes, the intermediate weighted population was adjusted for unemployment and, for counties, by a sparsity measure in the following way:

Let U_m = unemployed males

$\quad\ \ U_f$ = unemployed females

$\quad\ \ U = U_m + \frac{1}{10}U_f$ averaged over three years preceding the grant period.

$\quad\ \ P^a$ = average population over three years preceding the grant period.

$\quad\ \ R$ = number of miles of road.

Then, if
$$\frac{U}{P^a} > \frac{1.5}{100}$$

$$w_u' = \left(\frac{U}{P^a} - \frac{1.5}{100}\right)10$$

And
$$w_s = 1 - \frac{P}{200R} \quad \text{if } P/R < 100$$

$$ = 50\frac{R}{P} \quad\ \ \text{if } P/R \geqslant 100$$

The weighted population was then equal to

$$P_w = P_w^1(1 + w_u' + w_s) = P(1 + w_c + w_v)(1 + w_u' + w_s)$$

AMENDMENTS OF 1937

If $\dfrac{U}{P^a} > \dfrac{5}{100}$

Let
$$w_u'' = \left(\frac{U}{P^a} - \frac{5}{100}\right)5$$

Let $\quad w_s' = 1 - \dfrac{P}{300R} \quad$ if $P/R < 100$

$\quad\quad\quad = \dfrac{40}{P/R - 40} \quad$ if $P/R \geqslant 100$

Let $\quad\quad P_w^2 = P_w^1(1 + w_u' + w_u'')$

Then the weighted population for grant purposes was

$$P_w = P_w^2(1 + w_s')$$
$$= P(1 + w_c + w_v)(1 + w_u' + w_u'')(1 + w_s')$$

(II) THE EXCHEQUER EQUALISATION ACT OF 1948

The grant was also based on weighted population.

Let $\quad C = $ number of children under 15, and for counties if $P/R < 70$

let $\quad P' = 70R - P$

$\quad\quad S = \tfrac{1}{3}P'$

The weighted population of an authority is

$$P_w = P + C + S$$

An authority was credited rateable value if its rateable value (V) was less than its weighted population times the national average rateable value per head of weighted population $(\bar{V}_w)$. Thus the credited rateable value (CV) was

$$CV = P_w\bar{V}_w - V$$

The actual calculation was made not on the authority's rateable value but on the product of a rate of 20 shillings in the pound. This is equal to rateable value, minus the cost of collecting rates minus losses on bad debts and on empty property.

(III) THE 1958 FORMULA

(a) The Exchange Equalisation Grant was renamed the Rate Deficiency Grant with two major changes. First, children were excluded from weighted population and the sparsity weighting was changed to

$$S = \tfrac{2}{5}P'$$

(b)	The needs grant. This grant was based on the following factors: Population (P), the number of children under 15 (C), the number of children under 5 (T), the number of people over 65 (O), and the number of pupils (E). There was also a high-density payment based on population per acre (P/A); a low-density payment based on miles of road per head of population (R/P), and a declining population payment based on population relative to the base-year population (P_b); the base-year population was the population twenty years preceding the grant year. There was also a special payment to authorities in metropolitan districts, and a rate product deduction. We shall use small letters to depict the payment per unit of the variable depicted by the capital letters.

The first part of the grant was called the basic grant (B), which affected the size of the low- and high-density payments, the declining population payment and the special payment to the metropolitan districts.

(i)	Basic grant (B)

$$B = pP + cC$$

(ii)	$t(T + O)$ grant for children and old people

(iii)	$e(1,000E - 110P)$ education grant

(iv)	High-density payment (H)

Let $\alpha = (P/A - 18)\dfrac{1}{200}$ then

$$H = \alpha B$$

(v)	Low-density payment (L)

Let $\beta = 20R/P$ then

$$L = \beta B$$

(vi)	Declining population (D)

Let $\delta = 0.475 - \tfrac{1}{2}\dfrac{P}{P_b} \geqslant 0$

$$D = \delta B$$

(vii)	$0.05B$ special grant to metropolitan districts.

(viii)	dV rate poundage deductions.

## (IV)	THE 1966 FORMULA

The 1966 formula made two major changes to the 1958 formula and a few minor ones. The major changes were the introduction of a roads grant into the general grant and a change in the calculation of the education payment in the grant. Before looking at these we shall look at the minor changes.

(a)	In the low-density payment ((iv) in the 1958 formula) β was changed to $22.5R/P$

(b) In the declining population payment, the base-year population was changed to the population ten years before the grant year and δ (see (vi) in the 1958 formula) was changed to $0.995 - P/P_b$

(c) The sparsity weighting in the rate deficiency grant was changed to $S = \frac{1}{2}P'$.

The education payment was calculated on the basis of education units rather than the number of pupils. The education units were calculated by a weighted sum of the following (weights in brackets): primary and nursery-school pupils (1), training-centre child under 16 (1.9), secondary and special pupils under 16 (1.19), secondary and special pupils over 16 (3.05), further-education students (2.88), university and other student awards (3.32), 1,000 school meals (0.94). If we denote the number of education units by E', the education payment ((iii) in the 1958 formula) was changed to

$$e(1,000E' - 200P)$$

The roads grant was incorporated into the formula in the following way:

Let R = miles of road excluding trunk roads
R' = miles of principal roads
v = payment per mile of road
v' = payment per mile of principal road
d = reduction of payment divided by 100 if $P/R < 4,000$
d' = increase payment divided by 100 if $P/R > 5,500$

The roads grant was vR

The principal roads grant was

$$v'R' - 4,000d + \frac{P}{R'}d \quad \text{if } P/R < 4,000$$

$$v'R' - 5,500d' + \frac{P}{R'}d' \quad \text{if } P/R > 5,500$$

Appendix 1.7.A2 Standardised Grant Formulae

The various grant formulae discussed in this chapter look very different. The 1929 formula was based on weighted population. The Exchange Equalisation Grant of 1948 was based on weighted rateable value. The 1958 and 1966 formulae had explicit payments per unit of need. Though there are major differences among these formulae, there are also major similarities which are unseen when one looks only at the verbal description of them. In this appendix we shall convert the formulae in such a way that the similarities become more apparent. Such a conversion will also bring out the real differences between them. Throughout the appendix we shall use a letter with a subscript j to denote a variable for a local authority, without the subscript it will denote the same variable for the country as a whole. A letter with a bar on top will denote the per capita average of the variable. Thus, for example, G stands for the total grant given by the government, $\bar{G}$ is the per capita grant, G_j the grant received by a local authority, and $\bar{G}_j$ the per capita grant received by a local authority.

(I)   THE 1929 FORMULA

We shall only consider the weighting for children under 5 and for rateable value, although the general form of the result holds for the more complicated weightings of unemployment and sparsity.

Let: G = grant
C = children under 5
V = rateable value
g = grant payment per head of weighted population
P = population

Using the definitions and equation (1) in Appendix 1.7.A1 describing the grant:

$$G_j = gP_j\left(1 + 20\bar{C}_j - \frac{1}{£10}\,\bar{V}_j\right) \tag{1}$$

$$G = \Sigma G_j = g\left(\Sigma P_j + 20\Sigma P_j\bar{C}_j - \frac{1}{£10}\,\Sigma P_j V_j\right)$$

However: $\Sigma P_j\bar{C}_j = \Sigma C_j = C; \;\; \Sigma P_j\bar{V}_j = \Sigma V_j = V$

Therefore, $$G = g\left(\Sigma P_j + 20C - \frac{1}{£10}\,V\right)$$

and

$$\bar{G} = \frac{G}{\Sigma P_j} = g\left(1 + 20\bar{C} - \frac{1}{£10}\,\bar{V}\right) \tag{2}$$

From (1)

$$\bar{G}_j = g\left(1 + 20\bar{C}_j - \frac{1}{£10}\,\bar{V}_j\right) \tag{3}$$

Subtracting (2) from (3) gives:

$$\bar{G}_j = \bar{G} + 20g(\bar{C}_j - \bar{C}) - \frac{g}{£10}(\bar{V}_j - \bar{V}) \tag{4}$$

(Although the expression becomes more complicated, the same transformation can be used for all the factors in the 1929 and 1936 formulae.) From (4) we can see that the formula is a per capita grant of $\bar{G}$, adjusted for any difference between the authority's per capita number of children and the national average, and between the authority's per capita rateable value and the national average. An authority which had the national average of these variables would receive $\bar{G}$ per head of population.

In the first grant period, $\bar{G}$ in the above formula was £0.37 and g was £0.1445. The great weight given to children relative to rateable value can be easily deduced from the above formulation. As far as the amount of grant received by an authority was concerned, an extra child was worth the 'loss' of £200 of rateable value. The extra grant received from an additional child, holding everything else the same, was £2.89. In this period, average expenditure per head of population by local authorities was about £6.

If we now compare two authorities both with the same number of children per head as the national average and one with the same per capita rateable value as the national average while the other has, to take an absurd extreme, no rateable value ($\bar{V}_j = 0$). The first authority would receive a per capita grant of £0.37, the second would receive a per capita grant of £0.46. With such a low weight attached to rateable value, the formula did not achieve much in the way of equalisation of rate poundages.

(II)   THE EXCHEQUER EQUALISATION GRANT OF 1948

We saw in Appendix 1.7.A1 that the calculation of this grant was based on rateable value per head of weighted population.

Let C = children under 15
       S = sparsity measure
       P^w = weighted population
       $\bar{V}_w$ = average rateable value per head of weighted population

The credited rateable value of an authority is

$$CV = P_j^w \bar{V}_w - V_j = (P_j \bar{V} - V_j) + (P_j^w \bar{V}_w - P_j \bar{V}) \tag{1}$$

However,

$$\bar{V} = V/P$$

$$\bar{V}_w = \frac{V}{P + C + S}$$

Therefore,

$$\frac{\bar{V}}{\bar{V}_w} = \frac{P + C + S}{P} = 1 + \bar{C} + \bar{S}$$

and $\bar{V} = \bar{V}_w(1 + \bar{C} + \bar{S})$.

Also,

$$P_j^w = P_j(1 + C_j + S_j)$$

Therefore,

$$P_j^w V_w - P_j \bar{V} = P_j \bar{V}_w [(\bar{C}_j - \bar{C}) + (\bar{S}_j - \bar{S})] \tag{2}$$

From (2) we can see that the additional rateable value given to an authority depends on its number of children per capita relative to the national average and its sparsity measure relative to the national average.

(III)   THE 1958 AND 1966 FORMULAE

Let N^1, N^2 ... be the number of units of the needs variables entering the formula, n_1, n_2 ... the payments per unit of these needs; d is the rate deduction in the 1958 formula; and z is the per capita payment. Then

$$G_j = zP_j + n_1 N_j^1 + n_2 N_j^2 + \ldots - dV_j$$

$$G = z\Sigma P_j + n_1 \Sigma N_j^1 + n_2 \Sigma N_j^2 + \ldots - d\Sigma V_j \tag{1}$$

$$\bar{G} = z + n_1 \bar{N}^1 + n_2 \bar{N}^2 + \ldots - d\bar{V}$$

Therefore

$$z = \bar{G} - n_1 \bar{N}^1 - n_2 \bar{N}^2 + d\bar{V} \tag{2}$$

From (1)

$$\bar{G}_j = z + n_1 \bar{N}_j^1 + n_2 \bar{N}_j^2 + \ldots - d\bar{V}_j \tag{3}$$

Substituting (2) into (3)

$$\bar{G}_j = \bar{G} + n_1 (\bar{N}_j^1 + \bar{N}^1) + n_2 (\bar{N}_j^2 - \bar{N}^2) + \ldots - d(\bar{V}_j - \bar{V}) \tag{4}$$

In 1967, the rate product deduction (d in [4]) became zero.

Comparing (4) of the 1929 formula, (2) of the 1948 formula, and (4) of the 1958 and 1966 formulae we can see their similarities and differences. All base the grant on the differences between the average per capita measure of some factors in an authority, and the per capita average of these factors in the country. The differences in the various formulae lie in the factors chosen and in the flexibility available to change the amount of grant going to some types of authorities without changing the total grant while retaining the formula. In the 1958 and 1966 formula, the relative weight given to any factor could be changed by changing the relative payment made to the factors, thus changing the relative amounts of grant received by different authorities without changing the total grant given by the government. This could not be done with the 1929 formula.

8 Conclusions

We have now reached a stage where we can draw the threads of our argument together. We have described a system of local government finance which has slowly evolved over centuries. Though what local authorities provide has changed over the years, local expenditure has risen substantially as a proportion of gross domestic product (GDP). The rate as a local property tax financing local expenditure is among the most ancient of taxes. It has been changed by alteration in the definition of property and in other ways. Since the first half of the nineteenth century, local government has regularly been in receipt of central government grant; though the proportion of local expenditure financed by grant has risen almost continuously until it has reached about two-thirds.

For more than a century there has been intermittent discussion of the workings and improvement of local government finance. We have recounted what we believe to have been the more important issues and conflicts of opinion. It is easy to think we are learning that most boring and useless of history lessons: that history repeats itself. Worse still, to draw the conclusion from the undoubted similarities of the predicaments and debates that have recurred that nothing changes. This is not true, as we think the preceding chapters have shown. Neither is it quite true that the changes that happen owe nothing to any deliberate conscious intention. So often it seems to us the intentions of the governments of the day have been frustrated by an imperfect understanding of the mechanics, even sometimes the mathematics, needed to achieve their complex aims. The framework of local finance is not to be established by those impatient of minutiae.

What have we learnt from our excursion into the past? Conclusions to each chapter have already been set out. Here we go over those ideas that arise in more than one chapter and which seem to us to be of significance.

Consider first the scope and nature of local government. In a democratic nation, local government commonly means elected government. But as we remarked in Part One, Chapter 1, English local government evolved from a system that was partly, and curiously, elected, and partly appointed. Especially since 1946, there has been a growth of governmental function performed by two forms of localised central government — by local branches of central government and by public corporations with a local presence. This raises the issue of when these three forms of organisation are most appropriate. History gives little help. We find that the transfer of services to what we have called localised central government has been mostly of redistributive services, as we would have expected on theoretical grounds, but there has been no real consistency in this, especially since the 1940s. Social services have been the most rapidly increasing local services since 1960 and are plainly redistributive. Indeed, the majority of local services are carried on in ways which are redistributive. The main argument for transferring local services such as gas, electricity and water to public corporations has been that there are nationwide economies of scale that local government cannot realise. Later we will want to question the adequacy of the judgement and indeed the relevance of economies of scale to the allocation of services between central and local government.

What is the significance of election? Local elections seem to imply the freedom of local government to take its own decisions within given constraints. Our understanding of the past leads us to question any simple distinction between 'free' elected local government and 'unfree' localised central government. John Stuart Mill used the argument that it was convenient for some national functions to be administered locally under the auspices of elected local representatives. In some cases, central government may control a service very considerably but in its administration still wish to involve elected members who are responsive to local views. They influence what is going on, but do not necessarily have anything approaching absolute power over the service. Neither can one assume that the control of a localised central service need itself be strongly centralised. Local agents may be given much discretion, though one would expect the absence of local elections would make them less responsive to local views.

We looked at the allocation of power between central and local government from another standpoint. One often hears that the allocation is plainer in a federal than in a unitary system. We have argued that a model of pure federalism is not applicable to the British (and possibly any other) system of local government. However, even though a completely specified allocation of powers between central and local government is extremely difficult the confusion on this point need not be as great as it currently appears in Britain.

Despite the limitations of fiscal federalism as a description, some of its key ideas do suggest the basis of an efficient division of labour.

We start with the observation that some local goods and services are either non-excludable or non-rival or both: that is, charging is not feasible and inefficient.

Or they are local spatial monopolies which if privately provided would be provided inefficiently. Or they are provided with redistributive intent – either as a form of cash transfer, as a proxy for cash transfer, or paternalistically with the apparent intention of inducing households to consume more of a service than they would freely choose given an equivalent transfer of cash.

If they are non-excludable or non-rival they must be provided by government or not at all. The control of local monopoly and redistribution are also functions that cannot be undertaken by other than government. The argument for local rather than central provision is that what is provided can be better tailored to local needs if there is local choice. This will lead to a more efficient provision of public goods. But there will be secondary effects. Households with 'fiscal residues' – that is which pay out more than they get in benefits – may tend to move to areas which provide the goods and services they want. From this, one can get the notion of local authorities as a market competing to retain and attract households (and employment) – differentiating their product to suit local needs. The discipline of ordinary markets is replaced by the twin disciplines of election, and of emigration of those whose dislike of what is offered is enough to make them move.

From this, one can point to an efficient division of functions. Local government should concentrate on the non-excludable, non-rival and spatial monopoly goods which have a local reference, leaving the national public goods to national government. Redistribution should be left to central government. The essence of redistribution is that it leaves some worse off and others better off. If local authorities vary in their redistributive policies, the losers will be tempted to move to areas where they will be asked to contribute less to redistribution.

Historically one would not expect local government, therefore, to engage in redistribution, yet it always has done so. How does one explain this paradox?

Explanation is possible at three levels. Until extraordinarily recently virtually all civil government was local government. If there were services to be provided or redistribution to be engaged in, the only government to do it was local. We have seen how all civil government was left to local authorities between 1688 and until after the Napoleonic Wars. Thereafter came a change as central government interested itself in home affairs. Historians have told us how during the nineteenth century, *laissez-faire* ideas ebbed away until from 1870 onwards there was increasing belief that government should take positive action. More recently, historians and economists have stressed that even those early nineteenth-century economists whose reputation was as adamant advocates of *laissez-faire* really believed in some positive function for government. Yet in spite of this, the growth of parliamentary interest in home affairs and the growth of the civil service, even as late as 1913 such central domestic civil government as Britain had was on the cheap. Measured by expenditure it had remained small. It existed, but it spent remarkably little by comparison with local government. In the interwar period central expenditure overall grew relative to local expenditure. Most of the civil part of this growth (that was not grants to local authorities) was transfer payments − the assumption of responsibility for pensions, unemployment and poor relief. It was only after 1946 that central government really started providing goods and services.

At another level there were administrative reasons why civil government was local so long. Lack of communications made centralised administration more difficult. Neither did British government develop autocratic centralised machinery of government to overcome this. Thus if there were to be any domestic government − beneficial or redistributive − it had to be local, despite the difficulties of effecting redistribution locally. The danger of the emigration of vagabonds to areas where poor relief was generous and of the exodus of wealthy citizens from areas burdened with poor relief − the essence of the modern Tiebout hypothesis − was well understood in Elizabethan and Stuart England.[1] Despite this, provision had to be local.

At yet another level there is a further explanation of the paradox. Given that civil government in Britain started by being local for administrative reasons, it became easier for central government to exercise control using local government than to replace it by central government. More and more local activities became covered by general legislation in place of the local legislation which had once been the main basis of local action. There were inspectors and there were grants. Gradually there grew up the practice of issuing regulations and circulars by which central government sought to influence and occasionally to control local government. In Chapter 2 we found it difficult to come to any conclusion other than that the ability of central government to influence local government has increased almost continuously since the start of the nineteenth century.

What this means, in effect, is that central government has acted so as to neutralise some of the market-simulating properties that would arise if local authorities were free to express their own preferences. As one would expect from the Tiebout hypothesis, it is most necessary and evident for redistributive services. While some, such as poor relief, have indeed been removed from local government, others such as education, housing and more recently social services are operated within a structure of law, regulations and advice which seeks substantial though not complete uniformity in provision. This is necessary if the losers from local redistribution are not to be tempted to lighten their burdens by emigration to other areas where they are less burdened. The weight of redistribution has also been alleviated by increasing government grant. The feasibility of local product differentiation has been reduced. Both the money and psychic costs of migration have been increased by creating larger local authorities – a process which started with the joining of parishes into Unions for the administration of the poor law. Thus many of the centralising tendencies in British local government can be seen as the consequence of trying to resolve the paradox – to make local government better able to perform redistributive functions for which in a less centralised state it would not be fitted. Other countries have solved the paradox in other ways. For example, education and poor relief are local government functions in the USA. There is practically no central interference and very little central financial support. The most noticeable effect of this is indeed to put a limit on the redistribution that takes place. Not only are the central cities aware of the emigration of the more affluent to suburbs that tax them less, but the suburbs employ land-use zoning to keep out those who would be a particular burden on their services.

At the limit, a local government could be 'unfree', that is no more than an agent. The elected members could be like their ancestors, the justices of the peace, or perhaps more correctly jurymen or members of Royal Commissions. They are genuinely independent and representative with their own ideas and opinions, and in the case of jurymen they are not appointed. Nevertheless what they do is strictly limited in extent. They are safety valves acting as important checks on government but with little discretion over policy or management.

Another paradox is that there are very different views on the practical freedom of local authorities that obtains. Some argue that despite the increased ability that central government has to influence local government, much freedom survives. Others complain that local authorities are little more than mere agents. We cannot get closer to the truth by the historical inquiry we have conducted so far. Later we will return to see if one can come a little closer to the truth by an examination of the evidence.

If, as is true in Britain, local government has been the agent for redistributive services from earliest times, then ideals and habits of philanthropy and service prevail. What were beneficial services begin to be treated as redistributive services. One aspect of this is the decline of charging and the benefit principle in rating. We have shown how the ability-to-pay principle slowly became dominant until it financed almost all services except trading services and housing. Difficulties of measurement, administrative convenience, judicial notions of what was equitable, all had their part in this. But as we will show more plainly in Part Two the inevitable effect of this is to open up fiscal wedges between what households pay for services and the benefit they derive. This is yet another reason for central action or influence to make services more uniform to avoid the problems caused by migration.

We have seen how especially during the nineteenth century and until the First World War the financing of local services quite often caused political controversy. One reason was simply the relative importance of both local public expenditure and local taxation. Another was the deficiencies of the rating system. Seen as an income tax, both its restriction to land and immovable property and the growth of new sources of income, accentuated inequities as between individuals and classes. Where a class lost money as the landowning classes expected to do, and to some extent did, from the repeal of the Corn Laws, it was natural for them to seek compensation. Some alleviation of the rate burden was the most obvious method by which compensation could be made. But this was not the only reason why rating and derating was hotly contested. Throughout the nineteenth century there were struggles between land and capital which were over the sharing of political as well as economic power. The People's Budget of 1910, with its land taxes and its assault on the House of Lords, was not the only, though it was the most conspicuous, occasion when an attempt to shift the burden on to land provoked a major political controversy.

Though in this century we have ceased to think of rates as an income tax because of the growth of direct income taxation and have come to think of rates as a tax on certain kinds of property, there remains a belief that rates would be fairer if they were an income tax. This we will be looking into. But both the limitations of rates as an income tax and the acceptance of the idea that an income tax should be progressive not proportional have provoked some changes to mitigate its incidence. Rate rebates have been introduced to lighten the burden at the lower end. The Exchequer Equalisation Grant which survives as the resources element in Rate Support Grant exists to tend to equalise burdens between authorities rich and poor in rateable value per head. The increased share of local expenditure financed by grant and the growing relative burden of rating on the non-domestic ratepayer have all reduced the 'price' of local services to the domestic ratepayer, so that indirectly an increasing proportion of local expenditure has been financed through a generally progressive tax structure.

Without doubt, grant is the most complicated topic in local government finance. It has been suggested that this is deliberate: Parliament and public opinion may find it easier to accept what it does not understand. But there are good reasons why grant is inevitably complicated. A grant system raises very complex questions of equity, efficiency and control. Possibly this is where old arguments most repeat themselves. We have seen how ideas that were current years ago — especially those of Lord Balfour — became accepted long after. We have also seen how on every occasion tinkering, the political wish to square the circle by reconciling irreconcilable objectives, has led to flaws in the grant system adopted. In each one has been the seeds of its own destruction. The problem here goes back to one of purpose. If government were clear where it wished to influence the purpose of local expenditure and where it was merely concerned to provide local authorities with funds to use at their pleasure, a rational grant structure might be worked out. Evident in the grant structure is a failure to resolve — one might cynically call it a prudent failure to resolve — the separation of powers and division of labour between central and local government. Very curiously in the British system one of the casualties brought about by the actual development of grant is that a local authority scarcely ever gains if its property values rise relative to the national average (Rabinowitz, 1977). Whether this is the cause or effect of a local authority attitude that it does not exist to increase wealth so that it can reduce rate payments or increase expenditure is another complex issue.

There is interdependence between rates, grant, local expenditure and GDP. We have noted an unconscious habit, rather than a conscious rule, that average rate payments be within 2 per cent and 2½ per cent of personal disposable income. We have also found a relationship between the growth of local expenditure and GDP. Though this has changed over the long run, it has been remarkably stable for a number of years. It would seem to follow that if expenditure is related to GDP, and rates to GDP indirectly through personal disposable income, then grant will adjust to meet the difference. At one level, therefore, grant can be seen as performing a passive role. But there is also the question of how far grant itself influences expenditure. Both on theoretical and commonsense grounds — there is no essential difference between the two — we have argued that if grant reduces the price of local services to the domestic ratepayer, more will be consumed. The evidence we have reviewed has been qualitative and historical. More rigorous techniques are needed.

While grant may have been one influence on the growth of local expenditure, we have examined others. Because no clear set of principles distinguishes central from local government output, there is an arbitrary element inasmuch as growth has been influenced by what is in the sector at any one time. However, the demand for government output — local and central — has been highly income-elastic. Though some of the simpler hypotheses do not hold, there has been an undoubted tendency for central expenditure to increase in war and in preparation for war. There has been some tendency for local expenditure in peacetime to grow faster than central expenditure. Before the Second World War cyclical influences were stronger. There was a tendency for local expenditure to be counter-cyclical until the end of the 1930s. Earlier there was some evidence that local authorities adjusted their capital expenditure counter-cyclically. Until the 1930s, there was bound to be a counter-cyclical element in poor relief. Since the Second World War there has been a very moderate counter-cyclical tendency in current expenditure — the most obvious explanation being that local government used periods of relatively light demand for labour to take on staff — because in general they were more insulated from cyclical pressures. Capital expenditure movements have been erratic. Dominated by shifts in housing policy, it is still not easy to relate this to the effect of national change in political control.

We have looked for political explanations. At the national level, changes in party have affected the composition of expenditure and in recent years there has been some tendency for Conservative governments to favour the growth of capital, and Labour governments to favour current expenditure. Overall, however, Labour governments are no more distinguished by higher growth rates than are Conservative governments. Neither are those governments remembered as reforming administrations over those which are remembered as cautious.

Although there have been cycles in the degree of control exerted by the central government on local authorities, we believe that the trend over the period we have examined has shown a decline in local independence. Various inter-related reasons have contributed to this decline; the central government is not wholly responsible for it as local authorities have also played a part.

Until very recently the desire of central government to provide goods and services and to make income transfers was accompanied by a reluctance to undertake these activities directly, It has, therefore, used local authorities for these functions. The tax base available to local authorities has been too narrow to bear the burden of such growing expenditures and the uneven distribution of the tax base among authorities has led to substantial equity problems. Combined with this was the reluctance of the central government to give up any of its profitable tax sources to the local authorities. This resulted in an increasing proportion of expenditures being financed with grants. Moreover, both the central government and the local authorities were and still are reluctant to specify some coherent division of labour which could be used to allocate financial responsibility according to the activities undertaken. The chaotic division of labour that has emerged has been not surprisingly accompanied by a chaotic division of financial responsibility and of control.

History can tell us what has happened and to some extent why it happened, but there are limits to this method. In each period, the arguments used to introduce change or for that matter to maintain the *status quo* have been about the effects of changes or lack of them on the parties concerned. Even though the reasons for the use of such arguments were to promote the interest of some particular group or party, their validity is not unimportant. To come to grips with that problem we need answers to the following analytical questions. Who does bear the burden of rates? What is the effect of a particular grant formula? What is the relationship between the type of financing used and the degree of control available to the central government? History can tell us what people thought were the answers to such questions but not whether they were correct. For an attempt at such an evaluation we move to Part Two.

NOTES

[1] The preamble to the 1662 Poor Act spoke of unrestrained vagabonds who try to settle in a parish 'where there is the best stock, the largest commons and the most commons . . . and when they have consumed it then to another' (Clapham, 1949, p. 300).

PART TWO   ANALYSIS

1 Introduction

We now move from a historical study, both qualitative and quantitative, of the characteristics of the system of local government finance to a theoretical and statistical analysis of outstanding issues.

The order of Part Two is as follows: in Chapter 2 we attempt to construct a consistent theoretical basis for assessing efficiency in local finance. Some conclusions emerge on the desirable properties of a local tax. The argument in this chapter draws extensively on economic theory – some of it quite advanced, though its conclusions are central to much of the analysis in the rest of the book. The non-economist reader may omit the chapter but must be prepared to accept that its conclusions will be used later in the book.

Chapter 3 is also theoretical. It analyses the purposes of grant, making use of the framework developed in Chapter 2. The theory is then applied to the existing grant system as a basis for describing and evaluating it. This chapter, too, draws on economic theory, though only the first section is likely to present any difficulty to non-economists.

The growth of local expenditure was traced historically in Part One. In Chapter 4 of Part Two some recent studies of the determinants of expenditure are reported. These are interesting not only for what they reveal about the factors that may lie behind the often quite substantial variations in the amounts local authorities spend, but also because the current regression method of needs grant assessment is itself based on analysis of expenditure. This chapter is empirical rather than theoretical.

Chapter 5 is on the grant elasticity of expenditure. The chapter contains both a theoretical analysis of the relationship between grants and expenditure and a report of statistical work carried out. Parts of this chapter again make use of economic theory.

Chapter 6 is about rates. First, there is an examination of the relationship between market values and rateable values – as a factor contributing to the alleged regressiveness of rates – and also the extent to which benefits of local government services and rate bills themselves affect market values. Next the regressiveness of domestic rates and the burden of non-domestic rates on industry are considered, and how the relative burden has been shifted through the 'domestic element' of the grant. Finally, there is some economic theory as to the effective – as opposed to formal – incidence of rates.

The last two chapters of this part are both on the relations between central and local government. The first is the more general discussion. It considers the ways in which central government intervenes in local government and the apparent reasons for this. It then attempts an empirical test of the practical freedom of local government. By contrast, Chapter 8 is confined to one aspect of these relations, central government's responsibility for macroeconomic policy, and the relevance to that of local authorities' behaviour. Various ideas current on how central government can influence local government are analysed. Unlike other chapters in this part, this chapter goes on to consider how central government's control of the macroeconomic consequences of local authority behaviour can be improved. This seems sensible because we argue that it is a distinct topic, and improvement there does not depend on any of the reforms of local government finance to be canvassed in Part Three and Part Four.

2 Efficiency in Local Taxation

We are concerned in this chapter with the economic concept of allocative efficiency, or Pareto optimality (see, for example, Little, 1957; Mishan, 1960). There are, of course, other aspects of economic efficiency in local taxation — collection costs, ease of evasion, and so on — and some we shall consider later on (Part Four, Chapter 3). The argument of this chapter is primarily theoretical. Its purpose is to provide a rigorous demonstration of propositions that will be used in discussing the grant system (in the next chapter), the incidence of rates (Chapter 6), and the suitability of new local taxes (in Part Four). Readers with no special interest in economic theory can safely omit this chapter but they will then have to accept its argument on trust.

The economic concept of allocative efficiency or Pareto optimality means, very roughly, that the resources of a community are employed in producing those goods and services which best match the preferences of the people in the community. Productive resources are scarce, and producing more of one good normally entails producing less of another. Allocative efficiency, or Pareto optimality, is a state from which it is impossible, by reallocating production from one good to another, to make anyone better off without making someone else worse off.

It is a standard proposition of welfare economics that allocative efficiency requires that people pay a price for the goods and services they consume equal to the cost of production. In competitive markets the prices charged to consumers will, in principle, and neglecting taxation and externalities, equal the costs of production, and the allocation of resources will, therefore, be efficient. In this chapter we are interested in similar conditions for allocative efficiency in the local government sector.

The most obvious approach, by direct comparison with the private sector, is for local government to charge for its services. If local government were to charge for services a price equal to costs of production, just as private firms do, people's choices would be efficient in terms of resource allocation. From the standpoint of economic efficiency no more need be said: charging for services, where feasible, is the most efficient arrangement on economic grounds. The feasibility of charging is, of course, a different matter, and we take this up in more detail in Part Four, Chapter 4.

In this chapter we are concerned instead with local government services that are financed through local taxation. Such services may be beneficial public goods whose benefits are non-excludable or non-rival (see Part One, Chapter 3), so that charging would be inefficient. They may be goods whose purpose is redistributive and would therefore be negated by charging. Or local governments may have decided not to charge for some service, though it would be perfectly feasible to do so. When local governments finance services from taxation they typically provide the same types and quality of service to all their residents. An individual household resident in some community is thus faced with a given set of services and a given level of local taxation. It is not in a position to choose more, or better, local government services (and to pay correspondingly higher taxes) but as long as it is resident in that community it must accept the collective decision.

There are, none the less, two mechanisms whereby economic efficiency can be achieved in this system. One, which we have discussed in Part One, is the 'median voter' hypothesis, which argues that the level of provision of local government services in each authority approximates the preferences of the median voter. The other, with which we are more concerned in this chapter, is the 'Tiebout effect' which argues that people wanting a different set of local government services from those provided where they live can move to a different local authority providing the services they want (Tiebout, 1956). But if these mechanisms are to be economically efficient there must be a higher price – in the form of higher taxation – for better services. If people vote for more local government services, they divert resources into local government, thereby reducing output elsewhere in the economy. Only if their taxes go up to match the higher expenditure will their decisions be economically efficient. Similarly, in choosing where to live a household will make an efficient decision only if the taxes levied in the different authorities equal the costs of the services provided.

These arguments of allocative efficiency assume that local government services are beneficial. But many – possibly most – local government services are re-distributive. We need to recall how we have used these words. A ratepayer gets a beneficial service when the value to him and his household or family is equal to the price he pays for it in local taxation. A community provides a beneficial service to itself when the same holds for its median voter – or more loosely for the 'majority'. If local authorities were competitive as perfectly as Tiebout imagined conceivable, one would expect the prices of such services to equal the long-run marginal costs of their provision (if it were feasible to charge of them, that is if they were 'excludable' and 'rival'). However, because tax prices are only rough approximations to efficient charges (whether these be based on long-run or short-run, marginal or average costs), their financing will have redistributive impacts – which we have called 'fiscal wedges' or 'residua' following precedent. If the value of a beneficial service to a ratepayer is more than the tax price he pays, he gains a positive fiscal wedge. If he has to pay more for it than it is worth, his wedge is negative.

However, the accidental or at least unintentional wedges that are the con-sequence of imperfect charging mechanisms need to be distinguished from intentional redistribution. A locally determined redistributive service is one meant to redistribute in cash or in kind. It may be from the median voter or majority to minorities – such as the poor, the aged, the mentally handicapped and so forth – in which case it is altruistic; or it may be from other minorities to the majority or median voter when it is egoistic. A centrally determined re-distributive service, on the other hand, would use the local authority as an agent and would reflect central government policies which also might be altruistic or egoistic or some mixture of both. It is also possible to imagine either tier of government redistributing from one minority to another which might be called neutral redistribution. As a consequence, without deciding first whether it is centrally or locally determined, one cannot easily define the form of redistribution or even firmly distinguish between beneficial and redistributive services. However, currently the main candidates for consideration as beneficial services would appear to be police, fire, refuse collection, street cleaning and lighting, libraries, parks and other environmental services. The main redistributive services would appear to be education, housing and social services (though in many localities their beneficiaries may be in the majority). The second group, of course, constitutes the larger part of total expenditure.

Education, however, is a particularly difficult case and is often classified as beneficial. Someone looking back over their lifetime might be expected to regard the income generated by the education he has received as beneficial to him. A father or mother may identify sufficiently closely with the interests of their children as to feel a benefit to them is indistinguishable from one to the parents. Such redistribution as occurs may be regarded as between different periods in a person's life, or alternatively as between generations, rather than as in the more normal sense between persons. Even so if, for example, some authorities provide no schools, or very poor ones, there would be an incentive for childless households to locate there before and after their child-rearing years, but moving somewhere where the schools are better when they want to send children to school. Such mobility would be economically inefficient. Moreover, there is redistribution of a more normal kind. Some childless households will never have children and yet are required to contribute to the education of the children of others. They, too, will have an incentive to go where the provision of education costs them least. In sum, in a neighbourhood where most residents are families or those about to raise or who have raised families, education is probably best analysed as a beneficial service; but where the majority do not have children of school age it is probably better analysed as a redistributive service.

Since the taxpayer does not always benefit from redistributive services, economic efficiency requires that the tax he pays is independent either of the amount of the service provided in his local authority or of his choice of where to live. This can be attempted either through the choice of tax instrument or through an approximately designed grant or through a mixture of both.

The main purpose of this chapter, however, is to compare different possible local taxes from the standpoint of economic efficiency. We shall examine five taxes: a poll tax, a local income tax, a land tax, a tax on residential property, and a tax on all property (such as the present rating system). But first we shall examine the assumptions underlying the Tiebout hypothesis more carefully, since they run through the whole of the subsequent analysis.

THE TIEBOUT HYPOTHESIS

To Tiebout, local government could be considered as an institutional arrangement which enables people to choose the public services they want, in the same way that the market system enables them to choose private goods and services. The method of purchasing is, of course, different in that it involves a simultaneous choice of where to live. The two methods are equivalent only if a number of special assumptions hold:

(1) that there are numerous authorities providing a sufficiently wide range of services so that every household's preferences can be catered for;
(2) that households are indifferent about where they live except for the provision of local government services;
(3) that the mobility of households between localities is costless;
(4) that local authorities adjust their levels of provision of local government services in response to movements of population.

This last assumption, which is in fact slightly different from that made by Tiebout, requires some explanation. Let us say, for example, that the set of services provided in one locality suddenly becomes very popular. People will attempt to crowd into that locality. But the locality cannot expand costlessly — it has some factors in fixed supply (for example, land). Existing facilities will become congested, and existing residents will try to stop the in-migration by planning restrictions on new housebuilding. House prices will rise sufficiently to choke off the excess demand to live in that locality.

The outcome is that many of the people wishing for that set of local government services cannot get them. A further mechanism is required. Tiebout suggested that new communities would spring up providing the mix of services people wanted and could not get in existing authorities. In Britain there is no empty land where new authorities can spring up. So we assume instead that other existing authorities suffering a loss of population will adjust their provision of services to a more popular mix. The analogy, as with Tiebout, is with competitive industry where, in this case, firms seeing a decline in the demand for their product switch to more popular lines.

While these assumptions ensure that the provision of local government services matches household demand, they do not ensure economic efficiency. That depends on the relative prices households have to pay — in the form of taxation — for the different levels of services, which itself depends on the type of tax levied. We next consider, therefore, the allocative efficiency of different taxes in this context by means of a simple analytical model.

A POLL TAX

In the literature of public finance, the superior economic efficiency of a poll tax above other taxes is based on its not being a disincentive to work since its incidence is independent of how much work is done or income earned, and it does not distort how income is spent. But in local government finance it has another efficiency property. Let us assume:

(1) that all services produced by local authorities are beneficial;

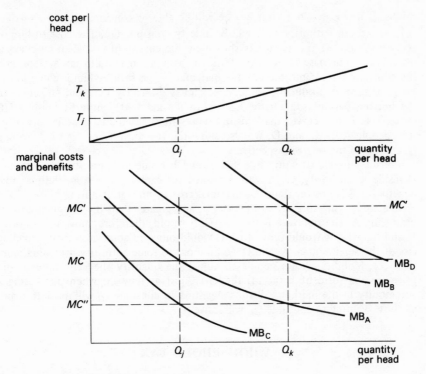

Figure 2.2.1. *Mobility to acquire benefits*

(2) that everyone receives the same beneficial services which are produced at constant (long-run marginal) cost;
(3) that the median voter's tax bill equals the long-run marginal cost of the services he consumes; and
(4) that all services are provided for persons (and none for non-domestic entities).

Then let authority j provide more services than authority k, but in each authority the services are financed by a constant per capita or poll tax. On the assumptions stated, the poll tax would be economically efficient.

In the top part of Figure 2.2.1 the per capita quantity of the good is measured on the horizontal axis, and the cost per capita which is also equal to the per capita tax on the vertical axis. As we move along the horizontal axis, changing the per capita quantity, we are moving across different local authorities which have decided to provide the per capita quantity shown. We show two authorities, j and k, which are providing the per capita quantities, Q_j and Q_k, to their residents. The per capita taxes are T_j and T_k, respectively. These taxes just cover the total costs of providing the services.

Consider a person choosing the quantity of the service he wishes to acquire. He can purchase any quantity he wants by choosing among the different authorities. If he locates in authority j he will be able to consume Q_j of the service. If he locates in authority k he will be able to consume Q_k. The cost to him of acquiring more of the service is shown by the change in tax when he changes localities to purchase more of it. With the assumed per capita tax system, and the constant cost of production, the marginal cost as seen by him is equal to the marginal cost of producing the service. This is shown by the solid MC curve in the bottom part of the Figure 2.2.1. (For the moment, ignore the dashed MC curves.) The four curves marked MB represent the marginal-benefit curves for four people A, B, C, and D. We also show the two authorities j and k providing Q_j and Q_k of the service respectively.

Consider first a situation in which C and B reside in authority j, and A and D reside in authority k. With the assumed per capita tax system, the marginal benefit for B is greater than the marginal cost to him of acquiring more of the service by moving to a different locality, and greater than the marginal cost of producing it. The opposite is true for C. B would, therefore, move to authority k, and likewise A would move to j. C would move to some authority providing less of the service than Q_j, and D would move to some authority providing more than Q_k. Mobility allows people to adjust the quantity they consume to the price (in the form of taxation) they pay, just as they do when purchasing a commodity in the market. All those wanting to consume Q_j will move to j, and all those wanting to consume Q_k will move to k.[1]

A HOUSEHOLD TAX

So far we have argued as if the consumption of beneficial services was the same for all persons in an authority. But the consumption of several may be better related to households or to dwellings than to the number of persons in a household or dwelling. For example, the investment needed to connect a house to power, water or sewerage may be so related as may be the amount of fire or police protection needed. If for any such reason a per household or per dwelling tax were preferable on grounds of economic efficiency, then the arguments of the last section would still hold except that 'households' or 'dwellings' should be substituted for 'persons' where appropriate.

One can imagine many modifications of a poll or household tax where the tax varied with age or other characteristics of the person or income in so far as they better reflected differences in the costs of providing services in the first case or with differences in the number in the household and various other characteristics of the household including its income in the second. The only ground we are at present considering for such a choice is superior efficiency (not equity). Other modifications of such a tax could relate to the physical dwelling – its ground area, volume, or building, its land. One could imagine a combination of such taxes reflecting the particular efficiency characteristics of different beneficial services.

The other taxes considered in this chapter can be considered as such modifications of poll or household taxes (local income tax) or dwelling taxes (land, housing and property taxes).

LOCAL INCOME TAX

Let us make assumptions comparable to those for a poll tax. They are the same except that the persons referred to are income-tax payers.

Let us consider now what would happen if we switch from the per capita tax system to a local income tax. To simplify the problem we shall initially assume that the average income in all the authorities considered is the same. In all authorities the tax rate times the average income in the authority will have to be equal to the previous per capita tax to provide the same total tax revenue. The cost of acquiring different amounts of the service is now different for different people. The cost of local government services in a locality is now the tax rate in that locality multiplied by the person's income. The cost of moving from one locality to another is the difference between the tax rates in the two localities multiplied by the taxpayer's income. On our assumption that average income in all authorities is the same, differences in tax rates among the authorities will reflect the differences in the amounts of services provided. Thus only for someone with the average income will the marginal cost as seen by him of acquiring more of the service be equal to the marginal cost of providing it. Only for such an individual is the solid *MC* curve shown in the bottom of Figure 2.2.1 relevant.

To bring out the kind of problem that this raises, assume that the people whose marginal benefit curves are shown in Figure 2.2.1 have different incomes. A and C have below-average incomes, B and D above-average. Now the marginal cost curves as seen by the two pairs are different both from one another and from what they were under the per capita tax system. The marginal cost curve as seen by B and D is the dashed marginal cost curve lying above the solid one. The marginal cost curve as seen by A and C is the dashed marginal cost curve lying below the solid one. Now C and B will choose to reside in authority *j*, and A and D will choose to reside in authority *k*. The location decisions of each person in our example are inefficient, even though each is equating his marginal benefit to his perceived marginal cost. The problem is that they do not perceive the true marginal cost of providing the service. (Such inefficiency will be called vertical.)

The basic reason for the misallocation in this case is that with services provided equally to all, but financed by a proportional tax system the provision of services necessarily involves a redistribution of income. All those whose tax base, in this case income, is above average, pay more for the services, all those whose tax base is less than average pay less. Earlier we referred to this vertical inefficiency as 'fiscal wedges' or 'residua' (Breton, 1965; Buchanan, 1949; see Part One, Chapter 3). Different people face different prices for the same service.

But there is a further problem with a local income tax. In general, the average level of income will differ between localities. The tax rate required to finance any given level of public spending will be lower in the locality with a high average income than in the locality with a lower average income. This creates an 'inefficient' incentive to migration, since everyone will wish to move into the high-income locality, not because it provides the public goods they want but in order to reduce their tax bill. (This inefficiency will be called horizontal.)

To examine the implications of this case in more detail, consider Figure 2.2.2.

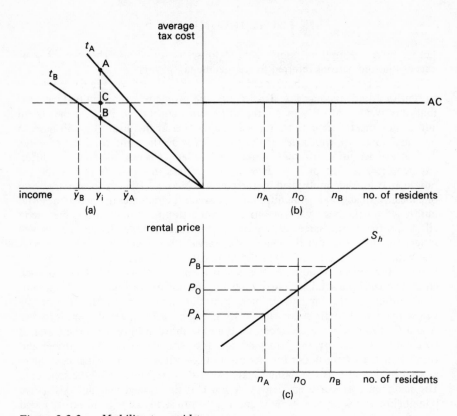

Figure 2.2.2.   *Mobility to avoid taxes*

The horizontal axis in the top right quadrant measures the number of residents in a locality. On the vertical axis of that quadrant we measure the average cost of providing the local government services and the taxes paid. Assume there are two authorities, A and B, which have identical average cost curves, so that the average cost curve shown in Figure 2.2.2 measures average costs in both authorities. In the bottom quadrant we show the housing market which, again, we assume is the same in both authorities. The curve marked S^h shows the supply curve for housing being a function of the annual rental price of housing (P_H) measured on the vertical axis. The horizontal axis measures the number of residents (n) in the authority, and initially we shall assume that the demand for housing depends only on the size of population.

Assume that initially the goods provided by the local authorities were financed by a per capita tax. The initial distribution of the population would then be such that there are n_O people in each authority. The annual rental cost of housing is then P_O in each authority. People will locate themselves among the two authorities, other things being equal, in such a way that the rental of housing will be the same in both. If the rental rate were higher in one authority than in the other, people would move from one to the other until the rental price of housing were equalised.

Assume now that we replace the per capita tax used to finance the locally provided services by an income tax. Assume that the average income in authority B, $\bar{Y}_B$, is higher than the average income in authority A, $\bar{Y}_A$. To finance the given quantity of the local good, authority A will therefore have to charge a higher rate of tax than authority B. This situation is shown in the top left-hand quadrant. On the horizontal axis we measure income, on the vertical axis taxes. The lines marked t_A and t_B measure the tax rates that have to be levied by the two authorities to finance the provision of the services. Thus $t_A \bar{Y}_A = t_B \bar{Y}_B = AC$. The tax rate times the average income in each authority is equal to the cost of providing the local services.

With the new tax system everyone living in authority A, in which the tax rate is higher, would now like to move to authority B, in which the tax rate is lower. As people move from A to B, the price of housing in B rises and in A it falls. Now when people decide whether to move from B to A, or the other way around, they have to consider two factors. The tax rate in A is higher, but the rental of housing in A is lower. It pays someone to move from authority A to authority B as long as the difference in the taxes he has to pay just compensates him for the differences in the rental of housing. However, the difference in the taxes he has to pay depends on his income. The higher his income, the larger is the difference in the tax he has to pay in the two authorities, and therefore the more willing he is to pay the higher rental for housing to move from A to B.

Consider a person whose income is Y_i shown in the top left quadrant of Figure 2.2.2. Assume we are now in a situation where, because of the movement of people from A to B, the rental rate of housing in A is P_A and in B it is P_B. The difference in the annual rental rate of housing is thus $P_B - P_A$. For a person with income Y_i the difference in his annual tax bill in the two authorities is $Y_i(t_A - t_B)$; this is shown by the distance AB in the left quadrant. If this distance is equal to the distance $P_B - P_A$, he is indifferent between the two authorities. For anyone with an income greater than Y_i it pays to move to authority B and pay more for housing. For anyone whose income is less than Y_i, it pays to move to authority A and pay more in taxes. Thus in equilibrium all those with an income greater than Y_i will live in authority B, and all those with an income less than Y_i will live in authority A.[2]

Two important points are brought out by the above analysis. First, the use of a local income tax to finance local services misrepresents the true cost of these services. The costs people face are the taxes they pay and the cost of housing. The taxes they pay depend on their income and on the average income in their locality which determines the tax rate. Thus not only do people with different incomes pay different amounts, but people with the same income residing in localities with different average incomes pay different amounts for the same services. It is exactly these differences which lead people to seek different localities, to avoid the tax burdens. Such mobility is inefficient. Relative house prices are affected, and thus the resources in the housing industry are misallocated. The other important point is that the relative burdens on people arising from the provision of local services depend not only on the actual tax rates across local authorities, but also on house prices. We cannot argue that because the tax rate is higher in one authority than in another, even though the services provided are the same in the two, the cost of local government services to people is higher in the one than in the other. That is to ignore the other important variable affecting the total burden, namely the differences in house prices which have resulted from the differences in tax burdens.

Consider a person with income Y_i in Figure 2.2.2. As we saw, he is indifferent as to whether he resides in authority A or B. In one he would pay higher taxes, in the other he would pay more for housing. If we looked at only the taxes paid and compared two people with an income Y_i, one living in authority A and one living in authority B, we would conclude that the one living in A is paying more for local services than the one living in B. As they are receiving the same services, we might think that inequitable. However, if we take account of the differences in house prices in the two authorities — differences due solely to the differences in tax rates — then we would conclude that both are paying the same amount for the services, but in different forms. One pays high taxes offset by low housing costs, the other pays low taxes offset by high housing costs. For anyone whose income is below Y_i, the higher tax rate in authority A is more than offset by the lower house prices in that authority, and the net cost of acquiring the local authority services is lower than it would be had they lived in authority B. Similarly, for anyone with an income greater than Y_i, the lower tax burden in authority B is not fully offset by the higher housing costs in that authority.

One other point is brought out by the analysis in Figure 2.2.2. There are different kinds of redistributions going on which are not at all obvious if one looks at only the local tax and benefit systems. We saw that the mobility of certain income groups arises because of the different amounts of redistribution that occur through the tax system in the two authorities. The mobility itself, however, leads to another set of redistributions which are more subtle. We saw that housing costs in B would rise and in A would fall. This means that the incomes of the owners of those factors used in housing which are in inelastic supply would rise in B and would fall in A. The higher rents paid in B will ultimately accrue in the form of higher incomes to the owners of factors in B. Similarly, the lower rents in A will show up as a fall in income to such factors in A. The fiscal benefits of living in B are, at least partially, capitalised into land values.

Consider again the individual with income Y_i who, as we saw, is indifferent as to whether he lives in authority A or B. In A he would be paying Y_iA in taxes for services whose cost is Y_iC. Thus he is paying AC more in taxes than the cost of the local services he is receiving. At the same time, he is paying $P_O - P_A$ less for housing services as compared to the pre-mobility situation. As a first approximation, this is the amount of income being transferred to him from the factors which are in inelastic supply.[3] Similarly, if that individual resided in authority B his payment in taxes would be less than the cost of the local services he would receive by an amount BC. However, he would be paying more in housing by an amount $P_B - P_O$. Again as a first approximation, this is the amount he would be transferring as additional income to the factors in inelastic supply in authority B.

As we saw, the net transfers for this individual are the same in the two authorities; that is why he is indifferent as to where he resides. But the recipients of these transfers are different in the two authorities.

Considered as an efficient local tax, there are thus two drawbacks to a local income tax. First, the Tiebout effect does not operate efficiently vertically because the tax cost of public services provided in different localities does not equal their costs of production but is affected also by the taxpayer's income. Secondly, differences in the average income levels of different localities create further incentives to migrate between localities which have no justification in terms of horizontal economic efficiency, and which tend to create localities segregated by income level.[4]

To combine these effects would require formal analysis beyond the scope of this book. What can be shown is that the resulting system is unstable (Wheaton, 1975).[5] There are always households who can better their position by moving from one authority to another. But as they move, they alter the relative advantages of different locations for other households, who then also wish to move. The outcome has been described as a game of 'musical suburbs', in which households continually follow one another around from place to place, all ending up no better off than at the beginning (Hamilton, 1975).

A LAND TAX

We next consider a tax on land, or site value rating. It is a standard proposition of economic theory that a tax on land is borne by landowners and not by the tenant or occupant of the land. The reasoning is as follows:

A landowner is faced with the choice of how to use his land. In general, it will be in his interest to put it to its most profitable use — be it industrial, residential, agricultural, or whatever. The landowner then receives as income the rent the land earns in its most profitable use. Now a tax is imposed on land rents. In consequence, the landlord's income, after tax, from each possible use of land is reduced. But, unless the marginal tax rate is over 100 per cent, the use offering the highest pre-tax income will offer the highest after-tax income also. The landowner has no incentive to switch his land out of the most profitable use. In consequence, the supply of land for each use remains unchanged, and therefore the market price of the land in each use does not change either. The land tax is neutral: it does not affect land use because it does not affect the market price of land, and it is entirely borne by landowners for the same reason. Land taxes have always been considered efficient because of this neutrality.

Analytically, the key feature of land is that it is assumed to be effortless or costless for the landowner to put the land to its most profitable use, rather than to some other. If the differential cost of maintaining the land in its most profitable use is zero, it will be put to that use however small the differential return net of tax. On the other hand, if there were higher costs in maintaining land in its most profitable use,[6] a land tax might reduce the after-tax return to such an extent that it did not cover the higher costs, and consequently the land would be taken out of its previously most profitable use. The supply of land to different uses would then change, and the tax would be neither neutral nor efficient.

For the rest of this chapter we will assume such costs are negligible, and that the rent of land is pure economic rent. And we will assume that a land tax is a tax on this pure economic rent, and that it does not affect the market price of land or the amount of land in different uses. The tax is paid wholly by landowners.

When the only function of a tax is to collect revenue, these efficiency and neutrality properties of a land tax are desirable. But where local taxation finances beneficial services, a land tax has a different function.

Let us consider what happens if local authorities provide different amounts of services which are financed by an *ad valorem* land tax. To understand its workings we need to make and then relax some restrictive assumptions. We assume:

(1)   that all services are beneficial;
(2)   that every household receives the same beneficial services produced at a constant cost per household;
(3)   that all householders are owner-occupiers;
(4)   that the median voter's tax bill equals the cost of services his household consumes;
(5)   that all land is residential; and
(6)   there can be no changes in the number of households through a change in household density.

All except the last are similar to the assumptions made for earlier taxes.

Then let local authority A provide more services than local authority B, so that households in A on average pay more land tax than those in B. It might be thought that a household considering whether to locate in A or B would prefer A because the burden of providing services is borne by landowners; but on the assumptions above that is not an advantage to him, since in order to benefit from such services he would have to become an owner-occupier and buy land (and a house) and pay land tax.

It might be thought that there was a vertical inefficiency analogous to that found with a local income tax, and that it would pay a household on our assumptions, the value of whose land was above average, to move out since it would be experiencing a negative fiscal wedge — paying more in tax than the cost of the services received. Conversely, one might expect lower-income households to move into lower-value land benefiting from a positive fiscal wedge. But if either were to happen there would be corresponding movement in house prices. The emigrating households from the higher-valued land would bring the relative price of the higher-valued land down, while those migrating into the lower-valued land would raise its relative price. After a disturbance there would be equilibrium when the differences in land values reflected variations in size, location and any other differences, but not differences in local fiscal burden. The fiscal wedges would have been capitalised by appropriate changes in land values. Therefore, on the assumptions set out above, there would in fact be no fiscal wedges and therefore no vertical inefficiency. They would be eliminated by capitalisation.

The same would be true of horizontal inefficiency between authorities. If for any reason authority A on average provided a better local fiscal package of beneficial services, then the house-price differential between the two would compensate precisely at the margin for the difference in the value of local government services in the two cases, since otherwise migration would take place until the two were brought into equilibrium. However — and this is the important point — migration will not take place because the effect of any fiscal wedge between authorities will be capitalised in land values. We therefore reach the conclusion that, on the assumptions made, differences in the burden of supplying beneficial services between authorities will not generate migration. If a household unexpectedly finds some change in the average benefits received or local taxes paid by households in its authority occupying land of its value, it will be locked in by a corresponding change in land values which will give no incentive to migration inward or outward.

Tiebout movements will only take place if there are differences in benefits which lead households to prefer to move from one authority to another as more congenial because of the services provided, and such movement is, of course, vertically and horizontally efficient.

These results obtain because the effect of the assumptions made is to make the supply of land, plots and household spaces completely inelastic. We may relax assumption (2) that all households in an authority receive the same beneficial services without materially affecting the result. If the costs of providing beneficial services vary with land values, then any fiscal wedges will be fully capitalised. There is no vertical inefficiency. If services vary between households occupying the same valued land, then fiscal wedges will be set up which should lead to Tiebout-style migration until adversely affected households have moved to preferred authorities.

Relaxing assumption (3) is not crucial either. In so far as tenants benefit from local services the cost will be borne by them, not by the landowner if the costs of services can be passed on to tenants. Despite rent control, the rate charges are passed on in Britain and the same might well hold of land taxes.

If asssumption (4) is relaxed, political power is divorced from the tax base in a different way. For example, one could well imagine that a democratic local authority might vote a package of local services to reflect the tastes of the median voter but the burden of which would fall on the richer voters. The effect of this might be sufficient to create a fiscal wedge for those occupying plots of higher value, but there is no difference in principle from those discussed under (2) above. Such a wedge will be capitalised, driving down the prices of higher-valued houses and plots in such areas.

The significance of this change is to alter the redistributive character of the services provided, since the implication is that beneficial services to the median voter may be subsidised by others. As in our analysis of other taxes, the consequence of relaxing this and similar assumptions made earlier is that a service can no longer be provided beneficially in the strict sense set down at the beginning of the chapter. It must be assumed to have some redistributive intent. In so far as it does, the analysis of the second section of the chapter is appropriate.

Relaxing assumptions (5) and (6) has more fundamental consequences. If some land is non-residential and the ratio of its value to that of residential land varies between authorities, then inefficiencies will arise similar to those identified in our discussion of local income tax. It will pay households to move to authorities with higher ratios of non-residential to residential land since, on the assumption that non-residential landowners derive no benefits from local services (or the weaker one that their benefit is lower relative to the taxes they pay), the cost of these services to the residential household will be lower. Migration will take place until land prices rise in the authorities with the more favourable ratios, and the house price differentials reflect no difference in efficiency.

Relaxing assumption (6) has a similar effect since there will be a tendency for subdivision of land and housing in any authority where the package is attractive. Households will move in and try to get the desired package at lower cost through occupying less space and so paying lower taxes. At the same time, households in the opposite situation whose fiscal wedge was negative might respond to the resulting fall in house prices by purchasing more housing. These changes will again be equilibrated through changes in land prices whose final outcome will also not be horizontally efficient.

As these arguments would suggest, what is crucial is the inelasticity of supply. A land tax on residential land alone is a more efficient method of financing beneficial services than is one on other land as well. This point will be taken further in Part Two, Chapter 6 when we discuss the place of non-domestic rating. But if it is possible to substitute non-residential for residential land and vice versa, the efficiency of residential land taxation will be reduced.

A HOUSING TAX

It is helpful to start with the extreme assumption that all households demand the same amount of housing. We again consider two authorities, A and B, A providing more local government services than B and levying a higher tax. The higher tax on housing in A lowers house prices in so far as it is capitalised. But the fact that households will prefer to live in A because of the greater quantity of local government services will tend to raise house prices in A. If the difference in the value of local government services equals the difference in the taxes levied, house prices, net of tax, in the two localities will be the same.

The horizontal inefficiency of the land tax — that of encouraging an increase in population or more strictly households — may also occur with a housing tax, but not if it is achieved by converting non-residential land to residential use, since each new plot may be supposed to be occupied by a new dwelling with a liability to pay taxes. Any fiscal wedges related to differences between the value of that house and the median house will once more be capitalised. Neither will there be inefficiency if more houses are built on the same land, provided the greater density is not reflected in lower taxes; nor if more households crowd into the same dwelling on the same assumption. However, if housing is taxed on an *ad valorem* basis, increased density on some plots or in some dwellings will lead to horizontal inefficiency.

Essentially, though, the assumption we have made, i.e. that all households demand the same fixed amount of housing, makes the housing tax not dissimilar from a poll tax. And, once this extreme assumption is relaxed, the housing tax becomes rather less attractive except in so far as one can assume differences in house prices parallel differences in service costs. Further, if average house values differ between localities the tax rate on housing will differ also, and this will encourage new housebuilding in areas of high average house values (and correspondingly low tax rates). And, of course, the tax on housing will reduce people's demand for housing as against other goods.

Since the land tax and the housing tax both lead to inefficiencies in principle, a comparison between them must depend on particular circumstances. We have, in effect, considered two kinds of housing tax. The first was a per house or household tax which in essence is similar to a poll tax. The second is *ad valorem*, in which case the only difference between it and an *ad. valorem* residential land tax will be its efficiency where non-residential land becomes residential.

A TAX ON ALL PROPERTY

A tax on all property, such as the present rating system, combines all the inefficiencies we have considered so far. We may again start with the case of one authority providing more goods and services than another. It will finance its higher expenditure by levying higher rates, part of which will be paid by households (domestic ratepayers) and is equivalent to a tax on housing, and part paid by industry, commerce, etc. (non-domestic ratepayers). Households, who receive the benefit of the higher spending, pay only part of the cost. People will wish to migrate into the authority.

The pre-tax rental on housing will tend to rise, and, given that only part of the cost of the additional services is borne by taxes on housing, the post-tax rental, and hence house prices, will tend to rise also.

The effect of the higher tax on non-domestic property is a little more complicated. It is necessary to distinguish whether it is employed in the production of goods for national or for purely local markets. If the former, the price the firm can charge for its product is given, and can not be changed just because the firm has to pay higher rates. But if the firm is selling to a local market it may be able to pass on higher costs in the form of higher prices. The tax can be 'shifted forward'.

We consider first a firm selling its products on the national market. We further assume that the particular local authority has not specific locational advantages in production, so that firms are indifferent as to whether they locate in that particular authority or in any other. The demand curve for non-domestic property in the area is on these assumptions perfectly elastic. An increase in the tax on non-domestic property will leave its pre-tax price unchanged. The effect of the tax will therefore be to reduce the post-tax price by the full amount of the tax. Landowners will obviously wish to take their property out of non-domestic use, where the return has fallen, and into domestic use.

Some firms will move out of the authority. The movement of firms out of the authority will lead to a fall in the demand for labour in the authority and if wages are flexible to a fall in wages. This fall in wages will to some extent offset the movement of firms out of the authority because of the property taxes, but it will not do so completely.

Thus if the demand for non-domestic property is perfectly elastic and the tax on such property is increased, we shall have the following effects: there will be an increase in the amount of housing, a movement of firms out of the authority, and a fall in wages within the authority. Who bears the burden of the tax? It is clear that the full burden of the tax will be borne by owners of non-domestic property and by wage earners in the authority. If all the non-domestic property is owned by residents of the authority, then the full burden will be borne by residents of the authority, either in the form of a fall in rental income on land, or in the form of a reduction in wage income.

Assume now that the demand for non-domestic property in the authority is not perfectly elastic but downward sloping. This assumption means that the authority has some special locational characteristics, which means that many firms in a particular industry are located there. The general effects are the same as in the previous case, except that now the pre-tax price of non-domestic property can, and will, rise. As firms leave the locality, the supply of the goods they were producing falls, and as they held a significant share of the market, the price of those goods rises. Now the tax is borne by owners of land and labour as in the first case, but also some of it is shifted forward in higher prices. The price of goods which benefited from the assumed locational advantage of the authority will rise relative to other commodities. One can treat the locational characteristics of the land as an input into the production of some commodities. When this input is taxed, the price of such commodities will rise relative to that of other commodities.

We can now deal very briefly with the case where firms produce goods for the local market and where the prices of goods in the local market can vary from those in the national market. Again the higher tax on non-domestic property will encourage firms to move out of the authority, but this will now reduce the supply of goods to the local market and as a result prices will rise.

The tax is therefore borne in part by owners of non-domestic property and wage-earners as before, but in part also by local residents who have to pay higher prices for the goods they purchase.

The source of inefficiency is the same in each of these cases – the movement of firms out of the authority and the change in land use. The only difference is that the equilibrating mechanism in the case of firms producing for national markets consists only of a fall in wages, while for firms selling in local markets the price of their products can alter as well.

This is the inefficiency we had already noted in the discussion of the general land tax. But rates also entail the inefficiencies of the housing tax. People with a high demand for housing will, other things being equal, tend to pay a large share of the tax bill, and hence prefer authorities whose expenditure is low. If average rateable values differ between authorities, tax rates will also differ and there will be an encouragement for both households and firms to move into the areas of high average rateable value.

CONCLUSION: BENEFICIAL SERVICES

The main point argued so far is that the tax levied to finance beneficial services should be as economically efficient as possible. The most efficient would not be a tax, but a charge set equal to long-run marginal cost for each service consumed by each consumer. That is the ideal against which taxes — by definition less efficient — must be judged.

The most efficient tax is a poll tax since such a lump sum does not affect the quantity of the tax base demanded. A comprehensive poll tax for each citizen in a locality would only be efficient if all citizens there consumed the same services which were produced at a cost equal to the poll tax. In practice, there will be vertical inefficiencies because some will value what they receive at more, and others at less, than what they pay. The main disadvantage of such a tax is that it offends against common perceptions of equity while not as efficient as a specific charge. Horizontal efficiency could only be achieved if there were many authorities and substantial migration.

A fixed household tax would be more efficient than a poll tax if long-run marginal costs of services provided were better related to this basis than that of a poll tax and vice versa. One could also imagine variable poll and household taxes that tried to relate the sums levied to the actual marginal costs of supplying each person or household. It would differ from a charge in that it would be a once-for-all payment on the basis of estimates of future consumption and would not thereafter depend on actual quantities. (If the calculations were retrospective, it would be a charge.)

A housing tax which varied with the value of the structure but not of the site would have some useful efficiency properties. Vertical inefficiencies related to above-average house values causing negative fiscal wedges (and their converse) would be capitalised in the short and medium run. Only in the long run might one expect consequential alterations in housing supply. Horizontal inefficiencies would also be capitalised. Every household moving in would have to pay the cost of the services provided in so far as it had to live in a net addition to the housing stock which paid the same amount of tax as existing households. But there would be a tendency towards horizontal inefficiency in so far as immigrating households were able to take advantage of services in a local authority by increasing housing density and so paying less tax.

A residential land tax has similar properties to those of a housing tax. Capitalisation limits the effect any vertical or horizontal inefficiency may have on migration. It, too, will be less efficient in so far as its burden can be reduced for some families without loss of services, by increasing population densities per unit of land so that their claim on services is partly financed by taxes on other land. However land, unlike housing, is in long-run inelastic supply.

A tax on all land including non-residential would lead to much greater horizontal inefficiency since there would be a tendency for households to reduce their burden by preferring areas with a relatively high proportion of non-residential land. (As we shall see in the next chapter the particular inefficiency can be, and indeed in Britain is, offset by an appropriate grant system.)

It is important to realise how capitalisation works in this case and indeed in any case where immigration leads to higher population density either by sub-division of plots, of houses, even the use of houses by larger families, or an increase in the proportion of residential land. Both the residential and the non-residential user already there is locked in by capitalisation. The locking in may not be perfect if the adjustment process is slow or if an individual has different, more pessimistic expectations on the future of his house or land value than that of the market (which, of course, he will only gain from if he is right). What happens is that immigration is encouraged whenever the immigrant households are able to pay less-than-average local taxes through economising on space and so on the tax base. Other households then have to pay more to cover the total cost of services. Zoning and other restrictions to prevent falling densities are therefore an entirely logical defensive tactic in such circumstances.

An analogous inefficiency would occur if a housing tax were to be replaced by a building tax since again there would be a tendency for locations to be pre-ferred where there was a high proportion of non-residential building (though this, too, could be offset by grant).

A property tax has some combination of the inefficiencies of a land and a building tax. Many other taxes have greater inefficiency in this context. We have here analysed local income taxes. They also create horizontal inefficiency; but their additional drawback is that they create vertical inefficiencies which will not be capitalised (or only to a more limited extent since there is a far from one-to-one correlation between higher incomes and higher land values in an authority).

We conclude, therefore, that an efficient local tax should fall on those who benefit from the local government services. On these grounds, we would prefer a poll tax, a local land tax or − on the assumption of owner-occupation − some form of housing tax. If housing is rented, the case for a housing tax is much less clear. For now tenants can vote for a higher level of local government spending financed by taxation levied on their landlords. A higher standard of local govern-ment services can, of course, make an area more attractive and hence allow landlords to charge higher rents, so that in part they may be able to recoup the tax.

This mechanism is clearly rather unsatisfactory. It is, however, based on the assumption that housing is rented at market rents. In practice, in Britain most property is rented out at below market rents, either as a result of rent-control legislation in the private sector or as a deliberate policy in the local authority sector. Housing taxes can be, and are, passed on in full to the tenant in both these sectors. Rather ironically, the case for a local housing tax on efficiency grounds is strengthened where there is rent control, because the costs of local government services are then borne in full by local residents.

REDISTRIBUTIVE SERVICES

We have seen that most local services are redistributive. Their efficient pricing raises more complicated issues.

Suppose first of all that central government wants to pursue a horizontally equitable redistributive policy defined as one which treats like individuals similarly irrespective of location; but that it wishes in part to use local authorities as its agent. Then if it finances these services by a 100 per cent grant, no special financing problems arise, but if it decides that such services should be financed partly by local taxation – possibly as an inducement to local efficiency – there will be differences in the unit cost of such services falling on the electors in different authorities and therefore on the horizontal inequity to be corrected by grant (see Part Two, Chapter 3).

If local authorities, not central departments, control such services, it follows that they are responsible for their organisation and efficiency. The local electors will have no incentive to be efficient unless they are substantially responsible for financing the services. Therefore to finance them, an efficient tax must fall on electors. It could be any we have considered for beneficial services or indeed any other local tax, providing it falls on those who decide the extent and pattern of redistribution.

Since in a democracy the majority is presumed to decide the local redistributive package, one would again expect it to reflect the preference of the median voter. One can regard it as a local public good by means of which the collectivity is assumed to derive utility both non-excludable and non-rival from the increased utility of the recipients (Thurow, 1971; and see Part One, Chapter 3). But this can seem disingenuous as it presumes a collectivity of purpose, or 'General Will', as Rousseau used the term, among the electorate which is scarcely ever likely to fit the facts.

Often a majority may indeed be voting redistributive services not altruistically but as a benefit to itself. The redistribution would then be a forced one from minorities to the majority. In other cases, there may be genuine altruism among the majority that makes it decide to redistribute part of its income to benefit some other group – for example, the poor. Such redistribution has been called Paretian and indeed satisfies the definition of Paretian efficiency stated at the beginning of this chapter (Hochman and Rodgers, 1969). Because the donors want to give, it makes everyone better off and no one worse off.

To decide what local tax would be most efficient would require complex analysis depending on whether such a local redistributive package was regarded as a local good, as really in the interests of the majority, as Pareto efficient, or in some other light. Normally, and rather inadequately, the decision on the form of tax is made on the grounds of what is thought equitable, either taken in isolation or in the context of a particular tax structure. Such differences over what is judged equitable we have discussed in Part One, Chapter 6. The most popular current opinion is that a progressive income tax is more acceptable than rates, or indeed a land, housing or poll tax. If equity alone were at issue there would be a strong case for financing redistributive services through a local income tax.

While there are a number of practical and other arguments against a local income tax to be reviewed in Part Four, the major shortcoming of such a tax relevant here is that it causes horizontal inefficiency, and so encourages inefficient migration. Unless one can believe that a local redistributive package is a public good with benefits which all value equal to their contributions to its finance, (which would logically imply no fiscal wedges at all) there will be losers in a locality who would gain from leaving it, as well as others who would gain from moving to it from elsewhere. It is the onerousness of the method of financing local services, both beneficial and redistributive – the redistributive consequences of both, that is – that motivates the equilibrating migration. The beneficial and redistributive cases differ in degree, but the inward migratory attraction of the explicitly redistributive case should be much greater since by definition the local redistributive package benefits some minority – usually the poor, the elderly and possibly some other minorities. If the package is particularly attractive so that its positive fiscal wedge is substantial, then it is the more likely to tempt members of such minorities to move into the neighbourhood. The analysis of the case will be more complicated for there will be different incentives to migration for the direct beneficiaries of the services and for tax-payers in general (Pauly, 1973).

Let us assume it is central (or federal) policy to permit local authorities to pursue their own redistributive policies. Such permission is easier to understand in a federation since it is often historically part of the pact made when the federation is established that its constituent parts should retain freedoms which imply the ability to pursue independent redistributive policies to some extent. Unitary states are much likelier to believe that local differences in redistributive policies are inconsistent with a more powerfully held belief that there should be substantial uniformity in the services provided. Where central government is sovereign, such decentralisation of the power to redistribute differently would in modern times have to be regarded as a deliberate act to encourage local variations – though such variations were accepted as natural and inevitable until less than a hundred years ago, as we have seen.

If there were such toleration of local differences – whatever its justification – financing such services through a land tax would eliminate horizontal inefficiency and discourage equilibrating migration. This is because the tax falls on economic rent and does not affect the allocation of resources, provided it is not levied at a rate of more than 100 per cent on that rent. The use of land taxes will maximise the ability of a local authority to pursue its own independent distribution policy without losing or attracting citizens. Of course, citizens may well have more important reasons for migrating outwards or inwards but they will only leave for this reason if their expectations of the future course of their own land price are different from the average. There will be in-migrants if such people are to gain by creating fiscal wedges in their favour through settling at lower than average densities and so paying less-than-average taxes while receiving services of greater value than those taxes, even after taking into account the capitalisation of those benefits in higher land prices.

While land taxes have this locking-in property, as we have seen in Part One, their equity has been more challenged in recent times than it used to be. It presumes that the onerousness of such services should be borne by landowners and be paid from their economic rent whoever they may be. Such a policy has become much less acceptable than it was when Henry George or later Lloyd George advocated site-value rating, partly because the growth of owner-occupation has meant that land taxes are likely to be less concentrated on the rich than was then the case.

Therefore, policy on the financing of redistributive services depends on the political trade-off desired between equity (which is normally likely to favour a local income tax) and horizontal efficiency (which will favour a land tax and to some extent rates). Or, at another level, it can be seen as a trade-off between a tax favouring local differences in redistribution even at the expense of some horizontal inequity (such as a land tax) and a tax which would discourage such diversity by increasing the likelihood of migration if there is much divergence (suggesting a local income tax). Where government is highly centralised so that uniformity is achieved through administrative means, it matters less on these grounds which tax is chosen.

To show the difference in the impact of the different taxes, we now consider the most important reason for differences in spending on redistributive services, that is differences in spending need. For example, assume that the service provided is education. Two authorities may provide exactly the same quantity of education per child, but the cost of this to an authority will be higher, the larger is the number of children in the authority. If the number of children per capita is higher in one authority than in another, the cost per capita, and therefore the tax per capita, necessary to provide the same service, a given quantity of education per child, will be different in the two authorities. Assume that the average cost of providing a given quantity of education per child is constant and the same in two authorities A and B. The average cost per head of population of providing education will then depend on the number of children per head of population.

In Figure 2.2.3 we measure the number of children per head of population on the horizontal axis in the right quadrant, and the average cost per capita of providing a given amount of education per child on the vertical axis. On that axis we also measure the per capita tax necessary to finance such expenditures. We show two authorities A and B, where A has a higher number of children per capita than B. The per capita tax in A (T_a) is thus higher than the per capita tax in B (T_b). It would also be true that if the taxes were raised by an income tax, the

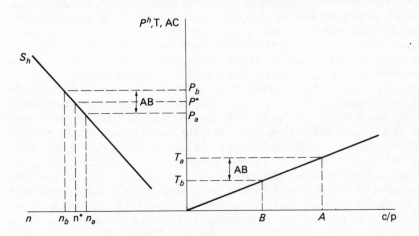

Figure 2.2.3. *Local taxes and differences in needs*

average tax payment in A would still be higher than in B and would again equal T_a. In the left quadrant of Figure 2.2.3, we again show the housing market which we assume is the same in the two authorities. S^h shows the supply curve of housing as a function of the annual rental rate of housing, P^h, measured on the vertical axis and the number of residents, n, on the horizontal axis. If education were charged for and not provided by the tax system, households would locate among the authorities in such a way that the cost of housing would be the same in the two authorities. However, if education is provided via the tax system, people in authority A who are paying higher taxes will want to move to authority B where taxes are lower. This movement of people from A to B will raise the rental rate of housing in B and reduce it in A. This movement will continue until the difference in the price of housing in the two authorities is the same as the difference in the tax payments in the two authorities.

We show this in Figure 2.2.3 where the distance marked AB is equal to the difference in tax payments $T_a - T_b$. Taxes are higher in authority A than in B, but this difference is offset by the differences in the cost of housing in the two authorities.

Assume we now replace the per capita tax by a land tax which is fully capitalised. Now the differences in tax rates do not induce any movement of people from authority A to B, and thus do not introduce any distortions in the housing market. However, if the per capita tax were replaced by an income tax or a tax on housing which was not fully capitalised, there would still be an inducement for people to move from A to B, and we would have the resulting distortion in the housing market.

A second case of differences in spending need for redistributive services is when there are actual differences in the costs of provision among the authorities. Assume that, because of certain characteristics such as sparsity of population or population density, the per capita cost of providing some local service is higher in one authority than in another. However, within the relevant range it is constant within each authority. This situation is shown in Figure 2.2.4. In the top quadrant we measure the number of people on the horizontal axis and average costs and per capita taxes on the vertical axis. We show two authorities, A and B, with average costs in A being higher than in B. In the bottom quadrant we again show the housing market which we assume is the same for the two, so the supply curve of housing S^h is assumed to be the same for both authorities.

Consider first a situation where there are n^* people in both authorities with the cost of housing being P^* in both authorities. The taxes paid in authority A are T_a and in B they are T_b. The difference in taxes will induce people to move out of A and into B. This movement affects the cost of housing in the authorities and will continue until the difference in the cost of housing $P_b - P_a$ is equal to the difference in taxes $T_a - T_b$, which is also equal to the difference in the average cost of providing the good. Unlike the previous case examined, this movement of people from A to B is not necessarily inefficient. The provision of the local good in this case is more costly in A than in B, therefore it is more efficient to provide the good in B than in A. There is a real saving of resources by substituting B as the supplier of the local good. If the households moving from A to B include beneficiaries of the service, the migration is efficient.

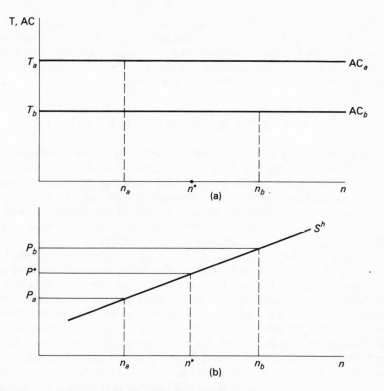

Figure 2.2.4.   *Local taxes and differences in costs*

Assume now that when there were n^* people in each authority we had used a land tax to finance the provision of the goods, and that this tax was fully capitalised. In such a case, though the tax rates are different in the two authorities, this difference does not induce anyone to move because the tax is fully capitalised. Thus the population will remain at n^* in each authority, and the provision of the local good will be less efficient than with a per capita tax (again on the assumption that some of the beneficiaries might migrate). The crucial difference between this case and the one previously examined, where the difference in per capita cost arose from differences in 'needs', is that in this case there are actual resource costs differences among the authorities, while in the previous case there were only perceived differences in costs through the tax system but not real differences in costs. In the present case, the movement of people from A to B may reduce the total resource cost of providing the good, if some of the beneficiaries move, even though it also affects the cost of housing in the two authorities. In the previous case the movement of people affected only the cost of housing.

If the per capita tax were replaced by an income tax, or a tax on housing which was not fully capitalised, the differences in tax rates would also induce people to move from A to B. Again such movement could be less efficient because of the real difference in the cost of providing the goods.

This complication — that the beneficiaries of a service may not be those paying for it — does not, of course, arise in the case of beneficial services. The argument of the last few paragraphs can thus be applied directly. With beneficial services that cost different amounts per unit to provide in different localities, a per capita tax is efficient and a land tax inefficient.

CONCLUSION: REDISTRIBUTIVE SERVICES

The requirements of a tax to finance redistributive services are different from those for one to finance beneficial services. The best tax for the first depends on who is controlling the provision of the services. If it is central government then there is an argument for their being financed through central taxation which is passed on to local authorities through grant; but the drawback of such an approach is that unless there is some burden or prospective burden on local taxes, there is no fiscal inducement to learn to be efficient.

The main efficiency requirement of such a local tax is that it should be such as to minimise the tendency to migrate. This holds whether it is central or local government that decides what is provided. If either takes a decision that a certain quantum of redistributive services is to be provided in an authority, then migration to avoid the consequential burden is to be discouraged. Therefore a land tax is a strong candidate for such a tax, and as there is no need to relate its incidence to benefits enjoyed by the median ratepayer, it could be a tax on all land. Therefore the optimal land taxes for beneficial and redistributive services are not the same, though one should not press the significance of this too far. The argument for restricting a beneficial land tax to residential land is based on the assumption that the occupiers of such land will derive the benefit from it. If other landowners, who do not derive any benefit, bear some of the cost, there will be more vertical and horizontal inefficiency and therefore more capitalisation and migration. If the services are redistributive, then there seems no obvious case in equity why some landowners should bear it and not others within the authority — that is, if landowners are intended to bear that burden. However, if capitalisation is not swift there may be substantial migration before it occurs: which would suggest it is in the interest of a government financing redistributive services in such a way to speed the process by announcing the expected consequences. The difference between the two situations may not be as great for another reason: the fact that the imperfection of a land tax (or indeed any other tax) as an efficient charging mechanism will mean that it will have redistributive consequences. But if a land tax is used for beneficial services only and there are no redistributive consequences, then the additional liability to land tax should have no effect on land values.

The choice of instruments is not easy. For beneficial services the most efficient is likely to be a poll tax. This is because the benefits of local beneficial services are not likely to rise in proportion with land, housing and income. It is generally a better approximation to assume they are constant per houshold than to assume they are proportional to any of the other tax bases. Though illogical, because such objections are not made to charging *per se*, the equity objections to a poll or per household tax to finance even beneficial services are likely to be overwhelming. If we assume, as seems likely, that the benefits from local services are no different in relation to a tax base of residential land or housing values, then the allocative inefficiency of the second would seem somewhat greater, and that of rates as a property tax will lie somewhere in between. (If any are modified by rate rebates for lower-income housholds, they will be less efficient.) If any of these also cover non-domestic property they will be less efficient than if they are confined to residential property. A local income tax is likely to be still less efficient for beneficial services, both because it creates more allocative inefficiencies and also because it is the most progressive, which will mean it will be still less efficient by comparison with a poll tax. The comparative efficiency of a poll tax in local government finance, because it depends on the assumption that beneficial services are of fairly constant value per household, is different from that argued ordinarily in public finance where the purpose to which the tax is put is not an issue. The efficiency argument used there, that it has less effect on someone's readiness to work, is also relevant here, though we have not discussed it.

The choice of tax instruments for redistributive services is different. A decision is first needed on the principle of equity to be adopted. If progressiveness is regarded as most appropriate, it should not be accepted without realising the effect this will have on inefficiency and migration. If it is possible still to except land values and regard them as taxable on equity grounds irrespective of the wealth of the owner, then on efficiency grounds, there is much to be said for site-value rating – the local land tax – as the best method of financing redistributive local services. Second to it, on the same basis, would be rates.

NOTES

1 We have examined a situation in which different authorities provide different quantities of the same service. It is clear that the same arguments apply to situations where different authorities provide different services and individuals have different tastes for such services.

2 This result depends on our assumption that all individuals purchase the same quantity of housing, irrespective of their income. If the quantity of housing demanded were positively related to income, the question who moves is more complicated. Individuals with higher incomes also purchase more housing. The net effect of the difference in the cost of housing between the two authorities will be greater for them. In this case, the actual income level at which someone is indifferent between the two authorities will also depend on the income elasticity of the demand for housing. Moreover some of the effect of the change will be capitalised. The result also depends on the assumption that people's incomes are unaffected by the locality in which they live.

3 As a first approximation because we are ignoring the aggregate loss in income arising because of the inefficient allocation of housing.

4 The second of these problems, but not the first, can be solved in principle by a system of resource equalising grants to local authorities – a point to which we return in the next chapter.

5 Aronsen and Schwartz (1973) examine evidence which, in their view, provides empirical support for the instability hypothesis.

6 It is in this context that the distinction between the 'pure' or economic rent of land, due to its location (or the 'inexhaustible power of the soil') and the market rent it commands (which may be affected by capital invested in it), is relevant. See Ricardo (1962, Ch. 10).

3 Principles of Grant Distribution

In this chapter we examine a question which has proved to be among the most difficult and contentious in grant policy. How should the relative amounts of grant going to different authorities be determined? In Part One, Chapter 7, we have examined how ideas on this subject have developed and how they have been incorporated into successive grant systems. In Part Two, Chapter 2, we have examined one of those ideas – the principle of economic efficiency – in more detail. We have shown how economic inefficiency can arise in a system of local finance. One objective of grant policy might be to offset such inefficiencies. In the first sections of this chapter we attempt to pull together these ideas to deduce some basic criteria for grant distribution.

The remainder of the chapter is taken up with a description and evaluation of the present (1978) Rate Support Grant system. While the analysis reveals some weaknesses in the present structure, we do not discuss specific reform proposals. In Part Three, Chapter 4, we discuss some changes that could be introduced within the present system, such as the government's unitary grant proposal. More fundamental reforms are considered in Part Four.

Grant distribution is not, of course, the only important feature of the grant system. In the following chapters in Part Two, we examine the relationship of grants and expenditure (Chapter 5), the use of grants as an instrument of central government control or influence (Chapter 7), and the role of grants in short-run macroeconomic policy (Chapter 8).

ECONOMIC EFFICIENCY AND GRANT DISTRIBUTION

In the last chapter we saw that two characteristics of the local finance system were typically associated with economic inefficiency. One was where the average tax base differs between authorities, which could be offset by a resource equalisation grant, and one was where the costs of providing onerous or redistributive services differ, which could be offset by a grant compensating for differences in such 'spending needs'. And these have indeed been the basic objectives of grant distribution since at least 1929.

But the argument of the last chapter is in fact rather more complex, and it is worth examining its implications in more detail. We first consider the case (1) where local authorities are only providing beneficial services. We also assume (2) that there is a single tier of authorities to avoid irrelevant complications; (3) that an authority provides the same services at the same cost to each of its households;

(4) there are no non-domestic ratepayers or consumers of its services; (5) that every authority provides the same services as every other; and finally (6) that no local services have appreciable public good or other externality characteristics so that the benefits are private to each household. We will shortly relax some of these assumptions.

Then, as we have argued, if payment for local services were made by a charge or poll tax equal to the cost of providing the services to each household, economic theory would say their provision was economically efficient.

Instead let us assume payment is made through an *ad valorem* property tax — rates — but that average rateable value is the same in all authorities. Then the average rate payment in each authority should be the same and still equal to marginal cost. Still there would be no horizontal inefficiency — meaning by that, economic inefficiency between authorities such that, setting aside any movement costs, it would pay households to move to another authority. (One might expect vertical inefficiency within authorities since households with above-average rateable values would have negative fiscal wedges or residua in that their payments were above marginal cost, and vice versa, for those with below-average rateable values. But these fiscal residua should be wholly or partially capitalised into property values).

Relax the assumption that local authorities provide the same services as each other, while keeping the one that they each provide the same services to all their households. As services are still beneficial there need be no horizontal inefficiency. Average rate payments will be higher where more services are provided. They should still always equal average cost.

Now let us alter the critical assumption and allow average rateable values to vary — as of course they do — between authorities. The reason why average rateable values vary is crucial. At one extreme we can envisage any household finding the rateable value of a similar dwelling the same wherever located. None the less average rateable values might vary because of differences in the mix of types of dwelling. Here there is horizontal inefficiency. The rate price to any household cannot be assumed to be equal to the cost of providing services whether or not all local authorities were to provide the same services to all households. There would be an incentive for households to move where average rateable values were high, and rate poundages low. Such an incentive would be inefficient and it could be eliminated by a system of differential grants to authorities which effectively equalised their tax bases. So there would then be a case in terms of economic efficiency for a resource equalisation grant.

At the opposite extreme is the situation where rateable values vary systematically between localities. If all dwellings in local authority A have rateable values twice those of dwellings in local authority B, a typical household would expect to find its rateable value twice as high in A as in B. If services provided by each authority are the same, and there is no resource equalisation grant, the rate poundage in A will be half that in B and the average ratepayer will expect the same rate bill in both authorities. Rate payments should equal costs of providing services. The reasons for rateable values being higher in A are immaterial, so long as the difference is systematic. It may have locational advantages so that people prefer to live there, house prices and rents being correspondingly higher. It is economically efficient that households enjoying greater locational benefits should pay more for housing to live in the locality, but there is no reason in terms of economic efficiency why they should also pay more for local government services. There is no efficiency case for a resource equalisation grant.

Reality lies between the two extremes. Average rateable values will vary both because of differences in mix and because of differences in locational advantage, so creating problems in designing a resource equalisation grant.

Let us now imagine rates replaced by a local income tax. There would be no horizontal inefficiency in circumstances similar to those we have analysed for rates. If local authorities provide the same services or different services, having equal average incomes, there would be no incentive for the typical household to move. (There will be vertical inefficiency between households within authorities which will not be effectively neutralised by tax capitalisation, though theoretically it could be removed by an appropriate but impracticable system of inter-household grants within each authority.) However, as we have shown in the preceding chapter, there would be an incentive to move to localities where incomes are high to reduce the price paid by them for the local services they consume. Such an incentive would appear inefficient and would be corrected by a resource equalisation grant.

This does not mean that where there is a local income tax there are no polar extremes and no mixed cases corresponding to the situation where local services are financed by rates. We usually assume that differences in income reflect differences in command over resources; but let us return to authorities A and B. Instead of explaining the systematic difference in land values as caused by differences in residential locational advantage, let us assume they are the same and that A's land values are twice those in B only because the demands of other activities are bidding up the price of land. In such circumstances, residents of A will have to have money incomes sufficiently higher than those of B to offset higher housing and transport costs if their real income is to be the same as that of the citizens of B. If that were the sole explanation of differences in average income between local authorities there would be no horizontal inefficiency and no incentive to population movement. In other words, one can only assume that a resource equalisation grant is always justified on efficiency grounds where there is a local income tax in so far as the levels of local incomes are independent of locational differences between places.

Returning to rates as the form of local taxation, the introduction of non-domestic ratepayers creates further complications. We assume services are beneficial, but that their benefits go mainly to households; commerce and industry derive little direct benefit from local government spending. Horizontal efficiency requires that non-domestic property be derated, and firms charged for the services provided directly for them. Failing that, there could be a separate non-domestic rate, apportioning the costs of services provided to firms amongst them on the basis of their rateable value. On either of these arrangements, domestic rates would be unaffected by the amount of industry and commerce in a local authority.

But if the same rate is charged on industry and commerce as on households there will be horizontal inefficiency. Even if domestic rateable values are the same in each locality, and services provided are the same, tax rates and tax bills for domestic ratepayers will differ because of differences in the proportion of non-domestic rateable value. This inefficiency can be removed by a resource equalisation grant. If horizontal efficiency for domestic ratepayers is assumed to follow from an equalisation of their rate poundages, then the form of resource grant would be simply one of equalising total rateable value per capita. If horizontal efficiency for domestic ratepayers has been defined in terms of equalisation of average rate bills across authorities, again a resource equalisation grant can be constructed although its form will be more complex.

Some form of resource equalisation grant may be able to achieve horizontal efficiency for both domestic and non-domestic ratepayers where authorities all provide the same standards of services, but no grant can do this if standards differ. Efficiency requires that domestic ratepayers pay higher taxes where standards of services are higher, but that non-domestic ratepayers should not, since they generally receive no direct benefit from better local services.

ECONOMIC EFFICIENCY AND THE MEDIAN VOTER

We have suggested in Part One that political pressures within local authorities will lead them towards satisfying the preferences of the 'median voter' in terms of the level of services they provide and the taxes they consequently have to levy. We will develop a model of local expenditure based explicitly on this assumption in Part Two, Chapter 5. Here all we need to note is that satisfying the preferences of the median voter will lead to an efficient allocation of resources into the local government sector only if the median voter has to pay in terms of higher taxation the full marginal cost of additional services from which he benefits. Even if the median voter occupies property of about average rateable value for the local authority, this condition will only be satisfied if there is no taxation of non-domestic property, except in so far as the median voter owns commercial or industrial property within the local authority, and there are no matching grants.

The argument based on horizontal efficiency for a resource equalisation grant implies an equalisation of fiscal capacity for any level of expenditure, that is a matching grant. It follows that there may be a conflict between horizontal efficiency and allocational efficiency.

CONCLUSION: BENEFICIAL SERVICES

If rates were levied only on domestic ratepayers, arguments of horizontal efficiency suggest that the case for a resource equalisation grant depends on the cause of differences in domestic rateable value between authorities. But if a resource equalisation grant is justified on these grounds it should take the form of a matching grant, which would conflict with the objective of allocational efficiency. The simpler solution of no resource equalisation grant, which satisfies allocational efficiency and may be just as satisfactory in terms of horizontal efficiency as a resource equalisation grant, has much to commend it.

Ideally, non-domestic ratepayers should be charged for the services provided for them, or have a separate rate levied on them. If the same rate is charged on non-domestic as on domestic property, horizontal efficiency requires a resource equalisation grant to offset differences in the proportion of non-domestic to domestic property.

INTERGOVERNMENTAL EXTERNALITIES

There are some services we would describe as beneficial, part of whose benefits are enjoyed by people living outside the jurisdiction of the authority providing the services. A public park maintained by one authority may be used by people living in other neighbouring authorities. Road maintenance benefits the traveller through a locality as well as its residents. The police may assist visitors to an area as well as people who live there. Another example is a central city authority which provides services to many people who work in the area but live outside it.

Since local government is responsible politically only to local residents it will be likely to provide less of services that benefit non-residents than would be economically efficient. To secure efficiency, matching grants are required to meet the difference between the cost of the services the local authority would provide if it followed its own local interest and that which it would provide if it followed the wider social interest. Such grants would also be specific — that is tied to the provision of services where intergovernmental externalities are thought to be important. In the UK no grants are explicitly designed to achieve this objective, but some part of the administrative pressure from central government for uniform standards may be justified on these grounds.

FINANCING ONEROUS SERVICES

With beneficial services, the cost falling on the ratepayer can be envisaged as the price paid for the services received. With centrally determined onerous services, the ratepayer normally receives no direct benefit, so the cost is more in the nature of a tax. We have shown in the previous chapter that where the costs of onerous services differ between authorities, such differences should be neutralised to avoid the inducement for firms and households to move to authorities where tax burdens are lighter. It would also be regarded as inequitable for people in one locality to have to pay more in taxes because the cost of onerous services is higher.

The first requirement of a grant system for onerous services, then, is a grant to compensate for differences in the costs of providing onerous services, or to use the more common name, a needs grant. We examine the problem of needs assessment later in the chapter. But even if we have such a needs grant there is a second stage. If the objective in terms of equity is to equalise tax burdens, how exactly is that to be defined?

By horizontal equity we mean that people in equal circumstances be treated equally irrespective of their geographical location. It seems natural to think that if there are two households receiving the same standard of beneficial services from local government, it is equitable for each to pay the same in local taxation, whatever the level of onerous expenditures they are also financing. It should be stressed that this principle of equity is an ethical principle and as such applies only to individuals and not to geographical areas or organisations such as local authorities. It makes sense to say that some person, A, is treated inequitably relative to some other person B. It makes less sense to say that a local authority, X, is in some way being treated inequitably relative to some authority Y. To say that an authority is being treated inequitably can only mean that some people within that authority are being treated inequitably relative to people not living in it.

Equity scarcely arises where all services are beneficial since the commonly accepted principle is that equitable treatment means an equal price for the same standard of service. As we saw earlier in the chapter, the problem was to find grants which would reduce the fiscal residua caused by the imperfection of taxes as means of approximating to marginal cost pricing. But if there are also redistributive or onerous services where some or all ratepayers bear the burden of services benefiting a minority — usually not the same minority for each service — a problem of equity arises in deciding how to share the burden of financing those redistributive services.

For purposes of taxation, equity means that taxpayers in equal circumstances should pay the same in taxation. But how is equality of circumstance to be defined? First, the tax instrument used should be the same. Let us imagine three taxpayers in local authorities identical in every respect and in the redistributive service they provide, except that in one case rates are levied, in the second a local income tax, and in the third a mixture of rates and local income tax. Then equity is not realisable. Later in Part Four, Chapter 3, we shall show formally that a grant system cannot be devised to achieve equity where there is more than one local tax. Horizontal equity requires that local services are financed by one tax and it must be the same tax. This implies also that the tax should be really, not merely formally, the same — for example, that property or income be assessed in the same manner in different localities. (One could have different taxes for separate services — provided one also had distinct grant systems — but not different taxes for the same service or bundle of services.) Otherwise tax payments are most unlikely to be the same for individuals in different authorities but in the same circumstances. Horizontal equity is not possible in a system like that of the USA where states and sometimes localities have considerable freedom in deciding what combination of taxes to employ. Indeed, a central decision whether local taxes should be identical for all authorities or not is one test of whether a constitution is federal or unitary. It is arguable that a federal system of government — created as almost all have been by a joining of separate governments — need not imply pursuit of the principle that equals should expect equal treatment for taxation in the different states of the federation (Scott, 1964).

However, while such uniformity is a necessary step, it is not generally sufficient for achieving horizontal equity because it is not related to people's circumstances. An obvious next step is that taxes on people should be equal in relation to their ability to pay, and that a person's ability to pay taxes depends on some measure of either his income or wealth or both. Equity requires, then, that people with the same income or wealth should pay the same amount in taxation as their contribution to the provision of redistributive or onerous services.

Even this principle can be ambiguous. If, for example, there is a tax on cigarettes, a man who is a smoker will pay much more in taxation than a man who is not, although the two may have the same income. But it could be argued that they are being treated equally because both face the same tax rates. The smoker could stop smoking and pay the same taxes as the non-smoker. The two are treated equally in terms of the tax structure they face, though they end up paying different amounts in tax.

If equity is defined in terms of actual tax payments, then there is not much scope for taxes on particular commodities, or on property. The only way that equity can be achieved is by taxes on some measure of income or wealth that most closely approximates a person's ability to pay. There is one exception. If the consumption of some commodity or the ownership of some asset is closely related to the measure of income that defines ability to pay, the use of that commodity or asset as the tax base can be justified as a proxy. Two people paying the same tax rate on the commodity or asset will be making the same tax payment relative to the income measure defining ability to pay, within the range of error of the relationship between the tax base and the measure of income. If this error is small, one may accept that the principle of horizontal equity is satisfied 'on average', and that the deviations from it are acceptable.

Consider now the problem of attaining horizontal equity across local authorities. If the tax base used by local authorities is the same as the base accepted as the measure of ability to pay, or is a good proxy for it, the solution is easy. Any grant system which equalises tax rates across local authorities will achieve horizontal equity. If, however, the tax base used by local authorities is not the same and is unrelated to the base used to define ability, the equalisation of tax rates will not achieve horizontal equity. Two people with the same tax base will be making the same tax payment, but these payments differ relative to the measure accepted as defining ability to pay.

Historically, the use of property as the tax base for local taxes was justified because property was considered as a good proxy for ability to pay (see Part One, Chapter 6). But it is doubtful whether rateable value, which is the base for local taxation, is so any longer (see Part Two, Chapter 6). If we revert to our alternative definition of equity – of equality of tax structure – we can still justify equalising tax rates across local authorities. But on the usual definition of equity, equalising tax rates across localities cannot be expected to achieve it at all accurately.

Rather than pay grants to equalise tax rates across local authorities, one could instead provide more grant to a local authority where people's ability to pay is relatively low. Such a grant will enable the local authority to reduce its tax rate to the benefit of everyone living in it. While most people in that locality may have low incomes relative to the rateable value of their property, so their tax burden would have been judged excessive, a minority in the same locality may well have higher incomes so their tax burden would already be light. But all benefit from the higher grant to the local authority. The essential point is that the source of the inequity is the poor relationship between income and rateable value for the individual or household. It follows that, if the local tax system is thought to be inequitable because of the weak relationship between rateable value and ability to pay, the logical answer is to replace rates by a more equitable tax. None the less, we examine in Part Three, Chapter 4 whether rates can be made more equitable, in this sense, by alterations in grant policy.

On the other hand, one might see rates as part of a national tax structure involving various taxes on specific commodities and assets. What matters, then, is that the tax structure as a whole should be regarded as equitable, rather than every component of it taken individually. With taxes on other forms of expenditure and other assets, a tax on property can add to the equity of the tax system taken as a whole in the sense of relating people's total tax payments more closely to their ability to pay, even if rate payments themselves are not closely related to ability to pay. On this interpretation, a resource equalisation grant to equalise rate poundages could be regarded as consistent with the equity of the tax system as a whole.

RECAPITULATION OF THE THEORETICAL ARGUMENT

To recapitulate, horizontal efficiency where there are beneficial services requires a resource equalisation grant to equalise average tax bases between authorities in so far as their bases differ because of differences in the mix of households, but there is no case on efficiency grounds for such compensation where the differences in tax bases reflect differences in locational advantages. The difficulty in deciding how far each causes differences in the tax base is a major theoretical problem in the design of a resource equalisation grant.

Intergovernment efficiency would require matching grants to offset the effect of intergovernmental public goods and externalities in leading generally to the underprovision of the services affected.

Horizontal equity requires that the burden of taxes for redistributive services be equalised for taxpayers in similar circumstances. Step 1 requires that the cost of different levels of services that must be provided in different authorities because of differences in 'needs' must be equalised. Step 2 requires that the tax system used to pay for such redistributive services satisfies some criterion of equity. This is more difficult for rates than for local income tax only in so far as rates are regarded as a less satisfactory tax in equity. A resource equalisation grant to equalise rate poundages can be justified to improve equity, particularly if one is concerned with the equity of the tax structure rather than solely the relationship of rate payments and income.

For non-domestic ratepayers, the principle of grant is simple and straightforward. It should equalise rate poundages irrespective of levels of local government spending, except in so far as there are local differences in the costs of services provided for them.

THEORY AND REALITY

As we have seen, the development of the British grant system has brought into being grants which in their current form broadly serve most of these purposes.

The aim of the resources element in Rate Support Grant is the equalisation of the tax base. The aim of the needs element is to equalise rate poundages irrespective of differences in the level of onerous services provided by authorities because of differences in 'needs'.

While resources and needs grant are quantitatively the most important, there is also the domestic element in RSG. We argue that this is not best analysed as a grant but as a modification of rates. It will be dealt with in Part Two, Chapter 6 below.

There are also specific grants. The most important and complicated is the set of capital grants towards the provision of public housing. They are too complicated and raise too many special issues to be treated here without distorting the purpose of the book. Lastly, there are the remnants of the old specific grants of which the most important is that for the police. They were analysed in Part One, Chapter 7. No further analysis is needed here. We will therefore concentrate on resources and needs grants.

THE RESOURCES ELEMENT

The resources element as it now exists is identical in principle to the equalisation grant introduced in 1947. Until 1974, however, equalisation was carried out in terms of the average rateable value per head in authorities. Local authorities below the average were effectively brought up to that level by payment of grant: those already above the average received no grant but retained the benefit of their above-average rateable value.

In 1974 the system was changed. Instead of equalisation in terms of the national average rateable value per head, an arbitrary 'standard' rateable value per head is prescribed in the Rate Support Grant Orders. The standard has been set significantly above the national average rateable value so that virtually all authorities qualify for resources grant. This means that the resource equalisation property of the grant is much more effective, applying to virtually all the authorities instead of only about half.

Where the standard rateable value is set is dependent on the total amount of grant available. The higher the standard, the more authorities will fall below it and hence be 'equalised' up to it, but at the same time the greater the amount of grant that will have to be paid out. Setting the standard so high as to include all authorities is impracticable because of the immensely high rateable value per head in some central London boroughs, and particularly in the City of London.

The drawing of the standard below these authorities means that the resources element is lop-sided. A true equalisation grant would imply taxing those authorities above the standard to reduce their rateable value per head to the standard. In practice, above-standard authorities outside London — of which there are eight non-metropolitan districts — are allowed to keep the benefit of their above-average rateable value.[1] Those in London – there are 19 above-standard London boroughs – suffer a penalty in the form of a 'clawback' from their needs grant related to the size of their 'excess' rateable value.[2]

We have already examined resource equalisation grants in terms of equity and economic efficiency. But there is another important consideration. If authorities can increase their income by permitting development which raises their rateable value per head they have an incentive to develop. But if there is a resource equalisation grant no such incentive exists. Any change in rateable value per head resulting from permitting or preventing development is 100 per cent compensated through the resources element. As Rabinowitz (1977) has pointed out, this absence of any incentive to develop for all but a very few authorities is the most striking difference between American and British local finance. In the USA and indeed in many other nations, a major preoccupation of local government is to increase its rate base to increase its revenues. Conversely, the fear of the central cities is that as jobs and homes drain away from them, their tax base falls and so do their per capita revenues. Most British local authorities are now insulated from such hopes and fears, which may help to explain their relative lack of interest in the economic well-being and development of their areas. Indeed, in many cases, there is a positive disincentive to development because local authorities are unable to recoup all increases in costs from the developer. While it can charge for the most direct costs, a new development may mean new schools, social services, recreational facilities and other expenditure which in many cases will increase the per capita cost of supplying local services without any corresponding increase in rate revenue.

This feature of the resources element follows directly from its success in achieving an equalisation of rateable values per head up to the standard. To alter it would mean modifying the objective of achieving horizontal efficiency and equity – a change whose consideration we postpone until Part Four.

One characterisation of the resources element is that it is a matching grant. Each local authority whose rateable value per head is below the standard level is accredited notional rateable value sufficient to bring its total rateable resources up to the national standard rateable value per head. The government then pays, as the resources element of the RSG, each qualifying local authority its level of rate poundage on its accredited, or notional, rateable value. The more an authority spends the higher the rate poundage it will levy, and the larger the grant it will receive. In this sense, the resources element is a matching grant, in that additional expenditure is matched by additional payments of grant.

It is not at all difficult, in principle, to remove the matching grant characteristic from the resources element. All that is required is that the resources element be paid on the basis of some standard rate poundage, rather than on the local authority's actual rate poundage. The resources element grant would then become a lump sum independent of a local authority's expenditure.

We have here, however, a conflict of objectives. Resources element is used to try to meet two of the objectives set out at the beginning of this chapter. For beneficial services it sets out to remove the inefficiency that arises from the effect that differences in the mix of properties, both domestic and non-domestic, have on the magnitude of the rate base per capita. In so far as it tries to remove this reason why local authorities might need to levy different rate poundages to meet the cost of providing the same services, it follows that it should be a matching grant. For the principle is as valid whatever the level of services a local authority provides. It should not benefit or lose simply because its rate base deviates from the norm. The resources element as a matching grant does not achieve an equalisation of rate poundages for any given level of services, but only does not do this because unit costs of providing the same level vary. Horizontal efficiency does not imply the removal of such costs differences.

At the same time there is the objective of allocational efficiency, which argues against matching grants. A lump sum resource equalisation grant can be seen as a compromise between these two objectives. If the standard of beneficial services provided in different localities is approximately the same, then a lump sum resources grant will neutralise the bulk of the potential horizontal inefficiency arising from differences in the local tax base. At the same time, because it is lump sum rather than matching, it should not distort the allocation of resources between private and local government goods and services.

A similar point can be made with regard to the finance of onerous services. Again we assume that such services are to be financed by equal rate poundages on all ratepayers. This again can be achieved by a lump sum resource equalisation grant (together with a needs grant). But what if some authorities provide onerous services to a standard higher than that prescribed by the central government? Again the arguments of horizontal efficiency suggest such additional expenditure be supported by a resource equalisation grant. (Otherwise two authorities each providing the same standard of services in excess of the national standard would be levying different rate poundages.) And again the arguments of allocative efficiency go against a matching grant.

The basis of the unitary grant recommended by the Department of the Environment, endorsed by the Layfield Committee and accepted by the government, is to reduce the matching-grant characteristics of the resources element. At the same time, unlike the simple lump-sum resources element, the unitary grant preserves the features of horizontal efficiency — equal rate poundages for equal services for all levels of services. A detailed discussion of the unitary grant is deferred to Part Three, Chapter 4.

THE NEEDS ELEMENT

The objective of the needs grant, as described earlier in the chapter, is more straightforward, at least in principle, than that of the resources element. It relates only to centrally determined redistributive expenditure. Different localities may well provide different levels of expenditure on such services, and in so far as those differences reflect obligations imposed on them by central government they should be compensated by needs grant. But differences in their spending do not necessarily reflect differences in their obligations; a local authority may have chosen to provide a higher (or lower) standard of services. It is, therefore, necessary to examine the causes of expenditure differences in more detail.

Differences in expenditure may arise for a variety of reasons, which fall, conceptually, into four major categories: quality differences, differences in needs, 'involuntary' cost differences, and 'voluntary' cost differences. In education, for example, differences in expenditure might be attributed to differences in the pupil—teacher ratio (quality difference); differences in the numbers of schoolchildren in the population (a difference in 'needs'); externally imposed salary differentials, such as the 'London weighting' (an 'involuntary' difference in costs); or to differences in the efficiency with which the education service is administered (a 'voluntary' difference in costs). The notion of differences in need essentially envisages some 'client group' for each type of local authority service, with the number of people in each client group constituting a different proportion of the population in different authorities. Cost differences are defined as voluntary or involuntary according to whether they are, in principle, within the local authority's control. Higher costs resulting from differences in land costs, the London weighting on pay scales, the effects of population sparsity, or other geographical characteristics are classed as involuntary, while voluntary factors include the effects of policy decisions on how services should be provided (for example, by direct labour departments or outside contractors) and the administrative efficiency with which they are operated.

The rationale for providing centrally determined services at the level of local (rather than central) government is one of encouraging efficiency in the provision of the service by making it the responsibility of people with knowledge of local cost characteristics. If it is the responsibility of the local electorate to 'police' the efficiency with which such services are operated, it follows that the needs grant should not compensate for variations in efficiency. Clearly there will be no incentive for local government to operate more efficiently if by so doing it benefits only central government and not the local ratepayer. In terms of the classification we have adopted, it follows that the needs grant should not compensate for 'voluntary' differences in costs.

Differences in quality of service present a slightly more difficult problem. The fact that our onerous service is being provided at all must imply, in some sense, that the population in general thinks it should be provided even though it is of no direct benefit to most of them. But as we have said, in some localities, people may think the service should be provided at a higher standard than elsewhere. It may reasonably be argued that if this is the preference of the people of that locality they should be free to express it but have no claim on the general taxpayer for additional finance through higher grants payments. On the other hand, if in another locality people wish to provide a lower standard of the service it seems rather less reasonable that they should receive all the cost-saving (in the form of having to levy lower rates), while those receiving the service end up with a lower standard of provision and no compensating benefit. Central government may be able, through the administrative and legislative means at its disposal (see Part Two, Chapter 7), to ensure some adequate (in terms of national policy objectives) minimum standards. If so, local authorities providing higher standards may reasonably be expected to pay the additional costs.

The other two categories of differences in expenditure — differences in needs and differences in 'involuntary' costs — are outside the control of the local authority and the above arguments do not apply. The needs grant should therefore compensate for differences in onerous expenditures due to differences in centrally determined needs or differences in involuntary costs.

By contrast, the principle for beneficial services is that they should be financed by taxes levied on the beneficiaries. It followed that differences in expenditure on beneficial services between local authorities should not be compensated by differences in grant. This follows even if differences in expenditure are attributable to differences in 'involuntary' costs. Economic efficiency implies, in general, that people should pay the costs of providing the services they decide to consume, and if the costs of providing those services is higher in some areas than in others this should be reflected in the prices people face. The prices of private goods and services and earnings opportunities differ between localities, reflecting differences in the characteristics of the different areas, and there seems no logical reason why the tax prices people pay for beneficial public services should not differ for these reasons also.

To summarise, the needs grant should, on the basis of these principles, compensate for differences in needs and for differences in 'involuntary' costs of centrally determined services. It should not compensate for differences in expenditure arising from other causes. As we said at the beginning of the chapter, the distinction between centrally determined and beneficial services is not clear-cut, and this may lead to a conflict between the different objectives of the grant. To take an example, consider the London weighting on teachers' salaries which is an example of an 'involuntary' higher cost. From the point of view of ratepayers without children in London there seems no reason why they should pay more (relative to their ability pay) towards the cost of educating other people's children because they live in London. On the other hand, parents with children at school in London might be expected to pay the higher costs since they are consuming a service which is particularly expensive to provide in London. There is no means of resolving this conflict of objectives given that there is no clear distinction between what is centrally and locally determined.

If the needs grant is to compensate for differences in needs it is, of course, necessary to define more precisely what is meant by needs, and how they can be measured. As we have seen in Part One, Chapter 7 this has always been the major difficulty in designing grants. We return to a discussion of definition of needs in the context of a reform of the needs grant in Part Three, Chapter 4. In the remainder of this chapter we examine the current (1978) system of needs assessment in England and Wales — the regression method.

The regression method is based on the assumption that differences in needs between authorities lead to differences in their expenditures that are systematically and consistently related to various types of local authority characteristics — demographic, geographical, socio-economic, etc. — and that other influences on local authority spending (levels of beneficial services, operating efficiency, etc.) are not systematically related to these characteristics. Then, in principle, the characteristics associated with differences in spending need and the weights attached to each can be identified by regression analysis. The needs grant can then be based on the regression formula.

A local authority's spending need ultimately depends on an immense number of factors, many of them unquantifiable even in principle, and many others for which data is unlikely to be available. Even if all the relevant data was available, the number of explanatory factors would be so great that it would be impossible to estimate the effect of each regression analysis. Instead the hope is that many of these factors are correlated with some quantifiable socio-economic or demographic characteristic, which can be used in the regression analysis as a proxy variable for a large number of true need factors.

For example, the number of old people living alone in an authority may be closely correlated with all sorts of other expenditure needs associated with areas of declining population. Regression analysis cannot identify each of these factors separately. The weight given to the 'old people living alone' factor thus takes account not only of the costs of a wide range of other services attributable to factors normally, but not always, correlated with the numbers of old people living alone.

It follows that the weight given to any particular factor cannot be regarded as representing the cost of services provided for that factor. For example, the weight on primary schoolchildren is not the average unit cost of primary education but the total effect on local authority spending on all services (which for some services could be negative) of an additional schoolchild in the population.

Even though the relationship between the underlying true need factors and local spending needs may be quite stable over time, the estimated regression equation may be unstable. Small changes in the data, or in other factors, can lead to completely different proxy variables being selected. There is no doubt that this instability is confusing to people, say in Parliament or local government, who naturally expect that if a particular factor is held to affect local spending need in one year it will continue to do so the following year.

A related problem is that there may be a number of different configurations of proxy variables which, on statistical grounds, account for differences in local expenditures almost equally well. Any one of a number of regression formulae may seem equally good. The choice of formula then becomes political, based on looking at the effects of different formulae on the distribution of the grant between local authorities.

One consequence of the instability of the grant formula is that the allocation of the grant to individual authorities has tended to vary quite substantially from one year to the next. To reduce this instability, since 1975/6 the grant has not been based solely on the formula calculated for that year but instead it has been 'damped', that is part of the grant has continued to be paid on formulae calculated for earlier years. By 1978/9 the damping had been extended to four years, so that three-quarters of an authority's needs assessment for that year is attributable to previous years' needs assessment, and only one-quarter to the current-year needs assessment. In 1978/9 also a 'safety-net' arrangement was introduced, limiting the amount of grant an authority could lose from one year to the next. Despite these arrangements, fluctuations in grant allocations from one year to the next remain a source of concern with the regression method.

While damping and, to a lesser extent, the 'safety net' reduce year-to-year instability in grant distribution, it is at the cost of slowing down the responsiveness of the grant to changes in the 'true' pattern of spending needs. Say, for example, there is a sharp increase in teachers' salaries. Then the spending need of authorities with many schoolchildren will rise, and this should be reflected in a higher weight on schoolchildren in the regression equation. But because of damping it will take four years for grants to adjust fully to the higher costs.

But perhaps the most serious difficulty with the regression analysis is in the assumption on which it is based — that differences in expenditure that can be accounted for by need factors represent differences in spending need. One could argue that standards of services, operating efficiency and other non-need factors are likely also to be related to socio-economic and demographic characteristics — possibly working through the political process. Then the regression equation may tell us what accounts for differences in expenditure between authorities, but not what accounts for differences in expenditure need.

To take one example, the population sparsity factor in the regression formula reflects largely the higher expenditure of some of the remote Welsh counties. The weight given to that factor represents the differences in the average expenditure of these counties as against the rest of England and Wales (taking other needs factors into account). The difference in expenditure may indeed be attributable to greater spending need associated with population sparsity. On the other hand, it could be that these Welsh counties are providing services to a higher standard than elsewhere, which might be traced back to the fact that an abnormally high proportion of their expenditure is financed by central government grants.

The technical name for this problem is 'omitted variables bias', that is if some relevant factors are left out of the regression analysis the estimated effects of the other factors will be biased. Ordinarily, the solution to omitted variables bias is to include all the relevant variables. And if we were attempting to estimate the true model of local government spending need by regression analysis the logical solution would be to include any factors that might influence the standard of services an authority might choose to provide.

It should be stressed that the purpose of including such discretionary factors is solely to achieve unbiased estimates of the effects of the needs factors. The estimates of the effects of the discretionary factors would, of themselves, be of no relevance for grant distribution.

The difficulty is that some of these discretionary influences — political preferences in particular — may derive from the same socio-economic or demographic characteristics that influence spending need. In consequence the discretionary variables may be quite highly correlated with the needs factors. Then regression analysis is an unreliable technique for estimating the relative influence of each. There can be no certainty that a needs-grant formula derived by incorporating such discretionary influences in the regression analysis will be unbiased, or even less biased, than one derived from a regression analysis from which discretionary factors had been omitted.

None the less, while conceding these difficulties, it cannot be denied that if discretionary factors are omitted, regression analysis is bound to produce estimates of spending need systematically biased in favour of authorities with a preference for higher standards of services. The regression method will be vulnerable to the criticism that it rewards high-spending authorities while penalising those that are more thrifty. It follows that some procedure for distinguishing between spending needs and local preferences is required.

A number of studies of the determinants of local authority spending have been carried out, which we examine in more detail in Part Two, Chapters 4 and 5. Most show that, in terms of statistical association, factors such as political control, local income levels and the effects of the grant system on local tax bills have an effect on local authority spending. *A priori*, these factors seem more likely to be related to the level of services provided than to spending needs. Our own results (see Part Two, Chapter 5) also show that omitting these discretionary factors affects the weights on the various needs factors.

Political constraints have so far prevented the testing of many of the more plausible discretionary factors in England and Wales. (Of those tested in our exercise, only the low-income factor has been incorporated into the regression analyses carried out by the Department of the Environment.) The exclusion of possibly relevant factors is a serious criticism of the regression method as a means of estimating expenditure need in England and Wales. It means that the method will have an overt bias in favour of authorities with a preference for higher spending – those under Labour Party control, or those where local tax bills are low. That overt bias must, at some stage, become unacceptable to central government.

In practice, the regression method has had a substantial impact on grant distribution. Each year has seen a shift of grant to London and the metropolitan districts at the expense of the 'shire' counties. London's share of the needs grant total has risen from 16.5 per cent in 1974/5 to 21.6 per cent in 1978/9. Over the same period, the metropolitan districts' share has risen from 25.3 per cent to 26.5 per cent while the shire counties' share has fallen from 58.2 per cent to 51.9 per cent. London's gain can be attributed largely to special arrangements made for it in the regression procedure rather than to changes in the formula itself. But the relative gains of the metropolitan districts, and losses of the shire counties, are attributable largely to changes in the regression formula (Jackman and Sellars, 1977*a*). Successive regression equations have tended to favour the cities because of their higher expenditure. Whether this higher spending is entirely a reflection of higher spending need is, of course, at the centre of the political battle which the regression method has precipitated.

While reform within the regression approach may be possible, it is unlikely that this central issue of the extent to which central expenditure measures spending need will ever be satisfactorily resolved. Discussion of the reform of the needs grant has thus concentrated on alternative approaches, some of which we consider in Part Three, Chapter 4.

CONCLUSIONS

What is most surprising about the British system of grants is how clearly the mechanisms that have developed over the years related to the objectives of horizontal efficiency and equity. As Part One, Chapter 7 showed, this used to be recognised. Recently there has been far less fundamental discussion of the principles of grant distribution.

The British system of grants seeks to achieve equal rate poundages for equal services. Yet, as we have shown, the idea that equal rate poundages, rather than equal rate bills, is the appropriate criterion of horizontal efficiency depends on the reasons why rateable values differ between localities. Whether equal rate poundages achieve equity depends on the definition of equity adopted. We have suggested a definition of equity in terms of a tax structure including rates as a tax on property. Within this definition the equalisation of rate poundages is equitable. But if the local government finance system is seen in isolation it may well appear inequitable that people should pay different amounts for the same local government services. Also the equalisation of rate poundages for all standards of services necessarily implies a matching resources grant, which is an incentive to higher local government spending.

The basic problem with the needs grant is the mounting confusion and irresolution of purpose in the division of function between central and local government observed in Part One, Chapters 3 and 4. There is no attempt to make even an approximate division between locally and centrally determined services, or parts of services, which could be made the basis of a rational grant system. Central government scarcely even sets standards upon which a needs grant could be based. The price paid for 'flexibility', for enabling central government to intervene or to refrain from intervening, is a high one. Hence the endless and ultimately hopeless search for a method of grant distribution which can achieve horizontal equity without making such distinctions. The regression approach is only capable of a pragmatic defence.

NOTES

1 The authorities in this position in 1978/9 were Slough, Beaconsfield, Ellesmere Port, Thurrock, Watford, Welwyn Hatfield, Elmbridge (Surrey) and Spelthorne (Surrey). All the metropolitan districts receive resources element.
2 The London boroughs with rateable value per head in excess of the standard are Camden, Hackney, Hammersmith, Islington, Kensington and Chelsea, Lambeth, Southwark, Tower Hamlets, Barnet, Brent, Croydon, Ealing, Enfield, Hillingdon, Hounslow, Kingston upon Thames, Richmond upon Thames and the Cities of London and Westminster. Not only are the London authorities with rateable value in excess of the standard more numerous but the excess itself is on average much greater than for the provincial authorities, which accounts for their differential treatment.

4 Influences on Expenditure

In Chapter 4 of Part One we described the growth of local government expenditure, both in total and on the major services, and examined some of the factors that might account for it. In this chapter we look at the current position in more detail. Some local authorities spend much more, per head of population, than others. We would like to know what factors influence the expenditure patterns of local authorities.

There are several reasons for being interested in this question. First, there is the relationship between actual expenditure and 'spending need'. Spending need is a concept we have made frequent reference to in our discussion of grants. Essentially it is defined as the amount authorities would need to spend if they were all to provide some given standard of services. In the course of this chapter we will indicate some ambiguities in this concept. In the present context if actual expenditures reflect spending needs, then a study of the pattern of actual expenditures may reveal a great deal about the factors causing differences in spending needs. Such factors could then be made a basis for grant distribution. Furthermore, such information could be used in predicting, say, the effects of a decline in the birth rate or of population movements between different types of localities on the total and composition of local government expenditure.

But differences in actual expenditure may not simply reflect differences in the costs of providing some given standard of services across authorities. There may be local variations in services or standards. Such variations may be due to differences in the financial resources of different authorities including their receipts of grant from central government. Any association between grant and expenditure would have obvious implications both for the structure of grant and the use of grant as a means of controlling aggregate local government spending. Local spending variations may also be associated with political factors – the ideology of the party in control of the local council, its willingness to defy central government guidelines, and so on. And the existence of local variations in standards of services is of itself of interest in the context of the relationship of central and local government. Significant local variations in services would be inconsistent with the view of local government as an 'agent' of central government.

In the first section of this chapter we set out the evidence on variations in current expenditure by type of authority and by service. There has been a number of studies of local government expenditure in the UK. The different approaches taken in these various studies are discussed in Section 2. In Section 3 we discuss the main results for each of the major services, drawing on our own empirical work as well as on other published studies. Section 4 examines

Table 2.4.1. Estimated current expenditure per head of population 1976–7

Service	All Authorities		London		Metropolitan districts and Counties		Non-metropolitan districts and Counties (England)	
	£	%	£	%	£	%	£	%
Education	113.02	(53.2)	127.66	(47.6)	113.82	(51.1)	108.30	(56.3)
Libraries, museums and art galleries	3.57	(1.7)	5.62	(2.1)	3.89	(1.7)	3.02	(1.6)
Personal social services	18.44	(8.7)	31.80	(11.8)	19.49	(8.7)	14.67	(7.6)
Police	15.84	(7.5)	19.04	(7.1)	16.70	(7.5)	14.45	(7.5)
Fire	4.41	(2.1)	6.23	(2.3)	4.59	(2.1)	3.87	(2.0)
Administration of justice	1.79	(0.8)	1.54	(0.6)	2.07	(0.9)	1.73	(0.9)
Transport	20.85	(9.8)	31.32	(11.7)	24.41	(11.0)	16.43	(8.5)
Housing a	8.65	(4.1)	22.98	(18.6)	9.09	(4.1)	4.77	(2.5)
Refuse collection and disposal	5.88	(2.8)	8.43	(3.1)	6.50	(2.9)	5.09	(2.6)
Environmental health	2.73	(1.3)	4.12	(2.5)	2.73	(1.2)	2.41	(1.3)
Baths, sports and recreation	2.51	(1.2)	4.31	(1.6)	2.42	(1.1)	2.03	(1.1)
Parks and open spaces	3.51	(1.7)	6.95	(2.6)	3.70	(1.7)	2.54	(1.3)
Town and country planning	3.89	(1.8)	4.40	(1.6)	4.14	(1.9)	3.65	(1.9)
Others b	10.09	(4.7)	11.86	(4.4)	9.21	(4.1)	9.24	(4.8)
Total c	212.47	(100.0)	268.42	(100.0)	222.76	(100.0)	192.20	(100.0)

Source: Return of Rates 1976/7 (CIPFA), table 5.
a   Rate fund contributions to housing.
b   General administration, precepts, revenue support for trading services (other than housing and transport), cemeteries and crematoria, un-allocated contingencies and all other services.
c   Total current expenditure, excluding revenue contributions to capital account, inflation provision, planned additions to balances and other adjustment.

aggregate local government spending, again drawing on our own work as well as other published studies

In the next chapter we examine the impact of economic factors — rateable values, central government grants and household incomes — on local government spending. In this chapter we concentrate, therefore, on social political and demographic influences on expenditure, leaving a more detailed analysis of economic factors to Part Two, Chapter 5.

EVIDENCE ON SPENDING VARIATIONS

The present allocation of expenditure between services is set out in Table 2.4.1. Local government spent over £200 per person in 1976/7. Education is far and away the largest service, accounting for over half of all current expenditure. The second most important service, in terms of current expenditure, is transport. This includes not only local authorities' traditional responsibilities for road maintenance and lighting, but also concessionary fares for old people and revenue subsidies to public-transport authorities. It is this latter component which has risen very sharply in recent years. Third, in current expenditure terms, is personal social services, another area of rapid recent expansion. Next is police, which is a service administered by separate police authorities which represent both central and local government, and are financed jointly.[1] The figure for housing expenditure represents only rate-fund contributions — the major part of housing expenditure being financed by rents and direct subsidies from central government. Next come refuse collection and disposal, and the fire service. No other individual service accounts for even as much as 2 per cent of total current expenditure.

The remaining columns of Table 2.4.1 show the allocation of expenditure in the different types of authorities. London authorities spend significantly more than the average, while the non-metropolitan counties and districts, covering mainly rural areas, spend significantly less. Furthermore, these differences are not simply a reflection of generally higher costs and prices in London and the other big cities. As the percentage figures show, the pattern of expenditure is significantly different also. The cities, and London in particular, spend proportionately more on personal social services, transport (as a result of bigger fare subsidies) and rate-fund contributions to housing.

These aggregate figures conceal very considerable variations. Amongst the metropolitan districts, for example, Manchester was spending £258.39 per head, while, at the other extreme, Dudley was spending only £133.32 (CIPFA, *Return of Rates 1976/7*). There are differences in expenditure on all services, but perhaps the most dramatic in proportionate terms are again personal social services (where Manchester spent £33.13 per head of population as against only £11.63 per head in Dudley). Differences in spending on education, though smaller in proportionate terms, are quite substantial — £133.89 per head in Manchester to £90.96 per head in Dudley. In some of the smaller services, too, there are interesting differences. For example, refuse collection costs £10.18 per head in Manchester as against £4.22 per head in Dudley, which seems a surprisingly large difference.

A similar pattern of variation exists in the London boroughs. Expenditure on personal social services ranges from £15.41 per head in Bexley to £61.24 per head in Tower Hamlets, and rate fund contributions to housing from only £1.59 per head in Havering to £63.85 per head in Camden. Again, variation in education expenditure is much smaller proportionately; the range is from £97.82 per head in Redbridge to £152.49 per head in ILEA.

Variations in expenditure are much smaller in the shire (non-metropolitan) counties. This is not surprising, for the more variable elements of expenditure — personal social services and rate fund contributions to housing — are, as Table 2.4.1 shows, much less important in the shire counties than in the metropolitan areas. There are variations — the range of spending is from £162.65 per head in Suffolk to £220.35 per head in Cleveland, but the main factor involved is education. Over half of this difference is accounted for by Cleveland's higher spending on education.

The spending of the Welsh counties is towards the upper end of the range of the English shire counties, with the exception of Powys, whose expenditure (£268.30 per head of population) is far greater than anywhere else. Generally the Welsh counties spend more than the English on education. Also the very sparsely populated Welsh counties — particularly Powys — have much above-average expenditure on roads.

To summarise these general points:

Education
This is by far the largest service in terms of expenditure, and there are significant, though in proportionate terms relatively small, variations between authorities. Of the 106 education authorities in England and Wales all but 9 are spending between £100 and £135 per head of population. The only authorities outside that range are, at the lower end, East Sussex (£87.85), Dudley (£90.96), Devon (£91.50), West Sussex (£92.60), Cornwall (£95.14), Dorset (£96.28) and Redbridge (£97.82), and at the upper end Powys (£135.28) and ILEA (£152.49).

Transport
There is some variability in expenditure per head on roads, but the only authorities which differ substantially from the average are the very sparsely populated counties, especially Powys. Public-transport fare subsidies, on the other hand, are a significant component of expenditure in London and the metropolitan counties, but very small in the shire counties and Wales.

Police expenditure
This is one of the most stable. No authority deviates from the average expenditure of £15.84 per head by more than about £4 per head.

Personal social services
By contrast show very great variations. Solihull has the lowest expenditure — only £9.15 per head of population. The shire counties in England and the Welsh counties are in the £10 to £20 expenditure per head range, while in metropolitan districts and outer London boroughs, the range is from £10 up to around £35

per head. The average expenditure in Inner London is nearly £50 per head, as against an average of less than £20 per head for the metropolitan districts, with a maximum of £61.24 per head in Tower Hamlets.

Housing

It is not surprising that the rate fund contribution to the housing revenue account is one of the most volatile components of expenditure, since it depends both on total housing outlays and on the proportion financed from rents or direct central government grants. Many authorities make virtually no rate fund contribution to housing, £1 or £2 per head, or even less in some cases. The range is up to about £20 per head in all authorities outside Inner London. In Inner London the range is much greater, from about £6 per head in Kensington and Chelsea to over £60 per head in Camden.

Other services

Expenditure on the fire service is relatively stable across authorities, but the other smaller services show significant variation. But, in expenditure terms, each of these other services is too small, taken individually, to make a large contribution to explaining differences in aggregate expenditure.

Clearly there is significant diversity in the spending behaviour of local authorities. We next outline the different approaches that have been adopted in analysing these differences in expenditures.

STUDIES OF LOCAL GOVERNMENT EXPENDITURE

While there have been quite a number of studies, particularly over the last ten years, examining the spending behaviour of local authorities, their results are not readily comparable since they have been intended to answer different questions. Before examining their results in detail it is therefore helpful first to outline the purposes for which they were undertaken.

The studies fall into five distinct groups:

(a)   The first group consists of the research studies undertaken for the Royal Commission on Local Government in England. These research studies were, of course, primarily concerned with the relationship between local government performance and the size of the authority. Most relevant in the present context is Gupta and Hutton (1968). Gupta and Hutton adopt a multiple-regression approach − that is, they investigate how far differences in the expenditure of authorities in particular services can be accounted for by differences in the size of the authorities and by various economic, social and demographic characteristics. If they were to find, other things being equal, bigger authorities spending less per head on a service they would interpret this as evidence of economies of scale. The approach does, however, also provide a great deal of interesting information on the relationship between expenditure and the various economic, social and demographic factors they considered.

The services Gupta and Hutton examined were highways, housing and local health services. Education was the subject of a separate research study (No. 4, undertaken by the Royal Institute of Public Administration, 1968). The results of the study on education are of less interest and value, however, as the approach adopted was to compare the expenditure on different parts of the education service of large and small authorities, without reference to other possible influences.

Research Study No. 5 (Woolf, 1968) also studied the relationship between service provision and various local authority characteristics. But she measured service provision by various direct indicators (e.g. overcrowded classes) and her results therefore can not easily be used in accounting for differences in expenditure.

(b)   The second group of studies consists of the work of Bleddyn Davies and his associates (Davies, 1968; Davies *et al.*, 1971; Davies *et al.*, 1972). The main aim of these studies is to relate the provision of services, as measured in part by expenditure, to the need for them, as indicated by the social, economic and demographic characteristics of the authority. Davies was not primarily concerned to explain what might account for the differences in spending between authorities but to find out whether expenditure is higher where needs are greater. But in some of the later studies (e.g. Davies *et al.*, 1971) Davies and his colleagues do put forward definite conclusions as to the factors responsible for the differences in spending they observe. Davies's work is, of course, mainly concerned with the personal social services, but he has examined education also.

(c)   The third set of studies are those of political scientists. They emphasise that local government expenditure is the outcome of policy decisions of a local council which is itself a political body and subject to political influences. They typically develop propositions on *a priori* theoretical grounds as to the factors that might influence such decisions and then test these propositions against the available evidence. The approach is well exemplified by Boaden (1971). He suggests that an authority's spending on some service will depend on the incidence of need in that locality, the local authority's disposition towards expenditure on the service and the financial resources available to it. Need depends primarily on social and demographic factors (the ideology of the party in power on the council and its willingness to defy central government guidelines), and resources or economic factors such as local income levels and central government grants. Other studies include Oliver and Stanyer (1969), Alt (1971) and Ashford (1974).

(d)   The next group consists of three studies commissioned by the Layfield Committee. Diane Dawson's study (1976) though entitled 'Determinants of local authority expenditure' presents empirical work only on education. Moore and Rhodes' study (1976) is of expenditure in the context of needs assessment. Both these studies are primarily concerned with the use of expenditure as a measure of need for grant purposes. The third study by the present authors is more concerned with the possibility of using differences in expenditure as evidence of the degree of local discretion in education. This study forms the basis of part of Chapter 7, on the role of central government, though we make some reference to it in this and the following chapter.

(e)   The fifth set of studies are those of the Department of the Environment.

Since 1974 the needs element of RSG has, in principle, been distributed according to a formula in which the assessed spending needs of authorities are estimated by regression analysis. A great deal of work goes into these regression exercises but only the final outcome is published in, or can be inferred from, the Rate Support Grant Orders. The choice of variables to be considered in these exercises is, however, severely constrained for political and administrative reasons. Nor does the Department publish any of the normal statistical tests of significance of the variables in the final formula. These limitations greatly reduce the value of its work for purposes of independent inquiry.

3. STUDIES OF SERVICES

The major services provided by local government are education, personal social services, police, housing and transport. In this section we examine each of these services in turn:

(a) EDUCATION

The first recent study is that of Bleddyn Davies (1968, ch. 12). He examined the educational expenditure of the county boroughs in 1961/2. He used a simple correlation approach, that is of seeing whether educational expenditure (or some part of it) was correlated with each of a large number of other variables, taken independently.

His first finding, as might be expected, was that educational expenditure per head of population in an authority was highly correlated with the proportion of schoolchildren in the population in that authority. Higher spending per head simply reflected more children in the population and not higher spending per child. Davies therefore went on to examine the factors correlated with expenditure per pupil. His results for primary and secondary schools are set out in Table 2.4.2 (Davies examined other aspects of educational expenditure also, but these are less important in the total budget and therefore of less interest in the present context.)

How are these correlations to be interpreted? Davies regarded these variables as indicators of social conditions, helpful or detrimental to a child's educational development. From this perspective the results are a little ambiguous. Children in localities with many immigrants from the New Commonwealth (assumed to be a disadvantage) received better educational provision (at least as measured by expenditure). Those in localities with poor-quality housing, or predominantly working-class areas, on the other hand, seemed to receive a worse provision, at least as regards secondary education. Davies does not attempt any explanation of these findings or of the other correlations he observes. Presumably part of the explanation is that immigrants are a minority group whom the majority of the community perceives as having additional educational needs. By contrast, a predominantly working-class community, no doubt with local councillors with working-class backgrounds, might well not share Davies's view that their children

Table 2.4.2. *Factors associated with educational spending*

	Primary	Secondary
Factors associated with high spending	Immigrants (+0.36) Shared dwellings (+0.27)	Immigrants (+0.32) Non-manual (+0.32) Rooms per dwelling (+0.30) Tertiary occupations (+0.24)
Factors associated with low spending	Population aged 5 to 11 (−0.26) *Housing lacking basic amenities (−0.21) *Small dwellings (−0.20)	Industrial occupations (−0.30) Dwellings of low rateable value (−0.25) Heavy industry occupations (−0.24) Population aged 11 to 18 (−0.24) Semi-skilled and unskilled (−0.23)

Source: Davies (1968), ch. 12, derived from tables 66 and 71.
Notes: On a sample of this size, a correlation of 0.22 is significant at the 5 per cent level, and one of 0.28 at the 1 per cent level. Variables marked with an asterisk therefore fall slightly below the 5 per cent significance level.

suffer 'educational handicaps' because of their 'unfortunate backgrounds' (p. 276). There may simply be less pressure for the improvement of educational standards than in middle-class areas.

Some of the other correlations may seem less easy to explain. It is not obvious, for example, why primary-school expenditure per pupil should be greater the higher the proportion of households in 'shared dwellings.' This probably illustrates one of the main difficulties that bedevils any analysis of local government expenditure, the intercorrelation of variables. Shared dwellings are particularly to be found amongst immigrant families, and, as we have seen, education expenditure is high where there are many immigrants. Thus education expenditure is high where there are many shared dwellings not because the proportion of households in shared dwellings as such has any effect on educational spending but, in all probability, because both are associated with a high proportion of immigrants in the population.

There are a number of possible interpretations of the finding that expenditure per pupil tends to be lower the higher the proportion of schoolchildren in the population. It may indicate some form of economies of scale — that school-buildings, teachers and equipment can be used more intensively where there are many schoolchildren. Another possible explanation is a financial one. The additional financial cost of having to provide education for a large proportion of children in the population, unless matched by a commensurate increase in income, may force a reduction in the standard of provision. Finally, it is possible that the correlation is spurious, the higher proportion of schoolchildren being associated with predominantly working-class areas where, as already observed, educational expenditure tends to be lower. Equally, of course, it is possible that the correlation between educational expenditure and social class is spurious, simply reflecting the fact that both are correlated with the proportion of schoolchildren in the population rather than being directly related.

Interesting though these findings are, they seem to raise more questions than they answer. Boaden's approach goes some way towards resolving these ambiguities by analysing the relationship between expenditure and variables which, on theoretical grounds, he suggests might be expected to influence it (Boaden, 1971, ch. 5). His study of the county boroughs in 1965/6 finds that, after adjusting for the proportion of schoolchildren in the population, expenditure was strongly correlated with political control. Labour councils typically spend more than Conservative or others. Further, this correlation remained even after making allowance for social, economic and other political factors. Boaden interpreted this result as a reflection of ideological preference. Labour councils were spending more, not because educational needs in their areas were greater, or because they had more money, but because they chose to.

Such a finding can hardly be regarded as conclusive, however. It is always possible that some other factor affecting the educational needs of schoolchildren is correlated with Labour control, and the higher expenditure results from this higher need rather than from political preference.

Boaden's other findings were negative. Total population size, other political variables (proportion voting at elections, number of committees, etc.) and financial variables (government grants, per capita rateable value) seemed to exert no independent influence on expenditure.

Alt's study also concentrated on political variables. He examined educational expenditure for a random sample of forty-four county boroughs for each of the ten financial years 1958/9 to 1967/8 (Alt, 1971). Like Boaden, he found a significant correlation between expenditure per pupil and Labour Party control, both for primary and in secondary schools. He found that total population size and the degree of party competition – small majorities on the council indicating a high degree of party competition – had little independent impact on spending. However, Alt found one financial variable to be significant, which he called 'wealth' and which was intended as a measure of average household incomes in the locality.

In the absence of any local incomes data, however, Alt measures 'wealth' by average per capita rateable value in the authority. Even if household incomes in an area were well approximated by rateable value per head, and we have no evidence that they are, the measure would be unsatisfactory since rateable value per head has an impact on local authority finances independently of any relationship with personal incomes. In the next chapter we set out an 'economic' model of local government expenditure in which the separate effects of household incomes, rateable value and central government grants are identified.

Two studies commissioned by the Layfield Committee examined education expenditure. Moore and Rhodes (1976) reached a conclusion, apparently in conflict with that of most other writers, that almost all variation in expenditure in primary and secondary schools in 1967/8 could be accounted for by the proportions of schoolchildren in the population and by the London weighting on teachers' salaries. Their study, though, does not examine spending by individual authorities, but only the aggregate expenditure of the main classes of authorities (county boroughs, London boroughs, English counties, Welsh counties). They did, however, carry out one simple regression on individual authorities to test for the existence of economies or diseconomies of scale. Like earlier studies, they found no significant relationship.

The study by Diane Dawson (1976) is based on evidence for all education authorities for 1975/6, and is thus the first study of the new authorities created by the reorganisation of 1974. Dawson shows that expenditure per pupil is influenced by the average size of schools in the authority, by the proportion of immigrants and the proportion of households 'suffering from multiple deprivation' (i.e. living in housing lacking basic amenities). Average school size was relevant both because pupil–teacher ratios tend to be lower in smaller schools and because teachers in smaller schools tend to stay longer and hence receive higher average salaries. Pupil–teacher ratios are also lower in areas with many immigrants or households in multiple deprivation, for these areas qualify as areas of 'special need'. A local education authority may request an addition to its quota for teachers in order to provide additional teaching for immigrants and in schools in educational priority areas. Dawson stresses, however, that local authorities varied very greatly in their readiness to take on the extra teachers they were allowed. But she does not attempt to explain the causes of these variations.

Our own study is concerned primarily with the effects of local economic factors – that is of average household incomes and government grants. We examined the educational spending of county councils and of county boroughs in 1972/3. Our results are discussed more fully in later chapters, but do seem to show some influence of economic factors on education spending, particularly in the counties.[2]

These studies present, by and large, a consistent picture. The main, and most obvious, finding is that variations in educational expenditure per head of population are mainly attributable to differences in the proportion of schoolchildren in the population. This is perhaps the clearest possible example of a 'needs' variable — an authority with more schoolchildren per head of population will have to spend more on education per head of population for a given standard of provision.

Second, there is no evidence of economies of scale in education authorities. Neither the total population of the authority nor the total number of schoolchildren significantly affect expenditure per pupil. Dawson finds evidence that costs tend to be higher in smaller schools, but small schools are more likely to be connected with the sparsity of population in an authority than with the total size of the education authority. Griffith (1966, for example, pp. 528–9) has suggested that large authorities, with more political muscle, may be more likely to defy central government by exceeding guidelines on standards of equipment, etc. It is therefore possible that there may be economies of scale, but the off-setting effects of economies of scale and higher standards on expenditure per pupil may roughly cancel out.

More interesting, perhaps, is the effect of 'social need' factors. As we have seen, Bleddyn Davies found a very mixed picture in 1961/2, while Diane Dawson found a clearer correlation between social needs indicators and expenditure in 1975/6. We examined the relationship between educational spending and various local authority characteristics for 1971/2. We were unable to find any significant relationship between expenditure and needs characteristics. Our best equations, for expenditure in primary schools per primary schoolchild and expenditure in secondary schools per secondary schoolchild, for county boroughs, were respectively:

$$XPRI = 107.50 - 0.24 PROPO + 0.008 Y + 0.11 PRI$$
$$\qquad\qquad (0.09) \qquad (0.003) \quad (0.05)$$

$$- 2.28 CON + 36.68 ILLEG + 3.29 LAB \qquad R^2 = 0.24$$
$$\quad (2.47) \qquad (24.58) \qquad (3.25)$$

$$XSEC = 222.94 - 0.59 PROPO + 0.022 Y - 7.05 CON$$
$$\qquad\qquad (0.25) \qquad\quad (0.009) \quad (5.31)$$

$$+ 67.27 ILLEG + 1.30 DEC - 10.65 HIGHD - 0.90 NEDGR \quad R^2 = 0.15$$
$$\quad (66.34) \qquad (0.78) \qquad (7.28) \qquad\quad (0.63)$$

where *PROPO* measures the proportion of owner-occupiers, *Y* measures household income (see next chapter), *CON* and *LAB* are political variables measuring the proportion of councillors in the Conservative and Labour parties, *PRI* is the total number of primary schoolchildren in the local authority, *DEC* is the rate of decline of population, *HIGHD* the proportion of the population in densely populated wards and parishes, and *NEDGR* the receipt of needs grant per head of population. (Full definitions of the variables are given in Appendix 2.4.A1.)

Despite all these variables, the explanatory power of the equations is poor (as indicated by the low R^2) and most of the variables are statistically insignificant. In fact only two are significant (the same two in both equations), *PROPO* and *Y*.

In what sense does an authority with many immigrants, or households in housing lacking basic amenities,[3] 'need' to spend more on education? Not in the same way as an authority with an above-average proportion of children needs to spend more — to provide some given standard of service — because the whole point is to provide additional facilities for these children in the hope of compensating for the assumed disadvantages of their home background. The amount of additional expenditure is a matter of judgement, and not of 'need' as the word is used in this context. Once a judgement has been made as to the amount of additional expenditure thought appropriate, then the extra expenditure in each authority will depend on its numbers of immigrant (etc.) children and this will again be a 'needs' factor.

Finally, both Boaden and Alt find a strong correlation between expenditure and political control. Both interpret this result as indicating local political autonomy, regarding education as a redistributive public service.

(b) SOCIAL SERVICES

Expenditure on the social services has increased very rapidly over the past twenty years. This expansion has been associated with major new legislation (Mental Health Act, Childrens' Act, etc.) and accompanied by reorganisation of social service departments following the recommendations of the Seebohm Committee. Before this reorganisation there were, in most authorities, three separate departments concerned with personal social services: welfare (provision for old people and the physically handicapped), childrens' services, and local health services. Because most published studies predate the reorganisation and because these categories still dominate expenditure,[4] we will examine expenditure on the three categories separately.

(i) Services for old people

Two major studies of local authority provision of old people's services have been carried out by Bleddyn Davies. In the first (Davies, 1968, chs. 8 and 9), he attempts to construct an index of need for local authority provision. The argument is that local authorities need only provide services for old people whose families are not caring for them — because they are too infirm, or have no surviving relatives, or whatever. Davies finds that the proportion of old people in old people's homes varies according to demographic characteristics, such as age, sex and marital status. As might be expected, the proportion in homes increases with age, but he also finds that, for any given age group, a greater proportion of men than women are in old people's homes and a greater proportion of single than married people. Davies then constructs an index of need for old people's services in each authority based on these demographic characteristics of its old people, called the 'family-care index'.

But lack of family care is not the only reason for old people going into homes. They may be ill, or have no suitable housing, or their family may be too poor, or have no space for them. Davies constructs a second index of need – a 'social-conditions index' – to take account of local authority characteristics such as overcrowding, infant mortality rates, proportion in working-class occupations, etc. This social-conditions index is correlated with the family-care index, but not very closely (the correlation coefficient is 0.29). There is no obvious way of establishing the relative importance of the two indices, however, so what Davies does is to leave out of the subsequent analysis those authorities for which the two indices are very different. (For example, the seaside-resort towns have many old people – mostly relatively affluent who have retired there – so the family-care index suggests high need while the social conditions index suggests low need.) For those authorities (fifty-two out of the eighty-three county boroughs) for which the two indices give roughly similar measures, the family-care index is adopted as 'the' index of need.

Table 2.4.3. *Correlation coefficients for old people's services – County Boroughs 1961/2*

Revenue Account net expenditure on	Index of need	Number of old people per thousand population
Residential Homes	+0.36	+0.37
Domestic Help	+0.08	+0.19
Home Nursing	+0.29	+0.29

Source: Davies (1968), ch. 9, derived from tables 32–7.

Table 2.4.3 shows that expenditure is related to the index of need, and significantly so except in the case of provision of domestic help. But the correlation between expenditure and the proportion of old people in the population unadjusted by any demographic or social factors is just as close. This result arises in part because the index of need is quite closely correlated with the proportion of old people in the population. But it also suggests variations in expenditure are not well accounted for by the particular demographic and social-need factors Davies considers.

The purpose of Davies's other major study (Davies *et al.*, 1971) is very different; it is specifically to identify the causes of variations in expenditure. The statistical approach is sophisticated and highly complex. The following example gives a simplified idea of the method. Assume that variations in spending are associated both with poverty and Labour control, factors which are themselves closely correlated. Then, the argument would run, while poverty might cause people to vote Labour, a Labour council is (presumably) not a cause of local poverty. The basic cause of the variations in expenditure, then, is poverty, and Labour control is only a manifestation of poverty and not an independent cause of high expenditure. But poverty is not perfectly correlated with Labour control, nor does it account for all variation in expenditure. We can then ask whether a poor locality with a Labour council spends more than an equally poor locality with a Conservative council. If so, this would indicate an independent influence of political factors.

The main cause of variations in expenditure on old people's services turned out to be needs factors and particularly the family-care index (described above). Additionally, politics had a strong independent influence, with Labour councils spending more than Conservatives. Also the existence of a separate, independent welfare department within the administration led to higher spending. The size of the authority (measured in terms of population) and its rateable value had no significant independent impact on expenditure.

Boaden's discussion (1971, ch. 7) of welfare services is, by contrast, short and simple. He finds expenditure correlated with proportion of the population over 65 and with poor housing amenities, broadly consistent with Davies' findings, but, unlike Davies, finds no independent effect of politics. Alt (1971, table 8) also finds spending on welfare services not significantly related to party control.

Welfare services are discussed briefly by Moore and Rhodes (1976, paras 47–50). Their concern is that county councils in 1967/8 were spending less in relation to their numbers of old people than the county boroughs or London boroughs. They interpret this as indicating that urban areas had 'identified their welfare needs more thoroughly' – a situation they expected to be put right by central government legislation imposing statutory duties on local authority social service departments. An alternative interpretation, of course, is that a larger proportion of old people in urban areas may need local authority welfare services, for the reasons examined by Bleddyn Davies.

We examined expenditure on old people's services in county boroughs in 1972/3. Though our study is based on more recent evidence, the results are broadly consistent with those of Bleddyn Davies. Demographic and social factors are the most important, political factors exert some influence, and economic factors are relatively unimportant. Our best equation was:

$$XOLD = 0.093 + 6.353\,OLD + 0.819\,CLF - 0.005\,CON \quad R^2 = 0.28$$
$$\qquad\qquad (1.602) \qquad (0.360) \qquad (0.004)$$

(figures in brackets are standard errors)
where $XOLD$ is expenditure on old people's services (per head of population), OLD is the proportion of people over 65 in the population, CLF is a 'social-conditions' index,[5] and CON is a political index of Conservative strength. The equation tells us that, in 1972/3, on average, an additional person over 65 added £6.35 to county borough expenditure on old people's services, and that expenditure tended to be significantly higher in areas with poor social conditions, and probably somewhat lower if the council was Conservative controlled, though this effect was not statistically significant. Economic factors seem relatively unimportant and we return to this in the next chapter.

(ii) Children's services
Children's services consist primarily of the provision of local authority homes for children whose families are incapable (or judged incapable) of caring for them. Again, the major studies on children's services are those of Bleddyn Davies, and they follow very similar lines to his work on old people's services.

Davies (1968, ch. 11) constructed an index of need based on the character-istics of families that are prone to having children taken into care by the local authority. The particular characteristics he thought important were immigrants, mobile families living in boarding houses, and families where the head of the household was unemployed. Areas with many such families, in his view, would need to provide more places in children's homes than areas with a more settled population. Davies constructed an index based on these characteristics, called the 'anomie' index. Expenditure per 'weighted population' was not significantly correlated with the anomie index.[6] Davies concluded that standards of provision of children's services were correlated with need to 'only a small degree' (p. 259).

The second study (Davies *et al.*, 1972) again concentrated on the causes of differences in provision of services. In this study, Davies found a limited, but not totally insignificant, influence of 'Wealth' (i.e. rateable value) on spending, and again, a significant political impact both on the total of spending and on its allocation within the budget for children's services. But most important was the strong correlation between expenditure and various socio-economic and demographic characteristics[7] of the local population. But there are different interpretations of this finding, which seems at first sight at variance with the result of the previous study. These local authority characteristics might influence expenditure because they indicate the 'need' for the service, they may affect the authority's ability to recruit qualified staff, or simply be correlated with the size of the authority and hence of the department. Davies clearly believes, for example, that size is important because it allows greater specialisation and hence the capacity to take on a wider range of problems, but since local authority size is highly correlated with some of his 'needs' indicators (such as overcrowding and the proportion of immigrants) it is impossible to establish the extent to which the higher provision is in fact a consequence of size rather than of these 'need' factors. This is, of course, the problem of multi-collinearity to which we have already referred in the previous chapter on grants, and which has bedevilled all attempts to construct indicators of spending needs for local authorities on the basis of socio-economic or demographic population characteristics.

Boaden (1971) also found that expenditure on children's services was strongly correlated with socio-economic characteristics (such as social class and housing amenities) and with Labour control.[8] The relationship between expenditure and rateable value is not reported, presumably because it was found to be insignificant. More interestingly, there is a strong negative relationship between expenditure and the proportion of rateable value represented by domestic hereditaments (households), which Boaden attributes to some form of 'ratepayer resistance'. We return to this in the next chapter.

Again our own analysis, based on more recent data, tends to confirm the finding that socio-economic factors are the most important influences on expenditure on children's services. For county boroughs, in 1972/3, we found that expenditure per head on children's services (*XCHI*) seemed to be influenced most by illegitimacy rates (*ILLEG*), over-crowding (*CRWD*), proportion of immigrants (*IMMIG*), proportion of owner-occupiers (*PROPO*), and inversely to the proportion of children (under 18) in the population (*CHI*). (Full definitions of the variables are given in Appendix 2.4.A1.) The relationship was:

$$XCHI = 0.675 + 57.824ILLEG + 13.441CRWD - 7.174CHI$$
$$(9.028)(2.654)(2.007)$$

$$+ 0.011PROPO + 0.277IMMIG \qquad R^2 = 0.67$$
$$(0.005)(0.390)$$

(figures in brackets are standard errors)
Neither political nor financial factors contributed to the explanation of differences in expenditure.

(iii)   Local health services
Local health service departments were responsible for a variety of services, including ambulances, health visitors, day nurseries and so on. Gupta and Hutton (1968) in their investigation of economies of scale in local government for the Royal Commission, examined three components of the local health service budget – ambulances, home nursing and administration.

For ambulances they found a positive correlation in county boroughs between expenditure and population size, which they interpreted as evidence of diseconomies of scale. Clearly Bleddyn Davies, faced with the same finding, would have interpreted it as evidence of greater need and/or more adequate provision in the larger cities, given the inter-relationship of population size and socio-economic characteristics. In the counties, Gupta and Hutton found expenditure correlated only with the proportion of the population living in urban areas – a correlation difficult to explain from a 'cost-of-service' standpoint, but, of course, consistent with a 'social need' approach. The 'social need' explanation also seems consistent with Gupta and Hutton's own results on home-nursing expenditure, where they find costs per visit lower in the big towns, for the social need factors would be expected to affect the number of visits rather than the cost per visit. Finally, on administration costs, there seemed clear evidence of economies of scale. Both for counties and county boroughs, the smaller authorities tended to have higher administrative costs per head of population than the larger authorities.

Boaden's results for local health services were very similar to his findings for children's services. The main influences were socio-economic characteristics (housing amenities, social class and population density) and Labour control. Again, the correlation between expenditure and party control was confirmed in Alt's study (1971, table 8). The correlation with population size is positive but not significant. Again there is a negative relationship between expenditure and the proportion of domestic rateable value in total rateable value.

(c)   POLICE

Variations in expenditure on the police are not as great as variations in spending on education or on the social services. Further, it is not difficult to account for such variation as does exist.

Boaden (1971) and Alt (1971) each find that police expenditure per head of population is higher in larger county boroughs than in smaller ones. This does not indicate diseconomies of scale in the police force as such, but the tendency for crime rates to be higher in the bigger cities. Boaden also finds population density associated with higher spending, and this is confirmed by Moore and Rhodes (1976), but again this probably only reflects the tendency for population density to be greater in the bigger cities.

Police expenditure also tends to be higher in cities with a high proportion of middle-class inhabitants, and lower in Labour-controlled cities. This could be either because the middle class are more threatened by crime than the working class, or because of political preference by middle-class people for a higher standard of police protection even though the benefits accrue as much to working-class people living in the locality. The first explanation suggests a greater 'need' for police in the better-off areas because the population is at greater risk. According to the principle of the needs grant, such additional expenditure need should be fully compensated by additional grant. It may seem odd that wealthier areas should attract additional grant at the expense of poorer areas in order to protect that wealth, but this is precisely what the logic of the grant system implies.

Perhaps even more ironically, if the higher spending is altruistic rather than self-interested, and much of the benefit does not in fact accrue to the wealthy, then the higher spending in principle should not attract grant. It represents a voluntary variation in quality rather than a higher level of need.

(d) HIGHWAYS

Current expenditure on highways (maintenance, minor improvements, cleansing, road lighting, etc.) depends primarily on the road mileage in the authority. Expenditure per road mile depends mainly on population per mile, presumably because it is a major determinant of road use. These findings are, of course, consistent with the idea that differences in local government spending on roads are primarily attributable to differences between authorities in the costs of maintaining roads to a given standard.

Gupta and Hutton (1968) additionally found an economies-of-scale effect in highways expenditure. Larger authorities, whether measured in terms of population size or of road mileage, tended to spend less per mile (after taking account of differences in population per mile) than smaller ones.

There seems relatively little evidence of 'discretionary' spending variations on highways. Gupta and Hutton, and also Alt (1971), found a positive correlation between spending and rateable value per head, but in neither case was it statistically significant. Alt also found an insignificant (negative) relationship between spending and Labour Party control. He did, however, find a significant negative relationship between spending and competitiveness, which could be interpreted as suggesting that councils with narrow majorities found road maintenance an easy service to cut back in order to hold down rates at election times.

(e) HOUSING

Local authority housing expenditure raises so many issues that it would take a book rather than a subsection of a chapter to deal with the subject at all adequately.

But we are here concerned not with housing policy but only with housing finance as it impinges on local government finances more generally. By housing expenditure we may mean one of three things:

(1)   Capital expenditure, that is the cost of land, building costs, etc. incurred in building new local authority houses or in acquiring housing stock.

(2)   Housing revenue account current expenditure, that is, primarily, costs of debt servicing for capital expenditure incurred, together with cost of maintenance and administration.

(3)   Rate fund contribution to housing revenue account. Expenditure on the housing revenue account can be met from rents charged to tenants, from specific housing grants from central government, or from the local authority's own revenues ('rate fund').

The various studies of housing expenditure have examined different aspects of this system. Gupta and Hutton (1968) with their concern with economies of scale, looked at differences in unit costs in housing between authorities.[9] They found unit costs were higher where the population was large and in areas with high population density and in building schemes with a high site density. More surprisingly, they found unit costs positively and significantly correlated with social costs and negatively and significantly with the use of direct labour (as against outside contractors). They suggested that this result was indicative of diseconomies of scale in housing departments. They also examined the rate fund contribution to the housing revenue account, which they found very significantly, and negatively, related to social class. This suggests that the 'higher-class' areas are building fewer council houses but to a higher standard, or less efficiently, and perhaps charging higher rents for them.

Boaden (1971, ch. 6) also examined differences in the rate fund contribution to the housing revenue account. He found a very significant correlation not only with social class, but also with Labour control, and with receipts of central government grant. Though these factors are correlated with each other their effects are so strong that Boaden is able to show that political control and grant each exert a significant independent influence (1971, table 6.6, p. 69), while the influence of social class is mainly attributable to its correlation with the other two variables. The correlation coefficients are very much higher than those found for the other services. The inference is clear – that the housing subsidy for the rate fund is determined by political and financial factors. Differences between authorities in this component of expenditure are a result of local discretion – the local council's political motivation and its financial resources – and not by any 'need' concept such as the difference in the cost of providing some given standard of service.

One obvious question is whether the rate fund contribution of Labour councils represents, as it were, a higher rent subsidy per dwelling, or simply a greater number of council houses in Labour areas. An earlier paper by Boaden and Alford (1969) had examined the activity of local authorities in housebuilding by trying to explain differences in the proportions of new housebuilding in different localities built by the local authority. Their findings are that political control and finance are the main factors, but that housing need also exerts an independent, though only marginally significant, influence. Alt (1971) also finds politics the main influence on housing expenditure, although he does not specify what measure of housing expenditure he is using.

A much more ambitious study of capital expenditure on housing has been undertaken by Nicholson and Topham (1971). They suggest investment in local authority housing, like any other investment decision, will depend on the return from the new investment (in this area the value of the benefit of the new housing which, in turn, will depend on the inadequacy of the existing housing stock), on the cost of the funds and on the motivation of the decision-maker. Despite starting from economic theory, they therefore end up with a very similar set of variables to those used by Boaden, that is variables indicating needs, resources and disposition.

Nicholson and Topham's findings are quite different from Boaden's, however. Their explanation is dominated by housing-need indicators, particularly over-crowding and lack of amenities. Neither political nor financial factors contribute significantly to the explanation of variations in capital expenditure. Unfortunately, various interpretations can be advanced for the variables Nicholson and Topham found most important. In particular 'housing judged unfit by the local authority' – their most significant explanatory variable – may indicate a council's ideological commitment to public housing as much as the physical condition of the housing stock. Likewise, the next most significant variable – 'impetus' – that is the size of the council's housebuilding programme in previous years, does not provide a satisfactory explanation, since the size of the programme in earlier years itself needs explaining.

Likewise, the financial variables used by Nicholson and Topham can be criticised as measuring primarily the cost to the ratepayers, and taking no account of the share of the cost borne by the tenants in the form of rents. Some authorities clearly do not intend to subsidise the housing-revenue account from the general rate fund,[10] and housebuilding in such authorities will, therefore, being self-financing, not be affected by the general state of the council's finances.

4. TOTAL CURRENT EXPENDITURE

One approach to investigating factors affecting the total current expenditure of local authorities would be to add together all the factors affecting expenditure on the individual services. But an alternative, and much simpler, approach is to cut through the detail on the assumption that the detailed characteristics of a locality may influence the distribution of its expenditures between different services but not the total.[11]

One such approach is by Oliver and Stanyer (1969). They use a composite measure to indicate the geographical, economic and social structure of an area, namely the proportions of rateable value in the area represented by domestic, commercial, industrial and other hereditaments. They find that the composition of rateable value is significantly correlated with spending, spending being lower in county boroughs with a high proportion of domestic to industrial property, and high where the proportion of commercial to other property is high. While this finding is of some interest, the explanation is not at all obvious, and may relate more to the ratepaying capacities of the different types of property than the socio-economic characteristics of the locality.

Oliver and Stanyer found no significant relationship between political control and expenditure. A more recent study, by Ashford, Berne and Schramm (1976) using data for 1967, only three years later than the period examined by Oliver and Stanyer, has reached a completely opposite conclusion. Their 'most important' finding is that political factors are significant in local government spending decisions. This latter finding is more in accord with the studies on individual services.

The other major set of studies on total current expenditure are those undertaken by the Department of the Environment annually since 1974 for the purposes of calculating the needs grant formula. We are here concerned with the results of the expenditure analysis *per se*, and not with the use of the results for grant purposes, which was discussed in the previous chapter.

The concept of differences of needs — of spending differences required to provide similar standard of services — can be applied easily in two services. In education, spending will depend primarily on the numbers of schoolchildren, and in highways on road mileage. Factors based on these two measures of need[12] have appeared in the needs grant formulae for each of the years from 1974/5 to 1978/9.

Indicators of socio-economic characteristics have, however, been included and in some cases dropped from the formula in a highly volatile way. The 1974/5 formula included two such factors, a population decline and 'personal social-service units', but the latter were in fact a measure of expenditure rather than an indicator of need. The number of these socio-economic needs indicators rose year by year until no less than eight were included in the 1977/8 formula.[13] The rate of population decline has been the only one included throughout, and its status is not at all clear — it may, for example, be indicating only that the reduction in the provision of services is lagging behind the decline in the population using them. Not only have the variables in the formula changed, but, as we showed in the previous chapter, their coefficients have also altered dramatically from one year to the next.

The DoE analyses do not examine the effects on total expenditure of politics or of grants. But one economic variable — the proportion of households with low incomes — is found to have an effect on expenditure. The greater the proportion of households with low incomes, the lower the local government expenditure. This is interpreted as an 'income' effect — that poorer households can less easily afford to pay the normal levels of rates, and councils in areas with many poor households reduce their spending in order to hold down their rate bills. We shall report similar studies in the next chapter.

While it is possible to infer the results of the DoE analyses from the Rate Support Grant Orders, it would be difficult to compare these results with those of other studies since, as we noted earlier, we have no tests of the statistical significance of the DoE results. Jackman and Sellars (1978) carried out a regression analysis using the main needs variables that have appeared in the Rate Support Grant formulae, for the shire counties and metropolitan districts for 1975/6. The results are:

Shire Counties

$$X = 47.45 + 4.40 SPR + 291.08 EDU + 396.56 MOC + 14.92 HBA$$
$$\quad\quad\;\; (8.29) \quad\quad (11.47) \quad\quad (3.74) \quad\quad\quad (1.25)$$

$$+ 1096.71 NH \quad\quad R^2 = 0.609$$
$$\;\;\; (4.56)$$

Metropolitan Districts

$$X = 70.33 + 24.79 DEC + 199.39 EDU + 371.36 OAL + 29.04 HIGHD$$
$$\quad\quad\;\; (0.90) \quad\quad\quad (2.36) \quad\quad\quad (1.61) \quad\quad\quad (2.80)$$

$$+ 448.07 MOC + 1456.82 LF \quad\quad R^2 = 0.700$$
$$\;\; (5.26) \quad\quad\quad (2.09)$$

where X is expenditure per head, SPR is a measure of sparsity, EDU is educational units, MOC is multi-occupancy rates, HBA is the number of people living in dwellings lacking basic amenities, NH is the number of new permanent dwellings constructed, DEC is a measure of declining population, OAL is the number of old people living alone, $HIGHD$ is a measure of population density, and LF is the number of single-parent families. (Figures in parentheses are t-statistics.) As can be seen, the level of explanation is high, 61 per cent for the shire counties and 70 per cent for the metropolitan districts, using the needs factors alone. The individual variables are significant excepting HBA in the first equation and DEC and OAL in the second.

5. CONCLUSIONS

There are two services for which the concept of 'spending need' has an obvious, operational meaning. In education, for a given standard of service, expenditure will be influenced primarily by the numbers of school children of different ages. Likewise, with highways, the costs of maintenance and minor repairs will be primarily affected by total road mileage. Empirical studies both of the particular services and of total expenditure support these expectations. Expenditure per head varies between authorities because of differences in the proportions of schoolchildren in the population and differences in road mileage per head.

The influence of social conditions on expenditure is far less straightforward. Spending on the social services, and also on education and housing, seems significantly related to various socio-economic characteristics, but the underlying processes of causation are not obvious. In terms of statistics, the problem is one of multi-collinearity, that because all the social-needs indicators are closely correlated with one another it is not possible to identify the effect of each independently. But this is only a symptom of a more fundamental difficulty. The nature of the services is not precisely or objectively defined — in legislation or elsewhere — and a great deal of discretion is left to the local authorities in the administration of the services and in how legislation is interpreted. Any correlations between expenditure on such services and the socio-economic characteristics of the locality are statistical regularities rather than underlying causal relationships. It may be that proportionately more children are taken into care in localities where the population density is high, but no child will be taken into care just because it lives in a local authority with a high population density. Equally, the concept of an equal standard of service between different authorities can have little operational meaning when the standard itself cannot be defined objectively.

The concept of a given standard of services applies with even less meaning, though, in housing to rate fund contributions to the housing revenue account. Even if it were possible to give any operational meaning to the idea of 'housing need' (Harrison and Webber, 1977), it is clear that rate-fund contributions depend not only on the amount of local authority housing but also on the extent to which rate subsidies are used to hold down rents.

On the balance of the evidence, political influences are also important. The main services affected are housing and the personal social services. There are remarkably few studies of the relationship between political control and total expenditure, but the recent study of Ashford, Berne and Schramm (1976), finding a significant relationship, seems more consistent with evidence on individual services and with the evidence on rate poundages (Part Two, Chapter 6) than with Oliver and Stanyer's result of no significant correlation. We present our own results on the influence of politics in the next chapter.

Most of the studies find little influence for economic or financial variables, personal incomes, rateable values, grants, etc. But few of them have made a systematic attempt to incorporate all the relevant financial variables. In the following chapter, we construct an 'economic' model of local government expenditure and discuss our empirical estimates of the impact of economic and financial variables — particularly central government grants — on local government spending.

NOTES

1　Except for the Metropolitan Police, which are responsible directly to the Home Secretary but are none the less financed jointly by central government and the London boroughs.

2　A recent study by Storey (1975) merits only a brief discussion, because Storey examines factors affecting the proportion of expenditure going on education. This proportion will clearly be as much (if not more) affected by variations in spending on other services (where there is often greater variability) than by variations in spending on education. Storey's finding, that the proportion spent on education is affected most by road mileage and the numbers of old people in the authority, is therefore unenlightening.

3　Housing lacking basic amenities is presumably a proxy variable for parental inadequacies. The idea that a child's educational prospects can be directly affected by the plumbing in its home is not to be taken seriously.

4   In our study of social service expenditure in 1972/3, which was during the period of transition, we find that 79 per cent of the variation in total expenditure can be accounted for by variations in expenditure on old people's and childrens' services.

5   The index in fact is based on single-parent families, which are a good indication of general social conditions, particularly poor housing and low incomes. Full definitions of all the variables are given in Appendix 2.4.A1.

6   Again, however, the analysis is confined to county boroughs where the incidence of need as measured by the anomie index is consistent with the 'social conditions' index, which, in this case, limited the comparison to twenty county boroughs. Weighted population is the total number of children under 18 in the authority weighted according to age group.

7   The characteristics considered were death rates, infant mortality rates, population density, proportion of immigrants, retail sales, occupations mix, population change, unemployment, proportion in boarding houses, overcrowding, households sharing, and so on.

8   Alt (1971, table 8) also found a significant influence of party control and also a positive influence of party 'competitiveness' (i.e. smallness of majority). Boaden, however, finds a negative correlation between expenditure and percentage turnout in local elections, another possible measure of 'competitiveness'.

9   The best cost variables were superstructural building costs per square foot of accommodation provided and supervision and management costs per existing dwelling.

10   Even by 1976/7, one metropolitan district (Solihull), four London boroughs and a large number of non-metropolitan districts were supporting their housing revenue accounts with rate fund contributions of less than ½p in the pound.

11   An analogy might be the spending of a household, where the composition of goods purchased will depend on the household's characteristics, but the total spent on its income.

12   The factors, in fact, are 'education units' — numbers of schoolchildren weighted by age to take account of differences in costs for different age groups, and population sparsity, which is closely correlated with road mileage per head of population.

13   The 8 factors were population decline, high population density, people of pensionable age living alone, overcrowding, housing lacking amenities, one-parent families, shared households and unemployment rates.

Appendix 2.4.A1   Definition of Variables

EXPENDITURE

X: Estimated rate and rate support grant-borne expenditure per head of population (for shire counties the expenditure figure applies to county services, while for metropolitan districts it includes both county and district services).

XPRI: Estimated primary-school expenditure divided by the number of primary schoolchildren in the authority.

XSEC: Estimated secondary-school expenditure divided by the number of secondary schoolchildren in the authority.

XOLD: Estimated expenditure on old people's services per head of population.

XCHI: Estimated expenditure on children's services per head of population.

Source: CIPFA statistics.

NEEDS FACTORS

CHI: Percentage of population aged under 18 years.

CLF: Average number of children per lone-parent family.

CRWD: Overcrowding: numbers in households with more than one person per room as a proportion of the total population of the authority.

DEC: Decline of population over previous five years as a proportion of current population.

EDU: Education units per head of population. Education units are weighted according to type of education. Primary schoolchildren have a weight of 1, the weight on secondary schoolchildren varies from year to year but is around 2, while students in further education have a weight around 3–3.5.

HBA: Numbers living in housing, lacking exclusive use of basic amenities at the time of the 1971 Census as a proportion of the population.

HIGHD: Numbers living in wards or parishes with a density higher than fifty persons per hectare at the time of the 1971 Census as a proportion of the total population.

ILLEG: Illegitimate births as a proportion of total births.

IMMIG: Number of immigrants as a proportion of the total population.

LF: Number of lone-parent families with dependent children as a proportion of the population at the time of the 1971 Census.

MOC: Number living in shared households in permanent buildings as a proportion of the total population at the time of the 1971 Census.

NH: Number of new permanent dwellings started between 1 April 1975 and 31 March 1976 expressed as a proportion of total population.

OAL: Number of people of pensionable age living alone at the time of the 1971 Census as a proportion of total population.

OLD: Number of people over 65 years as a proportion of total population.

PRI: Number of primary schoolchildren as a proportion of total population.

SPR: Sparsity, measured as the number of acres in excess of 1.5 per head of population, divided by total population.

OTHER FACTORS

CON: Index of Conservative strength on council, taking account of past as well as current political representation.

LAB: Index of Labour strength on council, taking account of past as well as current political representation.

NEDGR: Needs element grant receipts per head of population.

PROPO: Number of owner-occupied households as a proportion of the total number of households.

Y: Average household income in the authority. For method of calculation see Appendix 2.5.A1.

5 Grant Elasticity of Expenditure

By the 'grant elasticity of expenditure' we mean the responsiveness of local government spending to changes in grants received from central government. In Part Two, Chapter 3 we argued that a matching grant (such as the resources element of RSG) will tend to encourage higher expenditure than a block grant. The proposed unitary grant is also motivated in part by fears of excessive spending in authorities where the matching grant proportion is high. Our concern over the workings of the regression method for the needs grant is in part attributable to the belief that grant may influence spending. Clearly, a central element in the assessment of any system of grant or proposed reform must be the influence of that grant system on local government spending.

From the viewpoint of macroeconomic control, the relationship between grant and expenditure is of central importance. We discuss the principles involved in Part Two, Chapter 8; suffice to say here that central government policy makers are extremely concerned as to whether a cut in grant will lead to lower spending or to higher rates.

There is a more general argument about the relationship of grants and expenditure, which is emphasised in the Layfield Report. To Layfield, responsible government meant that 'whoever is responsible for deciding to spend more or less money on providing a service is also responsible for deciding whether to raise more or less taxation' (Layfield, 1976, ch. 4; see also Jones, 1977). But in local government there was no clear and direct relationship between spending and taxation because of the high proportion of local government spending financed by grant.

The Layfield argument is clear enough in relation to matching grants. If an authority embarking on an additional £100 of expenditure need only raise an additional £30 from the rates, the remainder being provided by a matching grant such as the resources element, it will not have to balance the benefits of its higher spending against the £100 it actually costs, but only against the £30 it has to raise from its ratepayers. This conflicts with Layfield's definition of responsibility for government decisions on public expenditure. In this context, political accountability and economic efficiency are very similar: both require that the authority balance the benefits of its additional spending against the cost incurred.

Layfield's argument is much less obvious, however, in relation to unhypothecated block grants such as the needs element of RSG. Because the grant is unhypothecated, local authorities can spend it as they wish. And additional expenditure has to be met, in full, from the rates, so that spending decisions are taken in full awareness of the costs involved. Of course, in practice, local authorities cannot spend the grant as they wish because central government constrains their freedom by various legislative, administrative and other instruments. But then it would be claimed that it is these other forms of control, rather than the grant, which limit their freedom. To Layfield, however, the high level of grant necessitates these administrative controls. Central government is bound to attempt to ensure that the money it provides will be spent in accordance with national policies and priorities. It is inconceivable that central government would pay out money of the order of magnitude of RSG — currently over £6,000 million — and then take no interest in how that money is spent.

To meet the objection that a block grant does not impose any constraints on local ability to spend that grant as it pleases, the Committee argued normatively that the situation did not meet its test of accountability: 'There is no means by which taxpayers and electors can hold local authorities collectively accountable for their expenditure. The contributions made to local government through national taxation . . . are not generally perceptible to the taxpayer . . .' (pp. 264—5). Against this, central government argues that accountability is achieved since the cost of marginal expenditure falls on local authorities: 'Parliament can then rely on local authorities' accountability to their own electorate to ensure proper stewardship of the total expenditure' (p. 265). In return the Committee will only argue that the government's arguments were unsound: 'Because Parliament can rely on the accountability of local authorities only if the grant is not a preponderant, and especially, not a growing part of their revenue. Where the grant is a preponderant and growing part of local revenue the government must accept increasing responsibility and ensure that it is spent in accordance with national policies and priorities' (p. 265).

The force of 'must' in the last sentence is not clear, and the weakness of the Layfield Committee's analysis at this point has caused widespread dissent from its conclusions. On it, the Committee rested its pivotal conclusion that local government must go in either one of two directions. Either the grant proportion is increased and it must become increasingly the agent of central government, subject to its accountability procedures; or the grant proportion is reduced and central government could then rely on local instruments of accountability. From this followed the two Layfield polar solutions, the centralist and the localist (using labels the Committee did not create but which were quickly attached to them by one of its members, Professor Day).

In this form, the Layfield argument on the significance of grant is unsatisfactory, as was pointed out by Professor Day in a note of reservation. The point was also argued in the powerful critique of the Report by Francis Cripps and Wynne Godley (1976). They accused the Committee of describing what in its judgement ought to be as what is. Since RSG is an unhypothecated block grant 'local authorities cannot, in the very nature of things, be called to account by central government for the way the grant is appropriated unlike a department where expenditure is voted under subheads by Parliament' (p. 7). Tempered by various non-financial central government influences, local authorities, therefore, had spending freedom, and the influences varied greatly with the service. Their description of how annual RSG negotiations were conducted reached the

conclusion that what emerged did not have the legal status of a central government budget estimate; but was a forecast of what local authorities would spend
by which they were not bound. That was the position until for the first time in
Circular 84 in 1976 (DoE, 1976*a*), the Secretary of State declared unilaterally
that he would regard the total of their estimates as a ceiling which, if exceeded
by local authorities, could result in a curtailment of RSG in subsequent years
below what it might otherwise have been. Cripps and Godley recognised this
innovation as a major invasion of local freedom. We would not disagree with
that description of the legal position.

Cripps and Godley then criticise the Committee's analysis, quoting 'The first
requirement of a financial system for local government is accountability: whoever is responsible for incurring expenditure should also be responsible for
raising the necessary revenue' (1976, p. 10). Cripps and Godley say this is simply
untrue, but it is surely unfair to criticise a normative statement for not being
descriptive. It was a major Layfield contention that responsibilities were confused and needed clarifying. But Cripps and Godley themselves put forward a
questionable statement of fact: 'Even if local government were entirely dependent for its income on central government money, provided the grant is not
hypothecated, the electorate is in a position to call its elected members to account and replace them with others if they would rather have the money spent
in some other way' (ibid., p. 11). While theoretically true, it is to miss the Committee's point. Cripps and Godley are arguing legalistically. To them accountability means the statutory need to present estimates to Parliament. Since
expenditure from block grant does not need to be presented to Parliament, *ergo*
there is no accountability to Parliament. The local electors can vote their councils
out. Legally the accountability is to them. But the Committee was protesting
against central government using the whole range of ways of influencing local
authorities − to be discussed further in Part Two, Chapter 7 − to get local
authorities to spend money as it wanted, whatever the formal arrangements of
accountability. Cripps and Godley could have answered that this made no
difference since, whatever the influences playing on local authorities, they could
still be turned out by local electors for policies for which they were legally
accountable though not really responsible. Even this would not have been a good
argument in its own terms because, as we have seen, the evidence suggests that
local elections were decided by national issues so that in present circumstances
local accountability is theoretical. Instead, Cripps and Godley relied on the
unsupported and irrelevant assertion that 'there is nothing seriously wrong with
the present system as far as the question at issue is the autonomy and accountability of the individual authority. Indeed it seems to work well and provide a
substantial degree of local autonomy while guaranteeing some degree of uniformity in the standards with which certain key services are provided' (ibid.,
p. 13). In other words, they believed it did not matter that real accountability
or responsibility was divorced from formal accountability. On the contrary, the
Committee argued that it did.

Surprisingly, what is missing from Cripps' and Godley's discussions and which
might have been expected from them as economists is any mention of incentives.
Both the Committee and Cripps and Godley argued politically or legalistically

rather than behaviourally. Plainly an unhypothecated grant *could* leave local authorities almost complete discretion. Local elections *could* be decided on local issues. It *could* be the case that the cost at the margin of additional expenditure fell 100 per cent on the local authority, yet that appearance also might not be the reality if, as until recently, every year the block grant increased so that a local authority could expect that if it spent more it would get more in grant next year, if not this. What would have made the Committee's position much stronger would have been a demonstration that, other things being equal, a higher proportion of grant encouraged the local authority to spend more, a lower proportion to spend less. Similarly, what would have strengthened Cripps' and Godley's case would have been a demonstration that the proportion of its revenue derived from block grant had no effect upon a local authority's propensity to spend. Accountability here is defined very much as the Committee saw it. They hypothesise that an increased grant proportion would reduce a local authority's incentive to control its expenditure, thus necessitating more central government interference to replace that loss of local discipline. There are two main aspects of this proposition. The first is that central government interference will increase and local discretion will diminish. We have attempted to test this proposition and report on our results in Part Two, Chapter 7. In this chapter we are concerned with the relationship between the amount and form of grant received by individual local authorities and their total expenditure.

It might be thought that further analysis of this question is unnecessary since a number of the studies discussed in the previous chapter have investigated the impact of economic and financial factors on expenditure. The results of these studies suggest that economic considerations are relatively unimportant. But the economic variables considered in these studies often seem inappropriate. The most commonly used is rateable value per head of population. The use of this variable seems to confuse two concepts: personal income of people living within a local authority area, and financial resources available to a local authority. Personal incomes are not well approximated by rateable value per head in an authority, or even by domestic rateable value per head, given the differences in valuations between areas. Nor, given the existence of the resources element of RSG, does rateable value per head affect the financial resources of an authority. The finding that expenditure has little relationship with rateable value per head therefore can tell us nothing about the impact of economic or financial factors, for these are not themselves related to rateable value per head.

In this chapter, therefore, our procedure is as follows. First, we construct an 'economic' model of local government in order to define more precisely the economic variables relevant to its spending decisions. Thus we can separate the influences of personal incomes, different types of rateable value and the different elements of grant. We then describe the data and estimation procedure used and present the main results.

AN ECONOMIC MODEL OF LOCAL GOVERNMENT SPENDING

Local government is democratic so that in principle its decisions reflect the preferences of the community it represents. Ideally, this democratic principle would be achieved through the electoral process, but, as we have discussed in Part One, local elections in Britain have been dominated by national parties and issues, though very recently inflation and high rate increases have at last had a demonstrable effect on local elections, and the tendency if maintained could transform the situation. Even so, local politicians are responsive to local public opinion.

We do not explore these political issues further in this chapter. We shall simply assume that local government expenditure decisions do reflect the preferences of the local community. We shall further identify the local community with some average or representative voter whose preferences and financial resources are taken as characteristics of the community as a whole.[1]

The last idea is that, in deciding on some additional spending, the local authority will balance the benefits of that spending against the additional tax burden that would fall on such an average, or representative, citizen. The better off the average citizen, the more easily he can afford to pay higher rates, so one might expect local government spending to be higher, other things being equal, where personal incomes are high. We have already documented (Part One, Chapter 4) how closely the growth of local government spending has been associated with the growth of income over time. A second important economic influence would be the 'price', in terms of higher rates, of local government services. A local authority would be more likely, other things being equal, to incur additional spending of, say £10 per head of population if it needed to increase rates by an average of say, £3 per head than if it needed to increase them by £8 per head. It is worth examining this relationship between additional expenditure and tax burdens in more detail, because it is where the influence of grants should be most important.

THE BUDGET CONSTRAINT OF THE AVERAGE CITIZEN

Let us first consider a system in which local government receives no grants. We may denote the disposable income (i.e. money income less central government direct taxes) of the average citizen as Y. We assume the average cost of private goods and services is p_x and the average cost of local government services is p_g per unit of service. Given his income, and these prices, the average citizen may decide how much to spend on private goods and services (say he buys a quantity x) and how much of local government services he wants provided (say an amount g). Clearly, he cannot spend more than his income, so the amounts x and g must satisfy the budget constraint:

$$p_x x + p_g g = Y \tag{1}$$

If his income, Y, is cut, he must spend less on x or on g, or, more likely, less on both. If p_g goes up, so that local government services become more expensive, he will demand fewer units of g (though total expenditure on g may in fact rise since the price per unit has gone up).

He does not, of course, purchase units of g directly. Rather they are provided by local government and financed through rates. If the rateable value of his house is V_i, the rate poundage, r, will have to be sufficient to finance the local government spending, that is

$$rV_i = p_g g \tag{2}$$

The picture is complicated, however, by the payment of central government grants to local authorities. In this chapter we consider only the RSG. Local authority income takes two major forms. First, there is the lump-sum grant provided by the needs element of RSG. Assume, for some authority, this amounts to £N per head of population. Then there is income related to the rate poundage it levies. If its effective rateable value per head is V, and the rate poundage is r, then this income amounts to rV. V will include domestic and non-domestic rateable value, and the resources element of RSG. For authorities in receipt of resources element — the great majority — V will therefore be equal to the standard rateable value per head. The local authority budget constraint can then be written:

$$N + rV = p_g g \tag{3}$$

The budget constraint of the average citizen will also be affected by the domestic element of RSG. If the rate-poundage deduction for domestic hereditaments is d pence, the average citizen's budget constraint can be written:

$$Y - (r - d)V_i = p_x x \tag{4}$$

The interpretation of these equations is as follows. If the local authority levies a rate poundage equal to d, the average citizen pays no rates and the local authority has an income equal to its needs grant plus the rates collected on non-domestic property and the domestic element of RSG. If it increases its rate poundage above d, the average citizen has to pay rates, and hence reduce his private expenditure, but local government receives more money so local government spending can increase. The rate poundage will be increased until the benefits to the average citizen of higher local government spending begin to be more than offset by the costs of reduced private consumption. But, as can be seen from the equations, every penny increase in the rate poundage reduces private consumption by V_i pence, while allowing local government spending to increase by V pence per head. As perceived by the average citizen, local government expenditure is subsidised by the non-domestic ratepayer, or by the resources element, or both.

We can combine equations (3) and (4), in the form of a budget constraint for the average citizen, incorporating private consumption and local government services. From equation (3), it can be written:

$$r = \frac{1}{V}(p_g g - N) \tag{5}$$

and substituting this into (4), and rearranging, gives:

$$Y + N\frac{V_i}{V} + dV_i = p_g g \frac{V_i}{V} + p_x x \tag{6}$$

Two features of equation (6) should be noted. First, on the left-hand side, the needs and domestic elements of RSG constitute, in this context, an income source equivalent to personal disposable income. In principle, a citizen's readiness to spend on local government services or on private consumption would be independent of the source of income. An increase in needs grant could be used to finance additional private consumption, through allowing a reduction in rates, just as additional private income could finance more local government services through higher rates. The use of the income should be independent of its source. Second, on the right-hand side, the equation confirms that, under the present system, the effective price of local government services to the average citizen is reduced by a factor V_i/V.

In defining the price variable in this way we are assuming local authorities are concerned only with the burden of rates on households and not with the effect on firms, or other non-domestic ratepayers. While non-domestic ratepayers have no votes by virtue of the ownership of non-domestic property, they may, in many cases (e.g. small shopkeepers and other small local businesses) be resident in the locality, and vote in response to the total rate bill they have to pay. Households may also be concerned about the level of non-domestic rates because of the effect on new capital investment in the locality and hence on employment prospects. But perhaps most important, as we mentioned earlier, local government may be as much influenced by pressure groups as by elections, and non-domestic ratepayers may influence spending decisions in this way. According to Layfield:

> local businessmen have a close concern with local authorities' affairs. This concern leads them to bring influence to bear on councils through local chambers of commerce, or directly through local elected representatives, or by seeking election to councils. Public accountability is not only a matter of voting rights. Consultation, representation of sectional interests and public protests all have a part to play. Because commerce and industry have both a concern with the provision of local services, and, through the rates they pay, an interest in the levels of local expenditures, the arrangements may be said to answer to tests of accountability. (1976, ch. 10, para 29)

It is not clear whether Layfield is suggesting that these opportunities to exert pressure put non-domestic ratepayers on a par with domestic ones. Such a suggestion would imply that local authorities might be as reluctant to levy additional rates on non-domestic as on domestic ratepayers. If so, we would have to define the price variable as the total cost in additional rates (both domestic and non-domestic) of an additional £1 of local government spending. For authorities not in receipt of resources element this will take on a value of £1, for others it will be the ratio of the authority's actual rateable value per head to the standard — that is, it would measure the extent of an authority's resources-element entitlement. In our empirical work, we have examined both definitions of the price variable.

LOCAL GOVERNMENT SERVICES AS PUBLIC GOODS

In Part One, Chapter 3 we discussed various aspects of the theory of public goods in relation to local government services. In the present context we are interested in one such characteristic, namely the provision of services at some given standard to all in the community entitled to those services. Even with this rather limited collective characteristic, local government services are not on a par with private consumption as has been hitherto assumed in this chapter. For we can no longer equate average expenditure on some local government service with expenditure to the benefit of the average citizen.

For example, in education the standard of service may depend on the number of teachers and other resources per pupil. If the number of pupils is greater relative to population in one authority than another, the same expenditure per head of population will imply lower educational standards in the first authority with the larger proportion of schoolchildren. The cost of providing some given standard of schooling will be larger, per head of population, in authorities with a high proportion of schoolchildren in the population.

To express this formally, let g' now denote, for example, educational resources (teachers, etc.) per schoolchild, and u the proportion of schoolchildren to population in the authority. We may rewrite equation (6) as:

$$Y + N\frac{V_i}{V} + dV_i = p_x x + p_g g' u \frac{V_i}{V} \qquad (7)$$

The effect on expenditure of an increase in u is, however, uncertain. Clearly if standards are unaffected (i.e. g' unchanged), expenditure will increase by an amount $p_g g'$ for each additional schoolchild. But the fact that the provision of any given standard of education has become relatively more expensive (as it has to be shared across more children) may encourage a reduction in standards, which might reduce expenditure. Furthermore, the supplementary factors in the needs grant are themselves based on factors such as schoolchildren, that is factors which affect the expenditure per head of population required to provide some given standard of services. Then an increase in u could lead to an increase in N sufficient in principle to allow g' to be maintained without increasing rates. In this simple example we could write the needs grant in the form $N = n_0 + n_1 u$, and then, if n_1 were to equal $p_g g'$ for each type of service, the increase in expenditure required to maintain g' with an increase in u would be fully compensated by an increase in needs grant.

The relationship between the budget constraint and the spending on local government services can best be illustrated by means of diagrams. In Figure 2.5.1, the amount of services provided by local government (g) is measured along the horizontal axis. The amount of private income, after taxes and rates, left to the representative citizen is measured on the vertical axis in terms of the quantity of private goods and services he can purchase (x). The line AB represents the budget constraint: it slopes downwards because the more services local government provides, other things being equal, the higher rates it must charge and the less money people will have for private spending. Assume the local

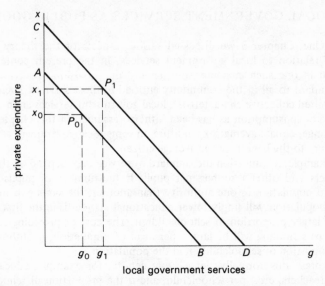

Figure 2.5.1.   *Local government spending: the effect of higher income*

authority decides on a level of spending of g_0, leaving private citizens, after payment of rates, x_0 to spend on private goods and services. On Figure 2.5.1, we may represent this decision by the point P_0 on the budget constraint. The local authority, as it were, chooses a position on the budget line reflecting its citizens' preferences for local government services and private spending.

If now there is an increase in the general level of incomes in the locality, for each level of local government spending, and hence of rates, people can afford more private spending. The budget constraint will shift out, from AB to CD on Figure 2.5.1. The local authority may then increase its expenditure, in so far as people want to see a higher standard of living reflected in the standards of public as well as private goods and services. The new position is P_1, with g_1 measuring the level of local government spending and x_1, private spending.

The impact of change in the other main element in the budget constraint, the needs grant, is less straightforward. If an authority receives a higher grant while its 'needs' remain unchanged, say as a result of changes in the grant formula, then the authority has more money available which can finance either a higher level of services, or, through a reduction in rates, a higher level of private spending. The budget constraint shifts just as with an increase in personal incomes, as shown in Figure 2.5.1. In principle, an increase in needs grant, with unchanged needs, and an increase in personal incomes should have the same impact on local government spending. In practice, people may be reluctant to part with higher incomes but prepared to allow local authorities to spend additional grant receipts – if only because they are unlikely to be aware of a change in grants and the opportunities it offers for reducing rates.

On the other hand, an increase in needs grant may be associated with an increase in 'needs' – for example, where an authority's needs grant entitlements rise

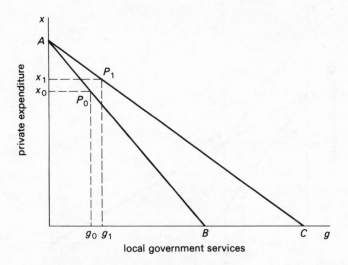

Figure 2.5.2 *Local government spending: the effect of matching grants*

because of an increase in the number of schoolchildren with a given needs-grant formula. We return to this case below.

We consider next the effect of the resources element. In Figure 2.5.2, we start from the same position as in Figure 2.5.1, with the same budget line AB, and the authority at point P_0 with g_0 local government services and x_0 private expenditure. Now consider the effect of an increase in the standard rateable value V. This will increase the local deficiency of rateable value on which the resources element is paid. The higher the rate poundage charged, the higher the resources element grant received. The budget constraint therefore swivels out to AC, to indicate that the higher the level of local government spending the greater the additional grant received. The flatter slope of the line indicates that the prices of local government services have fallen, in that more local government services can be provided at a smaller cost in terms of local taxes, and hence a smaller cost in terms of private spending. The new position will be P_1, with a larger increase in local government spending to take advantage of the 'cheaper price' (Wilde, 1971).

Thirdly, there is the effect of changes in spending 'needs'. The cost to an authority of, say, maintaining its educational standards with an increase in the number of schoolchildren, depends on how high its standards are; with low pupil—teacher ratios, more teachers will be required for a given increase in the number of schoolchildren if standards are to be maintained. An increase in 'needs' will, therefore, swivel the budget constraint inwards, from AB to AC in Figure 2.5.3. Both private spending and local government spending per unit of service are more likely to fall as shown in the figure. But as the number of people for whom the service is provided has risen, local government spending may well rise even though spending per unit of service has fallen.

If the higher spending needs are accompanied by an increase in the authority's

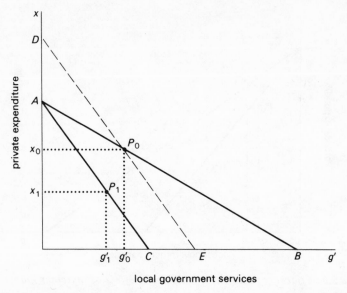

Figure 2.5.3.   *Local government spending: the effect of higher spending 'needs'*

needs grant, the budget constraint will be shifted out as shown in Figure 2.5.3 from AC to DE. if the needs grant payment per unit of need is equal to the amount per unit the local authority was originally spending (i.e. $n_1 = P_g g_0'$) the new budget constraint will go through the original point P_0. The authority will be able to maintain its existing standard of services without increasing rates, or having to reduce private expenditure.

In this case, the higher expenditure is due to a combination of higher needs and higher grant. We would expect each of these factors, taken on its own, to be associated with higher spending. But in practice they go together because the needs grant is based on needs indicators and it may, therefore, be impossible to distinguish their relative importance. Authorities with higher needs might spend more irrespective of their receipts of needs grant, so that it is the differences in needs that are the main determinants of spending differences. Alternatively, they may only provide for their higher needs because they receive additional grant.

As we have shown in the previous chapter, there is no objective way of measuring needs, and the concept is itself an ambiguous one in many respects. The needs grant is itself as good a measure as any of relative spending needs, so in part of our work we have used the needs grant as a variable measuring the combined effect of differences in needs and payments of needs grant. But we also consider the effects of needs variables separately in an attempt to identify the relative impact of needs factors as against grant payments.

PREFERENCES

So far, we have examined how local government spending varies in response to differences in resources and in needs which, as we have shown, alter the budget constraint. But spending variations may also reflect local preferences. Two local authorities faced with the same budget constraint may choose different levels of spending because in one locality people value public spending relatively highly, while in the other they have a preference for private spending.

The most obvious way to measure such preferences is by political allegiance. Traditionally, the Labour Party is the party of public spending. People voting Labour expect to see a high level of provision of public services, and local councils will reflect such preferences.

Preferences are not only reflected in politics, of course. Some areas may, for example, have a proud tradition in, say, education which any political party would respect. There may be all sorts of special local circumstances which influence spending. Important though these purely local factors are, they will have such a varied and unsystematic effect on expenditure that it is impossible to take them into account in a study of this kind.

EMPIRICAL ESTIMATION OF ECONOMIC INFLUENCES ON EXPENDITURE

DATA

For reasons of data availability at the beginning of our research study, the year examined in most detail was 1972/3. There are two advantages of using 1972/3 data. First, much of the relevant data is derived from the 1971 Census and will have become a less accurate measure of social and other conditions several years later. Secondly, in 1972/3 there were still single-tier authorities (county boroughs) responsible for all local government services. Under a two-tier system there are various estimation difficulties for which no completely satisfactory solution exists, for example how the benefits of services provided by the upper-tier authorities are distributed between the various lower-tier authorities. Nevertheless, we also report work on 1976/7, as in the previous chapter.

FIRST ANALYSIS

The data in the first analysis, unless otherwise stated, is drawn from the eighty-three county boroughs in England and Wales for 1972/3.

THE VARIABLES

The dependent variable, expenditure on local government services, is defined as estimated rate and RSG borne expenditure net of debt charges (CIPFA, *Return of Rates 1972/3*).

The first of the independent variables is average personal disposable income in the locality. There is no direct data on personal incomes by local authority area in the UK. We have, therefore, sought to construct a direct measure of personal incomes by local authority area. Our method is set out in detail in Appendix 2.5.A1. Essentially it is based on socio-economic groups. We have the composition of population by socio-economic group for each local authority, including for each county. But there is Inland Revenue data for personal incomes by county of residence. By associating population composition in terms of socio-economic group in each county with the average income level of that county we are able to infer a relationship between socio-economic groups and incomes. We can then use this to construct a measure of average personal incomes for each of the county boroughs.

The 'price' variable is easily computed from the figures for domestic rateable value per head, or total rateable value per head (depending which variant of the price measure is required) from *Rates and Rateable Values*, published by DoE, and from the figure standard rateable value per head derived from the Rate Support Grant Order.

Data on needs grant payments were supplied by the DoE, political variables derived from the *Municipal Year Book*, and other variables from the 1971 Census, except where otherwise indicated.

ESTIMATION PROCEDURE

We estimated three types of equation. The first was of the relationship between expenditure and the budget constraint variables — personal incomes, price and the needs grant — alone. The second set of equations incorporated political preferences. The third set included various needs indicators in an attempt to separate out the effect of needs indicators from the effect of grant payments.

In algebraic notation, the three equations to be estimated can be written:

$$X = a_0 + a_1 Y + a_2 RV + a_3 NEDGR \tag{8}$$

$$X = b_0 + b_1 Y + b_2 RV + b_3 NEDGR + b_4 LAB \tag{9}$$

$$X = c_0 + c_1 Y + c_2 RV + c_3 NEDGR + c_4 LAB + c_5 u \tag{10}$$

where X is local government expenditure per head of population, Y average personal incomes, RV the price variable, $NEDGR$ the needs grant per head, LAB a measure of Labour Party strength on the council, and u various indices of need. We therefore introduce last the type of variable considered in the previous chapter to establish fully how much of the variation can be explained by the economic and political variables.

RESULTS

The results for the first model for total expenditure are given in equations (11) and (12). In equation (11), price is measured as the tax cost to the average domestic ratepayer of each £1 of local government expenditure (DRV). In equation (12), price is measured as the proportion of expenditure financed by rates, including non-domestic as well as domestic ratepayers (TRV).

$$
\begin{array}{ll}
X = 83 - 0.013Y - 0.084DRV + 0.97NEDGR & R^2 = 0.29 \\
\quad\quad (0.006)\quad (0.14)\quad\quad\quad (0.24) & F = 10.43
\end{array}
\tag{11}
$$

$$X = 84 - 0.014Y - 0.034TRV + 1.02NEDGR \qquad R^2 = 0.29$$
$$\quad (0.006) \quad (0.079) \qquad (0.23) \qquad\qquad F = 10.26$$
$$\tag{12}$$

(figures in parentheses are standard errors)

The income variable is significant, but it has the 'wrong' sign — poorer localities in terms of household incomes seem to spend more rather than less on local government services, even after taking account of differences in needs. The price variable has the 'right' sign whichever way it is measured, but it is not statistically significant in either equation. The coefficient on the needs grant is significant and close to one, as might be expected, which is consistent with the theoretical model we have outlined.

We obtained similar results for this model in relation to social services expenditure. In equations (13), (14) and (15) XSS is expenditure per head of population on the social services, $XCHI$ expenditure per head of population on childrens' services and $XOLD$ expenditure per head of population on old people's services:

$$XSS = 1.13 - 0.003Y - 0.95DRV + 0.026NEDGR \qquad R^2 = 0.1$$
$$\quad (0.001) \quad (1.37) \qquad (0.042) \qquad\qquad F = 2.78$$
$$\tag{13}$$

$$XCHI = 0.97 - 0.001Y + 0.45DRV + 0.48NEDGR \qquad R^2 = 0.2$$
$$\quad (0.0004) \quad (0.47) \qquad (0.014) \qquad\qquad F = 0.48$$
$$\tag{14}$$

$$XOLD = 0.35 - 0.003Y - 0.22DRV - 0.025NEDGR \qquad R^2 = 0.15$$
$$\quad (0.004) \quad (0.46) \qquad (0.014) \qquad\qquad F = 1.20$$
$$\tag{15}$$

The explanatory power of the equations is consistently low, and the variables are typically insignificant.

We obtain a similar result for educational expenditure. In equation (16) XED denotes educational expenditure per schoolchild:

$$XED = 81.21 + 0.0028Y + 0.13TRV + 0.56NEDGR \qquad R^2 = 0.09$$
$$\quad (0.0054) \quad (0.07) \qquad (0.23)$$
$$\tag{16}$$

Interestingly, however, we find a very different result for education expenditure per schoolchild in the county councils, which is denoted by XED_{cc} in equation (17)

$$XED_{cc} = 75.86 + 0.032Y - 0.21TRV + 1.06NEDGR \qquad R^2 = 0.59$$
$$\quad (0.011) \quad (0.11) \qquad (0.18)$$
$$\tag{17}$$

In this equation both personal income and price have the sign predicted, and both are significant. We discuss possible reasons for the different results for the county councils and the county boroughs further in Part Two, Chapter 7.

Despite this result for the county councils, the attempt to account for differences in spending by local authorities solely by reference to the budget constraint is clearly unsatisfactory. The next step is to incorporate political preferences.

THE IMPACT OF POLITICS

The simplest way of introducing a political factor into the analysis is by means of a 'dummy' variable assigned a value of one for a Labour council and of zero otherwise. The coefficient on this variable will measure the extent to which Labour councils behave differently in their expenditure from non-Labour councils. But this approach is rather crude, and exploratory empirical work revealed that the variable was not significantly correlated with spending differences.

We have instead used, as an indicator of political preferences, the proportion of Labour members on the council. Where there is only a small majority, the political impact on expenditure may be moderated (a) by the greater effectiveness of opposition councillors, (b) by the greater electoral vulnerability of the ruling party and its consequent need to appeal to the 'floating' voter and (c) because, where majorities are small, the opposition is likely to have held power in the recent past, and spending may be as much influenced by past political decisions as by current ones.

In equation (18) we therefore introduce a political variable, LAB, the proportion of the councillors belonging to the Labour Party.

$$X = 83 - 0.006Y - 0.07TRV + 0.58NEDGR + 0.25LAB \qquad R^2 = 0.42$$
$$\quad (0.006) \quad (0.007) \quad (0.24) \qquad (0.05) \qquad\qquad F = 10.6$$
$$(18)$$

The political variable is not only highly significant in itself but adds considerably to the explanatory power of the equation as a whole. Income retains its negative sign but is no longer significant, which could be interpreted as suggesting that the negative relationship between income and expenditure in equation (12) might be spurious. A more plausible relationship would probably be that Labour councils tend to spend more, and where household incomes are low there is more likely to be a Labour council.

SPENDING AND INDICATORS OF NEED

Finally, we have considered a number of indicators of need:

DEC is the rate of decline of population. It is well known that local government expenditure per head tends to be higher in areas of declining population. The relationship is normally explained on the grounds either that it is the enterprising and self-supporting who move out of declining areas leaving behind a population consisting disproportionately of the old or other needy groups. But it is also sometimes suggested that local authorities may be slow to scale down their services in face of a declining demand for them when population falls.

POP is total population size. This may give evidence of economies or diseconomies of scale, or of the relationship between the size of the authority and the extent of service provision, or it may, as noted in the previous chapter, be correlated with various other social conditions affecting the demand for local government services.

OAL is the proportion of old people living alone, EDS is the proportion of schoolchildren in the population, and $CH4$ is the proportion of children under the age of 4.

The results using these variables in addition to the economic and political variables are set out in Table 2.5.1. Equation (19) is comparable to equation

Table 2.5.1. *Estimated effects of need, political and financial factors on local spending*

Equation Number		Y	TRV	NEDGR	LAB	Variable Constant DEC	POP	OAL	EDS	CH4	R^2
19	120	−0.002	−0.19	−	−	1.14	0.08	−2.08	−0.38	0.47	0.44
		(0.006)	(0.07)	−	−	(0.23)	(0.06)	(1.07)	(0.62)	(0.83)	
20	115	−0.007	−0.18	1.16	−	0.82	0.08	−1.90	−0.28	−2.09	0.49
		(0.006)	(0.08)	(0.42)	−	(0.24)	(0.06)	(1.00)	(0.80)	(0.87)	
21	95.7	0.004	−0.12	−	0.27	1.00	−0.105	−0.99	−0.44	0.39	0.53
		(0.006)	(0.07)	−	(0.08)	(0.21)	(0.100)	(1.11)	(0.58)	(0.79)	
22	91.3	−	−0.095	0.94	0.13	0.88	0.07	−0.96	−1.76	−	0.58
		−	(0.071)	(0.37)	(0.04)	(0.19)	(0.05)	(0.96)	(0.74)	−	−

(12), but using needs variables instead of payments of needs grant as a measure of need. The effect of income is now much less significant, but the effect of price becomes significant and of the 'right' sign. Of the needs variables only decline in population is clearly significant. None the less, the variables in the equation can account for 44 per cent of the variation in expenditure as against only 29 per cent for equation (12).

In equation (20), payments of needs grant are introduced in addition to the various needs variables. The needs grant is still significantly associated with expenditure and the overall explanatory power of the equation is improved. The coefficients on the needs variables are not much changed, suggesting there may be an independent financial effect on expenditure for needs grant payments.

Equations (21) and (22) include the political variable *LAB*. Again the explanatory power of the equations is improved, and the political variable itself is clearly significant. The income variable disappears and the price variable is barely significant, though it has a negative sign throughout. Declining population remains the most important of the needs variables.

SECOND ANALYSIS

The expenditure figures in the second analysis are the local authority estimates of rate and RSG expenditure per head in 1975/6. In the case of the shire counties, the expenditure per head estimates are applicable to county services only, but for metropolitan districts the estimates reflect county and district expenditure.[2] The definitions and sources of the data are generally similar to those for the variables in the first analysis, except that the percentage of those living on low incomes was derived from the Inland Revenue quinquennial survey of personal incomes (1969/70) modified by the Department of Health and Social Security earnings survey (1969/70) in the case of metropolitan districts. (Results, methods and data are described in more detail elsewhere, see Jackman and Sellars, 1978.)

Better and more significant results were obtained in this study of local expenditure after local government reorganisation than in that conducted for 1972/3. In the second analysis equations were first fitted using needs variables alone — already reported at the end of the last chapter. With such factors alone 61 per cent of variation in the shire counties' expenditure and 70 per cent of the variation in the metropolitan districts' expenditure could be explained. Including the proportion of households with low incomes as an explanatory variable increased the level of explanation slightly. The best equations, however, included low incomes, household rate bills, the Welsh differential domestic element, and the political variable (i.e. the proportion of Labour councillors).

Shire Counties

$$X = £84.66 + 5.84 SPR + 207.47 EDU + 361.64 MOC + 1,010.14 NH$$
$$(9.43) \qquad (7.01) \qquad (3.54) \qquad (4.33)$$

$$- 52.34 Y_L - 0.0085 DRV + 0.16 LAB \qquad\qquad R^2 = 0.644$$
$$(2.08) \qquad (0.41) \qquad (3.48)$$

Metropolitan Districts

$$X = 127.10 + 177.15EDU + 45.02HIGHD + 373.72MOC + 1,824.79LF$$
$$\quad\;\; (0.299) \qquad (5.79) \qquad\qquad (5.00) \qquad\qquad (3.44)$$

$$-92.06Y_L - 0.14DRV + 0.20LAB \qquad\qquad\qquad R^2 = 0.789$$
$$\;\;(1.53) \quad\;\; (4.02) \qquad\; (2.84)$$

Shire Counties allowing for differential domestic element

$$X = £96.91 + 4.67SPR + 166.23EDU + 667.77MOC + 1,400.82NH$$
$$\qquad\;\; (8.05) \qquad\;\; (6.05) \qquad\quad (6.53) \qquad\qquad (6.45)$$

$$-37.16HBA - 58.08Y_L - 0.016DRV + 0.11LAB + 13.82DDE$$
$$\;\;(1.98) \qquad\;\; (2.55) \qquad (0.69) \qquad\;\; (2.34) \qquad\;\; (8.07)$$

$$R^2 = 0.709$$

Y_L is the proportion of low-income households, DDE a dummy variable reflecting the higher domestic element in Wales. The other variables are as defined in Appendix 2.4.A1. The figures in brackets are t-statistics.

These equations are a considerable improvement upon those including only needs factors. The explanation in the variation in shire county expenditure has risen to 65 per cent and for metropolitan district expenditure to 79 per cent. The second shire county equation explains 71 per cent of variation. In the first shire county equation all variables are significant except DRV. In the metropolitan districts equation all are significant except low incomes. In the second shire county equation all are significant again except domestic rateable value. These are very satisfactory equations. The needs variables are not very different from those in the needs equation alone.

Not only are the results of the second analysis more significant but they are also more interesting than those of the first. An increase of 1 per cent of the proportion of low-income households in the shire counties would be associated with a reduction in expenditure of about 52p or 58p per head of population, which is consistent with what our economic theory on the influence of low incomes would suggest. The comparable figure in the metropolitan districts is 92p but is not significant. A possible reason for this is that the income data for the metropolitan districts is much less good, though we cannot be sure that this is the reason.

Though total rateable value was tested and found significant in the metropolitan districts, though not in the shire counties, the form of the price variable that performed better was domestic rateable value per household, suggesting, as theory would indicate, that local authorities take into account, consciously or unconsciously, the burden on the domestic ratepayer and are less influenced by the burden on the non-domestic ratepayer or on the Exchequer through resources grant. In the metropolitan districts the influence was highly significant. It is not in the shire counties, but a plausible explanation for this is that, while the main influence of variations in domestic rateable value per head in the metropolitan districts is the proportion of non-domestic rateable value, that proportion varies much less in the counties where the cause of variation in domestic rateable values per head is closely related to the quality of dwelling as reflected in the presence or absence of basic amenities, a needs factor. That the price variable is really as much at work in the shire counties as in the metropolitan districts is suggested by the impact, when isolated, of the extra domestic element received by the Welsh counties (*DDE*) where the domestic element is worth 36p as against 18.5p in England, and is associated with an extra £14 expenditure per head of population.

Finally, politics is as significant a variable as it had been in 1972/3. A council with 75 per cent Labour councillors would, on the basis of these estimates, be typically spending in the order of £7 to £10 per head more than a council with only 25 per cent Labour councillors.

CONCLUSIONS

On income, the evidence of the first analysis suggested that there was no significant relationship between the level of personal incomes and local government spending. We have not had available equivalent information for 1975/6 so we have no way of testing whether this still holds. But in 1972/3 the results seemed to conflict with that of the DoE who found that spending was lower, other things being equal, in a county with a relatively high proportion of low-income households. In 1975/6 we also have found this significant.

There were signs of the working of the price variable in both analyses, more especially in the second. In the metropolitan districts both total rateable value as a proxy for resources element and household rate bills were negative and highly significant, particularly the second. The implication is that while local authorities (at least metropolitan districts) are concerned with the impact of their expenditure on household rate bills, they are less concerned as to whether the rest is derived from commerce, industry or from central government grant. This is evidence that the higher the proportion of grant, the greater the propensity for a local authority to spend. On the basis of the estimates of the metropolitan districts a cut of 10 per cent in the national standard rateable value per head for resource element purposes would lead to a reduction in spending of around 2 per cent. In the shire counties neither were significantly related to expenditure. We conjecture that the reason for this was because lower rateable values are highly correlated with a needs factor — housing lacking basic amenities — whereas in the metropolitan districts it was variation in the proportion of non-domestic rateable value that had the main causal effect. However, we deduced that the price variable was likely to be powerful even if masked by this needs variable on the grounds that a particular price variable, the Welsh domestic element differential, did seem to have a powerful and significant effect on the expenditure. If this could be seen to be working, then it was rational to suppose that the other price variable would also be having its effect. Of course one cannot prove this, but it leads us to believe that the price variable works as economic theory would indicate.

There is a clear relationship between Labour Party control and spending which is consistent between shire counties and the metropolitan districts. An increase of 10 per cent in the proportion of Labour councillors will typically be associated with additional expenditure of £1.50 to £2 per head, an increase of about 1 per cent.

Quite apart from our analysis leading us to conclude that the grant elasticity of expenditure is positive, we also draw the conclusion that both needs and discretionary factors influence expenditure.

NOTES

1 There are a number of empirical studies of local government expenditure in the USA based on these assumptions. For good examples see Barr and Davis (1966); Bergstrom and Goodman (1973); Borcheding and Deacon (1972); Gramlich and Galper (1973).
2 The single-tier county boroughs were abolished in the reorganisation of 1974, so more recent analysis is necessarily based on the major-spending authorities in the two-tier system, i.e. shire counties and metropolitan districts.

Appendix 2.5.A1   Methods of Estimating Local Incomes

THE METHOD

The *Survey of Personal Incomes*, published by the Inland Revenue, contains a breakdown of income by county which allows an estimate of the mean income of tax units within a county to be calculated. Unfortunately there is no such breakdown for county boroughs. However, we do have two sources of income statistics for these authorities.

The first is the DHSS survey of manual earnings of men and women, *Regional Statistics of Earnings*. (The sub-regional tables from which data for the larger county boroughs was taken are unpublished.) The survey covers fifty-one out of the eighty-three county boroughs, so if this measure were adopted, we would be able to analyse influences on spending in only fifty-one rather than all eighty-three county boroughs. Nor would the fifty-one for which the data is available be a random sample for the eighty-three, but would include those authorities selected by the DHSS for its survey — mainly the larger and more urbanised authorities. It would therefore be misleading to make inferences from the sample of fifty-one about the behaviour of all county boroughs. Furthermore, we want a measure of average household incomes which is by no means the same as the earnings of manual workers.

The second source is based on car ownership, and has been developed by the Ministry of Transport. Their estimate is derived as follows: from *National Transport Survey* data published by DoE, a relationship between car ownership, an individual's weekly income, and the density of population in the area where he lives is calculated. (Data on car ownership and on the population density of local authorities can be obtained from the Census.) Using the estimated parameters and the Census information on car ownership and population density, an estimate of average income can be made for each authority.

The method we have adopted (for a full account, see Osborne, 1975) is based on the hypothesis that variations in mean community income can be explained by variations in the proportion of people in different socio-economic groups. If this hypothesis is found to be valid then we can calculate an equation whose parameters allow us to estimate how income changes with the socio-economic composition of different communities. As we have information on the socio-economic group composition of the population for each county borough we would then be able to estimate the mean income of tax units in each borough.

The credibility of the method rests on the assumption that income groups can be identified with socio-economic groups. More precisely, we require that the variance in income between socio-economic groups is greater than the variance of the incomes of individuals within a group. Intuitively, this assumption states that if we know the mean income of a particular socio-economic group to which an individual belongs we have a much greater chance of guessing his true income correctly, than if we have no information on his socio-economic group. The reason for basing the method on socio-economic groups is our belief that these do tell us more about a person's income than, say, his age, colour or rateable value.

To use the parameters obtained from the sample of counties to predict income in the county boroughs it must, in addition, be assumed that both samples are drawn from the same population.

THE RESULTS

The income data for the counties is derived from Inland Revenue statistics. The *Survey of Personal Incomes* is based on a 1 per cent sample of all tax returns. The income measure is income liable to tax, that is net of permissible deductions (such as mortgage interest relief) but before deduction of personal allowances. It is published in the form of an income distribution by county (place of residence of tax unit). From the distribution, a figure for the mean income of tax units in each county can be calculated.

The next step is to try and account for differences in the mean incomes of the counties by reference to proportions of their populations in different socio-economic groups. The method adopted was multiple regression analysis, and the results are presented in Table 2.5.A1. The Inland Revenue survey provides information on total income (Y_T), earned income (Y_E) and investment income (Y_I). The results for these three income measures are presented separately.

These results suggest that it is possible to account for over 80 per cent of the variation between counties in total mean income by reference to the

Table 2.5.A1. *Income and socio-economic group*

	Y_T	Y_E	Y_I
Constant	1,093.15	1,845.32	−1,888.94
	(519.50)	(704.36)	(3,668.60)
S1	+52.93	+52.39	+8.14
	(22.97)	(31.09)	(47.30)
S2	−1.84	+15.51	70.41
	(14.46)	(16.99)	(35.92)
S3	+73.41	−64.29	−8.33
	(49.95)	(64.38)	(64.00)
S4	+20.66	+12.00	−11.81
	(15.05)	(23.74)	(43.46)
S5	+26.75	+18.25	+75.52
	(19.00)	(22.73)	(51.97)
S6	−3.87	−16.61	+1.42
	(9.61)	(14.51)	(37.19)
S7	−12.73	−54.29	+72.50
	(26.58)	(30.70)	(52.77)
S8	+4.73	+16.85	−
	(28.34)	(39.06)	−
S9	−0.52	−13.81	+19.63
	(8.45)	(8.59)	(39.05)
S10	+13.47	−	+25.61
	(8.89)	−	(40.27)
S11	−9.58	−3.01	−
	(8.95)	(11.30)	−
S12	−	−26.19	−3.57
	−	(22.77)	(37.23)
S13	−5.45	−56.90	+64.14
	(18.29)	(32.86)	(47.30)
S14	−	+22.69	−1.85
	−	(10.35)	(39.94)
S15	+9.65	−	+4.45
	(7.44)	−	(37.51)
S16	−	+0.26	+32.74
	−	(11.97)	(35.83)
S17	−10.09	−21.11	+15.83
	(8.70)	(16.69)	(34.59)
$\bar{R}^2$	80.7%	72.8%	70.1%

Note: Figures in parentheses are standard errors.

socio-economic group composition of the population. Over 70 per cent of variation in both earnings and investment income separately can be accounted for in the same way.

The next step is to calculate the mean incomes of the county boroughs on the assumption that it bears the same relation to socio-economic group as that established for the counties and set out in Table 2.5.A1. The resulting income estimates are set out in Table 2.5.A2.

Finally, it is interesting to compare the resulting income estimates with the DHSS survey data for the county boroughs for which it is available, and also with the income estimates based on car ownership. In Table 2.5.A3 the first column, headed DHSS, records the income measured in the DHSS *Survey of Manual Earnings* of both men and women. The income of manual men derived from the same survey is set out in the third column, headed *MALEE*. The results of the present study are in the second column, headed Est. Net. Inc., and of the car ownership study in the fourth column, headed DoE Est. For most authorities the method we have adopted seems to give results closer to the DHSS figure for the earnings of manual men than the car-ownership study. The Spearman rank coefficient as against the DHSS survey was 0.64 for the estimates in this study as against 0.56 for the car-ownership study estimates. It should be stressed, however, that the DHSS figure is of male manual earnings, and not of average household incomes, so it should not be regarded as a 'true' standard of comparison.

Table 2.5.A2. *Income estimates obtained using regression coefficients calculated at County level and applied to County Boroughs*

£		£	
1,709	Luton	1,531	Leicester
1,625	Reading	1,505	Lincoln
1,565	Birkenhead	1,533	Grimsby
1,659	Chester	1,378	Great Yarmouth
1,560	Stockport	1,502	Norwich
1,697	Wallasey	1,587	Northampton
1,598	Carlisle	1,450	Newcastle-upon-Tyne
1,671	Derby	1,682	Tynemouth
1,706	Exeter	1,450	Nottingham
1,480	Plymouth	1,752	Oxford
1,551	Torbay	1,683	Bath
1,619	Darlington	1,428	Burton-on-Trent
1,424	Gateshead	1,585	Dudley
1,388	Hartlepool	1,376	Stoke-on-Trent
1 522	South Shields	1,532	Walsall
1,463	Sunderland	1,460	West Bromwich
1,636	Southend-on-Sea	1,609	Wolverhampton
1,584	Bristol	1,504	Ipswich
1,654	Gloucester	1,508	Brighton
1,491	Bournemouth	1,493	Eastbourne
1,484	Portsmouth	1,509	Hastings
1,574	Southampton	1,548	Birmingham
1,657	Canterbury	1,639	Coventry
1,535	Barrow-in-Furness	2,180	Solihull
1,417	Blackburn	1,422	Warley
1,402	Blackpool	1,601	Worcester
1,520	Bolton	1,384	Kingston-upon-Hull
1,251	Bootle	1,561	Teesside
1,413	Burnley	1,307	Barnsley
1,599	Bury	1,515	Bradford
1,424	Liverpool	1,525	Dewsbury
1,400	Manchester	1,579	Doncaster
1,459	Oldham	1,533	Halifax
1,268	Preston	1,696	Huddersfield
1,502	Rochdale	1,514	Leeds
1,303	St Helens	1,442	Rotherham
1,333	Salford	1,558	Sheffield
1,760	Southport	1,744	Wakefield
1,331	Warrington	1,545	York
1,414	Wigan	1,595	Cardiff
		1,548	Merthyr Tydfil
		1,613	Swansea
		1,520	Newport

Table 2.5.A3.   *A comparison of alternative income estimates (£)*

	DHSS	Est. Net. Inc.	MALEE	DoE Est.
Newcastle	1,081	1,450	1,434	1,259
Gateshead	1,095	1,424	1,473	1,215
South Shields	981	1,522	1,318	1,194
Sunderland	1,006	1,493	1,367	1,295
Bradford	971	1,515	1,283	1,299
Leeds	1,029	1,514	1,413	1,336
Kingston-on-Hull	1,082	1,384	1,438	1,339
Sheffield	1,106	1,558	1,484	1,435
York	1,091	1,545	1,555	1,446
Huddersfield	1,067	1,696	1,449	1,375
Leicester	1,105	1,531	1,500	1,516
Nottingham	1,034	1,450	1,404	1,459
Northampton	1,152	1,587	1,628	1,779
Derby	1,093	1,671	1,481	1,857
Norwich	1,032	1,502	1,360	1,696
Ipswich	1,039	1,504	1,459	1,798
Southend-on-Sea	1,077	1,636	1,472	1,750
Portsmouth	1,047	1,484	1,428	1,596
Southampton	1,141	1,574	1,594	1,798
Luton	1,240	1,709	1,703	1,958
Reading	1,231	1,625	1,704	1,756
Oxford	1,174	1,752	1,627	1,756
Bournemouth	1,080	1,491	1,359	1,837
Brighton	1,058	1,508	1,396	1,446
Plymouth	1,078	1,480	1,467	1,857
Bristol	1,111	1,584	1,558	1,857
Cardiff	1,147	1,595	1,566	1,777
Swansea	1,099	1,613	1,456	1,717
Newport	1,126	1,520	1,476	1,756
Stoke-on-Trent	1,031	1,376	1,386	1,499
Birmingham	1,129	1,548	1,598	1,616
Coventry	1,267	1,639	1,736	1,897
Walsall	1,054	1,532	1,503	1,659
Wolverhampton	1,239	1,609	1,639	1,739
Solihull	1,390	2,180	2,080	2,988
West Bromwich	1,017	1,460	1,476	1,579
Dudley	1,059	1,585	1,466	1,939
Manchester	1,047	1,400	1,415	1,295
Liverpool	1,061	1,424	1,477	1,339
Birkenhead	1,184	1,565	1,580	1,557
Stockport	1,132	1,560	1,541	1,610
Wallasey	1,135	1,697	1,662	1,629
Blackburn	1,053	1,417	1,411	1,366
Blackpool	1,020	1,402	1,313	1,516
Bolton	1,037	1,520	1,428	1,354
St Helens	1,158	1,303	1,460	1,375
Oldham	1,062	1,459	1,458	1,238
Preston	1,075	1,268	1,474	1,259
Salford	1,106	1,333	1,458	1,179

6 The Incidence of Rates

It is often asserted that rates are a particularly unjust and inequitable form of taxation (e.g. Layfield, 1976, ch. 1). In Part One, two principles of the rating system were discussed — the benefit principle according to which rate payments would bear some relation to the benefits the ratepayer received from local government services, and the ability-to-pay principle according to which rate payments would be related to the ratepayers' ability to pay. Dissatisfaction with the present system arises from the belief that rate payments seem quite arbitrary and unrelated either to benefits received or ability to pay.

In this chapter we attempt to explain the main factors determining the rates levied on households or firms, and account for the variations in rate payments between ratepayers. The rate bill facing an individual ratepayer is made up of three elements, (1) the rateable value of the property for which the ratepayer is liable, which is determined by the Inland Revenue Valuation Office; (2) the rate poundage set by the local authority; (3) various rate reliefs, for example the domestic element of RSG, rate rebates, partial derating of charities, and so on.

In this chapter we consider each of these elements in some detail, in the first part in relation to its formal, in the second, its effective incidence. We consider first the determination of rateable values, describing the principles of the valuation procedure and examining how it works in practice, drawing on our study of the determinants of house prices and rateable values, which is summarised in Appendix 2.6.A1 to this chapter.

FORMAL INCIDENCE

THE DETERMINATION OF RATEABLE VALUES

The rateable value of a property is assessed as the market rent that property could command less any costs to the owner of repairs, maintenance, insurance, and so on. It is the assessed net rental value of the property.

The valuation procedure is as follows: there are general revaluations of all properties — in statute every five years but in practice much less frequently — and at these general revaluations each property owner is asked to inform the valuers of the market rent for his property. The returns constitute the rental evidence on which the assessed rental values are based. Such rental evidence can be provided, of course, only where properties are in fact rented out in a free market. On the basis of the rental evidence, the valuers form an impression of the general level of market rents in an area, and of the factors that may affect the rents of individual properties relative to this general level. They then apply these criteria to assign rental values to each property in the area, which are called their gross rental values. There is then an arbitrary deduction — to take account of the landlord's costs of repairs and maintenance — to reach net rental value, which constitutes the rateable value of the property (for further discussion, see Part Three, Chapter 2).

Until 1950 valuation was carried out by local valuation officers, employed by local authorities. There was no mechanism to bring about uniformity of valuation procedure across authorities. In 1944, Sir John and Lady Hicks (Hicks, 1944) published a study which pointed to numerous geographical and other anomalies in the calculation of rateable value. They argued that a probable cause was that the valuation procedures which had developed independently in the different authorities had come to diverge over time and that there was a possibility that political pressures were influencing the relative valuation of different classes of property. The Hicks's recommended a national valuation service to achieve uniformity. To this end, the Inland Revenue took over responsibility for valuation in 1950. Despite this, local variations in valuation procedures persist. Indeed they may be as great as before 1950.

The key to the problem is the virtual disappearance of evidence on market rents. Before 1914 more than 90 per cent of all housing and by far the greatest part of other buildings were rented at free-market rents. Since then the percentages of dwellings by tenure have changed, and the majority of dwellings are now owner-occupied:

Table 2.6.1.   *Housing tenure 1914–76*

Percentage	1914	1938	1960	1971	1976
Owner-occupied	10	32	44	53	55
Local authorities and new towns	–	10	25	29	29
Privately rented and miscellaneous	90	58	32	19	16

Source: *Housing Policy Review Report* (DoE, 1977a), part 1, p. 37.

Even as late as 1951, 63 per cent of houses were rented. By 1976, rental housing had fallen to 45 per cent of the total. So that there is now no direct evidence on rents for more than half the dwellings. In the past, valuers looked for similar rented properties in the same neighbourhood when determining gross values for owner-occupied housing; but this becomes more difficult and the results more problematic as the numbers of comparable rented properties decline. Even this understates the valuation problem. Public-housing rents in general are of no relevance because their level has been affected by subsidy and by cross-subsidisation within local authorities so that they have little relation to the open-market rents required. This has left private rented housing, most of which is concentrated in a few central urban areas. There are many parts of the country in which privately rented housing has fallen to less than 2 per cent of the stock. If that were not enough, virtually all the private rental stock is rent controlled under a number of different statutes which have created different divergences between actual rents and those which might be expected in a free market. Under this strain, rent estimation for rating purposes had become almost completely hypothetical both for the public and privately rented proportions of the stock, while for owner-occupied stock valuers have been driven to increasingly ill-founded comparisons in their attempts to estimate what rents they might fetch in a non-existent free rental market (see Wright *et al.*, 1974, pp. 72–4).

Market rents should relate reasonably closely both to the benefits a person might enjoy from living in the property and to his income or economic circumstances.[1] If in spite of the valuation problems, rateable values are closely related to market rents, as they should be in principle, then there would be a broad correspondence of a person's ability to pay and the value of a dwelling, even though some people might live in dearer or cheaper housing than one would expect. If, on the other hand, due to absence of rental evidence, rateable values bear an erratic relationship to market rents they would bear equally little relationship to the ratepayers' ability to pay. We have, therefore, made an empirical study of the factors that appear to determine rateable value, to see whether in fact they are related to market values and if not how they differ. (The details of the study are presented in Appendix 2.6.A1 at the end of this chapter.)

We first examine how closely rateable values relate to capital values, or sale prices, of properties. The capital value of a property is not, of course, the same as its rental value. But its characteristics — both in terms of housing qualities such as floorspace, standard of decoration, facilities such as garden, garage, etc., and in terms of locational amenities such as neighbourhood characteristics, convenience of access to transport, shops, parks, etc. — will clearly be the major determinants both of rental and capital value. Indeed, in principle, the capital value of a property should be equal to the capitalised value of its market rent, and should, therefore, be more or less the same multiple of the market rent for all properties. For properties where it is expected that market rents might rise sharply, say as a result of redevelopment, the increase will be reflected in the current capital value, which will, therefore, be high relative to the current market rent. Similarly capital values will be low, relative to current market rents, if it is expected that the rental value of the property will fall.

This relationship assumes a free market, and will not hold perfectly in a market subject to rent controls and security of tenure where property owners do not in practice have the option to let their property at free market rents or sell it with vacant possession. Then the market value with vacant possession will be substantially greater than with a sitting tenant. In this case, the effective vacant-possession market value is shared by landlord and tenant. The relation between rental and capital values is further confused by the existence of important tax concessions to owner-occupiers relative to the private rented sector which increase the price a purchaser will pay above the value of it as housing.

Even so, one would expect the main factors accounting for differences in the capital values of different houses to be their housing and locational attributes. Such factors would also affect rental values in a free market. If rateable values reflect rental values, we would expect them to be quite closely correlated with capital values. This question was the first we examined.

Our finding was that the correlation between house prices and rateable values was rather weak. There is some tendency for more expensive houses to be assessed at a higher rateable value, but there is considerable variation in the relationship. Rateable values are not a good reflection of market rents.

Secondly, there seems to be a systematic tendency to assess higher-price properties more lightly, as a proportion of their value, than lower-price properties. In this sense, the valuation system is regressive — the rateable value of a £30,000 house will be less than twice that of a £15,000 house.

A number of explanations for this regressiveness have been suggested. Houses whose capital values are increased relative to their rental values because of the hope of redevelopment will appear more often in the higher price ranges. Similarly those in a state of decay will appear more often in the lower price ranges. Tax concessions to owner-occupiers are more important to the higher income groups, and they will increase capital values more relative to rental values in the higher price ranges. So far as these explanations stand it is the capital value rather than the rateable value which does not accurately reflect the market rent. But it is also likely that relevant rental evidence became scarce earlier for the medium- to higher-priced housing used by the higher income groups as owner-occupation increased. As a result valuers were particularly cautious about increasing valuation assessments for these properties in the absence of rental evidence.

Our study suggests, however, that other factors have been at work. While lower-price properties derive their value mainly from the provision of basic housing features (floorspace, etc.) such factors account for only part of the value of higher-price property. Much of the value of higher-price property seems instead to derive from particular attractive features — perhaps specific to an individual house or location — which, we think, valuers fail to take into account in making their assessments. We were unable to account to a greater degree for differences in house prices in the higher ranges on the basis of all the information used in our study, and we think it likely that valuers, often working with less information than we had, might similarly fail to account for these influences on market value.

The third issue we considered was the consistency of valuation practice in different local authorities. Rateable values tend to be higher, relative to house prices, in some local authorities than in others. But this finding might simply reflect the fact that house prices are higher on average in some authorities than in others. In Appendix 2.6.A1 we show the ratio of rateable value to house price for each range of house prices for a number of London boroughs, and this provides clear evidence of differences in valuation. We have also looked at the relationship between rateable value and housing characteristics. It is possible, for example, that rateable values might be systematically related to factors such as floorspace, location, etc. with a consistent valuation procedure, although one unrelated to capital values (or market rents). But the factors associated with variations in rateable value were different in the different authorities. Despite the centralisation of the valuation process since 1950 there seems little evidence of consistency in valuation practice being achieved — related or unrelated to market values. Further analysis shows a systematic tendency for rateable values to be higher relative to market values in the centre of conurbations than in the rest of metropolitan regions (Foster and Lynch, 1978). The most plausible reason for this is that geographical patterns of rateable value have been frozen much as they were before 1950 while land values have risen more towards the periphery of cities and towns than they have at the centre. Such a flattening of the urban rent gradient has been an almost universal phenomenon as urban areas have grown and their densities have fallen (Clark, 1968, ch. 9).

The basic cause of all these deficiencies is the absence of adequate rental evidence, or indeed of any rental evidence at all for some types of property. The imposition of further rent controls in 1974 can only have made this problem worse. The difficulty is of course well recognised. The adoption of assessments based on capital values was recommended by the Layfield Committee, and we examine it in Part Three, Chapter 2.

By comparison the assessment of commercial and industrial property presents few problems: there is an active rental market, normally unrestricted by controls and in consequence no shortage of rental evidence on which to base valuations.

VARIATIONS IN RATE POUNDAGES

The second factor influencing rate bills is the rate poundage levied by the local authority. The process of determining the rate poundage may be envisaged in the following way. The local authority estimates its expected expenditure, and deducts from it its expected receipts from specific and supplementary grants, and from the needs element of RSG. The remainder is divided by the local authority's 'effective' rateable value to give the rate poundage. The authority's 'effective' rateable value comprises both its actual rateable value and its notional or 'credited' rateable value represented by the resources element of RSG.

We showed in Part Two, Chapter 3 that, at a first approximation, the purpose of RSG is to equalise rate poundages for a given standard of services. It is intended that payments of needs grant should compensate for differences in expenditure per head of population, for a given standard of services, so that expenditure per head net of specific and supplementary grants and net of needs grant would be equalised across authorities. Likewise the resources element would bring all authorities up to some 'standard' rateable value per head of population, so that each authority would have to raise the same net income from the same effective rateable value, and hence each would set the same rate poundage.

We have seen in Part One, Chapter 7 that the dissatisfaction with the RSG system in the years immediately prior to 1974 was associated with an increase in the dispersion of rate poundages. Despite the reforms of RSG in 1974 significant variations in rate poundage have persisted. In 1976/7 rate poundages in non-metropolitan districts ranged from 56.0p in Blaby in Leicestershire to 109.4p in Afan in West Glamorgan. In metropolitan districts the corresponding range was from 61.5p in Leeds to 96.3p in Newcastle upon Tyne (CIPFA, *Return of Rates*, 1976/7). Table 2.62 shows the variation of rate poundages of major-spending authorities from 1971/2 to 1977/8.

To simplify somewhat, variations in rate poundages may arise either because of differences in expenditure per head uncompensated by needs-grant receipts, or because of differences in effective rateable value per head.[2] Since the increase in the resources element in 1974, virtually all authorities outside London receive it, so their rateable value per head is effectively equalised. Why, then, do such

Table 2.6.2.   *Coefficient of variation of rate poundages 1971/2–1977/8*

Authority (no.) Rate poundage:	1971/2	1972/3	1973/4	Year 1974/5	1975/6	1976/7	1977/8
County boroughs (83)	11.44	13.16	15.01	–	–	–	–
Metropolitan districts (36)	–	–	–	11.35	12.32	11.15	10.33
Rate precept:							
County councils (58)	18.34	18.62	17.19	–	–	–	–
Shire counties (47)	–	–	–	8.72	9.32	8.97	8.19

large variations in rate poundages persist, particularly in the metropolitan districts?

One explanation follows from our analysis in the last few chapters (see also King, 1973; Jackman and Sellars, 1977b). We showed in Part Two, Chapter 3 that since 1974 an increasing share of needs grants has indeed gone to authorities with above-average rate poundages, but that they have, for whatever reason, increased their spending rather than using the grant increases to hold down their rates. In consequence, the dispersion of rate poundages has not been reduced as much as might have been expected. A second factor follows from our analysis of the 'price' variable in Part Two, Chapter 5. By increasing substantially the standard rateable value per head in 1974, the extent to which local authorities were grant-aided or additions to their spending not only increased on average but the dispersion would have increased also. Authorities with low rateable values per head would benefit substantially from an increase in the national standard rateable value per head, and from the analysis in Chapter 5 we would expect their expenditure to increase. Authorities with high rateable value per head would benefit less (if at all) with a correspondingly smaller effect on their expenditure, so that the dispersion would increase.

Our argument is not that rate poundages should be uniform but that their variation should reflect the standards of local services. If ratepayers in one locality are receiving better services than people elsewhere, then the benefit principle – and economic efficiency – suggest they should pay more in rates. And provided the higher rate burden is compensated for by better local government services there is no inequity. But to identify variations in rate poundages with variations in standards of service implies a reliable means of needs grant. We have shown in earlier chapters that this is scarcely possible, even in principle, and has certainly not been achieved in practice.

THE DOMESTIC ELEMENT AND NON-DOMESTIC RATING

The basic rate liability on a property is the local rate poundage levied on its rateable value. There are, however, a number of rate reliefs. In this chapter we are concerned only with rate reliefs for domestic ratepayers (households). There are also reliefs for various non-domestic ratepayers (agriculture, charities, etc.) which are examined in Part Three, Chapter 3.

The formal incidence of domestic rates is reduced not only by rate rebates and allowances where these apply, but also now by domestic rate relief to all domestic ratepayers.[3] This is financed by a grant from central government and could be discussed as such. Since its sole purpose is to reduce domestic rate burdens, however, it is more relevant to examine it in a discussion of the incidence of rates. It has two impacts — to reduce the impact of domestic rates and necessarily to increase the share of rates paid by the non-domestic ratepayer.

The domestic element
The domestic element was introduced in 1967/8, prescribing a uniform reduction in rate poundages on all domestic hereditaments of 5 old pence (about 2p) in England and Wales and 10 old pence (4p) in Scotland. Its purpose was evident. As noted in Part One, Chapter 6, local government expenditure was expanding rapidly in the mid-sixties, and central government wished to protect domestic ratepayers from the rate increases implicit in that expenditure growth. By limiting relief to domestic ratepayers the cost to central government in terms of additional grant is held down; the scheme is essentially equivalent to mandatory super-rating of industry and commerce to provide the additional funds.

The domestic element proved very popular with central government, and it was increased every year, reaching its highest level (18½p in England, 36p in Wales, and 27p in Scotland) in 1975/6. Even these figures understate the increase, for the introduction of the new valuation list in 1973/4 substantially increased the value of a given rate poundage relief. In 1967/8 the domestic element cost £26 million, accounted for about 1.5 per cent of the aggregate exchequer grant and reduced domestic rate bills by around 3.6 per cent (England and Wales) and 4 per cent (Scotland). By 1975/6 the comparable figures were a cost of £650 million, 9.4 per cent of the grant in England and Wales, 4.9 per cent in Scotland, and a reduction in domestic rate bills of 27.5 per cent (England), 45.1 per cent (Wales), and 15 per cent (Scotland). Just as the domestic element was introduced at a time of rapid growth in local government spending, so its most rapid increase came in the early 1970s. Between 1972/3 and 1975/6, the cost of domestic element increased from £147 million to £651 million, more than quadrupling in three years (Layfield, 1976, annex 10, table 28). As a result, mainly, of the increase in the domestic element the yield of non-domestic rates has risen much more rapidly than that of domestic rates — a 142 per cent increase as against an 88 per cent increase for domestic rates, between 1966/7 and 1974/5 (Layfield, 1976, annex 10, table 27).

From 1975/6, however, the picture has changed. The domestic element has not been increased (except in Scotland), and since it is a fixed poundage, this means that any increase in rate poundage will lead to an equal absolute, but higher proportionate, increase in the domestic rate poundage. Whereas before 1975/6 the domestic element had been used to protect local authorities from the consequences, in terms of domestic rate bills, of their higher expenditure, since 1975/6 it has had the opposite effect of (slightly) intensifying that pressure.

None the less, the desire to restrain local government expenditure cannot have been the only motive for the change in policy on the domestic element. Central government could have put the same pressure on domestic rate pound-ages, at a substantial saving in grant to itself, by cutting back the needs and resources element while allowing the domestic element to increase further. The purpose of holding the domestic element constant, rather than letting it increase, is clearly to hold down the growth of non-domestic rate bills. With the sharp fall in corporate profits in the mid-1970s, non-domestic rate bills were absorbing an unprecedented proportion of corporate income. Whereas domestic rate payments as a proportion of personal disposable income have remained relatively static, at about 2 per cent to 2½ per cent, the yield of non-domestic rates has nearly quadrupled since the mid-1960s while corporate profits have less than doubled.[4] The differential rating of industry and commerce had gone far enough.

Non-domestic rating
While the undoubted effect of domestic rate relief is to increase the relative contribution of non-domestic rates to local revenue by comparison with domestic rates, let us consider the incidence of non-domestic rates. So far in this chapter we have assumed the 'forward' shifting of rates — that is that rates are ultimately borne by the tenant or occupant of the house. A similar assumption of forward shifting of non-domestic rates implies that rates on commercial and industrial property are similarly shifted forward to the consumers of the product in the form of higher prices. It is interesting to consider next the incidence of non-domestic rates by income group on this assumption.

The incidence of non-domestic rates by sector has been studied by Mair (1975; 1978) and also by Whalley (1975). From the *Census of Production* and Inland Revenue statistics, they are able to compute the payment of rates as a proportion of total input costs in each sector. Using the 1968 *Census of Production*, Mair (1975) calculates rate payments in excess of 1 per cent of total input cost in water supply (7.2%), distributive trades (4.8%), miscellaneous services (3.3%), electricity supply (4.8%), cement (2.1%), mining and quarrying, and communications (each 1.7%), iron and steel (1.4%), gas (1.3%), and building materials, pottery and glass and coke ovens (1.0%). Clearly these are sectors intensive in the use of land, buildings or fixed capital in the form of plant and machinery.

These figures are rate payments by sector, not by product. Each sector buys in various intermediate goods and other inputs from other sectors, which will themselves have paid rates. Input—output tables provide an approximate measure of the input of each sector per unit output of every other. It is thus possible to make an estimate of the total rate payment embodied in the final output of each sector, as a proportion of the price of the product. Information on expenditure by product of households of different income groups is provided in the *Family Expenditure Survey*, published by the Department of Employment.

Such calculations have been carried out by Mair. He finds a considerable degree of regressiveness in non-domestic rates, which absorb about 1.3 per cent of the income of the lowest income group (under £6 per week in 1968), but only just over 0.5 per cent of the income of the highest income group (over £60 per week). By contrast the regressiveness of 'gross rates' on domestic property (before rebates) according to Layfield (1976, table 36) varied from over 7 per cent in the lowest income group (under £20 per week in 1975) to only 2 per cent in the highest income group (over £100 per week). Clearly these figures do not allow direct comparison, but equally they provide no support for the view that domestic rates are more regressive than rates on industry and commerce.

THE RELATION BETWEEN RATES AND INCOME

Though historically the burden of rates fell on all ratepayers, it was likely to be light on the very poor – either because they were not ratepayers, or because they lived overcrowded in dwellings of low rateable value. Nevertheless there were sporadic attempts in the occasional statute to alleviate the burden of rates on the very poor. Later there was a more systematic measure of relief provided in the way in which arbitrary deductions were fixed for repairs and maintenance. This became proportionately larger for lower-rated property and so reduced the rate burden which was calculated on the assessed value after this deduction. There were a few other minor attempts to reduce the burden on the poor (Rating and Valuation Act, 1925, sect. 2[4] ; Money Payment [Justice Procedure] Act, 1935, sect. 10[2]). It was, however, the combined effect of the depression of the 1930s, the rapid growth of local capital expenditure in the late 1930s – much of it for civil defence – and resentment of changes brought about by the revaluation which was due to come about in 1939, which led to the establishment of the Fitzgerald Committee to look into problems of hardship caused by rates. They discussed several methods of alleviation including a form of rebate. The Report was completed in 1939, but it remained unpublished until 1944. Its recommendations were not acted on.

The revaluation of 1963 and the rapid increase in expenditure of the early 1960s brought further complaints of hardship. To examine them the Allen Committee was set up. The analysis they made confirmed that rates were regressive, being a greater proportion of the income of the poor than of the rich. As a result rate rebates and allowances were introduced in 1966. They were expanded in 1974. Essentially they provide that the poorest households in receipt of supplementary benefit receive a rate allowance to meet their rate bill in full, while other low-income households receive a complete or partial rate rebate dependent on their income, family circumstances and rate bill.[5]

The relationship between rate bills and income as a measure of ability to pay has been examined again by the Layfield Committee (1976, ch. 10).

They first consider the incidence of 'gross rates', that is domestic rate bills after deduction of the domestic element of RSG, but prior to deduction of rate rebates, etc. Like the Allen Committee before them, they find the incidence of gross rates uniformly regressive. The higher a household's income, the smaller the proportion of income it pays in rates.

They then examine the incidence of 'net rates', that is after deduction of rate rebates. As might be expected, rate rebates, provided they are claimed, significantly reduce rate bills for the lower income groups. As a result the incidence of rates becomes progressive in the lower half of the income distribution, roughly proportional in the middle income ranges, and regressive again for higher income groups, who, of course, are not affected by the rebate. This result is readily explained. As incomes rise, on average rateable values tend to rise but less than proportionately to the increase in incomes. This factor leads to a rise in rate bills less than proportionate to the increase in income, that is a regressive effect. At the same time, as incomes rise, rate rebates are reduced, so that rate payments rise more than proportionately to income.[6] In the lower income ranges this second effect dominates, so rates are progressive there while in the higher income ranges the former effect dominates, giving a regressive pattern.

The justification for rate rebates is not immediately obvious. Why have special means-tested rebates for rates and not for other items of expenditure of low-income families such as tobacco, bread, sausages, etc.? Why not simply provide higher cash benefits and allow households to meet their own rate bills? There are two issues involved here affecting both 'vertical' and 'horizontal' equity. The effect on vertical equity — or the redistributive effect — of rates is regressive. This regressive effect can be offset by rate subsidies (or rebates) to those with low incomes and, for symmetry, rate surcharges for those with high incomes. But the regressive distributional effect of rates could more easily be offset by making income tax more progressive rather than by introducing special rebates and/or surcharges. At the top end of the scale one can argue plausibly enough that the tax system as a whole is progressive and there is no particular cause for concern if one element in it is not.

At the lower end of the income scale, the argument is not so clear. It has so far proved impossible to introduce a comprehensive negative income tax/tax credit/social dividend scheme in Britain, although FIS is a step in that direction. But this argument does not apply in the case of supplementary benefits, where the cash payment could be increased and separate payment of rates bills withdrawn.

The second issue is one of horizontal equity — that is to say that people equal in their ability to pay may face very different rate bills. Clearly this horizontal inequity cannot be offset by any changes in the income tax schedules. But the question here is whether the horizontal inequity is in fact an inequity at all. The household with the higher rate bill will often be living in property of relatively high rateable value, itself reflecting the benefit of housing quality or location. Viewed as a tax on such benefits the higher rate bill is not inequitable. We would accept this argument in general, but it may break down for low-income households because mobility may be difficult. Many such households will be old people who are very reluctant to move even if they are deriving no material benefit from the proximity to employment of a central city location, yet the house it occupies will be rated to take account of this locational advantage. Hence it can be argued, in such cases, that differences in rates reflect differences in the cost of living to households to which there are no compensating differences in benefits to those households. There is, therefore, a case in equity for compensating for these differences in costs.

The normal economic argument against selective subsidisation of components of expenditure is that it encourages excessive expenditure on these items. But it is often very difficult to move home, and wastefully expensive if the period of low income may turn out to be temporary. Payment of rate rebates is unlikely to lead to a distortion of expenditure patterns, at least in the short run. In the longer run, of course, rate rebates may blunt the economic incentives to households to move away from areas where land is scarce and property values are high, or to give up accommodation which has become too large for them. Such economic incentives serve the purpose of releasing property for more beneficial uses, and it seems anomalous that low-income households should be partially insulated from this process by rate rebates. Rate rebates will also reduce the effective 'price' of local services to the voter which will weaken the electoral discipline on expenditure, especially where rebates are common.

CONCLUSION ON FORMAL INCIDENCE

The discussion so far has been on the formal incidence of rates. We find that anomalies in the methods used to value property do mean that there are significant variations in the formal burden of rates as a property tax. While some part of the declining ratio of rateable value to market value with higher prices is caused by differences in the factors that determine rents and capital values, the rest would appear due to the methods of valuation, and would seem difficult to defend, given the purpose of rating as a tax. The case for and against the introduction of capital valuation will be considered in Part Three, but the effect almost certainly would be to lower rateable values for the very lowest price and raise it for the very highest-price houses while leaving most houses – those between the extremes – not greatly affected.

The intention of the resources element is such that one would have expected a tendency towards equalisation of rate poundages, given also the function of the needs grant. No strong conclusions can be drawn from this since local authorities have discretion to vary their rate poundage to finance activities they want. Even so, the operation of the two grants achieves a more equal incidence of rate burdens between local authorities than would occur in their absence. It was shown also how from 1966 the formal incidence of rates has been altered very substantially by the introduction of the domestic element in RSG which has had the effect of derating the domestic relative to the non-domestic ratepayer.

Finally we have shown how rate rebates and allowances also modify the formal incidence of rates making it progressive for the lowest income groups. In their absence, the incidence of rates on those groups would be regressive as it has been in the past. The progressiveness and regressiveness of rates would be altered by capital valuation, but it could also be altered by the use of different house-price multipliers to be applied to different bands of rateable values. In the past rent allowances adjusting gross rateable values have been used to alter progressiveness. In principle, one could achieve any degree of progressiveness one wanted by selecting appropriate multipliers, though it would be an imperfect reflection of progressiveness in relation to income because rateable values imperfectly reflect differences in income.

EFFECTIVE INCIDENCE

In discussing the formal incidence of rates we assume that it is on the occupier in the case of domestic property and on the firm's customer in the case of non-domestic property. But rates need not necessarily be incident on these groups. A landlord faced with a higher rates bill may be able to pass it on to his tenant by charging a higher rent, but he may not. Similarly there is no basis for a belief that firms can always pass on higher rates in the form of higher prices to their customers.[7] The effective incidence of rates – who ultimately pays the rate bill – is much less obvious than the formal incidence.

The analysis of this problem necessarily entails economic theory, and can be omitted by those prepared to take our conclusions on trust. We start with a very simple set of assumptions – that all property is let out, bought or sold in free markets and that rates are levied at a uniform poundage on all types of property and in all locations.

ECONOMIC THEORY AND THE INCIDENCE OF RATES

A property owner will seek the best rent he can get, which will be determined by the return on the property in its most profitable use. If a property tax is levied, or increased, the rent the property owner can charge will not increase, for the imposition of the tax has done nothing to alter the profitability of the property in different uses, and hence has not altered the rent a tenant is prepared to pay. The tax then falls entirely on the property owner. The fact that the rent, net of tax, the property owner receives, has also fallen, will also reduce the capital value of the property, for if the property yields a lower net of tax return the price people would be prepared to pay to purchase it will fall correspondingly. This fall in property values will, however, affect new investment, for the fall in the price of existing capital will obviously reduce the price people are prepared to pay for new capital goods. For example, a fall in the price of the existing housing stock will reduce the price people are prepared to pay for new houses, and hence affect the rate of housebuilding. The rate of investment in new capital will therefore fall. But the reduction in investment demand will lead to a fall in interest rates, which will continue until investment becomes profitable again.[8] Interest rates will fall until capital values are restored to their previous level.

As a numerical example, assume some property were to yield £1,000 per annum and the interest rate were 10 per cent. Its capital value would be £10,000. If now a property tax with an effective rate of 25 per cent were imposed, the net of tax yield would fall to £750 per annum, and, with a 10 per cent interest rate, the capital value would fall to £7,500. Investment now becomes unprofitable and interest rates fall until, at an interest rate of 7½ per cent, the net of tax yield of £750 becomes equivalent again to a capital value of £10,000.

Who then pays the property tax in the long run? Nothing has happened to alter the gross market rents or capital values of property – supply and demand are both unchanged. Hence prices of goods and services are unaffected. The property owner receives a lower net of tax yield on his property. But if his ownership of the property is financed by borrowing, this is offset fully by lower interest charges. The tax is borne by the ultimate wealth owner, because the income from the ownership of wealth is reduced. Of course, if the property owner has not borrowed but holds his wealth in the form of property then he suffers the loss of income with no offset in the form of lower borrowing costs. In the same way, the owner-occupier of residential property pays rates only in so far as he owns the property; in so far as it is financed by a mortgage, payments of rates are offset by lower mortgage interest charges.

On this argument, it is clear that rate payments are unrelated to the incidence of the tax. Non-domestic rates do not, for example, affect the price of goods and services because they do not alter the cost of capital to the firm but only the distribution of that given total between interest charges and taxation. Likewise, the rate paid on domestic property let out on a free-market rental does not affect the total cost of the property but only the distribution of that cost between rent and rates. Similarly rates do not affect the total cost of buying a property for owner-occupation but only the distribution of that cost between mortgage-interest payments and rates. Rates are paid ultimately by wealth owners. The relationship of rates to income thus depends on the relationship of wealth to income. On average on this analysis, rates are progressive, as typically those on higher incomes have more wealth relative to their incomes than those with lower incomes. But there are groups, particularly the old, with low incomes but significant wealth, particularly in the form of owner-occupied housing, and these groups may well be heavily burdened by rates.

The argument so far has depended upon the assumption of a fall in the rate of interest sufficient to offset in full the effect of rates on capital values. Consider now the opposite extreme, where interest rates do not fall at all. Rates will now reduce the net of tax yield, and capital value of property and new investment will be discouraged. As interest rates do not fall, less investment will be undertaken, reducing the supply of capital goods. The reduction in supply will increase their market value, or pre-tax price and, as a result of the reduced supply, the higher price can be shifted forward into the prices of products (or the rent of housing). Not all property is reproducible capital: land, for example, is in fixed supply so its pre-tax price will not rise. Taxes on land will still be borne by landowners and will not be shifted forward into higher prices.

The extent to which interest rates fall, and hence to which property taxes on reproducible capital are shifted on to wealth owners, will depend on what happens to savings. If lower interest rates reduce the supply of savings, or divert it abroad, there will indeed be a less than fully compensating reduction in interest rates and a reduced rate of capital formation. It is generally thought that savings are not highly interest elastic. The incidence of rates will then depend on the degree of international capital mobility. If wealth is locked into the country it will bear the tax, but if not there will be a capital outflow until the pre-tax return has risen sufficiently to meet the tax charge.

But in the above discussion we have identified rates with a tax on all forms of capital goods. In fact, the tax is levied on immovable but not on movable capital. Clearly the imposition of a tax on one form of capital but not on the other will encourage investment in the untaxed forms. As long ago as 1817

Ricardo criticised rates for falling more on agriculture than on manufacturing: 'The farmer being rated according to the actual production he obtained, the manufacturer only according to the value of the building in which he works, without any regard to the value of the machinery, labour or stock which he may employ' (1962 edn., p. 260). He claimed this would lead to a distortion in the allocation of capital from agriculture to manufacturing because the heavier burden of rates in the former depressed the return on capital there, relative to that obtainable in manufacturing and commerce.

Ricardo's criticisms were valid. The formal analysis of the problem was developed by Harberger in 1962. Harberger was concerned with the effects of the corporate income tax, which is a tax on capital in the corporate, but not in the unincorporated, sector of the economy. The problem is exactly paralleled by the incidence of rates which is a tax on immovable but not on movable capital. Harberger showed that such a tax, with the total supply of capital given, would tend to shift capital from the taxed to the untaxed sector, causing the pre-tax price to rise in the taxed sector and fall in the untaxed sector, until the post-tax price was the same in both sectors. The price of the output of the taxed sector would rise and of the untaxed sector fall, leading to reduced output in the taxed sector, and higher output in the untaxed sector. As far as the consumer is concerned, the higher price of the taxed sector output is offset by the lower price of output of the untaxed sector. Though the tax affects prices it is not borne by consumers. The after-tax price of capital has fallen in both sectors, so the tax falls primarily on the owners of capital irrespective of whether their capital is held in the taxed or in the untaxed sector. There is, in addition, a welfare loss of economic efficiency due to the misallocation of capital between the two sectors.

Thus, even allowing for an untaxed sector – movable property – the incidence of rates is still on property owners, provided only that the supply of savings is unaffected. But rates do now cause a distortion in the allocation of resources between different sectors of the economy, according to the extent to which the sectors employ movable as against immovable property.

DIFFERENTIAL RATING OF DIFFERENT TYPES OF PROPERTY

On theoretical grounds, the impact of taxing different types of property at different rates is no different from the differential taxing of movable as against immovable property we have already considered.

The derating of agriculture, for example, as compared with uniform rating of the same total yield, will tend to increase resources in agriculture at the expense of production of other goods and services. The price of agricultural products will fall due to the increased supply, while the prices of other goods and services will tend to rise. Agricultural derating will not benefit the consumer or reduce the cost of living. But it will raise agricultural production.

Likewise, differential rating of commerce and industry at a higher rate than residential property will lead to an increase in land and building for houses, resulting in a fall in house prices and (market) rents, and a reduction in industrial and commercial building and capital formation leading to an increase in its price, and hence industrial costs and the prices of goods and services to the consumer.

In the UK in recent years there has been unprecedented investment in house improvements, conversions, modernisations, etc. while investment in industry has languished. At the time of writing (1978) there remains a substantial demand for building-society mortgages, despite record lending in 1976 and 1977. At the same time, the demand for bank loans from industry and commerce remains stagnant. Evidently there is scope for substitution between the two sectors, and it is unlikely that tax considerations are of no relevance.

What then is the incidence of the differential rate? If we were to replace a uniform rate on both domestic and non-domestic property with a differential rate which was higher on non-domestic than on domestic property, even if the whole rate bill in each case were ultimately borne in full by wealth owners, there would be a difference in that the relative price of housing would be lower, and other goods and services higher with differential rating. In this case, the effective incidence is the same as the formal incidence.

Whether, in the long run, a household is better off as a result of shifting the rate burden from domestic to non-domestic ratepayers depends, then, on the relative importance of housing as against other items of expenditure. Particularly now that there are rate rebates it does not follow that the relative reduction of domestic rates and the shifting of the burden on to other items of consumers' expenditure is necessarily progressive in the sense of reducing the total burden on low-income families. For total expenditure, as a proportion of income, is higher for low-income families, so the rate content of non-housing expenditure will also be regressive in relation to income (Mair, 1978). Second, non-domestic rates do not enter the prices of all goods and services equally, as noted above (p. 316).

Higher rating of non-domestic property, then, will benefit groups for whom housing constitutes an above-average proportion of expenditure (rather than income). It will be to the benefit of Londoners, and probably to the benefit of retired people and people living alone. Even then it will tend to discourage the provision of jobs in London. But it will not benefit low-income families in general to any significant extent.

It is unlikely that these distributional considerations were, in any case, the main reason for the introduction of differential rating. Non-domestic rates are a 'concealed' tax, hidden in the prices people pay for the goods and services they consume. Higher prices resulting from non-domestic rates are not attributed by the consumer to local government spending. Differential rating can, therefore, induce people to accept a higher level of local government spending than they would have done had the whole cost been borne on domestic rates. The advantage of domestic rate relief to central government is that it allows an expansion of local government services at no visible cost to the ratepayers and relatively little cost to the taxpayer, while the disadvantage is that the higher rating of non-domestic property will discourage industrial and commercial investment and work through into higher prices, and by reducing corporation tax receipts oblige central government to levy higher taxes elsewhere in the economy.

RENT CONTROL

At present British legislation provides for rate increases to be passed on to tenants in full in both public and privately rented sectors. Thus if the actual rent is enough below the open-market economic rent for this to be possible in full, all domestic rates will fall on occupiers. If the actual rate is too near to the open-market rent for full shifting, then the effective incidence would be partly on the owner and partly on the occupier. In practice, given the virtual ubiquity of rent control, one can be sure that formal and effective incidence coincide: both are on the occupier.

LOCAL VARIATIONS IN RATES AND EXPENDITURE

The conclusions we have reached on the incidence of rates in this chapter are different from those we reached in Part Two, Chapter 2. Here we are considering the incidence of a uniform rate across all localities while in Chapter 2 we were concerned with the incidence of differences in rates and in expenditures between localities. It is important to note the differences. Higher rates matched by higher beneficial expenditure in one local authority will be incident on people living in that authority. But higher rates matched by higher beneficial services in all authorities will be incident on wealth owners (Miezkowski, 1972; Aaron, 1975).

In Appendix 2.6.A1 to this chapter we have reported an empirical study of rateable values and capital values of property. The main purpose was to investigate the relationship between the two, but the data may also be used to examine the validity of some of the propositions advanced in Chapter 2. We there assumed that beneficial expenditure would tend to increase local property values while increases in local taxes would tend to reduce them. Such propositions have already been tested in the USA (Oates, 1969). There are considerable statistical problems in any exercise of this kind. Our results suggest there is some tendency in the local authorities we have examined for higher spending on education to be associated with higher property values, *ceteris paribus*.

CONCLUSION: EFFECTIVE INCIDENCE

In theory rates will ultimately be incident on wealth owners, and will not be shifted on to tenants in the form of higher rents or to consumers in the form of higher prices. Even this theory may not hold if capital is mobile between countries, for wealth owners can then escape the tax by investing abroad so that the tax would be shifted on to tenants or consumers.

In practice, however, the difference between formal and effective incidence is smaller than might seem at first sight. Domestic ratepayers typically either own their homes or are tenants with controlled rents. In both these cases, rates will be incident on the occupier of the property. We have also shown that the effective incidence of differential rating operates through its effect on prices and is, therefore, again the same as the formal incidence.

NOTES

1 The immobility in the housing market which results from controlled and subsidised rents and the high costs of buying and selling houses may significantly reduce these relationships in practice. This is an important element of the argument for rate rebates, see p. 318.

2 We are abstracting from changes in balances, revenue contributions to capital, errors in estimates, etc.

3 Since 1976 domestic ratepayers in several inner London boroughs get additional rate relief. This is one of the mechanisms in the current (1977/8) RSG introduced to replace the Greater London Rate Equalisation Scheme.

4 *CES Review*, vol. 4 (September 1978), table 3, pp. 78–9; and also pp. 45–7.

5 The mechanism is as follows: the 'allowable' income for any household is calculated according to the number of children, etc. If a household's actual income is equal to its allowable income it receives a rate rebate equal to 60 per cent of its rate bill. If its income exceeds its allowable income its rate rebate is reduced by 6p per week for each £1 per week its income exceeds the allowable level, while if its income falls below the allowable level it receives an additional 8p rebate for each £1 shortfall up to a maximum of its total rate bill, or £3 per week, whichever is the smaller.

6 An increase of £1 in income will reduce rate rebates by at least 6p at the margin while, on average, rates absorb about 2½ per cent of disposable income.

7 The Layfield Committee noted that 'Government departments were able to tell us very little about the economic effects of rating on commerce and industry, even though the yield is of the same order as Corporation Tax or VAT' (Layfield, 1976, p. 178). The argument for heavier non-domestic rates has often been couched in rather simple-minded ways referring to industry and commerce's supposed greater ability to pay. The quotations from the Crossman diaries in Part One, Chapter 6 suggest that those concerned did not doubt that the incidence of domestic rate relief would be such as to shift part of the burden of rates from the household to employers.

8 Neglecting possible monetary complications. The argument in the text will hold, for example, if monetary policy is conducted so as to maintain some given level of economic activity.

Appendix 2.6.A1   Residential Market Values, Property Tax Liability and Tax Capitalisation

INTRODUCTION

The purpose of this appendix is twofold: to examine the economic determinants of housing market values and property tax liability using the residential location framework of Alonso (1964) and Muth (1969); and to investigate the capitalisation of local property taxes using data for three classifications of variables: housing attributes; environmental–locational proxies; and levels of local government expenditure.

The conclusions are:

(1)   that price and rateable value are not determined by the same variables;
(2)   that rateable value is determined by different attributes from price in each taxing authority, indicating that it is not identical to the rental value of a dwelling but is arbitrarily determined;
(3)   that rates are a regressive form of taxation in that a lower-priced dwelling pays more in proportion to its value in rates than a higher-priced dwelling and that they are inequitable in that they vary for any given type of dwelling across local authorities;
(4)   and that local government expenditures do influence the value of dwellings, although the extent and importance of capitalisation of property taxes is not clear.

Residential location theory is based on capital theory which posits that in a perfect market the value of each property will equal the discounted sum of the expected net value of the flow of housing services generated by the property over time. That is, each property is a capital asset that is valued because it yields a flow of services over its capital life. This approach introduces several difficulties, however, in that the quantities of housing services and their prices, as developed in the theory of residential location, are not directly observable data. Thus in empirical analysis the market value for each property is related to the observable, measurable attributes of the housing stock. One way of doing this is through cross-section price-specification regressions. Data on such characteristics which are normally quantitative attributes do not necessarily represent the full complexity of residential services emanating from a house at a particular location. For example, two houses identical in a quantitative sense in the same neighbourhood are objectively the same, but they may differ in qualitative terms. If the choice of observable data does not implicitly or explicitly incorporate this type of information the effectiveness of estimation will be reduced. None the less, the attribute approach as a proxy for residential housing services, when appropriately specified, appears to capture a significant proportion of the variation in residential-housing market values.

The capitalisation of property taxes in the values of houses is dependent upon the incidence of such taxes and the extent of capitalisation of benefits derived from local government expenditure financed by these taxes. The effective incidence of property taxes is comprised of two effects: as a tax on land it falls on landowners since land is in fixed supply and the full level of taxation will be capitalised; as a tax on buildings it falls on the consumers of housing services. Such taxes may be shifted to capital since it will reduce the returns from investment but it is usual to assume that the effect in reducing the real return to capital is relatively small. Owner-occupiers thus bear all property taxes on their properties since they are both landowners and consumers of housing.

The incidence of rates and benefits are separate and distinct to the extent that property taxes are not a good user's charge — an individual's tax liability does not necessarily coincide with the level of consumption of specific services. Thus it is the difference between the level of taxation and benefit from expenditure which is capitalised and will vary between dwellings.

DATA

Two sets of housing data are used: cross-section data from a survey of estate agents in the Greater London area conducted for the Local Government Finance Project in December 1974, and cross-section data for local authorities in England from the Inland Revenue Purchase Docket (PD) forms for existing and new housing sold in the fourth quarter of 1974. The Inland Revenue data is analysed by London boroughs, counties and metropolitan districts.

The only attributes which can be used as proxies for housing services, and introduced into the regression analysis, are those on the house-description sheets which restrict them to those of a quantitative nature. In the estate agents' survey the variables are:

PRICE:	Sale (asking) price of the dwelling.
RATVAL:	Rateable value of the property.
BEDRMS:	Number of bedrooms.
BATHRMS:	Number of bathrooms.
RECRMS:	Number of reception rooms.
TOTALRMS:	Sum of *BEDRMS*, *BATHRMS* and *RECRMS*.
SQFTAGE:	Floor area in square feet.
GARAGE:	Size of garage by number of cars held.
GARDEN:	The size or existence of a garden.
TYPE:	Type of dwelling, i.e. semi-detached, detached, bungalow, or terrace house.
TENURE:	Freehold or leasehold tenure.
CENTREAT:	Central-heating installation.

Three additional variables — *RAIL*, *BUSRT*, and *PARKS* — are included by locating the houses by address and determining the distance in miles from them to the nearest rail/underground station, bus routes and parks.

The data from the Inland Revenue PD forms are rather more limited in quantitative attributes than is the case for the estate agents' survey:

PRICE:	Sale price of the dwelling.
RATVAL:	Rateable value of the property.

AGE: Age of the dwelling: pre-1919, 1919—44, 1945—60, 1961—70,
              1971 or later.
TYPE: Type of dwelling: bungalow, inter-terrace, end-terrace, semi-detached,
              detached.
SQMTRS: Floor area in square metres.
BEDRMS: Number of bedrooms.

There are two additional dummy variables which indicate whether a garage is
included (*GARAGE*) and whether the property is leasehold (*LEASEHLD*). Since
the Inland Revenue data are identified only to the borough/district level individual cases cannot be examined which eliminates the possibility of calculating
distance variables on a case-by-case basis.

The Inland Revenue data are utilised to obtain a more broadly based data set
which will accommodate the inclusion of 'environmental' and expenditure data
in the equations, thereby extending the study of house-price determination and
facilitating the investigation of capitalisation of local property taxes. To this end
twenty additional variables or groups of variables are considered.

Two variables are obtained from the 1971 Census which can be utilised as
proxies for environmental, locational, or qualitative characteristics:

OWNOCC: Percentage of private households which are owner-occupied.
SEG: Socio-economic group index.

The *SEG* index is comprised of the seventeen socio-economic groups which
are aggregated into seven groups as in the Census. These groups are then banded
into 'upper', 'middle', and 'lower' groups. The percentage comprising the middle
band is fairly constant in all boroughs, roughly 50 per cent of the total. Therefore *SEG* is defined as the ratio of the upper to the lower band.

Five additional variables for the London boroughs sample are taken from the
1971 *Annual Abstract of Greater London Statistics*, published by the GLC.

DENSITY: Population density per acre.
PARKS: Public open areas, in acres.
INDRV   Industrial and utility rateable value as a percentage of total rateable
              value in the borough.
SMOKE: Pollution index for smoke content in the atmosphere in micrograms
              per cubic meter (yearly average).
SULDIOX: Pollution index for sulphur dioxide content in the atmosphere in
              micrograms per cubic metre (yearly average).

Data on education expenditure and pupil—teacher ratios are taken from *Education Statistics — 1974—75 Estimates* published by the Chartered Institute of
Public Finance and Accountancy (CIPFA, July 1974). Detailed data are available
for all authorities except the Inner London Boroughs, where the Inner London
Education Authority (ILEA) reports average values for all the boroughs:

PED: Estimated costs per pupil of primary education.
SED: Estimated costs per pupil of secondary education.
TED: Total cost of education per pupil derived by averaging *PED* and *SED*.
PPTR: Primary pupil—teacher ratio.
SPTR: Secondary pupil—teacher ratio.
TPTR: Total pupil—teacher ratio, derived by averaging *PPTR* and *SPTR*.

Local government expenditure and rates are obtained from the *Return of Rates and Rates Levied per Head of Population (England and Wales) 1974–75* published by CIPFA (July 1974). Four categories of expenditure, expressed as estimated expenditure per head of population are utilised:

LIB: Public libraries, museums, and art galleries.
CLIB: Public libraries, museums and art galleries at county level.
PKS: Parks and open spaces.
RC: Refuse collection and disposal.
SS: Social services.
CSS: Social services at the county level.

Aggregates comprised of various combinations of these categories of expenditure are also utilised: *TEXP*, total expenditure defined as the sum of the *LIB*, *PKS*, *RC* and *SS*; *TCEXP*, the sum of *CLIB* and *CSS*; *PEXB*, the sum of *LIB* and *PKS*; and *NEXP*, the sum of *RC* and *SS*.

RP, the rate poundage levied in each authority is also taken from this source.

HOUSING MARKET VALUES AND PROPERTY TAX LIABILITY

Regression analysis is performed on five subsets of data from the estate agents' survey which correspond to London boroughs or sets of boroughs — two outer London boroughs, Bromley and Croydon, and nine inner London boroughs, Kensington and Chelsea and Lambeth separately, and Camden, Greenwich, Hammersmith, Lewisham, Southwark, Wandsworth and Westminster which are aggregated into one subset, Inner London Boroughs (7) (*INLB*7).

The procedure is to regress all independent variables against the two dependent variables, *PRICE* and *RATVAL*, using a step-wise inclusion method in which the independent variables are entered only if they meet certain statistical criteria. The order of inclusion is determined by the respective contribution of each variable to explained variance. The cut-off point for each equation is determined by the lowest value of the coefficient of variation attained.

A major determinant of house price, or of rateable value, is obviously the size of the property. Our data permit four possible measures of size: the first utilised the variables *BEDRMS*, *BATHRMS*, and *RECRMS*, the second, *TOTALRMS*, the third, *SQFTAGE*, and the fourth, *SQFTAGE* and *BATHRMS*.

A comparison of the *PRICE* equations for all five samples best highlights the differences among them. First, *BEDRMS*, *BATHRMS*, *RECRMS*, *TOTALRMS* and *SQFTAGE* enter their respective equations with a positive sign although not always statistically significant. With the exception of Bromley one or more of the above variables does not enter or does so at a statistically insignificant level. This could be due to the inter-relatedness of these variables as indicated by their correlation coefficients. None is sufficiently great to cause problems of extreme collinearity (the 0.8 to 1.0 range) but the degree of inter-relatedness is sufficiently important to question the validity of the coefficients, especially in the first equation. If multi-collinearity is present, the precision of estimation falls so that it becomes very difficult to disentangle the relative influences of the independent variables. The assumption of minimum variance estimators is no longer valid. This is not of crucial importance in the present study since we are interested in the signs and not the magnitude of the coefficients.

Of the remaining variables, *TENURE*, *GARAGE*, *CENTHEAT*, *BUSRT* and

PARKS enter with the same sign in each sample. *TENURE* enters only in Croydon equations (1) and (2) (negative and insignificant), being a constant for Bromley and Lambeth and not entering into the two other samples, indicating that a house with freehold tenure is more expensive than one with leasehold tenure. *GARAGE* is positive and significant in all equations for Bromley, Croydon and Lambeth. *CENTHEAT* is likewise positive but is significant only in Bromley, equations (3) and (4). The distance variables *BUSRT* and *PARKS* enter as negative values. The values of the coefficients for these variables are fairly stable in each sample. *GARAGE* is not only stable within each sample but across the samples as well. The remaining three variables — *TYPE*, *RAIL* and *GARDEN* — enter with different signs in the different samples. The sign of the coefficient for *TYPE* varies because of the ordering given to the dummy variable in conjunction with the distribution of types of houses in each borough.

In all five samples *PRICE* increases as one progresses from terraced to detached houses. Ignoring sign, the coefficient on *TYPE* is both stable within and across the samples. Being a distance variable *RAIL* might have entered the equations with a negative sign but such is not the case with the Croydon sample. There could be several explanations for this; there may be a nuisance factor involved due to the noise causing houses near to stations to be of lower price; Croydon may to a certain extent be a self-contained community with industrial, commercial and residential facilities which would eliminate the need for transport into central London for many local residents; or car ownership may be higher in outer London boroughs thus minimising the importance of the distance to stations.

By aggregating the data into two larger samples, outer London boroughs (*OLB*), comprised of the Bromley and Croydon samples, and inner London boroughs (*INLB9*), consisting of Kensington and Chelsea, Lambeth and the seven boroughs in the inner London boroughs (7) sample, the coefficients of the distance variables confirm a pattern which is only partly evident in the individual borough samples. For the outer London boroughs sample *RAIL* and *BUSRT* enter into each of the four equations with a positive sign whereas in the inner London boroughs (9) sample they enter with a negative sign. Therefore in outer London the proximity of public transport does not increase the value of a house as is the case in inner London. The nuisance factor is still present in both samples although to a lesser extent in *INLB9* since rail transport is for the most part below ground level. Bromley is basically a residential area for central London workers, as opposed to Croydon which is a more self-contained community, and could conceivably have different transport needs, but the equations do not substantiate this. Car ownership, road congestion and availability of parking is most likely to be the cause of the difference in sign between the samples.

The third variable which changes sign is *GARDEN*, entering with a negative coefficient in the inner London boroughs (7) sample. Again, looking at the aggregated samples, *GARDEN* has a positive coefficient in all equations for *OLB* and a negative coefficient for *INLB9*. This change is possibly due to the difference in definitions of the variable in the two samples: in the *OLB* sample *GARDEN* is measured in acres whereas in the *INLB9* sample it is a dummy variable with a value of (1) if a house has a garden and (0) if not. Returning to the *INLB7* sample 93 per cent of the cases have a garden. However, all those cases not reporting a garden are located in Westminster and thus the variable could be proxying for a locational or environmental attribute. The sign on the coefficient would therefore indicate that a house located in Westminster would be valued higher than a similar house in one of the other boroughs included in the sample.

In comparing the results of the best-fitting equations in each sample, the R^2 or percentage of variation explained diminishes as the mean price of the sample increases:

Borough	Mean Price (£)	R^2
Bromley	35,676 (4)	0.58 (4)
Croydon	26,726 (1)	0.79 (1)
Kensington and Chelsea	52,047 (5)	0.35 (5)
Lambeth	29,278 (2)	0.71 (2)
INLB7	32,948 (3)	0.64 (3)

This relationship between *PRICE* and R^2 may be due to the type of variables which are included in the regression equations as opposed to those omitted and represented in the error term. In general form the four equations can be written as:

$$P = a + d_1 Q_1 + d_2 Q_2 + \ldots d_n Q_n + u$$

where P is *PRICE*, a is a constant, d_1 to d_n coefficients, Q_1 to Q_n the independent variables and u the error term. The independent variables are all of a quantitative nature − total number of rooms, garages, size of gardens − which can explain only a certain percentage of the variation. The error term reflects the influences of omitted variables, measurement errors, and random variation. Assuming that there is no measurement bias the error term is:

$$u = b_1 q_1 + b_2 q_2 + \ldots + b_m q_m + b_n E + m \qquad (m = n - 1)$$

where b_1 to b_n are the coefficients, q_1 to q_m the qualitative and omitted quantitative variables, E an environmental variable, and m a random error. The qualitative variables would include indicators of the quality of construction and finishing work, modernity of kitchen and bathrooms, fully tiled bathrooms and the like; the environment variable would be an index of the quality of the neighbourhood. As the price of houses increases the qualitative variables are likely to have an increasing influence on *PRICE* since the quality of a house normally increases with its price. This is indicated by the relationship between *PRICE* and R^2. The sample with the lowest mean *PRICE*, Croydon, and thus least influenced by the qualitative variables in the error terms is also the sample for which the equations best fit the data. This relationships is valid for all five samples: R^2 decreases as *PRICE* and the influence of the qualitative variables increase.

DETERMINANTS OF RATEABLE VALUE

In the Bromley sample the *RATVAL* equations are similar to the *PRICE* equations − the same variables enter both sets of equations with the same signs except for *GARDEN*, which does not enter any of the *RATVAL* equations, and *BUSRT* which enters these with a positive sign. The degree of collinearity between variables is low although *RECRMS* is statistically insignificant in the first equation, due possibly to its relatedness to *BEDRMS*.

The equations for the Croydon sample differ from those for *PRICE*. Although there is a high degree of inter-relatedness among the variables *RECRMS* enters with a positive and significant coefficient which it did not in the *PRICE* equations. A second distinction is that *BUSRT* rather than *RAIL* enters and with a negative sign.

Although there is little evidence of collinearity between variables in the Kensington and Chelsea sample, two of the room variables *BEDRMS* and *RECRMS*, are insignificant in the first equation, and *BATHRMS* does not enter. It is unlikely that house size is not a determinant of rateable value in this sample since both *TOTALRMS* and *SQFTAGE* enter at a statistically significant level in their respective equations.

In the Lambeth sample the *RATVAL* equations are again similar to those for *PRICE*. In the first equation only *BATHRMS* enter due to collinearity problems with *BEDRMS* and *RECRMS*. Two additional variables, *TYPE* and *BUSRT* enter equations (1), and (1) and (2), respectively although not at a significant level. The fourth equation terminated with *SQFTAGE* as its only explanatory variable as was the case with *PRICE*.

Finally in the *INLB*7 sample the same problems arise as were found in the *PRICE* equations – probable multi-collinearity and a negative sign on *GARDEN*.

Problems of multi-collinearity among the variables were dealt with in relation to the *PRICE* equations. The conclusions reached at that point in the analysis are equally valid for the *RATVAL* equations and will not be repeated. Of the variables which do not enter consistently with the same sign the coefficients on *TYPE* and *GARDEN* vary for the same reasons as in the *PRICE* equations. Instead of *RAIL* altering its sign, however, it is *BUSRT* in the *RATVAL* equations which varies, having a positive (and insignificant) coefficient for Croydon and *INLB*7. Where the samples are pooled the sign of *BUSRT* is negative in all four equations for *INLB*9 and positive in equations (3) and (4) in the *OLB* sample, as is the case with the *PRICE* equations, but negative in equations (1) and (2), altering the pattern found in the *PRICE* equations.

The values of the coefficients are highly stable within each of the samples, varying by only a few pounds from the mean value of the coefficient. However, they are very unstable across the samples. To the extent that these variations reflect different percentages of the mean *RATVAL* of each sample, this stability across the five samples may indicate the non-conformity of valuation of housing attributes in different valuation areas.

In comparing the results of the best-fitting equation in each sample the R^2 or percentage of variation explained is not as closely related to the mean value of the dependent variable as was true with the *PRICE* equations:

Borough	Mean RATVAL (£)		R^2	
Bromley	519.65	(3)	0.48	(1)
Croydon	504.67	(2)	0.79	(5)
Kensington and Chelsea	1115.55	(5)	0.64	(4)
Lambeth	446.18	(1)	0.54	(2)
INLB7	640.06	(4)	0.59	(3)

Nor does it appear to depend upon the variability of the dependent variable or the independent variables *SQFTAGE* and *TOTALRMS* as indicated by their standard deviations relative to their means in each sample. It is often the case that the greater the variability of the data the better the fit of the regression line. In terms of the influence of omitted variables it cannot be qualitative variables alone which affect the explanatory power of the equations since the results differ so markedly from those for the *PRICE* equations. There is a possibility that locational and environmental variables are having a stronger influence than in the *PRICE* equations, but what they may be cannot readily be seen from the results. To the extent that the valuation of a house is a subjective measure of the value of a house, however, based upon observation rather than market forces, those attributes taken into consideration in the appraisal will vary from one valuation to another. Such non-standard valuation procedures would account for the previous results.

In comparing the *PRICE* and *RATVAL* equations there appear to be few differences between them. Nearly the same variables enter any one equation in both sets and usually with the same sign. No one type of equation best explains *PRICE* or *RATVAL* in all five samples, although the *SQFTAGE* and *SQFTAGE–BATHRMS* equations are best in four of the *RATVAL* samples and in three of the *PRICE* samples. The distinction which does emerge is that *PRICE* and *RATVAL* are not necessarily determined by the same variables in any one sample. *PRICE* being market determined, the variables enter consistently in each equation for each sample. Since *RATVAL* is subjectively determined, however, the variables which enter are arbitrarily chosen. By examining the valuation ratio, *LRATIO*, defined as *RATVAL* divided by *PRICE*, it is evident that the relationship between *PRICE* and *RATVAL* varies among the samples:

Borough	LRATIO
Bromley	0.0150
Croydon	0.0186
Kensington and Chelsea	0.0196
Lambeth	0.0160
INLB7	0.0193

RATVAL is not a constant proportion of *PRICE* which lends support to the proposition that *PRICE* and *RATVAL* are not determined by the same variables in any one sample. Regressions with *LRATIO* as the dependent variable for the five samples yield significant equations for all samples except Kensington and Chelsea. In the other four samples with *PRICE* as the independent variable each equation contains a positive constant and a negative and statistically significant coefficient on *PRICE*. This indicates that the proportion of the value of the house utilised as the rate base is not constant but negatively related to *PRICE*.

The London estate agents' survey consists of a random sample of estate agents listed in the London telephone directories. Due to the nature of the sample, however, the assumption of randomness may not be valid. The samples are restricted in size since a large number of house-description sheets do not include data concerning one or many of the variables that are included in the analysis. A bias is introduced if there is a certain type of house or price-range of house and a certain set of housing characteristics included on the description sheets associated with any one estate agent. The Inland Revenue data for London are thus utilised to provide a broader and statistically better data base and to allow the inclusion of qualitative/environmental and expenditure variables.

The sample for each borough from the Inland Revenue data is weighted according to the percentage of owner-occupied housing in each borough *vis-à-vis* London as a whole, and aggregated into three subsamples: all London boroughs; the inner boroughs; and the outer boroughs. The housing data from the PD forms is identified at the borough level but the census and expenditure data were available only as borough averages. One approach to the analysis would be to aggregate the housing data to obtain average values for the variables in each borough, making it compatible with the additional data. For such aggregate values to be representative of the data, however, it would be necessary to assume that all housing in a borough is fairly homogeneous and that the average values of variables are representative of the sample as a whole. To retain the amount of information present in the housing data, individual cases in each borough are utilised but the additional variables are entered as the same value for each case in a borough. Therefore borough-level equations can contain only housing data while at more aggregate levels all variables are included. The results of the borough equations are similar to those in the estate agents' survey and will thus not be discussed here.

The all-borough sample contained 2,293 cases. In the *PRICE* equations the housing variables – *AGE*, *TYPE*, *LEASEHLD*, and *GARAGE* – are regressed against the dependent variable and then the environmental variables are introduced. In this sample either *OWNOCC* or *SEG* is utilised plus *DENSITY*, *PARKS*, *INDRV*, *SMOKE* and *SULDIOX*. The results confirm the pattern found previously. The housing characteristics variables which enter do so with a positive sign as well: as population density increases so do land values and pollution levels. While not being statistically related these three variables are taking into account similar influences. *PARKS* is also positive; *INDRV* is negative in two equations and positive in a third. The negative relationship appears more reasonable in that the greater the proportion of rateable property comprised of industry, the lower the quality of the area. The positive sign in the third equation appears to be due to the inter-relatedness of *SEG* and *INDRV* causing a sign reversal.

The results for the inner London boroughs are broadly similar to those for London as a whole. The housing attribute variables are positive except for *TYPE* which is negative in the *PRICE* equations, penalising larger dwellings perhaps in conjunction with higher land values in inner-city, more densely populated areas. Again *SEG* is positive and significant while in most equations *OWNOCC* does not enter. Of the five environmental variables – *DENSITY*, *PARKS*, *INDRV*, *SMOKE*, and *SULDIOX* – only the first and the last enter, *DENSITY* with a positive sign and *SULDIOX* with a negative sign. This negative relationship may be taking account of varying levels of pollution within a highly polluted area. Since we are dealing only with the central densely populated area in which all the boroughs have high levels of atmospheric pollution, an area with somewhat less pollution would be preferable.

In both samples the explanatory power of the equation and its level of statistical significance were increased with the addition of the qualitative/environmental variables. Additionally, as the field of reference is narrowed from all boroughs and to the inner boroughs, and finally to individual boroughs, the explanatory power of the equations increased. This is due to the fact that housing characteristics, qualitative attributes and, especially, locational and environmental characteristics are area specific.

An additional result of the London study is evidence that rates are in fact a regressive tax. In a simple regression equation with *LRATIO* as the dependent variable and *PRICE* as the independent variable the intercept is positive and the slope, or coefficient on the independent variable, negative for each borough sample, indicating a negative relationship between the two variables. If the liability ratio is calculated for intervals of house prices the results are similar

Table 2.6.A1. *National economic planning regions. The regions corresponding to the national economic planning regions, excluding the GLC and the metropolitan areas.*

Region 2
Avon, Cornwall, Devon, Dorset, Gloucester, Somerset, Wiltshire.

Region 3
Cambridgeshire, Norfolk, Suffolk.

Region 4
Befordshire, Berkshire, Buckinghamshire, East Sussex, Essex, Hampshire, Hertfordshire, Kent, Oxfordshire, Surrey, West Sussex.

Region 5
Cleveland, Cumbria, Durham, Northumberland.

Region 6
Humberside, North Yorkshire.

Region 7
Cheshire, Lancashire.

Region 8
Derby, Leicestershire, Lincolnshire, Northamptonshire, Nottinghamshire.

Region 9
Hereford and Worcester, Salop, Staffordshire, Warwickshire.

Note: The data for the regions was collected at the county and county district levels and aggregated into the eight regions. These are numbered 2–9 to be consistent with the national economic planning regions.

with lower-valued dwellings paying a higher percentage of their value in rates than more expensive dwellings. Additionally, the liability ratio for any one price band varies from borough to borough, increasing the inequity of the rating system in spite of the fact that all valuations are calculated by a central authority, the Inland Revenue (see Table 2.6.A1).

The same procedure was followed for the counties and the metropolitan districts using the housing data only, with broadly similar results for each sample.

CAPITALISATION

To determine the extent of capitalisation of local taxes and expenditures, it is necessary to examine both the capitalisation of rates and the level of benefit derived from local services.

Benefits are difficult to determine since some index of quality of output is necessary. Due to the nature of local government services, however, such an index is extremely difficult to formulate. In its place, a specification of inputs is used but this is not an adequate indication of the benefits derived from expenditure. Typically the data used is expenditure per unit of service provided, ignoring the other inputs.

The first area of expenditure examined is education expenditure, the largest single item of expenditure in a local authority's budget. The initial set of variables considered are PED, SED, TED – primary, secondary and total expenditure per pupil. This is not an adequate indication of quality since the most important input, the quality of the pupils, is not known. Thus one authority could be spending more per pupil than another and yet be producing more poorly educated students. An attempt is made to overcome this difficulty by utilising pupil–teacher ratios – primary, secondary and total – *PPTR*, *SPTR*, *TPTR* – but again this formulation is comprised of quantities and not the quality of the input and is directly related to levels of expenditure.

The other services considered are expenditures per head of population on libraries and museums, refuse collection, parks and social services and combinations of these variables. All of these variables suffer from inadequate specification of quality of service.

With the Inland Revenue outer London borough sample, educational expenditure and pupil–teacher ratios were introduced. The housing variables are not discussed since all the variables enter with a positive sign and are statistically significant. The same qualitative–environmental variables were entered as before but only *SMOKE* and *SEG* in the *SQMTRS* equation are significant. The education variables are entered separately. In the *SQMTRS* equations for *PRICE*, *PED* and *TED* enter positively and significantly implying that an increase in educational expenditure per pupil increases the value of the dwelling. Likewise *PPTR* and *TPTR* enter their respective equations negatively and significantly so that a deterioration in the pupil–teacher ratio adversely affects house values. *SPTR* enters its equation positively and insignificantly but it is the last variable to enter the equation in the step-wise inclusion method and may thus be compensating for the influence of the other variables. In the *BEDRMS* equations only *TED* and *SPTR* enter significantly but with a positive sign. *SED* and *TPTR* are also positive but statistically insignificant. This switch in sign indicates relatedness among the variables which compensate for one another depending upon the order in which they enter the equation.

The last set of variables to be considered are the levels of local government expenditure – *LIB*, *PKS*, *RC*, *SS*, *TEXP*, *PEXP* and *NEXP*. Due to the interrelatedness of these variables, the level of collinearity with the previous qualitative–environmental variables, and the low level of relatedness with the dependent variables, the individual expenditure levels cannot be utilised. In an attempt to overcome these problems the expenditure variables are aggregated – *PEXP*, *NEXP* and *TEXP* – but their signs and level of significance continue to vary according to the other variables in the equation.

The data for the metropolitan districts is aggregated, first into the six metropolitan areas and secondly into one sample comprised of all six areas to permit inclusion of education expenditure data. The results for the housing variables alone are similar to those previously obtained and will not be analysed here.

In the Greater Manchester sample the educational variables are highly interrelated and thus only one can be used in any one equation. Four of the six education variables enter the equation: *PED*, positively and significantly; and the three ratios, each negatively and significantly. The expenditure variables are also highly inter-related and can only be introduced individually. Only *PKS* and *RC* are not multi-collinear with the three pupil–teacher ratios, but only *PKS* enters the equation – positively and significantly.

In the Merseyside sample, only *PED* and *TED* enter the equation but they are insignificant. All of the expenditure variables are highly correlated with one another and with the education variables. When introduced separately the expenditure variables do not enter the equation. None of these variables has influence in this sample.

In the South Yorkshire sample low levels of inter-relatedness allow groups of the education and expenditure variables to be included in one equation. Two sets of equations are tested — the first with *SED*; the second with *SPTR* — plus *TEXP*, *PEXP*, or *NEXP*. *SED* enters negatively and *SPTR* positively. The three expenditure variables each have a positive sign in the first set of equations and a negative sign in the second. The non-housing variables are the last three to enter each of the equations so it appears that multi-collinearity may again be causing changes in signs.

In Tyne and Wear the education variables do enter the equations. Several of the expenditure variables are not highly correlated, however, and can thus be entered in groups. In each case, however, they are statistically insignificant and all (*LIB, RC, SS, TEXP, PEXP, NEXP*) have a negative sign. *PKS* enters positively.

In the West Midlands sample *PED*, *SPTR*, *PPTR* and *PKS* are the only variables which influence the equation. All are statistically significant and all negative except for *PED* and *PKS*.

Aggregating the six metropolitan areas into one sample does not improve the results. Similar problems with multi-collinearity are encountered while the explanatory power of the equation is not as great as for the individual samples. To test whether this is due to several of the metropolitan areas being amalgamations of previously unrelated local authorities, the Greater Manchester, Merseyside and West Midlands areas which are characterised by a high degree of relatedness before the reorganisation of local government in 1974, are aggregated into a single sample. The results, however, do not differ from those previously obtained.

The data for the counties is aggregated into eight regions (see Table 2.6.A1), and again the education and other local expenditure variables are introduced into the equation. The education variables produce mixed results. In half the cases the coefficient is insignificant. In half of the remaining cases the variable enters with the opposite sign to that in the previous samples. This may be caused by there being too few observations of education expenditure and pupil—teacher ratios which vary only county to county. The best results are in those regions which contain a large number of counties.

The regional data provide the largest data base for the inclusion of the local services expenditure variable, including *CLIB*, *CSS* and *TCEXP*. The signs of the coefficients, however, are for the most part either all positive or all negative depending upon the region. The pattern which emerges is that for those regions which include a metropolitan area, the signs are positive and for those containing only rural counties the signs are negative.

The evidence as to the capitalisation of local government expenditure is inconclusive. The correlation coefficients between *PRICE* and the independent variables are of correct sign, but when entered into a regression equation problems of multi-collinearity make the coefficients unreliable. Tentatively it can be stated that education expenditure per pupil is positively related to *PRICE*, as is expenditure on libraries and parks, but the use of such expenditure levels per head of population are not adequate indicators of benefits derived from local government expenditure.

These results are similar to those found by Oates (1969) in his study of the effects of property taxes and local government expenditure on property values in the USA.

7 The Role of Central Government

In Part One, Chapter 2 two polar opposites of central and local relations were outlined: those of fiscal federalism and the agency theory of government. Both were admitted to be unreal. There is no example of pure federalism, and a straightforward comparison between a large firm and government misses important differences between the two. Again the polar notion that central government controls local government, even allowing the latter some freedom of action but only that given by central government, is as unreal a description of actual relationships between central and local government as is pure federalism.

Under pure federalism, central government would have no function towards local government. This follows from the definition of pure federalism as a state in which central and local governments are 'co-ordinate and independent'. Again by definition, even the decision as to which functions each should perform is the province of some supra-government to which both central and local government are subordinate.

In Part One, Chapter 3, the argument presented on the division of labour between central and local government suggested that central government would be better suited to providing what used to be called onerous, but which we prefer to call redistributive and paternalistic, public goods. Local government would be better suited to the provision of beneficial goods — both public goods and spatial monopoly goods (though there were examples even of these which might be better provided at the national level — public goods because their benefits extended so far and spatial monopoly goods because there were national economies of scale in production). We found that the actual division of labour bore little relation to this. Although there were traces of the influence of such ideas — as one would expect from the prominence given long ago to the distinction between onerous and beneficial — the effect of historical accident and contrivance seem to have been far greater.

While the framework developed in that chapter is therefore more normative than descriptive, and thus primarily for Part Four, it also has its consequences for our analysis here. Central government interferes in local government for three respectable reasons, which is to say the constitution departs from that of pure federalism for three such reasons. The seeds of all are to be found in that seminal quotation from J. S. Mill in Part One, Chapter 2, p. 51.

(1) First there is interference by central government merely to improve or ginger up local government. As Mill puts it, the excuse for this is superior intelligence and knowledge. One can add the argument of countervailing power. Even if central government were not superior, an external force scrutinising local government would make it less likely to sink into inertia and inefficiency. The

difficulty with pressing this too far is that it presumes a disinterestedness in central government which hardly seems reasonable. The apparatus that central government has set up to improve productivity and get value for money has — from the Chadwickian inspectorates on — also been used to influence local policy as central government wishes.

(2)   Secondly, there are what economists call intergovernmental externalities. Frequently mentioned in the theory of local government finance, they find less place in practical investigations. Such an externality exists when the costs and benefits relating to a decision to be made by one government do not all pertain to citizens of that government. The literature is full of examples of theoretical interest but of limited importance. Two neighbouring jurisdictions share a mosquito-ridden lake. The health of the one depends in part on the action of the other to keep down mosquitoes (Buchanan, 1968, ch. 2). An efficient solution requires the governments to negotiate, or that their actions be otherwise constrained, so that they act jointly.

(3)   In as much as local authorities are agents of central government in the provision of beneficial, redistributive or paternalistic services, one would expect central government to intervene just as any headquarters would interfere with its divisions in the hope of achieving greater efficiency in the realisation of the headquarter's objectives.

We cannot hope to settle how far central intervention is to be explained in terms of one or other of these 'respectable' motives or how far it is itself a result of confusion and muddle. At the end of Part One, Chapter 2, however, we said that one of the most difficult questions in local government finance was to decide how much freedom local government had from central government, not in theory but in practice (Griffith, 1966, pp. 49—94). In the next chapter, we shall be considering central government's interest in local government in relation to macroeconomic policy. In this chapter we shall concentrate on what signs we can establish of the extent to which local government acts independently of central government. Our results are modest but they may be useful in indicating what is relevant in this highly charged and contentious area.

To prove there is more rather than less freedom for local government is not to show that the federal principle is more powerful than the unitary or agency principle or vice versa. As well as the negative freedom that results from a clear demarcation between the roles of central and local government, there is the delegated freedom of action a superior may give a subordinate. This second freedom is revocable at the will of the superior. The first implies a right to freedom which, as under a federal system, persists until the supra-government alters the situation. By analogy, the statutory freedom of action a local government enjoys until Parliament alters the law is negative or 'federal' in spirit. The freedom a local government has at the discretion of a minister until he or his department changes its mind is more conveniently described as delegated freedom.[1]

In the next section we extend the theory of agency government (1) to develop the notion of delegated freedom, but (2) to show how far the agency theory seems to fit the facts of British local government. Recognising that the aims and methods of central government change frequently, we list the major instruments central government uses to influence local authorities and then examine the change in instruments used over time in one service – education. Finally, we look for signs of freedom – negative or delegated – in expenditure on education.

THE ORGANISATION OF GOVERNMENT

The agency theory of local government is far less well developed than the federal. In the 1930s Luther Gulick suggested government should model itself on a decentralised firm (Gulick, 1937; see also Williamson, 1967). His models were some of the largest firms of the time, such as General Motors or Dupont, already decentralised as holding companies. He argued that government should also be organised with divisions or subsidiaries. Central government should lay down policy for these largely autonomous divisions whose job should be to take day-to-day decisions executing these policies.

Under Roosevelt, Gulick was himself influential in helping establish the still characteristic form of American government, where the executives of domestic central government tend to be relatively small while the daily business of government is transacted by comparatively independent large agencies. The distinction between 'policy' and 'day-to-day management' on which this division of labour is supposed to rest is logically untenable (Foster, 1973, pp. 15–16). Yet it has proved useful on both sides of the Atlantic. In Britain the decentralised agency is far less common in the mainstream of government than in the USA – though there are exceptions such as the Supplementrary Benefits Commission or the Manpower Services Commission. However, there is a parallel. The same distinction between policy and everyday management has been attempted as a basis for separating the powers of minister over nationalised industries from the powers of the boards of those industries. The very imprecision of the distinction has helped to give it a long life.

In Gulick's scheme, the functions of central government were summed up in the acronym POSDCORB – planning, organising, staffing, directing, co-ordinating, reporting and budgeting (Gulick, 1937, p. 13). Decentralised bodies were set up on a basis reflecting their Purpose, Clientele, Process and Place, aiming at as much homogeneity in all these as possible. Thus there was a presumption against an authority with too many purposes, though this might be mitigated if its activities were concentrated in one place – like the local authority or the Tennessee Valley Authority or the Highlands and Islands Development Board – or if its clientele was spread throughout the nation but was relatively homogeneous – like the Federal Housing Authority or the Supplementary Benefits Commission.

Even as developed by Gulick, there is a major difference between a private corporation and a central government in these relations with their divisions. Although one can exaggerate the single-mindedness of firms – they have other objectives – financial objectives are normally dominant (Marris, 1964, pp. 46–109). There can be no dispute that the management objectives of government are almost always more complex than those of a private firm, and that because of it the monitoring of government performance is also harder. Naturally this also affects relations between the centre and its divisions, whether central or local.

Divisions within government are more likely to have a plurality of masters than those of firms (Ostrom, 1973, pp. 33–42). Again there is a parallel in private enterprise where the board may reflect different interests and so may not always be sending the same signals down the line; while in the background there are also the interests of the shareholders, workers and managers. But the problem is far greater in government. In a democracy at least there is usually a rapid turnover of masters. Moreover, any division of government knows that others have power besides those with formal responsibility for it. They may be other ministers, the Prime Minister or President, the House of Commons or Congress. Powerful heads of divisions, notoriously, have built up their own practical independence by playing one off against another. Even formally it is far from uncommon for a government division to have responsibilities to more than one superior.

Local government seen as a division introduces another complication. While earlier we have said that an agency theory of government is consistent with local elections, elections still make a difference to the balance of power. We take two cases. In the first, the rulers, central and local, belong to the same party. Though this is not always true we may suppose they share similar objectives. Even then it is a crucial difference that central government cannot dismiss a locally elected representative. He has to be worked with. One must not exaggerate this point. The power of ministers to influence nationalised industries through dismissing their chairman is in practice far less than might appear (Foster, 1973, ch. 7). Even so, dismissal is impossible in democratic local government. If local government is of a different party from central government, its instinct will be to oppose. Assuming central government aims to use local government as its agent, it must rely more on other instruments to get its way. A private firm can get a long way in imposing central will by judicious firing and hiring.

Moreover, the relations between central and local government will be less flexible than those between the headquarters and divisions of a firm. A board can take decisions to discontinue a product, introduce a new one, close down a factory or re-locate it. Despite growing union and other constraints on its actions, it will ordinarily have the formal freedom to take such decisions. By contrast, the relations between central and lower levels of government are more restricted by laws and the rights of various bodies. They are, of course, greater in a federal than in a unitary state – in the USA than in Britain.

If one supposes a central government like that of England in the eighteenth century which scarcely wants to intervene in local affairs, it does not matter whether the form of government is federal or unitary. Local authorities will have practical freedom. If by contrast one assumes a central government which does wish to impose its will and influence the policies of local government, then it will meet opposition from those who disagree with it, even in a highly centralised governmental system, where the lower reaches of the bureaucracy can act as an obstacle. Even within a unitary state, locally elected government will increase the difficulty central government has in getting its own way. The checks and balances of any division of powers between legislature, executive and judiciary or the existence of a federal system with a clearer distinction between the powers of central and local government would further reduce central powers of control.

Whatever the form of government, as its scope and the range of its interests increases, so does the countervailing power of these other interests. Indeed, it becomes harder for central government to get its way whatever its powers. Congestion reduces the time and effort central government can give to any one issue. The result is a paradox. Both minister and officers feel that despite constant complaints at increasing government intervention, their actual ability to get their policies adopted is being progressively reduced. As the business of government grows and affects more interest groups, both central and local government can simultaneously feel their freedom of action diminished.

In such circumstances a number of strategies are open to central government.

(1)   Because a command or request to local authorities becomes a less successful way of achieving central policies, central government multiplies the instruments it can use. The exercise of influence becomes more like a negotiation in which central government to get its way on some matters, is prepared to trade resources or permissions on others. Thus a statutory requirement that a certain course of action by local government requires central government approval becomes a way in which central government can influence not only that course of action, but others through delaying or threatening to withhold permission or resources for something else local government wants. One consequence of this is that it becomes harder to distinguish how a power is used from its apparent purpose. Another, less direct, is that as central government's instruments multiply, so the exact status of some of them becomes open to interpretation. This is particularly true in Britain where the interpretation of most of the statutory powers on which central government relies has never been challenged in the courts. However, there is a severe cost in this multiplication of instruments. More time and effort is needed to deploy them. The administrative cost of central government achieving a given end is likely to grow and add to central government congestion.

(2)   As a result central government is likely to try to simplify its task by reducing the number of local governments or other agencies with which it deals. This is easier in a unitary than in a federal system, though not always easy there as the opposition to the 1974 local government reorganisation in England and Wales showed. Reduction in the number of local governments will simplify its administrative tasks since it has to relate to fewer entities, but at the cost of the people being less able to get what they want from local government because individually they are further distanced from it. (The effect of size on the realisation of local preferences is discussed in Part Four, Chapter 6.)

(3)   Central government will also attempt to give local authorities more freedom where it believes this will have least effect on its influence on policy. The most obvious example of this in Britain has been the gradual withdrawal of detailed financial control. In the nineteenth century when grants were introduced, it was accepted as axiomatic that central public accountability required that central government should scrutinise in detail how each local authority

spent that money. This in practice meant a close interest in how it spent all its money. While this was a powerful means by which the professional interests in central government could influence local government — as we shall see in the next section — it was too cumbrous to be an easy vehicle of ministerial influence. Hence by the 1920s, one already heard the cry that local authorities needed more financial freedom. This argument has been used to support the introduction of block grants, and later their extension to cover more areas of grant.[2] Undoubtedly it has been a particular method of increasing local freedom; but not surprisingly opponents have maintained strongly that despite this, there has been ever greater centralisation.[3] It can be seen as a concession of freedom in one respect to make it administratively easier for central government to find the time and resources to use instruments which are more relevant to policy.

(4)   As expectations of what central government can affect have increased, so it has needed to intervene in more areas of policy. A recent example is that after many years in which the content of the curriculum taught in state schools was not often an issue, in the mid-1970s it suddenly aroused intense interest. The influence of this on the 1977 Green Paper was evident and profound. The Department of Education felt it must influence local authorities on matters previously left to local authorities, as influenced by the teaching profession. It did not want new legislation to give it new powers but reinterpreted old powers to give them this authority. Neither did it want an administrative apparatus to control curricula forever — when it was probable that in a few years political attention would pass on to something else. Hence one heard much then — and in particular in the Green Paper — of the need for central–local relationships to be a flexible partnership.

The Government accept that the dividing line between central and local responsibilities is not always clear. There are many reasons for this. The central/local relationship is changing all the time because national economic and social priorities can alter substantially even within quite short periods. It is not long, for example, since government policy encouraged rapid expansion in local services. Subsequent developments in the economy have meant restrictions on the growth of public expenditure in general and in the local government sector in particular. Nevertheless, the change in emphasis in the relative responsibilities of central and local government remains compatible with a well understood and accepted constitutional relationship. Any formal definition of central and local responsibilities would lack the advantages of flexibility and rapidity of response to new circumstances. It would be likely to break down under the pressure of events. The Government's view is, therefore, that while clarification of responsibilities wherever practicable is desirable, a fundamental redefinition is not necessary as a basis for solving the problems of local government finance. The disadvantages of both the centralist and localist approaches are clear, and the Government do not think there is a case for the adoption of either. (DoE, 1977*b*, Cmnd 6813, para. 2.8)

The most obvious interpretation of this is that central government does not want to define central–local relationships – that is, make any concession to the spirit of federalism – because not only ought central views on policy to predominate but also central government should be able to turn its attention to those policy issues which at any time it holds most important. At other times, on these same issues it may be ready for local government to exercise considerable freedom.

The outcome of all these influences is inevitably complicated, confusing and shifting. Central government wishes to give local authorities more freedom in certain respects to be more effective in getting its way in others. This element in the situation is the freedom of the 'agent' – delegated freedom. But the growth of the scope of government creating congestion within Whitehall and also raising up increasing numbers of pressure groups has reduced the freedom to act, the negative freedom, of central and local government. These obstacles to action have more affinity to the checks and balances of a federal system which also act as obstacles to the free exercise of power by either level of government. What is different is that, in principle at least though far less in practice, the division of labour within a federal system is based on a cool appraisal of what is best done at each level. In Part One, Chapter 3 we showed how hard it was to rationalise the scope of local government in any similar rational way. What we observe is both more confused and shifting – though at any one moment in time we can try to understand which way the system is moving.

CENTRAL GOVERNMENT AND EDUCATION

If the powers of government cannot be defined and are changing both in form and content, then to consider how they are used requires observation over a period of time. We cannot attempt this for all services. Education is, however, by far the most important, accounting for more than 50 per cent of local current expenditure. Central–local relations in education have a long history and illustrate most forms of control. It is also relevant to the exercise we undertake in the last section of this chapter.

The potential power of the state as defined in various statutes has always been extensive in education, even in the nineteenth century. Its first major financial contribution was a £20,000 grant authorised in 1833 to be supervised by the Privy Council, which appointed two inspectors for the purpose in 1835. Possibly, to quote West, 'the State had simply leapt into the saddle of a horse already galloping' (1970, p. 138), as the first objective may well have been merely to support the educational work of the National Society and the British and Foreign Society rather than to take a firm grip of the reins. By 1846, policy had become more directed to influencing the outcome. A Privy Council minute of that year to assist teacher-training colleges awarded certificates to all students who successfully completed the prescribed course. A certified teacher employed by a school inspected by the government and satisfying the inspection was paid one-half of his salary by the government. The outcome was a system of payment by results which made it blatantly obvious to the teaching profession who set the standards and therefore the pattern of expenditure. The first instruments were the inspectorate and grants.

The voluntary system had so far failed to provide universal elementary education. As Cannan put it

the State, seeing the goodness of the working endeavoured to assist and encourage it . . . at last finding that the voluntary system was never likely to be thoroughly effective in particular parts of the country, it enacted that rates should be levied where the voluntary system had failed to provide adequate schools — the natural and inevitable result soon followed: voluntary effort slackened and now provides for only a trifling proportion of the whole expenditure incurred. (1927, p. 136)

This second stage where central government sought to persuade all local authorities to provide education was initiated by the 1870 Forster Education Act. The Elementary Education Act of 1870 also divided the country into school districts (consisting of municipal boroughs and parishes) and introduced the principle that the grant was to be allocated in relation to both resources and needs. Even where local authorities were unwilling, the government did not accept full responsibility for the financial burden it had imposed upon them. The districts were to be supervised by school boards elected by local ratepayers, whose duty it was to ensure that sufficient accommodation was provided for all children up to the age of 13, either by the voluntary organisations or by the boards themselves (Keith-Lucas, 1952, pp. 213—18). Government grants contributed the major share of expenditure by school boards (93%), while rates provided the rest (7%). Section 97 of the Act introduced the principle referred to above, in that special account was to be given to areas with below-average resources by paying each local authority which failed to produce 7s 6d per scholar (the unit of need) from the product of a 3d rate, the difference between this sum and the amount raised. The main body of the grant was distributed in relation to the number of pupils and teachers.

Many historians of the period emphasise the continuing role of the state as a mere source of subsidies with very little interference in the determination of the quality or quantity of service. This opinion discounts one important means of intrusion which the provision of grants, and the consequent spending of public monies, introduce; namely, the requirement that each local authority must achieve a prescribed standard of efficiency in the provision of the service to be eligible for a subsidy. As Cannan points out,

the general principle of the terms of partnership between the State and the localities in regard to education has been that the State should pay definite sums for definite quantities of particular services — for example, so many shillings for each child taught such and such subjects to the satisfaction of the inspectors — while the locality makes up the balance. (1927, p. 137)

Indeed the 1871 Code gave each school 6s per pupil for attendance, and 4s for passing in all of reading, writing and arithmetic — the three Rs — plus a further 3s for some additional subjects (Eaglesham, 1956, p. 12). At this period we see grant used quite specifically for central government to buy education from local authorities. Central government set the standards. If these were not reached, the money was not paid. To an economist with a prejudice in favour of specific grants which are a price for services rendered this has great attractions.

The system of *ad hoc* school boards was abolished by the Act of 1902 when the counties and county boroughs (established in 1888) became the education authorities. Payment of grants to both provided and voluntary schools were conditional upon conformity to restrictions laid down as minutes of the Privy Council. The overall management and enforcement of standards of local schools continued as the Board of Education (established 1899). The Board of Education had responsibilities not simply with respect to the individual local authority but for every individual school and college within a local authority.

The system gradually broke down as both central government and some local authorities widened and diversified the curriculum. The more varied teaching needs became, the less easy it was to devise standards by which to continue payment by results. The grant became a less effective instrument by which central government could establish uniform standards.

Inspectors' reports became more important than the number of pupils passing precisely set examinations. Mysteriously, this shift in criteria was referred to as one towards 'block grants' (Eaglesham, 1956, p. 51). The power of the inspectors meant that although in theory local authorities were free to vary their rate contribution, in practice they did not do this very much.

While the interwar period saw a continuation of the earlier system of finance, the Ministry of Education began to place greater reliance on securing greater uniformity in the numbers and quality of the teaching staff. The Burnham Committee was first set up after the First World War and quickly became an important force for the unification of both the salaries and qualifications of teachers.[4] Its first Report imposed a system of payment based on four scales relating to rural areas, London and other urban areas. The second Report of the Committee dealt with the pay of higher elementary teachers. Burnham removed the determination of pay from individual local authorities to the national level, of special importance as wages account for such a large proportion of total education expenditure. The Act of 1918 also introduced the two main grants which were to continue to 1944, in the form of specific percentage grants for both higher (secondary) and elementary education. The elementary education grant originally gave 36s per unit of average attendance plus 60 per cent of expenditure on teachers' salaries plus 20 per cent of all other expenditures less the product of a 7d rate. Again the principle of combining needs and resources within a single grant was maintained. In the case of higher education, the grant was to total 50 per cent of total expenditure. To prevent unnecessary extravagance, a limit was set on the total amount of grant that any authority could receive. The grant could be likened to a conditional matching grant given the strict imposition of standards by the Board of Education. The board argued successfully to prevent Chamberlain from including education in his block grant when he was reforming local government finance in 1928.

Since the Second World War, statutory and administrative developments have made greater centralisation possible. Beginning with the 1944 Education Act and the McNeil Report in the same year on the Burnham system, there has been an increase in the ways in which central government could act to influence local educational policy. The 1944 Education Act gave particularly wide powers to the minister of the new Ministry of Education. The Act begins with the following declaration of ultimate authority in that, 'it shall be lawful for His Majesty to appoint a Minister whose duty it shall be to promote the education of the people of England and Wales . . . and to serve the effective execution by local authorities, under his control and direction, of the national policy for providing a varied and comprehensive education service in every area'. While the Ministry of Education and its successor the Department of Education and Science have issued a stream of circulars on every aspect of educational policy, administrative control seems to be particularly well established in two major areas: teachers' salaries and pupil—teacher ratios, and school-buildings.

The determination of teachers' salaries remains the responsibility of the Burnham Committee which adopted, at least in principle, the recommendations of the McNair Committee that 'the salary scale of a teacher [should] be the same in whatever type of school he or she was servicing, except for servicing in the London area'. The determination of the distribution of posts of special responsibility requiring particular qualifications is not at the discretion of the local authorities nor is the number of pupils per teacher, both being decided by the points and quota system. The 1945 shortage of teachers led to the introduction of the points system whereby both the number and distribution of posts of responsibility are determined.

The points are allocated on the basis of the number and ages of pupils within schools and the total score of points determines the allocation of posts between schools. A certain degree of discretion is left to the local authority in appointing heads of departments, in so far as they take full advantage of possible openings. As many of these proved reluctant to do so the scope was widened in 1956 by doubling the points for 13 to 15 year olds in order to improve the number of posts in secondary schools. It should be noted that in so far as any local authority fails to take full advantage of the number of posts allocated, both the National Union of Teachers and the Department of Education and Science (DES) are likely to object.

The quota system was introduced after the Second World War because of the uneven incidence of teacher shortages. As with all other arrangements in this area it is a voluntary system closely watched by the DES. The basic objective is to limit the total number of teachers a local authority can employ, so forcing teachers in surplus areas to move to those of acute shortage. According to the DES the system has worked in so far as the variation in pupil—teacher ratios has fallen from 40 per cent to 13 per cent from 1956 to 1970. The quota is determined by the total pupil population, the incidence of immigrants and Welsh-speaking communities.[5]

The other major area of detailed administrative control is school buildings. School buildings are capital expenditure, and hence require loan sanction from central government. Loan sanction is only granted if the proposed building satisfies departmental requirements, which specify in considerable detail the type and design of school, classroom size, and even the area of playing field. This very detailed control over school buildings affects current educational expenditure both directly through the interest charges on the debt incurred and indirectly in that expenditure on staffing and maintenance is influenced by the type and design of school buildings.

The main institutional relationship by which this control is exercised is through the building branch. The minister, in combination with the building branch, traditionally has extensive powers in three main areas: the approval of projects in building programmes, the imposition of minimum standards of accommodation, and the limitation of costs. Not only is the minister responsible for choosing between specific projects within a local authority (he also chooses the total sums allocated for construction purposes to any given local authority), but he also lays down the average minimum space per child and the maximum cost of a given unit of accommodation per pupil.

At the same time as this increases the scope and sophistication of the instruments to lead local authorities to accept national policy objectives, the payment of the grant is no longer explicitly linked to the provision of nationally accepted levels of expenditure. In 1958, the education grant was completely subsumed into the needs element of RSG. The divorce between responsibility for financing and the power to control educational policy seemed to have been achieved.

Thus the relevant statutes and the extent and nature of the administrative apparatus give the Secretary of State very great powers over local authorities — sufficient to make it possible in law to reduce them to his agents. But, as has often been pointed out in relation to British government, a potential for power as defined in statutes does not necessarily imply that such power is exercised. Thus on the surface it appears that power not only exists but is seen to be exercised by the minister. The extent to which this has totally removed the discretion in the actual determination of expenditures from local authorities to central government is the concern of the last sections of this chapter.

Usually the minister has been able to avoid drawing on the apparently supreme power given him in the 1944 Education Act. But when in 1976, a Secretary of State for Education did rely on this to try to prevent a local authority refusing to execute plans for comprehensive education after a change of party at a local election, the local authority tested the minister's power in the courts, which decided that the secretary of state had exceeded his authority.

This account of relations between central and local government in education illustrates the diversity of instruments central government has used. There is the formal power as laid down by statute, circulars, voluntary co-operation over quotas, specific grants, loan sanctions. It also shows how control has moved — less fast than in some areas — from exact controls to ones which rely more on a number of instruments. The replacement of specific by block grants has been an increase in freedom; but central government had retained the influence it most needed over the training of teachers, quotas and the specification of schools. Now that there is a greater interest in the content of curricula it is finding powers for that, as it did to speed comprehensive education.

Thus one finds virtually every instrument deployed that is listed in the next section.

CENTRAL GOVERNMENT'S INSTRUMENTS

The diversity of instruments central government uses is very great. Their kind and uses vary widely between and even within central departments. Some are not under the control of ministers but they do have their effect in increasing the relative influence of central government's policies.

(1) Congestion in Parliament and the development of the party system has almost eliminated the passing of locally inspired Acts of Parliament to allow local authorities to undertake policies which they want and which differ from the norm.

(2) As a corollary, with very few exceptions legislation that local authorities operate under has passed through Parliament at the initiative of central government. Not only does it reflect the policies of that government but almost invariably it gives ministers powers in some form or other to supervise local authorities in their execution of that legislation.

(3) Such statutory provisions are extended by the practice of issuing regulations in circulars. Their status varies. The power to issue them may itself be provided for by statute. Or its basis may be less formal. If the base is statutory, what is circulated may be instructions or advice to local authorities. If its base is non-statutory, its status will be that of advice. But as Professor Griffith has pointed out, it is often exceptionally hard to tell what if any is the legal basis of what is written to local authorities (1966, p. 58). A habit has grown up of issuing circulars and writing letters as if they were advisory, even where central government may believe it has power to issue instructions. Because few such statutes have been tested in the courts, there is often genuine doubt what the law is. Central government often tends to assume that its wishes should be overriding unless the law expressly provides the contrary. It would seem as if local authorities have generally become used to accepting most of the advice of central government and often to ask the advice of its officials even when there is no statutory requirement that they should do so.

(4) The old Benthamite inspectorates survive and have multiplied. To them have been added a host of central government officers whose duty it is one way or another to deal with local authorities. They are found in almost all the major home departments — Environment, Health and Social Security, Education, the Home Office, Agriculture, Transport, Employment, the Scottish and Welsh Offices. Many are professionals — architects, engineers, planners, doctors, etc. Others are professional administrators. They exist to watch what the local authorities are doing. Their interest is of three kinds. There is first a professional interest which derives directly from John Stuart Mill's view of local authorities as simply less well informed. In various ways they have a view of professional standards to which local government should aspire. Second, they wish to persuade local authorities to adopt policies consistent with those of their ministers. Third and more recently, there is an interest in affecting local government finance in the interest of macroeconomic policy. Thus these officers can be seen both as an independent influence on local behaviour and as keeping watch on or using the other five main sources of influence to achieve the policy aims of their ministers.

(5)　Financial control in its more obvious forms has had a diminishing importance. The use of grant common in the education department which tied its payment to the results achieved by schools disappeared early in this century. The gradual reduction in specific grants has meant that that method of influence has declined, though its actual influence has always been much exaggerated, since a grant provided for one purpose by central government need not necessarily be fully reflected in local expenditure on that item, when local authorities could use it to release resources for expenditure elsewhere. Movement towards a block grant has meant that local authorities have had fewer financial restrictions on their ability to spend grant as they pleased. The overall level of grant, on the other hand, can have an influence on the quality of local authority current expenditure and therefore be an instrument of national macroeconomic policy.

(6)　Central government does exercise more control over capital expenditure through its power to give or withhold loan sanction, the power to borrow money for specific purposes. Loan sanctions are granted by individual central departments to develop services each in its area. Beginning as an instrument like the district audit to check improper expenditure − in this case, borrowing to an extent which might endanger solvency − it drifted into an arrangement through which central government could control the details of local expenditure (Layfield, 1976, pp. 69, 242). Despite changes in recent years which have enabled local authorities to get 'block' loan sanctions for certain generally minor categories of expenditure, capital control remains a constraint on their freedom in the opinion of local authorities. Central government seems prepared to relax detailed control still further by moving towards block approvals for capital expenditure also (DoE, 1977*b*, Cmnd 6813, ch. 5). As with current expenditure grants, it is the total that is becoming the object of interest for purposes of macroeconomic policy.

(7)　There is consultative machinery, which has existed in some shape or form for many years, to discuss the distribution of grant and to predict local authority expenditure. It has been elevated since 1975, when a Consultative Council was established chaired by the Secretary of State for the Environment and attended by ministers and senior officials of departments dealing with local authorities as well as by representatives of the local authority associations and the GLC. Its activity was to cover England and Wales for RSG, but England alone for other matters since Wales has its own council chaired by the Secretary of State for Wales (Layfield, 1976, annex 14). Besides RSG which, carrying over from its predecessor, was its prime reason for existing, its function was to review the economy, consider the financial implications of major policy changes and discuss any other questions of local government finance its members decided on.

It is a body in which central government expects and is expected to take the lead in initiating most of what is discussed. Besides the traditional activity of deciding the basis of RSG − most of the work on this goes on in subordinate committees − its main function so far has been as a forum in which ministers can persuade and cajole local authorities to reduce expenditure and restrain the growth of manpower. This spreads the burden of unpopularity among ministers whose purpose is strengthened by the presence of the Chief Secretary of the Treasury. His role is recognised as that of a critic of public expenditure.

Since ministers have to present an agreed front at the council, it becomes harder for them to perpetrate the inconsistency for which they have been so often censured in the past by the local authorities: individually encouraging local authorities to spend even at a time when overall government policy is restrictive. As the interest of departmental ministers is almost invariably to want local authorities to spend more on those causes they rate highly, direct discussions between departments and local authorities frequently reflect this. Local authorities complain that they have often been under pressure to develop services even when overall they have been asked to restrain growth. Ministers and officials have urged them to switch resources from elsewhere without having indicated what they would be ready to see cut back. Or they have simply been told to implement legislation. While from central government's standpoint a major result of the council must be to bind ministers together, the local authority associations find it useful to be able to question central government on the consequences of its legislation. They have successfully pressed central government to state its views on the expenditure and manpower implications of all legislation and other measures that affect local government. They have presented local government views on these implications, often arguing that the financial resources and manning they will need will be far higher than the central government predicts. It is reasonable to wonder whether the Consultative Council will be as important when the economy moves into a phase where there are no macroeconomic reasons to restrict expenditure. Central departments could then easily revert to a situation in which they deal directly with local authority associations to discuss what expenditure increases are to be encouraged.

A major result of the growth of this consultative apparatus has been to enhance the influence of the local authority associations. There are separate associations to represent the shire counties, the urban areas and the districts, and London, that have developed from similar associations that existed before the 1974 reorganisation of local government. In general the Association of County Councils and the Association of District Councils, which represent the less urban areas, are likely to have a Conservative majority at all times. The Association of Municipal Authorities is more volatile and likely to change its dominant allegiance, as is the London Boroughs Association. It is hardly surprising that central government has tended to favour local authorities of its own political complexion. It is odder but not unsurprising that it has come also to favour associations of its own political complexion even though it will always have a minority of opposed authorities. Inevitably out of this has emerged a conception that non-urban authorities are of a greater interest to the Conservative Party and the urban areas to the Labour Party. As we saw in Part Two, Chapter 3 the recent mechanism of RSG has reinforced the common purpose of these blocs. Collectively these urban, non-urban and London groupings are able to influence the distribution of RSG.

While the local authority associations are necessary if there is to be a Consultative Council — all 2000 local authorities can hardly be present — the system itself creates stresses. It divides members and officials into two. There are those who are caught up in the activities of the associations and take part in the negotiations with central government, and there remain the majority who are

not. As the issues discussed in the council and its committees are often complicated and most of the papers are confidential there is a disparity of information.
The minority feel they understand the processes by which central government
reaches its decisions on local authorities. The majority are remote from it, and
may be forgiven for thinking that closeness to central government means greater
influence over its decisions. Inevitably this sets up strains within local government. There is the suspicion that because of this some councils are privileged
and more influential, and the opposite concern that being drawn into the process, they become more amenable to central influence.

How long can the machinery exist in its present form? The associations are
being given a representative role far more important than in the past. One can
anticipate that authorities of one political complexion, that find themselves
permanently in a minority in an association of opposed persuasion, will become
increasingly restive. Various developments are possible:

(i) A regional grouping might replace the present associations; or
(ii) a political grouping in which a change of party at a local election was
followed by a change in association; or
(iii) the local authorities might combine into one association so that they
could settle most of their differences out of sight of central government.

(8) Central government power is also indirectly increased by the *ultra vires*
principle ensuring that local authorities may only do what the law positively
permits them to do. No longer are they able to do whatever the law does not
forbid.

(9) The district auditor has developed from a mere auditor into someone
whose duty it is to see that local authorities do not breach the *ultra vires* principle. They are also starting to develop a role as watchdogs of efficiency (DoE,
1977*b*, Cmnd 6813, para. 7.6).

The main influences that exist to limit the freedom of local government are,
therefore, the replacement of local private by public Bills as the instruments of
legislation; sections in Acts of Parliament conferring powers on ministers; powers
conferred on them and their officials by regulations and more informal locus
given them by custom; the inspectorates and the other departmental civil servants there to watch and influence local authorities; grants; local sanctions; and
the consultative machinery, backed by the *ultra vires* principle and the district
auditor.

To which must be added the influence of professional associations who interest themselves in standards of services in such a way as to encourage uniformity
and limit the freedom of local authorities to vary their decisions.

THE FREEDOM OF LOCAL GOVERNMENT

Professor Ryle told a story of some peasants terrified by their first railway train.
Their pastor explained to them how it worked whereupon the peasants said
'We understand what you say. But there really is a horse inside, isn't there?'

(Ryle, 1950, p. 75). Men often wish to believe that action cannot be explained scientifically but rather — to use Professor Ryle's famous phrase — there is a ghost, or horse, in the machine who is really responsible for what occurs.

Similarly one might ask if there is a need for the concepts of freedom or lack of it to describe a local government's behaviour. A local authority pursues various policies, and spends its money in particular ways. Why ask if it does so freely? If indeed the argument about the presence or absence of freedom in local government were like the argument about free will versus determinism in persons, then there would not be profit in it. Instead the argument is about the effect of constraints on the ability of local authorities to pursue their own policies. Even this presents grave problems. An old tradition regards freedom as the ability of an individual or a government to do what it wants to do. An increase in freedom becomes an increase in the ability to maximise satisfaction. Unfortunately this is contrary to a common-sense notion of what freedom is. It is possible for a slave to have every want satisfied — to be utterly content with his lot provided, of course, he wants what his master gives him and does not want not to be a slave. That, as a matter of observation, slaves were rarely so contented does not destroy the possibility that a man could be both slave and free — if freedom is defined as having one's wants satisfied. Similarly, it is possible that a local government whose every move and expenditure is dictated from above could be a free authority in that its wants were better satisfied than if it had more choice. Indeed this notion is one we found rooted paradoxically in John Stuart Mill's division of labour between central and local government. The superior knowledge and intelligence of central government means that in many respects — all those that did not actually require local knowledge — it could satisfy local wants better than local politicians. This is the motive force of well-intentioned paternalism and is still powerful, often being used to justify central intervention. If central government knows best, then want maximisation could mean a local government relinquishing much or even all of its freedom to central government — or more plausibly, relinquishing that freedom which central government does not itself decide to give back to it as an agent.

Professor Barry (1965, p. 137) has pointed out that in a more widely accepted meaning of freedom it is defined as the absence of certain restrictions on the ability to satisfy wants. He quotes Graham Wallas (1908, p. 158):

Common usage refuses to say that the liberty of a Syrian peasant is equally violated if half his crops are destroyed by hail or locusts, half his income is taken by a Turkish tax-gatherer or half his working hours are taken for road construction by a German or French commander . . . The reactions to human obstruction take the form, first of anger, and an impulse to resist and then if resistance is found to be, or felt to be, useless, of an exquisitely painful feeling of unfreedom; and similar reactions do not follow non-human obstruction. Wounded self-respect, helpless hatred and thwarted affection are, that is to say, different psychological states from hunger and fatigue, though all are the results of obstructions to the carrying out of our impulses. When Shakespeare wishes to describe the ills which drive men to suicide he gives

'The oppressor's wrong, the proud man's contumely,
The pangs of despised love, the law's delay,
The insolence of office and the spurns
The patient merit of the unworthy takes'

As Barry says, the difficulty of this is that freedom then depends on whether a man or government thinks itself free. On this basis undoubtedly the volume of local complaint that its freedom is constantly infringed is enough to prove lack of freedom; while a slave could be free if he has no 'exquisitely painful feeling of unfreedom'. Two notions war in the Wallas commonsense definition. The first is what the person or entity in question feels. The second is what common usage thinks. The latter may refuse to accept a slave can be free but is likely to be more equivocal over the state of local government. If one asked any citizen other than one active in central or local government whether local government had much freedom, he would probably be puzzled how to reply.

One answer might be to consider how far local politicians achieve their manifestoes. 'A sincere declaration of intention', says Stuart Hampshire, 'is the most reliable of all sources of information about a man's future actions, if he is a free agent' (1959, p. 177). By this test most government, central and local, is unfree. But both a man and a political party can make a sincere declaration of intent and fail because of unpredicted events and forces. In politics, one also has to reckon with manifestoes which are insincere in the sense that they are meant as attractive compromises which no one expects will be adequately realised.

When one turns to negative freedom, other problems arise. The classic John Stuart Mill definition of liberty simply will not do in this context, which may explain his less than forthright defence of local liberties: 'The only part of the conduct of any one, for which he is amenable to society is that which concerns others. In the part which merely concerns himself, his independence is, of right, absolute. Over himself, over his own body and mind, the individual is sovereign' (Mill, 1910*a*, p. 73). While one can imagine a state of affairs in which central government shows no interest in some local activities, all local government involves 'others'. There have been attempts to argue that some matters are of purely local interest. This is the basis of a division of labour in a federal constitution and underlies the difficult distinction between national and local public goods. Yet if central government says, as 'another' or representative of 'others', that it is interested in any local activity, such a declaration of interest makes Mill's definition of freedom useless. Indeed, in the 1977 Green Paper central government makes protection of the interest of minorities a reason for its interest in local affairs (DoE, 1977*b*, Cmnd 6813, para. 2.2). As in a democracy there are always minorities, on this basis a central government could always find a reason for interfering with local freedom (Barry, 1965, pp. 141–8).

However, we have shifted our ground because of the peculiar implications of Mill's concept of freedom. Any definition of freedom which restricts its operation to acts which do not infringe the interests of others has a very limited scope. The absence of freedom has to consist in a feeling of lack of freedom. In that respect very different degrees of unfreedom are felt by different local politicians and officials in different places and at different times. An economist's defence of freedom is likely to be in terms of the satisfaction of wants.

Given there is a role for government, demand is more likely to be satisfied if the provision of beneficial local goods is localised — a question we shall enter into more in Part Four, Chapter 6. But all such arguments are defenceless against an assertion of paternalism or protection of minority interests from central government — or anyone else for that matter. So that we are left with a conflict between central and local government over the most desirable extent of autonomy — a conflict which is not overt, as central government protests that it too desires local autonomy.[6]

What evidence of freedom can be found? There is abundant evidence of central government instruments for intervention, but as we have pointed out (1) their existence does not mean they are all used; (2) of course many of them are used but this does not necessarily destroy freedom, only limit the freedom left to local authorities. However, all persons and entities have restrictions on their freedom of action — human as well as non-human. Considerable intervention could still be consistent with considerable freedom. Even then one is in a quandary. It is not uncommon to hear local government give as examples of freedom its ability to settle what seem quite petty matters of detail.

What we can look for is something else again. In so far as local authorities are free, one would expect them to make different choices. This is an empirical observation based on the general argument that when allowed, human beings, singly and in groups, do behave diversely. More direct evidence is found in the USA where different local authorities do choose very different packages of local goods and services. Of course, local government could use its freedom to conform. There are pressures to conform. Powerful professional bodies argue to this effect. Central government's persuasion is often directed to this end. So we come to the opposite of our earlier paradox of the free-feeling slave. This is the slavish free man — who chooses to conform. Certainly there is no way of proving local governments do not choose to be similar, so that what we attempt can only be a partial test of freedom. If we reveal considerable uniformity in behaviour, we cannot prove it was not freely chosen. But where there is diversity, there is greater likelihood of free choice. It is conceivable that central government could impose diversity on its agents; but we have no evidence or any real reason to believe that this is central government's intention. Of course, there are elements in diversity which cannot be attributable to local choice, but we shall try to distinguish them.

Our aim, therefore, is to identify diversity in expenditure which would lead us to believe there is a presumption of the survival of some local freedom. The data and the technique — multiple regression analysis — will not allow us all the manipulations we would like. But we believe we are able to make limited progress. We have examined many more equations and variables than are reported here. We have had to identify variables which on *a priori* grounds we would expect to be associated with local rather than central choice. While we have looked at political differences, in education we have found that differences in local income and in the 'price' of services to the ratepayer are more powerful in explaining expenditure differences among those variables we believe reflect local choice.

VARIATION IN EXPENDITURE AS A SIGN OF LOCAL FREEDOM

In this section we examine the evidence as to whether central controls have in fact brought about a reduction in the variation of education expenditure across authorities. It is easy enough to measure the extent of expenditure variation.[7] The difficulty is in finding an appropriate standard of comparison that might give some indication of the extent of variation that could be expected in the absence of controls. We consider two types of comparison: (1) with US data, and (2) with earlier data on educational expenditure.

In the USA, local education authorities have considerable autonomy and there is no attempt by the federal government to impose detailed administrative guidelines and controls in the manner of central government departments in the UK. There are, however, difficulties in interpreting a direct comparison of US and UK data. First, it might be expected that the greater size and diversity of the USA might lead to greater expenditure variation irrespective of the extent of federal government intervention. Second, school districts in the USA are typically smaller than local education authorities in the UK. In fact, we only have data for average school-district expenditure for those counties and metropolitan areas with population in excess of 50,000 people. Such units are similar in population size to local education authorities in the UK, but the comparison conceals the possibility of substantially greater expenditure variation between different school districts within a county or metropolitan area in the USA than within a local education authority in the UK.

An attempt to allow for the greater size and diversity of the USA was made by dividing the observations into four major regions – the East, Central, West and Southern States – each region somewhat more homogenous than the nation as a whole. The coefficients of variation of educational expenditure per head of population for counties and metropolitan areas in the four regions are set out in Table 2.7.1. For the UK, we have used data for England and Wales only, as different arrangements for local government apply in Scotland and Northern Ireland. The year 1972/3 was adopted as the last clear year before local government reorganisation, both in order to facilitate comparison with earlier years and because data for the years of reorganisation may be distorted by transitional factors.

The figures in Table 2.7.1 show significantly greater variation in the USA than in England and Wales. The coefficients of variation for the USA seem consistent with the results of earlier studies. Fisher (1964) reported a coefficient of variation of average expenditure on local schools across states in 1960 of 22.2 per cent.[8]

The fact that there is less variation in England and Wales may, as suggested earlier, be the result of greater similarity of conditions in different authorities rather than of conformity imposed by central agencies.

Next we examine the pattern over time in the variation of education expenditure within England and Wales. Earlier it was suggested that the administrative control most likely to encourage equalisation of expenditure is the quota system. It is, therefore, interesting to see whether the variation of expenditure has

Table 2.7.1. *Expenditure variation in the USA and in England and Wales*

	Year	Number of Observations	Coefficient of Variation
USA [a]	1970/1		
Central		74	24.55
East		55	21.42
South		59	18.56
West		41	18.80
England and Wales	1972/3	141	12.77

[a] The regions are constituted as follows: *Central region*: Illinois, Indiana, Michigan, Minnesota, Nebraska, Wisconsin. *East*: Connecticut, Delaware, Maryland, Massachusetts, New Jersey, New York, Ohio, Pennsylvania, Rhode Island, Washington DC. *South*: Alabama, Arizona, Florida, Georgia, Kentucky, Louisiana, Missouri, N. Carolina, Tennessee, Texas, Virginia. *West*: California, Colorado, Oklahoma, Utah, Washington.

Sources: *Local Government Finances in Selected Metropolitan Areas and Larger Counties: 1970–1* (US Dept. of Commerce, 1972); and for England and Wales, *Education Statistics 1972–3* (CIPFA, 1974).

Table 2.7.2. *Variation in average expenditure per pupil 1959/60–1972/3*

Year	All authorities outside London	County boroughs	County councils
1959/60	12.39	7.13	13.52
60/1	11.72	6.32	12.88
61/2	11.58	6.45	12.67
62/3	9.06	5.58	10.73
63/4	9.36	5.47	10.68
64/5	8.43	5.92	9.99
65/6	7.92	5.47	9.49
66/7	7.89	5.61	9.13
67/8	7.85	5.69	9.14
68/9	8.03	6.03	9.22
69/70	7.76	6.09	8.72
70/1	7.93	7.28	8.26
71/2	7.88	7.33	8.22
72/3	–	7.52	7.51

Source: *Education Statistics* (CIPFA, relevant years).

in fact been reduced since the introduction of the quota system in 1958.

The figures are set out in Table 2.7.2 which presents figures for all authorities (outside London) and for county councils and county boroughs separately for each year from 1959/60 to 1972/3. London is excluded due to the reorganisation of its local government in 1965.

While the figures in Table 2.7.2 show a general reduction in the variation of expenditure, they call for further comment. If one looks at all local authorities the coefficient of variation declined to the mid-1960s and remained steady up until reorganisation. The fall in the coefficient has been virtually continuous in the county councils. The county borough coefficient fell to the mid-1960s but thereafter rose to levels above those at the start of the period. A possible explanation is that central control over counties grew, while that over county boroughs grew then declined. But such discrimination seems inherently implausible.

If one looks at the county councils above one might argue that they lost the opportunity for high spending in 1958 when a block grant replaced a specific education grant, including a 60 per cent matching grant for relevant expenditure. Thus it could be argued that this matching grant had led to greater diversity, and that counties were restrained by the block grant, with no matching element, to achieve greater uniformity. A possibly more plausible explanation is in terms of the pupil—teacher ratio. As a generalisation, pupil—teacher ratios have always been lower, that is better, in counties than in cities. (The ratios were 26.6 and 20.6 for county primary and secondary schools in 1958/9 compared with 31.0 and 21.3 in county boroughs.) Since the quota system has operated over time to bring below-average authorities up to average, while leaving above-average authorities unaffected, this may have had some effect on county councils. This would indicate that central policy — the quota system — has reduced local freedom to vary the pupil—teacher ratio. A final explanation would be to say that in other policies besides the quota, central government has moved to control county councils more in the interests of uniformity. Taking these last two together we believe tentatively that they give some indication that our hypothesis is likely to be correct.

The county borough data is more difficult to interpret. The post-1958 effect could have been operating into the mid-1960s, as could the quota system, in reducing variation except that the early 1960s were a period of sustained teacher shortage which made it harder to correct their quotas, especially in the cities which were in general less preferred by teachers. We need to look at the quota more closely.

Table 2.7.3 shows the mean quota deficiencies of county boroughs and county councils over the period, the quota deficiency of each authority being defined as the deficiency (−) or surplus (+) of quota-qualifying teachers[9] hired to quota-qualifying teachers allowed, expressed as a percentage of the quota allowed. As can be seen from Table 2.7.3 the deficiency of quota-qualifying teachers falls up to 1968/9, when, in response to the easing of the teacher shortage, quota allowances were increased.

The interest of Table 2.7.3 is that county boroughs, despite their inferior

Table 2.7.3   *Mean quota deficiencies*

Year	County boroughs	County councils
1965/6	−0.4	−1.1
66/7	−0.1	−0.8
67/8	+0.7	+0.1
68/9	+1.9	+1.1
69/70	−0.2	−0.8
70/1	−1.1	−1.3
71/2	−0.3	−1.0

Source: Department of Education and Science data.

pupil—teacher ratios, have had a consistently smaller quota deficiency.[10] In so far as the quota system has had any effect, it will have had more of a restrictive influence on teacher recruitment in the county boroughs than in the county councils. But it is not clear that it has had any effect of this type, in that the differential in the mean deficiency between the county boroughs and the county councils has not narrowed over the period.

It is often suggested that central control implies the equalisation of education expenditures per pupil across local authorities. This may be the objective of central government, but other objectives are equally, if not more, plausible. For example, central controls may be designed to achieve a uniformity of standards across local authorities (in terms of pupil—teacher ratios and such like). The cost of provision of such a standard may differ between local authorities due to differences between different areas in the price of labour or land, in the age distribution of pupils, in the age of school-buildings or of numerous other factors. These cost differences will lead to differences in expenditure levels fully consistent with the central-control hypothesis.

Furthermore, the objective of central control may not simply be one of ensuring uniformity of standards. It may be directed towards the objective, enshrined in the 1944 Act, of equality of opportunity. Given the differences in innate ability, etc., between individuals, such a policy objective might imply compensating differences in educational provision. In so far as differences on educational expenditure between local authorities can be attributed to national policy initiatives along these lines, they clearly provide no evidence of local discretion.[11]

For these reasons, the observed value of coefficient of variation of educational expenditure across local authorities does not provide an unambiguous measure of the extent of local discretion. It all depends on what factors appear responsible for the observed variability in expenditure.

LOCAL AUTHORITIES' USE OF FREEDOM

In this section, we investigate a model in which variations in expenditure are attributed to local economic factors. A number of studies of this type have been carried out in the USA.[12]

The main economic factors that might be expected to influence expenditure on education (like any other service) are income and relative prices. But these variables have to be defined carefully in the context of local government expenditure. As we have shown in Part Two, Chapter 5, the relevant income measure consists of (1) block grants, which are paid direct from central to local government and (2) the level of household disposable incomes, part of which can be collected in local taxation (rates) and used to finance local government services. The more grant local government receives, or the higher general level of household incomes in the area, the greater the availability of financial resources and hence the more may be spent on education. While, in principle, the two sources of income are equivalent in that a local community's preference between expenditure on local government services or on private-consumption goods should not depend on the source of its income, in practice local governments may be less reluctant to spend additional grant income than to raise rates when household incomes rise. Thus in the regression analysis we have retained the two income measures – block grants and household income – as separate variables.

The relative price variable measures the cost to the local community of provision of education in terms of other goods and services foregone. There are two components of this cost, first the actual marginal cost of provision of educational services relative to the price of other goods, and second the payment of matching grants. The first of these components will depend on relative factor cost differences in different local authorities, and factor intensities in education as against other services. In the absence of the relevant data it is not possible to estimate differences in this relative cost factor across local authorities. It is unlikely that this will introduce significant errors, for it is not clear that the relative cost of education will vary in any systematic manner across authorities. The absolute cost of education may, of course, be higher in central city than in rural areas, but other goods are more expensive in cities as well, so the relative cost may not differ very much.

The second component of the relative price is the payment of matching grant. The resources element of RSG is a matching grant in that the central government acts as a 'notional' ratepayer on each authority's deficiency of rateable value relative to a given 'standard' level of rateable value. The more an authority spends, the higher its rate poundage and the more resources element grant it collects. An authority whose rateable value is, say, 40 per cent below the standard level can finance an additional £1,000 of expenditure by increasing its rate poundage to raise £600 from its local ratepayers and £400 in additional resources element grant (equivalent to the collection of rates on the notional rateable value). The cost of the £1,000 of additional expenditure to the local community is thus only £600. Local authorities differ in their rateable value deficiency and hence in the relative cost of local government services to the local community.

Our first test was to regress educational expenditure per pupil on these three economic variables, using data for 1972/3. The notation is as follows:

XED: Educational expenditure per pupil, net of debt charges (£). Source: *Education Statistics* (1974).

Y: Household income (£). For the county councils this is the average income per tax unit, published by the Inland Revenue, *Survey of Personal Incomes, 1970/1*. No such direct measure is available for the county boroughs, so we have adopted a measure constructed on the basis of socio-economic groups. (See Appendix 2.5.A1 to Chapter 5.)

NEDGR: Block grants, measured as the needs element of RSG per head of population (£). Source: Department of the Environment.

TRV: Relative price variable. An authority's rateable value expressed as a percentage of the standard rateable value. An authority whose rateable value is in excess of the standard will not receive resources element, nor will it be charged 'negative' resources element, so the price variable takes the value 100.

The results for the county councils and the county boroughs were:

County Councils

$$XED = 75.86 + 1.06\ NEDGR + 0.032Y - 0.21\ TRV \qquad R^2 = 0.59$$
$$(21.61) \quad (0.18) \quad\quad (0.011) \quad\quad\quad (0.11)$$

County Boroughs

$$XED = 81.21 + 0.56\ NEDGR + 0.0028Y + 0.13\ TRV \qquad R^2 = 0.09$$
$$(15.01) \quad (0.23) \quad\quad (0.0054) \quad\quad\quad (6.07)$$

(figures in brackets are standard errors)

On normal criteria, the equation for the county councils seems satisfactory. A significant proportion of the variation is explained and the variables are significant and the signs of their coefficients are consistent with the theoretical argument. On the same criteria, the equation for the county boroughs is not satisfactory: the R^2 of the equation is low and, of the variables, only the needs grant is significant. But the purpose of the exercise is to discover what factors account for expenditure variation. The model tested, which is based on local discretion, includes local economic factors, and the finding that such factors do not account for expenditure variation is as valuable in the present context as a finding that they do.

It is interesting to compare the coefficient estimates with those obtained on US data. Although there have been many empirical studies of local government expenditures in the USA, relatively few contain estimates of expenditure elasticities in education. Hirsch (1960) calculated an income elasticity of demand for public-education expenditure of about 0.60, but this estimate may be unreliable as he used local property values as a proxy for local income. More recently, Borcheding and Deacon (1972) and Peterson (1975) have estimated income and price elasticities for education, using models similar to that adopted in this chapter.[13] Borcheding and Deacon estimate the determinants of aggregate expenditure on education in across states, while Peterson estimates the determinants of expenditure on education across school districts in four states and in one metropolitan area. In Table 2.7.4, we compare these elasticities with those derived here for the county councils in England and Wales (computing elasticities at the sample means).

The expenditure elasticities show that the effect of income and relative prices in England and Wales is far from negligible, but the elasticities are significantly lower than those estimated for the USA.

Why should the results for the county boroughs be so different? One approach to this question is through more detailed statistical analysis. We tried disaggregating expenditure into its main components (e.g. teachers' salaries), including additional variables (e.g. average school size) and running separate regressions for primary and secondary schools. The results of the more detailed analysis are broadly consistent with the simple, aggregate equations. In each case, local economic factors are significant in the county councils but not in

Table 2.7.4. *Expenditure elasticities*

		Income	Price
USA			
Aggregate state expenditures		0.94	−1.13
(*Source*: Borcheding and Deacon, 1972)			
School districts:	California	0.84	−0.36
	Michigan	1.22	−0.51
	New Jersey	1.23	−0.25
	New York	1.35	−0.55
	Kansas City	1.10	−0.70
(*Source*: Peterson, 1975)			
England and Wales			
County councils		0.32	−0.33
(*Source*: Authors' own estimates)			

the county boroughs. The equations are set out in Appendix 2.7.A1 to this chapter.

An alternative approach, along the lines discussed earlier in this chapter, might be to consider any differences in circumstances of the two types of authorities. It has been shown that county boroughs were hiring more teachers relative to their quotas than the county councils. This suggests that the quota system might have had a greater effect in restraining the influence of local factors in the county boroughs. Further the teacher shortage, which had not disappeared by 1972/3, seems to have been more pronounced in the county boroughs. This might mean that the observed variation in expenditure is attributable more to supply than to demand factors.

CONCLUSIONS

The results are not easily interpreted and as was stressed initially one cannot prove the effect of central control or persuasion. The strongest evidence would seem to be that the coefficient of variation is less than in the USA, has been declining over time in the counties; and again that in the counties, in particular, income and price — variables that one would expect to be influential if local authorities had freedom — have an influence on expenditure, though generally a weaker one than in the USA. If the last result is accepted, there are signs of local diversity but considerably constrained.

NOTES

1 Negative freedom is used because the use of the concept is similar to its use in political philosophy. Delegated freedom is not the same as the more ambiguous concept of positive freedom in political philosophy. What matters is how far the superior can itself alter the constraints on the freedom of the inferior.

2 Neville Chamberlain, *Hansard* (1928), vol. 223, col. 104; Henry Brooke, *Hansard* (1957), vol. 579, col. 902.
3 Col. Wedgwood, *Hansard* (1928), vol. 223, col. 273; Michael Stewart, *Hansard* (1957), vol. 579, col. 1,087.
4 The Burnham Committee consists of representatives of local education authorities, central government and teachers' unions.
5 Department of Education and Science, Circular 11/67, 10 January 1967: 'para (6) The quotas for January 1968 . . . as in previous years . . . indicate the total number of full-time teachers of all kinds, including head teachers, supply teachers, peripatetic teachers, supplementary teachers and uncertified teachers, that each local authority should be employing in their primary and secondary schools and practical instruction centres in January 1968.' 'para (9) As hitherto the Secretary of State will be prepared to consider requests by individual authorities for minor adjustments to their quotas where these are justified in special circumstances. He has in mind, in particular, the special staffing arrangements which some authorities may feel it necessary to make for schools servicing districts with a substantial immigrant population.'
6 Recent examples include the White Papers, *Reform of Local Government in England* (Ministry of Housing and Local Government, 1970, Cmnd 4276) and *Local Government in England* (DoE, 1971*b*, Cmnd 4584); and the Green Papers *Future Shape of Local Government Finance* (DoE, 1971*a*, Cmnd 4741) and *Local Government Finance* (DoE, 1977*b*, Cmnd 6813).
7 The most suitable statistic is the coefficient of variation, which is the standard deviation of a set of observations divided by its mean.
8 Rozenthal (1960) similarly found a coefficient of variation for 1957 data of 17.3 per cent, though this result is not directly comparable as he had defined the coefficient of variation as the semi-interquartile range divided by the median.
9 Some teachers (for example, the part-time) do not qualify under the quota system.
10 One possible reason for this is that the county councils are allowed higher quotas because their average school size is lower. (Primary schools are normally smaller in rural areas, which come under county council authorities.)
11 The increasing emphasis of central government policy in respect of encouraging the provision of additional educational facilities in 'educational priority areas' and in areas with high proportions of immigrant pupils has been evident in DES circulars since the late 1960s. Previously policy had concentrated simply on the equalisation of input measures such as the pupil–teacher ratio.
12 For example Fisher, 1964; Borcheding and Deacon, 1972; Peterson, 1975. There has been a number of empirical studies in the UK which we have reviewed in Part Two, Chapter 4. None is primarily concerned with estimating the influence of discretionary economic factors.
13 Ohls and Wales (1972) have also computed an income elasticity of educational expenditure (of 0.59) but they use a slightly different model.

Appendix 2.7.A1   Education Equations

The four tables in this appendix summarise the main regression results. The dependent variables in the four tables are respectively (1) total educational expenditure per pupil, (2) expenditure on teachers' salaries per pupil, (3) expenditure net of teachers' salaries per pupil, and (4) expenditure on school transport. The independent variables, in addition to the economic variables discussed in the text, are average school size — measured as the average number of pupils per school (AV) — the proportion of schoolchildren aged 16 or over ($K16$) and, in the school-transport equations, a measure of low density of population (LDP).[1] In the tables, separate equations are presented for the county councils and the county boroughs, and for primary and secondary schools.

Table 2.7.A1 shows that neither the disaggregation into primary and secondary schools nor the addition of the non-economic variables materially affects the results discussed in the text. The purpose of Tables 2.7.A2 and 2.7.A3 is to distinguish between expenditure on teachers' salaries and expenditure net of teachers' salaries, in that the former is more obviously influenced by central administrative controls. The results in Table 2.7.A2 are, however, very similar to those of Table 2.7.A1, while the explanatory power of the equations in Table 2.7.A3 is significantly lower. This suggests that, for the county councils, local economic factors play a greater part in the determination of expenditure on teachers' salaries than on other expenditure. This result again casts doubt on the effectiveness of administrative controls in equalising expenditures.

Finally, in Table 2.7.A4, there is an analysis of expenditure on school transport for the county councils. (School transport is not a significant item of expenditure for the county boroughs.) The explanatory power of the equations is good, but this is almost entirely attributable to the low-density variable. The equations in the second part of the table omit the economic variables and a comparison of the results shows that the economic variables add little or nothing to the explanatory power of the equations.

NOTE

1   The measure adopted is the proportion of the population living in wards or parishes with population density below 0.5 persons per hectare. Source: unpublished DoE calculations based on the 1971 Census. The data source for all the other variables is *Education Statistics* 1972/3, published by the Chartered Institute of Public Finance and Accountancy.

Table 2.7.A1   Education spending: Total expenditure

	Constant	NEDGR	Y	TRV	K16	AV	R^2
County councils							
Primary schools	54.92 (21.04)	0.97 (0.18)	0.024 (0.011)	−0.23 (0.11)	–	–	0.60
	65.59 (20.00)	0.69 (0.19)	0.032 (0.011)	−0.14 (0.11)	–	−0.11 (0.04)	0.66 –
Secondary schools	96.79 (34.35)	1.16 (0.29)	0.041 (0.018)	−0.18 (0.17)	–	–	0.37
	81.43 (21.19)	0.92 (0.19)	0.029 (0.011)	−0.24 (0.11)	2.51 (1.23)	–	0.62 –
County boroughs							
Primary schools	81.21 (15.01)	0.57 (0.23)	0.0028 (0.0054)	0.13 (0.07)	–	–	0.09
	84.53 (16.28)	0.52 (0.24)	0.0030 (0.0055)	0.14 (0.07)	–	−0.11 (0.20)	0.09 –
Secondary schools	202.53 (39.89)	−0.23 (0.62)	−0.0021 (0.0142)	0.18 (0.19)	−1.07 (1.11)	0.012 (0.013)	0.04 –

Table 2.7.A2 Education spending: Teachers' salaries

	Constant	NEDGR	Y	TRV	K16	AV	R^2
County councils							
Primary schools	60.82 (15.49)	0.54 (0.15)	0.018 (0.008)	−0.055 (0.082)	– –	−0.13 (0.03)	0.75
Secondary schools	84.07 (20.69)	0.73 (0.19)	0.017 (0.011)	−0.19 (0.11)	3.06 (1.20)	– –	0.56
All schools	76.49 (12.54)	0.56 (0.12)	0.013 (0.007)	−0.16 (0.07)	3.48 (0.74)	−0.040 (0.020)	0.81
County boroughs							
Primary schools	69.65 (9.62)	0.077 (0.13)	0.005 (0.003)	0.067 (0.045)	– –	−0.016 (0.011)	0.08
Secondary schools	169.85 (26.00)	−0.64 (0.35)	0.003 (0.009)	0.068 (0.120)	−37.00 (65.35)	−0.020 (0.031)	0.06
All schools	117.60 (15.14)	−0.26 (0.21)	0.004 (0.005)	0.060 (0.070)	−17.34 (38.06)	−0.010 (0.018)	0.05

Table 2.7.A3 Education spending: Expenditure net of teachers' salaries

	Constant	NEDGR	Y	TRV	K16	AV	R^2
County councils							
Primary schools	4.76	0.15	0.014	-0.082	—	0.021	0.21
	(8.87)	(0.09)	(0.005)	(0.047)	—	(0.017)	–
Secondary schools	16.36	0.38	0.022	—	-1.93	-0.004	0.15
	(19.63)	(0.14)	(0.009)	—	(1.14)	(0.008)	–
All schools	7.34	0.31	0.017	-0.057	-1.15	0.021	0.21
	(12.77)	(0.13)	(0.007)	(0.069)	(0.75)	(0.020)	–
County boroughs							
Primary schools	31.68	0.16	0.002	0.058	—	-0.004	0.02
	(12.55)	(0.17)	(0.004)	(0.059)	—	(0.015)	–
Secondary schools	60.87	0.49	0.003	0.14	-88.37	-0.015	0.07
	(26.04)	(0.36)	(0.009)	(0.12)	(65.46)	(0.031)	–
All schools	51.02	0.27	0.004	0.10	-80.37	-0.020	0.09
	(16.67)	(0.22)	(0.006)	(0.08)	(41.91)	(0.020)	–

Table 2.7.A4   Education spending: School transport

	Constant	NEDGR	Y	TRV	K16	AV	LDP	R^2
County councils (including economic variables)								
Primary schools	−5.30 (4.48)	−0.022 (0.077)	0.001 (0.002)	−0.025 (0.024)	– –	0.031 (0.011)	0.26 (0.06)	0.76 –
Secondary schools	−6.70 (7.14)	−0.023 (0.118)	0.007 (0.004)	0.004 (0.037)	−1.20 (0.43)	0.006 (0.003)	0.46 (0.07)	0.85 –
All schools	−7.09 (5.15)	−0.014 (0.085)	0.004 (0.003)	−0.016 (0.028)	−0.71 (0.30)	0.024 (0.009)	0.39 (0.06)	0.86 –
County councils (omitting economic variables)								
Primary schools	−6.63 (2.13)	–	–	–	–	0.027 (0.009)	0.26 (0.03)	0.75 –
Secondary schools	8.13 (1.68)	–	–	–	−0.73 (0.40)	–	0.39 (0.02)	0.82 –
All schools	−2.88 (2.79)	–	–	–	−0.63 (0.27)	0.025 (0.008)	0.38 (0.03)	0.85 –

8 Macroeconomic Policy

Macroeconomic policy is concerned with the aggregates of economic activity, with total output and employment, the balance of payments, economic growth and inflation. It is only in so far as it affects these aggregates that local government is relevant to the conduct of macroeconomic policy.

In this chapter we first outline central government's approach to macroeconomic policy, as it affects local government, in terms of the evolution of ideas and their practical implementation. We then examine the use of grants as an instrument of macroeconomic control, and then of loan sanctions for capital expenditure. We then consider the effects of inflation, first on local authority finances and then on the operation of central government policy towards local authorities.

THE FRAMEWORK OF MACROECONOMIC POLICY

Before the Great Depression of the 1930s few disputed that the finances of governments should be conducted on the same principles as those of private individuals and enterprises. Current expenditures should be financed from current income receipts, and capital expenditures by long-term borrowing to be paid off out of the income generated by the capital.

Thinking on macroeconomic policy was dominated by the arguments of the classical economists, most simply encapsulated in 'Say's Law' — that there is a general tendency for the level of aggregate demand in an economy to be equal to productive capacity, or that 'supply creates its own demand' (see, for example, Mill, 1848, bk 2, ch. 14). People were aware, of course, that Say's Law did not hold exactly at all moments of time. There was considerable concern and discussion of the trade cycles that dominated economic activity in the nineteenth century. But those fluctuations were typically ascribed to changes in the state of business confidence which the government was powerless to prevent. Indeed the most government could do was to avoid itself being a cause of changes in business confidence by pursuing 'unsound' financial policies.

Local governments are obliged to balance their budgets to this day in part on the basis of this thinking. Indeed the only problem from the point of view of central government, given this approach, is with the payment of grants. If grants are tied to local government expenditure, and local authorities in aggregate spend more than expected, central government grant payments will have to rise, with the result that central government may be in difficulty balancing its own books. As we have argued in an earlier chapter (Part One, Chapter 7) this concern was a major factor leading to the introduction of block grants. A block grant, such as the present needs element of RSG, is almost entirely unaffected by local spending decisions, and the total financial commitment of central government is therefore quite precisely predetermined.

In this 'classical' system, all local authority current expenditure is financed from taxation – either directly through rates or indirectly through grants themselves financed from central government tax revenues. The classical approach assumes that taxes reduce demand in the private sector to the same extent that public expenditure increases it, and hence that changes in the total of local government current expenditure have no effect on the total level of demand in the economy. Likewise, capital expenditure is financed by borrowing, and it is assumed that money borrowed by local government would otherwise have been lent to some private borrower. Local government capital expenditure thus simply displaces private capital expenditure and the total of demand is unaffected. None of this implies that the level of local government expenditure is a matter of indifference, for clearly in this approach the more local government spends the less is available for private consumption or investment. But the issues raised are those of resource allocation – of the competing claims of different sectors for scarce resources – and not those of macroeconomic policy.

The Great Depression was a period of unparalleled crisis in government finances. The sharp fall in economic activity led to a correspondingly sharp fall in government revenues, while on the expenditure side the introduction of 'redistributive' expenditures, in particular unemployment benefits, around the time of the First World War meant that expenditures tended to rise in the slump. Quite apart from the political problems of cutting benefits, or increasing taxes, in the midst of a severe depression, there was also a collapse of intellectual confidence. The alleged self-righting mechanisms in the economic system had evidently failed. On a simple commonsense view it seemed absurd to cut back spending further as a deliberate act of government policy when the very low level of spending seemed the obvious cause of the whole problem. None the less there was no way to argue with the 'Treasury view' that to run a budget deficit would mean more borrowing which would not only 'crowd out' an equivalent amount of private borrowing but also depress business confidence and hence would be more likely to reduce than increase the overall level of demand.

The depression created difficulties in central government's relation with local authorities since their expenditures under the Poor Law inevitably rose at a time when many authorities wished to cut back their expenditure and others wished to increase it. Within the Labour government there was a sharp division between the Prime Minister, Ramsay MacDonald, and the Chancellor of the Exchequer, Philip Snowden, who favoured local expenditure cuts and others, like Oswald Mosley who anticipated Keynes and urged local government to spend more.

In economic theory, the turning point was the publication in 1936 of Keynes's *General Theory of Employment, Interest and Money*. Keynes not only attempted a theoretical rebuttal of the classical position that demand would always tend to equality with productive capacity, but provided a new way of thinking about macroeconomic issues. According to Keynes, the self-righting mechanisms on which the classical approach relied were weak and unreliable, and there was no tendency in general for demand in the economy to be adequate to maintain full employment. Furthermore, intervention by government might be able to influence the level of demand. The policy prescriptions of the *General Theory* were in fact rather less radical than its theoretical innovations – an 'easy money' (low interest rate) policy and if that did not work more public investment to make up for the unwillingness of private investors. But four years later, in *How To Pay for the War* (Keynes, 1940) the full potential of deficit financing was recognised, and the principle introduced that the balance of the budget should be determined by the state of the economy and not by the classical principles of sound finance. On this principle, if there is unemployment, government expenditure should be increased, or taxes cut, which will stimulate demand and reduce unemployment. Likewise, if the problem is inflation (as it was during the war), taxes should be increased, or government expenditure cut to reduce demand and hence reduce inflationary pressures. These principles were enshrined as official government policy in the 1944 White Paper on *Employment Policy* (Ministry of Reconstruction, 1944, Cmnd 6527).

For purposes of practical administration, the Keynesian approach was translated into the idea of 'demand management'. The government would attempt to steer the actual level of demand towards the level it desired (which would be determined by its macroeconomic objectives of full employment, price stability, balance-of-payments equilibrium, and so on) by use of macroeconomic policy instruments (principally taxes, and monetary policy). To begin with, decisions on public expenditure continued to be made according to more or less traditional criteria, while macroeconomic policy guided the budget judgement on taxation and the conduct of monetary policy. The conventional links between public expenditure and taxation were broken.[1] The total size of the public sector and the tax burden was determined less by a decision on the relative benefits of public as against private expenditure than as a by-product of macroeconomic management. None the less, in this phase, local government was not much affected by central government's pursuit of its macroeconomic objectives.

But with the growth of public expenditure it became increasingly invidious that the burden of macroeconomic adjustment should be thrown wholly on to taxation. In principle, macroeconomic restraint could be achieved as effectively by expenditure cuts as by tax increases, and macroeconomic expansion by expenditure increases as by tax cuts. The procedure eventually adopted by central government in the 1960s of relating public expenditure to the medium-term economic assessment followed the recommendations of the Plowden Committee (1961). It is based on 'regular surveys of public expenditure as a whole, over a period of years ahead, and in relation to prospective resources', and is generally known as the PESC system, after the committee (Public Expenditure Survey Committee) which takes charge of it. But if central government wishes to use public expenditure as an instrument of macroeconomic policy it is immediately confronted with the fact that it does not itself have the powers to control a large part of public expenditure, namely that part undertaken by local governments. This disparity became evident towards the end of the 1960s and even into the early 1970s when central government reined back real central expenditure, but was unable to influence local expenditure in the same way.

THE PESC SYSTEM

The basis of the PESC system is that each central government department prepares estimates of public expenditure within its sector on the basis of unchanged policies normally for the next five years. At the same time, the Treasury prepares its medium-term assessment for the economy over the coming five years, estimating the likely growth of productive capacity and the various claims on that productive potential. Normally the balance of payments and investment are held to have prior claims on productive capacity because the government has committed itself to balance-of-payments or growth targets which take precedence over public expenditure or private consumption. But once these prior claims have been met, the remainder of the growth in output is available to provide for growth in public expenditure or private consumption. The government then decides on the balance between private and public spending. If, for example, it wishes to give priority to the growth of public expenditure, the system will tell it by how much private expenditure needs to be cut back, and hence what tax increases would be required.

More significant from the standpoint of local government is the opposite case. If the government wishes to give priority to the growth of private expenditure, public-expenditure growth would need to be cut back. Suppose that the PESC system has produced estimates of a relatively fast growth of public spending on the basis of existing policies. Then policy changes would be required to reduce public expenditure to the desired level. While central government can normally change its own policies it has no power to compel local authorities to change theirs. In short, the present system of macroeconomic management assumes government can control the total of public expenditure while in fact it has no formal powers to do so. In his note of dissent to the Layfield Report, Professor Day cites a 'high Treasury Official' describing 'local government finance as it is at the moment as the "Achilles' heel" of the Treasury's control over aggregate public spending' (Layfield, 1976, p. 307).

We argued in the last chapter that the absence of formal powers does not necessarily imply the absence of effective control. There are many sanctions central government can use to encourage local authorities to comply with its wishes, including the threat of legislation. It is not always obvious which authorities are conforming to the policy guidelines. For if central government, in discussion with representatives of local authority associations, agrees to a reduction of, say, 2 per cent in the planned growth overall of some service, there is no direct implication for the growth of expenditure on that service within any particular authority (Layfield, 1976, ch. 13, para. 16). Existing service standards, costs, population characteristics and all sorts of special factors, vary widely between authorities. An overall reduction in planned expenditure growth of 2 per cent may be fully consistent with an actual increase in expenditure of 10 per cent in any particular authority or a reduction of more than 2 per cent. Others may completely ignore guidelines for some services but end up with no increase in overall expenditure because other elements of expenditure have been falling for quite independent reasons. Moreover, any attempt to penalise rapid growth of expenditure tends to bear as heavily on authorities who are behind national standards and are attempting to catch up as on those who are ahead. For the purpose of macroeconomic policy, what matters most is not generally a small minority of authorities in open defiance of central government policy guidelines, since their effect on the total may be small, but that a large number slightly overspend, amounting in aggregate to a significant increase in public expenditure.

Central government has other means at its disposal for influencing capital expenditure. It requires loan sanction which provides a means for its control. We consider both instruments in greater detail.

THE RATE SUPPORT GRANT AND MACROECONOMIC POLICY

Payments of grants to local authorities have for a long time been based on estimates of how much local authorities are likely to spend. Calculations of such expenditure ('total relevant expenditure') antedate the introduction of PESC. Indeed for many years during the 1960s the two systems continued side by side, but quite independently, the estimates of total relevant expenditure on which grant was paid being significantly greater than the figures of local government expenditure derived from the public expenditure surveys for PESC.

Estimates of total relevant expenditure for RSG used to be forecasts of what local authorities in aggregate were likely to spend. They took account of existing service levels and expected improvements, as well as demographic and policy changes. The forecasts were made on a service-by-service basis by working groups ('expenditure subgroups') of representatives of central government departments and local authority associations. But their purpose was to forecast and not impose predetermined expenditure targets. Thus their forecasts were frequently proved incorrect. Since 1975, RSG negotiations have been incorporated into the PESC system. Instead of attempting to forecast local authority expenditures, the subgroups have been asked to examine the implications of complying with the expenditure targets in the annual public expenditure White Papers which are the outcome of the PESC system. While this goes some way to ensuring that the estimates of total relevant expenditure for grant purposes are consistent with PESC targets, it does not of itself imply that actual expenditure will be any closer to those targets.

If the grant is to be used as a means of restraining expenditure, what is required is a reduction in total grant paid. This reduction can be brought about irrespective of estimates of total relevant expenditure by appropriate adjustment in the proportion of that expenditure financed by grant. There are two major objections to the use of grant for controlling aggregate local government expenditure:

(1) It is indiscriminate. A cut in grant penalises authorities who keep to the expenditure guidelines as much as those who defy them.
(2) It may be ineffective, even creating worse problems than it solves, since a cut in grant may not lead to reductions in expenditure but to rate increases, whose unpopularity rebounds on central as well as local govern-

ment, and which could in turn result in higher wage demands and so more inflation.

Cutting grant is meant to put pressure on all authorities to hold back their spending. Those that do will be able to cope with the reduction in grant without imposing exceptional rate increases. Those that do not, on the other hand, with rising expenditure and falling grant will have to levy exceptionally large rate increases. Though the cut-back in grant may be indiscriminate, it should cause major difficulties only for the overspending authorities.

But the way in which the mechanism works is complicated by the fact that the resources element is a matching grant. Authorities in receipt of resources element receive grant in proportion to their expenditure. If they spend in excess of the policy guidelines they still receive the additional grant, forcing the government to cut back on the grant going to other authorities which may have kept within its expenditure guidelines if the overall grant ceiling is to be preserved. We have already pointed (in Part Two, Chapter 3) to the anomalous feature of the resources element whereby the central government is committed to support a large proportion of the expenditure of many authorities with an open-ended grant, however much they spend. Quite apart from the consequences discussed there, a matching resources grant weakens the effectiveness of altering grant levels as an instrument of macroeconomic policy.

We have also argued (Part Two, Chapter 3) that the present regression method of calculating needs grant tends to reward high spending. So that authorities which defy expenditure guidelines will, if the regression analysis is able to identify any common characteristics amongst them, also receive more needs grant in the subsequent year's needs grant allocation. And these additional receipts of grant will again in all probability in future years be at the expense of authorities that have held back their expenditure, if the overall ceiling is to be maintained.

But these arguments are criticisms of the actual structure of the grant and not of its potential effectiveness as a macroeconomic instrument. Such inequities in the way in which the grant system operates do not make changes in grant levels any the less effective in implementing macroeconomic policy; and if, as will be discussed later, resources grant were to lose its matching characteristic over the relevant range of expenditure or *a fortiori* if needs grant were replaced by another which did not reward expenditure increases, inequity would no longer be a deterrent to greater reliance on changes in grant as a macroeconomic instrument.

The other objection is more fundamental. It is that if grants are cut, local authorities will not reduce their expenditure but instead increase their rates. There is no clear evidence on this question. But we have shown in Part One that rates, as a proportion of disposable income, have remained remarkably constant over time, and this suggests that local authorities might encounter significant ratepayer resistance, should they attempt to increase their rates too fast. Nevertheless one would expect some part of this fall in grant to be reflected by increased rates or the running down of balances.

But we must now ask a much more fundamental question. From the point of view of the government's macroeconomic objectives does it matter whether the cut in grants leads to a cut in expenditure or to an increase in rates? For Keynesian demand management purposes, either will reduce aggregate demand.[2] But their equivalence was rejected by the Treasury in its evidence to the Layfield Committee (Layfield, 1976, ch. 13, para. 7), because:

(i) An increase in rates is likely to reduce private sector savings as well as expenditure so that the demand on resources, from the public and private sectors together, will be increased.

(ii) The government has a proper concern with the overall balance between public and private spending . . . Severe restraint on personal spending is liable to lead to pressures for further wage increases which can only exacerbate the problem of inflation.

The Layfield Committee accepted these arguments, but to us both seem dubious. The first is familiar from elementary economic textbooks, where it is known as the 'balanced budget multiplier' (Haavelmo, 1945). The argument is simple. A hundred pounds spent by the government on goods and services creates demand for £100 worth of goods and services. But £100 raised in taxation may only reduce consumers' expenditure on goods and services by, say, £70, the remaining £30 coming out of savings. In total, therefore, the demand for goods and services increases by £30.

However, for all its distinguished intellectual heritage there is something inherently questionable about the balanced budget multiplier. Is, for example, an increase in the number of restaurants, or clothes shops, of concern for macroeconomic policy on the grounds that part of the money spent in such establishments may come out of private savings, and so the total demand on resources will increase? But why should this be any different from the provision of additional services for residents of some locality by the local authority, and financed from rates? On the conventional argument, if people employ private contractors to clear away rubbish there is no effect on aggregate demand. But if the local authority provides the service, total demand on resources is thought to increase. The weakness in the conventional view is that it assumes (correctly) that taxes impoverish people but does not allow for the possibility that public expenditure may provide offsetting benefits which will reduce their private consumption. A household's decision on how much to save is determined by the balance between current and future living standards, and will not be significantly affected by whether the goods and services that contribute to its standard of living are provided by the public or by the private sector.

On the above argument the balanced budget multiplier would be zero: there would just be a substitution between private and public spending. But we would not go as far as this extreme position. First, the argument only holds for what we have called beneficial expenditures. Where the ratepayer receives no direct benefit from the services local government provides, it is reasonable to assume he will pay part of his rates out of savings. Second, the main part of the rate burden falls not on households but on firms. That taxes on households reduce their spending is well known, and supported by numerous econometric studies. The impact on aggregate demand of taxes on firms is much less well understood.

Non-domestic rates could be passed on to the consumer in the form of higher prices, or could affect profits, wages or rents. As we have seen in Part Two, Chapter 6 there is considerable uncertainty as to the incidence of non-domestic rates, and the effect on demand must also therefore be uncertain.

For the purpose of macroeconomic strategy, what is important is the prediction of aggregate demand and changes in aggregate demand resulting from changes in policy. How such changes are distributed among different elements of aggregate demand is not relevant to macroeconomic control but an issue of resource allocation. If we can be reasonably sure what change in local expenditure resulted from a change in grant, a balanced budget multiplier effect would pose no problems for macroeconomic management. All that would be required is that the change in grant be such that the sum of the local expenditure effect and the consumption effect of the change equal the desired change in aggregate demand. For example, if a cut in grant of £100 leads to a cut in local expenditure of £50, an increase in rates of £50, and the marginal propensity to consume is 0.8, private spending will fall by £40. The grant cut of £100 will only have an aggregate demand effect of £90. So if the objective were a change in aggregate demand of £100, the change in grant would have to be £111.

A problem may seem to arise if the effect of the cut in grant on expenditure is not known with certainty. In our example the effect of a cut in grant of £100 would have an effect on aggregate demand of £100 if local expenditure dropped by the full amount of the cut in grant, or of only £80 if rates were increased by the same amount as the cut in grant. To estimate the likely effect of such ignorance on the ability to predict the effect of changes in grants on aggregate demand we look at the relationship between the errors in predicting changes in aggregate demand and those in predicting how a cut in grants is allocated between cuts in local expenditures and increases in rates. Simple algebraic manipulation shows that

$$e_d = \frac{e_a s}{1 - s\bar{\alpha}}$$

where e_d is the percentage error in predicting a change in aggregate demand resulting from a change in grant, e_a is the percentage error in predicting what proportion of a change in grant will result in an increase in rates, s is the marginal propensity to save, and $\bar{\alpha}$ is the predicted proportion of the change in grant which will result in a change in rates. Thus if it is predicted that rates will change by half the change in grant ($\bar{\alpha} = \frac{1}{2}$), and the marginal propensity to save is equal to 0.2, a 20 per cent error in the prediction will result in a 2.2 per cent error in predicting the change in aggregate demand arising from the change in grant.

The effect of such an error on the predicted level of expenditure is, however, much smaller and depends on the relationship between the predicted change in expenditure and the actual level of expenditure. If the predicted change were 10 per cent of the actual level then an error of 2.2 per cent in predicting the change in expenditure would result in an error of less than one-fifth of 1 per cent in predicting the level of expenditure. If the predicted change was merely 5 per cent of the level, the error of 2.2 per cent in predicting the change would result in an error of about one-tenth of 1 per cent in predicting the level of expenditure. Errors of this order of magnitude are trivial in comparison with the actual errors habitually made in predicting central government expenditure, which are more easily controlled by central government. These have ranged between 1969/70 and 1975/6 from 1.5 per cent to 8.1 per cent with a mean error of over 5 per cent (Perlman and Lynch, 1977). As a result it seems absurd to suppose that the government's responsibility for overall management of the economy is threatened by such relatively small errors in predicting balanced budget effects.

In the above argument we have assumed that local expenditure can be financed either with grants or rates. In the long run that is true. However, in the short run expenditure can also be financed by running down the accumulated balances held by local authorities. In the past years these have averaged about 7 per cent of local expenditure. A cut in grant can thus have a smaller effect on aggregate demand than we have assumed. The analogy is with the situation in which private consumption depends on permanent income rather than current income. In such a case, a change in taxes will have a small effect on consumption if it is considered a transitory change. Similarly, a transitory change in the grant may have a small effect on local expenditure and rates. In the former case consumption is maintained by running down savings, in the latter case it is maintained by running down balances.

The possibility of financing expenditure with balances complicates but does not change our previous conclusions. Now a prediction has to be made about how a change in grant will affect expenditure, rates and balances. The appropriate change in grant to achieve some given change in aggregate demand will now also depend on its effect on balances. Any error in predicting the change in balances will affect the outcome. Again, however, we do not believe that such possible prediction errors provide a sufficient case for central control over local expenditure on the grounds of the government's responsibility for overall management of the economy.

The second argument is closer to the heart of the issue. Central government, it goes, has a 'proper concern with the overall balance between public and private spending' (Layfield, 1976, p. 239). The reason for this is the fear that increases in local government spending financed from rates will lead to higher wage claims. It is not clear whether this fear of inflation is the only reason why the central government is concerned about local government spending. In any event, we consider the inflation argument next, and the more general argument later in the chapter.

The claim advanced by the Treasury that 'a severe restraint on personal spending is liable to lead to pressures for further wage increases' is widely believed and has some econometric support. In a well-known study, Sargan (1961) demonstrated the tendency of money wages to keep up with prices, and this relationship has been confirmed for later years by Henry, Sawyer and Smith (1976). One interpretation of this result is that trade unions insist on increases in money wages sufficient to keep up with price increases. An alternative interpretation, for which Parkin, Sumner and Ward (1974) find supporting evidence, is that price increases lead to an increase in firms' revenues and hence in the amount they are prepared to pay their workers. Personal living standards depend not only on wages and prices but also on direct taxes. Wilkinson and Turner (1972) and Johnston and Timbrell (1973) have found evidence that increases in direct taxation are associated with higher wage claims.

These studies take no account of any benefits of public expenditure. One may well argue that a fall in the standard of living leads to higher wage claims, but it is not obvious that an increase in public expenditure need always imply a fall in living standards. If the people of a locality vote for councillors favouring higher public expenditure, an increase in expenditure must be assumed to reflect those preferences and cannot, therefore, at the same time represent a reduction in living standards. However, the existence of redistributive impacts – the fiscal wedges – analysed in Chapters 2 and 3 of Part Two – means that one cannot exactly assume that even taxation to support beneficial services reflects the preferences of all citizens affected.

There is also a slightly more technical point in this context: rates figure in the retail price index which is generally taken as the relevant price index for wage negotiations. An increase in rates, therefore, pushes up the price index and may thus feed directly into wage claims. But rates are not a price but a measure of expenditure. If people consume more of a private good at a given cost per unit, their expenditure on that good will increase, but the retail price index will be unaffected because the price of the good has not changed. But if people want more of a service provided by local government, again at a given cost per unit of service provided, rates will increase and this will appear as an increase in the retail price index even though no prices have gone up. This anomaly is due to faulty accounting procedures and not to any fundamental difference between private and public expenditure. It would be both possible and sensible, for example, to deflate increases in rate bills by the increases in the quantity of local government services (derived say from PESC estimates) to arrive at an average increase in the price paid by the household per unit of local government services provided.[3,4]

There is, however, a further problem with the use of grant for macroeconomic purposes. If grants are cut, and rates rise in consequence, it is argued that much of the political unpopularity of the higher rates will rebound on central government. On this argument, even if central government were satisfied that the control of grant was an adequate instrument for purposes of macroeconomic policy, it would be an instrument it could not use for fear of its political consequences.

Evidence supporting this view is somewhat slight, and prompted only by the atypical experience of 1974. The changed needs grant formula introduced in that year altered the grant distribution substantially in favour of the urban authorities. The then Conservative government proposed a variable domestic element to offset the very large increases in rate bills that would otherwise have fallen on domestic ratepayers in the rural authorities. This variable domestic element was scrapped during March 1974 by the incoming Labour government, leaving authorities no time to adjust their expenditure or rate demand before the start of the new financial year in April. The outcry from rural ratepayers led to the payment of a special rate relief in October 1974.

It would be unwise to regard this example as a precedent. The large rate increases in 1974 were, clearly enough, the consequences of last-minute changes in grant distribution and not of local spending decisions. Ratepayers were right to regard central, rather than local, government as responsible. And central government's concern with the burden on rural ratepayers in October 1974 may not have been unconnected with the general election held in that month.

The more general argument that central government will not cut grants for fear of the political consequences is belied by more recent experience. The proportion of total relevant expenditure financed by grant was reduced from 65.5 per cent in 1976/7 to 61 per cent in 1977/8 which proportion was retained again in 1978/9 despite strong local protests. Local authorities were given plenty of warning that a severe settlement was to be expected well before the formal announcement in November, 1976. They were able to adjust to the settlement and increases in rate bills averaged around 10 per cent to 15 per cent, slightly below the prevailing rate of inflation.

Finally, it should be noted that disillusionment with orthodox Keynesian policy in recent years has led to far greater emphasis on the financial or monetary aspects of macroeconomic policy. In place of the Keynesian emphasis on 'real' magnitude, macroeconomic policy now centres around financial variables such as the Public Sector Borrowing Requirement, Domestic Credit Expansion, etc. As far as these variables are concerned it does not matter whether a cut in grants to local authorities leads to an increase in rates or a reduction in expenditure.

It is hard to avoid the conclusion that central government's involvement in discussing and attempting to influence the composition of local authority current expenditure cannot logically or practically be defended as necessary for macroeconomic control. Instead, the government seems to believe that local authorities are not always responsive to the wishes of the communities they represent, that they tend to increase their expenditures beyond their ratepayers' willingness to pay for them, and that people look to it (the central government) to control this undesired expenditure growth. There is some political and economic evidence in support of this view. But to confuse resource allocation and macroeconomic control is dangerous because policies to achieve one do not necessarily achieve the other, and vice versa. A ceiling imposed on increases in rate poundages, for example, would limit local authority income and hence current expenditure. Thus it achieves macroeconomic control. But the consequences of such a policy on the allocation of expenditure between services and across authorities might be wholly unacceptable and would certainly be a major further encroachment on local autonomy. On the other hand, arrangements which provide for control over resource allocation may imply a loss of macroeconomic control (as has been the case with housebuilding, see below).

Our conclusion is that the most straightforward and effective method of controlling local current expenditure is to alter the grant percentage to a greater extent than has been usual in the past, except from 1976/7 to 1979/80. Central government should, therefore, only allow for leakages in the local authority current expenditure multiplier by increasing the overall percentage cut or increase in grant accordingly. We have argued that there is no substantial macroeconomic case for central government being further concerned how far local authorities react to changes in grants by altering expenditure or their tax yields. If there are some activities which central government wants to favour or discourage, this is a separate matter which is not easily catered for within the present grant system, though we have seen in the last chapter that there are many other ways in which central government exercises its influence over local patterns of expenditure. Changes in the grant system as instruments of such influences will be discussed in Part Four.

If grants are so used for macroeconomic policy local authorities must not expect always to receive as much warning of central government's intentions on RSG percentages as it has had in the recent past if macroeconomic exigencies require this. The general tendency in macroeconomic stabilisation is to avoid too frequent changes in policy as likely to be self-defeating. The same holds for changes in grant as such an instrument. Nevertheless, there may be circumstances when the Chancellor needs to act quickly and there is no obvious reason why local government should be any more immune than personal or corporate taxation.

CAPITAL EXPENDITURE

Capital expenditure is financed largely from borrowing. In demand management terms, expenditure financed by borrowing has a far greater effect on aggregate demand than that financed by taxation, as there is no offsetting fall in private consumption. Increased borrowing tends to raise interest rates, and hence reduce private investment demand, but the offsetting effect here is probably small. And, in any event, the government is highly sensitive to the behaviour of interest rates which have an immediate effect on the balance of payments and private housebuilding, as well as on private investment and its own borrowing costs. While we could make a case that changes in local authority current expenditure financed by taxation would have no significant macroeconomic effects, the same cannot be said for changes in capital expenditure financed by borrowing.[5]

For this reason, local authority capital expenditure is more closely controlled than current expenditure. All capital spending requires loan sanction. The present procedure was introduced in 1971. Capital expenditure is divided into four types of which two — key sector schemes and locally determined schemes — are of major importance. The key sector covers those areas of local government activity with which central government is most closely involved, and includes education, housing, principal roads, police and personal social services. Within this sector all capital projects have to be approved individually by the relevant central government department, but there is no limit on the total expenditure of any given authority. The locally determined sector covers street lighting, libraries, parks, improvements to secondary roads, and suchlike. Each authority is given a total capital allocation for each year, up to which it can borrow, and spend as it chooses amongst projects in the locally determined sector.

For purposes of macroeconomic control, the question is how well these arrangements control total capital expenditure by local authorities in any given year. The locally determined sector lends itself very well to macroeconomic control. Each authority is given an allocation and these can be summed to indicate the likely total of capital expenditure. If this total is too high in terms of macroeconomic policy objectives, the allocations for individual authorities can be reduced.

With key sector schemes it is more complex. Some departments may work to an overall budget of the total of loan sanctions they are prepared to grant. Others may be more permissive and grant loan sanctions to all schemes meeting certain criteria irrespective of how many are brought forward. School-building has come into the first category while housebuilding used to follow the second. It is clearly necessary for macroeconomic purposes, if the existing procedure is maintained, that all departments operate with fixed total capital allocations, and this has now been introduced.

Of course, capital expenditure is not normally completed within the year the loan sanction was granted, and many capital projects may take many years to complete. A sudden cut-back in loan sanctions may only show up in reduced capital spending with some delay. For this reason, changes in the granting of loan sanctions may not be an appropriate instrument for short-run stabilisation, or 'fine tuning', of the economy.

In their study commissioned for Layfield (1976, app. 6) the National Institute of Economic and Social Research found little evidence of instability resulting from local authority capital expenditure, except for housing, which as we saw in Chapter 4 of Part One had a major destabilising effect on the economy. Central government has wished to encourage local authority housebuilding and as a result loan sanctions have been readily available. But it has not been able to forecast accurately at what rate they would be taken up and, given the importance of housing in total capital expenditure, as a result total capital expenditure has deviated significantly from forecast. The benefits of council housebuilding are no longer unquestioned and controls on this sector have now been introduced.

LOCAL AUTHORITIES AND INFLATION

Inflation has important effects both on local authorities' own finances, and on central government policy towards them.

THE EFFECTS OF INFLATION ON LOCAL AUTHORITIES

We consider the effects of inflation first on authorities' current income and expenditure, and then on the capital account.

First, there is the question of whether inflation squeezes local authority revenues. Assume, for example, a year in which on average prices, wages and other incomes were rising, in money terms, by 20 per cent. The cost to an authority (excluding debt charges) of providing existing services would be likely also to rise by about 20 per cent. Assuming the proportion of expenditure financed by grant is unchanged, rate increases of the order of 20 per cent will be required to meet these higher costs.

Now it might be said that if ratepayers' incomes were rising, on average, by around 20 per cent and the prices of other goods and services rising at the same speed, rate increases of around 20 per cent would be perfectly acceptable. And in the long run this argument is no doubt true. Once people have come to realise that higher prices have come to stay and adjusted to the falling value of money, they will come to accept the higher rate bills. But this process takes time. In the short run, if there is an unexpected acceleration in the rate of inflation, people will regard their higher rate bills as a greater real burden on them and attribute them to an expansion in local government services. This confusion may be described as 'money illusion', that is the illusory belief that money is still worth what it was when in fact its value has fallen.

Because, at least in the short run, ratepayers resist rate increases which do no more than keep up with inflation, local authorities may be under pressure to hold rate increases below the rate of inflation, even if this means cutting back services. Local authorities are worse off than central government, whose tax revenues tend to rise automatically and imperceptibly with inflation because they are concealed in the prices of goods or in deductions from pay. With the exception of vehicle excise duties, rates are the only form of taxation levied independently of any receipt, or expenditure, of money and hence whose revenues are not automatically buoyed up by a general inflation of money incomes and prices.

Further, because rateable values are fixed in money terms and revalued only infrequently, the increase in rate bills takes the form of an increased rate pound-age. If rateable values were revised annually, and property values were to rise with inflation, it would be clearer to ratepayers that the increase in their rate bill was the consequence of general inflation — as reflected in their increased prop-erty value — rather than of higher real expenditure by the local authority. Increases in rate poundages would then again reflect changes in service provision rather than general inflation.

Annual revisions of the rateable value of each property are impracticable, but a possible compromise is indexation of rateable values. Indexation would imply increasing all assessments on the basis of one, or a small number, of indices of property values. Regular revaluations would still be required to take account of changes in the relative values of specific properties. But under such a system, average assessment would not be much affected by revaluation. For most properties only a relatively small adjustment (up or down) would be required. So a second advantage of indexation is that it might increase the frequency of revaluations by reducing the unpopularity associated with them, a matter to which we return in Chapter 2 of Part Three.

While there would be continued dispute and disagreement as to which index to use, and to how many different indices for different types of properties on locations,[6] the main objection to indexation in this context is that it would be no more than a 'cosmetic' change. What matters to the ratepayer is the increase in his rate bill. How that increase is split up between rateable value and rate poundage is a secondary concern.

The only way of overcoming the problem is through replacing rates by a more buoyant and less noticeable source of tax revenue. We consider arguments for new sources of local revenue in Part Four, Chapter 3, and examine the 'buoyancy' issue in more detail there. But we must note in conclusion here that the problem is only a short-term one. Domestic rates, as a proportion of disposable income, have remained remarkably steady over the last few years (Layfield, 1976, annex 10, table 27). The outcry in 1974 reflected money illusion rather than an increased average real burden. That outcry is now over, without real rate revenues having suffered relative to personal disposable incomes.

Turning from the income to the expenditure side of the budget, there is no general reason why the prices of goods and services purchased by local government, or the wages paid to local government staff, should increase more rapidly relatively to other prices in times of inflation. The item of expenditure most affected is debt charges. Interest rates, though affected by many other factors, normally rise with inflation to compensate for the fall in the value of money. If, say, the rate of inflation rises from 3 per cent to 8 per cent and there is a corresponding rise in interest rates from 5 per cent to 10 per cent, interest charges double, thus increasing very sharply relative to other costs. This element of expenditure may then rise much more rapidly than the general rate of inflation. On the housing revenue account, for example, interest charges constitute the main part of expenditure, and while it is quite possible for interest rates to double within a year, it is hardly conceivable that the rents charged to tenants could be doubled between one year and the next.

In fact the issue is much more complex than this suggests. If capital expenditure is financed by long-term borrowing at fixed interest, as has been traditional, interest charges on that borrowing are fixed in money terms and thus do not increase with inflation. The effect of inflation on total debt charges thus depends on the proportion of new borrowing (on which the higher interest rate must be paid) in total debt outstanding. With the increases in interest rates in recent years, long-term rates have been at historically high levels, and local authorities have responded by increasing their short-term borrowing in the hope that interest rates would fall and they could then reduce their borrowing costs. This shortening of the debt has, however, increased the proportion needing to be refinanced in any year, and hence increased the vulnerability of local authorities to further increases in interest rates. Local authorities have now agreed to a voluntary code for lengthening their debt. Before examining this question there is a more fundamental point to be considered.

The increased interest charges which accompany inflation do not constitute an increased real burden for local authorities. They compensate lenders for the fall in the real value of the money they have lent the local authority. From the standpoint of the local authority, the higher interest payments are offset by the erosion in the real value of their outstanding debt. The inflation component of the interest charge is more in the nature of capital repayment than current expenditure. Inflation accompanied by high interest rates can be envisaged as placing a heavy burden of debt repayment in the early years of a loan to compensate for the erosion of the real value of the capital by the time of redemption.

Now inflation does not alter the benefits over time provided by some capital investment, and there seems no good reason why it should bring forward the effective burden of debt charges. An investment with a life of twenty years should be financed by revenue contributions over the whole twenty years of its life, and not almost wholly in the first four or five years as will be the case with inflation and fixed-interest borrowing. A simple reform that would deal with this problem would be to allow local authorities to finance part of their interest charges from new borrowing, provided only that the real value of their outstanding debt was not thereby increased. The basic objection to financing interest payments with new borrowing is that it leads to an ever-increasing debt burden. But the erosion of monetary debts by inflation allows a limited amount of new borrowing without the real burden of debt being increased.

Alternatively, local authorities might be allowed to follow the lead of the national savings movement, and borrow on indexed terms. Experience with the national savings schemes suggests that the interest rate offered could be very low, or even negative, with borrowing of this form. The interest payments would not fluctuate as a result of inflation, and this would protect local authorities from serious financial disruption in the event of sudden changes in the rate of inflation. It must be recognised, of course, that with indexed debt, the lender's capital is protected in real terms, so it follows that the local authority's debt is not reduced in real terms by inflation. In money terms it increases at the same rate as inflation, but this does not represent an increase relative to the authority's income or expenditure or the value of its capital stock.

The absence of any schemes of this type to take account of the inflation component of interest charges has meant that central government has had to step in with higher grants – particularly in housing – which has further confused the issue of financial accountability. It would be absurd, for example, to attempt to balance the housing revenue account year by year if the main component of expenditure is interest on short-term debt which fluctuates wildly. But the abandonment of this principle and the fact that rents now form a relatively small part of housing revenue account income implants the notion that council tenants cannot be expected to pay 'economic' rents and that the determination of council rents can only be resolved as a political issue. In fact, with proper inflation accounting, or with indexed borrowing, the principle of balancing the housing revenue account would be quite practicable and could reintroduce economic criteria into council housing policy.

High interest rates associated with inflation do not only lead to difficulties on the current account, they raise questions as to the appropriate form of local authority borrowing in times of inflation. Local authorities have traditionally relied on long-term fixed interest debt as their main source of borrowing. But long-term fixed interest debt is a highly risky investment in times of rapid and varying rates of inflation. People lending money on such terms require high interest rates to compensate for the risks involved, that is the risk that they may lose their capital as a result of rapid inflation during the period of the loan. It follows that if inflation does not accelerate as anticipated, borrowers have to pay twice over both through repaying capital and through high interest rates to compensate for the unrealised possibility of capital erosion. In the circumstances, local authorities have fought shy of long-term borrowing.[7]

The alternative is short-term borrowing. But there are problems here, too.

First, as noted above, short-term borrowing means that interest charges are highly vulnerable to short-term interest rate fluctuations. Second, the large amount of refinancing required may create difficulties for monetary management. The government's response – the 'voluntary code' – is to encourage authorities back into long-term borrowing with the attendant high costs and risk that involves.

We have already discussed measures that could help local authorities deal with instability in interest charges. If the main worry is the difficulties that may potentially be caused for monetary management by the volume of refinancing that short-term borrowing implies, there seems a good case for encouraging local authorities to issue variable rate bonds. The interest payments on such bonds are linked to short-term interest rates, so that a borrowing authority need not fear that because interest rates are historically high at the time of issue, it will have to continue to pay an abnormally high interest rate over the whole life of the loan.

A second possibility is indexation, which protects lenders from the risk that their capital will be eroded by inflation. One might expect that long-term indexed debt need carry no risk premium. If local authorities were to borrow on indexed terms, they would in all probability find that interest payments on long-term debt would be no higher than on short-term debt (assuming both were indexed). Such a narrowing of interest rate differentials could well be more effective than the 'voluntary code' in encouraging authorities to revert to more long-term borrowing.[8]

A more radical approach is equity financing. Local authorities could sell shares in the ownership of their capital. There are many schemes, for example, whereby council tenants are able to share in the ownership of the housing they occupy. Likewise, council office premises, vehicles, and so on could be rented, hired or leased rather than purchased outright. While these arrangements raise many issues other than those of financial management, they may provide a useful means of reducing the burden of debt charges and hence partially insulating authorities from the disruptive effects of inflation.

INFLATION AND CENTRAL GOVERNMENT POLICY

While the rate of inflation was low, the procedure for dealing with it was of little consequence. The grant total was increased each year[9] to allow for price increases, but the mechanism for calculating the increase was not a matter of great concern. With the acceleration of inflation in the late 1960s and early 1970s a more systematic procedure was required.

The principle is that increases in costs and prices between the time of RSG settlement and the year in which it is paid should qualify for grant as in the Rate Support Grant Order. In the RSG settlement for 1974/5, for example, the government decided to finance 60.5 per cent of total relevant expenditure with grant. The actual figures in the Rate Support Grant Order, published towards the end of 1973, were calculated on the basis of November 1973 prices. The figure for total relevant expenditure would then be revised to take account of price and cost increases between November 1973 and November 1974, and a new grant total calculated as 60.5 per cent of total relevant expenditure at the new prices. The difference between the old and new grant totals would be distributed on the basis of a Grant Increase Order.

This arrangement raises difficulties both of practice and of principle. The practical difficulties concern the measurement of price increases from one year to the next. The information is provided by local authorities who are asked to estimate the increase in expenditure over the past twelve months in providing services to the standards implicit in the aggregate figure for total relevant expenditure. It is, of course, very difficult to distinguish what part of an increase in expenditure is attributable to higher prices and what part to changes in the type or quality of service provision. Nor is it always easy to interpret the precise expenditure implications for a particular authority of the aggregate figure for total relevant expenditure. It follows that Increase Orders may in fact be providing grant for increases in real expenditure in addition to cost and price increases.

An alternative would be to base the Increase Orders on some centrally compiled index of costs. Cost indices specific to local government spending have proved difficult to compute and are not currently available. There are cost indices for the economy as a whole, which could be used, but costs in the local authority sector may rise at a different rate from costs in the rest of the economy. That raises a question whether, in principle, the grant increase should compensate for increases in local authority costs or simply the rate of inflation in the economy as a whole. Historically, local authority costs have risen faster than costs and prices in the rest of the economy, a phenomenon which has become known as the 'relative price effect'.

The relative price effect
It is often claimed that local authority services are labour intensive, and offer few opportunities for cost-reducing technical innovations. While this may be so, it is rather puzzling for there seems nothing inherent in the nature of public provision of a good that would link it to these technological characteristics. A related argument is that there is productivity growth in local government services but it has taken the form of improvements in the quality of services provided with given inputs (which is difficult to measure and remains unrecorded) rather than reductions in the costs of providing services of given quality. And, of course, many would argue that local authorities are not exposed to competition and do not have the same incentives as private firms to innovate and reduce costs. It has been calculated[10] that in recent years costs in local government have been rising at just over 1 per cent per annum on average faster than costs in the rest of the economy. It may seem that this figure is small relative to the general rate of inflation and the relative price effect can be ignored. But it is possible that this increase in relative costs may be, in part, the result of the automatic compensation of local authority cost increases by central government grant. Local authorities are more likely to concede wage increases or any of the other pressures which may lead to higher costs (better staffing standards, etc.) if they expect the additional costs incurred to be borne largely by central government. Increase Orders do not compensate individual authorities for increases in their

own individual costs, but any general increase in costs will attract additional grant.

If the relative costs of providing some service rise, it is by no means clear that central government will wish to continue to support that service at least to the same standard. If a service becomes very expensive, it may feel the scale of provision should be reduced. It will not wish to support services to a given quality irrespective of the costs involved. It follows that local authorities should not expect to receive grant automatically to compensate for increases in relative costs.

On the basis of this argument, there is a case for linking the Increase Order not to an index of local authority costs but to an index of the general rate of costs increases in the economy as a whole, for example, the GDP deflator or an index of wage costs. Local authorities cannot insulate themselves from general inflationary trends in the economy (except very temporarily), and there is no reason why grants should not be increased to take this into account automatically.

Cash limits

In practice, a much more drastic solution has been adopted. 'Cash limits' have been applied to the Increase Order, limiting the amount that can be paid out in grant to a given money sum irrespective of the rate of increase of costs either in the local authority sector or in the economy as a whole. Provided cash limits are based on an accurate prediction of the rate of inflation, they can provide a clear and straightforward indication to local authorities of the magnitude of cost increases that will be supported by grant. In practice, cash limits have worked quite well because they have been introduced at a time of effective incomes policy, and the increases in costs have not exceeded predictions.

But governments have a chronic tendency to underpredict inflation, and incomes policies to break down. It is not clear how cash limits would survive in a situation like that of 1974 when local authorities were told to base their calculations on a 9 per cent rate of inflation and the actual rate turned out to be close to 20 per cent. If local authorities were to face cost increases of 20 per cent while being limited to an increase in grant based on an assumed inflation rate of 9 per cent the outcome would be a financial crisis. Few local authorities have balances sufficient to tide them over a deficit of this magnitude. Central government would be bound to intervene and the credibility of the cash limits undermined.

It might be argued that local authority costs do not rise of their own accord, but consist mainly of wages and salaries which go up only to the extent that increases are granted by the employers. If cash limits restrict cost increases to 9 per cent, will not local authorities have to restrict wage increases to that figure? Again the 1974 experience is relevant. It is hard to believe that the unions representing local authority staff would accept a cut of over 10 per cent in the real pay of their members, particularly when other unions are suffering no such reductions. A sharp cut in wages, even if accepted by the unions, would have harmful effects on morale, recruitment and staff structure. It is neither feasible nor desirable to impose on local authorities a requirement to restrict cost increases to a rate significantly different from that prevailing in the rest of the economy.

CONCLUSIONS

The main conclusions of this chapter are:
(1)   Central government cannot justify meddling in current expenditure on the pretext of its responsibilities for macroeconomic management.
(2)   The best method of controlling local authority use of national resources in the interest of macroeconomic policy is through varying the grant proportion.
(3)   Controls, or rationing, of capital expenditure may be justified but the existing system of loan sanctions provides an adequate mechanism.
(4)   Some measure of inflation accounting should be introduced to prevent local authorities being overburdened by interest charges which reflect inflation rather than a real increase in borrowing costs.
(5)   Grant Increase Orders should not be subject to 'cash limits' but instead be linked to an index of increases in costs in the economy as a whole.

NOTES

1   Curiously, in British parliamentary procedure, government expenditure and taxation have always been subject to separate votes.
2   Of course, central government may wish to reduce local government expenditure for reasons unconnected with macroeconomic policy. We are not concerned with such arguments here.
3   The notion of a 'unit of local government services' should not be regarded as fanciful. The PESC system assumes the possibility of separating 'volume' and 'price' elements of an increase in expenditure and presents estimates in volume or constant price terms. If, in some year, average rate bills rise 15 per cent while local government spending in volume terms rises by 5 per cent it is perfectly sensible to deduce that the average cost per unit of service to the ratepayer has risen by 10 per cent.
4   The retail price index is misleading in many ways. There would be advantages, in any case, in paying more attention to other price indices, for example the wholesale price index or the GDP deflator. Rates do not figure in either of these indices.
5   Capital expenditure on onerous services financed by borrowing will result in higher rates in the future to finance the debt. If these tax payments are capitalised in local property values, house prices will fall and consumption may be reduced in consequence. This is another application of the argument that with perfect discounting of future tax payments there is no difference between tax and debt financing. Both will have, at most, a balanced budget multiplier effect. It could thus be argued that even capital expenditure need not be controlled for macroeconomic policy purposes. Though there probably is some offset from such tax capitalisation the future is much too uncertain for complete capitalisation, especially in the short term.
6   These practical difficulties should not be thought overwhelming. The French government is proposing to introduce a form of indexation for revising assessments for the local property tax in France. See the Evidence of the Rating and Valuation Association to Layfield (1976, app. 9, pp. 267–9).
7   Private firms have abandoned long-term borrowing for the same reasons. There were no new debenture issues during the mid-1970s, for example.

8　Indexation raises a whole range of issues for which there is not enough space to discuss here. But a strong case exists for indexed long-term debt which offers security to the lender as well as being efficient for the borrower. This argument, and other aspects of indexation, are discussed in Jackman and Klappholz (1975).

9　Except in special circumstances when no increase was paid as a deliberate act of policy, for example in 1968.

10　The calculations have been made by the National Institute of Economic and Social Research, and are quoted by Layfield (1976, ch. 2, para. 30).

9 Conclusions

The chapter on the incidence of local taxes depended on a clear distinction between taxes levied to pay for locally determined beneficial and redistributive services and to pay for centrally determined redistributive services. This distinction is crucial to much of the argument of the remainder of the book. A local tax can be looked on as the price people pay for services they receive from local government. If they are beneficial services, then the ideal tax is one which approximates as closely as possible to a charge. If they are redistributive services, then the ideal tax is one which conforms as far as possible to established canons of equity and efficiency in taxation. The comparative merits of various taxes were reviewed. In various ways local income taxes, a tax on housing or a poll tax would have merits as methods of raising revenue for beneficial services. A tax on land, though attractive as a national tax and as a tax to finance centrally or locally determined redistributive services — because of the absence of incentive effects — for that reason would be less good as a way of paying for locally determined beneficial services.

The same distinction was crucial to our understanding of the purposes of the grant system. Many of its current tribulations and the discontent of those involved in it result from the failure to follow through or even to make the same distinction. Where taxes are used to finance locally determined services the main aim of a grant system is to achieve horizontal efficiency, that is to say grant should be used to reduce the differences in the discrepancies between the cost of provision and the average tax payment levied in each authority. This objective can be achieved by a matching resource equalisation grant. Where local taxes are used to finance centrally determined local expenditure, the corresponding grant aim is horizontal equity, so that grant is used to equalise so far as is possible for each local taxpayer the payment made by him towards such services. The appropriate grant is a unitary grant which combines an (unmatching) resource equalisation grant and a needs grant. Both the objectives of horizontal efficiency and equity are traditional in British local government finance though they are far from realised in practice. Until the distinctions are carried through into practice, attempts to measure needs are doomed to failure. Currently, regression analysis purports to measure differences in spending needs but in fact only measures differences in past spending.

Part Two, Chapter 4 contained an examination of factors that seem to account for differences in local expenditure, both on specific services and in aggregate. The chapter summarised much material both from other analyses and our own. Part Two, Chapter 5 used some of this material to analyse one question of major importance: the influence of grant on expenditure. The data used was cross-section. There has been a tendency in Britain to deny the possibility that increasing the proportion of local expenditure financed from grant and so reducing the effective 'price' of that expenditure to the local citizen has any effect in encouraging additional expenditure. Such insensitivity to price does not only run counter to our ordinary generalisations about economic behaviour, it also appears to be contradicted by the evidence. The evidence suggests that to increase the grant proportion does encourage local spending.

Old allegations take long to die. While early in the 1960s rates were regressive, the introduction of rate rebates in the mid-1960s has got rid of regressiveness for the poorest ratepayers. Nevertheless, the allegation is still common. Part Two, Chapter 6 argues as well that regressiveness is less worrying among the relatively affluent ratepayers because what matters is the net incidence of all taxation (and ideally all benefits). The chapter also demonstrates how the burden of rates had shifted from the domestic to the non-domestic ratepayer so, in its turn, reducing the 'price' of local services to the local elector. The economic consequences of the shift were examined.

Part Two, Chapter 7 tried to get to grips statistically with the difficult question of how far local authorities could be regarded as 'free' and how far as agents of central government. The instruments central government uses to influence local government were set out and the problems of defining 'free action' in this context illustrated. The changes in the institutional practices used by central government in education were used as an example of the problems of reaching any conclusions in this area. Nevertheless the statistical approach − if its premises are regarded as sufficiently valid − does suggest a conclusion which seems to fit *prima facie* intuition − there is not as much freedom as, for example, in the USA, but there are signs of expenditure patterns which suggest some freedom or non-conformity.

In the last chapter the problems central government faces in the macroeconomic control of local authorities' expenditure were analysed. It was argued that many of the controls, actual and proposed, seem redundant or unnecessary. A more relaxed regime was advocated for current expenditure, as were more systematic arrangements to take account of the effects of inflation.

PART THREE   AMELIORATION

1 Introduction

'If there is such a thing as growing human knowledge', wrote Sir Karl Popper 'then we cannot anticipate today what we shall only know tomorrow.' (1957, p. x.). We cannot anticipate in advance all the consequences of any proposed social reform, and some we may realise only after the reform has been put into effect. Because of this ignorance, there is a case for a 'gradualist' or 'piece-meal' approach to social reform:

> Social life is so complicated that few men, or none at all, could judge a blue-print for social engineering on the grand scale; whether it be practicable; whether it would result in a real improvement; what level of suffering it may involve; and what may be the means for its realisation. As opposed to this, blueprints for piecemeal engineering are comparatively simple . . . If they go wrong, the damage is not very great, and a re-adjustment not very difficult. They are less risky and for this very reason less controversial. (Popper, 1966, Vol. 1, p. 159)

It is in this spirit of trying to set right anomalies and imperfections in the present and familiar system rather than venturing into the unknown that Part Three of this book has been written. The reforms we suggest here may come about because the faults they are designed to rectify are generally recognised, and there is the prospect of reasonable agreement as to what should be done.

More radical change is unlikely to take place as a result of reasoned argument: it is too disruptive and too risky. Radical change occurs only when some crisis with which the existing system is unable to cope is sufficient to overcome the inertia of maintaining what is. These changes are, however, directed at the believed source of the momentary crisis, rather than being considered reforms related to features of the system that were responsible for its breakdown. At the end of Part Three we ask whether the ameliorative reforms we examine would make the system more resistant to crises in the relationship of central and local government than it has been in the past. Our answer is that they would not, and that at some stage more radical reforms will be required. It is to these we turn in Part Four.

Part Three, then, is to be regarded as 'piecemeal social engineering'. Through-out, it is assumed that rates remain the sole local authority tax. But there are improvements to the rating system to consider. In Chapter 2 we examine valuation and recommend a procedure that could make rates more equitable, more progressive and more buoyant than they are now. In Chapter 3 we argue for levying rates at a uniform poundage on all types of ratepayers within a locality. The present arrangements of differential rate poundages are complex, have unintended and inefficient economic effects and encourage central government political intervention in local government finance. These reforms we see as being consistent with rates providing about the same proportion of local revenues as now.

Charges are given no greater prominence than now. The remaining source of local revenue is, therefore, the grant from central government. The main question (Chapter 4) is whether the method of grant distribution should be revised. Here we argue that a significant reform of grant requires more radical reform of local government. Within the constraints of the present system there is not much that can be done. We do, however, see virtue in the government's proposed unitary grant, mainly because it attenuates the high matching grant implicit in present resource equalisation arrangements which we have shown encourages too high a level of local government spending. Changes in the organisation of local government, or in its relationship with central government, could be accompanied by more radical reforms of grant, but these are issues we leave to Part Four.

2 Assessment of Rateable Values

Historically, rating has changed its tax base from a widely defined and imprecise concept of property including movables, intended as a practical proxy for income and wealth, to a narrower definition as land, buildings and fixed plant. In the chapters of Part Three we accept that tax base. This chapter and the next are concerned, therefore, with modifications of the *status quo* which would still preserve the traditional character of the English system of local government finance by preserving the traditional form of the rating system.

The entire discussion in this chapter is concerned with making rates the *ad valorem* tax they are intended to be through purging the tax base of the anomalies that are now pervasive because of past and current methods of assessment. The chapter will concentrate on the assessment of dwellings, where the problems arise. We shall refer briefly at the end to the valuation of non-domestic property.

1. RENTAL VALUATION

It would be convenient if we could treat valuation as a purely technical question; and indeed that is how it is often regarded, as for example in the Layfield Report (Layfield, 1976, pp. 168–77).[1] But there are more fundamental issues.

Superficially, the main problem discussed is technical: the adequacy of the evidence available to establish rateable values. British practice has been to use rents as the evidence and tax base for rating. Rates paid R by a ratepayer are a proportion, a, called the rate poundage, of a measure of rent RV, the rateable value; so that

$$R = aRV$$

The rate poundage a is determined by the rating authority (as modified in effect by any other authority with the right to precept). The Local Government Act, 1948, led to the Inland Revenue assessing rateable values in England and Wales from 1950, independently of the authorities levying rates.

For most properties rateable values are reached by first estimating what are called gross (rental) values and adjusting these to calculate net (rental) values.[2] The gross value is defined as the rent at which the dwelling might be expected to be let 'from year to year if the tenant undertook to pay all the usual tenant's rates and taxes and the landlord undertook to bear the costs of repairs and insurance and other expenses, if any, necessary to maintain the hereditament in a state to command that rent'. (General Rate Act, 1967, sect. [19]6). This gross rental value does not include the cost of any services provided by the landlord –

for example, central heating or lifts. Legally it would appear that any improvements made by owner or tenant should be fully reflected in the occupier paying more rent to match the increased value of the property, and that the rent should be an open-market rent in the most profitable use for which the dwelling has planning permission.

In practice, the application of the law seems obscure. Someone may have planning permission to alter the existing use of a dwelling which could require him to pay more rates, but he may not be charged more until he actually alters the use. Valuers are required to get what is called 'the tone of the list' by omitting variations in value caused by changes in supply and demand since the last general revaluation.[3] During the currency of the list, ratepayers cannot get their rateable value altered because of general changes in the neighbourhood property values unless they can argue that values have fallen below the level at the last revaluation, themselves estimated two years before a new list becomes effective.

To get the net value, an allowance is deducted from the gross rental value that represents the cost to the owner of repairing, maintaining and insuring the building. The net value is the rateable value (RV) and is the tax base for rating.[4] This means that in principle rates paid are proportional to the market rent net of operating, repairs and maintenance costs. Net rents so defined are not true owner's or landlord's profits as they allow no deduction for depreciation. In this, valuation practice follows British law, which does not allow landlords or other owners any tax-deductible depreciation provisions. Such rateable values (which are hypothetical rents) must be estimated for all properties even for those which are not, and never have been, rented.

Even so, these rateable values are notional in two important respects.

(a)   The allowance for repairs and maintenance is not merely arbitrary. As a declining proportion of rateable value, it is implausible.[5] There is no good reason for supposing that the costs of repairing, maintaining or insuring a building are a falling proportion of the rent charged. If two similar dwellings command different rents and, therefore, rateable values because one is in an urban area of high property values and the other is in the country, it is not impossible that repairs, maintenance and insurance could be very similar. But a difference between town and country is only one reason for a difference in rents and rateable values. They will also vary because one dwelling is larger, and there is no reason to suppose that repairs, maintenance and insurance are a declining proportion of size. Costs will also vary with age, type of building, materials used, climate, the tastes of the occupier, the past maintenance record, and such environmental matters as exposure to vibration and pollution. The repair, maintenance and insurance allowance is arbitrary and implausible because it apparently assumes that all reasons given for higher costs under these three heads operate so that these costs are a falling proportion of rateable value. But few of them are likely to do so, and there will be great variation in the relation of these costs to rateable values, according to circumstances.

If it is the genuine intention of the law to make such adjustments, either of two courses would seem logical:

(i)   The first would allow ratepayers to set actual expenses against gross rents to establish the net rent or rateable value on which they must pay tax.

But this is hardly practical since it would entail a considerable administrative burden of checking to avoid false claims and so greatly increase the costs of rate collection. It would also mean that ratepayers could reduce, and even eliminate, their contribution to the cost of local services if they decide to spend more on these rate-deductible items. This problem is made much worse in practice by the fact that rateable values are below market rents.

It is similar to the position that existed when there was an imputed income tax on owner-occupied housing (Schedule A). Householders generally found it easy to do enough repairs and maintenance to reduce their tax payments to zero. Allowing a similar offset against rates could well mean the end of the rating system.

(ii) More practically, standard deductions could reflect some objective characteristics of dwellings. Just as it is standard in the USA for valuers to work with tables relating building and depreciation costs to age, size and condition of the building, so standardised tables could, in effect, mean variations in repairs, maintenance and insurance costs also relating to age, size, condition and other measurable factors. While still arbitrary in their treatment of any individual building, they would be fairer and more rational than the present fossilised British deductions.

But it may be misleading to take the deductions at their face value. Their practical effect has always been to introduce some progressiveness into the rating system. The relationship of gross value to net rateable value is shown in Table 3.2.1.

The table shows that, despite the rather cumbersome formula, the average rate of statutory deduction declines fairly smoothly as gross values increase, implying that the higher the gross value, the higher is rateable value as a proportion of gross value.

Progressiveness has never been proclaimed as the true rationale of the provisions for statutory deductions. However, even if this were the intention it is one of three mechanisms which affect the progressiveness of rates. The other

Table 3.2.1. *Relationship of Gross Value to Net Rateable Value*

Range of Gross Value	Formula for Statutory Deduction [a]	Marginal Deduction	Average Deduction Rate (%)	
			Lower end	Upper end
0–65	45%	45	45	45
66–128	£29 + 30% of excess over £65	30	44.4	37.4
129–330	£48 + one-sixth of excess over £128	16.7	37.3	24.7
330–430	£80 + one-fifth of excess over £330	20	24.2	23.2
430 and over	£100 + one-sixth of excess over £430	16.7	23.2 approaches 16.7	

[a] The formula is set out in the Valuation (Statutory Deductions) Order (1973). See also Hepworth (1976)

two are, as will appear, the assessment process itself and rate rebates. No co-ordination of the three would appear to exist.

(b) A second and more important reason why net rental value is national is the sparsity of evidence on rents themselves discussed in Part Two, Chapter 6. As we there saw, rent estimation for rating purposes had become almost completely hypothetical both for the public and privately rented proportions of the stock, while for owner-occupied stock valuers have been driven to increasingly tenuous comparisons in their attempts to estimate what rents they might fetch in a non-existent free market (Wright *et al.*, 1974, pp. 72–4). As a result, rateable values do not reflect market values: higher-price property is generally undervalued and there are severe geographical discrepancies.

Despite this, there have been many who hoped that the rental basis could be retained by moving over to 'fair rents' as an aid to estimating gross values. The notion of a 'fair rent' is broadly that of a market rent, except that scarcity is to be ignored in its calculation. The concept was introduced in the 1965 Rent Act and extended by the 1968 Rent Act and the 1972 Housing Finance Act.[6] For a time, it seemed as if the concept of a 'fair rent' had won bipartisan acceptance; but in 1974 the use of a rent freeze[7] as a counter-inflationary measure and the repeal of the 'fair rent' provisions of the 1972 Housing Finance Act made it far less likely in future that the principle of 'fair rents' could be used by valuers as a basis for calculating gross values.

Even if 'fair rents' were not likely to disappear in the public sector, replacement of market by fair rents in estimating gross values would have had its drawbacks. As 'fair rents' are statutorily defined as rents which do not reflect scarcity, so gross values would also come not to reflect scarcity.[8] As property values do reflect scarcity, rating based on 'fair rents' would have departed further from the original purpose of rates as a property tax.[9] (Indeed, one can take the argument still further. As pure land values are demand determined and reflect nothing but the scarcity of land in relation to demand in a particular location, logically, gross values would have moved towards becoming property values, excluding the value of land, that is a rate on buildings.) Another drawback is practical. In many parts of the country 'fair rents', especially for public housing, have been calculated by reference to gross values so that the use of 'fair rents' to estimate gross values would have been circular.

As we saw in Part Two, Chapter 6, local variations in assessment persist even between contiguous local authorities and could be as great as they were before 1950 when the Inland Revenue took over valuation. Thus the incidence of rates and the resource element in grants will be unfair, though to an unknown extent.

If there were no central government grants influenced by local rates and rateable values, the inequity would merely be a problem within each authority.[10] A local authority which rated costly property higher relative to cheaper property than did another, would be effecting different redistributive policies through its rating system; and that might be a cause of concern to central government. If a local authority estimated its rateable values lower on average than those of its neighbours, it would have to have a higher rate poundage to raise a given sum and vice versa. But the resources element means that the grant a local authority receives depends in part on the level of rateable value per head.

An authority whose rateable values appear systematically lower than those of another authority will receive more resources element without good reason. That this is not the result of deliberate tinkering by the local authority, but appears to be the inadvertent effect of non-uniformity in Inland Revenue valuation procedures does not make the outcome less unfair. What may have happened is that the growing decline in information on rents has frozen the inequities that existed before the Inland Revenue took over in 1950. Especially over the last ten to fifteen years, there has been a convergence of house prices for similar types of housing in different regions, but no such convergence of rents. Therefore, valuation based on the surviving rental data does not reflect changes in regional land values.

The evidence considered in Part Two, Chapter 6 makes it unlikely that that explanation is the only one. That evidence suggested that possibly because of lack of rental evidence, valuers were strongly influenced by certain objective factors – the number of rooms, the existence of a garage, garden or central heating – in ways which were poorly related to either rents or prices.

The difficulties of using a rental basis for calculating rateable values have, therefore, become exceedingly strong, and will become increasingly so as owner-occupation increases and private renting declines, while either government subsidies or rent control or both affect the rental property left.

The remaining arguments for retaining the present basis of calculation are administrative and legal. The system has worked well for many years. Court decisions over a long period have clarified how the relevant concepts should be estimated in a great many odd and difficult cases. Despite the artificiality and arbitrariness, many thousands of ordinary ratepayers have understood the principles well enough to argue their cases before local valuation courts and the Lands Tribunal. Moreover, if the old rent-based system were kept for some but not all types of property, the co-existence of more than one basis for valuation would create an inconsistency within the system which itself could cause difficulties in equity. None of these arguments are negligible, but it is hard to argue that they outweigh the near absurdities caused by lack of evidence.

2. NOTIONAL CAPITAL VALUATION

The problems have been recognised by the Inland Revenue and the various professional bodies who have recommended the replacement of rental by capital values as the basis for assessing rateable values (Layfield, 1976, p. 169). As 55 per cent of dwellings in the UK are in the owner-occupied sector and are on average sold once every fourteen years, this may seem no more than common sense and a technical change raising no issue of principle. For the owner-occupied majority of housing, the capital value used for assessment would 'conform as nearly as possible to the actual conditions under which the majority of transactions take place so that the values produced bear a reasonable correspondence to market figures at a relevant date' (ibid., p. 171). In parallel, valuers would make their best assessment of the likely vacant-possession price of rented property, and so establish capital-based rateable values in those tenures.[11] They would be helped because there are sales of privately and, in growing numbers, of publicly rented stock.

Such a replacement of rental by capital values for the assessment of dwellings would be an undoubted gain provided the new capital values are actual. However, the Department of the Environment put a definition of capital value to the Layfield Committee which was as notional as the old notional rental value it was suggested it might replace.

> The value of the hereditament shall be the amount which the hereditament might be expected to realise if sold by a willing vendor in the *open market freehold with vacant possession at the relevant date* with the benefit of any easement or other right inuring for the benefit of the hereditament and subject to any easement or other right subsisting for the benefit of other land and to any other restriction statutorily imposed upon the hereditament *and on the assumptions that the use of the hereditament would be permanently restricted to that existing at the time of the valuation, including any change of use for which no planning permission would be required*, that no alteration to the hereditament would be made other than any alteration for which no application for planning permission would be required, *and that the hereditament was in the state of repair at the time of valuation which might reasonably be expected by an occupier of the particular property having regard to its character, its environment and to the neighbourhood in which the hereditament is situated*. (Layfield, 1976, p. 441)[12]

Those adjustments which would not be reflected in a free-market price have been italicised by the authors. Thus valuers would be required

(1) to adjust to the open-market level any actual sales values which are too low and preferential, for example, because they represent a favourable transaction to a relative, as they adjust preferential rents;

(2) to convert to freehold values where relevant;

(3) to discount any reduction in sale value because of a sitting tenant;

(4) to adjust sale prices to the values that would have obtained two years before the 'relevant date' of the last general revaluation — the 'tone of the list principle';

(5) to exclude any part of prices reflecting 'hope or development value' — that is any increased income from a change in use with or without planning permission;

(6) to adjust sale prices to offset an unusually good or bad state of repair.

(7) that 'banding' should be adopted and small variations on prices for similar properties be eliminated, 'so that properties falling within each band of values are assessed on the same figure'.

The Committee did not mention one modification of rental values which traditional practice suggests would also be applied to sale prices:

(8) Valuers have also normally tried to adjust to eliminate idiosyncratic rents – where, for example, someone has 'fallen in love' with a house and paid well above the market rent or a vendor has priced low for a quick sale. Again one might expect a similar adjustment of idiosyncratic sale prices.

(9) Even these traditional adjustments would leave behind at least one element of what is owner's rather than occupier's value: the effect of mortgage-interest relief and other tax advantages on house prices and, therefore, on rateable values if capital values are used for assessment.

As a consequence of such adjustments, notional capital values would be even further removed from actual sale prices than rental values have been from actual rents.

All this must make it debatable as to whether the replacement of notional rental by notional capital values will achieve the great improvement in assessment claimed or required. One can now see why until very recently there was vigorous opposition to changing to capital values, despite a dearth of rental evidence;[13] and also the force of the argument that the basis for making adjustments to rental values has been well tested by performance and so has become widely accepted and understood.

ACTUAL SALE PRICES

Rather than work from definitions of capital value which derive by analogy from definitions of rental value used in the past, it is worth considering a more radical change with the virtue of simplicity: not to replace one notional value by another, but to replace notional rental values by actual sales prices, keeping adjustments to the minimum. Let us start with the proposition that 'the rateable value of a hereditament shall be the actual sale price realised in the market' and then go through the adjustments considered above to judge how many can be resisted. Of the nine adjustments considered above, we argue that three should be accepted, one is optional, while the remainder can well be rejected. The basis of the new system, therefore, is that whenever a property is sold, freehold or leasehold, that transaction price should become the rateable value, so that a house sold for £12,000 in any year would have a rateable value of £12,000 in that year. The rate poundage would be directly levied on that value. Thus revaluation would be automatic on sale. One consequence of such a direct relationship is that it should increase the intelligibility of the rating system. It would make it clear that rates were an *ad valorem* tax on property. Purchasers of domestic property would realise that in deciding how much to offer, they were determining an important dimension of their rate bill since it would be proportional to the price paid.

Some adjustments are necessary:

(a) If the principle of an *ad valorem* property tax is to be preserved, the rateable value must be the value freehold. Otherwise some part of the property value will not be rated. Conversion of leasehold sale prices to their freehold equivalent would not be difficult or contentious.

(b)   The same principle requires that the sale value be an open-market value. Where a property is sold to a relative or friend, it is not uncommon for the price to be a preferential one below market levels. To use a preferential price as a tax base would confer an unfair advantage on the purchaser as ratepayer. The law could require that any preferential transactions are declared. Whenever the valuation office has reason to suppose that a sale is a preferential one, then a special valuation to establish the appropriate open-market value should be undertaken at the vendor or purchaser's expense. Similar action could be taken where a price is apparently preferential because a vendor agrees to accept some part of the price as a side payment, not as part of the formal price for the house. Side payments could be made illegal with the same effect as for premia on rental property; any purchaser would be entitled to retrieve any such payment.

(c)   The value must be that with vacant possession if rent-controlled tenants with security of tenure are not to be under-rated. Such a tenant benefits from rent control which reduces the open-market value of the property to the landlord. If the open-market value without vacant possession were to be the rateable value, the tenant, if he contributes to the rate bill, would in effect get a second subsidy — from the rating authority as well as from the landlord. But the vacant-possession value is needed if the whole value of the property is to be rated. To avoid special valuations, the most practical approach might be to use a standard multiplier of sales value to calculate rateable values for such property.

If those three adjustments can be defended as consistent with the status of rates as an *ad valorem* property tax, the remainder are not susceptible of that defence.

(d)   There is no need to value at a 'relevant date' determined in relation to infrequent periodic revaluations. Instead all properties would be revalued annually.

Each year, between sales, a dwelling's rateable value would be adjusted by an appropriate multiplier reflecting the change over the year in the sale prices of property of that type within the local authority. The multipliers could probably most easily be established by district valuers' staff surveying a running, small, stratified sample of the PD (Particulars Delivered) dockets they receive whenever there is a sale.[14] Thus over the course of a year they would observe the change in prices of houses of different types and establish a mean change for the year. These samples would automatically give the annual multipliers or price indices appropriate for revaluing each type of property in each local authority area. Every year a new valuation list would come out giving the actual sale price for every dwelling sold during the year and an appropriately up- (or possible down-) rated value for every other property. Individual valuations based on visits by valuers would only be necessary where a special assessment was needed, for example because of change of use, a major structural change in the property, or a major change in the environment. An example of the last might be movement in values caused by a new motorway.

If it were still true, as it was before 1963, that decennial revaluations were based on individual inspection of every property, this new proposal could be argued to be radical in replacing individual by statistical assessment. But recent revaluations have themselves been based on valuers using quasi-statistical procedures where they have altered the value of classes of property by using 'multipliers' calculated for that class. What we are suggesting, instead, is both more frequent, that is annual, up-dating and a more systematised statistical basis for estimating multipliers.

A further argument for annual revaluation is that since capital values are capitalised rents, capital values may be more volatile than rents if both are calculated on the same basis because of changes in interest rates or expectations. However, since capital values also reflect the investment good, the tax-advantage aspect and the development value of property — which rents do not — greater volatility of capital values could result if these elements were more volatile than the housing-consumption good component. The practical departures from open-market rents caused by the growth of regulation and control could have had the effect of reducing the volatility of rents, while capital values continue to fluctuate more because they better reflect fluctuation in real rents, current and anticipated, as well as the alternative use value of capital. Such fluctuations would be a problem if annual revaluation were impossible or extremely difficult. However, the abundance of information on house prices should make it reasonably easy to construct appropriate house-price indices to allow annual revaluations.

An additional advantage from annual revaluations would be to eliminate the sudden discontinuities in the present system. There is an outcry after each revaluation — as in 1963 and 1973 — which is especially loud from those whose rateable values have risen more than average, and who therefore find their rate bills have risen. They would be less likely to complain if every year they had experienced a smaller increase. It would be less of a jolt and they would see more clearly how they had benefited from capital appreciation. Conversely, those whose rate bills had fallen would see that this was caused by the relative depreciation of their property.

(e) Where there are prospective advantages to the owner, with or without planning permission, reflected in the price but not in the rent that could be charged an occupier, it is often argued that sales prices should be adjusted to exclude any such hope or development value before being used as rateable values.

But a property with development value is bought at a price reflecting that value only because the purchaser believes this to be a profitable investment. This element in its price is the investment aspect of the property, and if rates are a tax on property, there is no obvious reason for not raising rates on it. Once again a liability to be rated would be taken into account by a prospective purchaser and would be reflected by his offering a lower price than he would if this part of the value were not rated.

Yet this would be to introduce into the rating system a taxing principle which in the past has been vigorously excluded from it. One argument is the alleged inequity of taxing a capital sum — that is a prospective net worth — before an income stream accrues to it (Davenport, 1917, p. 4). However, this is an argument against all capital taxation, and can be met by the recognition that if the purchaser of a property knows he will be rated on the investment (development or hope) value of his purchase, he is rational if he offers a price less by the capital (present) value of the annual amount extra he expects to pay in rates, than if he were not to be so rated.

It is often argued as if it were incorrect to rate on the development value of a site or building. But there is nothing right or wrong about it. Where rateable values are based on rents reflecting current income streams only (actual or imputed), development value should be excluded; it does not yield a current income stream. When rateable values are based on capital values as reflected in the sale price, it is the value (wealth) which is taxed not the current income stream. All elements of that wealth should then be taxed.[15]

(f)   A more difficult question is presented by a property's state of repair, which will be reflected in the purchase price. A ratepayer would be financially better off buying a property in a poor state of repair and then repairing it, than buying the same in a good state, because his price, and therefore his rateable value, would be greater in the second case[16] – unless some special adjustment were made. The adjustment could be made through designating a property at point of sale by its condition. Thus one could designate a property as category A, B or C and, for example, alter the rateable value of a property as reflected in its sale price by some percentage. Thus if a property were in above-average condition (A) its rateable value would be less than 100 per cent of its sale price and vice versa.[17] Such an approach means that the unrepaired property is treated as though its 'true' value is the same as that of a repaired property, because on the margin the difference in their prices is exactly equal to the repair costs.

Such an approach raises two difficulties. The first is practical. Someone, either the estate agent, or possibly an independent valuer, would have to decide the state of repair at the point of sale. If an estate agent or other accredited person seriously mis-stated the state of repair, a sample check with heavy penalties might work as a discipline, provided the rewards of misclassification were not too great. What would be more difficult would be to decide what was relevant to the definition of a repair. Decorations are usually thought to be of negligible importance in determining a house's value – given the frequency with which they should be undertaken and differences in tastes. What are relevant are the improvements of bathrooms and kitchens, rewiring as well as reroofing, repointing, damp-proofing and other major repairs. It would be extremely difficult to decide what proportion of the difference in the price paid for a house is due to a difference in relevant repairs. With all their problems, notional values would again be introduced into the equation.

The other problem in such treatment is one of equity. The tax base would become a potential value conditional on additional expenditure on repairs. It would blur the nature of the tax as an *ad valorem* tax on the market value of a property. Such treatment would also introduce addtional uncertainty and incomprehensibility into the rating system.

If the sale price without any adjustment for state of repair is used as the rateable value one might revalue the house whenever there was an improvement or major repair, or indeed a deterioration in its condition, but the practical difficulty of checking on repairs after sale is very great. Before a government valuer is able to visit many repairs may have been undertaken – indeed as they may be after a single visit. In any case, he needs to know what improvements have been made and this will not always be obvious. He will then adjust the sale value upwards to reflect the enhanced rateable value, so allowing the value of a house to rise and be reflected in its rateable value as it is improved. Against this must be set a common hostility to improvements being reflected in rateable values, already resented when someone builds a garage or installs central heating and finds his rateable value increased. He feels he is being asked to pay twice over (or at least more than once).

This last point should make one reflect whether adjustment for state of repair is the best approach and whether it would not be more sensible *not* to alter rateable values for changes in the state of repair. Improvements which require planning permission might lead to increases in rateable value as at present, but other improvements need not. Like decorations they could be regarded as maintaining the home. Any improvements in quality could be ignored until resale. As a compromise one could require home-owners to notify the local authority only when certain major changes take place. The installation of central heating is the most obvious and perhaps the only case worth action, especially as it normally leads to an increase in resale value exceeding its cost. Conversely, owners might ask for their rateable value to be reduced if the state of repair was such that they could argue that for this reason the resale value was substantially reduced.

But whether or not one allowed for certain exceptions, there would be an advantage in not generally adjusting the sale price by the state of repair to determine the rateable value. It would save valuation time, and confusion about the valuation process. Its practical effect would be to act as a deterrent to poor maintenance and an inducement to home improvements since this would not result in any increased liability to rates until after resale.

(g) The Layfield Committee suggested that rateable values should be rounded through 'banding'. Thus houses of value £12,000 to £12,500 might be assumed to have the rateable value of the mid-point of the range – £12,250 – and so on. One of the greatest difficulties valuers have in accepting actual open-market values to establish rateable values comes from the fact that perhaps the main reason for appeals against rateable values is the discovery by one ratepayer that one of his neighbours in an apparently identical house has a different rateable value.

(h) The present valuation practice assumes that ratepayers should be protected from the effect of personal preferences and external influences on their property.

It is argued that sale prices are influenced by the personal preferences of purchasers, and are idiosyncratic to some extent, so that they should be adjusted to eliminate the effect of such preferences. However, in a broad sense the price of property is determined by the interaction of buyers' and sellers' preferences, sometimes diverse, sometimes similar. Practically it is very difficult to decide what proportion of a house price reflects a purchaser's special 'idiosyncratic' preference as opposed to any other preference. Indeed, how can one really draw such a distinction? One supposes the case in mind may be where someone 'falls in love' with a house or values a feature of the house so much that they are ready to pay substantially more than anyone else would for it. But *caveat emptor*. Either there was an under-bidder, in which case at least one other party was ready to pay almost the same price; or the purchaser was carried away into paying an unnecessarily high price. If someone is ready to pay highly for a property and knows in advance that the more he pays for the house, the greater his rate payments in proportion, he can hardly object since he is being rated in accordance with his own valuing of the property.

The use of sales values will mean that identical dwellings — even twin semi-detached houses — will have different rateable values and pay different amounts in rates. This may happen even if both are sold at the same time. One vendor may settle for a quick sale. Another may hold out for a higher price. This, it is said, will often be judged as unfair by ratepayers who have come to expect similar dwellings to have the same rateable values. Indeed, such discrepancies are now the main reason for appeal against rating assessments. All we can say against this is that the notion of equity will have changed if public opinion accepts that it is the price paid that determines the liability to rates. The prices and the liability to rates will vary for the same dwelling at different times. The value of a particular dwelling may rise or fall more than would be indicated by the particular price index used for its annual revaluation. In some cases, as at present, it may be reasonable for ratepayers to ask for a revaluation where there has been a material change in circumstance — for example, a major build-up of congestion or pollution — but, in general, the point should be met by the realisation that provided a buyer recognises that the price he pays will determine his liability to rates, he has gone into a purchase with his eyes open.

(i)   Lastly, there are the differences between rental and capital values that arise because of tax advantages to owners. Mortgage-interest relief, which itself varies with income-tax rates, and treatment for capital-gains tax have an effect on house prices, raising the price which it is profitable to offer for a house. The more expensive a home, the greater the proportion of its price that reflects its advantage not as a home, but as a method of saving which attracts tax advantages through mortgage-interest relief and exemption from capital-gains tax. Similarly, in the past forestry and farm land have been higher priced because of their tax advantages in respect of death duties. The capitalised value of the rent such homes can fetch — since the tenant does not derive such advantages — will be below their sale value in the open market. The effect of moving from rental valuation to sales prices will raise the rateable values and, therefore, the rate burden of those properties whose prices are most influenced by such tax advantages — the higher-priced properties for the most part. In effect, increased liability for rates will reduce those tax advantages. Trying to adjust market values to exclude this element would be almost impossible. Besides, there is no obvious reason why an *ad valorem* property tax should not be levied on the full value of the property to the owner whatever its cause.

We have argued for capital valuation on the grounds of availability of direct evidence and of comprehensibility to the ratepayer. But there is a significant part of the housing stock, namely local authority housing, to which these arguments do not seem to apply. The present principle is that council housing, like other housing, should be rated on the rent it would command in a free market. If capital valuation were adopted, council housing would be rated on its free-market sale value. We believe it would be easier to estimate free-market sale values than free-market rents for council properties for three reasons:

(1) Sales of council properties do take place, while virtually no council property is let out at free-market rents. In assessing rateable value, no allowance would be made for the discount at which houses are sold.

(2) The capital value of a property can also be derived, in principle, from the historic cost of construction (revalued by means of a price index). One problem here is that as public housing often costs more to build than private housing of similar type and size, the historic cost may overstate the current market value.

(3) Comparability with owner-occupied property, for which capital valuation is more accurate and reliable.

Some consequences of replacing rental by capital values — notional or actual — are worth mentioning. It will reduce rateable values on old property in a bad state of repair whose rental value may still be high. Towards the end of its life the sale value of such property tends to decline relative to its rental value. This is particularly true of poorly maintained slum property. To down-rate such property would seem to be a positive advantage of capital valuation. Second, valuers have had a tendency, from caution, to ascribe lower values to the type of property where rental evidence is comparatively scarce. Thus it can be argued that owners and occupiers of flats have been more highly rated than owners and occupiers of houses; and of large, atypical houses more than of smaller standard houses. This is one reason given also for thinking that, in general, rateable values of non-domestic property — for which again rental evidence is more abundant — may have risen relative to those for domestic property generally. Third, geographical anomalies in existing valuations would be removed, leading to higher selective valuations in some areas, and lower in other (Foster and Lynch, 1978).

As with all changes, there are problems of transition to the new system, though in many ways it would be easier than the transition from notional rental to notional capital values. Suppose it was announced to come into full operation five years ahead, then everyone who bought a property would realise that that price, up-dated by the appropriate multiplier, would be their rateable value after the appointed day. Each year before introduction, the indices might be published so that those interested could become aware of how they were calculated. On average 7 per cent of owner-occupied houses change hands every year (DoE, 1977a, part 3, p. 240). For those that were not sold by the appointed day, when the new system was finally introduced, one would go back through the PDs to see the last price at which it was sold and apply an appropriate price index from then on. Or one could follow the normal valuation practice of establishing a comparable value by comparison with properties which had recently been sold. Or where the property was particularly unusual or had not been sold for a very long time, there would be a special individual valuation to establish a hypothetical market value. But, whichever was done, it is unlikely that the problem would be any greater than that of transition to notional capital values.

In conclusion, on domestic rating if these arguments are accepted there would seem to us to be a strong case for getting rid of rental valuation; but instead of replacing it by much-adjusted capital valuation of a notional kind, to replace it by actual sales values which we suggest should be defined as follows:

The rateable value of a hereditament shall be the amount which the hereditament has realised on the assumption that it was sold by a willing vendor in the open market freehold with vacant possession with the benefit of any easement or other right inuring for the benefit of the hereditament and subject to any easement or other right subsisting for the benefit of other land and to any other restriction statutorily imposed upon the hereditament, and that no alteration to the hereditament would be made other than any alteration for which no planning permission is required.

The discussion so far has concentrated on domestic property, which is where the absence of rental information makes capital valuation sensible. For most types of non-domestic property, rental information is more abundant than sales data. There is, therefore, no case in terms of availability of evidence for arguing for capital valuation of non-domestic poperties.

Yet there are are arguments in terms of comparability. We have shown that the capital value of a property may include 'investment' as well as 'consumption' value, while only the latter will affect its rental value. It is, in part, for this reason that capital values are more volatile than rents. It would seem anomalous to tax domestic property on one basis, and non-domestic on another. Ideally, and provided sufficient sales evidence is available, non-domestic property should be rated according to the same principle – of actual capital values with annual revaluations – as we have recommended for domestic property.

Both Layfield (pp. 168–77) and the government, in its Green Paper response (DoE, 1977*b*, Cmnd 6813, paras 6.14 – 6.22) regarded capital valuation as a technical issue, and they do not seem to have been aware that the proposal entails a change in the tax base. In consequence, they were not worried about the anomaly implicit in recommending a continuation of the rental basis for non-domestic property. Hence Layfield recommended, and the government accepted, the idea of a 'divisor' which would be applied to the capital value of dwellings. No doubt the divisor would be set, initially, so as to maintain the relative contributions of domestic and non-domestic ratepayers at existing levels.

A more logical way of determining the 'divisor' to achieve comparability between domestic and non-domestic properties would be as follows. First, the average investment yield on non-domestic property could be calculated from the tables already published derived from estate agents' data. Say the average figure is 8 per cent, so that a commercial property with capital value of £50,000 might typically attract a rent of around £4000 in the current year. Then the same figure, 8 per cent, would be used as the divisor. The argument would be that a given capital sum would then attract the same assessment for rates whether used in the purchase of domestic or non-domestic property.

The investment yield on commercial property fluctuates with the general level of interest rates, and if the divisor were to move with it, the relative burdens on domestic and non-domestic ratepayers would be stabilised to some extent – the fluctuations in house prices being offset by changes in the divisor. This arrangement, however, introduces an unwelcome additional uncertainty for local authorities. Presumably the divisor would be decided annually at the same time as the annual revaluations on which each year's valuation lists would be based are completed, so the two sources of uncertainty would be combined.

There would also be a case for annual revaluation of non-domestic property even if its assessment remained on a rental basis. Otherwise the relative contribution of non-domestic ratepayers would always fall between revaluations, and by quite substantial proportions in times of inflation.

Finally, there has been discussion of whether the divisor should be used to determine the relative rating of domestic and non-domestic ratepayers in lieu of the domestic element of the Rate Support Grant. In the next chapter we shall argue against the differential rating of domestic and non-domestic properties, but even if this argument is not accepted it seems illogical to muddle together valuation procedures and tax structures.

CONCLUSIONS

The conclusions of this chapter are:

(1) The arguments for introducing capital valuation are overwhelming if rates are to be a credible *ad valorem* property tax. Although in its 1977 Green Paper the government proclaimed its intention to introduce capital valuation in time for the next revaluation in 1982, that plan was subsequently dropped. The 1982 revaluation was to have been on a rental basis, despite the government's view that 'there is no longer enough evidence of free market rental values to support another revaluation of domestic property on the present basis' (DoE, 1977*b*, Cmnd 6813, par. 6.15). In 1979 the Conservative government postponed revaluation even on a rental basis, and the passing of time can only make current anomalies worse.

(2) There is a strong case for using actual sale prices (or where relevant their freehold equivalents) rather than assessed capital values as rateable values.

(3) There should be annual revaluations, based on local house-price indices. The first step in the transition should be the construction of such price indices, and the preparation of hypothetical valuation lists to illustrate the new basis of assessment.

(4) While, ideally, non-domestic property should be taxed on the same basis as domestic, if the rental basis is maintained, the divisor should be derived from the investment yields on industrial and commercial property. Non-domestic property should also be revalued annually, and if differential rating is wanted, it should be achieved by subsequent adjustments rather than made part of the valuation process.

NOTES

1 The district valuers responsible for valuation in England and Wales are civil servants in the Inland Revenue. They regard their role as purely technical. They execute policies which are the DoE's prerogative.

2 Net values are calculated directly for some buildings. See Wright *et al.* (1974), chs 5, 6; Hepworth (1976), pp. 85–8. Our discussion concentrates on residential dwellings, but,

as will appear, the conclusions apply to all buildings. 'Hereditament' is a term used to describe the unit of land to be rated plus any building on it.

3 There are exceptions to this. See General Rate Act, 1967, sect. (19) 6.

4 See Wright *et al*. (1974), chs 5, 6 for variations on this practice.

5 The Secretary of State is free to change the formula by order under the General Rate Act, 1967.

6 There was a precedent for it in the rating system itself. The Valuation for Rating Act, 1953, sect. 2, required valuers to use 1939 values as their base but to ignore the effect on values of postwar scarcity.

7 Counter Inflation (Private Sector Residential Rents) England and Wales Order, 1974. Rent Act, 1974.

8 As we have seen, the Valuation for Rating Act, 1952, did ask valuers to disregard scarcity. It is now the regular practice in Scotland to base rateable values in Scotland on local authority rents which do not reflect scarcity. The very high proportion of dwellings owned by local authorities is the justification for this.

9 The proposition that scarcity should be eliminated in assessing rateable values was put to the Fitzgerald Committee on Valuation for Rates. Their comment still seems sound: 'We are unable to accept this proposal. It would entail a fundamental revision of the law of rating . . . The proposal would involve a departure from the statutory definition of 'gross value' inasmuch as it would be necessary to find not the rent at which the premises might reasonably be expected to let but the rent at which they might reasonably be expected to let if conditions were otherwise than they are. It would moreover raise extremely difficult questions as to what constitutes an abnormal shortage of accommodation which is the class that is likely to occupy the accommodation, what are the economic circumstances of that class and what are the rents appropriate to those economic circumstances, and as to what would be the appropriate bodies to determine such questions' (Ministry of Health, 1939, published 1944). The opposite view in which can be seen the germ of the notion of fair rent was put by Lady Simon in a minority report of the same committee.

10 Fitzgerald (1939, published 1944, pp. 8, 9) gave grants and precepting as the reason why uniformity had become of much greater importance.

11 This might be supported by other methods of valuation. For example, the 'contractors' method' might be used for local authority property without comparable owner-occupied dwellings, It is basically cost plus profit. It is not used for any dwellings at present. See Wright *et al*. (1974, p. 72).

12 This was suggested by the valuers of the DoE.

13 For example, in the local authority associations' evidence to DoE preceding the Local Government Finance Green Paper (DoE, 1971*a*, Cmnd 4741).

14 One could use techniques of a kind similar to those used by statisticians and called 'category' analysis. And one could use multiple regression analysis to examine what are the important factors affecting differences in price trends over time. But simplicity might suggest no more than the following characterisation within any given local authority. House type (detached, semi-detached, flat, bungalow, etc.); by size; by age band; by geographical subarea – all data which is on the PD, or that the Valuation Office otherwise possesses.

15 We shall examine this issue further in connection with site value rating in Part Four, Chapter 2.

16 This would be the case unless the tax were completely capitalised.

17 Assuming the same degree of capitalisation the relative price of repaired and unrepaired properties would remain the same, if the relative tax rates were such that the tax payments on the two types of properties were the same.

3 Abolition of Differential Rating

By differential rating one means any departure — whether by derating or super-rating — from the principle that a local authority levies a uniform rate poundage on all rateable values within its boundaries, that is, any departure from rates as a uniform *ad valorem* property tax. This principle was accepted by both the Layfield Committee in its analysis of derating (Layfield, 1976, pp. 165–7) and also by central government in its reply to the Committee. If the principle is accepted, then arguments for exceptions must be grounded on considerations of efficiency, equity or expediency and convenience.

The most conspicuous departures from the principle of a uniform rate are in agriculture and Scottish industry.

Agriculture was progressively derated in stages from the 1890s until it was completely derated in 1929. Present central government policy is to keep it derated in spite of the Layfield Committee recommendation to the contrary. More curious is the case of Scottish industry. All industry in the UK was derated fully from 1929 to 1958. In that year, English and Welsh industry was fully rated again, while Scottish industry became only half-rated. While one argument for this was regional, another was that domestic rateable values were so low relative to market values that Scottish industry had to be half-rated if it were not to be over-rated by comparison with the domestic ratepayer.

Since the introduction of the domestic element in RSG in 1966 the relative burden on non-domestic property has increased. The domestic element is a method of super-rating all non-domestic rateable value. It has made the position of Scottish industry even more curious, since it is derated by half and super-rated on the other half. In London, the super-rating of the non-domestic rate-payer has been taken still further. For many years a pooling arrangement has existed through which the richer London boroughs such as the City, Westminster and Camden have made over part of their rate income to help the poorer ones. Since 1976, this has been modified so as to increase the contribution of the non-domestic ratepayer to the pool, by comparison with the domestic ratepayer. The domestic element has also been much higher in Wales than in England since 1974.

Another oddity is the special position of churches and charities. Churches are derated. Since 1961, charities have had to be no more than half-rated, but local authorities have the discretion to reduce their rates further to zero if they choose. Until 1977, charities were different in another way. Whether half-rated or fully derated they were not removed from the valuation list so that their existence did not reduce the reckoning of a local authority's rateable value per head and so did not affect its entitlement to resources element. One of the few

Layfield recommendations accepted and executed has been to rectify this (DoE, 1977*b*, Cmnd 6813, p. 31).

CHURCHES AND CHARITIES

If the principle of an *ad valorem* property tax is accepted, one still needs to ask what it is about property that is being taxed. The straightforward answer is that it is being taxed because property yields an income. This may be in cash, or it may be imputed: the income in kind that an owner-occupier derives from occupation of a house he owns. The special cases of churches and charities arise, however, because a property may yield an income, yet this accrues neither to owner nor to occupier. Rating either will seem unfair.

The rating history of churches is peculiar. They have never been rated. Indeed, they were supported by rates from earliest times and it seemed reasonable that church rates like poor rates should be levied according to ability to pay. All parishioners were liable because all were churchgoers and all were assumed to benefit from what was in fact a public good. But after the schism with Rome and the growth of dissent, the forced payment of church rates by members of other congregations naturally became a major grievance, ultimately put right in the nineteenth century by the abolition of the compulsory church rate. Since churches are no longer a public good, in economists' language, logic might have suggested that they should have become rated. Yet they never have been. Tradition is the most likely explanation. Another justification is that the imputed income, that is the benefit from the existence of a church, does not go to its owners, nor to well-defined occupiers, but to its congregation. One is on the threshold of difficult semantic questions here – in what sense does a congregation' occupy or own a church? – as well as difficult theological ones – who derives benefit from a church?

The case of a church shades into that of rating charities. First, let us consider the case of a non-residential charity – for example, the headquarters of a famine-relief organisation or of a body helping the disabled. Again the benefits, if the charity is genuine, go neither to the technical owner, or tenant of the building, nor to the staff who 'occupy' it. No charge is made for its services in so far as it is a charity. The beneficiaries who enjoy 'income' from the charity – in cash or kind – are the objects of its charity. Thus rating such a charity as if it were an income-yielding property again seems misconceived.

Many charities, however, are residential. Their residential occupiers enjoy some or all the benefits or income from the charity in cash or in kind. Therefore in logic they could be rated, but this would be against common sense. They do not pay (at least in full) for the benefits they get from the property. Indeed, the essence of a charity is that the beneficiaries are given services and shelter, and to make them pay tax on the charity they receive naturally appears perverse, though gifts (if not called charity) are taxable.

One can, however, look at the matter in a more complicated manner if one is so minded. The income received from a charity is not in an economic sense that of the beneficiary. The gains are what the National Income Accounts call an income transfer — a transfer from someone who has earned or otherwise gained it, to someone else who does not provide any service or good in exchange for it. One can add to this a further complication. Philanthropists would not give to charity unless the satisfaction of doing so outweighed the cost. This is no more than a truism if the charitable gift is voluntary. (If the contribution is forced we would not call it a charity.) Thus the income in an economic sense is the imputed or psychic income gained by the philanthropist who feels better off, a better man, or that he has appeased his conscience, or done his duty, by being charitable. Thus one could argue that if there were any income accruing from the property (as distinct from income transfers) it is psychic income to the donor, and that that should be rated. The implication that donors should be taxed or rated on their gifts is also against common sense.

Where a charity benefits local inhabitants alone, full derating may be justified as the benefits are all enjoyed by ratepayers. Even then there may be distributional biases. Charities benefit atypical groups — the poor, the disabled, even the local rich, or local animals. If not offset by resource grant, obligatory derating — complete or partial — is a subsidy from the collectivity of ratepayers to such a group. If derating is fully compensated by an increase in resource grant, it is a subsidy from the collectivity of taxpayers to such a group.

Still more questionable is such a subsidy from derating or under-rating when the beneficiaries of the charity are national or international. A local authority may incur substantial costs in providing services for which it does not receive rates and from which the benefits accrue to persons mainly or wholly outside its jurisdiction. In this case, compensation via the resource grant transfers the burden of the subsidy from the ratepayers of a local authority to the collectivity of taxpayers. Moreover, because charities are completely or partially exempt, they will gravitate to high-rated, central-city areas where their rate-exempt status helps them undercut other bidders for property. This has been found to be a common experience in the USA and in some cities has affected their revenue-raising powers considerably. If this happens the central subsidy through the resources element will be all the greater.

Local authorities would suffer no financial loss if charitable rateable value (or 50 per cent of it) were excluded when resources element is calculated. Until 1978, charities were included in the Valuation List at full assessment. Their derating or under-rating did not increase local authority entitlement to resources element (Layfield, 1976, p. 167). This is no longer the case. They are now fully compensated via the resource element for the 50 per cent obligatory derating.

The present treatment of charities is more consistent than it was in the past. The 50 per cent compulsory derating offset by the resource element is a method by which the central government gives a tax concession to charities. The percentage is arbitrary and is a choice for central government. As the derating is compulsory, it is equitable for local authorities to be compensated via the resource grant whatever else may be the purpose of the grant system. There is no reason why ratepayers should be forced to give charity to charities, as they were in the past.

Allowing local authorities to derate charities by more than 50 per cent without any compensation via the resource grant raises a different issue. Should local authorities be allowed to rate different properties at different poundages? We discuss this issue below. Our general conclusion is that they should not be allowed to do so. If they wish, they can make direct contributions to charities rather than giving hidden subsidies through the rating system.

THE COMPENSATION AND HARDSHIPS ARGUMENTS FOR DERATING

The historical arguments for derating were that the interests in question had suffered a loss for which they deserved compensation, or they were in such dire straits that they needed to be subsidised, and that derating is a convenient form of this. So the landed interests argued that before 1846 their rating was a price they were prepared to pay for the Corn Laws that protected them; and that was especially suitable because the poor relief their rates largely financed was some compensation to the poor for the higher cost of bread caused by the Corn Laws. After these were repealed and bread prices began to fall, the landed interests argued in reverse: since the poor had gained cheaper bread and they had lost rents, the agricultural interests deserved compensation. What, they felt, could be a more appropriate form of compensation than the derating of their land. By 1929 when agriculture was fully derated, the argument was not so much one of compensation but rather that, like industry, agriculture was suffering.

But, whatever the force of such arguments in the past when rates were a major tax, they mainly no longer apply. If there is a case for relieving any such economic activity, then there will always be national taxes that can be reduced or subsidies that can be increased. Moreover, so uneven is the incidence of rates as a proportion of final consumer prices, that derating – partial or complete – will have a distortionary effect on the activities affected by comparison with a cut in VAT or corporation tax. In general, it would give the greatest relief to activities which were most land and capital-intensive which would be perverse if, for example, the aim were to stimulate employment. If agriculture and Scottish industry are not fully rated as a deliberate result of government policy to subsidise them, re-rating these properties would have to be accompanied by an offsetting reduction in other tax burdens or increase in other subsidies. This would at least have the advantage that the form and amount of subsidy would be explicit.

The persistence of both agricultural derating and the half-rating of Scottish industry may be more complex. The government response to the Layfield Inquiry rejected re-rating of agriculture. The most plausible, if not honest, reason for retaining agricultural derating is that it is a way of by-passing EEC rules limiting the subsidies a member nation may give to its agriculture.

The case for half-rating Scottish industry arises because the assessment of rateable values in Scotland works to produce a ratio of industrial to domestic rateable values on average twice that in England and Wales. So half-rating industry is to compensate it for this result of the Scottish valuation process. Either the ratio reflects the truth, in which case half-rating seems unjustified, or this is yet another anomaly in current valuation practice which could be remedied by the move to actual sale prices as rateable values which we discussed in the last section. The most plausible explanation is that the great predominance of local authority housing with their low rents in Scotland, coupled with an almost total absence of open-market rental evidence, means that rateable values bear no relation to open-market values. Thus the truth may be, not that Scottish industry would be heavily rated by comparison with English or Welsh ratepayers if they were fully rated, but that Scottish domestic ratepayers are lightly rated because of the valuation process. In the absence of industrial half-rating, industry would carry an especially disproportionate share of the rate burden. Logically, this amounts to an argument for assessing Scottish rateable values on the same principles as in England and Wales.

DOMESTIC AND NON-DOMESTIC PROPERTY

In Part Two we developed arguments based on considerations both of efficiency and accountability leading to the view that non-domestic rates were an unsatisfactory local tax. It migh seem logical, therefore, to recommend at this stage that non-domestic rating be abolished, or at least made into a national tax levied at the same rate in all authorities. But such a recommendation, which would wipe out more than half of a typical authority's local tax base, cannot be contemplated without consideration of other more fundamental reforms (e.g. the introduction of new sources of local revenue), and so goes beyond the scope of Part Three. But we shall take up the case for the removal of non-domestic rates from the local tax base in the context of a more radical package of reforms in Part Four.

If local authorities continue to levy rates on non-domestic property, the general principle of rates as an *ad valorem* tax suggests that the same poundage should be levied on non-domestic as on domestic property. Despite its general endorsement of the principle of uniform rating, the Layfield Committee felt that the relative burdens on domestic and non-domestic ratepayers should not be determined on that principle, but rather be fixed by central government 'on the basis of national considerations' (1976, p. 177).

The present domestic element provides a standard reduction in the poundage paid by domestic ratepayers. While it was born of political expediency (see Part One, chapter 6), its existence can be defended on a number of grounds:

(1) That industry and commerce can typically afford to make a larger contribution to local government than can households.
(2) That industry and commerce can set their rates against tax while households cannot, and the domestic element partially compensates for this differential tax treatment.
(3) As a form of domestic rate relief, the domestic element provides greatest asssistance to households where rateable values are highest, hence it helps to reduce geographical disparities in rate bills.

Each of these arguments may be questioned:

(1)   Special taxation of business is often justified at the national level by the argument that there should be some redistribution of income from them to the beneficiaries of public expenditure. A politician may well comfort himself with the argument that non-domestic rates have the effect of passing the burden of local services from the poor to industry and commerce, and therefore to the more affluent. Even formally, this is only partially true since many small shop-keepers and firms are far from rich. However, this is to fail to distinguish formal from effective incidence. Rates on non-domestic ratepayers will in the long run be passed on in higher prices and will become another form of indirect taxation. Indirect taxation is regressive. Thus the net distributional impact of non-domestic rates will be regressive, the more so the more the super-rating. In the long run this could offset the effects of rate rebates.

(2)   The differential tax treatment of domestic as against non-domestic rate-payers suggests that the domestic element can be viewed as a form of tax relief. If the rate poundage is 80p. and the domestic element 18.5p, the domestic rate-payer pays an effective poundage of 61.5p, a reduction in his rate bill of about 23 per cent. This could be contrasted with an effective reduction of the standard rate of income tax (currently 33 per cent) if the ratepayer were allowed to set his rates against his taxable income, and with an effective reduction of the rate of corporation tax (currently 52 per cent) for a non-domestic ratepayer paying that tax.

If the domestic element is envisaged as an indirect form of tax relief, it might seem more logical to make household rates tax deductible. Commenting on this possibility, the Layfield Committee rightly pointed out that it would benefit those in the higher tax rates most, while it would not benefit at all those below the income tax threshold (1976, p. 163). To maintain roughly the present degree of progressiveness at the lower end would require an adjustment in rate rebates. But even if this were done, and a high rate of take-up of the rebates achieved, the overall effect would still be to make the rating system more regressive.

There are other arguments against tax deductibility for domestic ratepayers. If a local authority increases its expenditure, the additional cost will be borne in part by central government through the additional tax relief the higher rate bills will attract. One can view tax deductibility as an indirect central government grant to local authorities, but taking the form of a matching grant. Such grants typically reduce the incentive to control expenditure. On the other hand, the fact that ratepayers' gross rate bills would be larger might instil a greater awareness of the cost of local government services, particularly as there would normally be time lag before a higher rate bill became incorporated into a person's tax code. There is also the possibility that for institutional reasons central intervention in local government would be less if the effective grant took the form of tax deductibility to households rather than direct payments to local authorities.

An interesting variant of tax deductibility has recently been suggested by the Conservative Party. This is that all ratepayers would be entitled to a fixed deduction from their income-tax bill as a contribution towards their rate bill. Such a scheme would benefit all taxpayers equally, though again there would have to be increases in rate rebates to provide equivalent assistance to those below the income-tax threshold. Further, because the deduction is a lump sum, there is no incentive for local authorities to increase their spending knowing the part of the higher cost will be borne by central government through increased tax deducibility. One difficulty with this proposal is that of determining which taxpayers are eligible for the rates allowance, for example in a multi-occupied property. Additionally, the proposal does nothing to reduce regional disparities in rate bills, although it could be modified to do so.

It follows that if the domestic ratepayer is to be given some relief, the present domestic element is probably preferable to any form of tax deductibility. But more fundamental is the question of whether domestic and non-domestic ratepayers ought to receive similar tax treatment of their rate bills. Economic logic suggests that resources should be taxed at the same rate in whatever sector they are employed (see Part Two, Chapter 6). Buildings and land employed in industry and commerce attract two taxes: non-domestic rates and corporation tax (or income tax in the case of non-incorporated businesses). Buildings and land employed in providing dwellings attract only one tax, domestic rates. The imputed income from dwellings used to be taxed under Schedule A of the income tax. If schedule A were still to exist, there would be a case for allowing domestic rates to be set against the imputed income. But given the absence of Schedule A, there is a case for rating domestic property higher than non-domestic, given that the return of the latter is also liable to income or corporation tax. At the very least, the fact that non-domestic rates are tax deductible provides no justification, on these grounds, for rate relief for domestic property.

(3)   While it is true that the domestic element provides greatest assistance to areas where rateable values are highest and hence reduces geographical disparities in rate bills, it is hardly a very efficient means of achieving this outcome. At a first approximation, the domestic element reduces all domestic rate bills in the same proportion. More fundamentally, one could argue that if one accepts the objective of the grant system of equalising rate poundages, one cannot logically object to the disparities in rate bills which inevitably arise, while if one does not accept that objective it is more sensible to argue for reforms of the grant system than for differential rating.

Our arguments here recapitulate those of Part Two, Chapter 6 where we have shown that the higher rating of industrial and commercial property is likely to be economically inefficient and regressive. But there are more political arguments against the domestic element. It is the cheapest way of hiding the costs of higher local government services to the local electorate. We showed in Part Two, Chapter 6 how the domestic element had been increased substantially during a period in which ratepayers were rebelling against the rate costs of the increased services central government had ordained. It is for this reason that Layfield recommended that its divisor, which would take the place of the domestic element with capital valuation, should be unchanged between revaluations (Layfield, 1976, p. 178). This proposal was accepted by the government (DoE, 1976, Cmnd 6813, p. 19).

The domestic element has permitted other anomalies, specifically in the treatment of Wales and of London. A higher domestic element for Wales was originally introduced on the grounds that water rates were higher there than in England. While this is no longer the case, the Welsh domestic element has not been correspondingly reduced. In London, a higher domestic element has been introduced for the central boroughs in order to hold together inappropriate equalisation arrangements between the London boroughs (Jackman, 1979).

We therefore see no case for the departure from the principle of uniform rating achieved by the domestic element in the present grant structure.[1] We would, therefore, recommend the ending of this differential rating, either by phasing out the domestic element or, should capital valuation be introduced, by choosing a divisor on the basis of uniform treatment (see Part Three, Chapter 2). Under present arrangements, the ending of the domestic element, and transferring the money released to the needs and resources element, would lead to average increases in domestic rate bills of around 10 per cent, and reductions in non-domestic rate bills of about the same order. Clearly, it would not be impossible to introduce a change of this magnitude over a period of years.

LOCAL FREEDOM TO DIFFERENTIATE RATE BURDENS

The differential rating we have considered so far has been the consequence of central policy (except partially in the case of charities and the peculiar instance of the London Equalisation Scheme). In recent times, British law has been firmly opposed to allowing local authorities the freedom to under-rate or super-rate certain classes of property, or particular properties, as they decide.

The historic argument against allowing local authorities to ape central government and rate different types of property at different poundages is two-fold. There is first what follows from the ancient notion of a rate as only a means of raising money to meet expenditure and not as an instrument of policy to influence the behaviour of the income groups, or firms, taxed. The second comes from the real fear that as small a populace as that of a local authority might hold minorities and even individuals to ransom. A super-rate on chemical firms, for example, might affect one firm in a local authority area but because it was large and costly to move, it might prefer to pay extortionate costs rather than migrate. It would be caught in a trap. Similarly, a poor area might try to super-rate the houses of a minority of rich people. In the past the same effect was achieved sometimes by the valuation process when local authorities were responsible for it; but the nationalisation of assessment by the Inland Revenue and the removal of the freedom from local authorities to rate differentially have both been aimed in part at preventing local authorities from discriminating against any minorities or individuals.

While this notion of equity does seem wise as between various groups of domestic ratepayers and indeed generally, there is one exception that is widespread in many countries, but particularly in the USA. That is the freedom to entice industry by granting full or partial rate exemption usually for a limited period of time. Some states in the USA allow exemption to all establishments within industries specified by law. In Alabama and Kentucky individual local authorities may grant exemptions. In Arkansas and Louisiana exemptions can be made by individual contract. In Alaska they must be ratified by the state. Many other states have some kind of exemption, though in a variety of forms, and if some of the most oblique methods are included – for example, the construction of state or local factories for lease which are themselves exempt from property tax – almost all practise some form of under-rating.

It has often been argued against this that any distortion of free trade through discriminating subsidies will lead to a less efficient allocation of resources. This view on its own is no more or less valid than other anti-protectionist arguments at the national level. The protection of industries can be defended on the 'infant industry' argument which says that it is justified until an industry has grown to a stage where it realises economies of scale that enable it to compete without protection. Such protection can also be justified where there is unemployment of men and resources to the point where such derating is equivalent to a compensation reducing the cost of such inputs to their shadow price – the real cost of employing which will be below the money cost of doing so. There may be other externalities which justify a measure of subsidy. But the danger is always that competing local authorities will engage in beggar-my-neighbour policies which reduce the well-being of each though improving the profits of the benefiting firms. A rash policy of stimulation through rate reductions may reduce local real incomes. However, it should be noted that while rates exceed the cost of benefits of local services supplied so that industry or commerce have negative fiscal residua, it will always be in the immediate financial interest of local authorities to permit any reduction of rates for new industries unless that falls below the cost of service provision. Indeed, an argument for allowing this discretion is that over time it will tend to pull industrial and commercial rates down to their marginal cost levels.

But a quite different argument is that it would permit an unprecedented degree of local autonomy. At present in Britain regional and other spatial location inducements are nationally determined. To allow local authorities this discretion would reduce the national ability to conduct this programme. Which is the more desirable policy is largely a political question. Local authorities, faced with the pressure to improve services and strong opposition to increases in domestic rates, have often argued for powers to super-rate non-domestic property. The 1971 Green Paper (DoE, 1971a, Cmnd 4741) suggested that the then government was taking the possibility seriously. However, the opportunity of introducing super-rating amongst the various other reforms of 1974 was not taken up. The Layfield Committee did not even consider the possibility.

The basic reason for not allowing local authorities the power to levy discretionary rates on industry and commerce is again one of accountability and efficiency. Higher rates levied on non-domestic ratepayers will, as we have argued, end up in higher prices for the consumer. The shareholders or consumers may well not be aware of the extent to which the profits they receive or prices they pay are influenced by rates. Even if they are, they will not normally even be resident in the local authority imposing the rates and thus have no means of influencing the decision. By imposing rates on non-domestic ratepayers, local authorities can provide benefits to their local community at the expense of people living elsewhere who have no say in the matter.

It does not follow from this argument that, given discretion, local authorities would increase non-domestic rates without limit. As we have seen, there is countervailing pressure in the form of tax competition.

The relative strength of these influences on non-domestic rate poundages is likely to differ between authorities and over time. Discretionary super-rating is, therefore, likely to be associated with a greater variability and instability of non-domestic rate poundages. Differences in rate poundages between authorities will have some influence on the location of new investment, an influence for which there will normally be no justification in terms of economic efficiency (see Part Two, Chapter 2). Efficiency requires that investment be located where profits are highest – because costs are low, or where there is a strong market demand, etc. – and not in areas where it secures a tax advantage. The variability and instability of non-domestic rates under a discretionary system may then lead to greater uncertainty and inefficiency in the planning of new investment.

CONCLUSION

In this chapter we have argued against differential rating. In so doing, we argued from the standpoint of the tax structure and not in terms of revenue effects on particular authorities because we are implicitly assuming the grant system will continue to equalise resources between local authorities. We believe there is no justification for treating agriculture differently from other industries, save for the desire to evade EEC policies. The rating of churches and charities poses more intricate questions. We would prefer government to give assistance to such organisations directly, rather than altering the tax system. If central government wishes to give rating relief it should fully compensate local authorities for the revenue they forego by removing such properties (wholly or partially) from the valuation lists. If local authorities wish to make further contributions to charities they should do so explicitly and separately.

We see no case for the differential rating of domestic and non-domestic property. We therefore propose that the general domestic rate relief provided by the domestic element of RSG be ended. On the same grounds as we favour uniform rating as a general policy, we do not believe that local authorities should be allowed to levy different poundages on different properties within their boundaries.

We find only one valid argument, and that a presentational one, for allowing domestic rates to be tax deductible. Otherwise such deductibility is merely a hidden grant to finance local expenditure with distortionary effects in the overall tax system. Such a hidden grant can only be justified if it is believed that higher gross rate bills will increase accountability even though net costs are the same, or if it were to reduce central intervention in local government.

NOTE

1   We might add that the domestic element causes some practical administrative difficulties. See Layfield (1976, p. 179).

4 The Reform of the Grant System

In the discussion of grants in Part Two it was argued that the principal objectives of the grant system were horizontal efficiency and equity and that this required resources and needs grants. Resources grant was required to equalise the tax base and to equate rate poundages for any given level of services provided at the same cost. Needs grant was required to equate rate poundages where there were differences in the costs of services to be provided, that is what is customarily called differences in needs.

Various difficulties were discovered. It was argued first that the objectives of the system required that differences in tax base should be equated where their cause was a difference in the mix of properties of similar value so as to result in a different average rateable value per head, but not where such a difference was due to systematic differences in land values because of locational preference. This difficulty is virtually insuperable because there is no practical way of distinguishing between the two sets of causes of variation in average rateable value per head. Among the most important causes of variation in rateable value per head is the proportion of non-domestic property, but if this were effectively excluded from the grant system and either taxed according to a common rate poundage or charged on a cost-of-services basis, then it is arguable that most of the variation left would reflect differences in locational preference. If so, then there would be a case for abandoning the objective of resource equalisation, that is the resources grant for beneficial services to which these above arguments relate. Systematic differences are relevant to the objective of horizontal equity for centrally determined onerous services.

Thus this distinction itself turns us back on another dilemma: a rational grant system requires a clear distinction between locally determined beneficial and redistributive services for which needs element should not be paid, and centrally determined redistributive expenditure of an agency type for which needs element is appropriate. But to move towards a clear distinction on these matters would require a fundamental change both in a readiness to recognise that such clarity is desirable — which is far from the current wishes of central government — and probably also in the division of powers between central and local government. They are, therefore, questions to be analysed in Part Four.

The arguments of this chapter are essentially negative, saying that within the parameters of the present system there is very little that can be done to better it. Rate Support Grant and, in particular, the regression approach to needs assessment is a brilliant device provided one does not inquire too closely into what it means. Inquiry does go on, however, and the grant system does contain within it the seeds of its own destruction.

The resources element as such is not much of a practical problem because the incoherence to which we have drawn attention is not generally recognised. On the other hand, there is persistent criticism of the regression approach to the estimation of needs. Most of it is from local authorities who note, first, that the equations estimated vary substantially from year to year, and that this means that some authorities always experience sizeable changes in grant despite the damping introduced by averaging the current equation with a number of those from past years. The cause of this is multi-collinearity between variables. Secondly, local authorities often complain that their 'needs' are insufficiently recognised. It may be because some of the data on which the variables are based are out of date, or are never collected in an appropriate form. But sometimes there is a confusion over who or what is the arbiter of needs. The idea that needs are what an equation estimates them to be seems mysterious, as indeed it is. It is the mystery that keeps this part of the system going. Yet another difficulty is with the distinction between variables which are accepted as needs variables, and those that are regarded as discretionary. In Part Two, Chapter 5 it has been argued that a greater part of the variation in expenditure can be explained as due to discretionary influences — income, price and politics — than central government activity. But any distinction between two such sets of variables is a pale and fragile reflection of that between centrally and locally determined expenditures. Finally, and possibly most damaging of all, local authorities who spend most, provided they have characteristics in common with other local authorities who are high spenders, will progressively shift the grant in their direction. In practice, this means that as the years roll on, a greater proportion of grant will tend to go towards urban and towards Labour authorities.

While central government is readier to accept regression analysis as the least evil, many central departments, but particularly Education, dislike the fact there is no requirement that local authorities should spend according to the policies agreed in reaching the estimate of total relevant expenditures as set out in the Rate Support Grant Order. Education, as the largest expenditure block, has suffered particularly from raids in the expenditure cuts of the mid and late 1970s.

All these difficulties cast a dark cloud over the future of the needs element. This chapter is negative because it doubts if any better method can be devised without radical specification of the roles of central and local government. It also dismisses the sense of trying to improve the equity of the resources grant by redefining it in terms of income, which was recommended by the Layfield Committee.

REFORM OF THE NEEDS ELEMENT

The purpose of the needs grant, as we have seen, is to compensate local authorities in full for differences in the costs of providing centrally determined redistributive services — to some given standard — in order to equalise tax burdens on local ratepayers. The problem is of deciding what spending comes into this category and what does not. In its Green Paper in response to the Layfield Committe Report, the government 'recognise the impossibility of absolute precision in the assessment of the relative spending needs of authorities' (DoE, 1977*b*, Cmnd 6813, p. 29). The wording may give the impression that what is lacking is absolute precision, but that some degree of precision is possible. This is misleading because it suggests needs are objective, and all that is lacking is a method of measuring them accurately. But the concept of need is normative. A judgement has to be made on the services central government requires local authorities to provide and the standards it wants to see.

One definition of need is statutory obligation. Local authorities need to spend money on education because they have a statutory obligation to provide it. It may sometimes be feasible to define the statutory obligations imposed on authorities but impossible to measure exactly the expenditures these obligations impose. Legislation is seldom, if ever, formulated precisely enough in terms of the standards required. Thus even though the obligations are imposed, there may be great variety among authorities in terms of the actual expenditures undertaken to carry them out. Sometimes minimum standards are indicated by the central departments responsible for services, and some controls imposed. Over time some typical standards and expenditure levels may become expected as 'normal'. Sometimes there are departmental or government reviews which lead to revisions of these standards, often again without very precise formulation of what is required. But certain questions remain to be answered. Are expenditures greater than the standard (whether defined as a minimum or norm) 'needs' that the general taxpayer should be expected to help finance? Are such expenditures (which are in some sense centrally or socially acceptable) to be distinguished from other expenditures which do not merit a central contribution? Different answers imply different grant systems. Different views can be taken on these questions. But in order to translate concepts of need into an actual grant system some view must be taken. And every grant system implicitly gives an answer to these questions: an answer which it is useful to make explicit.

One approach is that legislation or regulation imposes some minimum standards. For example, in education there are minimum standards in terms of pupil-teacher ratios and requirements on facilities, books, and so on to be made available. Beyond the minimum standards implied by such requirements, any expenditures could be considered to be locally determined, leaving open the question as to whether any or all such above-minimum standard expenditures should merit grant. This concept of a minimum standard has a long history. As we have seen (see Part One, Chapter 7), it played a major role in Webb's suggestions for a grant system. Of course, the actual expenditures required by a particular authority to achieve the given minimum standard may depend on other factors − for example, the cost of providing the inputs or its geographical peculiarities. In terms of defining needed expenditures in this sense, one would want to take those into account. Given this concept of needed expenditure, what it is that one wants to measure to determine an authority's needs is clear, though how to do so may be extremely difficult. Consider the following procedure. We first define the units to which the service imposed by the legislation is to be applied. For example, the number of children of the age group to be educated. We then define the standard imposed by the legislation either explicitly or via departmental advice. There are two ways of doing this. First, in terms of output

– for example, a standard of education to be achieved (presumably on average); second, in terms of inputs – for example, the required student–teacher ratio. We then look at the costs within each authority or determine the variables affecting these costs and determine the needs of the authority. Here we know clearly what is meant by needs. It is the amount of expenditure imposed on the authority by legislation, given the characteristics of the authority that affect those expenditures it has to undertake to achieve the standard imposed.

As is clear from the above outline of the procedure, it may be very difficult to specify all the characteristics determining the minimum expenditures required to carry out the imposed activities. An alternative method is to use regression analysis to determine these characteristics. To use regression analysis involves a particular assumption: that, on average, authorities are providing services to the standard imposed.[1] If so, the regression analysis will, in principle, identify those characteristics of authorities which affect the amount they need to spend to provide services of the required standard.

The mechanics of the regression analysis yield a definition of locally determined, or non-standard, expenditure, but of a curious kind. Standard expenditure, on this definition, is the expenditure that a local authority would spend if it conformed to the regression formula – that is, spent the average of authorities which had the same characteristics. Non-standard expenditures are by definition the amount an authority may spend above that standard expenditure, or indeed below. This concept of non-standard – which is a statistical one – is not easily related to our definition of needs which is more fundamental for grant purposes. Yet it is an attractive simplification. The 'needs' of a local authority are easily measured. There is no better representation of them than past expenditures of other local authorities with the same characteristics. Thus the notion of a central government imposed standard has been translated into that of standard expenditure as determined by a regression formula, and non-standard expenditure becomes the difference between that and actual expenditures.

There is a second important difference between the regression approach and an approach based on statutory obligations. There may be many areas of expenditure which central government may wish to encourage and support with grant, but which it does not wish to impose by statute – for example, provision of assistance to the mentally handicapped, or of recreational facilities. If the provision of such services is related in any systematic way to the characteristics of local authorities, it is likely to attract needs grant under the regression approach.

There is a third category of expenditure which local authorities are allowed to undertake, but which central government would not wish to support by grant. Under the regression approach all expenditure counts equally, and central government may well find itself supporting this category of expenditure with grant also. In the attempt to avoid this outcome, the regression approach is confined to variables plausibly related to need – that is to factors affecting expenditure on the services central government wishes to aid and *relevant* expenditure.

The search for variables which will be good proxies for some notion of needs is as old as the attempts to devise block-grant systems. We discussed some of these attempts and failures earlier (Part One, Chapter 7). We now turn to examine in more detail the concepts of needs implicit in two approaches: regression analysis and the client-approach.

REGRESSION APPROACH

The regression analysis approach uses past expenditures of authorities to determine their relative needs. What is the implicit concept of needs underlying such an approach? Consider first a service such as education which is imposed on authorities by statute. Such statutes do not specify the exact expenditures that should be undertaken. The actual expenditures undertaken by authorities represent an interaction between three factors: first, their interpretation of what is imposed and how much they want to do in the area so imposed; second, the exhortations and advice given by the departments responsible for the service, for example in terms of acceptable student—teacher ratios; and third, local circumstances which may affect the costs of providing a particular level of service. We now run a regression which gives us some relationship between actual expenditures and various factors, and find how much on average, given these factors, authorities spend. We now define this as the standard amount to be spent. It is this amount that we insert into the blank space left by the statute, and though it is still not statutory, it is what is expected. In a sense, the regression tells us how the statute and the regulations have been interpreted on average through the interaction of local decision makers and the departments. Of course, we would exclude variables which on *a priori* grounds we do not consider as needs variables, for example the political party in power.

We might believe, for example, that a particular political party interprets the statutes and regulations too enthusiastically, and therefore its higher expenditure represents its preference rather than needs. The regression analysis could be interpreted as asking the following question. How have local authorities interpreted the statutes and translated them into expenditures? The answer given by the regression analysis is then taken to define what was left undefined in the statutes. The regression could be interpreted as telling the government what it has actually imposed on authorities when it formulated the particular statutory obligations and regulations.

This interpretation is implicit in the government's response to Layfield, when it states that existing expenditure is used (to determine needs) 'because it represents and reflects the combined influence of the Government's policies acting through legislation control and advice on particular services and of the policies of individual local authorities expressed in their budgeting and expenditure decisions' (DoE, 1977*b*, Cmnd 6813, p. 30).

The use of regression analysis on total expenditures, rather than only those where there is a statutory or other obligation, is more difficult to rationalise. It implicitly views all local authority expenditure as equally worthy of grant. It assumes that local preferences for expenditures always reflect those of central government. On the one hand, this is useful for local authorities. With such an interpretation, part of the cost of local wants can be passed on to the general taxpayer through attracting grants. However, as in most areas, a price has to be paid. If all expenditures are to be treated as needs, all expenditure decisions should represent the interaction of local decisions and the control and advice of central departments. It is clear and, we believe, correct, that if all local authority expenditure is considered for needs grant, the degree of local autonomy with respect to such expenditure is going to be decreased.

THE CLIENT-GROUP APPROACH

There have been many suggestions for using more precise and *a priori* defined measures of needs independent of the expenditures of local authorities. Roughly speaking, the most favoured approach attempts to determine the needs of an authority by enumerating in some fashion the individuals within that authority who need a particular service and then estimating the expenditures necessary to attain some standard of provision for that service, and thus defining the needs of an authority. This approach is independent of the actual expenditures of authorities. It has been called the client-group approach. There are two strands in the approach which must be distinguished. One of the purposes of measuring different characteristics of a local authority might be to use these measures as an explanation of the actual expenditures of authorities. For example, one may derive some social-deprivation indicator based on poor housing conditions, the number of old people living alone, the number of one-parent families, and so on. Because local authorities provide services for such groups, it follows that their expenditures may be related to the size of such groups within the authority. The purpose is essentially similar to that of the regression-analysis approach. We are searching for better explanations of local expenditures. The test of whether such an index should be used rather than, say, a density index or a declining population index depends on whether this measure does better statistically in explaining expenditures. The essential point is that expenditures are still considered to be the measure of needs, but we are searching for a better explanation of them.

A quite different approach is to use such indices to determine needs independently of actual expenditures. In contrast to the above approach, these measures would be important even if it turned out that there is no relationship between them and the actual expenditures of authorities.

The objectives and limitations of this approach can be seen by examining one such attempt. In his book, *Social Needs and Resources in Local Services* Bleddyn Davies presents an alternative to the use of expenditure as a measure of needs. He wants to base such a measure on studies 'of the needs of individual persons for services, and the factors that create or accompany individuals' needs, [which] are the main evidence from which one must make deductions about the relative needs of areas' population for services' (1968, p. 16). There is one crucial difference between this and the regression approach. The regression approach is essentially localist, not only because it gives local authorities a great deal of discretion about their expenditures, but more fundamentally because it accepts the collective expenditure decisions of authorities as defining the criteria for their needs and thus their claim on the central government. On the other hand, the Bleddyn Davies approach is essentially centralist. The whole aim of the approach is that of securing what he calls 'territorial justice', which is defined as 'to each area according to the needs of the population of that area' (ibid. p. 16). Moreover, it is not just a measure of need for attracting grants, but one which also requires the local authorities to meet the needs measured. It is up to the central government to achieve this: 'territorial justice requires local authority conformity to a standard not only with regard to the amount of service provided but also with regard to its quality' and such a requirement 'must limit the autonomy of individual authorities to some extent' (ibid., p. 25). This general approach starts at exactly the opposite end of the spectrum from the regression approach. The former asks what variables are a good proxy for expenditures, and calls them needs variables. The latter asks what expenditures should be reflected in the needs variables already defined? And how can we make sure that such expenditures are undertaken?

Of course, such an approach requires an *a priori* definition and measure of needs. Two such approaches of defining needs are used by Davies. As these have slightly different implications for grant systems and, as we shall see later, for control, it is useful to examine both. The first approach is essentially to define needs in terms of averages of what is actually done. This is exemplified by his analysis of the needs for residential homes for the aged.

We start with an analysis of the type of aged who are currently in old people's homes in the country as a whole (that is, those in particular age, sex, and marital categories). This defines the proportion of old people of a particular category who need to be in residential homes. From this, one can derive an index for each authority in terms of its proportion of old people in a particular category to define how many places in residential homes it needs. To convert such an index into an expenditure-need index, one would have to incorporate a variable measuring costs per place. This approach essentially defines an authority's standard expenditure need in terms of the average standard of provision. It differs from a regression-analysis approach only in so far as actual expenditures are not taken into account to see whether such a definition of need is justified in terms of the actual expenditures of authorities. For example, Davies finds very little correlation between his measure of need and expenditures on these services.

The second approach used by Davies essentially measures needs without taking into account what is being done to satisfy such needs. This approach is exemplified in his measure of needs for children's services. He derives an index of need (the anomie index) from a set of characteristics which are assumed to generate needs for children's services. Thus, from particular studies of the children who appear in juvenile courts or are deposited in local authority homes, he derives certain social characteristics which, he believes, result in the need for children's services. The index is composed of such variables as various categories of people born outside the British Isles, the proportion of the population living in boarding houses and hotels, the percentage of males unemployed, etc. Thus this index and this whole approach does not define need in terms of what is actually provided by local authorities. For this index, it is unnecessary to look at any actual expenditures of local authorities.

The client-group approach would be consistent with the regression approach if there were a relationship between local authority spending and the various indices of needs. They differ if actual expenditures and the chosen measures of needs are unrelated. In such a case, the regression approach taken strictly would throw out the needs index as not being a good proxy for needed expenditures. The needs approach would, on the other hand, deduce that the authorities were not providing the needed services. It is in such a situation that one has to specify more precisely the concept of needs. If there is no relationship between expenditures and the chosen index, one may say that the index does not measure 'needs' as seen by the authority. If one believes that local decision making is the major consideration, then the revealed preference of authorities is that the chosen needs index is wrong. If, however, the needs index is chosen on the *a priori* ground that it is in the social interest that the needs measured by it should be satisfied, and that it is up to local authorities to provide for such needs, then the lack of relationship between needs and expenditure is a measure of the failure of local authorities to provide for these needs. Either their concept of needs is different from that measured by the index, or they are not willing to carry out the dictates of the general will. Should we then base a grant system on such measures of need? In their evidence to Layfield, Moore and Rhodes (1976) construct such a grant system. Their attempt exemplifies the problems involved.

They define standard expenditure on a particular service as the national level of the service provided at the national average unit cost. To measure the national level of a service provided they use the same approach as that used by Bleddyn Davies for old people's services. They define the group receiving the service and find the national participation rate of that group. For example, the national level of provision of resdental homes for old people is measured by the proportion of old people in residential homes in the nation as a whole. The needs of a local authority are then measured by the number of old people in the authority multiplied by the national proportion of old people in residential homes. The expenditure need of the authority would then be derived by multiplying this number by the average cost of providing a place in a residential home. Moore and Rhodes then look at the differences between this measure of needed expenditures and actual expenditures by local authorities. They break up the difference in each service to show how much is due to differences in participation rates, and how much to difference in unit costs. They find that a large proportion of the differences arise from differences in participation rates.

In an earlier part of their paper, they stress that the objective they set for the need element of the grant system is that the grant 'which individual authorities receive should be such as *to make the rate burden in these authorities invariant to the need to spend*' (ibid., p. 87, their italics). With this aim of the grant system and their measure of needed or standard expenditures, the next step should be simple. The grant should be distributed on the basis of the type of calculation described in the last paragraph. They do not, however, recommend this. One major element in their proposed grant system is the number of social-service units in an authority multiplied by average expenditure per unit. The social-service units, which were used in the 1974 regression formula, are the actual number of units of a particular service provided by an authority. They include the number of people in residential accommodation, the number of home helps and day-care places, etc. They are thus a measure of the services actually provided by local authorities, not the services local authorities need to provide, as previously defined. The dilemma they face is one which is faced by all client-group approaches. The approach is based on defining needs objectively. When this is done, there is, however, a reluctance to base the grant on such needs if the authorities do not provide for them. Whether a low participation rate arises because potential clients do not wish to become actual clients, or because the local authority does not wish to accept them as clients, there is a reluctance to give a grant based on the estimated potential clientele rather than on the number for whom services are actually provided.

Education is one area often set up as an example of the client-group approach, and it is one area in which such an approach is feasible. The reason for this is clear, as is the reason why one should not generalise from education to other services. In education, there is a captive client group. Not only is the authority obliged to provide the service, but the clients are obliged to participate. For other services, we need much more information about the causes of different participation rates to be able to disentangle needs from standards of provision. Of course, the expenditure approach, whether using averages or regressions, whether it is done service by service or on aggregate expenditures, often seems less satisfying than objective measures of need. But Aristotle's dictum that 'It is a mark of an educated man not to look for more precision than the subject matter admits of' (1934 edn, bk 1, ch. 3) surely applies also to governments.

Does this imply that there is no alternative to the use of regression analysis? It all depends on what is wanted. The departures we have considered all appear to imply more central control; but again one must appreciate why this is so. Suppose Moore and Rhodes had carried through their apparent intention and had devised a grant system related to some politically based notion of need. Moreover, suppose it were adopted and authorities got the grant implied by their needs so defined irrespective of what they actually spent. Thus a local authority would get a substantial grant because it had large number of elderly people, though it provided practically nothing for them. Such a grant system is technically possible. The political reality is that it would be difficult to adopt such a system without the growth of a corresponding belief that central government should make laggard local authorities provide the services for which they receive grant, even if they do not want them. Therefore, embodying notions of territorial justice or other normative notions of need in a grant formula will without doubt encourage the growth of central intervention.

But the problem of defining territorial justice or normative needs for such a grant system is likely to lead to centralisation of another kind. Someone has to define such notions of justice and such norms. Though it is technically possible to imagine devolving this to some independent commission, or even to negotiations between local authorities, in practice central government ultimately must take responsibility, whoever it may consult on the way. In itself, this imposes a cost on central government which has to be far clearer about its priorities than at present if they are to be embodied in a formula. From such a formula one could read off in very precise terms the relative importance central government attached to, say, services for the elderly against recreational facilities or libraries. Moreover, the naked political context of such a formula would mean that an incoming government with different political values might feel obliged to change it, which could lead to greater instability in the distribution of grants.

Many of the criticisms of the expenditure approach arise fom the ambiguities surrounding the use of the word 'needs'. To most people what is a 'need' is a subjective judgement. When used to refer to the needs of large groups, it appears self-evident that defining needs is a moral or political judgement. But on the expenditure approach, needs are defined differently. It might be less confusing if the needs grant were called the 'determinants-of-expenditure' grant instead. It is only because what is spent collectively by local authorities can be assumed to be the product of political interaction within authorities and between local authorities, their associations, professional organisations, public opinion and central government, that it can reasonably be argued that both the pattern of expenditures and the equations found by regression analysis reflect a political process. The use of 'need' in such a context is virtually tautological: what they spend they may be assumed to need to spend.

A possible merit of the regression approach is that by concentrating attention on the objective facts of past expenditures and ignoring ideals and aspirations, it could, in principle, lift grant distribution out of politics, in a way which would be hard to achieve by any other means. In practice, for reasons we have already discussed in Part Two, Chapter 3, there is political bias in the regression method, and in consequence it has been associated with unprecedented political controversy.

If a determinant-of-expenditure basis for grant distribution is to be kept, then regression analysis seems statistically the best way of estimating the required formula. But if one abandons the determinants of expenditure – miscalled needs approach – then the real problem is not statistical or methodological. It is to decide who is going to set the norms – the needs or ideals of territorial justice – that will be required. It is hard to see the outcome as other than an increase in central government intervention.

Thus we reach our conclusion that alternatives to regression analysis either turn out to be trying to achieve what regression analysis can do better, or represent a shift towards greater central determination, as with the client-group approach. We reject that here, only as incompatible with the present system because it would mean a substantial change in power.

At another level there are clearly changes that could be made in the definition of expenditures relevant or reckonable for RSG. Something of the kind is done already but only to exclude services financed by 90 per cent specific grants. This, too, would require an unprecedented clarity of distinction between centrally and locally determined expenditures, or rather between locally determined 'wants' and collectively determined 'needs'. What could be done is to rely more on the distinction between 'needs' and 'wants' or discretionary variables as being some reflection of the differences between locally and centrally or collectively determined expenditure. We believe that equations should include such variables as evidenced in Part Two, Chapter 5, but they should not be used to distribute grant (Jackman and Sellars, 1978).

Finally, there is a change that could be used to help overcome a particular disadvantage of the regression approach. It is essentially backward looking. It looks at the past to predict the future. Any major change in the present will therefore not be taken into account. The problem we have in mind is legislation which imposes new obligations on local authorities. The expenditure required to carry out such new obligations will not be incorporated into the needs grant, which is determined by past expenditure patterns. One method of avoiding this problem is to provide a specific grant whenever new obligations are imposed on local authorities. Such a grant could be specified for a fixed number of years, so that it does not acquire the sanctity of an irrevocable tradition, but long enough for actual expenditures to adjust to the new impositions.

THE RESOURCES ELEMENT

As we have seen, the principle of the needs grant entails some concept of 'standard' expenditure. Whether we define standard expenditures in terms of the obligations imposed by the central government on local authorities, or by the acceptance of the results of the local and departmental interaction revealed through regression analysis, the idea is that these expenditures represent an obligation on local authorities. Moreover, in terms of services they are the same for all local authorities. Differences in standard expenditures occur only because of differences in local authority characteristics which affect the expenditures necessary to provide the same services. On this approach, any individual, whatever his geographical location, can expect to receive the same services. It therefore seems just that he should be liable to the same tax rate, wherever he lives. Thus one could argue that the aim of the resources element should be to equalise the tax rate (whatever the tax base) across all local authorities. In this way, an individual with the given tax base will pay the same tax whatever his geographical location. Individuals are treated equally wherever they live.

Under the present system, the local tax is on rateable value so, if the objective is to equalise tax rates, the resource grant would be based on rateable values. If the local tax were a local income tax, then the resource grant should be based on income. On this approach, a rich authority is one whose average tax base is higher than the national average, a poor authority one whose average tax base is lower. A change in the tax base can change the ranking of rich and poor authorities. The aim of the resources element would be the same whatever the tax base used. It would be to equalise the tax rates on that base across all authorities. With the use of one tax base, authority A may receive more grant than another authority B. In terms of the aim of the grant, the equalisation of tax rates, that is perfectly sensible. It can achieve equality, in that people with the same tax base are treated equally whatever their geographical location, though the people whose taxes are equalised will be different in the two cases.

There has recently been a resurgence of criticism of the use of average rateable value as the criterion for the resource grant, even though rateable value is the local authority tax base (Godley and Rhodes, 1973). The Layfield Committee has proposed a change in the criterion used for distributing the resource element of RSG. The proposal is to use average incomes rather than average rateable values. It is clear from Layfield that the aim of the proposal is to improve horizontal equity defined in terms of individuals' ability-to-pay taxes. Their criticism of the existing method of distribution is that 'the value of the property they occupy is a worse measure of some peoples' ability to pay taxes than their consumption of other goods and services' (1976, p. 222). In the following paragraph they justify their proposal by concluding that 'Families with similar incomes would still not necessarily pay the same amount of rates in different areas, but they would no longer have to pay substantially different amounts by reason of the variation in the level of property values between areas' (ibid.).

The first point to make about this proposal is that it is based on a different equity objective. The objective of the present system — to equalise tax rates — can be defended on grounds of what we earlier called equity of tax structure. But as we showed in Part Two, Chapter 3 an alternative, and more common, definition of equity is in terms of the relationship between taxes and ability to pay. And while a household's income might be taken as a good measure of its ability to pay, its rateable value might not be.

If we were to adopt a local income tax, and a resources element equalising local income-tax rates (for 'standard' expenditures), both definitions of equity would be satisfied. Tax rates would be equalised and household tax bills would be directly related to their income and hence to their ability to pay. The case for basing the resources element on local income while the local tax base is rateable value is much less powerful. The proposal would increase the dispersion of rate poundages — the aim would be low rate poundages in authorities where rateable value is high relative to income, and high rate poundages where rateable value is relatively low. More important, it would not necessarily achieve its objective of bringing about a closer relationship between a household's rate bill and its ability to pay.

We can consider first a very simple example — two households identical in terms of income and rateable value, but living in different authorities. Under the present system, in principle rate poundages are equalised (for 'standard' expenditures) so their rate bills are also the same. Under the Layfield proposal rate poundages in the two authorities would in all probability differ as a result of the changed basis of grant distribution. The two households would end up paying different amounts in rates.

While this example shows that the Layfield proposal will not lead to an unambiguous improvement in equity, it is reasonable to ask whether or not equity will improve 'on average'. More precisely, will the variation in the rate bills of households of any given income level be reduced or increased by the proposal? There is no simple answer to this question, and we set out an illustrative example in some detail in the appendix to this chapter. If rateable values vary systematically relative to income between areas (for example, for reasons of locational preference or advantage) then the Layfield proposal will tend to improve equity. But if the variation is due to differences in the mix of income levels and rateable values, so that a household of given income might expect to live in accommodation of similar rateable value in the different authorities — the averages differing due to differences in the mix of households — then the Layfield proposal would tend to worsen equity.

One might think that — whatever its effects on equity — the Layfield proposal would at least be progressive in terms of shifting a greater proportion of the tax burden on to higher income groups. But the proposal benefits people living in authorities where incomes are low relative to rateable values. The actual level of income in such authorities may, in fact, be higher than in other places.

In practice, rateable value differentials tend to be greater than differences in average income levels, so the areas which would benefit most from the Layfield proposal are those where incomes are already relatively high − in particular, London. Indeed, the main impact of the proposal would be to benefit London.

At this stage we must consider the treatment of London more explicitly. London has rateable value far in excess of other authorities, and of the standard rateable value per head for the resources element. Logically, the objective of the present system − of rate-poundage equalisation − should imply a symmetrical resources element, so that London's excess rateable value would be taxed away. This happens only in part − through the 'clawback' of London's needs element entitlement (Jackman, 1979). Clearly the government has not been prepared to accept the logic of rate-poundage equalisation as applied to London where rateable values are typically exceptionally high relative to incomes.

If the main effect of the Layfield proposal − as opposed to rate-poundage equalisation − is to benefit London, but London already escapes rate-poundage equalisation through the present *ad hoc* and asymmetrical arrangements, there might seem little point in the reform. But at present the determination of London's grant share is a matter of arbitrary political judgement as to the size of the clawback. As we showed in Part Two, there has been a very substantial increase in London's share of grant in recent years, and a corresponding belief that the grant system has been politically manipulated to the benefit of London. If the Layfield proposal were adopted, special grant arrangements for London would no longer be required.

THE RESOURCES ELEMENT AND 'NON-STANDARD' EXPENDITURE

We have so far considered a resource equalisation grant for 'standard' expenditures. Such a grant would be a lump-sum grant. For example, if standard expenditure after deduction of needs grant were £100 per head, and if standard rateable value were £200 per head, then the rate poundage local authorities would need to levy would be 50p. Their resources element would be 50p multiplied by their deficiency of rateable value, irrespective of how much they actually spent.

The present system is to pay resources element on all expenditure, that is including locally determined or 'non-standard' expenditure. We discussed the case in terms of equity for a resource equalisation grant on beneficial expenditure in Part Two, Chapter 3. There we argued that there was a conflict of objectives. There is a further point we should make here. If local authorities expect to receive grant on non-standard expenditures, it is inevitable that those who provide the grant will seek to influence local authority expenditure decisions. The more local authorities demand autonomy with respect to such non-standard expenditures, the weaker the case for a matching resource equalisation grant.

A proposal for different grant treatment of standard and non-standard expenditure makes sense only if it is possible to distinguish reasonably accurately between the two. We have already discussed some of the difficulties of needs assessment. This might suggest that a margin of error should be allowed. Local authorities spending up to a given amount more than their assessed standard expenditure could be allowed resources grant on all, or part, of the excess on the grounds that the excess might well represent an underestimate of their 'true' spending need rather than 'non-standard' expenditure. But the greater the excess, the less likely it can be explained by an underestimate of spending and the more likely it is to be non-standard, or locally determined expenditure. The implication is that there should be a 'tapering' resources element: the more local authorities spend in excess of their assessed spending needs, the greater the proportion of the cost they have to finance from their own resources. If, for example, the estimated rate poundage to finance standard expenditure were 50p, the resources element might instead be based on the authority's actual rate poundage up to a maximum of, say, 60p multiplied by its deficiency of rateable value. A more sophisticated proposal along these lines is incorporated in suggestions for a unitary grant, to which we now turn.

A UNITARY GRANT

The unitary grant is a government proposal, which it presented to the Layfield Committee and later argued for in its Green Paper in response to the Layfield Committee Report. The proposal is to combine the needs and resources elements into a single grant. The grant paid to each authority would be the difference between its centrally assessed spending need and its rate product at some standard rate poundage, set by government. The grant could be a lump sum, or local variations in spending could also attract grant. In the Green Paper proposal, authorities deviating from their assessed spending needs by some given percentage would be able to finance their spending at some higher rate poundage, again set by central government. The higher the spending in excess of assessed spending needs, the sharper the increases in rate poundages.

One advantage of this proposal is that it would allow a simpler and more effective equalisation of rate poundages. In the absence of any grant, three authorities might need to levy rate poundages of say 65p, 85p and 95p respectively to finance their standard expenditures. If these authorities now receive needs grant on the basis of all the various needs factors affecting their spending it might reduce their rate poundages to, say, 40p, 50p and 60p respectively. If standard rateable value is set equal to the rateable value per head in the first authority, payment of resources element will bring the rate poundage in the other two authorities down to 40p also. The requirements of equalisation have not only equalised rate poundages, they have reduced what was already the lowest rate poundage by 25p. It is this cost which is unnecessary for equalisation. In practice, there may not be sufficient grant money to achieve full equalisation, so the standard rateable value might have to be set lower than the rateable value in the first authority. This would result in rate poundages of say 40p, 45p and 45p.

With the unitary grant proposal the standard rate poundage could be set at 50p, or 60p, or even 65p. Rate poundages would be equalised and the amount of grant needed much smaller. There is a second point: full equalisation under the existing system would require a high standard rateable value, which would, in turn, imply a high rate of matching grant for many authorities. There is no such implication with the unitary grant proposal. There need be no matching grant component and, if there is, its rate need have no relation to the extent of grant support for standard expenditure.

The unitary grant does not presuppose any particular system of needs assessment. But it does expose a problem if central government wishes to restrain local government spending by cutting the grant total. Under the present system, the government can reduce the grant total while still using an essentially 'localist' procedure — regression analysis — to determine the relative amounts of grant going to different authorities.

We can distinguish two cases. First, total local government spending is unchanged, but central government wishes to see a larger proportion financed by the ratepayer and a smaller proportion financed by grant, leaving the grant-distribution procedure unaffected. Under the unitary grant, it can similarly leave each authority's assessed spending need unchanged, but increase the standard rate poundage. The fear is that central government might shirk this outcome because it would attract the blame for the rate increases.

The second case is one where central government in fact does want to reduce local government spending, as a result, say, of policy changes set out in a public expenditure White Paper. The grant proportion may not be changed. Under the present system the grant total would be reduced but its distribution unaffected. Under the unitary grant system it would be necessary to reduce the assessed spending needs of authorities. But how are such changes to be fitted into a regression system of needs assessment? Indeed, the unitary-grant approach seems to require some method of reconciling the current systems of localist relative-needs assessment and centralist determination of aggregate expenditure.

The most contentious aspect to the unitary-grant proposal, however, is the increased emphasis it gives to the concept of assessed spending need, or standard expenditure. In part, this is presentational: under the present system it is possible to calculate authorities' assessed spending needs from their needs-grant allocations, but such calculations are not carried out, and there is no publicity attached to spending above or below this implicit figure of assessed spending need. By contrast with the unitary grant such figures would be explicit and public and this would undoubtedly create additional pressure for local authorities to conform to them. But, second, central government would be in a position, by setting a large increase in rate poundage for even a small increase in spending over the standard, to impose a heavy financial penalty on authorities exceeding their assessed spending need, providing an additional incentive to conform to that assessment. Given the difficulties in accurately assessing spending needs, which as we have seen are substantial and insuperable, a grant system placing greater emphasis on this concept must be viewed with considerable suspicion.

THE TWO TIER SYSTEM

In the present two-tier structure, RSG may not be able to achieve equalisation because not all authorities receive both needs and resources grants. Resources grant is paid to the rating authorities, that is to the metropolitan and non-metropolitan districts and the London boroughs. The higher-level authorities, the county councils, police authorities, and so on precept on the rating authorities, but the precepts qualify for resources element grant so the outcome is the same as if every authority received its own resources grant.

The needs element is more complex. It is paid to the London boroughs, the metropolitan districts, the non-metropolitan counties and, starting from 1979/80, the non-metropolitan districts also. The regression analysis is carried out on the expenditure of the non-metropolitan counties (including the expenditure of each county's constituent districts), the metropolitan districts (with metropolitan county expenditure apportioned between districts in proportion to their populations), outer London boroughs (with GLC expenditure apportioned on population basis) and on inner London as one unit (because of the difficulty of apportioning ILEA expenditure between the inner boroughs).

What happens next is different in each of the main groups of authorities. In London, the needs grant entitlements of the outer boroughs and of inner London, derived from the national regression analysis, are pooled together. Then separate needs assessments are made for the GLC, the metropolitan police, ILEA and the outer and inner boroughs separately, and the total London needs grant is split up between the different authorities on this basis. So that in London both the boroughs and the precepting authorities have a needs grant entitlement. For legislative reasons, needs grant is in fact only paid to the boroughs, the needs grant entitlements of the precepting authorities being shared between the boroughs in accordance with their rateable values – that is in proportion to the amounts they contribute in precepts. (There are a number of additional complications, see Jackman, 1979.)

In the metropolitan counties and districts outside London, the counties receive no needs grant allocation. However, the needs grant received by the metropolitan districts must be, in part, supposed to contribute towards county expenditures. Since all metropolitan districts receive resources element, the precepts they pay to the counties are made essentially on a per capita basis. Since county expenditures are apportioned to the districts on a per capita basis in the process of determining their needs—grant entitlements, the whole system operates consistently.

Until 1978/79, the situation for the non-metropolitan authorities was less satisfactory. The counties received all the needs grant, even though some must be supposed to contribute towards the expenditure of the districts. In a sense the counties received 'too much' needs grant, and so reimbursed the districts by levying lower precepts than otherwise. But again, with the vast majority of non-metropolitan districts in receipt of resources grant, the benefits of lower precepts are shared between the districts on a per capita basis. It is equivalent to their receiving a needs grant based only on their population. That is to say, the arrangements up to 1978/9 made no allowance for differences in expenditure need between districts within a county.

Before coming to the new arrangements for the non-metropolitan districts introduced in 1979/80, it is worth considering some more comprehensive suggestions for reform. The Layfield Committee wanted both tiers of authority to receive both needs and resources elements of the grant, and levy rates. They suggested that for both metropolitan and non-metropolitan authorities the needs grant, as currently estimated, should be divided between counties and districts in proportion to expenditures. (Layfield, 1976, p. 227). In the non-metropolitan counties about 15 per cent would go to the districts and 85 per cent to the county, while the metropolitan counties would receive about 20 per cent and metropolitan districts 80 per cent. The allocation of needs grant to districts in non-metropolitan counties would be in proportion to population, while the metropolitan districts' needs grant would be reduced on a per capita basis to provide the county needs grant.

With the Layfield proposal, each ratepayer's rate bill would be the same as under the present (1978/9) arrangements.[2] But that rate bill would be made up of two different tiers. Its purpose was to improve accountability, to allow ratepayers to distinguish the tax levied on them by district and county authorities.

In its evidence to Layfield, the Department of the Environment (Layfield, 1976, app. 7) had suggested a somewhat more adventurous proposal which could affect rate poundages. Essentially, the proposal was that each county with its districts come to an agreement about how their needs grant allocation be shared between them. This is what now happens in London. This proposal clearly founders on the impracticality of expecting authorities to agree to one procedure on needs assessment rather than another, when clearly each procedure will favour some authorities at the expense of others. Nor would central government be likely to accept a simple majority vote, which would almost inevitably go along political lines. London has been allowed to distribute its own needs grant, in part because there are sufficient authorities to allow the use of regression analysis, rather than some more overtly subjective and political procedure. Also, the London boroughs have had thirty years of experience with rate equalisation schemes in which to learn the issues, and political compromises, involved. Even so, central government has been closely involved with the London needs grant arrangements.

From 1979/80, the non-metropolitan districts will receive needs grant. The total needs grant for each non-metropolitan county will be divided between county and districts in proportion to their expenditures. Then that part of the grant allocated to the districts will be shared between them on the basis of their assessed spending need. For 1979/80 the districts' assessed spending needs will be determined three-quarters on the basis of their population, and one-quarter on the basis of their past expenditure.

The high weight given to population can be justified in the first year in terms of reducing sharp year-to-year fluctuations in grant distribution. (It will be recalled that the previous system was equivalent to paying needs grant to the districts on a per capita basis.) Such a justification cannot be used in subsequent years. Equally, there are obvious objections to basing the grant wholly on actual expenditure. To be consistent, the government should run a national regression analysis on non-metropolitan district councils' expenditure and base their grant on that. But such an approach is unacceptable to the district councils themselves, the large majority of which are rural authorities and opposed to regression analysis. A reform of the needs assessment procedure – for example, towards the client-group approach – could break the deadlock. Otherwise, even as a stop-gap, the present arrangements seem likely to become increasingly unsatisfactory over time.

As far as London and the metropolitan counties are concerned, present arrangements satisfy the equalisation objectives of the grant, at least in terms of the way the two-tier system is treated. We do, however, see advantage in terms of accountability in following the Layfield recommendation in paying grant directly to the metropolitan counties, as proposed by Layfield, and to the GLC and ILEA on the basis of their need assessments that are already calculated for the London needs grant distribution procedure.

CONTROL OF EXPENDITURE

Two aims of control have shaped grant systems. In the early period of grants the issue was control over particular services. In the later period the issue was one of general macroeconomic control (see Part One, Chapter 7). Most recently, a third aim has emerged: the reduction of the public sector *per se*.

We have noted already the apparent incongruity of a grant system moving increasingly away from specific grants toward the present, unhypothecated, block grant at a time when detailed central government involvement in the provision of specific services has been growing. We have shown that central government has so many other instruments to hand with which to influence local authority behaviour that to use the grant system for this purpose is, in a sense, superfluous (see Part Two, Chapter 7). Within the confines of the present system, we do not see any justification for a significant extension of specific grants.

In terms of the control of aggregate local authority expenditure, we need to distinguish between the long-term influence of grants on the size of the local government sector, and the short-term use of grant in demand management policy. As far as the former is concerned, we would argue in favour of lump-sum rather than matching grants, on the grounds that the latter are likely to encourage too high a level of local government spending. It is for this reason that we have argued against the open-endedness of the present resources element, and have looked favourably on the government's unitary-grant proposal.

For short-term demand management, we have argued that it is essential for central government to be able to determine the grant total, as changes in this total are in our view a legitimate instrument of macroeconomic policy. The present resources grant presents a problem in this respect, for while its total is fixed, as far as individual authorities are concerned it is an open-ended grant. The conflict is resolved by a 'clawback', so that if the total of local authorities' claims for resources element exceeds the total available, each claim is scaled down in the same proportion to give the right total (Lynch, 1977).

CONCLUSION

Throughout this chapter the argument has been hampered by the dilemma noted at the start. In place of an explicit statement of what local expenditures are standard, that is centrally (or collectively) determined, the grant system has to fall back on a variety of oblique and faulty contrivances. In a pure federal system this would not happen because, as we have seen, it is a defining character- istic of federalism that the division of functions between central and local government is explicit, as are the powers and responsibilities exercised by each. It should follow that the purposes of particular expenditures could clearly be assigned to the federal or the local level. A unitary government could be as ex- plicit as it chose. British government does not choose to be, and the role of law in Britain and the convention of central government power are such that it does not have to be clear. This is defended, as we have seen, on two grounds. The first is democratic. In a unitary state, central government is sovereign and has a right to impose its will on local government, which is another way of saying that Britain has so far not found it desirable to have federal elements in its law protecting local from central democracy. Second, there is the more prag- matic doctrine of ministerial or administrative flexibility which believes that ministers, as the superior government, should have the right within very broad limits to change their minds and intervene in local government when it is their policy to do so, and refrain from doing so when they do not want to intervene. As we have seen, this doctrine was clearly stated in the 1977 Local Government Finance Green Paper (DoE, 1977*b*, Cmnd 6813).

Given this irresolution of powers, the only changes recommended for the needs element were, first, the free use of discretionary variables such as income and politics for estimation though not for grant distribution. They ought to be included when found statistically superior. Second, because of the backward- looking bias of the regression approach there is a case for a temporary or seed- corn specific grant for new centrally determined expenditure. The client-group approach to the estimation of needs was rejected on the grounds that it would represent a fundamental shift of power towards central government. Conversely, very simple approaches like a percentage grant on all expenditure, or a fixed per capita grant, can be rejected because they would imply in the first instance that all locally determined expenditures would be grant-aided, while authorities would not be fully compensated for differences in their needs, and in the second because it means abandoning the attempt to equalise rate poundages for needs.

The Layfield recommendation that the resources element should equalise in terms of the average incomes of the inhabitants of a local authority was rejected because, as chalk and cheese, such an amalgam would fail to achieve any of the desired objectives. The belief that equity is better satisfied in terms of incomes than rateable values is an argument for altering the tax base, not for inserting an incongruous element into a system based on rateable values.

It was then pointed out that the very improvement of the needs-element dis- tribution, first by introducing regression analysis and then improving it so that it explained an increasingly higher proportion of expenditure, had changed an important presumption. In the past, there was a presumption that central government was being less than generous, grant-aiding a lower proportion of expenditure than could reasonably be regarded as centrally or collectively determined. Now the presumption is the other way. The probability that locally determined expenditures are grant-aided by the needs element is increasing because, in effect, the regression approach treats the residual or statistically unexplained expenditure as non-standard or locally determined; and that proportion is diminishing. The arguments for and against grant-aiding locally determined expenditure were gone into more deeply in the context of the operation of the grant system, but the conclusion reached was the same as that reached in Part Two, Chapter 3 that such expenditures should not qualify for a needs-element grant. But given the inexplicitness already referred to, not much could be done about it.

The grant system set out in this chapter is not very different from the unitary system proposed by the DoE, because it also unifies the resources and needs element in the interests of equalising rate poundages for a given standard of services – the difference being fairly minor in practice, as set out above, though the reservations about the efficiency or equity of the system, even of its capability of survival, remain great.

NOTES

1 Formally, it is also necessary to assume that deviations from the average bear no systematic relationship to the characteristics of local authorities which affect their spending needs.
2 This would be strictly true only if all non-London authorities were receiving resources grant: a handful of non-metropolitan districts do not, see Part Two, Chapter 3.

Appendix 2.4.A1　Definition of Variables

With the present resource grant system, based on rateable value, rate poundages are in principle equalised across all authorities with the same per capita expenditure (net of needs grant). With a resource grant based on average incomes, rate poundages will differ even when per capita expenditures are the same. The change in rate poundages will depend on the relationship between standard rateable value (the present base for the resource grant) and standard income (the

Table 3.4.A1.   *Example of the effects of an income-based resource grant*

	v/y	y	v	v_s	r_y
A	0.05	3,000	150	0.6	0.36
B	0.04	4,500	180	0.6	0.45
C	0.025	3,000	75	0.6	0.72

income base for a resource grant) and the relationship in each authority between its average income and its average rateable value. If r is the rate poundage in an authority with the present resource grant and r^y is the rate poundage with an income-based resource grant then

$$r^y = r(^vs/y_s)(y/v) \qquad (1)$$

where $^vs/y_s$ is the ratio of standard rateable value to standard income and y/v is the authority ratio of income to rateable value.[1]

Table 3.4.A1 shows three hypothetical authorities A, B and C which are assumed to have the same per capita expenditure. The first column (v/y) shows the authorities' rateable value income ratio. The second and third columns show average incomes and average rateable values in the authorities. The fourth and fifth columns show the rate poundages under the two grant systems. The last column is constructed on the assumption that $^vs/y_s$ is 0.03 and with the use of column one and equation (1) above.

In our example, the move from rateable value to income as the resource base has decreased rate poundages in authority A and B and increased it in authority C. The reason for this is that A and B have a higher rateable value income ratio than standard, they thus receive a relatively larger resource grant when it is based on income as compared to rateable value.

The top row of Table 3.4.A2 shows individual incomes ranging from £2,000 to £5,000. Section I of the table shows rateable values in the three authorities of individuals with the incomes shown in the top row. We have assumed that within each authority there is a positive relationship between income and rateable value, but for all income groups rateable values are highest in authority A and

Table 3.4.A2.   *Effects of an income-based resource grant on hypothetical households*

	2,000	2,500	3,000	3,500	4,000	4,500	5,000	
$\overset{*}{V}_{iA}$	140	145	150	155	160	165	170	
$\overset{*}{V}_{iB}$	155	160	165	170	175	180	185	(I)
$\overset{*}{V}_{iC}$	65	70	75	80	85	90	95	
$v_s\overset{*}{V}_{iA}$	84	87	90	93	96	99	102	
$v_s\overset{*}{V}_{iB}$	93	96	99	102	105	108	111	(II)
$v_s\overset{*}{V}_{ic}$	39	42	45	48	51	54	57	
$v_y\overset{*}{V}_{iA}$	50.4	52.2	54	55.8	57.6	59.4	61.2	
$v_y\overset{*}{V}_{iB}$	69.75	72.0	74.25	76.5	78.75	81.0	83.25	(III)
$v_y\overset{*}{V}_{iC}$	46.8	50.4	54.0	57.6	61.2	64.8	68.4	

lowest in authority C.[2] Section II of the table shows the rate payments for the various income groups if the resource grant is based on rateable value, Section III shows the rate payments if it is based on income. These are derived by applying the appropriate rated poundages from Table 3.4.A1.

With the rateable value based resource grant individuals in A pay nearly twice the amount in rates as those in C with the same income. The move to an income based resource grant reduces this difference. Individuals with the same income still pay higher rates in A than in C, but now the difference is much smaller. The change has improved horizontal equity across these two authorities.

Let us now compare authorities A and B. With the grant based on rateable value, individuals in B paid higher rates than those in A with the same income. The move to an income-based grant nearly doubles this difference. Across these two authorities horizontal equity has become worse. The difference between A and C is that rateable values are systematically higher relative to incomes at all income levels — the average income levels in the two authorities being similar. The difference between A and B is in the mix of income levels and rateable values — while rateable value at each income level is approximately the same.

NOTES

1 With the present resource grant system $r_j = e_j(1/v_s)$ where e_j is the per capita expenditure and v_s is standard rateable value. With an income-based resource grant we would have $r_j^u = (1/v_j)e_j(^y j/y_s)$.

2 We have assumed that there is a linear relationship between rateable value and income within each authority of the form $V = a + bY$. The calculations in Table 3.4.A2 were made on the assumption that the regression coefficient b in the above relationship is 0.01.

5 Summary of Recommendations and Prognosis

The recommendations made in this part have been pitched to be ameliorative, not fundamental. They accept the system as it is, that is they accept

(1)   that rates will continue to be the sole local authority tax;
(2)   that there will be no greater reliance on charges;
(3)   that the objectives of the grant system will continue to be horizontal efficiency and equity; but
(4)   there will be no fundamental change in the balance or explicitness of re-lations between central and local government. In the phraseology of Part One, Chapter 2 there will be no 'federalisation' of British local government finance.

Even within these limits, substantial changes are desirable. Our proposals re-late to the rating system and the grant system, the two major sources of finance for local authorities. It is useful to recapitulate these and examine more closely the costs and the expected benefits of introducing the package we propose.

1   RATES

(a) DOMESTIC PROPERTY

The rateable value of domestic property is to be based on the actual purchase price of such property or the currently estimated price derived from annual indices of house prices. Only minor adjustment to the sale price would be made, primarily to convert leasehold to freehold values.

We would suggest that this proposal should be introduced with an advance notice of about five years. The Inland Revenue should start constructing property price indices from current sale prices, and from any information of the recent past that was available. The period of five years would give valuers time to learn to cope with any new problems that may arise, and to devise methods to over-come them. About two years before the introduction of the new system each local authority should announce the rate poundage on sale price that would be levied if the new system were in operation. This would give purchasers at least an idea of the order of magnitude of the relationship between sale prices and rates. The benefit of doing this would be twofold. First, house purchasers would have two years in which to take account of the effect of rates on their offer price. With the knowledge that the new system would actually be introduced in the near future, purchases made before its introduction will take account of the prospective change. House prices will adjust accordingly. The second advantage of giving a period of two (or if possible more) years of advance notice about the effects of the new system is that information will become available about its distributional cost. For example, we would know that property in certain price brackets would be affected greatly by the new system by comparing over the two years the rates actually paid under the old system with those that would be paid under the new. Such information will be crucial in deciding whether any transitional arrangements should be made and how such arrangements should be formulated. We discuss such possible arrangements below.

The major adjustment we have accepted to sale prices and the one that may affect a large number of purchasers is the conversion of leasehold to freehold values. For very long leasehold property such an adjustment will be trivial. However, property with short lease could be affected quite drastically. We would propose that tables of such adjustments, even if approximate, should be easily available to all who want them. A purchaser of a short leasehold property would then easily be able to calculate the rate bill to expect given the adjustment to be made.

Advantages of the proposal

The major advantage of the above proposal is that it would make rates an *ad valorem* tax on the value of property rather than what they have become, namely, a tax on a very notional value of property more and more divorced from the reality of value. As the evidence on rents has become scarcer and scarcer, rateable value has become more and more a mythical concept. Given the length of the periods between revaluations, the relationship between rateable value and actual value is almost non-existent. Rateable value is now what it is because five or eight years ago somebody calculated a hypothetical rent on the basis of little or no evidence, on property which may never have been rented. The slow disappearance of rented property makes it totally inappropriate to use rents as the basis for estimating rateable value.

Differences in rateable value, both geographical and quantitative, will be based on differences in house prices. Just as it is accepted that a house in one area of the country is more or less expensive than in another, even though they are in some sense alike, it will be accepted that the rates will be different if they are based on the value of the house rather than on notional rents.

There will, of course, be some problems. There will still be rented property for which the sale price had it been sold would have to be estimated. This is, of course, the problem with the current system in which the rent of sold property, had it been rented, has to be estimated. For such properties hypothetical sale prices would have to be estimated. However, the greater abundance of evidence on sales would make these hypothetical values more closely related to actual ones than is the case with the present system. The other problem will be with council housing. With these, neither sale prices nor rentals are related at all closely to market values.

But it would be no more difficult, and, in all probability, easier to estimate hypothetical sale prices for these than it is to estimate hypothetical rents.

(b) NON-DOMESTIC PROPERTY

Ideally we would recommend that non-domestic property should be valued on the same basis as domestic — namely, on freehold market values, with annual revaluation by means of price indices. Unless consistency between domestic and non-domestic valuations is achieved in this way a number of anomalies can result.

At the same time, rental evidence for non-domestic property is widely available, and the arbitrariness of the valuation procedure which is the main reason for advocating capital valuation of domestic property does not apply to non-domestic. A hybrid system, of capital valuation for domestic and rental valuation for non-domestic, as recommended by Layfield, is feasible and in our view a clear gain on the present arrangements. But — unlike Layfield — we do not believe the 'divisor' under such a system (determining the relative tax burdens on domestic and non-domestic ratepayers) should be determined by central government. Instead, we believe the same rate poundage should be levied on all ratepayers — domestic and non-domestic — within each authority. We recommend the abolition of the domestic element which effects a super-rating of non-domestic property in the present system. Under a system of capital valuation of all properties, we would want to see a uniform rate levied on all types of property within a local authority. With the hybrid valuation scheme we would recommend a divisor determined by market rental yields and not by government, again in order to achieve a uniform rate burden.

2. THE GRANT SYSTEM

We have considered different ways of specifying needs and resources for the purpose of distributing grants among local authorities. The most appropriate conceptual definition of needs also happens to be most difficult to measure. We looked at the client-group approach to the measurement of needs and the current regression method. Though the client-group approach has certain attractions, its implementation would require a much better specification of the imposition on or expectations from local authorities than is currently made. At one level, we believe that the client-group approach represents an indirect attempt to improve the regression approach; to find better proxies for the determinant of actual expenditure. In the regression approach one is looking for the variable which will best explain total expenditures of local authorities. One could look at specific services, for example education and the social services, and see whether these can be explained separately; this would be a regresssion approach on a service-by-service basis. One could go further and look at subservices within any major service, for example expenditure on the aged or on children in care, and we would have one form of client-group approach. All these approaches are, however, fundamentally the same in that they are looking for explanations of actual expenditures undertaken by local authorities. Which approach is then to be chosen depends on their relative ability to provide such an explanation.

A client-group approach which defines the client groups in advance and, moreover, defines what it is that the client groups should be provided with is different. For such an approach, standards have to be defined and probably enforced. Such an approach would have major implications for the relationship between central and local government. It would have certain advantages in clarifying the areas of responsibility among the two tiers of government. If feasible, it would be a tempting solution to the problems of central/local relationship which have bedevilled local government since at least the beginning of the nineteenth century. It seems more likely, however, that if such a solution were introduced it would be in the form of an actual transfer of services between the two tiers of government.

We have, therefore, accepted the regression method of defining 'needs' though it would be less misleading if it were overtly recognised as an expenditure-determining approach rather than as a needs approach.

We argued that for the purpose of the resource grant, the definition of resources should be whatever is used as the tax base for local authorities. As long as rateable value is the local tax base, the resource grant should be based on rateable value. We examined the Layfield proposal to use average income for the purpose of the resource grant. We showed that this would not necessarily improve horizontal equity. Moreover, it would result in different tax rates across local authorities with the same expenditure per head and lead to all the efficiency and equity problems that this may involve.

The grant based on the regression-derived definition of standard expenditure and using rateable value as the measure of resources should be a unitary grant, as proposed by the government in the 1977 Green Paper (DoE, 1977b, Cmnd 6813.

PROBLEMS OF TRANSITION

Of all our proposals, the one which will have the biggest distributional effect and therefore raise the biggest transitional problems is the move to capital valuation. People in more expensive houses will face much higher rate bills than under the present system, and therefore the sale price of these will fall relatively. As soon as it is announced that capital valuation is to be introduced and the tax rates are set, purchasers will take this into account and the burden of the changeover will fall on the present owners. Because rates are not completely capitalised there will also be a long-run effect increasing the rate burden on those owning more expensive houses. The equity considerations of these two effects may be different.

Let us look at the long-run effects first. Whether the increase in the tax burden on those in more expensive housing is considered equitable or not depends on one's view of equity and on the relationship between the value of a house owned by an individual and whatever is considered as the base for judging ability to pay. Given the relationship between house values and incomes and the present regressive relationship between house values and rateable values, the move to capital valuation would make the rating system and, therefore, the whole tax structure more progressive. If it is believed that the tax structure should not be made more progressive then the move to capital valuation should be accompanied by a reduction in the progressivity of the income-tax system. In this way, the progressivity of the tax structure will be maintained, even though that of the rating system has been changed. An alternative would be to make rate poundages explicitly regressive or to make rates tax deductible. What should not be done is to get the desired result by manipulating assessments of rateable values. One of the major arguments for capital valuation based on sale prices is that it gets away from the notional values that have become prevalent because of lack of rental evidence and the various adjustments made. If the valuation process is to be used to make the tax structure more equitable it could easily become as notional as is the present one.

A more difficult problem is the short-term one; the once-and-for-all effect on present owners. Transitional arrangements could be made, but these should not be related to the assessment process itself. We have seen in our examination of the history of local government how easy it is for transitional arrangements to become enshrined into a new system. Lump-sum transfers to compensate for the changeover to the new system are in many ways the best method of solving the problem. For example, the estimated capital loss on a house arising from the transition to the new system could for one year be treated as a tax-deductible capital loss. Similarly, a capital gain could be taxed. With our suggestion that there should be a two-year period in which proposed tax rates will be announced, there should be some information from the price indices constructed for local authorities on the effect on house prices. There would also be information of the difference in rates under the two systems. A rough capitalisation of such differences could be made and this would be considered as the sum which would count for capital gains or losses. Such adjustments would, of course, not be perfect. However, often the search for perfect solutions to present inequities can introduce great and continuing inequities in the future.

If such changes are adopted, will they be sufficient to preserve the system? If they are not made, will it make any difference to its survival?

As we write, it is difficult to predict the immediate future of local government finance, as it is of local government. Two stages are over of the crisis which led to the setting up of the Layfield Committee in 1975. There was, first, the rapid rise in rates in 1974 and 1975. Despite the unprecedented grant, both absolutely and as a proportion of local revenue, inflation brought about an increase in rates in 1974/5 of 27 per cent over 1973/4; and of 29 per cent in 1975/6 over 1974/5. Besides inflation, local government reorganisation in 1974 also increased local expenditure in several ways. The was, first, the additional expense of reorganisation itself. There was also the tendency among many authorities doomed to extinction to embark on spending sprees. Many built recreational facilities believing that if they did not do it, they had no reason to suppose the larger authorities would into which they were swallowed up. They also ran down their reserves rather than increase their rates. The new incoming authorities, therefore, had reserves to rebuild, in many cases capital works to operate as well as the effect of inflation. They were seriously misled by the

Treasury's optimism over the inflation rate in 1974 and 1975. Despite large extra increases in grant during these years to compensate, the increases in rates were necessary. A very few authorities had to increase their rate call during the year. But the protest of the ratepayers was intensified by three factors. First, there was inflation itself which is a redistributionary agent impoverishing especially the elderly and others on fixed incomes. Secondly, there were the effects of the 1973 revaluation which, like all revaluations, inevitably raised some rateable values more than others. Thirdly, there was the grant system which was moving in favour of the urban areas at the expense of the rural areas. This led to a concentration of protest among elderly retired ratepayers outside the urban areas though there were protests everywhere.

The first stage of the crisis was ending towards the start of 1976 to be replaced by a period in which central government was engaging in fiercer public expenditure cuts than ever before. Gross domestic product per head in real terms fell. The growth of local authority manpower slackened. In 1977, manpower actually fell. Even so, local expenditure relative to gross domestic product rose in the mid-1970s because local expenditure fell less than private expenditure, remaining more insulated from fluctuations in the economy (as indeed it had been in the 1930s, though then local expenditure included poor relief). As we have seen earlier, most of the cuts of local expenditure were on capital expenditure and so fell on the private sector, rather than on public-sector employment.

In 1978 and before the General Election of 1979 there was a modest reflation of public expenditure in which local government appeared to share. Without a change of government a greater increase in local expenditure than in GDP per head seemed likely. But the Conservative election victory has brought into being a government for the first time undertaking action to bring down local expenditure not only immediately but in the long run as part of the process of reducing the public sector. What is less clear as we write in August 1979 is whether there will also be reform of local government finance. If so, this will principally be because central government wants it and probably will increase central control. The absence of well-worked-out plans makes coherent reform unlikely.

Yet it seems to us that the long-term case for reform remains strong. The recession of the mid-1970s may have broken the pattern of the local expenditure growth so that in future it increases at a lower rate than in the 1960s and early 1970s. But we have no confidence that this will be so. When government is as powerful as it is in Britain, and when so many politicians, professional associations and trade unions have an inevitable interest in the growth of local expenditure, we doubt whether present economising will be maintained. If it is not and there is also, as seems inevitable, political pressure to keep down rate increases, then we foresee continuing growth in grant and, therefore, in the grant proportion. By lowering the price, this will induce further increases in local expenditure. But that is not the end of the matter. We also see most local expenditure as redistributive, reinforcing central government's wish to intervene to ensure some uniformity in provision. The erosion of local autonomy will go on.

We have discussed various changes. Some seem to us an almost unequivocal gain. If rates are retained, then unless capital valuation replaces rental valuation the absence of information on rates will go on eroding the credibility of rates as a property tax. This has happened already to too great an extent. Rates are in danger of becoming too arbitrary a tax because of it. We believe also that the super-rating of the non-domestic ratepayer through the domestic element of RSG is hard to defend. It is sacrificing economic development and jobs to short-run political expediency. If we are to retain a grant system of roughly the present kind, then there seems a strong case for making it more consistent as a unitary grant.

What these changes will not achieve, however, is any protection of local government finance from a long-run tendency for the central government grant proportion to increase, which we have argued will have both economic and political effects. Neither are we sure that the objections on the grounds of equity to rates as the local tax have died away forever. It seems also that the growth of public expenditure should bring about a greater interest in the efficiency with which it is spent, which should reflect again on the design of the grant system and the possibility that charges might replace some part of local taxation. More critically, the virtual impossibility of reforming the grant system within the present regime, coupled with the intensifying irritation of local authorities at it, means that it could break down and would have to be replaced, which could scarcely be done rationally.

Finally, to return to some of our preconceptions at the start of the book, it is far from clear that there is an optimal division of labour between central and local government in extent or kind.

All these arguments are reasons why this is not the last word of the book, nor the last book on this subject.

PART FOUR   REFORM

1 Introduction

More radical proposals for reform are likely to be prompted by one or other of these beliefs:

(1) that local authorities need more than one local tax if their revenues are to be buoyant enough to finance their activities;
(2) that rates are an indirect tax on buildings at a high rate and, therefore, not only a deterrent to new constructions and rehabilitations but lead to too high densities and overcrowding;
(3) that rates as a tax no longer conform with modern notions of an equitable tax;
(4) that it would be more efficient if rates were replaced as far as possible by charges and
(5) that changes are needed in organisation – in the areas, hierarchy or scope – of local authorities and they are thought to entail changes in financial arrangements.

All except one of these arguments are interesting and may be the grounds for well-argued cases for reform. They will appear extensively in the chapters that follow. The exception is the first which happens to have been the commonest in most previous writings on reform and to have been influential in achieving reform in the USA. Even so, it is an insidious enemy of local autonomy and responsibility. More sources of revenue are not necessary to finance more expenditure. Extra expenditure can also be financed by increasing the share financed by central grant. Greater buoyancy is the cry of the hard-pressed local politician or official who wants to spend more but does not dare persuade the local electorate to pay more through rates because he fears the answer will be no.

As our examination of the past has shown, this has been the British way. While there have been periods of stringency when local governments have been protesting at the shortage of revenue, they have been relatively brief. Grant has always been increased to accommodate central government's views on the rate of expansion of local expenditure – not, of course, enough to satisfy the ambitions of all local authorities.

Other regimes have relied more on multiplying taxes. We have not yet done this in Britain. Taxes other than rates available to local government have always been of negligible importance. Goschen's assigned revenues which looked like taxes were not so at all, as we have seen (Part One, Chapter 5, p. 130), but grants. Local authorities had no freedom to set the rate at which these were set. Whether or not local authorities should rely on more than one tax raises several considerations, some of which we shall go into later. But on the additional buoyancy provided by the multiplication of taxes we shall make only one point.

There is evidence from the USA that *ceteris paribus* a local authority with more taxes will be able to raise more revenue per head than one with fewer taxes, even when adjustment has been made for differences in income and other factors. A plausible explanation is that multiplying the number of taxes reduces the amount of information available to the local taxpayer by confusing him. The cost side of the 'fiscal wedge' is blurred. He is less able to estimate what he pays for the local goods and services provided for him. While noting the advantage of this for a cynical local government which sets its spending decisions above those of its ratepayers, as economists we would find it impossible to recommend such a change to increase buoyancy through diminished information. It can scarcely lead to greater efficiency in local government.

A closely related question is that of noticeability. The complaint is sometimes made that rates are a less buoyant tax because they are paid by most ratepayers in two large half-yearly instalments. The sheer size of each rate demand – often not fully anticipated – evokes protest which coerces the town hall into spending less than it otherwise would. This was one of the arguments that brought about the change that has made it possible for ratepayers to pay monthly, on the principle that ten small shocks will be less noticeable than two large ones. A rational man should not be affected by differences in timing (provided any implications for interest payments are reflected in the demand). If he is, it implies that his intelligence is reacting as if there were differences in the information available to him. Presumably one can defend monthly instalments as giving him more frequent information. If that is the explanation, the objection to six-monthly rate demands cannot be defended as particularly democratic. Any inefficiency is the consequence of the ratepayers not planning their own financial affairs sensibly.

The chapters that follow relate to topics other than buoyancy and noticeability. Part Four, Chapter 2 discusses an old idea: site value rating whose chief current rationale is argument (2) above. Its adoption would remove the deterrent effect of rates on building.

Part Four, Chapter 3 discusses other local taxes. In the past most arguments for more local taxes have had their source in a desire for more buoyancy. If we discount that, the main serious argument is that other taxes could be more equitable. Views on what would be more equitable are infinitely various. We continue to concentrate on one notion which has been reserved as an ideal throughout the history of rating: that rates should approximate to a local income tax. We have discussed how far rates could be adapted to become more like an income tax. But there are limits to the adaptation of rates. Other taxes are considered but in not as much detail as by other writers (Hildersley and Noltage, 1968). The main reason for this follows from our down-grading of buoyancy as an objective. It is not easy to make a case for other local taxes on the grounds of equity. Generally they seem less equitable since most will export part of the burden of taxation outside those areas where services are provided. A local sales tax, for instance, has the net effect of favouring areas where people shop at the expense of the areas in which they live. Payroll taxes, business taxes and other excise taxes have similar effects.

The case for charging (Part Four, Chapter 4) is that it is more efficient than taxing. A local income tax or rates need not be more appropriate for redistributive services, though they will be for genuine public goods.

The chapter suggests that current redistributive objectives may be better achieved by charges combined with new forms of grant.

Efficiency in the provision of local services can be increased where rates are replaced by charges. Again, there is much more detail on particular charging mechanisms elsewhere.[1] Neither have we been able to find elasticities of demand to give us a confident basis for estimating the effect on expenditure of substituting charges for rates. What we do in Part Four, Chapter 4 is (1) to explore how far non-excludability and non-rivalness deter the introduction of charging and, finding they are characteristic of few services, then (2) to explore which seems to be the fundamental policy conflict between the greater efficiency of charging and the political will to use local services to redistribute.

Part Four, Chapter 5 discusses a number of topics to do with the uses to which grant may be put. Some are consequential on the introduction of site value rating, local income tax or charges. Another use would be to modify the age-old objectives of horizontal efficiency and equity in favour of giving local authorities a positive incentive to allow development or at least neutralise present cost disincentives. At a more fundamental level there are changes in grant arrangements that would promote either central or local powers.

The next two chapters are on the consequences for finance of changes in the structure of local government. Part Four, Chapter 6 is on their size. Part Four, Chapter 7 discusses special-purpose authorities, the numbers of levels of government and the transfer of functions to or from local government.

NOTE

1   Bird (1976), and the vast literature referred to there; Institute of Municipal Treasurers and Accountants (1968); Maynard and King (1972); Harris and Seldon (1976); and Seldon (1977).

2 Site Value Rating

In discussing the history of site value rating in Part 1, Chapter 6 we saw that interest in it had waned in the last fifty years. Indeed the Layfield Inquiry considered it very briefly and concluded that the 'passing of the Community Land Act [in 1975] providing for development values to be realised by local authorities has now effectively removed site value rating from consideration' (Layfield, 1976, p. 170).

Yet this last judgement is too dismissive. A partially locally received tax on development values is not equivalent to site value rating, which in its pure form has three crucial differences from the *ad valorem* property tax form of rates:

(1) it taxes development values;
(2) it taxes 'the hope value' of underdeveloped land;
(3) it taxes land but not buildings.

Only the first is a feature of the Community Land Act. As it happens both the Lloyd George and the Snowden versions of SVR were 'impure'. They were meant to achieve (1) and (2) but as they were additional to ordinary rates, their practical effect would have been that land would have been rated at a higher level than buildings — in other words a super-rating of land by comparison with buildings.[1]

THE ARGUMENTS FOR SITE VALUE RATING

The essential economic argument for SVR remains Ricardo's, already discussed in Part One, Chapter 6. Economic rent is unearned increment created by the demand for a relatively scarce factor, land. Because demand, not cost of production, determines land values, a land tax will not affect the use to which land is put provided (1) the tax does not exceed 100 per cent of that rent and (2) landowners do not anticipate a reduction in land tax in the near future (Foster and Glaister, 1975). If either proviso does not hold, land will be withdrawn from the market. Otherwise there will be no distortion in the allocation of resources.

With minerals, land was widely held to be the only non-reproducible scarce factor of production which because of that scarcity would create economic rent. Competition determines the rewards to those factors of production which are reproducible so that their opportunities for earning rent are far more limited in duration. Taxing such reproducible factors as labour, capital and material inputs would distort the allocation of resources. The argument for a land tax has lost force as land has declined in value as a proportion of national wealth, and as it has become recognised that the power of the modern corporation is often such that it may create conditions which enable it to preserve monopoly power and, therefore, scarcity which itself is a cause of economic rent.

But from Ricardo's analysis until the 1930s, economics did suggest to many thinkers, conservative and radical, that land rent was the most economically efficient source of tax revenue. Underlying the economic argument was often a moral argument that what was 'unearned' should not be retained. 'To affirm that a man can rightfully claim exclusive ownership in his own labour when embodied in material things', wrote Henry George, 'is to deny that anyone can rightfully claim exclusive ownership in land' (1886, p. 238). Curiously, he believed that the expropriation of rent by the society that had created it, and its proper use could cure the ills of poverty almost whatever their cause. But the idea that, since society created the demand for produce that created the unearned increment, it should have the right to use it, continues until this day as a mainspring of social and political attitudes towards land ownership and development. Herbert Spencer, a profound conservative, and Joseph Chamberlain, a liberal turned conservative, believed it (Garvin, 1932, Vol. 1, pp. 385–6). So did Lloyd George. Snowden, introducing SVR, used the same kind of language: 'The principle underlying this Bill is to assert the right of the community to the ownership of land. I have never made any question about that nor that the right should be expressed in the from of a rent paid by the occupier, or rather the owner of the land to the community (Long, 1939, p. 36).

It would be idle to suppose that SVR will ever be as emotional an issue again, both because the so-called aristocratic stranglehold over land has much diminished; and because industry and more affluent persons generally are now seen as more important providers of income and wealth. But there is a direct logical relation between the animus against the landed proprietor and that against property developers and others now accused of making vast profits from the development of land. The language of George and Snowden was echoed in the White Paper introducing the 1975 Community Land Act.

The 1886 Royal Commission began to turn men's minds away from the belief that rent was almost exclusively associated with agricultural land. As the economist Sidgwick noted 'Ricardo's conception of rent as increasing independently of any outlay on the part of the landowner as society advances in population and wealth is much more clearly applicable to the case of building land in towns than it is to the case of agriculture which Ricardo chiefly had in view (1887, p. 291). One implication of this is financial. A more recent student of land taxation has said that 'to restrict the tax to the site value of agricultural land — assuming such a restriction to be administratively feasible — would probably condemn it to virtual oblivion as a revenue raiser (Wald, 1959, p. 142). Not only is there more money in developed land, but the recognition of this paved the way for a separation of the two. In 1909, SVR was presented as a measure to tax the landowner, both urban and agricultural. But in times of depression, the agricultural landlord was asking for and getting relief from existing rates. By 1929, agriculture had been derated and the enthusiasm for SVR, despite Snowden's emotive language, became diverted to a more limited enthusiasm for a tax on development gains. Since the Second World War, development gains have generally increased in political importance and real value, while there has been little impetus to rerate agriculture.

Let us now consider, in turn, the three issues that we have said distinguish SVR.

1. DEVELOPMENT VALUE

'Development value' is an artificial concept that has no special meaning in relation to the concept of economic rent. Normally what is called the existing
use value of land and property rises with population and prosperity. In the long
run little of this will be a rise in the real value of existing buildings. Most real
increase in existing use values will reflect increased land values. They will be a
Ricardian phenomenon − the effect of secondary increased demand on the value
of the relatively scarce factor, land. In Britain, this existing use value element in
increased land rent is taxed (a) through increased rateable values following
periodic revaluation; (b) through capital gains tax on sale or transfer of all property except the main residences of owner-occupiers (and also local authority
housing on the rare occasions this is sold) and (c) through capital transfer tax.

Rateable values also rise to reflect development gains defined as the difference
between the existing use value of a site and its value after development,[2] that is,
its 'development value'. There is no capital gains tax on development gains, but
instead a special development gains tax, currently called development land tax
(1978). It can be regarded as a capital sum equivalent to annual super-rating. Its
justification is Ricardian, a high tax on the unearned increment in land values
associated with development. It is not levied on buildings. Provided it is less than
100 per cent of economic rent of the site and provided landowners do not anticipate repeal of the legislation, or some other effective reduction in the tax rate,
any tax rate up to 100 per cent which leaves some profit incentive to the landowner should not affect the use or allocation of land. That is the principle.[3]
Objections to its practical truth will be considered later in this chapter. The
provisos are important. It would be foolish to plan a 100 per cent tax rate because changes in values and difficulties in its exact measurement may make the
effective tax rate exceed 100 per cent. Since such taxes are politically contro-
versial, hope of repeal or tax-rate reduction is a powerful reason for landowners
refraining from development.

The Ricardian argument for high rates is as relevant to increases in existing
use value as it is to development gains. Probably existing use values are not
super-rated, for one reason because of a greater difficulty of measurement. The
amount of development gains can be estimated fairly easily. Where there has
been redevelopment, it will be market value in existing use plus development
costs subtracted from development value less new building costs. But where the
appreciation has been in existing use value one has to estimate how much of the
change in value is attributable to land and how much, positive or negative, to
changes in the value of existing buildings.

A second reason is that it is widely thought fairer for society to tax new
income from new 'unearned' sources at a higher rate than increased income from
an old source. A discrete decision is needed to make a development investment.
A landowner making such a decision should make it knowing that he will be
liable to development gains tax. If the development is a failure, development
gains tax will be a burden if assessed and collected on its predicted value, but
this is a calculated risk for the developer. Changes in existing use value are
more continuous and arguable more reversible. Neither argument is especially

compelling. Both the difficulties of assessing land values and the question of achieving an acceptable transition will be discussed later in this chapter. The former point only gains weight if landowners do not anticipate a tax on increases in economic rent whether it accrues as enhanced existing use value or as development value. Nevertheless in Britain, though not in many other countries, a development gains tax is likely to be the nearest approximation to a land tax at a high rate which a government is prepared to levy.

The earliest protagonists of SVR wrote at a time when there was no system of planning permissions. Without planning control, changes in land values will be continuous, even if generally upward. Land values will rise as the prospect of successful development emerges, as land approaches the point of development and the risks and uncertainties diminish. The often multiple change in land value that takes place when permission to develop is granted is a consequence (a) of the number of permissions being rationed to a number below that which would hold in a free land market and (b) of it being not completely predictable if and when a given land parcel will receive permission to be developed to another use. In the context of a planning system it is more feasible to tax development gains at a higher rate than any other appreciation of land values.

The existence of planning control makes it easier to estimate development gains as it introduces discontinuities in land values when planning permission is granted which are easier to estimate. It is in assessing 'hope value' that planning creates more problems.

2. HOPE VALUE

SVR logically implies the rating of all land value. The market value of a piece of land may be higher than the present value of its earning or renting power in its existing use because of the prospect of development. Until development takes place, this prospective value is called 'hope value'. In any system of zoning or planning permissions, this 'hope value' may be divided in two. Before the land is zoned or granted planning permission for a more remunerative use, its market value may still reflect a hope or probability that the zoning will be so revised or the planning permission granted. We shall call this the pre-permission hope value. After the permission is granted, the probability and nearness of redevelopment will rise steeply so that post-permission hope value is likely to approach closer to development value. SVR would rate both species of hope value.

The main argument for rating hope value put by the 1885 Royal Commission on the Housing of the Working Class was that it would hasten development. They believed this would bring down all land values in urban areas by extending the land supply available to meet the given demand, and thus make it possible to build homes more cheaply. They were chiefly interested in reducing the cost of housing to the poor.

More recently, a similar argument has been used by Gaffney (1972*a*, pp. 247–50; 1973, pp. 18–23). He argues that the taxation of hope value is needed because it will increase the efficient use of land by wealthy landowners who are least likely to borrow and most likely to ignore the imputed opportunity cost of the capital tied up in land. Moreover, the wealthy are likely to be able to borrow at a lower interest rate than the poor, either because of capital market imperfec-ions or because interest payments are tax deductible, so even if they borrow to finance land transactions the cost to them will be lower. He concludes, there-fore, that the taxation of hope value would reduce the price of development land by substituting an actual tax cost for notional interest foregone. Moreover, the rating of hope value would have more effect on the large and wealthy land-owners because the real cost now of holding development land idle is higher to the small landowner.

These arguments seem to us to be at best of a second order of importance. It may be true that the wealthy are less rational than the poor, though this is not obvious. It may also be true that because of capital market imperfections, whether induced by the tax system or not, the opportunity cost of holding land is lower for the wealthy than the poor. Though if such is the case, one would expect the wealthy non-landowners to purchase land from poor landowners and become wealthy landowners. But surely the arguments for taxing hope value and the effect of such a tax on the supply of development land are much simpler. Individuals may decide not to develop land or sell it at the current price for development for two reasons. They may want to consume the services of the land in its non-developed use, for example as a park or hunting reserve. Or their expectations about the future value of the land are more optimistic than those of the market and therefore they want to hold the land as an investment. In either case not taxing hope value would introduce a distortion. Land in one use (developed) would be taxed at a different rate from land in another use (still undeveloped). Such a distortion will lead to substitution effects. The arguments for the efficiency of a land tax are only valid if land is taxed at the same rate in all its uses

One common argument against the taxation of hope value is the alleged un-fairness of taxing or rating someone on a property value before the higher level of income actually begins to accrue.[4] But those who argue thus have forgotten tax capitalisation. If someone buys land with hope value, he will pay a lower price if the tax arrangements are such that he will be rated on that hope value; the difference being equal to the purchaser's estimate of the discounted present value of the extra tax liability, discounted for risk.

The unfairness may seem greater when there has been no sale and a landowner finds upon revaluation of his land — suppose it is a farm — that he is paying substantially more in rates, though neither its use nor its income has changed. But this is no more unfair than the experience of a public company that holds assets that it under-utilises and then finds itself taken over. The analogy is almost exact. A public company which does not make the most profitable permissible use of its assets runs the danger of having a majority of its shares bought out by those who will use them more profitably. But take-over can be avoided by the original management employing those assets profitably. Similarly, SVR induces landowners to put their land to the most profitable permissible use. One can bolster this argument by the supplementary thought that since it is unearned increment created by the demands of society, not by the landowner, it is not unreasonable for society to share in the hope value it creates whether or not the landowner hastens to react to it. But this last thought is not a necessary one.

It is widely asserted that there is such an inconsistency between SVR and a system of planning controls. In its Evidence to the Layfield Committee, the Rating and Valuation Association followed a number of predecessors in stating that SVR would require a complete recasting of planning law so that the owners of every parcel of land in the country could know with some exactness what development would be permitted (Layfield, 1976, pp. 9; cf. Ministry of Housing and Local Government, 1952, and RICS, 1964, para. 49). Thus it would seem to go against a tendency in British planning to move away from development plans that map zones in which various uses will be permitted — from experience, themselves mutable — towards more flexible, that is less exact, structure plans which do not map prospective permissions.

The main point surely has already been made. Provided market values are used as a guide, hope value will be sufficiently discounted by the land market to adjust for such very great uncertainties — until actual permission is granted. The more a local authority announces its permission policy in advance and sticks to it, the greater the certainties and the higher hope value. From one standpoint, mind changing and procrastination are depriving a local authority of a source of revenue, albeit a small one.

The comments of an American assessor or valuer, Beach, are interesting here. He complains that in zoning

the professional land planner may create a monster that not only conveys false impressions of value but may also act to destroy the present tax base. Most professional planners have, with a great deal of planning and foresight, chosen to zone all land adjoining swamps and railroad tracks, especially those with sidings, industrial. They also determine that every major intersection must have all four corners zoned commercial and the dying downtown areas must have more land zoned to encourage 'economic' development in an orderly fashion. In order to protect himself from the irate homeowner, the professional planner fringes all of his plan with buffer zones of lesser density industrial development or apartment use. After lengthy hearings that no-one except the speculator and large landowners attend, the local news media praise the plan as a giant step for progress and encourage its adoption. It does not matter that there is little labor available for industrial plants or that all the homebuilders for fifty miles in every direction would not be able to develop the land for twenty years it they tried. The zoning is here, so let the furor begin.

The local assessor 'sees' the potential in the zoning; therefore, highest and best use being the criteria for assessment, he increases all favourably zoned land. The owner of this land puts it on the market, and, although he may be ten miles from sewer and water, he offers his land for sale at prices comparable with fully developed industrial sites . . . Perhaps assessors should keep out of the planners' way, but it would seem to me that land that will not be utilised in the foreseeable future should only have suggested zoning indicated and not be zoned to encourage speculation. Suggested zoning provisions might leave the control of orderly development with those in government who must stay behind and weep when the planner leaves . . . How can agricultural land be assessed as farmland when zoning allows a one-hundred storey high-rise apartment, or how can a swamp be assessed at a salvage value when zoning allows the erection of a multi-billion-dollar industrial complex. Perhaps the assessor's crystal ball has a little more judgment in it if his homework is up to date. Perhaps the ball predicts that the highest and best use at the present time, and for a reasonably foreseeable time, is agricultural on the farmland, and that prohibitive costs of draining and/or filling the swamp indicates that a salvage value is the most reasonable value to establish at this time. (In Holland, 1970, pp. 94–6)

Beach here is reporting a common situation where planners zone land over-optimistically and valuers reinforce that over-optimism by assuming it is right and reflecting it in impossibly high assessment values. Beach's answer is surely the right one. The assessor or valuer must not allow the planner to persuade him to fix those impossible land values. He must insist on realism and follow the indications of the market. Untold damage has been done by valuation practice in Britain which has blighted large tracts, especially in central cities, by insisting on unrealistically high land valuations. The fault there is not with SVR but with the valuation method used. All this reinforces the argument that actual market values should be used as far as possible in assessment, not the notional values which *inter alia* create this kind of distortion. It is allowing planners to talk up values – nothing else – which leads the Rating and Valuation Association to say that if SVR were to be adopted, planners must designate land uses more exactly. If anything, this would make the matter worse should it mean a greater tendency to designate impossible land uses with the effect of encouraging valuers in more unrealistic assessments.

It has to be admitted that the general tendency is away from the use of market values towards a situation in which the planner or assessor has to make a forecast of development potential in lieu of the market. No wonder this is placing a strain on the practicality of SVR in Australia where it exists.[5] But the same strain is being placed on the rating system in Britain in so far as planners here encourage unrealistic hopes and forecasts.

A similar problem arises with the objection that SVR 'would tax land values . . . often when it would be quite impracticable to realise them – for example, when there were several interests in the land and none of the individual owners could redevelop because he could not acquire the other interests (DoE, 1971a, Cmnd 4741, para. 2.75). But the principle is in fact different. No law stops these interests collaborating to achieve the profitable development. What does so must be readiness of one or more owners to forego a profit; or more probably to extract a higher share of the profits by hanging back. This is an example of the Prisoners' Dilemma paradox to be analysed later in this chapter. As Gaffney has argued, where there is such interdependence, a powerful lubricant is essential if there is to be any semblance of an optimal comptetitive outcome: 'Taxing rent . . . loosens everyone's hold on land, especially land with monopoly potential' (1973, pp. 28, 29). Gaffney would like land valued at its unrestricted value – in the absence of planning controls – because he believes passionately in market forces. Relying on market valuations which reflect the difficulty of site assembly would fit better with the approach we have adopted here.

Thus much depends here on the process envisaged. If hope values are established by reference to real market values, the problems should never arise. If someone buys land for which planning permission has not been granted, he will pay very substantially less than if it had development permission because of the risks involved. If any hope value is to be rated, the price will be still lower by the discounted present value of this extra rating liability. Then no hardship arises. Moreover, one can expect that with such a liability, hope value will almost always be small, even negligible. It will only not be small if the probability of permission being granted seems very high to the purchaser and if the development value also promises to be substantial. But, whatever the circumstances, a purchaser will only pay a price reflecting hope value if he judges it to be in his financial interest. By analogy, the same considerations will hold for land that is not sold but acquires hope value. If planning permission is problematic, the hope value will be correspondingly small or negligible. The only unfairness would arise if a valuer attached a hope value to a property which did not fairly reflect the uncertainties of securing planning permission; but that would be a failing of the valuation process, not one implicit in SVR.

An apparently more telling objection to SVR is its inconsistency with the planning system at a more fundamental level. The 1971 Green Paper suggested the rating of hope value to encourage the best use of land had 'more force in relation to under-developed countries [where] the need is to channel and organise development in the best possible way' (DoE, 1971a, Cmnd 4741, para. 2.73). This is surely a false antithesis. In the first place, planning controls do raise the cost of developed land by restricting its supply and so increase the costs of housing and all other development. That is as true now as it was when the 1885 Royal Commission noted this consequence. It is a social judgement implicit in there being such planning controls — though not explicit in Acts of Parliament or White Papers — that we have now reached a stage where the positive benefit of such planning controls is worth the higher price of developed land, as it may not be in poorer nations. The benefits in question may be of several kinds: the positive benefits of a green belt, of the preservation of farmland, and other factors whose sufficient value is questionable though it will not be questioned here. Let us assume that planning controls that raise land prices by restricting land availability are socially desirable.

Netzer has argued that a neutral tax is often not regarded as socially optimal (1966). Society wants to encourage lower densities than the market would achieve because higher environmental quality is associated with lower density. But if this is a social judgement it should be reflected explicitly in zoning controls or planning permissions; or more optimally through explicit taxes and regulations to correct for the assumed divergences between social and private cost.[6]

The main point that needs to be made is the irrelevance of the argument to the point at issue. It would be relevant if, and only if, the valuation and the planning system contradicted each other — if land was valued at a hypothetical free-market value which could not be realised within the planning system. But that would be absurd. Otherwise once planning permission has been granted, what is the objection to taxing hope value? Surely it is not then in the social interest to delay development if permission for it has already been granted? If permission has not been granted, then there is no greater difficulty. The Green Paper said that 'a site might be taxed for several years on a high development value that might then be lost through a change in planning proposals, or for some other reason, before the ratepayer had realised any part of it (DoE, 1971*a*, Cmnd 4741, para. 2.75). It is not made clear if the changes are before or after planning permission has been granted. If the second, compensation would be justified which is not unreasonable when the state changes its mind and alters the extent or type of development it has once permitted. Apparently more difficulties arise where the applicant changes his mind. If he goes for a still higher-valued development, there is no problem. If he voluntarily prefers a lower-valued development when a higher could be achieved as at first intended, it is difficult to see why society should lose by his foregoing a profit. If external circumstances change and reduce the profitability of what he first intended, then it is vital that this should be reflected as quickly as possible in the rateable value assumed, even though this means he gets no refund on the rates paid on an earlier assessment value before he changed his mind. Despite this, he must still be better off from the change. Otherwise he would not have made it.

If such doubts arise before permission is first granted, this uncertainty must affect the likelihood of planning permission being granted and should already have depressed pre-permission hope value. Thus such vagaries are already allowed for in the purchase price of properties with hope value, and cannot be the grounds for any allegation of inconsistency between SVR and a planning or zoning system.

Therefore, the case for rating hope values has nothing to do with any alleged inconsistency between SVR and planning. If economic rent on land is to be taxed or rated, then there is a logical case for including hope value. There is also the positive argument that it will stimulate landowners to develop their land quickly once it has been zoned or otherwise granted permission for development. It will discourage landowners withholding their land. Where the uncertainties are great − whether or not these are caused by the planning system − the market value of hope value to be taxed or rated will be low, and the rate on it correspondingly low, even probably excluded as *de minimis* in most cases. Provided local authorities mean what they say when planning permission is granted and do not wish to delay it, the rating of hope value should lead to a more efficient planning process. What one cannot do, however, is to set up an SVR system which is deliberately inconsistent with the planning system, so that it sets higher values than the system wants realised. The only outcomes, then, are either palpable unfairness or a fiercer war by the landowner to over-persuade the politicians who control the planning system.

It is questionable whether hope value should be super-rated as development value so often is. The danger is that the total tax may amount to more than the increase in economic rent from development. For example, if development gains are taxed at 75 per cent of development values a law which requires that the tax should be paid in advance of actual development − for example, when planning permission is granted – could easily, given interest charges on the advance tax payment, amount to demanding a more than 100 per cent tax on the present value of the development gains.

As an administrative simplification it might be worth levying a tax on hope value only when zoning has been accomplished or planning permission granted, since the amount of hope value that will be taxable before then is likely to be small in any individual case. But that is only an administrative convenience, not a question of principle.

These arguments imply no conflict between SVR and planning, provided land values reflect market values The arbitrariness and artificiality of some valuation practices can create injustices where none need exist. Human improvisation of values is rarely a better substitute for the test of the market place. Many of the practical problems that are often thought to arise are not the fault of SVR but of the valuation process. We shall return to various questions in the actual assessment of land values later in this chapter.

3. DERATING OF BUILDINGS

The Ricardian argument for taxing land does not apply to the taxing or rating of buildings.[7] Buildings do not ordinarily earn economic rent. The relatively rare examples that do, are generally particularly beautiful buildings whose beauty has a scarcity value that is a cause of rent. Ordinary reproducible buildings are generally valued by the market on a basis that recognises a fairly elastic supply of buildings except in the very short run. If demand increases and bids up the price of buildings then more will be built until building prices are in equilibrium again. Rates as a tax on buildings reduce the price a purchaser is ready to offer for a new building, so reducing the price at which buildings can sell profitably. This, in its turn, must reduce the supply of new buildings and the stock of all buildings below what would exist in the absence of rates.

Taxing or rating buildings will have other distorting effects on the use and construction of buildings. By putting up the cost, it will encourage higher densities of construction and occupation than otherwise. It will increase the marginal cost of every kind of building. Thus buildings will be lower, less well finished and less well provided with built-in services than would otherwise be the case. Similarly, rates like any other tax levied on built property discourage maintenance, so leading to a lower level of housing quality. Again, they raise the marginal cost of rehabilitating and improving old property. So building rates create more slums than would otherwise exist.[8]

Not only can rates on buildings, if sufficiently high, prevent redevelopment, but in the USA local property taxes have contributed to the abandonment of buildings which became derelict partly because the returns on any improvement or repair would not be worthwhile given the local taxes that would then be payable, even though a rent could be paid which would cover the resource cost of the building.[9] If the building cannot be improved so that its use is profitable, then if the rates are payable whether the building is used or not, it will pay the owner to abandon it. If rates are not payable on the building, he may retain ownership but let it rot. Abandonment is exacerbated by the fact that as one building is abandoned the marketability and prospective return from the improvement of its neighbours declines. This is a situation which can lead to cumulative abandonment.

Indirect taxation affects many goods. If buildings were rated at the same effective tax rate as other goods, there would be no allocative distortion. However, building taxation and subsidisation is sufficiently various and obscure to make comparison difficult.

In Britain, owner-occupied housing is rated, but if mortgaged the interest on that mortgage is tax deductible (unlike any other interest on personal borrowings). There is no capital gains tax and the owner is not taxed on his imputed income from his home. If rates are set against this, the net effect is a substantial subsidy on a mortgaged house which varies with the marginal tax rate of the mortgagor. If there is no mortgage, rates are likely to be greater than the amortised value of any exemption from capital gains tax. The position of a local authority tenant will be different and usually amounts to a net subsidy, unless the tenant lives in an old building. Most other owners of buildings — private rental, commercial, and industrial — pay rates but receive no subsidies. As a measure of its incidence, a rate of 2 per cent to 4 per cent on the market value of a building, against a net return of 10 per cent appears as a tax rate of about 20 per cent to 40 per cent on income — considerably higher than current (1978) rates of value added tax.

This is not a completely satisfactory exposition of the position. In an article written at the time that the 1906 Liberal government was contemplating introducing SVR, Cannan made an important objection to the elimination of rates on buildings. He agreed that rating buildings deterred builders, but argued that this was 'obviously because of the cost, not only of land and bricks and mortar, but also the cost of maintenance, furnishing and services of all kinds' (1907, p. 41). Among these services are those provided by local authorities. So Cannan objected 'that at present if he puts up and occupies a big building . . . and thereby puts the local authority to large expense in providing all sorts of services, he will have to pay large rates. Under the new scheme he would not pay directly a penny more if he put up and occupied a sky-scraper than if he put up and occupied a one storeyed cottage' (ibid.). So he pleaded that British proposals should follow New South Wales and Australian practice, where buildings were taxed but in effect at a lower rate than land.

The Cannan argument surely has force so far as beneficial expenditure is concerned. Beneficial rates are not a tax, as we have seen, but a charge for services provided. We have also argued in Part Two, Chapter 6 that there is evidence that in Britain and in the USA this beneficial expenditure increases rather than reduces house prices. For this reason and also on *a priori* grounds it cannot be said that such a charge for services is a deterrent to building. In Part Four, Chapter 4 more efficient methods of recouping this beneficial expenditure will be discussed. Nevertheless Cannan's argument and our own in Part Two, Chapter 2 suggests that SVR could be used to finance beneficial services in the absence of more efficient charges and would be more efficient than rates or a local income tax. To recapitulate, the advantage of SVR for this purpose is the costs of such services should be borne by the occupier in so far as he benefits;

but the vertical inefficiency caused by occupiers in some property price ranges either gaining more from such services than they pay, or vice versa, will be capitalised. This will avoid horizontal inefficiency and also, as a result, inefficient migration. If SVR is on both residential and non-residential land, a resource equalisation grant will be necessary to achieve horizontal efficiency on the assumption that non-domestic ratepayers derive disproportionately few benefits. But in line with our general conclusion on this matter in Part Two, beneficial services to domestic ratepayers should be financed by SVR confined to such ratepayers.

In Part Two, Chapter 2 it was argued that rates on land were particularly suitable for the financing of redistributive local expenditure on certain assumption. Because the capitalisation on average by property price band will deter mobility, local authorities will be able to finance their own redistributive programmes with less fear that the outcome will be a flight of adversely affected taxpayers. However, it is possible that central government might positively wish to limit a local authority's ability to redistribute, in which case that advantage would become a disadvantage. SVR could be used to finance centrally determined redistributive expenditures; but in that case clearly appropriate grants are needed to achieve horizontal equity which makes SVR less appropriate.

Before drawing final conclusions on SVR, we need to consider, first, how its introduction would affect tax incidence, second, tax buoyancy, and third, the practical problems of assessment and transition.

INCIDENCE

In its pure form, the introduction of SVR will mean a shift of local taxation away from buildings to land. The ratio of land to building value tends to be most towards the centre of cities and least in the suburbs. However, there is some evidence that assessors undervalue land in Britain, as in the USA, so that areas of low building density may find their rates rising relatively, as in general with properties with large gardens. For the same reasons one will expect the rateable value of bungalows to rise relative to houses, and houses relative to flats. All these tendencies will be diminished somewhat if rates on buildings are retained for beneficial services.

In so far as such changes in incidence lead to a change in the relative burden of rates between local authorities, the resource element in Rate Support Grant would compensate local authorities which lose and pay out less grant to those which gain.

In Britain two special assessments have been undertaken at Whitstable in 1963 and 1973 to establish the practicality of SVR (Wilks, 1964 and 1974). Both exercises estimated the change in incidence that would result. The 1973 exercise calculated that there would be a 10 per cent reduction in the incidence on houses, nearly a 60 per reduction in the valuation of flats, a 55 per cent reduction in maisonettes, and a more than 40 per cent reduction in the valuation of council houses. But there would be an 11 per cent increase in the valuation of bungalows and not far from a 300 per cent increase in the valuation of caravan sites. These large changes reflect an arbitrary undervaluation of land in present procedures, as well as the derating of buildings. This underassesssment of land was also an implication of our analysis in Part Two, Chapter 6.[10] In Whitstable there was a slight (1 per cent) increase in overall residential valuation and a 10 per cent reduction in rates borne by commerce and industry. The rating of industrial properties, however, was almost halved while there was a big increase in the rating of commercial property other than shops — offices, garages, petrol stations, etc. Almost no weight should be put on these particular figures because the land intensity (and relative underassessment of land) of different uses will vary very greatly. Again changes in incidence will be damped as long as the rating of buildings is kept for beneficial expenditures.

Turning from incidence between classes of property to that between persons, SVR is generally held to be more progressive than property rates (Hicks in Holland, 1970, pp. 14, 15). This is because buildings usually decline as a proportion of house plus site value as incomes rise. How important this is, of course, depends on what other measures are taken to affect income distribution through other changes in the rating system or in other ways.

BUOYANCY

In 1934, the Treasurer of Johannesburg wrote that 'there must be a stage at which the value of land reaches its apex; it will thereafter remain static or decrease. When this apex has been reached . . . the income from rates will also remain static or decrease (Lewis quoted by Long, 1939, p. 2). Yet Gaffney, writing nearly forty years later, could point to Johannesburg and Sydney as among the most rapidly growing and thriving metropolises dependent on SVR 'both booming with reported high land values' (in Holland, 1970, p. 157). With similar forebodings a 1964 report of the Royal Institution of Chartered Surveyors feared 'that a stage would soon be reached when, in order to meet the necessary expenditure, the local authority would need to levy a rate of more than 20 shillings in the pound' (RICS, 1964, p. 5). This predicament they reasonably thought to be incompatible with a tax on economic rent.

While it is unlikely in Johannesburg or elsewhere that real land value will reach a ceiling, land values could rise faster or more slowly than the values of other tax bases — income or other capital goods — and also than gross national product per head. No tax base can be guaranteed to rise at a particular rate or more in value than other tax bases.

One must distinguish between land values in general and the position of a particular authority. In any nation with growing population and rising prosperity, average land values will rise. It is conceivable that both could be associated with declining land-intensive residence and production but experience argues against this. The demand for food grows and increases the demand for agricultural land despite improvements in productivity. Affluence impels households to buy better houses on larger sites. Industrial production and offices tend to provide more space per worker. The demand for recreational land increases.

However, as Beach pointed out, a local authority can ruin its tax base and its land values by unwise planning and unrealistic assessment. Some areas — particularly old industrial areas of relatively poor environment — will lose their attractions and their land values will decline. But this will not be so very different in tendency, though it will be in amount, from what happens under the current rating system.

Whatever the long-term prospect, there is a short-run fear that reducing the tax base of rates by eliminating building will lose more revenue than will be added by integrating hope and development value taxation into the local rating system.

However, the extent of the decline in tax base is easily exaggerated. Gaffney has pointed out that the definition of rent or land value used by national income statisticians substantially undervalues land (in Holland, 1970, *passim*). In spite of a recent tendency to write up property book values and the subsequent recent fall in such values, it is highly probable that most companies still put property in their books at less than market value. There are also disadvantages in using rateable values to estimate land values. There is the difficulty of disentangling land from capital value, as well as the general problem of under-assessment. Attention has been given to this in the USA. For example, Gaffney reports that in Milwaukee careful analysis showed that the value of assessed land was 3.2 times its assessed value (ibid., p. 177). Perhaps the most useful study is Wilks's of Whitstable. The first showed his fears:

> It was soon noticed that the figures of rateable value we were producing were very much lower than those in the current orthodox valuation list. Indeed at one time it was feared that the total rateable value would be so low that to produce the same income as at present a rate poundage of well over 20 shillings would be needed . . . our fears were groundless, for the loss in rateable value in the outer-lying residental areas was more than made good by the increase in other areas. (1964, p. 12).

Only, it must be added, by bringing in land that under the present system is underassessed — in particular a golf course. But the general point holds that there is a tendency to underassess land.

The most comprehensive assessment has been that done by Manvel (1968, pp. 1–17) for the USA who estimated that 40 per cent of the market value of taxable real property is accounted for by land alone, and that land values have been rising at about three times the annual rate of the general price level. On that basis, Netzer argues that a 4 per cent average tax on land values would be enough to replace the entire present tax on land and buildings (1970, p. 198). Given that the theory implies the efficiency of high rates of tax on land values, taxes of this order of magnitude are about 25 per cent of a hypothetical net return of 15 per cent on land (inclusive of rates). On the basis of such figures, it seems doubtful if a transition to SVR would be associated with such a decline in the tax base that it would be imprudent to raise overall as much revenue as under the current system. Thus in conclusion it seems unlikely that buoyancy will be a problem.

ASSESSMENT

Whatever conclusions the reader may have reached on the merits of SVR, two important practical issues must be faced. The first is assessment. How does one separate land and building values as is required by this tax? What is the base upon which the tax is to be calculated? Earlier, a strong case was made for using actual market values as a basis for assessing rateable values. If that were to be adopted, then SVR would inevitably imply a more complex valuation process because of the need to separate land from building values. But if notional rental values remain or notional capital values become the basis for assessing rateable values, then there is force in a point some valuers have made that it is actually simpler to assess land values than property values.

ASSESSMENT OF AGRICULTURAL LAND VALUES

Since agricultural land is by its nature bare of buildings, it might be thought that it would present the least valuation difficulty. The main objection made is that contrary to what Ricardo supposed, experience shows that a land tax is not always borne by the landlord but is passed on to the tenant. This is Lady Hicks's judgement on the experience of the Indian land tax (in Holland, 1970, ch. 1). There seems no question but that landlords were able to pass on some part at least of the burden with often disastrous consequences of starvation and famine. But the interpretation placed on this by Lady Hicks, and which is the most damaging to Ricardo, is not the most plausible. In the 1830s a careful survey was done, each field being classified by soil quality. Assessment was based on this, the yield and revenue from each field, and an analysis of changes in the area under cultivation. The tax was deliberately aimed to fall on economic rent, but as Lady Hicks makes clear, Indian landlords quickly passed the tax on to tenants. The hardship was not great immediately, but as population growth increased during the century, holdings became more subdivided and the fertility of the land declined, the burden on the peasants became greater and has never been forgotten.

Now, if landlords were able to pass on the land tax, then the implication is that *ex ante* rent levels were less than the highest then compatible with efficient land use. This is borne out by the early experience that while the tenants were obviously poorer than if the tax had not been shifted on to them, the shifting did not at once affect the efficiency level of agricultural production. It is more plausible that there were cultural and ethical reasons why landlords did not charge profit-maximising rents; and indeed Sir Henry Maine gave precisely this explanation of what happened not many years afterwards (1871, lecture VI). Thus when the tax was imposed, landlords felt that this alien practice released them from their ethical obligations and so passed it straight on to their tenants.

While this is still relevant in deciding whether and how to introduce a land tax in many undeveloped countries, it has a relevance wherever rents are held below their economic level and the law permits rates to be passed on to tenants. For example, in Britain private landlords are prevented by rent control from charging an economic rent but are allowed to pass on rate increases. Thus any increase in rates will be passed on to the tenant, at least until the sum of rent and rates equals the maximum economic rent the tenant can pay.

Lady Hicks also argues that the Indian experiment made the mistake of assuming that Ricardo's famous phrase, 'the original and inexhaustible powers of the soil' was true. But, as she says, these powers may not endure. Especially in the province of Bombay, the original valuation was most careful and attempted to measure those powers on quality of the soil, but thereafter it took 'inexhaustible' literally. In fact, as population grew and land was subdivided, land productivity fell and at different rates in different places. Since these changes were not reflected in any downward land revaluation, not only were acute questions of geographical equity raised, but it is more than probable that the tax climbed to become more than 100 per cent of economic rent. If so, then one would have expected the tax to have been shifted on to the tenants, land use to have been affected, and agricultural output to have declined.

The moral is that agricultural land requires investment to maintain its fertility and that a land tax or SVR should never be set so as to exceed 100 per cent of the true rent which excludes the 'cost of production' of maintaining the productivity of the land.

THE VALUATION OF BUILT LAND

Valuation problems bulk large in the literature and have been allowed to create more difficulties than they should. Indeed, it is frequently claimed that SVR has failed in many cities for this reason; though equally the survival of SVR elsewhere shows that the valuation problems can be overcome. Lady Hicks has argued that valuation is relatively easy in a young and rapidly growing city where there are many land sales (in Holland, 1970, ch. 1). One might add that there are more sales and more bare sites in cities, young or old, which are freer of planning controls. Lady Hicks argues also that SVR has either broken down or experienced protracted problems in many Australian and African cities as these have matured and the volume of sales per acre has fallen. In Whitstable also, the valuer found that valuation was easiest towards the outskirts where there were many bare sites and sales, and harder in the commercial centre where both were less frequent. Without doubt, valuation is more difficult the older the city and the lower its turnover of land sales. The famous question which stumped the Valuation Committee set up to consider how to start the Lloyd George land tax was of the form: what would be the value of a bare site in Regent Street covered only with grasses, sedges and rushes if one were to assume that neighbouring sites were developed, as in fact they are?

Yet even this question admits of an answer. There are three broad categories of valuation problem, often overcome, but not always settled satisfactorily in either the valuation, or the relevant economic literature.

(1) how to separate site from building value;
(2) how to allow for changes in the original value of the land when caused by the landowner;

(3)   how to allow for such changes when they are caused by the community or third parties.

(1)   *Site and building value*

Valuation practice sugggests four basic methods of valuing land. There is first the reliance on land sales already mentioned. Secondly, one may try to establish capital values from derived income by using an interest rate. Apart from the vexed difficulty of deciding on an appropriate interest rate, little land is rented so that it is not of much use, at least in Britain.

More important is the sale of property for demolition. Clearance remains not uncommon in built-up areas. The land value is the sale price plus the cost of demolition. The first and third of these methods usually make it possible to construct a land-value map of an urban area which values land by implication at its alternative-use value.[11] Where a zoning system or planning controls exist, it is important that the map or the individual values are also adjusted to reflect this. An exercise of this kind does require that the assessor has available all data on sales in his area. Because of the weight given to sale values, it is often suggested that these need to be published; but this would not seem to be strictly necessary. The valuer will require some more information than he has now in Britain — for example, on the cost of demolition, but the Whitstable experiments have shown the comparative ease with which such maps can be prepared.

The fourth valuation method, used in Whitstable, values the building plus land and then deducts the value of the building (see Wilks, 1964 and 1974). This is plainly easier if one starts with actual market values than with notional rental or capital values. The real difficulty is the separate valuation of the building.[12] It would seem that valuation procedures are sometimes enforced that require valuers to make 'mistakes'. A common source of error is to assume that some of the economic rent accrues to the building, not all to the land. As Gaffney has shown, this is a common reason for the underassessment of land. The mistake is encouraged because valuers wish to be generous to landowners — where land is taxed at a higher rate than buildings or under regimes where depreciation is allowed on building.

Another approach is to estimate a replacement value of the building. The sense of this is that the stream of funds needed to maintain or replace the building is not part of its economic rent. Valuers have developed manuals to help them. Sometimes they work on a simple basis of the relevant cubic footage times a cost multiplier, depreciated to allow for age and condition. But the estimating can become more complicated than this.[13]

The method is far from perfect:

(a)   It will overvalue buildings where actual value is reduced for some other reasons, for example extreme ugliness.

(b)   Conversely it would mean the undervaluing of buildings which were particularly beautiful or old. There would be cases where the building as well as the land earned economic rent because of its rarity. Thus one could argue a special case for taxing this element in economic rent also.

(c)   A problem could arise where buildings were suffering from functional obsolescence. For example, a home may have been adapted for a disabled occupier. The extra cost is not normally fully reflected in the market value, but it would be in the replacement cost strictly interpreted. Another example would be a special-purpose factory which had outlived its functions.

Some adjustments are made for cases like this; but they are sufficiently rare not to complicate the administration of SVR very greatly.

A combination of these methods should make it possible to separate building from site values, not perfectly but as in Whitstable and in the many areas practising SVR, adequately enough to be practical.

(2) *Changes in the 'original' value where the landowner is the cause*

Much rarer are a number of special situations all of which may be analysed as involving externalities, normally pecuniary but sometimes technological. Various conundrums illustrate the points at issue.

There is first the second of Lady Hicks's Indian problems already mentioned: the exhaustion of the original powers of the soil. More formally, the land needed to be 'maintained' if its productivity were not to decline. The notion of a land tax may simply be represented as follows:

$$Y_o = (r + t_o)$$

where Y_o is the present value of the yield given its original powers; r is the present value of the landowner's rent stream, and t is the present value of the proportion received by the government as taxes. If t is proportional to r (or Y_o) then action – such as undermaintenance – by the landlord which caused Y_o to fall also reduces the present value of the tax stream. One might want to argue that since the decline in value was caused by the landowner's inaction, there would be no fall in tax. In other words, it is his liability to compensate the government. All depends on the initial tax rate. If it equalled or exceeded Y_o so that there was a more than 100 per cent tax rate, then the landlord can hardly be blamed when he had no financial interest in maintaining. But if the tax rate was less than 100 per cent and it was in the landowner's financial interest to maintain, one has to ask why he did not do so. It is very important that the causation is established where there are rundown houses or areas, just as much as where there is agricultural land of declining productivity. If original value is correctly assessed, the situation should not arise so it cannot be the basis of an objection to the use of original value.

A more interesting but similar problem is Professor Vickrey's redwood conundrum (in Holland, 1970). Should someone pay higher land taxes now because his land originally had a stand of giant redwoods? There are two issues here. The first is exactly the same as just discussed. If an owner cuts down a giant redwood forest he reduces the present value of the land while realising a profit. If he has been taxed for years at a value which reflected that prospect of profit, clearly he was being taxed on 'hope value' – that is prospectively before the income accrued. If the tax was rational, the present value would bear some relationship – for example, proportionately – to the present value of the expected revenue from the forest. If so, it is not unreasonable to go on exacting the land tax after the profit is realised. The prudent owner should invest a part of the proceeds in order to yield an annual sum necessary for this purpose. Or he might try to compound the payment. Indeed, as with mining royalties which possess precisely the same characteristic, the usual practice is to take tax as a proportion of the value realised when it is realised. However, if the redwood forest were cut down long ago, it would be pedantic and silly to refer to the 'original' value of the soil in assessing it for land tax or SVR. This would be retrospective taxation and iniquitous.

Although the Indian land tax and Professor Vickrey's redwoods might seem an oblique approach, the issues raised are very similar to the Regent Street conundrum that defeated the pre-First World War valuers. What was the bare site value, they asked? Should it be valued as covered with natural vegetation or with whatever pasture or crops occupied it before it was first built on? Such questions are surely pedantic. It would seem more reasonable and relevant to ask what price the site would command if the buildings were demolished and the site were ready to be built on again.[14] There are still ambiguities. Sites vary in load-bearing capacity which will affect their site value. If this was 'original' no difficulty of principle arises; but investment may have been made to increase that load-bearing capacity. If such a cost has been incurred, it should be deducted, at historic cost plus some profit if the expenditure is non-recurring. If the investment has a 'life' then some asssumptions must be made about amortisation.

It is common when assessing bare site value — it was done in Whitstable — [15] to assume that basic services — for example, water, sewerage, power — are available on site. If these have been provided at the expense of the landowner this contradicts the principle just laid down. It would only make some sense where all these costs had been borne by the local authority. Whatever they are, however, they are 'costs of production' not rent. If the principle is SVR and these services are to be met through SVR, it would seem more logical to exclude them from rateable value and raise the rate poundage to cover these expenses. But, as will be argued later (Part Four, Chapter 4) a strong case can be made for charging the landowner for such costs on a cost-of-service basis as they are incurred. It will be objected to this that someone would pay much less for a site in Whitstable or Regent Street unserviced than serviced, and by more than the cost of providing it with services. Nevertheless, the right principle would seem to be that an approximation to the historic cost of these services should be deducted from the serviced bare site value if the landowner either directly or through past rates has paid; or should not be deducted in the rather unlikely eventuality that he has not. He should be rated on all economic rent including any that may attach to a site being serviced, if that is a scarce factor.

One purpose of propounding these conundrums in the past has been to try to discredit SVR by pointing to conceptual circumstances imagined to raise impossible problems. Another of the conundrums Professor Vickrey tried to solve is certainly of this kind. What is the original value of a site, when as in the case of the New York Trade Centre, it was originally under water? The original value was surely zero. The principle we have been adopting suggests that one establishes the bare site value after reclamation and then deducts all the costs incurred in reclamation and site preparation to estimate the surplus or economic rent.

What is emerging is a recommendation that one should treat both investment and disinvestment symmetrically for establishing base or rateable values for SVR.

A further problem presented by Vickrey, but not solved by him, is less tractable in the general case. It is well established that while it may not pay an individual landowner to improve his property, it could be profitable for all if a whole neighbourhood agreed to be improved simultaneously. This is known in the literature as the prisoners' dilemma paradox (Davis and Whinston, 1962). If one house is improved in a dilapidated row, the price its owner can extract may not be much more and could easily not be worth the investment. Every other house, however, may gain some extra value from the presence of one shining home in a row — at no cost to its owner. But if all owners develop, the price of every home may easily rise to justify the investment of everyone. How is this to be achieved? Rarely through voluntary co-operation. Usually someone begins such a process of site assembly, but unless he is peculiarly skilful in hiding his identity, he will find the price rising against himself as he acquires more of the row and the surviving owners suspect the profit he will make if he acquires the lot. This is precisely analogous to a situation discussed earlier in this chapter. The rateable value and rates such an owner faces rise before he is able to secure a return. He is being rated on hope value. If his intentions do not require planning permission, that hope value will reflect the commercial risk that he may not be able to assemble what he needs. If he does need planning permission then hope value will be still further discounted; but for reasons already discussed, there is no obvious reason why he should not be rated on any hope value that survives, providing he knows his liability before he acquires.

One may constrast this with a rather different valuation problem. A landowner owns all the properties *ab initio*. He has leased them and he is waiting for these to fall in, before redeveloping them all. At what point should it be inferable that the hope value of his land has risen and that he is liable to rating on a higher base? Logically, it should presumably be as each lease falls in and increases the market value of his interest in the whole site. To establish this would probably need a series of special assessments. In practice, it may not be easy to be so logical.

(3) *Allowing for changes in the original value of the land where the landowner is not the cause*

By implication the principle has already been discussed where value is contributed by the local authority. One of the justifications for SVR is that economic rent is created by society. This may be a general phenomenon, as when population and property increase land values; or it may be more specific. For example, the building of a particular road may raise neighbouring values, as a similar road would have done eslewhere; or as may the provision of various services, such as education and health services which are beneficial and raise land values. In all such cases, logic suggests that such economic rent or betterment is properly recouped through SVR.

A more difficult practical problem arises when other, or 'third parties', are responsible for increases in land values. Again this is an externality or prisoners' dilemma problem. Suppose a neighbourhood is blighted by a factory which then moves, so raising values throughout the neighbourhood it has left? This is a rise in economic rent uncaused by the landowner, so that there is no case for his not being taxed on the increase. And consideration of economic efficiency suggests that a local authority might make financial payment to such a factory to move, and recoup this from the increase in SVR.

The best evidence of the practicality of land assessment must be the Whitstable experiment in Britain and overseas practice. Enough perhaps has been said to suggest that the Green Paper need not be right in its opinion that problems of valuation and litigation 'would be greater and more extensive than with the present basis of a free market rental because of the scarcity of evidence of site values' (DoE, 1971a, Cmnd 4741, para. 2.77).

PROBLEMS OF TRANSITION

There are possibly three main difficulties in moving to SVR should the end result be thought worthwhile. First, the valuation profession would have to be persuaded that the valuation problems could be overcome. Both widespread experience in the countries that practise SVR and the two Whitstable experiments have shown land valuation is feasible. As Back, an American valuer, has said

> from a technical point of view, land values can be established and maintained with reasonable accuracy provided the assessor is not asked to calibrate his 'crystal ball' so finely as to directly force a desired market objective in the valuation process. It is one thing to project a potential use and market value based upon legal effective zoning but quite another to disregard the forces of supply and demand and project a use and market value in accordance with someone's social or economic objectives. (In Holland, 1970, p. 37)

Even so, the reception of the Whitstable reports by the valuation profession was defensive and hostile (*Rating and Valuation Reporter*, 14 and 21 March 1974). This is not really surprising. The expertise of valuation is not a clear set of principles or scientific laws that can be set down in and expounded from textbooks and taught in the lecture hall. It is far more like a craft mystery, passed on from generation to generation by practice, and learnt by doing. The traditions of such professions are always hardest to change. Witness how long it has taken the valuation profession to recognise the case for replacing notional rental by notional capital values, though the free-market evidence for residential rental values, at least, has virtually disappeared. If there is to be any chance of persuading valuers that land assessment is indeed feasible, we should probably do what is common in most other nations but virtually unknown in British government, invite foreign experts on to the inevitable exploratory committee who have had actual experience of valuation for SVR.

The second problem would be that of the valuation itself. The Whitstable experiments may have shown — though not to the satisfaction of every valuer —

that land valuation is easier than the present notional valuation. Inevitably there are severe difficulties in passing from one system to another. Valuers would have to prepare for the new system while continuing the old. The transition could not be quick. Evidence would have to be accumulated on land sales and sales for demolition. Manuals would have to be written to provide factors for obsolescence, age and any other characteristics judged relevant. Then land maps would have to be prepared. The planning and some other laws would have to be changed — not fundamentally we have argued — but to make sure that the particular circumstances of tenancies and leases did not lead to inequity and inefficiency. In all it would be a formidable task. Perhaps the only way of lightening it might be to start in certain areas or types of property where the the benefits of introducing SVR would be greatest. One possibility would be to introduce it for commercial and industrial property where (1) rates amount to the highest percentage tax and (2) it is arguable that there is the greatest need to stimulate new building and modernisation to supplement existing investment incentive. Another possibility would be to start first in the local authorities with low real land values and a high proportion of rundown buildings to stimulate redevelopment and rehabilitation. But the disadvantage of moving first to help those who will benefit most is that it will thereafter be harder to introduce it where losers outnumber gainers. Thus the net effect of introducing such a partial SVR would be to reduce the rate revenue of certain authorities and presumably to lead to pressure for a compensating increase in government grant.

The third transitional problem is the familiar one of compensating the losers. A shift to SVR would mean an increase in the rateable value per head of areas of high land values per head — central business districts and some low-density suburban areas — relative to areas where the ratio of building to site value is higher. Though complex, it would be possible to alter the basis of the RSG resources element to offset this so that local authorities which had lost relative rateable value per head were compensated for this and vice versa. This could be a transitional arrangement spread over several years or it could be permanent, with some violence to logic. Within each local authority, the shift of burden from the less land-intensive uses to the more land-intensive could be cushioned by transitional arrangements which made the alteration in rate burden gradual, but these offsets could hardly be permanent without destroying the incentive effect of SVR on land utilisation and building.

DEMOCRATIC RESPONSIBILITY

One other argument should perhaps be mentioned. It is easy to slide from an assumption that SVR is a tax on land values accruing to the owner to the proposition that rates must actually be paid by the owner. From this, it is an easy step to arguing practically that owners are often difficult to trace and democratically that they are frequently not residents and electors in that particular authority, and so many do not have a vote. No problem arises for owner-occupiers, residential, commercial or industrial. Neither is there any real problem for premises whose rent or leases are settled in a free market. The occupier may continue to be legally liable for the rates. What matters is that he then pays the owner the economic rent which represents his offer price for the property on the assumption he, the occupier, pays the rates. If the SVR rises, the rent he pays goes down. We have already said that laws on leases and tenancies need to be changed to admit this flexibility. If the SVR rises because land values have risen, the owner will be no worse off because his income in a free market will have risen more than his rate liability has increased. But if the rate poundage has risen, then the owner will be worse off; and the democratic argument has some force. Current rents bear on both owner, so far as they are a tax on sites, and on tenants so far as they are a tax on buildings. SVR would mean that in a very few cases – because the free market is currently small – expenditure decisions would be divorced from rating responsibility to a greater extent than at present. Private and local authority tenants present a more difficult case because of rent control. As we have already argued, part at least of the incidence of SVR might be expected to be shifted to the tenant in such cases. Because of rent control, this argument against SVR does not have the force it would otherwise possess. But in any case, in so far as it is valid, it is also valid against the current rating system which in reality taxes owners for the most part, not occupiers.

CONCLUSIONS

What is the case for SVR? We tax development value. It is unlikely that under a system of planning controls there would be much revenue to be gained from taxing hope value. While there would be an elegance in unifying land taxation – of existing, hope and development value – as SVR would permit, the principal practical effect of SVR would be to derate buildings. If this is thought to be sufficiently advantageous, then SVR may be worth attempting. By this, one of two things may be meant. The first is a literal derating which would run into Cannan's objection that there would be no relation between the cost of services provided for a building and the cost to the owners or occupiers of that building. The second would meet this by retaining some cost-of-services or charging system for beneficial services which is not a tax, while derating buildings to the extent that all onerous expenditure not met by grant would be met by rates on site values. Thus eliminating the taxation of buildings would have undoubtedly favourable results. It would encourage building everywhere and this may be especially useful in dilapidated rundown areas. For example, it would follow that a factory set up in London docklands or some of the most blighted parts of Liverpool would pay a small site rate because the market value of the land would be low and there would be either no rates on its buildings or rates that might actually reflect the cost of services provided. However, one must not exaggerate the magnitude of this effect.

On an £8,000 house, let us assume arbitrarily that half its value is site value and half building. Then the effect of SVR might be to keep the same rate payment but to attach this to the site. As long as the existing building remains and is unimproved, the effect is negligible, unless at the next revaluation the value of land proves to have moved very differently from the value of buildings. But the net cost of any improvement will be less by the capitalised value of the rate increase that would currently follow improvement, but which would not do so if there were SVR. If the building were demolished and another £12,000 house built on the same site, then £8,000 would *ex hypothesi* be the building cost, but the rate liability would be the same as for the £8,000 house. The actual saving to the owner from SVR might be about 2 per cent of the difference between £12,000 and £8,000 or £80 per annum, equivalent to a present value of £800 at a 10 per cent interest rate.

It would not be necessary to introduce SVR to achieve such an effect. A special subsidy or rebate on building or improvement could achieve a similar one. Yet, if as seems likely, the demand for local services will rise with real income per head, and if it is agreed that there are strong arguments for devolving services to local authorities and for reducing grant absolutely, then the deterrent effect of rates on building and improvement will increase. However, judged from the standpoints of efficiency and equity, it follows from what has been said that the case for SVR depends on the purpose for which it is used. Less economically efficient than charging for beneficial services, it is more so than rates or a local income tax. It is particularly suited for re-couping increases in land value caused by society. Less equitable from many points of view than a local income tax, nevertheless as a tax on unearned increment there is a case for it as a tax source for redistributive services, especially local ones where its capitalisation acts so as not to stimulate Tiebout migration as a check on local redistribution. Thus, if it were not for the practical difficulties, SVR would be preferable to any other *single local* tax — which reinforces the case for it in a new area. But in a mixed system in which, for example, beneficial services were charged for, and centrally-determined redistributive services were financed, say, by a local income tax or grants, SVR might well be the ideal revenue source for locally determined redistributive services.

Against this the major arguments are administrative and practical: and these are never negligible. On balance, our conclusion is that if these could be set aside, there would be an advantage in SVR. We would recommend this for any country starting a rating system, partly because of its efficiency properties and also because it should be administratively simple.

In Britain we feel that the hold of the valuation process is such that we believe it most unlikely that any simplicity would be achieved. Experience suggests that valuers would be unlikely to allow rateable values under SVR to reflect market values. In particular, we believe there is a high probability that, in practice, values would reflect planners' overoptimistic valuations rather than the truth.

NOTES

1   The 1910 Act provided for (1) an incremental land value duty of £1 in £5 to be paid on the sale of any freehold or leasehold exceeding fourteen years; (2) a reversion duty of 10 per cent on the incremental value of houses; (3) an undeveloped land duty of $\frac{1}{2}$d in the £. The 1931 Act provided for a 1d in the £ annual duty on the capital value of land.

2 The base value in fact will normally be existing use value adjusted for various allowances. However, these will vary with changes in legislation and scarcely affect the
   principles, only the progressivity of development tax with the size of the gain realised.

3 See Foster and Glaister (1975) for a demonstration of this.

4 DoE, 1971a, Cmnd 4741, para. 2.74, which makes almost the identical point made by
   Davenport (1917, pp. 3–6).

5 This is brought out by the judgement of an Australian justice on a particular case that
   'since the commencement of the County of Cumberland Planning Scheme Ordinance,
   involves an artificial and most elusive enquiry. The valuer's role, which before the
   Ordinance was difficult, is probably now an almost impossible one. He and/or some
   other expert must now, it woud appear, assume the role of a forecaster as at a particular date of the uses to which the responsible authority, or the Court on appeal, would
   be likely to consent. The making of such forecasts, if limited to a consideration of
   decisions of the Court, would be essentially a matter for a lawyer who was a specialist
   in the particular field. However, the making of forecasts as to the decisions of a responsible authority whose decisions are not reported and whose consents are not appeal-
   able, involves problems of even greater difficulty. The ascertainment of unimproved
   capital value has from time to time been described in the decisions as a most artificial
   and unreal enquiry. With the advent of the town planning provisions of the County of
   Cumberland Planning Scheme Ordinance and the imminence of local planning schemes
   the position is, and must become still more, unreal and artificial.' Quoted in Australian
   Commission of Enquiry into Land Tenure. Final Report (Else-Mitchell, 1976), pt 4,
   ch. 2).

6 There are interesting externality arguments associated with this argument. See Foster
   in Rothenberg and Heggie (1974).

7 Moral arguments are also possible. The Treasurer of Durban in 1935, explaining the
   attractiveness of SVR there, wrote that the 'rating of buildings . . . is considered to be a
   confiscation of private property which is the product of private enterprise'. Quoted by
   Long (1939, p. 57).

8 A tax on buildings 'if the tax is high enough to matter . . . biasses owners . . . against
   supplying new floor space and shelter, and in favour of billboards, gas stations, junk-
   yards, open storage, parking lots, baronial estates, obsolescence, speculation and dilapi-
   dation. In general it favours old over new and ranks high among factors that retard
   urban renewal' (Gaffney, 1972a, p. 143).

9 Less likely in the UK because of the existence of rate rebates.

10 Note the comment of the *Rating and Valuation Reporter* (21 March 1974): This
   'highlights the grave criticism of site value rating that it bases liability on the size of the
   ratepayer's garden with which he may be stuck and may not want, instead of in the
   size and quality of his main source of enjoyment of life, the building'. Why should
   he be supposed not to enjoy his garden equally or be stuck with a house too large for
   him? Such an argument misses the whole point of SVR.

11 Beach in Holland (1970) has a very interesting discussion of how these are prepared.

12 Notional rental values as a basis for rateable values means another problem. An interest
   rate has to be assumed. The *Rating and Valuation Reporter* (14 March 1976) pointed
   out the difficulties. More curiously it objected to this method of valuation on the
   grounds that the ratepayers would often 'not be able to collect the sale price and
   deduct for age and obsolescence, and cube the buildings as found necessary at Whitstable'. Ratepayers do not now find their rateable values easy to understand. The
   manuals used in the USA to establish such adjustments are intelligible.

13 Black in Holland (1970) shows how this approach works out in practice.

14 Demolition cost should not be deducted on the assumption that the site is in its most
   profitable use, and redevelopment is not envisaged.

15 Following the phrasing of the 1936 LCC Bill.

3 Other Taxes

This chapter reaches one conclusion which is the same as a conclusion of the Layfield Committee: the only new local tax worth considering is a local income tax. But the reasoning is in many ways different, and ultimately the case for introducing a local income tax appears to us narrower. The Committee was anxious to add a local income tax to rates in partial replacement of grant; but it scarcely touched on the great difficulties of combining more than one local tax and central grant into a unified system of local government finance achieving horizontal equity. For this reason, we see a new local tax as a replacement for rates rather than as an addition to them. Thus the case to be made is for local income tax in lieu of rates.

The first section discusses the merits and drawbacks of the main candidates for other local taxes considered singly. The list of candidates is far from exhaustive; but many can be eliminated on the grounds that they are unlikely to raise enough revenue relative to the needs of local authorities to be worth the thought; while others plainly also have other drawbacks which lead us to reject all except local income tax. To go through them separately in detail would be unnecessary (see Hildersley and Nottage, 1968; Layfield, 1976, ch. 11). The second section discusses the severe problems of combining more than one local tax.

A SINGLE TAX

CRITERIA FOR NEW LOCAL TAXES

In the 1971 Green Paper, three criteria were suggested for new local taxes: administration, suitability and economic effects (DoE, 1971a, Cmnd 4741, app. 2, para. 7). The criterion of administration is self-explanatory: the actual collection of the tax, bearing in mind that it would be levied at different rates in different localities, should not present substantial new administrative problems nor be excessively costly.

The second criterion, suitability, involves two considerations. First, the tax should have a large base, so that the revenue derived from it could make a significant contribution to local finances. The size of revenue yield suggested by the Green Paper for a tax additional to rates was about 10 per cent of local government expenditure, and Layfield (1976, ch. 11, para. 5) suggested a similar figure of £1500 million in relation to local government spending of £13,000 million (1975/76). The required yield of a single tax would be at least 40 per cent of local government spending. The second element of suitability is much less straightforward. The tax should have sufficient buoyancy so that the revenue yield could be increased over time, either because of growth in the tax base with given tax rates, or because of the ease with which the tax rates could be raised. But, at the same time, the tax should fall on local electors 'in such a way as to impose some discipline on local expenditure decisions' (DoE, 1971*a*, Cmnd 4741, app. 2, para. 9). Since these requirements conflict, it is hard to see how any tax could satisfy both (Foster, 1973, esp. p. 6). On this question, the Layfield Committee were much more rigorous. They saw the issue of local taxation primarily in terms of 'accountability and perceptibility' — that local taxes are, ultimately, paid by, and perceived to be paid by, local electors. In contrast to the Green Paper concept of 'suitability' the Layfield criterion is both consistent and operational.

The third criterion in the Green Paper was called 'economic effects' — that is 'the impact of the tax in national as opposed to local terms' (DoE, 1971*a*, Cmnd 4741, app. 2, para. 12). This criterion raises issues generally described as macro-economic, that is to say the effect of new local taxes on economic management, inflation, the balance of payments, etc.

It is sometimes suggested that a national tax be given entirely to local government. This need cause no problem for the tax structure, but it may cause difficulties for national demand management if the tax in question had desirable administrative properties as an instrument of stabilisation policy. If, say, deflationary fiscal policy is required midway through a financial year, some taxes can be adjusted quickly and with little administrative cost: for example, customs and excise duties. If such a tax were given to local government, the means of conducting fiscal stabilisation policy are reduced, and the potential for such a policy is limited. If, say, a local petrol tax were introduced, and central government's excise duty on petrol abolished, central government would lose one of the major taxes whose rates can easily be adjusted (at least in administrative terms) for the purposes of demand management policy.

Our earlier discussion in Chapters 2 and 3 of Part Two indicated two additional criteria by which to judge possible local taxes: efficiency and equity. Efficiency could be best advanced by a poll tax or household tax — that is, a tax whose burden approximates to the distribution of benefits from the service. We do not, however, consider such taxes further here because they run counter to current notions of vertical equity.

By vertical equity we mean that taxpayers within any locality are effectively paying the same amount for the (equal) services they receive. We saw that a local income tax would be vertically inefficient and lead to an incentive for wealthier households to migrate to areas of low local government spending. By contrast, a land tax was vertically efficient because of capitalisation, as was a housing tax.

Horizontal efficiency means that a given taxpayer would pay the same in tax for any given standard of local government services in any local authority. Here we saw the advantages in taxes falling only on households, such as local income taxes, housing taxes or residential land taxes over taxes on all property such as the present rating system or site value rating. We also showed that horizontal efficiency could be remedied by means of resource equalisation grants — albeit at the cost of concealing the 'price' of local government services to the average elector.

LOCAL INCOME TAX

The Layfield Committee regarded local income tax as the 'only serious candidate for a new source of local revenue' (Layfield, 1976, p. 190). A local income tax (LIT) would easily provide a substantial yield. A tax rate on their calculations of only 4p in the pound would yield around £1,500 million (at November 1975 prices). Further the tax would meet one of the criteria of accountability, in that its final burden would rest on local residents and could not be substantially shifted on to persons resident outside the authority. It is for that reason that, in their view, the LIT should be levied on persons on the basis of their place of residence rather than their place of work.

But accountability requires not only that local residents pay the tax but that they are aware of the tax they are paying — the criterion of perceptibility. Here the case for local income tax is less obvious. Whether a local income tax would be perceptible depends mainly on how it is collected. And this immediately raises the main drawback of LIT, namely its administrative complexity, or high costs of collection. Layfield estimated that LIT would cost around £100 million to collect, that is close to 7 per cent of its prospective yield. This proportion is much higher than for other taxes, which generally have collection costs of $1\frac{1}{2}$ per cent to 2 per cent of their revenue yield. The reason for these very high collection costs is not inherent in the LIT itself, but rather in the national system of income taxation in the UK. Local income taxes are levied in many countries in Western Europe and North America without prohibitive administrative costs. We therefore first set out a system of income tax collection — based on self-assessment — under which a local income tax would be an attractive option. We then show how the UK system of tax collection differs from the self-assessment system and the problems this leads to.

The basic system of self-assessment is one in which the taxpayer, at the end of each tax year, calculates his gross income from all sources, deducts the allowances to which he is entitled, to arrive at his taxable income, calculates his tax liability by reference to tax tables, and sends off a cheque to the tax authorities. LIT can be grafted on to this system very easily. Local authorities, in addition to central government, would notify the taxpayer of the tax rate they had imposed, so the taxpayer could compute his tax liability and make the appropriate payment. For example, a taxpayer may have a gross income from all sources of £4000 and allowances of £1500, making a taxable income of £2500. Under the present system, central government might levy a tax of, say, 30 per cent so that the taxpayer's liability would be £750. With a local income tax, central government might levy a rate of, say, 25 per cent and the taxpayer's local authority a rate of 5 per cent, so the taxpayer's liabilities would be £625 and £125 respectively, and the only difference is that two payments would have to be made instead of only one. Under either system, the tax authorities would have to introduce checks to avoid tax evasion by under-reporting of income by taxpayers. With LIT it would also be necessary to check that taxpayers reported the same income to local as to central government, but the work involved in doing this is obviously not great.

The drawback with this system is that it entails very large lump-sum payments.

To smooth out tax payments, a system of instalment payments is generally adopted. These instalments can be calculated according to one of a number of rough-and-ready methods — an exact estimate being unnecessary because underpayment or overpayment of tax is corrected at the end of the tax year. LIT could similarly be paid in instalments, with an adjustment at the end of the year once the taxpayer's actual taxable income for the year was known.

The main administrative difficulty in the self-assessment system is that of calculating, and verifying, total gross income, from all sources, for each taxpayer. The British system avoids this problem altogether for the great majority of taxpayers. It is based instead on the principle of deducting tax from all income payments. Taxpayers' allowances are set against their income in their primary place of employment by means of their PAYE coding. Thereafter, income of all taxpayers is taxed at the same rate, so that tax can be deducted at source from all income payments at this standard, or basic, rate without reference to the total income of the taxpayer. It is necessary to compute total taxable income only for the small minority of taxpayers who are liable to tax at higher rates.

It is clearly not easy to graft a system of local income tax, allowing local authorities to levy different tax rates, on to this system. What Layfield suggests, essentially, is a local earned income tax. Each employee would be given a tax code indicating their local authority of residence. There would be a separate set of tax tables for each LIT rate, and employers would apply the appropriate tax table. Clearly the administration would be a little simplified if local authorities could confine themselves to large discrete steps in their LIT rates, for example to 3p, 4p or 5p but not 3.72p in the pound. Where secondary earnings are taxed at source the employer could again be informed of the local authority code, and where they are not the tax authorities would themselves apply the appropriate rate (as, for example, with the self-employed). This system could not easily be extended to cover dividends, interest, etc., and the suggestion is that these should pay a 'composite' local tax rate, presumably reflecting some average of tax rates actually being charged.

The LIT would be paid direct to the Inland Revenue, who would then calculate, presumably by means of a sample survey, the income tax base of each authority. It would then pay each authority, as a lump sum, its tax rate multiplied by its assessed tax base. Thus the LIT collected from individuals would not be passed directly to the local authorities.

The trouble with this system, apart from its administrative costs, is that the arrangements seem to obscure LIT payments by collecting them in conjunction with the much larger national income tax. Tax deductions under PAYE are affected by all sorts of factors and it is not clear that the effects of changes in LIT would be particularly obvious. Changes in LIT rates would be introduced at the beginning of the tax year, when tax allowances, national tax rates, individuals' PAYE coding are also often changing, and it would be difficult to disentangle the relative effects of each. Layfield suggests employees could be informed of their LIT payments periodically, but it is by no means obvious that this information would generate great interest. It is partly on these grounds that central government, in the 1977 Green Paper, rejected the proposal to introduce LIT.[1]

Under the present UK system of income-tax administration the balance of arguments seems to go against the introduction of LIT. On the other hand, under a system of self-assessment, the tax would both be cheaper to collect and more perceptible. There would then be a good case for its introduction. We do not wish to go into the arguments for and against introducing self-assessment in the UK tax system here (See Barr, James and Prest, 1977), suffice to say a case can be made on the grounds of the high costs and inflexibility of the present system. But should such a change be made, the case for local income tax should be re-examined.

Nevertheless, while this suggests a powerful administrative case and also a case on the grounds of accountability against LIT until self-assessment is introduced, and as a corollary an argument for the feasibility of LIT if there were self-assessment, it does not amount to an argument for LIT as such. The Layfield Committee did not have to argue this since their main concern was simply to find another tolerable tax to substitute for central grants on the assumption that it would be intolerable to raise substantially more in domestic rates. We think that LIT is better than the present rating system, because it falls wholly on households. If rates were levied only on households, however, there would be less of an argument for LIT.

We have already shown that though the efficiency properties of LIT are different from those of domestic rates, no strong case can be made for preferring one to the other on those grounds. The essential case for replacing domestic rates by LIT is one of equity. We have shown how rates were the best approximation to an income (and wealth) tax before a national income tax was possible. We have seen how even as late as the Royal Commission of 1901 it was confirmed that rates had this traditional function. Moreover, the yield from rates was very much higher than that from income tax until the First World War. Until then, for the majority, it remained the most important tax citizens had to pay. We have also seen how from time immemorial there have been struggles to improve the equity of rates as a quasi-income tax by the standards of the time. From the 1930s the regressiveness of rates − a notion derived from thinking about its incidence in relation to income − caused increasing concern until the problem was relieved by the introduction of rate rebates in the 1960s and their extension in the 1970s. We have also shown how many of the criticisms of rates amount in fact to objections that it does not have some of the properties of an income tax. We have argued that rates could be made to approximate more closely to an income tax, if that were what is desired, but only with difficulty. Administratively, there are great problems in altering rates to reflect the existence of additional earners in the household, for example. But we have also said that it seems to us that it is the progressiveness of the whole tax structure that matters, not the progressiveness of one component. Nevertheless, even if somewhat irrational, it is clear that there is growing concern with equity which finds its expression in a belief that individual taxes (and indeed services) should be made equitable by current standards independently of the whole, presumably on the reasonable grounds that we lack the means to evaluate the equity of the provision and finance of government services as a whole or the means to correct this in any certain manner. If LIT replaces rates, it will be because of the strength of this desire that local taxation should have the equity properties of an income tax, and, as an extension, that the horizontal equity of the system should be achieved in terms of local incomes rather than rateable values. If the notion of equity is sufficiently powerful and if self-assessment is introduced, there must come a point where it is more sensible to introduce LIT than to meet diminishing returns in trying to modify rates to become what they cannot: a simulacrum of an LIT.

So much for vertical equity. A suitable grant system can be devised, as we have shown elsewhere (Part Two, Chapter 3, pp. 424–5), to achieve horizontal equity with such a tax. But before commending its introduction, its major theoretical drawback must be faced: the problem that Part Two, Chapter 2 showed it posed for horizontal and vertical efficiency. While horizontal inefficiency can be met by a resource equalisation grant, in the absence of such a grant, an LIT would encourage more migration than would domestic rates because of the far less perfect capitalisation to be expected. As we also saw, there would be much less tendency to capitalise out vertical inefficiencies, and here no obviously feasible grant system could come to the rescue.

From this follow some important consequences. It is unlikely that an LIT would be the best method of raising money to finance beneficial services. It would be intrinsically no more efficient than domestic rates, bearing no better relation to benefits received. The fact that vertical inefficiencies would be less capitalised would be more likely to set up migratory movements as taxpayers sought to escape excess burdens. As a corollary, it would tend to encourage migration if used to finance locally determined redistributive services, and thus reduce the scope any local authority had for such redistribution. On efficiency grounds, such consequences could be argued to be in its favour but it would be a value judgement whether they should or should not outweigh the implications for the scope of redistribution. If used for centrally determined redistributive services, their tendency towards uniformity should avoid such inefficiencies.

TAXES ON FIRMS

(1)   *Corporation tax*

A major disadvantage of a corporation profit tax is the difficulty of assigning profits of a multi-authority company to a particular authority. There are many devices by which profits can be changed round between branches of a company, and different operations of a company. Thus the tax would be easily avoided unless the cost of overseeing it were very high. The greater the complexity of the rules governing the allocation of profits among authorities, the smaller would be the connection between tax and expenditures in a particular authority. The burden of the tax would have no connection with the benefits derived from the expenditures. It would not therefore be horizontally or indeed vertically efficient. It would be difficult to secure horizontal equity and its connection with any normally accepted canon of vertical equity would be remote.

(2)   *A company turnover tax*

A corporation tax based on the sales or output of a company does not have the disadvantages of a company profits tax. The value of the output of the part of the company located within a local authority is reasonably easily defined. There would still be possibilities of avoidance. For example, if a company produces an intermediate product for its own use within a particular locality, it could purchase this from its branch at a low price and thus reduce the value of sales of the intermediary. This kind of avoidance could be more easily checked and simple rules could be formulated for such cases, though there would be costs for companies and government.

Consider, first, a situation in which the company sells the goods it produces on a national market, and not only in the locality in which it produces the goods. Assuming the goods are also produced by other companies located in other authorities, the company cannot sell the goods at a higher price because its local authority raises its tax rate above others. In this case, forward shifting of the tax in the form of higher prices is not possible. Backward shifting will occur on to the various factors of production. The factors which will bear the tax are those that are fixed within the locality, and the tax will be borne by the owners of such factors, whatever is the location of the owners. The three factors which we may consider are labour, movable capital, and land. In the short run, both land and movable capital are reasonably fixed within the authority, while labour, especially the effective supply of labour rather than the population, is presumably variable. Thus in the short run we would expect that such a turnover tax would be borne by all the factors depending on their relative supply elasticities. Of these factors, labour is presumably local, the land may be local but could be owned by outsiders, and capital could be owned completely by outsiders but, of course, may also be owned by residents of the authority. In the long run, however, the situation is changed. Capital would be transferred to other localities where its rate of return is higher. The demand for labour and land within the authority will fall. If, for the moment, we assume that prices and wages are reasonably flexible then the wage rate and rents within the locality will fall, until the net return to the mobile factor capital is the same in the higher tax locality as in others. The tax will thus be borne by local labour and the owners of local property (who of, course, may not be residents). If wages do not fall as a result of the imposition of the tax, the tax will be borne by owners of local property and unemployment will occur.

From the above analysis of a turnover tax on companies which sell on a national market, we can see that such a tax does have the property that its burden falls on either local residents, in the form of lower wages, or local property in the form of lower rents. It therefore satisfies the condition that the beneficiaries of the expenditures financed by the tax, bear the burden of the tax. The disadvantage of this tax is, however, that its burden is not at all obvious. It is unlikely that the resulting lower wages will be perceived as arising from the tax on turnover and thus from the expenditures financed by the tax.

LOCAL SALES TAXES

It is convenient at this stage to consider local sales taxes. By this we mean taxes on the sale of commodities within the locality. Such a tax can be shifted forward if there are costs involved in transferring purchases into other localities. This tax could be avoided by residents if it were easy to shop in lower tax areas. If there are costs in doing this, then prices of goods sold locally will rise and the tax will be partly shifted forward and partly shifted backward, on to factors of production. The analysis of the backward shifting is the same as in the above case of a turnover tax. Locally immobile factors of production will bear the burden or rather some of the burden of the tax. As far as the forward shifting is concerned, locally immobile consumers will bear the burden of the tax. Thus in this case, the full burden of the tax will be borne by local residents or local property, either in the form of higher prices or as lower factor returns.

LOCAL PAYROLL TAXES

The analysis of these taxes must again distinguish between payroll taxes on locally produced goods, which are sold on the national market where forward shifting is not possible, and payroll taxes on locally produced goods which are sold in the local market where there are immobile consumers and into which there are transport costs. In the former case, the payroll taxes will be shifted completely on to the locally immobile factors, namely labour and local property. The effects will be the same as those of the locally imposed turnover tax or output tax on commodities sold in the national market. In the latter case, there will be also an effect on the prices of locally sold commodities and therefore some of the tax will be borne by local consumers.

Looked at from the standpoint of horizontal and vertical efficiency and equity such a tax suffers from the problem that besets all use of profits, sales or payroll taxation as a source of revenue. As we shall see, if combined with other local taxes it is impossible to devise an appropriate grant to achieve resource equalisation. On its own, none is likely to be a sufficient source of revenue without having severe long-run effects on the location of businesses. None is therefore likely to be acceptable on grounds of horizontal and vertical efficiency or equity.

TAXES ASSOCIATED WITH MOTOR VEHICLES

Among the most commonly suggested alternatives for local revenue has been various sorts of taxes levied on motor vehicles or their use. This has been partly due to the fact that local authorities maintain the roads cars use. Therefore, why not raise the tax to finance local expenditures from cars? The two major candidates for this have been licences and motor fuel taxes. These were considered by both the 1971 Green Paper and the Layfield Committee. They both reject the transfer of the fuel tax to local authorities. Both argue that there is much scope for substituting low-tax areas for high-tax areas as purchase sources. The Layfield Committee also argues that such a tax would not foster accountability because the tax would be hidden in the price of the fuel and so not noticed. The 1971 Green Paper argues, as well, that the fuel tax is a major tax used as a regulator of the economy by the Chancellor and allowing local authorities to levy their rates on it would make that more difficult. The 1977 Green Paper in response to Layfield mentions that the tax had been considered and rejected on the grounds that it does not foster accountability and the government agreed with the Committee's view.

The dismissal of the fuel tax by Layfield is somewhat brief. Much work had been done on the way such a tax should be collected by local authorities (or for them by the central government) which worked through adjustments in the rateable value of fuel outlets in relation to fuel throughput (see, for example, IMTA, 1968). In this way, it may be true that consumers of fuel will only see the tax as a higher price and therefore in Layfield's terminology it would not be a perceptible tax, but sellers of fuel would see it as an increase in their rateable value for the assessment of rates.

Given Layfield's acceptance of non-domestic rates on accountability grounds (1976, ch. 10, para. 29, p. 153) a tax on sellers of motor fuel might appear to satisfy the same criterion. In our view, the objections we have suggested to non-domestic rating would apply, *a fortiori*, to this proposal.

The other form of motor taxation − the vehicle licence ('road fund' licence) − could be transferred to local authorities. Payments of this tax would be clearly perceptible to the local electorate and hence it would satisfy the test of accountability. Its yield, however, is rather small (currently around £600 million). Furthermore, it is a somewhat inequitable tax, levying the same charge irrespective of the size or value of the car, or the amount of use it gets, let alone of the owner's income or wealth. This means that it would be difficult to increase the yield of vehicle excise duties at all substantially.

One way around this might be an excise duty graduated according to the engine capacity of the vehicle. Such a scheme is currently (1978) under consideration in the USA. People with bigger cars might reasonably be expected to pay more tax.

Whatever its merits for fund-raising it would rank low in relation to horizontal and vertical efficiency and equity. Indeed, it would only be likely to make sense as a rough approximation to a charge to meet local costs associated with the construction, maintenance and use of roads. Even as such, it has the disadvantage that local roads are used by non-local people. In that dimension, they are non-rival and therefore public goods. Moreover, the government proposed in 1978 to abolish such excise licences on the grounds that they were unduly expensive to collect in relation to their yield.

A more ingenious scheme would be for motorists to pay part of the petrol tax duty through the vehicle licence. The idea would be that the licence would be graduated in relation both to the engine capacity of the car and to the mileage travelled. Then the motorist's licence duty would be quite closely related to the petrol consumption of his car. An increase in excise duty with a corresponding reduction in petrol tax, as currently levied, could bring about a substantial increase in the local authority tax base without significantly altering the total burden on any taxpayer.

The scheme has a number of advantages: it is clearly perceptible to the local elector (at least if he owns a car), it creates no incentive for shopping around among authorities for low-tax petrol, and it does not impede the use of that part of the petrol tax left with central government as an instrument of national demand management. Thus it meets the objections of the Green Paper and Lay-field to other sources of revenue associated with motor vehicles.

Would such a tax be feasible in practice? The only additional information motorists need supply with their annual licence renewal forms is that of mileage travelled. What would be required is that each car be equipped with a 'secure' mileometer, which could not be tampered with, and that motorists report its readings on their licence renewal forms, and that there be some form of spot check for evasion.

It would be very difficult to devise a feasible tax which did not require ex-pensive equipment and many checks to prevent false reporting. A similar prob-lem would arise if petrol sold in different localities bore different local tax rates since then it would also entail all the problems of local sales taxes in general, in encouraging people to buy petrol wherever it was cheapest.

Thus the conclusion on the suitability of different taxes is indeed that of the Layfield Committee. LIT is the only strong runner, but only if self-assessment is introduced and only if the equity arguments make the upheaval worthwhile.

We have not gone into the use of other business taxes as an alternative to non-domestic rates since we argued earlier for the abolition of non-domestic rates and their replacement by charges. Alternatively, however, one could imagine a tax on businesses set to cover the average cost of services provided to businesses in general, or to particular categories of business. It is not immediately obvious, however, that any would be more efficient in relation to services provided than rates are. It is possible that some services — for example, for commuters — are provided more in relation to number employed than in relation to property values. If so, there might be some merit in recouping the cost of services pro-vided to businesses through a payroll tax. But setting that aside, the difficulties pointed out if such taxes are thought of as an alternative to non-domestic rates are mostly the same as those discussed above when they are considered as alternatives to rates in general. But for a discussion of attempts to overcome the problems of multi-jurisdictional business taxes see McClure (1977).

MORE THAN ONE TAX

If there is to be more than one tax, it follows that the prime candidate will be a combination of rates and LIT. The objections to any multiplication of local taxes are:

(1)   that it will make demand management more difficult and adversely affect the tax structure, both being seen as aspects of macroeconomic policy;
(2)   that it will pose severe problems for accountability; especially in a system that tries to achieve horizontal efficiency and equity.

While the main arguments which are used in favour of such multiplication are:

(3)   that it would increase the buoyancy of local revenues; and
(4)   that local dependence on central grant could be reduced.

The arguments are of very different weight. We will first discuss (1) and (3) which seem to us to be almost entirely misconceived, then consider (2), the severe problem introduced by increasing the number of local taxes, before turning to how one might secure (4), less dependence on central grant, the only valid reason for wishing more than one tax.

MACROECONOMIC IMPLICATIONS OF NEW LOCAL TAXES

The Green Paper argued that additional local taxes would make 'the task of predicting the impact of local taxation for the purpose of managing the economy . . . much more difficult' (DoE, 1971a, Cmnd 4741, app. 2, para. 6). There are two possible sources of concern here:

(1) That with more local taxes it would become more difficult to predict total local government expenditure. Confining local governments to a single tax source constrains their flexibility on the revenue side, and hence constrains their capacity to vary their expenditure at all substantially out of line with central government expectations.

(2) That, with several local taxes, even if the government can predict total local government spending, it will not know the relative yields or rates of the different local taxes.

On point (1), the argument is essentially the same as that of Part Two, Chapter 8. There we argued that, as long as local government spending is financed by taxation, the level of local government spending need be of no concern from the viewpoint of demand management. The additional local government spending would be offset by reduced private spending. The same argument applies to new local taxes.

But even if this argument is not accepted, it still does not follow that new local taxes necessarily make the prediction of local government spending more difficult. One outcome of making additional sources of revenue available to local authorities is to reduce the inequality of taxable capacity between them, and hence to reduce the need for resource equalisation grants. A local authority may well feel more rather than less constrained in increasing its spending if for every additional pound spent it has to raise 50p from rates and 50p from, say, LIT tax than if, as at present, it may have to raise 50p from rates, the other 50p coming from the resources element. Clearly, the key issue again is one of perceptibility: if the new local taxes are as perceptible as rates it is not clear that they will in fact provide local authorities with significantly greater revenue flexibility than they have at present.

(2) The second source of concern is one of tax structure. Local authorities may decide to switch from one tax source to another. The concern here is not only with orthodox demand management but also with longer-term considerations of the effect on the overall tax structure in the economy.

The difficulty for demand management arises if it is thought that, for a given yield, different taxes have different effects on aggregate demand. Then it will be more difficult to predict the effects on demand of a given increase in local taxation because it will also be necessary to predict how the total will be split up between the various local taxes. But the idea that different taxes have different effects on demand assumes they are paid, in part, out of savings. If, on the other hand, taxes are seen as a payment for local government services they will not be paid out of savings, as we have already argued (Part Two, Chapter 8), and these demand effects, therefore, will not arise. But whatever assumptions are made as to the demand effects of different taxes, it is hard to believe that errors in forecasting on this score could be significant in the context of macroeconomic policy.

Turning to questions of tax structure, it is useful to stress at the outset that the relative yield of different taxes is quite independent of which are assigned to local government. If a local income tax is introduced, for example, the total yield of income tax need not rise. If local authorities raise £x million through local income tax, their grants from central government can be reduced by that amount, reducing central government's revenue needs by £x million, and allowing it to reduce its collections of income tax by the same amount. If the new local tax is introduced in place of rates, its total yield still need not rise. If, for example, government wished to replace the revenue lost by reducing rates by, say, VAT, it need not introduce a local VAT. Instead it could introduce LIT in place of rates, reduce the national income tax and make up the lost central government revenue by increasing the yield of VAT. It is illogical, for example, to argue against the introduction of LIT on the grounds that income tax is already too high, or that increases in the rate of income tax might have disincentive effects or lead to higher wage claims (Layfield, 1976, app. 8, pp. 211–14).

While central government can always offset the effects of local tax yields on the total revenues collected from the different taxes, it cannot counteract differences in tax rates between different authorities. Assume, for example, that there were some tax where the government thought the most desirable rate was a per cent, and the maximum acceptable rate was b per cent. If local authorities were allowed to levy a local tax on this base, they might on average with to levy a rate of c per cent. Central government could then levy a rate of $(a-c)$ per cent, so that the average taxpayer would still pay, in total, a per cent (c per cent to local government plus $(a-c)$ per cent to central government). But some authorities might levy the tax at a rate well in excess of the average; say $(c+d)$ per cent. Taxpayers in that authority would be paying a total tax of $(a+d)$ per cent. This total might well be in excess of b per cent, the maximum acceptable rate. Central government might then feel obliged to reduce the national tax rate to below $(a-c)$ per cent, though this would mean collecting a less than optimal amount from the average taxpayer from this tax, and consequently having to increase other taxes. Even if $(a+d)$ per cent is below b per cent, the central government's options for raising the tax rate are limited to the gap between $(a+d)$ per cent and b per cent rather than to the gap between a per cent and b per cent.

It must be asked first whether there are any examples of taxes where an increase in the rate of a few percentage points (as a result of local variation) would approach any sort of maximum limit. Government departments like to depict the tax structure as a highly sophisticated apparatus, sensitively balanced in accordance with all sorts of optimising criteria, and which must be protected against any sort of change. In fact, in the last few years, effective tax rates have been shooting around all over the place under the impact of inflation. There is no reason to believe that any tax is currently at a level that might be regarded as optimal according to any objective criteria, and equally no reason to believe that local variations in tax rates would cause any serious problems.[2]

There is, however, a more fundamental point. If some local authority levies a tax rate significantly above the average, making a combined rate unacceptable to taxpayers, why is it for central government to intervene? Local authorities have discretion in levying taxes, and they are responsible to their electorates. Why then should they impose a tax rate significantly in excess of the rate imposed by other authorities, if it implies imposing unacceptable burdens on local tax-payers? In a system of local democracy, local political pressures would constrain local governments from levying excessive taxes. Central government would not then be obliged to alter the national tax structure to offset excessive local taxes.[3]

On the other hand, if central government believes local authorities are not democratic, and may impose taxes beyond their citizen's willingness to pay, and that those citizens will look to it (the central government) to protect them from excessive tax burdens, then its control over the national tax structure may be endangered. In these circumstances, it is not surprising to find that central government will seek to limit local authorities' discretion over the tax rates they may levy (Treasury evidence to Layfield Committee, 1976, app. 8, pp. 711–14). The argument again is a political one as to the accountability of local authorities to the communities they represent, rather than an economic issue of macro-economic control.

THE BUOYANCY OF LOCAL REVENUES

Buoyancy of local revenues is a common objective of local, and even of central, governments. Broadly, higher tax revenues can be secured in three ways.

First, automatically, through a buoyant tax base, which itself generates increased tax revenues. Thus the yield of income tax rises automatically with incomes, and progressive income-tax yields rise progressively (unless tax rates are lowered and thresholds raised). Sales-tax yields rise with sales, profits-tax yields with profits, and so on. But the automatic buoyancy of rates is confined to the revenue generated by increased rateable value.

In Britain total rateable values increased from £370 million in 1947/48 to only £835 million by the time of the first major revaluation in 1963. In that year rateable values rose to £2,185 million, but then rose to only £2,770 million by the time of the next revaluation in 1973. The average growth of rateable values between the two revaluations is only around 3 per cent compared with a growth of about 8 per cent in GDP in nominal terms over the period. But this lack of buoyancy between revaluations is made up by very sharp increases at revaluation. As a source of tax revenue, rates are not buoyant in the short run, but, taking revaluations into account, they are buoyant in the longer run.

A second source of tax buoyancy is through changes in tax rates. Local reliance on property rates means almost inevitable tax-rate increases every year between revaluations. (When revaluation occurs, tax rates fall and then start to rise again.)

A third source of revenue buoyancy is through multiplying the number of local taxes either by transfer of some taxes from central government, either fully or in part, or by the creation of new taxes.

Many systems of local government finance are criticised for having a low income elasticity such that local expenditures are rising faster than local taxes, creating a 'revenue gap' between local revenues and expenditure. By this is usually meant that the automatic buoyancy of the local tax revenue is insufficient to close this gap. The contrast is often drawn between national and local revenues. Typically, central government relies more on taxes like income taxes which have high income elasticity, while traditionally in many countries local authorities had to depend on taxes with low income elasticity like property taxes. In the 1960s this became particularly noticeable, not only because of a very general acceleration in the growth of local expenditure but also because inflation had tended to increase the buoyancy of central relative to local revenues. As the American economist Walter Heller has put it: 'At the Federal level economic growth and a powerful tax system interacting under modern fiscal management, generate new revenues faster than they generate new demands on the Federal purse. But at the state–local level, the situation is reversed. Under the whiplash of prosperity, responsibilities are outstripping revenue' (1966, p. 118). Indeed, Professor James Buchanan has formulated the hypothesis that 'in a period of rapidly increasing national product, that tax institution characterised by the highest elasticity will tend, other things equal, to generate the largest volume of public spending' (1967, p. 65).

In any simple sense, this hypothesis is often falsified. For as we have seen in Part One, Chapter 4, in Britain and indeed in most nations, local expenditure has tended to grow faster than central government expenditure, even though there is a general tendency for local governments to have less income-elastic taxes. In Britain, low automatic tax elasticity has been met both by tax-rate increases and by rapidly increasing government grants. In the USA there has been pressure for more grants, that is revenue sharing, and tax-rate increases, but also for new local taxes. For example, between 1957 and 1969 'every state but one raised rates or adopted a major new tax: there were 230 rate increases and 19 new tax adoptions in this period' (Heller and Pechman, 1970, quoted by Oates, 1975, p. 142). Britain is one of the relatively few countries which has stuck to maintaining only one local tax source, and which has refused to create new local taxes in spite of spasmodic pressure for them.

Most of the argument about increasing the buoyancy of local taxation has centred on giving the local authorities taxes with higher income elasticity through adding sales business and especially income taxes to property taxation. The notion that a local government can raise more revenue if its taxes are altered so as to increase the income elasticity of its revenue may seem common sense; but as Oates has argued (1975, p. 141), it is more puzzling than may at first appear. Why should people care about the income elasticity of the tax structure? If they do, it would seem to imply that they mind more if tax rates are increased than if the same increased taxation is taken from them less perceptibly through automatically rising tax bills. It would seem to mean that a person is more ready to accept increased public expenditure if financed through automatically rising taxes than through increased tax rates. This is inconsistent with our ordinary ideas of economic rationality. One explanation is that taxpayers are subject to a form of fiscal illusion. People do notice changes in tax rates more because they are publicly announced and agonised over. Tax increases without tax-rate changes take them unawares. But as Oates argues (1975, p. 143), it is always unsatisfactory to base any long-run phenomenon upon an assumption of human irrationality. The second explanation is that politicians find the cost to them of tax-rate changes requiring more public debate and justification great enough to prefer taxes which avoid such debate or require it less frequently. But this only shifts the problem one stage. Why is it that governments arrange their affairs so that some taxes yield more revenue without the need for public debate than do others?

A rather different argument Oates uses relates to one used in Part One, Chapter 1 in discussing the nature of local democracy: Downs's (1957, esp. ch. 14) contention that a rational man would neglect local politics and either not vote or vote without deliberation, if the costs of acquiring relevant information were disproportionate to the benefits he receives from casting his vote one way or another. To discover information about the yield of automatically buoyant tax revenue is difficult, while the publicity necessary to tax-rate changes means that it would involve the taxpayer in less time and effort to be informed. Thus he might oppose an increase in one but not in the other, even though if the costs of acquiring information were the same in both cases, his attitudes would be identical to equal tax changes in both.

All this argument cuts both ways. While one can see how a politician or official could welcome more automatically buoyant taxes because they raise revenue with less fuss, this only happens because it is more difficult for the taxpayer to find what is going on and so to relate tax and expenditures to decisions. Since the principle of local democracy means that the electors should be supreme, this amounts to a very strong argument against adopting income-elastic taxes for the sake of automatic buoyancy, which is not diminished rationally by observing that a very large part of central government revenue is automatically buoyant.

A further possible explanation not mentioned by Oates is that the greater relative popularity of income taxes depends not on a difference in information costs but on perceived differences in equity. If local income taxes are more progressive than rates, a greater proportion of the burden of any tax increase falls upon the relatively affluent. The median-voter hypothesis, or indeed majority rule, would imply increased taxation and increased expenditure because the burden on the median voter would be relatively less.[4] It is, therefore, through making taxation more onerous relative to benefits that the higher income elasticity is secured. Not too much weight can be placed on this argument since sales taxes are probably as regressive as rates and yet have a higher income elasticity, which should not be the case if differences in incidence were the whole explanation.

In the same article, Oates (1975, p. 144) performed a number of tests to discover whether reliance on more income elastic taxes will have been associated with higher growth of local expenditure. Such an inquiry is possible in the USA because local authorities vary greatly in the tax sources upon which they rely.

So he related percentage reliance on income taxes with growth of expenditure within the context of a multiple regression analysis. Looking at the expenditure of state governments between 1960 and 1970, he found a relation such that a state government which generated 35 per cent of its revenues through individual income taxes would, other things being equal, have experienced an expansion in expenditure per head of roughly $35 per head more than a state which collected no revenue from income tax. He found very similar results when he analysed the growth of city expenditures. Thus he concluded that whatever the reason for it, the reliance on local income taxes would appear to be associated with higher rates of growth of local expenditure.

It follows from our arguments that this is a bad, because undemocratic, reason for introducing LIT or multiplying the number of taxes.

As we saw at the beginning of the chapter, the Layfield Committee lay great importance on the principle 'that local authorities should be accountable to their electorate for their decisions on revenue to be raised and expenditure to be incurred' (Layfield, 1976, p. 184). They therefore conclude that 'the level and most importantly the change in the level, of any local source of revenue, should be set locally, be related clearly to local expenditure, and the effective burden should not be borne substantially by people outside the area concerned' (ibid., p. 184).

One of the problems with both Layfield's discussion of accountability and that contained in the 1971 Green Paper is that they look at local taxation as though it operated in a vacuum, rather than as being part of a fiscal structure with certain goals besides that of raising revenue. If the only function of the combined grant and local tax systems were to finance local expenditures determined locally the various criteria for alternative sources of revenue used by Layfield would be acceptable. However, as we have seen, the functions of the combined grant and local tax system is to achieve some semblance of equity and to eliminate some inefficiencies in a government structure in which local expenditures are not purely locally determined. Government constraints work not just on the revenue side but also on the expenditure side. As Layfield argues, 'the 1960s saw a growing national political concern with the objectives and extent of education, health, welfare, housing and transport services' (1976, p. 65). As we saw in Part One, Chapter 7, such concern was also shown in the nineteenth century and many activities were imposed on local authorities. The extent of the expenditure so imposed is extremely large. When discussing the possibility of defining minimum standards for which the central government would accept explicit responsibility, Layfield believes 'that any defined minimum standards would be likely to account for . . . over two thirds of rate fund expenditures (ibid., p. 73).

One of the reasons for the extent of central government financing of local expenditures in exactly the large proportion of these which are somehow centrally imposed. This is also one of the reasons for needs and resources grants, the former to compensate for differences in needs, the latter to compensate for differences in resources among local authorities. To achieve these goals, especially for what we have called standard expenditures, the grant system would have to be such as to equalise tax rates across authorities. Thus the actual tax rates set by local authorities are determined by a whole set of factors outside the control of local authorities. Changes in the amount of finance provided by the central government do not by themselves change the expenditure imposed by the central government nor the aim of the grant system to equalise rate poundages across authorities. These aims are independent of the proportion of local expenditures financed from a local tax source.

To bring this point out and its implication for local accountability, consider a unitary grant system based on standard expenditures. Such a system would equalise tax rates across local authorities (on whatever is the tax base used by the authorities). We shall for the moment assume a single tax base in the authorities. With such a grant system the government chooses the amount of grants it is willing to give to local authorities and simultaneously it therefore chooses the standard tax rate which is

$$r_s = \frac{E^s - G}{B_L}$$

where r_s is the standard tax rate, E^s is the total of standard expenditures of all authorities, G is the total amount of grants to be given by the government, and B_L is the total local authority tax base.

To equalise rate poundages across authorities each authority would receive a grant such that

$$g_j = E_j^s - (E^s - G)\frac{B_j}{B_L}$$

where g_j is the grant received by authority j, E^s its standard expenditure, and B_j its tax base.

With this grant each authority would finance its standard expenditures at the standard rate poundage, r_s. Thus even if at one level the authority can choose to set its tax rate at whatever level it decides, in the sense that there is no legal constraint on it, if it spends its standard expenditure it will set its tax at the standard rate. This result holds even if G is zero, that is that the government does not give any grants to local authorities. The grant system would still operate but it would be self-financing. Some authorities would receive grants, others would be paying for these transfers. There may still be a question of accountability and perceptibility. But the parties involved are not just the local electorate *vis-à-vis* the elected.

Assume that the grants given by the government to local authorities are raised by some tax (r_c) on some tax base (B_c), this may be an income tax or a corporate profit tax or, of course, different taxes on different bases. We thus have

$$G = r_c B_c$$

Thus there is a unique relationship between the standard tax rate on the base used by local authorities and the tax rate levied by the central government to finance its grants to local authorities. This relationship is

$$r_s = \frac{E^s - r_c B_c}{B_L}$$

By varying the tax rate on its tax base the government will vary the amount of grants going to local authorities and thus the standard tax rate on the local authority tax base. The two groups involved in this trade-off are those who possess the tax base B_L and those who possess the tax base B_c, and, of course, those whose interactions determine the total level of standard expenditures E^s. These interactions and trade-offs are much more complicated than those between just the local electorate and its local representatives. The aim of equalisation in the grant system cuts off the direct links between the standard expenditures of a local authority and its tax rate. The only link is that between the total of standard expenditures and the standard tax rate.

The problem of accountability is still present but is much more subtle. The question now becomes whether it is useful to have different tax sources for different kinds of expenditures. This issue arose historically with local government expenditures because these have always been linked very closely with one particular tax base, while, say, defence expenditures or currently expenditures on the health service, are not linked to a particular tax base. It may well be argued that a close link between particular tax rates and specific expenditures would give the voter better information about the consequences of his decisions. He would be better able to associate a change in a particular tax rate with a decision about specific expenditures. This applies to local authority expenditures and possibly to subcategories of local authority expenditures as much as to any other expenditures. Thus the argument may be that if a large proportion of local expenditure is financed through grants, namely through taxes which are not associated directly with the purchase of the services provided by local authorities, individuals will demand more of such services, because they do not see their full costs. The demand for these services may either show up as a demand on the individual local authority or a demand via the central government on the local authority. For example, it may be a demand on the central government to impose some new obligations on the local authorities.

On this concept of accountability one may want to have a tax base reserved for local authority expenditures to provide the information to voters about the cost of these services. Consider the example shown by the relationship shown in the equation above, in which the government was giving a grant to local authorities by having a tax rate r_c on its own base B_c. Assume that now the government assigns the tax base to local authorities. The assignment of this tax base does not, however, imply that the government has given up its other aim of the fiscal system, namely to equalise tax rates across local authorities and to make transfers between authorities so as to allow each authority to provide its services at these tax rates. Assume that the government picks the same tax rate it previously had so that r_c and r_s are the tax rates on the two tax bases B_L and B_c which are now both tax bases for local authorities. Therefore for each local authority j it will be true that

$$r_s B_L^j + r_c B_c^j = E_j + g$$

where g is the transfer, negative or positive, which allows all local authorities to finance their standard expenditures at the two standard tax rates r_s and r_c. Now it may be argued that the transfer of the tax base B_c to local authorities has led to the financing of all their expenditures via their own taxes in the aggregate.

For each local authority its expenditures are financed by taxes levied both on its own taxpayers and on others, if it receives a positive grant. If it receives a negative grant its taxes are higher than required to finance its own expenditures. Nothing has really changed. Every taxpayer is paying the same taxes as before and receiving the same services as before. However, if they all know that the tax base B_c has been reserved for local authority use they now all have information about the cost to them of local expenditures. Previously when B_c was a central tax base they did not know that these taxes went to finance local expenditures. They may have thought they financed, say, defence. Now they realise that this is not so and may react differently.

We have so far discussed accountability and perceptibility in terms of that large part of local expenditures which are standard expenditures. Of course, for the expenditures which are purely locally determined we would want to have accountability of the elected to the electors and perceptibility by the electors of the costs of local goods. The possibility of achieving this is as much dependent on a reasonably well-defined differentiation between standard and non-standard expenditures as it is on finding a perceptible local tax source.

As the transfer of an existing tax source to local authorities has been considered as an alternative source of revenue either to replace grants or rates we shall now consider this alternative. Such an alternative was tried in 1887, has not been much favoured since then but has recently had some advocates (Evidence to Layfield by the Association of District Councils, 1976, app. 2, pp. 221–2).

THE ASSIGNED REVENUE SYSTEM

In comparing the assigned revenue system with the present system we do not have to consider the equity and efficiency aspects of the taxes involved. These taxes are by assumption already being levied and their equity and efficiency properties will not be affected by their transfer from the central government to local governments.

Consider now an assigned revenue system which is to be used as a substitute for grants to be distributed on the basis of place of collection rather than by some formula system. An argument which may be made for such a system is that the distribution of such a tax will be more efficient in achieving the purpose of the grant system than the distribution of the grant via some existing formula. Consider the following example. Assume that expenditures on roads required by local authorities are closely related to the number of cars using the roads. Cars using roads belong both to residents of the local authority and to residents of other local authorities passing through the local authority. Car users pay a petrol tax to the central government and this is related to the amount of use they make of roads. One could argue on the benefit principle of taxation that such users should pay the tax because it is related to the extra cost they impose, namely the expenditures on road maintenance arising from their use of roads. However, road maintenance is carried out by local authorities. They do get a grant from central government, but it may be considered that such a grant is not sufficiently geared to the amount of expenditures they have to undertake;

that the formula used to distribute the grant does not sufficiently reflect the need of local authorities for such expenditures. An alternative would be to assign the petrol tax or some proportion of the petrol tax to local authorities. For example, to divide up the total petrol tax into some proportion reflecting the proportion of road expenditures financed by the central government and that undertaken by local authorities.

Ideally such assigned revenues justified on the above basis should be distributed to local authorities on the basis of the number of miles travelled by cars using the roads within the authority. Of course, the same end could be achieved if a grant formula included such a variable. An assigned revenue system could also be used to replace or supplement rates. The distinction is not, however, that great in a system in which the aim of the fiscal system is to equalise taxes and to enable authorities to finance their standard expenditures with the same tax burden. As we saw above in our discussion of accountability, such a system would result in various transfers among different taxpayers but would be the same as the grant system. It is the equalising goal of the fiscal system which determines who pays for the local expenditures and what the burdens will be on the various taxpayers, not the details of which level of government collects which taxes, and exactly how and by whom these revenues are collected. From the point of view of the tax burdens, the assigned revenue system has no advantage over the grant system. As far as accountability is concerned, an assigned revenue system may have advantages over the grant system in as far as taxpayers are informed about the cost to them of the services provided by local authorities because they can relate a particular tax to these expenditures.

Layfield rejects the assigned revenue system on the grounds that 'It would not make apparent the link between local expenditure decisions and the consequent need for revenue. Such revenue would not provide any direct relationship between each local authority and its electors' (1976, p. 185). As far as the latter point is concerned Layfield is, of course, right, assigned revenues do not relate individual local expenditures with their revenue. However, as far as the former point is concerned, it is not right. Assigned revenues do provide a link between local authority expenditures in the aggregate and the consequent need to finance them. Such a link may be more important in a government system in which such a large proportion of local expenditures is not locally determined, but imposed via the central government.

One of the characteristics of an assigned revenue system is that the tax rate is set by the central government and is therefore the same across all authorities. Some of the other alternative sources of local revenue that have been considered do allow for the possibility of different tax rates across authorities. We shall, therefore, consider this issue.

DIFFERENCES IN TAX RATES

One of the issues arising in the discussions of alternative revenue sources is that of the effects of differences in tax rates across authorities. Before facing this problem, it will be useful to see what degree of freedom is available to local authorities to differentiate their tax rates. If we assume that a resource element will still exist in the grant system the aim will be to equalise the tax rates across authorities. The aim of the grant system, as we saw, was twofold. First, it was to allow all authorities to finance standard expenditures at the same tax burden. Second, we argued that given the unitary nature of the whole concept of standard expenditures, there were arguments from both efficiency and equity considerations for equalising tax rates across authorities. These two are, however, independent goals of the grant system. With more than one tax base for authorities there is a problem. One could equalise the total tax burden necessary to finance standard expenditures without at the same time equalising tax rates across authorities. Or one could also require authorities to levy the same tax rate on each base.

With more than one tax base in an authority, the very question of how much it is necessary to transfer to an authority to allow it to finance its standard expenditures at some particular tax burden depends on the authority's choice of taxes, how much it will levy on each of the tax bases it has. Similarly, the government itself has to choose among different tax rates to decide what transfers to make. Given the total amount of grant the government wants to transfer to local authorities (this may be zero) the government is constrained in its choice of tax rates on the various tax bases. If, still assuming a unitary grant system, the government sets a standard tax rate r_1 on tax base B_1 (say rateable value), and a standard tax rate r_2 on tax base B_2 (say, LIT), its grant payment is given by $G = E^s - r_1 B_1 - r_2 B_2$. From this it follows that

$$r_1 = \frac{(E - G) - r_2 B_2}{B_1}$$

The government can choose any combination of r_1 and r_2 which satisfies the above condition.

The trade-off between r_1 and r_2 available to the government can be shown in Figures 4.3.1 and 4.3.2 below, by the solid lines. Assume that the government chooses some combination $\bar{r}_1$ and $\bar{r}_2$ as the standard rates on which it pays grants to local authorities. Assume that on the basis of this decision, local authorities A and B receive grants of an amount G_a and G_b respectively. Given these grants, they can finance their standard expenditures with some combination of tax rates on the two tax bases. For the individual authority j the combination of tax rates with which it can finance its standard expenditure is shown by

$$r_1^j B_1^j + r_2^j B_2^j = E_j^s - G_j$$

The trade-off for our two authorities is shown if Figures 4.3.1 and 4.3.2 by the dashed lines. The slope of these lines depends on the relative quantities of the two tax bases in the authorities. If the ratio of the two bases for an authority is the same as the ratio of these tax bases in the country, the slope of the authority's line is the same as that of the government's. In our example we have shown two authorities whose tax bases are different from those of the country as a whole. In Figure 4.3.1(a) we have authority A which has a larger proportion of tax base 1 (B_1) relative to tax base 2 (B_2) than the national average. In Figure 4.3.1(b) we show an authority which has a higher proportion of B_2 relative to B_1 than the national average. With both authorities their constraint lines must

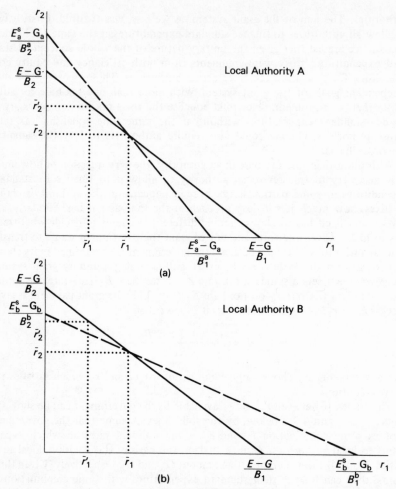

Figure 4.3.1   *Differences in relative tax bases*

pass through the points $\bar{r}_1$ and $\bar{r}_2$, the choice of standard tax rates made by the government. The reason for this is, of course, that the government has given grants to the authorities on the bases of these tax rates to enable them to finance their standard expenditures at these standard tax rates. Even though they can do so, they can also finance their standard expenditures with various other combinations of tax rates, all the combinations shown by the dashed lines.

Two points are brought out in Figures 4.3.1(a) and 4.3.1(b). The first is that the choice by the government of the two standard tax rates affects the amount of grant received by different authorities. In our example if the government had chosen the tax rates $\bar{r}_1'$ and $\bar{r}_2'$ instead of $\bar{r}_1$ and $\bar{r}_2$, authority A would get a lower grant and authority B would get a higher grant. Their constraints would be shown by lines passing through the new tax-rate combinations. The reason for this is clear. Authority A has a higher ratio of tax base B_1 relative to B_2 than the national average. Therefore an increase in r_2 relative to r_1 such that in aggregate the total quantity of relevant expenditures less grants can be financed (i.e. along the solid line) would allow it to finance more than its standard expenditures if its grant remained the same. The opposite is true for authority B. The choice of standard tax rates even for the same amount of grants the government is willing to provide can affect the allocation of the grants to local authorities.

The second point shown by Figures 4.3.1(a) and 4.3.1(b) is that even though the grants given to the authorities are such that they are able to finance their standard expenditures at the standard tax rates, they have the possibilities to finance their expenditures at different combinations of tax rates; the combinations shown by the dashed lines. If the purpose of the grants system were just to enable authorities to finance equal services at equal tax rates, then it would be sufficient to provide the grants determined by the government's choice of standard tax rates, and allow each authority to choose the tax rates it desired. Tax rates across local authorities would then vary, but the variation would be due to the authorities' decisions about relative tax burdens on different groups, not because they had to levy different tax rates to finance their standard expenditures.

We have argued that there are both equity and efficiency considerations for equalising tax rates to finance standard expenditures. With only one tax base, this can be achieved by providing the authority with a grant sufficient to do that, with more than one tax source that is not enough. To achieve the same tax rates the authorities would have to be constrained to levy the tax rates chosen by the government to finance their standard expenditures. This raises some major difficulties.

If all authorities only had standard expenditures it would be a simple matter to constrain them to the standard tax rates decided on by the government. However, if authorities make non-standard expenditures, their tax rates will not be equal to the standard tax rates anyhow. We then have a problem of whether to constrain them to a particular combination of tax rates with an accompanying grant system such that every authority which changes its expenditures by some amount should be able to finance this by applying the imposed combination of tax rates. Or we could allow the authority to choose within some range the combination of tax rates to finance the non-standard expenditures.

Consider Figure 4.3.2 below. For some authority A the solid line shows the combinations of tax rates it could use to finance its standard expenditures given the grant it receives on the basis of the government's choice of standard tax rates $\bar{r}_1$ and $\bar{r}_2$. If we constrain the authorities to charge the standard tax rates the authority will be at a point O. Assume now that the authority spent more or less than its standard expenditures. The first possibility is shown by the dashed line lying above the solid line, the second by the dashed line lying below the solid line. The line from the origin marked R shows all the combinations of tax rates such that

$$r_1^j B_1^j + r_2^j B_2^j = E_j^s - G_j$$

One could devise a grant system such that for equal expenditures above standard all authorities should be able to finance the increase in expenditures while

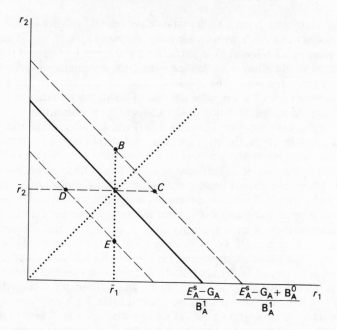

Figure 4.3.2　*Rate poundages in a two-tax system*

keeping the ratio of the standard tax rates the same. They could finance the increase in expenditures with the same increase in the standard tax rates. However, it would again not be sufficient to provide such a grant; one would also have to constrain the authorities to charge the same tax rates. This is similar to what happens with the current grant system where the grant is such that equal tax rates are levied for equal expenditures above standard. Alternatively, one could argue that for non-standard expenditures no grants should be given and constrain the authorities to charge a tax rate between the points marked B and C for those spending more than standard, and between the points marked D and E for those spending less than standard. Thus all deviations from the standard tax rates would be associated with deviations of expenditures from standard expenditures.

The various arguments for one or other of these solutions are similar to those discussed previously with respect to the function of grants. On the one hand, one could argue that non-standard expenditures are purely locally decided on and, therefore, that they should not be grant-aided. On this argument, the tax rates charged to finance these expenditures should be left to the local authority. Of course, its choice of tax rates has distributive consequences in that some groups will pay higher taxes than others to acquire the non-standard expenditures. Such redistributions will have consequences on locational choices, which we may consider as being inefficient or inequitable. However, to avoid these problems one does have to constrain local decisions. Such constraints, through grant transfers, and in the case of more than one tax base through impositions of tax rates, do reduce the autonomy of local governments and their accountability to their electorates. The inefficiencies and inequities may be the price that has to be paid for an autonomous and accountable local government system.

CONCLUSIONS

Most of the prolific argument for multiplying the number of local taxes has been based on a wish to increase the buoyancy of local sources of revenue. But on analysis this argument turns out to be one of very doubtful political morality. It amounts to encouraging local authorities to deceive their electorate by making it more difficult for them to appreciate the costs to them of the local services provided. Moreover, multiplication of local taxes makes it virtually impossible to sustain two current objectives of the British system: horizontal efficiency and equity. Each seems to us a sufficient reason against multiplying local taxes in a unified system of local finance.

Inevitably this conclusion weakens the case for introducing local income tax, because it would have to be in replacement of, rather than as a supplement to, rates. No other tax seems worth considering in this role either on efficiency or equity grounds, but a powerful case for a local income tax instead of rates can be made out, and has been touched on at various points in this book. We have seen historically how rates were once intended as the most feasible approximation to an income tax and indeed were generally developed on ability-to-pay principles. We have also seen in this century that rates have been modified in a number of ways to approximate more to the equity characteristics of an income tax, particularly through the introduction of rate rebates. Yet some of the most frequent criticisms of rates still made have their origin in some of the remaining differences between rates and a local income tax. Against this we have argued that what really matters are the equity characteristics of the whole tax structure. If we were to pursue the implied logic of the wish to substitute local income tax for rates, one might question why at the national level there is not exclusive reliance on direct taxation (except in so far as it is explicit policy to affect the consumption of particular commodities). It does not seem to us worthwhile recommending the replacement of rates by local income tax, given the upheaval it would cause, though if we were designing a system of local government finance on a clear slate, we would argue for it. Yet in spite of the irrelevance of some and the slenderness of other arguments for a local income tax, we would not be surprised if eventually it were introduced after national income tax had been reconstructed on a self-assessment basis, so insistent in the public mind is the model of it as an equitable tax.

The conclusion reached against multiplying taxes leaves us with the problem which led the Layfield Committee to argue for a local income tax in addition to rates: their belief that local dependence on central grant should be reduced. To this we return in Part Four, Chapter 5.

NOTES

1 'It seems highly questionable whether the great majority of electors could be made so aware of the LIT element in their normal PAYE deductions as to achieve the Committee's objective of securing an effective local discipline on local authority expenditure decisions' (DoE, 1977*b* Cmnd 6813, para. 6.11).

2 There is one possible, but unimportant, exception. The highest tax rate on investment income has been 98 per cent. If local authorities had then been given income tax, at an average rate of 4 per cent, central government income tax would be cut by 4 per cent giving a top rate of 94 per cent. Some authorities might levy a local income tax at an above-average rate, say 7 per cent. Taxpayers liable to the top rate in such authorities would then pay a combined tax rate of $94 + 7 = 101$ per cent. If tax rates in excess of 100 per cent are unacceptable, central government might have to reduce its top rate to, say 91 per cent, making the top rate in an average tax rate local authority 95 per cent instead of 98 per cent. If this consequence were thought undesirable, then administrative measures would be feasible given the small number of taxpayers involved (for example, a *pro rata* grading down of central and local tax liabilities to a ceiling marginal rate of 93 per cent).

3 We are not here concerned with tax differentials between localities. The effects of such differentials depend on the type of tax, and are discussed in that context.

4 Strictly, this argument depends on income distribution being skewed such that the median lies below the average. Empirically, this seems generally to be the case.

4 The Use of Charges

The case for charging for local government services rather than financing them through the rating system is the same as the general case for economic pricing. Charging a price that measures the costs of providing a service means that the consumer takes into account the resource costs of the alternatives open to him when he decides what to consume.

Economists argue that the relevant costs are marginal costs. An optimal pricing system is one in which all prices equal marginal costs. In practice, pricing systems which depart somewhat from marginal cost pricing (for example, average cost pricing, full cost pricing, and so on) are nevertheless in most actual circumstances likely to lead to a more efficient allocation of resources than providing goods and services free or heavily subsidised through the tax system.[1]

Pricing serves another extremely important but often forgotten function. It provides a method by which consumers can reveal their preferences among various services. Prices transmit information to producers where resources should be allocated if they are to be allocated in accordance with consumer preferences. Without such information, some other system of revealing preferences must be established or the services would be allocated according to the preferences of some other group, or according to the decision of some other group about 'true' preferences of consumers.

Consider the present situation in which charges for most of the services provided by local government are zero. The services are provided 'free' to consumers and the demand for them at zero price will be at that quantity at which their marginal utility is zero. Of course, goods are seldom provided in such abundance. Resources are, after all, scarce and therefore they must be rationed and allocated among the various services. How should it be decided whether, for example, more resources should be put into meals-on-wheels or into old age homes? At zero price there is an excess demand for both. If we want to take account of consumer preferences among these services we might possibly use queueing as a measure of the relative demand for the services. If the waiting list is longer for one of them we might decide that the relative demand for that service is greater than for the other, and reallocate resources from the one for which the queue is shorter. Would that be a correct decision? That a queue for one service offered at zero cost is greater than the queue for another offered at zero cost only tells us that at these relative prices there is a greater excess demand for one of them. It tells us nothing about the relative demands for the services if the knowledge of the true alternative costs were taken into account. A queue represents a voting system by the actual consumers of services. The problem is that the alternatives being foregone when something is being chosen are not known to the voters unless the relative resource costs of the alternatives are given to them. In our example, they have to know how many meals-on-wheels are given up for an extra place in an old age home. Moreover, there has to be an incentive for them to act on such knowledge. Inevitably when services are provided at a zero price the decisions about how much to provide are made by the producer groups who may decide on the basis of their conception of the true preferences of the consumer groups. But the latter seldom have much say in the decision.

A pricing system allows and forces the consumer group to choose among the alternatives, and the closer the pricing system approaches marginal cost pricing, the closer the choice is made on the basis of the correct information about the real alternatives available. Now consumers can determine which of the services they prefer and, moreover, can transmit the information to suppliers. This limits the suppliers' control over the quantities of services provided and leaves much of that in the hands of consumers. Of course, this also reduces the power of the suppliers to determine what will be supplied. Now they would be in the same position as suppliers of market services. They would have to use advertising or exhortations to convince consumers that the service they are providing is important.

While local authorities do charge for a variety of services — housing, public transport, school meals, home helps, and so on — almost all these services are subsidised, often heavily so. Even so, rate-borne services are a far more substantial proportion of local expenditure than are services for which a charge is made. In 1973/4 English and Welsh local authorities raised about 15 per cent of their current expenditure in fees and charges of which about half came from housing rents (Layfield, 1976, p. 133). Why is economic pricing not adopted more widely in the provision of local services? One argument for financing services completely or partially through the tax system is that it is technically or economically inefficient to price in certain cases. It is not efficient to charge economic prices if either one or both of two conditions obtain. We discussed these in Part One, Chapter 3 (and Appendix 1.3.A1). The first was non-excludability, which we defined as a situation in which the costs of using the price mechanism were expected to exceed the benefits from doing so; that is, the return from pricing was negative. The second was non-rivalness. At the limit, non-rivalness implies that the marginal cost of providing a service to additional consumers is zero. Costs do not increase as the number of consumers increases.[2]

The theoretical economic literature on local government finance and indeed on public finance generally tends to be written as if governments exist solely to provide public goods (i.e. displaying non-rivalness and non-excludability) and usually pure ones at that. This is ironical. It would hold up the argument to go into detail now, but later in this chapter we shall show that a comparatively small proportion of local expenditures — the same could be said of central government goods and services — is on public goods so defined. Externalities are far commoner than public goods; but the failure to charge for most local goods and services — again the same could be said of central goods and services — cannot usually be attributed either to public-goods characteristics or externalities. The existence of the latter, after all, only implies that some benefits or costs escape the pricing mechanism. What matters, therefore, is the likely magnitude of these in relation to the costs of providing the services.

Rather the reason for the failure to charge economic prices is redistributive or paternalistic. Yet this is not always explicit. Often it would seem circumstances have drifted into services becoming rate-borne. As we saw in Part One, Chapter 6 all rates were gradually assimilated to the ability-to-pay model of the poor rate, often for what was presented as administrative convenience. Beneficial rating was a form of charging. As it died out the implicit motive for providing rate-borne services became redistributive, though it was not always a conscious development.

Even though the initial assimilation of rates may have been more for reasons of administrative convenience that from a conscious desire to redistribute, subsequent governments have come to engage more in redistribution. Thus society has tended to accept that many services should be provided at less than cost to some ratepayers and, in effect, at more than cost to others.

As many local (and central) goods and services are provided at zero cost because of explicit redistributive considerations, it is useful to examine briefly why goods and services should be used for the purpose of redistribution. Such a consideration will at least clarify the issues in an area where there is much emotive thinking. Many of the services provided by local authorities were initially so provided explicitly for the poor sections of the population. The Poor Laws were so named correctly. They were explicitly redistributive in nature and were introduced in a period when there was no central machinery for redistribution. Similarly, education was initially provided free of charge to the poor. Today the services provided by local authorities are consumed by all or most income groups. Education, housing, social services for the elderly and the ill are used by most income groups. The arguments for the provision of these services are usually in terms of 'needs' and 'rights' and when pressed they are still basically redistributive arguments. But the basis of the redistribution and even the amount of redistribution and its direction are no longer clear. Many of the services now provided are not means-tested and as the client groups become larger and larger the income groups represented by the consumers become more varied. Similarly, the payments made for these services indirectly via rates and the taxes that finance the grant system all have to be taken account of when considering the actual amount and even the direction of the redistribution that occurs. There has also been much more redistribution in the direct form of cash payments and through the tax system. The question that must be asked especially when the range of goods being provided by the government, both central and local, increases is why should redistribution be in the form of goods rather than in the form of income? If the income distribution were perfect (here every reader can decide what he believes that to be) should the government still provide some goods and services without charging for them and financing them through the tax system? Given the assumption of an existing 'correct' distribution of income, some other reason must be given for such additional distribution in kind. If poverty is the main reason for distribution, there is very little reason for redistribution in kind and therefore little reason for the government to provide services directly except for those that have public-goods characteristics. Yet both in Britain and in other parts of the world, both central and local governments do provide a wide range of goods whose public-goods characteristics are, to say the least, not at all obvious.

Many of the goods provided by governments, though by no means all, are related to some particular characteristics of the individual; for example, being blind, having diabetes or being old and disabled. It may be believed by society that with such characteristics an individual with the same income as another would still be poorer. Because with these characteristics an individual must or will want to spend part of his income in ways that others do not; for example, to purchase a seeing-eye dog, insulin or home help. Such reasons for additional redistribution do not, however, imply that the redistribution should be made in kind. One solution is to give the individual additional income just sufficient to allow him to purchase what is necessary to alleviate the particular characteristics, with enough left over for his income to be the same as that of another. By redistributing income in this way, he will have the opportunity to acquire some specific goods and services and still be as well off as others who do not have these characteristics. With this approach, the amount to be redistributed takes account not only of income but also other 'relevant' characteristics. This is, of course, done already when the number of children, age, and so are taken account of in the amount of tax paid by individuals.

What if the individual in question decides to use his income to purchase commodities which are of no use to alleviate the specific characteristic which was taken account of when he received the extra income? For example, the partly disabled pensioner decides to use his extra income to buy a colour television set or drown his problems in champagne rather than get a home help? In so far as he makes this choice he is better off given his preferences and his well-being as he sees it. If the purpose of the initial additional redistribution was to make him, given his particular characteristics, as well off as another without such characteristics his choice should be allowed. If our concern is only with the well-being of the individual, as he sees it, there is no reason for his choices to be over-ruled.

Two views, not usually well articulated, are put forward against allowing the scope of choice implicit in the above argument. The first is paternalistic. It assumes that the giver knows best what is in the interests of the receiver. People can be induced to consume certain goods by forcing them to pay for them through the tax system, and then offering the goods 'free'. In this case, unless the goods have a negative marginal utility, people will be willing to acquire them. If in the consumers' view the goods do have a negative marginal utility one can, of course, go even further and pass a law forcing the consumption of the good. Compulsory education or compulsory treatment under the Mental Health Act are two examples. Thus it is argued that drug-treatment units or centres for treating alcoholics should be provided 'free', otherwise nobody would be willing to use them even if income were distributed perfectly.

There is another argument for redistribution in kind. This is based on the idea that the function of redistribution is not in terms of the utility of the recipient but that of the donor. There are certain characteristics which we do not like to see in our society. Our moral or aesthetic sense is offended by certain states of our fellow men. If what offends us is poverty we can redistribute income. If what offends us are certain characteristics of individuals, for example illness or slum dwelling, we want to eliminate these. If we distribute income and this is not used by the recipient to eliminate the characteristic that offends us, the individual who receives the income may be better off but the main purpose of the redistribution is negated. The knowledge that by spending his income in a way which he finds most desirable makes him better off is not sufficient to allow such expenditure. The redistribution was not made to make him better off in general, but to make him better off in a particular way which also satisfies the initial motive for the redistribution. In this case, as in the paternalistic case, the redistribution is made in kind.

These arguments for redistribution in kind do not necessarily imply that the government must actually provide goods and services. All that must be assured is that if income is redistributed, it has to be used for specified purposes.

The above considerations apply in general to the question of whether redistribution should be in the form of income or in the form of goods. There is a further question as to whether redistribution, in whatever form, should be undertaken by local government at all, or whether it should be left to the central government. We have previously argued against the suitability of using local government finance as an instrument of central government redistribution policy. The dilemma analysed was that central government has a choice. Either it accepted the Tiebout-style inefficiency that resulted from local authorities engaging in redistribution, or it had to impose controls eroding local freedom to secure some uniformity in overall redistributive policy. Moreover, adding redistribution through local government finance to that through the tax system does make it extremely difficult to estimate the net effect on the distribution of income of central and local redistributive policy taken together.

THE INTRODUCTION OF CHARGING WITHOUT COMPENSATION

The argument for reconsidering the policy on charging for local goods and services where it is feasible is, therefore, the standard efficiency one for economic pricing, but one must also take into account the redistributive impact of any such changes. Economists nowadays are careful to qualify advocacy of efficient, that is marginal cost, pricing by admitting that it is a valid ethical or political position to prefer a non-efficient price if it leads to a preferred income distribution, providing one allows for all the consequences of such a position and provided there is no more efficient method of distribution. If it were decided to charge for many services now heavily subsidised through the rate system, the immediate effect would be a substantial, though not easily predictable, change in the distribution of income.

As always when considering redistributional effects the reformer must recognise that any significant change will alter the expectations of those adversely affected and be a basis for claiming compensation. This issue is distinct from any opinion one may hold on the desirability of the effect that departure from marginal cost pricing has on the distribution on income. It is logically possible to disapprove of that, while admitting the case for compensation on the grounds of the disappointment of legitimate expectations.

To charge a price covering the full cost of a local service implies eliminating grant. It also logically implies eliminating the cross-subsidisation which keeps down the 'rate price' for some, in relation to the costs of the services provided for them.

In that case, the net distributive effect would be the product of two forces. Both ratepayers who consume more in relation to their rateable values and those ratepayers whose rateable values were relatively low would pay more, and vice versa. The net effect would certainly be a redistribution away from the poor and to the rich. The poor who now benefit from rate rebates would be especially badly affected.

Quite a number of arguments in favour of introducing charges are crudely redistributive. They come from people who in general feel that redistribution has gone too far in favour of the poor. This has tended to associate charging with anti-redistributive political views.

While the introduction of charging would be used to such an end, it is not a necessary implication. As we have said before, what really matters to an individual is his net position − his pre-tax income modified by the taxes he pays and the value he places on the government services from which he benefits. The redistributive impact of introducing charging could be mitigated by appropriate taxes, though never exactly. For simplicity, in analysis we shall argue as if government's interests in introducing charging were, so far as possible, to introduce at the same time offsetting changes to preserve the *status quo ante* income distribution.

We shall consider various changes in machinery which could be used to try to preserve the *status quo ante* income distribution while replacing rates by charges for those local services where this is feasible. The introduction of charging would be intended to have the beneficial effects on efficiency claimed at the start of this chapter. Demand for local services which are now provided far below cost would decline more than that for services that were comparatively less subsidised. A redistribution of income so constructed that it neutralised the introduction of efficient pricing preserving the existing pattern of consumption of local services would be pointless since it would achieve nothing. Neither would it be practical. Rather the purpose of compensating redistribution must be to leave individuals as near as possible in a situation where their incomes are adjusted so that their purchasing power is no less given the new and higher prices being charged for local services and the reduction in rates levied.[3] The individual faced by new prices is then able to readjust his purchases so as to get what he believes to be the best value for his money.

In what follows, we shall consider three mechanisms of compensation. The first is via the general tax system. The ratepayer faced by charges where previously he paid rates will nevertheless find that, left at that, he is better or worse off from the change. In general, the richer he is − paying higher rates − the better off he will be; and the poorer, the worse off. Other taxes are to be adjusted to make him as far as possible neither better nor worse off from the change. (Of course, as we have said, a government may wish to change the distribution of income at the same time as it introduces charging; but we shall not discuss that possibility here.) An economist would defend such an income adjustment as giving the maximum freedom to the consumer. He can spend it as he pleases between the local goods now charged for and private goods. Because, by assumption, local goods prices have been raised to him and raised relative to private goods prices, there will be some tendency for the consumption of local goods to fall.

Such an adjustment via the tax system is the appropriate one if the motive for the redistribution is the poverty of the individuals to whom income is redistributed.

The second mechanism to be considered will be the 'voucher' system, whose leading characteristic can perhaps be best described as a new currency or income that the recipient can only spend, depending on its form, on local goods or services in general or on some goods and services in particular. Thus by comparison with the first mechanism, consumers' satisfaction will be reduced because their freedom to spend will be restricted; but as a direct consequence, there will be less reduction in demand for local services because the consumer will be unable to spend the 'income' on private goods (or in some cases on only a restricted set of private goods).

This mechanism is the appropriate one if the motive for redistribution is paternalisistic or egoistic. In this case, the redistribution is to be accompanied by the recipients' consumption of specific goods.

The third mechanism varies in another way. A grant system is introduced so that, in effect, the local authority is able not only to reduce charges on average so that a household or non-domestic hereditament's aggregate of bills for charges equals average rate payment, but also to adjust relative prices so as to provide some compensation for those — especially the poor — who were particularly hit by the introduction of charges, for example through rebates. The main feature of this solution is, of course, that compensation does not go to individuals who have some freedom on how to spend it, but to local authorities who decide (with or without central directive or advice) how it should affect the pattern of charges it makes. This last mechanism would be pointless unless there was some intention to move towards a pattern of charging which reflected relative costs better than the current rating system does.

Thus at the limit, the introduction of charging could be accompanied by the elimination or overall reduction of government grants; or by the elimination or reduction of grants to authorities and their replacement by grants to persons. We shall have to discuss many features of the voucher system in this chapter, but we shall need to return to these issues when we discuss the reform of the grant system.

COMPENSATION THROUGH TAX CHANGES

The redistributive impact of introducing charges could be mitigated by appropriate tax changes, as well as by reductions in rates. Exact compensation through the tax and rating systems is impossible. Heavy consumers of services are almost certain to lose and light consumers to gain. But it should be possible to achieve approximate compensation for each income group. Tax allowances for children, the elderly and the disabled could, for example, be increased where the introduction of charging particularly affected such groups.

Compensation by income group would be most difficult for the poor. Not only would they lose most from charging in relation to their incomes, but reduced rates would reduce the relief they could receive through rate rebates and, if they receive supplementary benefits, rate allowances. Since they also pay little or no direct tax, it would generally be impossible to compensate them by remission of such tax. It would be difficult to compensate the poor without introducing some new means of compensation. If the tax system is the mechanism, this would mean combining the introduction of charges with that of a negative income tax (NIT) whose basic principle is as set out in Figure 4.4.1.[4] Those with annual incomes above an arbitrary chosen level (X) pay tax at a rate indicated by the slope BE in relation to OC. If a family has an income less than this level, instead of being taxed it receives cash (NIT) to make up its income. If it is decided to make BX the minimum income, then the NIT will be the difference between OA' and Pre-Tax income (OB). However, such a fixed minimum gives no incentive to a family to earn more income since it is all claimed back in reduced negative taxation. Therefore, instead of an absolute minimum, a sloping floor (AB) is fixed which does give some incentive. The shallower the floor, the greater the disincentive to escape from poverty – the so-called 'poverty trap'. The steeper the slope of AB, either the lower the absolute minimum income, AO, with what that implies for the poverty of the very poor, or the higher and the further to the right the cross-over point, BX, which will greatly increase the cost of the system. In a simplified system in which all NIT is paid for by higher positive income tax on the less poor, the shallower BE must become in relation to BC.

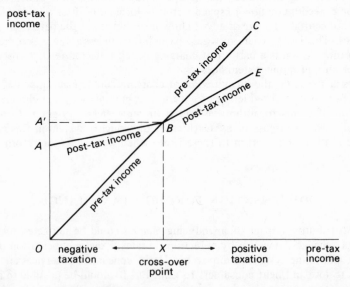

Figure 4.4.1 *Negative income tax*

In Britain there have been several attempts to introduce NIT or its near equivalent which have foundered on problems of administration. For example, many advocates of NIT have argued that it would be easier to avoid fraudulent claims by comparison with a welfare system which gives out a variety of payments in cash and kind according to circumstances. There is something to this. Especially in the USA where a variety of agencies provide overlapping welfare allowances, many apparently claim more than they are entitled to from different agencies. Even in Britain where the provision of welfare is less fragmented, the Supplementary Benefits Commission, the Department of Employment, and others involved employ elaborate and expensive checks to check fraudulent claims. If all other allowances were abolished and replaced by a single NIT, obtained from a single agency, one opportunity for fraud would be eliminated — claiming from more than one agency. But there would still be the problem of ascertaining the actual pecuniary circumstances of the individual or family. Even if self-assessment were generally introduced, the deterrent of punitive penalties if wrong declarations are made will be much less to the poor. Moreover, there is another difficulty often ignored. This is of a type familiar to students of RSG. NIT is a method of levelling up or altering — not, of course, equalising — 'resources'. But the question then arises: resources in relation to what? Families with children 'need' more than those without. Arguably single parents need more than families with two parents, the disabled more than the able, those who live in high-cost areas more than those who live in low-cost areas. How far a resources grant should be modified by 'needs' is as difficult and similar an exercise in political judgement for NIT as it is for RSG.

At present, local government finance itself contributes to the anomalies in the financial position of the poor in Britain, both on the tax and benefits side. Rate rebates have a different slope and cross-over point from many other social benefits. Not only does this have no obvious rationale, but it means that the financial position of the poor is affected by where they are and in what housing they have. Rateable values, as we have seen, are higher in the centre of large cities but this can be defended as a basis for rating on the grounds that where the fixing of wages and salaries is sufficiently free, this must be associated with corresponding differences in incomes for the same work. But the poor are peculiarly affected. First, though their rate call is higher where rateable values are higher, the poorest are likely to benefit by larger rate rebates tailored to reflect this. However, the cross-over point on rate rebates is likely to vary from place to place so that in practice the cross-over point will fall on people in different places at different income levels in a way which cannot be rationalised. As a consequence, the slopes of the rate rebate entitlement — the equivalent to AB in relation to DB on Figure 4.4.1 — will be as irrationally variegated.

On the benefits side, the variation in provision of various services is very great. The prices at which various social services are provided vary from zero upwards, even when these services are provided for the same group. To take a particularly vexed case, it is impossible to justify the prices attached to the various local authority and NHS forms of provision for the aged by reference to their different marginal costs. Shortage of facilities introduces an extra inequity, for example the well-being of poor old people can be greatly affected by whether relatively cheap public accommodation is available for them or if instead they have to pay much more for private accommodation not infrequently of lower standard because unsubsidised.

Similar anomalies affect the provision of housing for the poor. The subsidy received by a local authority tenant will vary depending on his authority's policy on pooling rents between its tenants, its policy on reflecting quality differences in rents, its policy on supervision and maintenance (which is outside the tenant's control), the subsidy regimes under which it built housing in the past, the effect changing interest rates and its funding policy has had on its average interest rates, as well as anomalies caused by quirks in central government policies on rent-fixing and the local authority's own policy on making rate fund contributions to its housing revenue account. The cost of housing, even more the actual cost of the dwelling inhabited by a tenant, has comparatively little to do with the rent paid. A poor person in an owner-occupied home with a mortgage comes under a different subsidy scheme with a quite different incidence. A poor person in private accommodation will get much less, even no subsidy at all. Even within the local authority sector, relative rents bear little relation to relative costs of provision.

These are only a sample of the problems that would arise if charges were introduced for local services and the tax system plus an NIT was used to compensate the losers. It would mean substantial changes in tax rates, threshold and allowances. Introducing an NIT would imply rationalising the structure of benefits for the poor, so that it became less incoherent than it is. One could argue that a positive benefit from introducing charging would be that if it were possible at the same time to introduce NIT, or at least a more rational system of social credits, both together would entail a very considerable enhancement of the tax structure.

The administrative difficulties that so far have been fatal to the introduction of NIT have been of two kinds. There is, first, the straightforward difficulty of expanding the size of the Inland Revenue staff to establish the incomes of all those now below the income-tax threshold, which self-assessment for the taxpayer should alleviate. While the numbers who do not pay income tax are far smaller than they used to be, the Inland Revenue have kept down their administrative labours by Pay-As-You-Earn – in effect by making employers the agents for collecting tax which is only thought possible if the great majority of direct taxpayers are taxed at a single standard rate. The Supplementary Benefits Commission exists to estimate the incomes of the very poor. But there is a host of intermediate poor who would have to have their incomes estimated if NIT were to be applied to all those not paying income tax. It means some expansion of the Inland Revenue or Supplementary Benefits Commission to cover these intermediate cases; and some merging or rationalisation of the operations of the two, so that persons who pass up or down the income scale could be dealt with consistently, especially when they pass the cross-over point. Frequency of job change, casual and unrecorded employment, the advantages of concealing, all, in any case, make the estimation of income complex for most who do not pay income tax. For all these reasons, the administrative costs of NIT would be high.

There is also a higher-order administrative or political problem. A whole

variety of administrative apparatus operating an inconsistent variety of rules
has developed to deal with different kinds of need of those in poverty. All manner of government services make provision for the poor by administrative devices
whose slopes and cross-over points vary in a baffling and confusing manner (in
the terms of Figure 4.4.1). A number of writers have tried to estimate the slope
and cross-over characteristics of the whole system and have found it apparently
irrational and variable — the variability increased by the different adjustments of
various apparatus to inflation. The higher administrative problem is simply that
the creation of a unified NIT implies grappling with all these inconsistencies and
trying to achieve a logic and order which would mean that the system as a whole
could be described in terms of a consistent slope and cross-over point. This problem has been avoided by most protagonists of NIT who have assumed that NIT
would be a relatively simple mirror image of income tax, with the comparatively
few allowances an income-tax system provides. But one of the characteristics of
poverty is that needs vary enormously, as do the costs of meeting those needs.
A single cash sum modified by spouse's, children's and other dependants' allowances is unlikely to be able to buy similar services for individuals or families
in very different physical and geographical circumstances. We do not need to go
more deeply into a complex problem. Most relevant to our argument is the
observation that the difficulty of establishing an NIT is likely to jeopardise any
attempt to compensate the poor through the tax system for the introduction of
charging, for both kinds of reason.

So far we have assumed that the purpose of departing fom economic pricing
is pure redistribution. Local government finance is being used to effect change in
income distribution, so that any tax change which put an individual in an equivalent cash position would be acceptable. But this ignores paternalistic motives.
Central government may wish to encourage greater consumption of local government services in general, or some services in particular, than individuals would
choose if they received an equivalent amount of cash.

VOUCHERS

A 'voucher' as used in this context is an ear-marked allowance or grant to persons entitling them to 'spend' some predesigned amount on a good or service.
How specific a voucher is made, depends on the reason for giving vouchers. A
voucher could be made redeemable by anyone for a specific amount of money.
Such a voucher would be identical to an income transfer. There may be administrative reasons for using vouchers rather than direct-income transfers. By comparison with introducing NIT in a PAYE system of taxation, vouchers appear
administratively simpler. Administrative simplicity is achieved because the apparatus that now deals with various income-related rebates could presumably deal
with vouchers. As always there is a cost. The rationalisation of benefits that NIT
is intended to achieve would not be attempted. There is no reason to suppose
any greater consistency between redistribution through local government finance
and other redistribution than exists currently. At the other end of the spectrum,
we could have a voucher which can only be redeemable for a specific service of a

specified quality. For example, an education voucher which must be used in exchange for services provided by an approved supplier. A voucher for the disabled might be used only for those services which are considered to alleviate the conditions for which the voucher was initially distributed. Such a limitation implies a degree of paternalism in so far as this 'income' or currency may be 'spent' by its recipients on certain designated purposes and not as freely as cash. Depending on how one regards the objects of paternalism — whatever these may be and they are usually far from clear — this is either a gain or a disadvantage.

In introducing 'vouchers' we are describing a possibility which has wider ramifications than merely for the subject-matter of this chapter. Those who advocate them see them more as substitutes for central grants, or even in some cases as a means of eliminating some local government activities and replacing them by private ones (Maynard, 1975). Because a 'voucher' is an ear-marked grant to an individual as distinct from a grant to an authority, central government could use them to eliminate or reduce grants to authorities and replace them by grants to persons. Citizens then have to pay charges or rates to cover all the cost not met by any grant that remained.

The most universal or general form of voucher in local government finance would cover all chargeable local services. Thus one might suppose a tri-partite change (neglecting any change in the central government grant proportion or form of grant):

(1) Charges would be introduced so that relative charges reflected relative resource costs.
(2) Rates would be eliminated in respect of those services.
(3) Vouchers would be issued to those who were particularly adversely affected by the change to restore their position as far as possible. In particular, the 'poor' might be issued with such vouchers. Again the principles for allocating vouchers would seem similar to those for RSG. Relative 'needs' must be established.

However, past discussion has been terms of vouchers confined to particular services. Separate vouchers could be issued for all the different services. Indeed, this does not fully describe the possibilities since one could if one so wished break services down into pieces and give separate vouchers for small subservices even to the same individuals.

Most has been heard of education vouchers and we shall use this to exemplify some of the issues involved.

To introduce such vouchers would require an administration able to hand out the right number (and value) of vouchers to the parents or guardians of those entitled which would seem no great problem. As paternalism it would mean the state requiring parents and guardians to spend this 'income' solely on education.[5] In education such paternalism can be bolstered by a special argument. It is that the state is standing in *loco parentis* to some extent. While most parents might be assumed eager to spend as much out of their income on the education of their children, there are weak, greedy, or sadistic parents, rich and poor, who would spend such money for their own purposes if they could. It is less easy to use this argument elsewhere where the recipient of the 'income' is also the direct beneficiary, but the argument that the interests of the recipient is not that of the beneficiary and, moreover, that the latter cannot be expected to know his own interests, has force for children, some mentally sick and handicapped, and possibly some elderly people who cannot look after their own affairs.

Most protagonists of education vouchers would like parents to be able to use vouchers at any school, private or state. At present the fact that fees have to be paid entirely out of their own pockets at private schools is a major deterrent to sending children to such schools. The protagonists of vouchers tend to assume that their introduction would go with eliminating all direct government grants so that all schools had to meet their expenditure from fees. But even if vouchers only replaced the rate contribution, this would alter the relative price of education in favour of private schools. Demand for them would be bound to expand. Clearly views on the merits of this will be divided politically.

Both vouchers and specific grants are of particular use when the national purpose is to ensure minimum standards, allowing either local authorities or individuals to pay for higher standards if they so wish. Thus in the provision of care for the elderly, a voucher system might enable the individual to purchase a certain quantum of services, divided between, say, meals-on-wheels, home cleaning, residential care, or even an extra cash supplement as the elderly decide for themselves. Then if the local authority should wish to provide more it could do so from its own funds, or the 'voucher' or grant could be topped up by the individual. Few of those who support vouchers would argue against an individual or a local authority buying better services than the national minimum out of their own resources. It seems clear that if the function of the voucher system is to allow a certain amount and kind of redistribution there can be no no argument against allowing individuals to purchase more of the commodity than is supplied indirectly by the voucher. This seems obvious if the purpose of the voucher is essentially redistributive, whether the redistribution is motivated by poverty, or paternalism, or egoism.

The 'topping-up' issue has arisen where the motives for redistribution have been different. Certain conceptions of equality of opportunity and of egalitarianism require that not only a certain minimum standard by achieved by all, but that a maximum is also imposed. If levelling up cannot achieve these goals, it is to be accompanied by levelling down. This issue has been raised most forcefully in education where equality of opportunity has been the motive for redistribution, but it has also been raised in the provision of health services and other areas. If such egalitarianism is the goal the only way it may achieve it is for the government to control the supply of the services involved and provide them equally to all. Within such a scheme, vouchers have no interesting role to play. Neither individuals nor local authorities should be allowed to purchase more of a particular commodity than is provided or decided by the central government. Topping up by local authorities should be as disturbing to such notions of equality as is topping up by individuals.

Though most has been heard of education vouchers, one could imagine vouchers being introduced for all local services in so far as they are not non-excludable or non-rival — that in as much as they are not public goods and to the extent they do not generate externalities. To give a few instances, one can imagine vouchers for the elderly which might be confined to local government services or could be extended to cover private homes and services. A greater rationalisation would be in provision for the elderly under the Supplementary Benefits Commission. On very similar lines there could be vouchers for the disabled, the handicapped, the blind and the deaf. In rather a different category would come vouchers for library services and for various other personal social services for less specific client groups. One particular form of voucher which has received considerable attention but which will not be discussed here because it presents very special problems is the housing voucher or allowance which may be universal or again confined to the local authority tenant.

Any voucher system would differ in its effect depending on whether local authorities were allowed to make rate fund contributions. If they were, then a ratepayer would be a net gainer or loser depending on his rateable value relative to his consumption of the subsidised service. The position would be still further obscured if the rate-fund contribution itself were grant-aided through the RSG as is the case at present with rate fund contributions for some purposes but not for others. Two issues are raised by such rate fund contributions. The first, is the 'topping-up' question which we have already discussed with respect to additional contributions by individuals themselves. The second issue is whether local authorities should undertake redistributive policies differing from those of the central government. What one feels about this will vary with the service. Let us consider again education, where attitudes are likely to depend on three issues.

The first is plainly moral or political. Some would argue that there is no reason at all why those who are childless or without children at a state school should contribute to the education of those with children. Taken to its limit, this is likely to be an argument against any subsidisation of education. If education is to be subsidised, or even if the education of the poor is to be subsidised, it is difficult to see why the burden of this should fall alone on wealthier parents with children at a state school. However, this is really not the point at issue. One can argue that those without children at a state school can make their contribution through central taxes and the vouchers, if such a contribution is to be made. It is far less obvious why, in addition, there should be a specific local contribution through a rate-fund contribution from the childless, those without children currently at a state school and, indeed, from the non-domestic ratepayer. Against this, as a matter of redistributive ethics, all one can put is the much weaker proposition that those without children at school in a community should be expected to contribute to the children of neighbourhoods as a form of forced altruism, again in addition to what they contribute as taxpayers. As this would mean that they would, *ceteris paribus*, have to make the greater contribution the smaller the proportion they were of the population, it is not easy to see the justice in this requirement which would lead to unequal burdens being placed on such individuals depending on the mix of population in their place of residence.

The second argument for a rate fund contribution among those without children is that it becomes a way of spreading the burden of school payments over a citizen's ratepaying lifetime, with some similarity to the purchase of life insurance to meet school bills in the private sector which also spreads payments over time. But there are various inequities in using the rating system to this end. Individuals and families move. There are areas from which there are high rates of outward migration when education is complete, especially for those who achieve most educationally. There are other areas to which people tend to migrate later in life after their children have gone through school. This gives rise to a particular form of intergovernmental externality whereby areas which receive a high proportion of highly educated people with higher incomes and expectations and living in higher-valued property benefit at the expense of other areas who provide the schooling for such children before they move, but do not benefit from them (Williams, 1966). Not only is there unfairness between persons in different areas because of this, but it leads to inefficiency. A local authority system with local freedom to vary the provision of education will normally provide a less than optimal level of education because the return to the citizens of the providing community from investing in education is less than the social return which includes the benefits that accrue to citizens of those authorities to which the educated have moved. Thus use of the rating system is both an inequitable and inefficient method for spreading educational payments over the parents' or beneficiaries' rate-paying lifetime. Once again, the national tax system working through a voucher or grant would seem both more equitable and efficient, making any rate fund contribution an unnecessary and inferior addendum unless, as argued above, there is held to be a case for an independent local redistribution policy.

Besides these two redistributive arguments for sharing the burdens locally through a rate fund contribution, there may be a further efficiency one. It would be that all the citizens of a local authority benefit from better-educated local children. This might be more compelling if there were a closer inverse relationship than seems likely between expenditure per pupil on education and juvenile delinquency, or if one could argue that local employers would benefit from higher expenditure on education or education over and above any benefit they may derive from paying higher wages to more highly educated or trained labour. While there probably are some externalities of this kind, they are hard to quantify and intuitively seem unlikely to justify much contribution to education finance from the citizens at large.

Thus if there were to be an education voucher system of the type described, on balance the arguments would suggest that the difference between the value of education (the fees), and the voucher value should be met by the parent (net of any government grant); and there would be no rate fund contribution. Central government would decide any variations in the value of the voucher to reflect the personal circumstances of the parent — for example, means-testing — or differences in the cost of providing education. The principal argument for such a system would be to clarify the relationship between cost of education and subsidy for all ratepayers. As the Tiebout argument suggests it would help take redistribution out of local government finance with the advantages we have claimed for that; and that in an area where redistribution and equality of treatment are widely held to be especially important. Once again the question of rate fund contribution to redistributive services raises broad issues to which we must return, concerning the relations between central and local government.

COMPENSATION THROUGH GRANTS

It is worth considering whether a scheme could be devised which used grants to or within local authorities instead of vouchers to tackle the relatively narrow question of any additional compensation that would seem equitable in so far as charges are substituted for rates. There are strong arguments against this in terms of horizontal efficiency and equity, but their consideration is postponed to the next chapter. Let us suppose education vouchers were introduced at a uniform rate per pupil and that the net effect of this was to lead to considerable discrepancies among authorities in fees (defined as the difference between the full costs per pupil and the value of the voucher). Presumably, these could either be met by rate fund contributions or, if the policy and the law were changed, by parental contributions. But the effects could be mitigated by central government grants designed to take into account such differences in costs and as near as possible to equalise rate fund contributions per pupil (at zero or some higher level). Let us take the process a stage further and suppose that instead of vouchers, such increases in central grants were adopted to offset the effect of introducing charges. If the design were perfect — which is virtually impossible — and the level of grant sufficient, the fees would be zero because met 100 per cent by a grant exactly equal to the fees. Taken to such an extreme, the exercise would be pointless but it does show the relation between a voucher scheme and the use of specific grants. As compared with a voucher system, the specific grant does not give any freedom of choice to the individual. It is analogous to a voucher system which limits the use of the voucher to a specific service provided by a specified supplier; in this case the local authority. As we argued above, such a specific voucher has at most a cosmetic effect. Secondly, by comparison with a voucher system, a grant system cannot easily reflect the financial or any other relevant circumstance of the parent, in the case of education, or more generally the consumer of the service specifically grant-aided.

This last scheme is of more interest to point up the analogy between the use of vouchers and grants as well as the differences. A grant system which went so far as reducing charges to zero might have some didactic value within the authority or for central government, but it would, of course, negate the efficiency case for charging as far as it affected the individual.

Despite these difficulties, housing grants, when rent rebates are added to them, have some of the characteristics of a grant system which does allow for differences in the personal financial circumstances of recipients. They are specific grants and reduce the cost of housing to all local tenants. Rent rebates reduce it most to those who are poor, especially if they have large families. Special grants for the construction of housing for some categories of the disabled and elderly have special redistributive effects. Finally, charges are made through rents, though the rent pattern usually obtaining in a local authority is a poor reflection of differences in marginal cost.

To recapitulate, the introduction of charging will have redistributive impacts. In general replacing rating by charging will throw an increased burden on (1) the poor and (2) those who tend to be heavy consumers, and vice versa. Such a change in distribution may be intended; and indeed many protagonists of charging seem as interested in this as in its effect on efficiency.

However, one could introduce charging mainly for its effect on efficiency and try to neutralise the redistributive impact.

(1) One method of doing this would be through offsetting changes in taxation. While rough compensation could be achieved for most income groups and possibly for those with differing numbers of children, dependants, disabilities, etc., one can never get perfect compensation. There are bound to be some gainers and losers. In particular, there is the problem of the poor. Services provided free or at less than marginal cost are a substantial fraction of the income of the poor who do not pay enough direct taxes to be remitted in compensation. If they were to be charged the full cost of services, negative taxation, that is cash transfers, would be needed to compensate them. But the practical and political difficulties of introducing an NIT in Britain have so far proved insuperable.

(2) Similar compensation could be achieved through a voucher system. This would entitle individuals or households to vouchers with a value determined by central government. These could be used to purchase local services. One could imagine a general-purpose voucher which could be used by its recipient to purchase the service the recipient chose. It would, in effect, be like having a special government income which could only be used to purchase local services. More familiar is the notion that individuals would receive vouchers according to their needs. Most has been heard of education vouchers, for parents with school (or university) children; but one can imagine vouchers for the elderly for various kinds of disabled or infirm persons. Vouchers seem most suitable where needs are likely to be fairly uniform and where an individual or a family can plan ahead. Thus elderly persons could use such a voucher to purchase the public services they want.

But a voucher system would be less sensible for health care where needs are far less predictable in timing and amount (unless accompanied by an insurance system).

In discussing vouchers we have been at pains to separate out various features of schemes which are widely seen as politically biased. If desired it would be possible to devise voucher systems under which the individual could not treat the voucher value as a minimum which he could top up to buy more expensive services to the extent that he could afford. Use of vouchers could be confined to public-sector provision. What seems central to the notion of vouchers is that the individual should have some choice on how to spend the vouchers. This should lead to greater satisfaction on the part of the individual as well as acting as a competitive discipline on the providers of services. Logically, the voucher can be seen as a way of making grants through individuals rather than through authorities.

(3) A third way of neutralising the redistributive impact of introducing charging would be through appropriately tailored specific grants. Instead of a block grant each authority would receive a grant in relation to a service with the implication that the difference between this and the full cost of the service would be met probably out of rates, but conceivably wholly or in part by an uncompensated charge levied on the individual.

The efficiency case for introducing charges is far more clear-cut and is the same as that for market pricing in general, so the whole discussion so far has concentrated on distributional questions. This seems inevitable because of the nature of the case that is usually mounted against the introduction of charging into public finance.[6] Harris and Seldon (1976, p. 93) give a related instance of one of them attending a meeting with a minister and his officials on NHS prescription charges where the officials argued that lower charges would not be worth collecting while high charges would disturb household budgets and would be socially unacceptable. Similar attitudes have their echo in the Layfield Report. Those who distrust charging may feel they have its defenders on the horns of a dilemma but this is only true as long as the two isssues of redistribution and efficiency are muddled. The case for replacing rates by charges is grounded both in efficiency and redistribution. The efficiency case is that already made for pricing. The redistributive case is indeed at the heart of the reasons for which the Layfield Inquiry was set up. Right at the beginning of the Report, the Committee went into the reasons why there had been recurrent attacks on the rating system over a long period. First, the complaint was made that there was a poor relation between rating liability and ability to pay, but secondly 'it was frequently pointed out that the rating system took no account of calls made on local services made by various types of household . . . There was a general feeling in much of the evidence that payment for services should be related more closely to the use made of them' (Layfield, 1976, p. 4). This is nothing but the expression of a case for charging: it seems unfair to many people that rates paid do not reflect use of a service. A rating policy which reflected the use of a service and therefore of the resources consumed in providing that service would be beneficial rating — that is charging. If it did so perfectly, it would be marginal cost pricing. Thus widespread views on avoiding what appears inequitable also provide a case for charging in local government finance. Not that this distributive criterion is the only one at work. There is also the widely held view that poor people and some other groups — the elderly, the disabled, large families — should *ceteris paribus* be put in a position to acquire local services more easily than otherwise would be the case. Thus if this second set of redistributive criteria is to be respected, some means must be taken of mitigating the efficiency and what we may call the first redistributive argument for introducing charging. Of the various methods of doing this, vouchers seem the most promising. They appear more feasible than reform through the tax system requiring an NIT. They can be made responsive to the personal circumstances of the recipient. Thus one could escape from the dilemma the civil servants thought they faced over prescription charges.

Table 4.4.1 shows the proportion of various local services that is financed by charges. It can be inferred that charges are fairly widespread but that for the most part they are set at levels which are low in relation to cost. Hence the force of the first horn of the apparent dilemma. There is indeed not much to be said for introducing or often for retaining nominal or derisory charges, the fossilised residue of past practice. On the other hand, the second horn of the dilemma is not as solid. Through vouchers or some other equivalent method, it should be possible to get the efficiency and what we have called the first and second redistributive benefits from charging. That is, not only could charging so introduced

Table 4.4.1. *Proportion of services financed by pricing – England and Wales, 1975/6*

(a) MAIN GROUPS OF RATE FUND SERVICES

Service	£m Expenditure	£m Fees and charges	%
Education	5,640.0	173.3	3.1
Libraries	156.2	6.5	4.2
Museums, Art Galleries	21.8	0.6	2.7
Personal social services	963.4	134.3	13.9
Police	860.0	21.6	2.5
Fire	216.2	2.5	1.2
Justice	99.6	1.4	1.4
Passenger transport	205.6	2.5	1.2
Highways, other transport	829.2	48.8	5.9
Housing (non-HRA)	737.9	49.2	6.7
Employment	32.9	0.9	2.7
Refuse	290.5	11.5	4.0
Recreation, parks, baths	360.9	40.2	11.1
Total	12,619.7	583.9	4.6

(b) TRADING SERVICES

Service			
Passenger transport	90.6	76.6	84.5
Harbours, piers	24.0	20.5	85.4
Markets	28.6	17.1	59.8
Slaughter houses	8.7	5.5	63.2
Aerodromes	28.8	18.1	62.8
Corporation estates	42.9	13.2	30.8
Total	366.6	199.0	54.3

(c) HOUSING REVENUE ACCOUNT	1975.2	891.7	45.1
GRAND TOTAL	14,9615.5	1,674.6	11.2

Source: Local Government Financial Statistics – 1975/6 (DoE).

avoid the objection to the rating system that in equity (as well as for efficiency), payment should be better related to use but it should also help derive a system which, far better than the one that exists now, would mitigate this by vouchers designed to give help where and to the extent society decides is needed.

This leaves what in this context may be called the third set of redistributive impacts: the paternalistic. Logically, the *status quo* can always be defended by such arguments. Rather than let beneficiaries have income or vouchers to purchase services they want, one can always argue that the relative prices that exist and the particular redistribution through rates and taxes affecting a particu-consumer getting a service represent a paternalistic judgement on what is the best balance between payment and subsidy. But while it would be logically poss-ible no doubt for an ingenious man to do this, the table just presented throws up no obvious pattern. Neither has there been any consistent or concerted attempt at rationalisation. Finally, we cannot pretend that what exists reflects any set of rational and consistent judgement. It just grew.

All this amounts in our judgement to a substantial case for altering local government finance by introducing charges and vouchers as probably the most feasible supplement. As we have already indicated such a conclusion is bound to be affected by the change in arrangements for grant which we discuss later. Their operation will also be influenced by political views on the extent to which consumers are allowed freedom of choice, especially whether they may use vouchers to buy private as well as public services. As economists we offer no opinion on the political pros and cons of this.

The remainder of this chapter considers a number of matters:

(1)   which services have public-goods characteristics;
(2)   which services have substantial external effects and how this might affect their financing;
(3)   at this point we shall pause and consider the extent of what might be achieved by financing on a number of different policy assumptions.
          There are a number of other issues that still need some discussion:
(4)   the use of charges as instruments of local policy except in so far as this can be justified by externalities; and
(5)   the financing problems posed by intergovernmental externalities.

PUBLIC GOODS IN LOCAL SERVICES

As we have noted, despite the usual assumption in so much of the relevant econ-omic literature that local authorities provide public goods, few local goods and services here, or in the USA or, to the best of our knowledge, elsewhere actually have the defining characteristics of public goods: non-excludability and non-rivalness. In this section we go through those services which do have the charac-teristics of non-excludability or non-rivalness, or both.

NON-EXCLUDABILITY

Among the examples of non-excludability are:

(1)   *Street lighting* which is the local equivalent of that classic example of a public good, the lighthouse. Like a lighthouse it confers its benefits on all who pass by, not merely lighting their way but reducing the chances of accident and indeed crime. There has been talk of scrambler devices which would enable passing ships to activate the lighthouse if they had a meter or some such mech-anism by which the lighthouse providers could bill them. Quite apart from the

difficulty of more than one ship passing at once, not all with scramblers, such devices would surely cost far more than could be justified by the return. *A fortiori* the same would be true of any conceivable device for street lighting which must be as pure an example of non-excludability, and therefore of a public good, as exists. In 1976/7 street lighting was 0.5 per cent of total rate fund expenditure.

(2) The *police* are a more complicated case. Who are the beneficiaries? Those whose life, limbs and property are not as much endangered as they would be in the absence of the police. Since the benefits of police protection are characterised by the absence of crime, there is no easy test of such benefits. Economists sometimes suggest in such a case that individuals might take out insurance or pay directly for police protection. But aside from the existence of partial non-rivalness, externalities make the attribution of benefits difficult. If it were conceivable that some householders in a road did not pay for police while others did, the payers would surely be worse off than if they lived in a neighbourhood where everyone had police protection. Thus even if we were to imagine a beneficial police force, that is one that was set up to provide services for which the consumers paid and had no redistributive or paternalistic element in its operations, the practical problems of charging are great enough to make police non-excludable and therefore a public good. (In 1976/7 police expenditure was 3.3 per cent of total rate-fund expenditure.) There are some services of a special kind for which police can be and are paid — for example, attending football matches — but all charged services were only 6.5 per cent of police total expenditure in 1976/7.

Similar arguments can be used to justify local expenditure on (3) *justice* as a public good which is 0.2 per cent of total local expenditure.

A rather more difficult case is presented by expenditure on (4) *planning*. Many of those who advocate charges suggest that planning permission could be charged for. However, such a 'charge' would not be a charge but a tax. Indeed, as has been argued earlier in Part Four, Chapter 2, it would be a form of land tax or site value rating. This holds because those who gain planning permission are not the beneficiaries of the system of planning control. In most cases, one can reasonably assume that those who want planning permission would be better off, directly at least, if they did not have to get it. The putative beneficiaries of planning controls are the citizens at large who in a democratic society must be assumed to benefit from the enhancement of environmental quality obtained through the planning system. It is extremely hard to attribute the benefits to particular individuals. Therefore there is non-excludability, and therefore the planning system is a public good. To charge for permission is not to charge the beneficiaries but to tax those whose gain might be greater or smaller without the planning system, depending on how far the planning system restricts supply relative to demand. Expenditure on planning is formally 1.4 per cent of rate fund expenditure (in 1976/7) though there will be other administrative expenditure which can be attributed to overall planning and policy formulation and cannot be attributable to particular services; while there may also be items within planning that are not public goods.

Among other relatively small items likely to be non-excludable are (5) some

part of expenditure on *pollution control*, though in some cases it may be possible to achieve efficiency through charging polluters.[7] Expenditures attributable
to pollution are 0.03 per cent expenditure.

Expenditure on (6) *land drainage* (0.3 per cent of rate fund expenditure), (7)
national and countryside parks (0.04 per cent), (8) *civil defence* (0.01 per cent),
(9) the *registration of electors* (0.07 per cent), (10) *council elections* (0.04
per cent), and (11) the costs of *rate collection* (0.05 per cent) is mostly non-
excludable.

A much more difficult case is that of (12) *roads* (just under 4 per cent of
local expenditure). Roads can in a sense be priced through fuel duty, vehicle
licences and parking charges but not very efficiently. The problem is, therefore,
one of partial non-excludability. We shall return to consider the very difficult
problems of transport pricing when we come to non-rivalness and to externalities. Our provisional conclusions will be that it is probably efficient to charge
for a high but not unknown proportion of local transport expenditure, including
expenditure on roads.

If we exclude roads the estimates are imprecise, but it is hard to see, however
generously interpreted, that non-excludable services could sum to more than 7
per cent of gross revenue expenditure.

NON-RIVALNESS

Non-rivalness is a term used to describe a good or service whose cost does not
increase with the number of those who use or consume it. In pure cases the
marginal cost is zero. In less pure cases it is very low — far below the level needed
to meet the costs of the service. The meaning to be attached to marginal cost
can cause difficulty here. For example, the cost of street lighting, police and
justice will be greater to an area with a larger population than in one with a
smaller population, and there will be other factors — like population density —
affecting the costs of its provision but, at any given moment, an additional
person will only affect cost slightly or not at all. The clearest example is with
street lighting. No extra cost will be incurred because ten cars drive down a
street rather than one.

Street lighting, police, the administration of justice, much expenditure on
pollution control, land drainage, national and countryside parks, civil defence
and council elections are non-rival and some of these are non-excludable.

Parks and open spaces other than national and countryside parks (1.04 per
cent of rate fund expenditure) are usually non-rival but not non-excludable.
A charge could be made of those entering the gates where these exist, and it is
not unlikely in most cases that the revenue it would raise would not exceed the
out-of-pocket costs from collecting it. Museums and art galleries (0.2 per cent)
are also non-rival to some extent. We shall see in the next section that while it is
likely that some costs of these should be recouped through fees, if we were for
the moment to count these as fully non-rival, not much more than 2 per cent
of local authority gross revenue would not be charged on the ground of non-
rivalness.

A more difficult case is again the provision of roads. Looked at in terms of providing road space, it is often the case that an additional vehicle on the roads imposes virtually no extra costs on the local authority.

If we exclude roads, then taking both non-excludability and non-rivalness together, it is likely that less than 9 per cent of local gross revenue expenditure should not be charged for on economic grounds. If we were to adopt charges wherever practically possible, this would be the irreducible minimum which should be raised in taxation.

EXTERNALITIES

A complete discussion of externalities and local policy requires a far fuller treatment than can be given in this book. We have already suggested Baumol and Oates (1975) for those who are interested in this matter.

Our attention is concentrated on those externalities which seem of special importance because their existence can be argued to have major implications for the financing of services. Two types of externality seem to be of special interest.

The first of these is on the model of the epidemic. This is the oldest and most traditional externality argument justifying local subsidies for local services. One can find it in the origins of public-health legislation. It pays the rich to subsidise the provision of a safe water supply, sewers, proper graveyards, vaccination and other measures of prophylactic public health in poor areas, even if they were never to enter them — not altruistically but in terms of pure self-interest to prevent the generation of epidemics which can spread elsewhere in the city and threaten all, even those living in sanitary housing and salubrious neighbourhoods. The same argument was used for subsidised housing. Merely forcing private landlords to provide their houses with decent sanitation and to make them healthy to live in, as always, merely led to the drying up of the supply of such houses. To get healthy housing for the poor, subsidies were required from the more affluent.

Trickier is a related argument which relies on the effect of subsidised improvement on labour supply. For example, it has been argued that public health and good housing not only prevent epidemic effects but, by making people fitter, provide a more productive workforce. Inevitably this raises the question of why employers do not pay enough to enable their employees to have sanitary homes and healthy conditions, if it would pay them to have the resulting more productive workforce. They surely would if they could. One argument may be true but can only be of limited significance. Until someone provides a healthier workforce, employers are too ignorant or myopic to pay a higher level of wages, even though it would be profitable for them and their workforce to do so. But like all arguments of a pump-priming or infant-industry type, even if valid they can only justify an initial subsidy. If they really have the benefits claimed, they should be self-perpetuating without subsidy thereafter.

A more likely long-term argument is the epidemic argument in miniature. One cannot make a house sanitary and health-giving unless neighbouring houses are improved simultaneously, because whatever one owner may do the disease — through rats, vermin, effluvia — will come on to his property and reduce the effect of any improvements. Indeed, unless all properties in a neighbourhood improve simultaneously, it will often be unprofitable for the individual landlord to improve, and therefore for the individual employer to pay higher wages, since neither will achieve the improvement in living conditions needed to realise a return on investment in the first case and higher productivity in the second. The return from investment in house improvement will be very much higher if all in a neighbourhood improve simultaneously; but this is so unlikely to be spontaneous that government action and subsidy is required.[8]

However, the practical effect of this argument is much diminished in comparatively affluent societies which already have high standards of living conditions and public health. As an argument for subsidy and cross-subsidy, it is a prime example of traditional financing arrangements outliving their original usefulness. Except in a very few areas in developed countries where slums and poor health persist (in Britain these are generally covered by special area subsidy schemes anyway) it is probably not too much to suggest that there are no subsidies which can be justified in terms of 'epidemic' effects. To take another even earlier example, when buildings were usually made of wood or other highly combustible material (as is still the case in many areas of the world), there is an 'epidemic' case for a general subsidy to fire-fighting. A fire that started in Pudding Lane spread and burnt down the whole of the City of London. But technical improvement in building construction and in fire-fighting equipment now mean that fires started in one building rarely spread to another. Thus there is much less of a case for subsidy to fire fighting on these grounds than there used to be (Carter, 1967). Similarly, one can argue that affluence and technical development reflected in better living conditions have for this reason ruled out the need for local subsidies to public health and housing expenditure. Where a particular householder or landlord acts in such a way as to threaten public health, it is now not unreasonable to make a specific intervention or to enforce a regulation to put the matter right, except possibly in a few comparatively small areas where some area-based intervention is needed. It is often argued, especially in housing, that standards of what is socially acceptable rise. While this may be true, one has to recognise first that there are instinctive tendencies in the professional groups concerned as soon as one standard is greatly met to raise it higher; but second, and more relevantly, whatever the justification for these standards they do not involve the risk of what we here call epidemic externalities. For example, to provide every dwelling with a water closet will reduce the risk of epidemic effect, but to insist it is inside rather than outside is a benefit to the household not to society at large, and the same can be said of the requirement that there should be central heating or insulation.

Discussion is sometimes confused by failure to distinguish between this and income-redistribution arguments for subsidy. Though paternalistic, one can understand the argument that on grounds of greater equity in income distribution, the poor should be provided with housing that does not fall below a given minimum level of quality; yet it may in modern conditions fall far below that level and yet have negligible external side-effects on other members of society. If this argument is accepted, then it will be rare that one can rely on such externalities as an argument for not charging marginal costs. There may

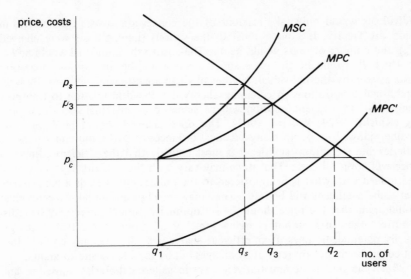

Figure 4.4.2 *Private and social costs*

be certain pollution examples where this is so, but at present at least they do not create an appreciable burden of local expenditure.

A more important cause of externalities is congestion. This may occur in museums, art galleries, parks, libraries and roads, which in the previous section we have characterised as public goods on account of non-rivalness. However, while marginal costs to the local authority may be zero or near zero, there may be non-zero marginal social and private costs after the facility has become congested. The point is illustrated in Figure 4.4.2.

In Figure 4.4.2 various costs and prices are measured on the vertical axis and the number of users of the facility, art gallery, museum, or road is measured on the horizontal axis. The curve marked p_c measures the marginal resource cost (assumed constant) of maintaining the facility as the number of users increases. This would measure, for example, the expenses on keepers, exhibits and administration in an art gallery as the number of users increases, or the expense of maintaining roads as the number of users increases. To users of the facility, however, there are also the costs that may be imposed by congestion. For numbers less than q_1, visitors are not affected by other visitors nor drivers by others on the road. Beyond q_1 people begin to experience inconveniences and delays as the facility becomes congested and these become progressively worse, the greater the congestion. The curve marked *MPC* represents the total costs including such inconveniences due to congestion. *MPC'* is the difference between the *MPC* and the *MC* curves. As soon as congestion occurs, the marginal social cost is different from the marginal private cost. Though individuals may take account of the effect of congestion on themselves, and therefore the cost to them, they also impose costs on others when the facilities become congested. These costs are shown by the curve marked *MSC*.

If no price is charged for the facility, the number of users would be q_2.

Individuals would only take account of the congestion costs to themselves in using the facility. If a price equal to the various running costs were charged (P_c), the number of users would be q_3. The cost to the individual would be P_3, of which P_c would be the price and the rest would be the various congestion costs as seen by the individual. Neither of these are efficient solutions. By well-established propositions in economic theory developed in relation to transport congestion, an efficient solution will be achieved by marginal social cost pricing (Knight, 1924; Walters, 1961). The price charged should be P_s and the number allowed in, q_s. In many practical instances of parks, museums, libraries galleries and recreation facilities it is most unlikely that the efficient admission price will cover all costs. That price may vary with times of the day, the season and indeed with what is being offered to the public; but there is a high chance that some overheads will be left.[9] They may even by substantial. An economist would argue that the price should be set optimally, though there may be redistributive arguments or not charging some or all groups the efficient charge, usually paternalistic ones. If an efficient charge is made, then any costs it does not cover should be covered not by charges but by local taxes and/or grants.

While charging is administratively easy in galleries, libraries, museums and some (fenced or walled) parks, it is notoriously difficult on the roads except through the very crude imperfect mechanism of fuel tax and annual vehicle taxes. To go into this any further is the special province of transport economics (Walters, 1968; Beesley, 1973, chs 9 and 10; Foster, 1975). But a number of issues do arise for local government finance which should be referred to.

If efficient prices could be charged through road pricing, then it is probable that the road system would make a profit in cities and a loss in the countryside because urban roads face increasing costs and rural roads declining costs (Walters, 1968). But instead, parking charges are resorted to. Recently, in Britain, parking charges have been increasingly used to help reduce traffic flow. Thus the finding in Table 4.4.1 that parking charges on average cover only 71 per cent of costs directly attributable to providing parking is the more remarkable. While this is an average, wherever there is serious congestion one would expect parking charges to make a profit if they are to have an efficient effect in reducing congestion. Generally in cities, road pricing even supplemented by parking charges is below the efficient price. With the further consequence for transport finance, that if the price of one of two closely competing services is below marginal cost, then general efficiency considerations suggest that the other price should also be below the marginal cost to achieve an optimal relation between them.[10] This is the proposition which justifies urban public-transport subsidies, though in Britain the extent of such subsidies has been pushed far further than can be justified by the principle.[11]

The principles and problems of efficient charging on transport become very complicated and have been very fully treated in the literature of transport economics. Even if they were to follow these principles as closely as possible, most local authorities will find that they will raise less than enough to meet their costs of providing transport. This problem is made worse because in most nations, including Britain, fuel tax and vehicle licence taxes accrue to central government while the costs are shared.

Here we cannot go deeply into this, but only suggest that charges should be set equal to marginal cost as far as is efficient. There remains the truly public-good aspect of transport where it is non-excludable and non-rival. This poses a difficult problem in intergovernmental externalities since the beneficiaries of any roads are partly local and partly people who live or work elsewhere — the former being in the majority. As we have seen, the notion that some roads are of greater national importance has been reflected in a variety of grant schemes, the rest of the funds being found from local rates.

In financing terms, it is difficult to think of any externalities from local services potentially of comparable importance. The conclusion must be that externalities are probably of relatively little importance in local finance despite their importance for policy. Indeed, the net outcome of the discussion is that even the 8 per cent of gross revenue expenditure postulated as non-excludable and non-rival would be reduced by efficient charges, but to an extent we cannot estimate in ignorance of the relevant demand curves. Some proportion of local-transport expenditure should also be borne on taxes, but again it is not estimable and is probably small. Thus it seems probable that some 90 per cent of local gross revenue expenditure could be priced if it were not for redistributive considerations.

CONCLUSION ON CHARGING AND LOCAL FINANCE

A major reform indeed could be achieved in local government finance if charging were widely adopted — possibly for up to 90 per cent of gross revenue expenditure. But it would mean quite a major change in redistribution unless special steps were taken to offset it. Though so far it has defeated reformers, a tax package including a negative income tax could do it. So could a system of vouchers. So probably could a system of ear-marked or specific grants. The basic case for such a charge is the general one that charges that reflect costs lead to more efficiency and consumer satisfaction than financing through taxation. It follows that the incidence of rates could be reduced to about a tenth if charging were adopted to the maximum extent. This would reduce many of the objections made as to the unfairness of the rate system, though, of course, the revenue would be found instead through charging. Since greater use would result in higher payments, there would be an incentive to economise. Thus one would expect some overall reduction in local expenditure.

In a few cases which we have not really explored, it might be argued that the costs of pricing might exceed the revenue raised. Though it is now outside local finance in the strict sense, water supply has been a local service and could become one again. The pricing of domestic water consumption might be uneconomical. Even there, it is far from unlikely that a crude charging system based on square or cubic footage or on the number of persons in the household might be more efficient than charging based on rateable values.

Others will no doubt argue that charging for domestic refuse collection would cost more than it would yield in efficiency. In the USA much thought has been given to this and there are many schemes working. One possibility would be a voucher scheme where each household bought the right to have so many dustbins emptied each week and was billed once a quarter for any additional dustbins or containers that had to be emptied.

While doubts on the profitability of introducing charging in some cases might be responsible for reducing its coverage to less than 90 per cent of gross revenue expenditure, various redistributive and paternalistic judgements are more likely to be responsible for any such exclusion. We have already discussed this in relation to education. While a voucher system could be restricted to state schools, and even be used merely as a method of charging — without giving greater parental choice even within the state system — Harris and Seldon (1976) have noted another source of opposition, that is from the professional groups involved, especially teachers who might dislike the transfer of power to parents which would be implied if they had greater freedom of choice over schools. If education were excluded, about an extra third of gross revenue expenditure would have to be financed from taxation.

Objections are also likely from the professional groups concerned with the social services. One argument that will be heard is that it is unreasonable to ask some groups, say the elderly, to exercise the choice implied either by an NIT or by vouchers. This would seem to treat all beneficiaries as if they were in the position of the few who undoubtedly because of age or disability cannot choose how they wish to spend vouchers. It will also be argued that giving vouchers will increase the demand for services because some who make no claim will do so in future. If desired this could partly be met by making vouchers taxable to reduce their value to the more affluent; but the pride which at present stops some from applying for various rebates and supplementary benefits, might stop the same people from using vouchers. But this cuts both ways. If there are social-services clients who need services, then socially it is desirable that they should be encouraged to use them. Another cause of some professional opposition is the uncertainty that will be caused to those who run services if clients are able to make choices, particularly between different providers, public or private, of the same services. But this is the means by which both efficiency and consumers' satisfaction is increased. Exclusion of social services from charging would remove a further 10 per cent to 12 per cent of gross revenue expenditure from the operation of charges. If health services were also excluded for similar reasons, a further 4 per cent to 5 per cent would be omitted.

The two matters that remain are of some interest, though neither is likely to raise substantial revenue for local authorities.

LOCAL CHARGES OTHER THAN FOR LOCAL SERVICES

The charges we have discussed so far have been for local goods and services and may be expected to yield substantial revenue to set against the cost of providing those services. But charges may also be used for regulation. The difference between such regulatory or instrumental use of charges and the parallel use of taxes is a matter of definition and therefore open to dispute, but it is probably most convenient to call such a levy a charge when it is based on an estimation of marginal social costs and a tax when it is arbitrary. In many cases, the distinction is fine. For example, penal taxation on cigarette smoking might be related to the marginal social cost of smoking, but many of the relevant magnitudes and values are incalculable. Nevertheless, such a tax could conceivably be based on a best estimate of social cost or it could be no more than an arbitrary political judgement. Therefore, the distinction between a tax and a charge in this context only becomes meaningful where there is reasonably sound evidence on marginal social costs. The difference between this type of charge and those discussed earlier is that marginal costs are not those of the provider. From the provider's standpoint they are externalities and the local authority is acting as an agent of society if it charges to to attempt to achieve a better, more economically efficient outcome than if the free market was left to its own devices. Even then the distinction can be blurred. We have already discussed the use of congestion charges as a means of pricing roads. From the point of view of the local authority as provider and maintainer of the road system, congestion is an externality, but it so happens that in that case there is a fairly direct intuitive connection between charging for congestion and using the proceeds for providing and maintaining the roads that are congested. In other instances no similar connection can be made.

Parking charges would probably represent an intermediate case. If they are seen merely as servicing the costs of providing parking space, then in urban areas parking charges set at an optimal level to reduce traffic congestion should raise more than enough to cover puely parking costs, especially when it is street parking that is being metered.[12]

Optimal parking charges should earn large profits. But if parking charges are seen in relation to the costs of providing road systems as a whole, they appear one means of charging for its use along with fuel and vehicle duties.[13]

The other instrumental uses to which charges may be put are various; and they are less used in Britain than in the USA. Here we have in the past relied more on regulation than on charges to control externalities, though charges for the purpose are becoming more common. One example is charging to control industrial effluents into rivers. To ban effluent may be impractical and very costly. It could lead to a loss of jobs as firms decide to migrate to areas where they do not have to meet such costs. Regulation can be time consuming and may also impose certain costs. Rather it may be more efficient to calculate the approximate marginal social costs per output unit of effluent and charge accordingly. The marginal social cost charges would reflect such costs as the additional cost of water treatment, effects on fishing, effects on property prices of any smells or other noxious consequences of water pollution, and so forth (avoiding double counting). Charging on this basis gives the polluter an incentive to invest to reduce pollution if it is profitable to do so. Even if he moves, the community knows that the net effect is beneficial if the calculations have been done properly. While it loses in net income generated by the firm, it more than gains in the benefits of reduced pollution. If the polluter stays and pays the charge, the community at large as represented by the local authority gains by an amount at least equal to the cost of pollution.

What it does with the revenue is another question. Morally, there is a case for it compensating the actual losers. Practically, it may treat the proceeds as additional, though almost certainly small, revenue source.

A similar justification can be used to replace other regulations by charges. Building regulations, safety regulations, all sorts of regulations, can impose very substantial costs by requiring more expensive forms of construction and maintenance. The point is that such costs can vastly exceed the social benefits of the regulation and that there is little incentive to the devisors of regulations to estimate whether this is or is not the case. Fire regulations are one example. Thus it might not be unreasonable to allow property owners in some circumstances to continue using or even construct buildings with lower fire standards, provided they pay a charge reflecting the higher costs that could be calculated as likely to fall on society on a probabalistic basis. Such a calculation is no different from that of an insurance premium against risk; and indeed liability could be expressed as a requirement to take out additional insurance. Because fire regulations so often are arbitrary and unfair, in many cases reductions in standards can be allowed without significant increases in insurance being needed. If charges are used, the distributional question again arises as to how the proceeds are to be used: whether to compensate the losers as far as possible or as an addition to local authority revenues.

Fines may also be employed to supplement local revenue. Fines for returning library books late, minor traffic or parking offences, even minor criminal offences, such as causing a disturbance, cannot be easily seen as charges to be set against costs, though fines for dropping litter or allowing one's dog to foul the pavement can more easily be related to some costs of street cleaning. While such fines are imposed as a deterrent, they also raise revenue. Whether the revenue goes to local authorities or elsewhere is a distributional question for central government.

CHARGES AND INTERGOVERNMENTAL EXTERNALITIES

Many local authorities supply services for others or combine with others to provide joint facilities. The principles of charging in such cases should provide no particular problem; but a greater difficulty is presented when there are intergovernmental externalities.

In practice, environmental externalities are likely to provide the most important examples of intergovernmental externalities. A smoke-creating factory in one authority, A, might discharge some or even most of its smoke into another, B. It would not pay authority A in the interests of its citizens to impose a substantial charge on that factory or make a substantial inducement to alter its technology to one which produced less smoke. But if A and B were to operate together, a rational charge or inducement might on a marginal social cost basis be large enough to lead to a beneficial change in the factory's operations. Similar examples can be found in water and noise pollution where there are similar boundary problems.

A rather different but theoretically identical case could be where one authority wishes to attract industry, but cannot do so unless it can provide housing for key managers and workers. Let us suppose that its environment is such that managers or supervisors will not want to settle there, but there is a neighbouring authority with an environment they would prefer, which for some reason will not make land available for new development. Then it could be in the interests of the first local authority to pay the second to do this for it.

Another example commonly found in the literature which we have already referred to is education. The problem arises because those who get education in a community do not all go on to live there. Some local authorities characteristically are net suppliers of educated people. Overall, there is net outmigration. Others are net acquirers of such people. Often it is the most educated who are least able to stay where they have been educated and who move on.

If there were no central government controls on or grants for educational provision, one can see how a relatively poor local authority area would not be ready to pay for a standard of education from which other parts of the country would derive much of the benefit. In such circumstances of freedom, there is a tendency for such local authorities to concentrate on providing basic education more suited to their own local employment needs. Since the areas which have a deficit of such people and import them cannot influence the policies for educational provision elsewhere, the net effect is likely to be underprovision of educated persons (see, however, Williams, 1966).

Financing of the road system can be analysed in the same way. If we consider again the public-goods proportion of roads expenditure that is left after as much as possible has been charged for by the best possible approximation to marginal cost pricing, a difficulty is dividing the burden between governments. Just as A and B were interested in each other's pollution control or provision of schooling, so citizens of A use B's roads and vice versa. If the overhead or public-good costs of roads in A were to be met through A's rates only, and by reference to the social return to A's ratepayers, then there would be underprovision of roads in A; and indeed for similar reasons there would also be underprovision in B.

What are the implications of this analysis for charging? A progression of difficulty can be illustrated by the examples we have chosen. Where two or a handful of neighbouring authorities are concerned, it should be possible to achieve efficient provision through negotiation (Coase, 1960). Where one authority would be helped by another investing more in pollution control or highway provision, it ought not to be any less negotiable than joint arrangements over the provision of special schools or residential homes. In the private sector, the presumption that any firm will engage in an activity which will make a legitimate profit is usually thought sufficient to ensure that negotiations can take place. In the public sector, there may be at least two problems. The first is that one local authority refuses to spend on the initiative of another, even if it were to be paid in full for it. The second is that as a monopoly provider one authority can hold a customer authority up to ransom, making a large monopoly profit at its expense. There would seem to be a strong argument for central government to devise and monitor rules of conduct governing such situations. The first problem should be that by some requirement a local authority should agree to provide services for another, or to take into account what the second authority is willing to pay whenever there is an intergovernmental externality. The second could be met by the first local authority being required to charge a price which reflected the costs involved, plus a reasonable profit, whatever that may be decided to be.

Negotiation, which is comparatively straightforward when a small number of authorities is involved, becomes extraordinarily complicated when there are large numbers. It is possible to conceive of one authority which is a net provider of educated people tracking down the residence of those who have left after education — provided they have not moved abroad — and billing the gainer authorities retrospectively for the costs of education; but it is hard to imagine that the revenues would be worth the costs, even if the policy were found politically acceptable. It is scarcely even imaginable that a similar check could be made on the domicile of those who use an authority's roads. Almost inevitably where there are large numbers, central government has to come in yet another role, standing in for the collectivity of 'other' authorities. Indeed, one can justify some part of the education grant as compensating the net provider authorities, though no item in the rate support grant formula reflects this particular factor. The traditional percentage road grants contributing to local expenditure can in principle be seen as the central government contributing to a local authority in proportion to the use of its roads by the citizens of other authorities.[14] Dearth of information, however, brings these cases near or over the border line separating a charge from a tax system. If the money received by one authority from another, or from central government approximately reflects the marginal cost of doing something for that other authority or central government, either in its own right or as an agent for other local authorities, then it is a charge; but if the contribution is arbitrary, then it becomes a way of distributing expenditure without regard to costs — that is it becomes a question of distribution and a tax. Thus, ironically, what is called a grant from central government may be represented as a charge made by a local authority for services provided to central government (as the representative of others), or it may in fact be a tax on central government (instigated, of course, by it) to help finance local expenditure, from which central government derives indeterminate benefit. Thus the wheel of definition comes round full circle. A service where benefits are national and indivisible between places is a national public good and by definition the cost cannot be divided between local authorities; local authorities cannot be charged, any more than can individual consumers. If a local authority provides such a service then it must be an agent. But if the marginal costs of providing a service within or to a local authority can be distinguished so that charges may be made reflecting such costs of provision, then the service is a public good as far as consumers are concerned. Nevertheless it is a local not a national good.

NOTES

1 In other words, economists' jargon, second-best problems are rarely of practical importance. Fishlow and David (1961); Misham (1971).
2 Readers will recall there is a much fuller discussion of these definitions in the appendix to Part One, Chapter 3.
3 See Hicks (1956). We are talking here in terms of what he calls the equivalent variation.
4 For a more detailed discussion of NIT see Green (1967).

5   Vouchers may or may not be tax deductible depending on the effect on income distri-
     bution to be achieved.

6   See the arguments used and sources quoted by Harris and Seldon (1976, part 2) in
     their convincing demonstration that the Layfield Inquiry did not take charging seriously
     enough.

7   The argument that efficiency can be achieved either by charging those who cause a
     negative externality — a social cost — or by compensating those who lose from it;
     and that the difference between the two is distributional if both are applied equally
     efficiently is a familiar one in economics. See Coase (1960). There are exceptions to
     the symmetry: see Baumol and Oates (1975).

8   This argument for intervention is known in the literature as the Prisoners' Dilemma:
     see Davis and Whinston (1962), Rothenberg (1967).

9   One can demonstrate that with constant returns to scale, in the long run the efficient
     price should cover all costs, short and long; but most, though not all, of the facilities
     local authorities provide of this sort will be subject to increasing returns to scale,
     particularly in cities and towns.

10 This assumes, as generally seems correct, that perverse 'second-best' effects are not
     important.

11 For the principle, see Foster and Beesley (1963). For arguments that question the
     empirical argument see DoE (1976*b*, Vol. 2).

12 That, as we have seen, parking charges meet only 70 per cent of such costs is a reflec-
     tion of the actual policies that *on average* determine parking charges.

13 Semantics dog us throughout this discussion. The Treasury always maintains that these
     duties are taxes and that they are unhypothecated. As a matter of tax philosophy, this
     is intended to reflect the Chancellor's right to set these at levels he determines so as to
     raise the revenue he requires, irrespective of the effects of these tax levels on relative
     prices. But for some years both vehicle and fuel duties have been set wih some regard
     to their effect on the allocation of resources. Thus, whatever Chancellors may say,
     these duties are in part being used as charges, especially in determining the relative
     vehicle duties paid by road freight vehicles of different weights.

14 This was far clearer when there were more gradations in percentage road grants. The
     more national the use of a road, the higher the central grant percentage was. Moreover,
     the Ministry of Transport used to modify the classification of roads so that a road with
     a greater proportion of national traffic might receive a higher grading, and therefore
     more grant, than another of the same quality but with less national traffic.

5 The Uses of Grant

This chapter covers a range of topics, important to the argument but often without close connection reflecting various issues raised for grant by earlier discussion and the diversity of purpose to which grant may be put. Section 1 states briefly how horizontal efficiency and equity can be achieved if rates were replaced by site value rating, a local income tax or charges. Section 2 goes through the case for reducing local dependence on central grant and considers how this could be done. In section 3, the objectives of horizontal efficiency and equity are relaxed in favour of giving local authorities an incentive to permit development.

The remaining sections discuss the connection between the form of grant and changes in the balance of power between central and local government. Grant systems which enhance the role of central departments and give them more power are considered in section 4, while section 5 is on forms of grant which would encourage local autonomy.

SECTION 1

In Chapter 3 of Part Two we argued that the basis of resource equalisation was less secure than often supposed. Indeed, the main argument for resource equalisation under the present system was to compensate for differences in the proportion of non-domestic to domestic rateable value. If, as we have recommended, non-domestic properties are exempt from local rating, the case for a resource equalisation grant is much less powerful. Horizontal efficiency and equity would require a resource equalisation grant with rates levied only on households, if differences in average rateable values between localities were attributable to differences in the mix of properties but not if due to systematic differences in property values.

Similar considerations would be relevant if rates were replaced by site value rating. Again, if all site values were rated there would be a strong argument for an equalisation grant to compensate for differences in the proportion of non-domestic to domestic site values. The grant would become a mechanism for equalising, or levelling up to, some standard site value per head. But if local site value rating were confined to residential land, the argument for a resource equalisation grant would be less clear-cut, for the same reasons as with domestic rates.

With a local income tax, horizontal efficiency becomes more important because it will be less fully capitalised than rates and hence there will be more of an incentive for people to migrate between authorities, as discussed in Part Two, Chapter 2. Resource equalisation would require a grant equalising, or levelling up to, some standard level of income per head. Because income levels vary much less between authorities than do rateable values, an equalisation of income-tax bases would entail much less grant than the present equalisation of rateable resources.

Horizontal inefficiency only arises for beneficial services in so far as the tax payment for the service differs from an efficient charge, as explained in Part Two. It follows that if charges were introduced, resource equalisation grants would become redundant for the charged services.

SECTION 2

At the end of Part Three it was argued that a weakness of the current system was that upward pressure on the grant proportion was likely to return when local expenditure began to grow again. In Part One, Chapter 4 it was shown that in the recent past there had been a tendency for a 1 per cent increase in GNP per head to have been associated with a more than 3 per cent increase in local current expenditure; and over a much longer period its increase on the same basis had been at least $2\frac{1}{2}$ per cent. While this relationship has no behavioural basis, it does seem likely that the income elasticity of local current expenditure is substantially positive. This is not surprising given the services local authorities generally provide are generally thought of as income-elastic, that is with demand rising faster than incomes. Possibly the restraint of the mid-1970s will be reflected in a less rapid growth of local expenditure in the future than in the recent past, though one cannot be sure of this. At the least, one can expect that, say, a $2\frac{1}{2}$ per cent per annum increase in GNP per head would be associated with two and a half times that annual increase in local current expenditure. The future of local capital expenditure is harder to predict. Possibly that will stay reduced as the shift of emphasis from construction to services is more likely to last.

There is no necessary connection between local expenditure rising more rapidly than incomes, and a growing grant proportion. This will happen if it continues to be the practice to increase grant so as to keep rate burdens a more or less constant proportion of personal disposable income. The more progressive income tax and the less it changes to reflect inflation the more pressure there will be on grant. Earlier it was argued as a Part Three conclusion that at the least the ratio of non-domestic to domestic rate yield should not be allowed to increase further and should preferably be reduced. Such a change would eliminate one mechanism through which the grant system can act to keep domestic rate burdens down. What would be left would be the more straightforward tactic of raising the RSG proportion as a whole. To illustrate, suppose that the income elasticity of local current expenditure is either $2\frac{1}{2}$ per cent or 3 per cent and that there is $2\frac{1}{2}$ per cent real growth per annum in GNP from 1979, then on the first elasticity assumption – and assuming no change in the proportion of income tax – the grant proportion would have to rise from 61 per cent to 70 per cent in ten years and to 76 per cent in twenty years. On the second assumption they would become 71 per cent and 78 per cent respectively.

The easiest way of preventing such a rise would, of course, be to alter the practice and allow the domestic rate burden to rise at the same rate as local current expenditure. Though recently it has been anathema to fix such matters by legislation, requiring grant to be set at such a level so as not to raise the grant proportion might be the only way of achieving such an objective and could be the only way of avoiding the political pressures which in the past have led politicians to cushion the domestic ratepayer as described, since nationally and locally they have an interest in hiding rising costs of local services from the local electorate.

The Layfield Committee took a much stronger line and argued for a major reduction in the grant proportion. Arbitrarily it said that 50 per cent – the proportion of the 1950s as it happened – was in its view consistent with local autonomy.

The Department of the Environment had told the Committee that a grant proportion of about 40 per cent was consistent with achieving equalisation with a unitary grant (Layfield, 1976, p. 218). This was taken as setting a lower bound to the grant proportion. The weakness of the arguments the Committee used for reducing the grant proportion were shown in Chapter 5 of Part Two. It argued as if it were plain that an increasing grant proportion as such implied more central government intervention and less local autonomy. On this it based its distinction between what have been called its centralist and localist solutions: 'Where the grant is a preponderant and increasing part of local revenue the government must accept increasing repsonsibility and ensure that it is spent in accordance with national policies and priorities (ibid., p. 265). Alternatively a dash for local freedom could be gained by a drastic reduction in the grant proportion from about 61 per cent to 50 per cent. That argument and the dilemma based on it has been shown invalid, given the formal basis of accountability for a bloc grant. The arguments gone over in that chapter do not need to be repeated.

Nevertheless, the formal argument is not the real argument. Over time there is no question but that central government has on balance intervened more in local affairs, though examples can be found of reduced intervention. But other explanations of this are plausible that have had nothing to do with grant.

The conclusion reached in that chapter was that there was sufficiently strong cross-section evidence that a higher grant proportion did increase local authorities' expenditure so that a cut in that proportion would lead to a fall in local expenditure, other things being equal. Even if it had been shown – which it has not – that local expenditure was invariant to 'price', as we have defined it, we would not infer there was no connection between price and quantity. Rather we would argue it was evidence that central government had so fettered local government by non-financial rules and regulations and the toils of persuasion that it had no freedom left to respond to price and was, indeed, no more than an 'agent'.

It still does not follow that the grant proportion should be reduced. It could be central policy to encourage expenditure; but if this is so, there must be another objective over and above horizontal efficiency and equity. Indeed, one could argue that by central government recommending the replacement of the present RSG by a unitary grant, a reduction in the grant proportion is implied. RSG is an inefficient and ultimately imperfect method of achieving the equalisation of rate poundages between authorities for a standard level of services. One cost of its inadequacy as a means to that end is that it requires a high grant proportion. The unitary grant can actually achieve the objectives of horizontal efficiency and equity with a grant proportion of about 40 per cent. Therefore, the traditional objective can be achieved with a lower grant proportion. While one can always manufacture or impute a different objective entailing a higher grant proportion, it is not easy to see what it might be, given ordinary principles of public finance. Such a subsidy is not a good way of altering income distribution, as has already been argued. It is difficult to see it as other than a diffuse paternalistic desire to encourage the consumption of local services relative to other services. Once horizontal efficiency and equity are achieved, why should one subsidise local services more, say, than the private output or the products of nationalised industries for which no problems of horizontal efficiency or equity arise? We have already discussed how far one can justify grants to authorities rather than to persons. It is more efficient the more prices tend to equal marginal cost.

With these provisos, and not expecting that in itself a reduction in grant proportion would necessarily increase local autonomy, we would argue for a reduction in the grant proportion on the grounds that it would both bring 'prices' of local services nearer marginal cost and lead to 'prices' that were more rational in terms of the relevant distribution policy of achieving horizontal equity.

The 40 per cent grant level required for horizontal efficiency and equity relates to rates. As land values are likely to vary more between local authority areas, the grant needed to achieve these objectives will have to be a higher proportion if there is site value rating. As in Britain average incomes between local authorities vary less than land values, or rateable values, a local income tax would imply a lower grant proportion than 40 per cent. However, the 40 per cent or its equivalent for other taxes is itself calculated on two assumptions reflecting particular and alterable ideas on the nature of the redistribution to be achieved. The first is that, as we have seen, some authorities are omitted as having a rateable value per head above an arbitrarily chosen 'standard'. Raise the standard and a higher grant proportion is needed and vice versa. Second, the British system assumes that the cost of the grant falls on central government. Horizontal equity could be achieved at zero cost to central government if the authorities with the higher tax base per head were taxed to pay for the grants that remained, but this would be to introduce another type of inefficiency into the system. The cost of services in the taxed authorities would be above marginal cost. While not attaching any real value to the two assumptions, we shall not assume any change in this respect in how the system works.

How could the grant proportion be reduced to 40 per cent or its equivalent for other taxes? The Layfield Committee experimented with assigning different taxes to the two different tiers of local authorities.

It was anxious to assign one tax to each tier (Layfield, 1976, pp. 270–80). The Committee argued that local authorities should not be allowed to choose their own combination of income tax and rates because it could lead to high rate poundage and low local income tax (LIT) rates in some areas and the reverse in others. The Committee saw this as 'unacceptable', though it is an example of local freedom accepted, for example, in the USA where different localities vary greatly in the mix of taxes they levy. We have argued both that multiplying local taxes in an authority leads speciously to greater buoyancy by confusing the electorate, and that it makes horizontal equity practically impossible. The Committee, pursuing its line of argument, was reluctant to give LIT to counties and rates to districts because of the great difference in the expenditure per head of metropolitan and non-metropolitan authorities in each tier. Thus LIT rates (or rate poundages) would be much higher in non-metropolitan than in metropolitan counties and vice versa — depending on which tax was assigned to which tier. Such an assignment would be a central imposition, and granted the different distributional impact of LIT and rates it would be odd to force a different income distribution in this respect on people simply because they lived in a metropolitan rather than a non-metropolitan county. For example, if the non-metropolitan counties had LIT and the metropolitan districts had rates — both being the major-spending authorities — the relative taxation of heads of households would be heavier in the latter and of earning non-heads of household in the former.

Understandably, the Committee next considered giving LIT to the major-spending authorities, reserving rates for the non-metropolitan districts and metropolitan counties. (The reverse was not considered since it would reduce the required yield from LIT below the level where it was worth incurring the costs of collection.) The difficulty here was that this would so much lower the yield from non-domestic rates as to require either a greater net burden of rates plus LIT on the domestic ratepayer, or some other consequential changes in national taxation to offset the loss of non-domestic rates. Rate poundages would be reduced by two-thirds.

Our analysis suggests that this is a positive advantage, as we have recommended the abolition of non-domestic rates. A reduction of non-domestic rates to one-third would not bring it down to a cost-of-service level — which we calculated to be approximately 20 per cent, but it would still be a very substantial reduction. To eliminate non-domestic rating, the Layfield Committee calculated that the rate poundage would have to stay at 80 per cent of the then rate poundage plus an additional 15p in the £ LIT.

On our analysis, the fatal difficulty for a solution which involves assigning different taxes to different tiers is that it prevents the achievement of horizontal efficiency and equity unless the tiers are entirely distinct in the services they provide, only one tax is given to each tier, and the same functions are provided by the upper and the lower tiers respectively throughout the country. It would require a more radical reallocation of powers than the Layfield Committee was able to consider and could not be consistent with the present situation where in urban areas the main powers and expenditure lie with the metropolitan districts, while elsewhere they belong to the shire counties. Without such a change a mixed solution of this kind is ruled out.

What are left are solutions which continue to assume a single local tax.

If rates remained the sole local tax, the most straightforward method of lowering the grant proportion would be through raising rate poundages. If both domestic and non-domestic rates were to be raised, about a 70 per cent increase in rate poundage would be required; but there would be no great efficiency advantage in much of this, since in part it would be replacing grants from central government with forced grants from the non-domestic ratepayer. Only the rise in domestic rates could be regarded as an effective increase in the 'price' of local services. If the rise were to be concentrated on domestic rates, then they would have to rise by about 150 per cent. Even if the reduction in grants was fully reflected by a fall in direct and possibly in indirect taxation, there would be hardship which one would expect to require transitional arrangements in mitigation. If, for example, lower grants were matched by income-tax cuts, the losers would be those who had high rateable values relative to their incomes, whether because they lived in large houses or because they lived where house prices were high. The gainers would live in small or otherwise low-valued properties relative to their incomes and, of course, those with taxed incomes who lived in others' houses — for example, young earners living with their parents. In the longer run, a more serious objection to replacing grants by rate increases is that it would intensify the inequity of rates — by comparison with income tax — and their inefficiency, because of the discouragement of building which we have already noted. Practically, however, any increase in rate yields relative to incomes would probably have to be phased over a long period and probably could not take place to the extent required if concentrated on domestic rates, even though income tax were reduced.

If site value rating were introduced, the problems would not be very different except there would be no additional discouragement of building. It is doubtful if a very great increase in site rate poundages would be acceptable in equity, or on efficiency grounds in some locations because of the possibility that it would amount to a more than 100 per cent tax on land values.

No such problems arise if local income tax were to replace grants. Indeed, if it were the aim to reduce grants, this would be another argument for an LIT. The least distributional change would achieved by (1) transferring rates to the Exchequer as a national tax at a uniform rate poundage to help finance central government services and raising as much revenue as it did when a local tax; (2) making over a sufficient proportion of the income-tax system over to local authorities to yield what they raise in rates and to compensate them for the required cut in grants. The redistributive impacts would be comparatively trivial, being confined to the effect of substituting a variation in local income-tax rates for a variation in local rate poundages.

Were a grant cut to be financed by more charging, the losers and gainers would be below and above average consumers of charged services, except in so far as they were compensated by vouchers. However, reducing grant overall would imply some under-compensation of the above average consumers. To finance a greater reduction in grant, the sums could be done assuming no or a less than offsetting reduction in rate burdens. This would have the advantage of preserving the efficiency and equity implications of the rating system, though the ratepayer would be worse off, especially if a substantial consumer of charged services.

SECTION 3

One feature of the present system is that except for a few authorities with above-standard rateable values per head, it removes all incentive to grant planning permission. Any increase in rates from a new development is offset by a 100 per cent equivalent reduction in resources grant. So far we have imagined this feature continued, even if the revenue source were changed because it is an implication of the objectives of horizontal efficiency and equity. The British tradition is that local authorities should not make money from granting planning permission – stigmatised as 'selling planning permissions'. Rather, local authorities should be financially neutral and take a cool disinterested view on the best use of land without it affecting their finances. The first major departure from this has been the practice that has grown up over the years of local authorities getting various benefits – planning gains as they are called – as a result of a negotiation to grant planning permission. Thus a developer might agree to provide some land free for street widening or to provide a site for recreation or space for a nursery school or clinic, beyond that required for the development itself. It is a way of transferring profits from developer to the local community; but it has the disadvantage that the local community can only gain within the context of the development. Ordinary consumer theory suggests that a local government should prefer cash to an equivalent value of land or space. It can spend the money more freely according to its priorities. The 1975 Community Land Act was a major step because for the first time it introduced legislation that provided for local authorities making a profit from development – a profit it was to share three ways with the Exchequer and other local authorities (through a pooling system). In effect, previous development taxation had accrued solely to national government. For the first time local government was to have a cut. When deciding, for example, whether to allocate land for housing or schools or to commercial development, it would have to bear in mind that it would make some profits from the income-generating development that it would not from social development – plainly a positive inducement to such development.

At the time of writing, there has been very little development under this Act and there is a high chance of repeal. But this is not the only reason why it is arguable that it has not been a sufficient inducement to authorities. One has first to remember that until 1974 all local authorities with rateable values above the average per head did not get resources element and had a strong financial inducement to develop, since they would gain on rate income even though they did not from development taxation. Thus one would hypothesise, other things being equal, a disinclination to develop among authorities who have gained resources element since 1974.

There is a difficulty here, because local government reorganisation occurred at the same time as the base of average rateable value per head was replaced by that of standard rateable value per head, so increasing the number of authorities in receipt of resources grant. But the general picture is fairly clear. Before 1974 in London, only Waltham Forest and Lewisham received resources element. In 1974, Greenwich, Wandsworth, Bexley, Bromley, Haringey, Havering, Redbridge and Sutton were added; in 1975/7 Merton and Newham; in 1976/7 Hackney, Barking and Harrow. Before 1974, Birmingham, Brighton, Chester, Eastbourne, Norwich, Oxford, Reading, Solihull, Southend, Torbay, Walsall, Warley, West Bromwich, Wolverhampton and Worcester did not get resources grant, neither among the counties did Bedford, Buckingham, Essex, Hertford, Surrey and West

Sussex. Since 1974, all metropolitan districts have received resources element except for Trafford in 1975/6, and so have most of the shire districts. The interesting consequence is that the spread of entitlement to resources element, combined with the London equalisation scheme means less incentive to develop.

However, an even more important reason is that without such an income gain, many authorities will be out of pocket from development. While developers are charged for roads to and on a site and for other immediate infrastructure, a new housing development can substantially put up the costs of providing local services. New schools may be needed or new facilities for social services, more capacity in the sewage system or the refuse disposal service. The local authority will not lose provided the cost per head of providing services does not rise; but this will be infrequent. New services generally cost more than old and not infrequently there are diseconomies of scale also. It is no accident that some of the strongest complaints against the regression approach are that it does not reflect costs of provision associated with extra population or shifts of population within an authority. Putting this right is no simple matter of incorporating a variable or two into the formula – partly because much of the expenditure is investment, but also because there are very great variations in the economies or diseconomies of scale associated with development even in different parts of the same local authority. Therefore, there is a strong case for charging developers and, in some cases, rehabilitators with both direct and indirect costs specific to their development which would otherwise have the effect of raising costs per head within the authority. Since the indirect costs could be susceptible to the exercise of considerable judgement in the allocation of costs, there is probably a case for any such estimates being subject to appeal if the developer charged feels that charges levied on him are excessive in relation to the costs he imposes on the authority. If this could be done, then local government finance ought to become neutral to development instead of being financially prejudiced against it.

The argument for going further than this would be to encourage development. This could either be seen as putting the clock back before 1974 or as a more general incentive to development. Whether this is desirable is a policy question for central government. We would argue that there is a case for it on the pragmatic grounds that local authorities tend to be biased against development, tending to hope that it will happen elsewhere. Frequently the benefits from an industrial or commercial development spill over a wide area. The immediate multiplier effects on the surrounding area may not be great. Thus the presence of intergovernmental externalities could justify a change to a system where the loss of resources element grant did not equal the revenue gain derived from an increase in rateable value per head, but rather were set at, say, 90 per cent of it, and vice versa for a loss. Ninety per cent is a purely arbitrary proportion. However, if such a system of development charges is not introduced to compensate local authorities fully for increases in their costs caused by new development, the efficiency case for a less than 100 per cent resources grant increases. The percentage below 100 per cent should at least be high enough to make it certain that any local authority does not lose from granting planning permission. We are inclined to go further than this and suggest that there is a cost of overcoming inertia in local authorities which inclines them against development in most cases, even when the financial effects are not adverse. It is related to the presence of intergovernmental externalities, but distinct from it. The intergovernmental externalities mean that while the benefits justifying a development tend to be diffused over many authorities, not only the cost of providing local services but also the social costs in terms of loss of amenity will tend to be concentrated near the development which, given the form of the planning system, will tend to have special weight in being able to resist change. The inertia argument is that any change is a costly process both in terms of planning effort and political or administrative time. The existence of both is likely to lead to a sub-optimal level of development in the absence of some offsetting inducement, even if the financial system were neutral, which it is not.

SECTION 4

So far no change has been assumed in the balance of power between central and local government. Now is the point at which to consider how changes in the use of grant could affect that balance, deliberately or less consciously. We begin with what, given all the trends of recent years in Britain, seems most likely: a tendency to increase the influence of central over local government.

In Part Three, Chapter 4 some well-canvassed substitutes for the current use of regression analysis to distribute grant were rejected on the grounds that they would alter central–local government relationships. The first was that RSG should be distributed in relation to the unit or standard cost of a particular service. The method was advocated by Godley and fellow economists from Cambridge. In outline, it resembles the method used in the 1950s and early 1960s when the pre-regression formula was loosely and obscurely based on something of the kind. Then the relevant cost was held to be that of a 'typical' low-cost authority who, while not at the bottom of the range of costs in providing a service, was in the lowest cluster of authorities above the bottom. In general, it could be assumed that there was always a substantial cluster of authorities at some such point whose average costs could be taken as a standard, it being assumed that local authorities spending substantially more were doing so voluntarily. Such a point's selection required judgement, but the implications of the method seem to have been profoundly obscure to local authorities. A more rational open use of this approach would require central departments to specify and cost a standard of service which they would be ready to grant-aid at a high, possibly even a 100 per cent rate, any costs above standard costs being grant-aided either at a much lower rate or being borne entirely by the local authority. This would be making explicit the distinction between standard and non-standard expenditure that we have found endemic in the discussion about grant.

A fairly close precedent has existed in housing. For many years central government has devised a housing cost yardstick. It requires the estimation of the standard cost of a house of standard characteristics. Grant is paid on a percentage of this standard cost with a small margin of tolerance. Any excess costs fall on the authority. The difficulties of such an approach are great. Central government has had to diversify the standard progressively to recognise different types of public housing — it is only on public housing that grant is paid in this form. Houses and flats of different sizes require different standards; and cases are always being made for new standards. For example, arguably different kinds of users — the elderly, the disabled — require different housing and different dwellings. Costs of provision vary between areas, particularly in the centre of major conurbations, and most of all in London. This is met by a high-cost provision which allows for higher costs in certain areas. Not only does this mean more cost estimation, but policy falls easily between two stools. On the one hand is the argument that social policy requires that higher costs should be met. On the other hand is the argument that it is not efficient to encourage building where costs are high. Usually the first argument has got the better of the second, so that there are London areas where the cost of providing housing is very substantially greater than normal, imposing a burden which may not easily be justified in either economic or social terms. But there are other administrative drawbacks. Policing this form of grant means that local authorities have to put all their building schemes to central government for approval. An army of architects and estimators is at work vetting plans and cost estimates. There is no real incentive to produce a house at less than the cost yardstick.

Arguably, architectural and bureaucratic pressures lead to over-design. While it is disputed as to how far the 10 per cent average excess in building costs of public housing over roughly the same-sized private housing represents a difference in quality, and quality desired by the occupant, that there is such a cost differential is hardly disputed. However, when one considers the practicality of extending the method to other spheres, there are more than administrative costs to consider. While it does not have this form the Department of Education's approval of school-building requires a detailed specification of standards, cost estimating and inspection, but is not made directly a basis for giving grant. The method is easiest to operate, albeit inevitably cumbrous, where new capital expenditure is concerned and the product in question can have a fairly standard form. The Department of the Environment has found it far harder to adopt a cost yardstick for the rehabilitation of existing dwellings which are non-standard and very various in the costs required to achieve a given standard. In many cases, it does not make sense to modify a building to a rigid standard. The development of a cost yardstick for current expenditure is likely to be still more difficult. The Home Office has done something of the kind for the police where very detailed cost control is exercised — even to the point of specifying the types of car the police can buy — but to extend this method in general would mean a large increase in staff and effectively the determination of local authorities procurement programmes and staffing standard in many respects. In effect something of the same kind is approximated in education where central government sets teacher quotas and salary structures are determined through the Burnham system, though there is some flexibility both in meeting quotas and in the choice of scales on which teachers are appointed.

The advantage of this approach is that central government can always hire technical staff of a kind who can administer such processes; but it moves government intervention in a direction which is undeniably bureaucratic and inflexible.

The sorts of considerations which determine the yardsticks and any grant system based on it are unlikely to have much to do with what is usually thought to be policy. Despite the tendency of some departments in some areas – housing, police, the school-building programme – to retain such an approach which was the one favoured in the early days of public education, the movement towards block grants has been favoured by central as much as by local government because the kind of detailed control is in general not the kind that either ministers or policy-minded civil servants want: and would be very hard to administer in most circumstances.

The second replacement for the regression method of grant distribution was to identify the client group for a service and pay grant according to the numbers of such clients. As was pointed out, such a method is most easily achieved in education, since the clients – the children who must be educated – are easily specified. Indeed, both this and the regression approach tend to coincide here since education expenditure variations are largely explained in practice by differences in the number of children in the population of a local authority. The rationale of such an approach is what we have seen called 'territorial justice'. It is certainly a centrally determined, redistributive concept and almost invariably a paternalistic one. Central government aims to ensure that children get the same standard of education wherever they are – even if, in practice, central government never quite achieves this. Similarly, the standard of public housing should be similar everywhere – even if, in practice, the variation in rents is substantial and, because of frequent variations in subsidy systems, bizarre. Not unexpectedly, most of the research into the design of formulae related to such an approach has been financed by the central department responsible for social services interested in the problem of securing the same provision of standards for its client groups in different parts of the country. Territorial justice is not secured if the elderly, the blind, the disabled, the mentally handicapped and other such groups do not receive the same standard of service. The problem is bedevilled, first, because there is such a variety of client groups; secondly because the rate of take-up varies far more than with public education which affects only a small minority – being influenced not only by differences in affluence but also by local differences in the strength of family relationships and by the number of clients in relation to the size of the population; and thirdly by the great differences in the kind of services provided – domiciliary or non-domiciliary, for example – which in some cases reflect as great differences in professional approach, often backed with passion. Conformity of view is frequently hard to achieve.

Unlike the first approach of standard costing, the rationale of the client-group approach – territorial justice – is something which ministers and policy-making civil servants frequently want, and not seldom use their powers of persuasion to achieve. It must be the explanation of much of the conformity in expenditure observed in British local government. As has already been shown, it would be technically feasible to distribute grant on this basis. The difficulties are threefold. The first is that, in practice, it has proved difficult for central government, or even the academic protagonists of such a scheme, to suggest that grant should be paid in respect of clients who are not actually using a service –

the elderly, for example, who look after themselves or who are looked after by relations. Yet this is implied. At the least it would be difficult to avoid a situation where there was pressure put upon central government to stimulate local government to go out and provide clients with services. This would be a major step into turning local authorities into agents. The second is that if grant were to be paid on this basis, it would be difficult to avoid central government taking a view on how the service should be provided, since it would affect cost. Closely connected with this, in practice, is that a decision would have to be taken on the weight to be given to different services in grant distribution which is not required under the regression approach. While an attempt could be made to achieve consensus on this between central government and the local authority associations, difference of views, both political and professional, are likely to be so extensive that ultimately such a decision would have to be taken by central government. While the grant might still take the form of a block grant, it would seem internally inconsistent for central government to specify the purpose for which grant was to be spent, as this method implies, and then take no interest in how it is actually spent.

One can imagine central government seeing some merit in a movement in this direction, since it could be represented as helping ministers to achieve their policies without undue interference in detail. However, it would not be achieved without difficulty. Central government would have to take a view — as it does not at the moment — on how its grant is to be divided between the client groups that are the interests of different central departments. This presumably would become part of the annual expenditure review, though it would be complicated by the undoubted desire of local authorities, represented by their associations, to make their observations on how the money should be allocated. Both within central government and between central and local government such negotiations would mean a substantial increase in the work that had to be done by the Treasury and other departments, and probably in the workload of ministers since many conflicts over the allocation of resources might be expected to come to the Cabinet. Even when the departmental division of grant had been decided, there would be the problem of allocating grant between the different client groups which are the responsibility of each deparment, a problem which would be greatest for the departments concerned with social services and with the environment since they have the greatest diversity of services. Indeed, it is unlikely that an allocation between departments could be settled unless each had first made a provisional allocation within each department, so complicating and probably extending the period of negotiation required.

It might be difficult to reconcile with retaining a block grant if ministers proposed a division of expenditure between client groups which local authorities decided to use differently after the grant had been distributed.

An intermediate scheme would replace RSG by departmental block grants. The effect would be to require central government to decide how grant was to be divided between these block grants, a decision ultimately taken by Cabinet, for which it would be responsible to Parliament. The block grants need not be departmental. Sometimes there would be a case for subdepartmental grants where a single department covered areas where expenditures are not particularly closely related, as, for example, the Department of the Environment covers housing, and a whole miscellany of infrastructure and other expenditures. One would not expect local authorities to have much to say in these decisions, though there could be preliminary discussions with local authority associations. Thereafter, the departmental or subdepartmental block grants could be allocated between the relevant local authorities on a variety of principles: by regression analysis, using a standard cost approach, or on the basis of client groupings.

To take regression analysis first.

The statistical advantages of such a change would not be very great. It would be unlikely to improve statistical significance tests above their already high level. But it could solve the problem posed by the existence of more than one tier of local authorities; since the regression analysis would be performed on all authorities performing a given expenditure function. It is also likely that the resulting formulae would be less likely to vary from year to year beccause of multi-collinearity and that for this and other reasons it is probable that the formulae would be more intuitively meaningful. For example, educational expenditure would depend of the number of children at different stages of education, sparsity and a number of variables which all could be seen to have a rational connection with the expenditure programme in question.

An advantage of such a change is that it could lead to greater rationality in central government expenditure decisions. Instead of departments arguing about formulae, the proportion of the total available for rate support would be divided between departmental block grants (or any other subdivision) as a result of political decisions taken by the Cabinet and discussions over formulae would be internal to each department. It is not necessary that because a local authority is given £x million in, say, education block grant that it is forced to spend that money on education. It could remain as free as it is now, only it would perhaps be clearer how its priorities related to those of central government.

Or it could insist that money received as a departmental block grant was spent of the purposes to which that grant related, though allowing freedom within that area (as is the avowed purpose of the new proposals for housing subsidy).

A major step, again, would be taken if the regression approach were abandoned and some of the alternative methods of distribution considered in Part Three Chapter 4 were introduced. At the limit, central government might pay departmental block grant on the basis of formulae, explicit or implicit, which reflected its priorities and had no regard to past expenditures or any local priorities. If the block grant form were retained, probably on a client-group basis but also possibly using a standard cost approach, then local authorities could still be free to spend within the total grant given them for each block, but the amounts they receive would be determined by central notions of their case for spending. Alternatively, central government could become more *dirigiste* and return to a position akin to those of the early educational grants where it was paying for services rendered. There would no longer be any question of block grants. We would have reached the realm of specific grants where control over what is actually provided is at least as strict as that currently exercised by the Home Office over local police expenditure through the existing specific grant for police.

Even specific grants can be handled in a variety of ways with different implications for central—local relationships. It could be similar to that between a nationalised industry and central government, where central government now has a policy of what amounts to making a specific grant for a specific service rendered. An example is the payment of subsidies to the railways for unremunerative rail services where, in effect, government is a bulk customer ordering and paying for services provided. In similar terms, central government could be seen as buying social services, education and other onerous services from local governments. This would be the apotheosis of the agency role for local authorities. As a monopoly buyer, central government would exercise very great influence in the provision of services. As monopoly supplier within their geographical areas, it would be difficult to avoid central government exerting influence to keep costs down within local authorities. Like a nationalised industry, a local authority might be a contractor or agent in respect of some services — the centrally determined onerous ones — while providing others — the locally determined onerous and beneficial services — as it decides. Central government might buy minimum standards of provision, anything more being a local option. There would still be important differences, because ministers do not appoint the members of local authorities and because local authorities traditionally have not received 100 per cent grant so that they might have an inducement to keep them efficient. Moreover, the relationship would be different if the local authorities had the discretion to decide whether or not to supply a service, or central government, in some cases, could choose between a local authority and another public body, or even a private one, when ordering a service.

SECTION 5

While much is heard of devolution, the tendency is towards more government activity and more of it being by central goverment either directly or through exerting greater influence over local government or other decentralised units of government like the nationalised industries. How could one attempt to reverse this trend so far as it could be done through altering the arrangements of local government finance?

We have already argued that reducing the grant proportion over a comparatively small range — from 61 per cent to 40 per cent — will not necessarily change the balance of power between central and local government. It may have some effect, however, and should not be discounted completely, in that the lower the grant proportion, the higher the 'price' to local electors and therefore the greater the incentive to local authorities to stand up to central government when resisting persuasion to increase expenditure as well as possibly a greater readiness to stand firm on how the money is spent. Even though there may be some range of grant proportion where changes will not affect central government's wish or ability to influence local authorities, it remains difficult to imagine that, at the limit, if grant were abolished altogether this would not affect central government's influence; but this as much because it would only make sense as evidence of central government's will to allow local authorities more freedom as because of the change *per se*.

It is the loose connection between particular changes in grant arrangements and political will that makes much of the argument of this section speculative. For example, a change which one would expect to be associated with greater local freedom would be for the needs element to be abandoned, resources element being retained. One would expect this to be a signal that central government was only interested in compensating local authorities for differences in their per capita tax base and, because it had given up grant-aiding to compensate for differences in 'needs', it was no longer interested in how the grant money was spent by local authorities. But it is possible to imagine central departments continuing to strive after the uniformity of provision they try to get, for example in education through teacher quotas, control over salary scale, and other powers they now use. Nevertheless, once again, such a change would not make sense except as a move towards giving local authorities more freedom. However, that particular change would also seem to imply that central government was changing its mind on distributional policy, since local authorities that had disproportionately high numbers of schoolchildren, social-welfare cases or other clients for local services would be hard hit. Therefore, it would have become more difficult for central government to use local authorities as its agents for the provision of centrally determined onerous or redistributive services, or to expect the disadvantaged local authorities with disproportionate needs to provide of their own volition as good services as those authorities with fewer needs per head.

A more constructive approach which would start to divorce the distributional question from that of local freedom would be to replace grants to authorities by grants to persons. But one would have to take care what incentives were built into a scheme. For example, the simplest form of this would be to make tax payments deductible from income-tax liability, as discussed in Chapter 3 of Part Three 3. Rates would rise so that net rate payments by the average ratepayer paying a basic rate of tax would not be very different from what he pays at present. Central government would be able to reduce RSG correspondingly, in effect, replacing the cut by grants through the income-tax system. It would not imply a reduction in the proportion of grant, only in how it is paid. The presumption is that it would reduce central government's ability to influence local authorities because it would be taken as evidence of a wish to disengage. After all, it is not an ordinary use of words to regard a reduced liability to income tax as central government grant. If it were, central government could try to presume to influence all persons and organisations on the grounds that by not taxing them more, it was giving them grants which gave it a right to try to influence their pattern of expenditure – which would be absurd. The drawbacks to tax deductibility as a method of increasing local freedom are (1) the distributional complications reviewed in our earlier discussion, (2) the fact that it was also not distributionally neutral in that it did not allow for either resources or needs equalisation, and (3) that, in any case, the reduction in the grant proportion achievable would be less than 10 per cent. Therefore, one must assume that even a unitary grant would require topping up if there were not to be a very large further increase in local taxes, so that, in effect, the relevant signals from central government would not have changed.

Nevertheless, pursuing the same line of argument, the most effective method of increasing local freedom would seem to be through replacing grants to authorities by those to persons. Vouchers could be used by central government to give those whom it intends to be beneficiaries of local services the command over resources it wishes, given their resources and needs. As has been demonstrated, a voucher system could, in princiiple, completely replace the needs and resources elements for those centrally determined onerous or redistributive services for which it is technically reasonable to charge. The direct cash nexus between central and local government would have been broken for such services (though resources element might still be paid in respect of local beneficial public goods). The presumption would be that both through their buying power and through the voting system, the local beneficiaries of such services would exert enough influence on local authorities to get a service acceptable to them and to central government. However, the cost of such local freedom would have to be recognised. Local authorities would, within their areas, in effect be monopoly suppliers of services (except in so far as there were also private suppliers as discussed above in Chapter 4). In many authorities, the beneficiaries of such services might be minority groups. Central government could hardly be disinterested if a local authority did not provide a particular service at all. Presumably there would have to be a statutory duty on an authority to provide such services. Even so, because the service affected only a minority, a local authority might try to provide — as it could at present — a poor service in relation to the price charged. This can and does happen with nationalised industries and local authorities at the present moment with no very effective discipline from the market in most cases. But, in principle, this is no different from the problems that always exist where there is a monopoly.

CONCLUSIONS

However, the main argument remains one of political will, and provided central government accepted that it would interfere less, a combination of other measures to reduce the grant proportion — unitary grant, charges or less grant in the context of introducing LIT — could have a similar effect in encouraging local freedom.

SECTION 1

(1) If rates were to be replaced by site value rates or by LIT alone the resources element could be redefined in terms of the new tax bases, but
(2) if taxes are replaced in part by charges there is little or no case for retaining a resources element for such services.

SECTION 2

(3) There are various ways in which the grant proportion could be reduced. The distributional consequences would be easiest to deal with if LIT replaced rates.

(4) One argument for reducing the grant proportion is that the present RSG is an extravagant and imperfect method of achieving horizontal efficiency and equity. The same objectives could be better achieved through a unitary grant which would imply a substantial reduction in the grant proportion. To argue for a grant proportion above that needed to achieve those objectives would mean importing a new distributive objective. Almost certainly it would have to be paternalistic. Therefore, one can argue for a reduction in the grant proportion. An alternative way of looking at this is to say that there would be greater efficiency in the provision of local services and the objectives of horizontal efficiency and equity would be better achieved if the grant proportion were cut and the 'price' of services allowed to rise towards marginal cost.

(5) The argument, however, used by the Layfield Committee that a cut in the grant proportion *per se* would increase local autonomy does not seem valid.

SECTION 3

(6) The objectives of horizontal efficiency and equity conflict with another objective, that of giving local authorities an incentive to develop. When resources element was calculated in relation to average rateable value per head before 1974, all authorities with above-average rateable value per head had such an incentive. Since then, virtually only some central London authorities have had such an incentive.

(7) But it is not just a question of lack of incentive. Local authorities are often not able to recoup all the costs caused them by development. Therefore there is a positive disincentive to develop.

(8) The incentive could be made neutral if a proper system of development charges were adopted. Failing that there is much to be said for reducing the resources element from 100 per cent to some lower percentage, say 90 per cent, as a rough balance. Even if there were no net development costs to local authorities, a reduction in the percentage could be justified on policy and efficiency grounds as a central govenment response to intergovernmental externalities likely to reduce development below the optimum.

SECTION 4

(9) In various ways, and serving rather different central government interests, replacing regression analysis by a client-group or standard-cost basis for grant distribution replacing rate support grant by departmental or subdepartmental block grants, or by specific grants, would all increase central government influence over local authorities.

SECTION 5

(10) The most effective method of increasing effective local autonomy is by replacing grants to authorities by grants to persons. This could be done through appropriately designed systems of vouchers reflecting resources and needs characteristics for services capable of being priced, without basically affecting the redistributive aims of central government, but in the right context other measures to reduce the grant proportion could help.

6 Optimal Size

Some of the ideas we have used so far can be adapted to analyse three related but distinct questions from those examined earlier in the book. We have hitherto taken the existing structure of local government as given — that is, so far as Britain is concerned, the two-tier system of counties and districts which was established in England and Wales in 1974 and with minor modifications in Scotland in 1975. Not that it has mattered particularly what structure is assumed. Most of what has been said is as relevant to the structure of local government that existed from 1894 to 1974 as to that which has succeeded it. One reason for this is the sheer arbitrariness typical of local authority boundaries. This is as true of federal as of unitary systems. As one writer has observed, 'federating is the strongest tie that previously unorganised, colonial or Balkanised regions are prepared to accept' (Scott, 1964). Traditional ties to particular lands are one reason why they will not further submerge their identity in a unitary state. Similarly in unitary states, boundaries between local government areas are steeped in history. While changes do occasionally occur — as in England and Wales in 1974 — they are piecemeal. Each tier in a federal or unitary system is composed of areas of substantially different size, wealth and population. Even a Napoleon with the advantage of a revolution behind him cannot impose an entirely uniform system of equal local government authority areas against the forces of tradition. If it could be done, it is not clear how equal would be defined — whether in terms of area, population, natural resources and wealth, or more complex criteria.

All the same, economic analysis can be used to help illuminate the issues relevant to feasible changes in local government structure. The 1969 Royal Commission on Local Government in England which was the basis, albeit modified, for the 1974 reforms, did use economic arguments to support its general recommendation that local authorities should be larger; and that powers should be shifted from lower to higher tiers (Cmnd 4040, e.g. pp. 68–70).

This chapter will comment on one structural question, the optimal size of local government, at some length; the next chapter will comment on the argument for vertical separation of local authorities covering the same areas but with different functions, and for there being more than one tier of local authority.

OPTIMUM SIZE — THE ALL-PURPOSE AUTHORITY

Since the Second World War, several American economists have written on the theory of optimum size in local government. They have not presumed to define an exact optimum. In practice, the debate has been between those who have argued, often quite politically and even emotionally, for smallness in local government, and their opponents who see the greater advantage in enlarging local government populations and areas.

Those who argue for smallness — the Little Local Governmentmen — are much in the tradition we have already mentioned of Toulmin Smith, T. H. Green and Alfred Marshall — if one dare lump such different thinkers together — who in England in the second half of the nineteenth century saw local government as a bulwark of civil and personal liberties against the centralising tendencies of national government. They realised that *laissez-faire* had become an insufficient doctrine and that there must be some government intervention, but looked for a middle way between *laissez-faire* and a powerful paternalistic state. The arguments we are about to consider are different, first, because the authors are all economists and second, because the power of central government even in the USA has increased so much that what they are hoping for is not a middle way as an alternative to a dominant belief in *laissez-faire*, but a reaction against centralising national government. Even so, there is a similarity in spirit. Henry Simons, who was one of the earliest of this school, wrote in 1948 that

> Good political structure should be closely similar to the informal organisation or federation of large societies, cultures or civilisations. The range and kind of governmental authorities and legislation at different levels should reflect the different range and kind of consensus, attained or unattainable. As one moves from primary groups through small to large communities and so on to inclusive society, the range of moral consensus becomes narrower and its content at once more fundamental or abstract and more vague or ambiguous. Government in a free society must at different levels, adapt itself to the existing hierarchy of moral consensus and try to build or to facilitate society's building a strong, bottom heavy moral structure . . . Large governments, like giant corporations . . . [may be] instruments of progress; but they lack the creative powers of a multiplicity of competitive smaller units. (pp. 12, 13–14)

The language may be different but many of the sentiments are similar to those expressed fifty and a hundred years earlier.

Among the arguments the Little Local Governmentmen commonly deploy are these:

(1)   It is easier and cheaper for citizens to understand political issues in a small community and, in particular, to acquire information on alternative policies (Tullock, 1969*a*, Oates, 1972).

(2)   The smaller the local authority, the closer will be the relation between decisions on expenditure and on the revenue required to finance it, and this will make for greater efficiency (Oates, 1972).

(3)   The more numerous local governments and the more trained elected members there are, the better nursery local government will be for national government (Mill, 1910*b*; Oates, 1972).

(4)   The smaller the population the better local authorities can reflect the wishes of their inhabitants.[1]

(5)   The smaller local governments are the greater their number. There will be

more competition and more innovation in the provision of local goods and services, and therefore a wider choice for the citizen.[2]

Against this the Large Local Governmentmen argue:

(6) that there are economies of scale in the provision of many local goods and services which justify large jurisdictions;[3]
(7) that local authorities need to be large to be able to employ high-quality staff and to attract high-quality councillors; (Royal Commission on Local Government, 1969, Cmnd 4040)
(8) that there are economies in the administration of local by central government if there are not too many authorities for it to have to deal with (ibid.);
(9) that the more local authorities there are, the more boundary problems — that is, intergovernmental externalities — there will be to create friction;[4] and
(10) national government is the appropriate level at which redistribution and paternalism should operate; and it is the delegation of such policies to local government on an agency basis that is responsible for much of the pressure for larger-sized local government.[5]

Lastly, there is one argument only relevant for the provision of onerous public goods:

(11) that the larger a local authority is, the more feasible is redistribution from rich to poor within its borders. (Tiebout, 1961; Rothenberg, 1970; Oates, 1972)

Many of these arguments need further illumination and some are contradictory. Grouping them together, there are a number which rest directly[6] on assertions of the existence of economies or diseconomies of scale (1, 2, 6 and 7). Others are concerned with intergovernmental externalities (5, 8 and 9). Two important ones are concerned with maximising consumers' surplus, that is the utility ratepayers gain from goods provided (4 and 5). Rather than go through these arguments seriatim or in these groups, we shall approach the problem by first building as strong a case as possible for smallness in local government and then considering criticisms of that conclusion. The arguments are very different for beneficial public goods than they are for onerous goods. Each will be examined separately.

THE ARGUMENTS FOR SMALL LOCAL GOVERNMENTS: THE BENEFICIAL PUBLIC-GOODS CASE

(1) CONTROL-LOSS

In a famous passage, Aristotle said that 'a state cannot be made out of ten citizens, and one which is made out of ten times ten thousand is no longer a state'

(Aristotle, 1948, bk IX, ch. X, para. 3). He argued that members of an effective political community needed to know each others' characters and fitness for office; and to be able to meet together in the market place to discuss business. As he also said, 'a state composed of too many . . . can hardly have a true constitution. Who can be the leader of a mass so excessively large? And who can give it orders unless he has Stentor's voice?' (ibid., bk VII, ch. IV, para. 11, p. 342).[7] Even if we had not accepted the military and economic inevitability of large nation-states, almost universal literacy, newspapers, radio and television have greatly increased the range of Stentor's voice. Yet something remains of Aristotle's argument. The media are a form of communication, yet all but the most serious newspapers do not wish to bore their readers with the details of national issues which most of them will find too abstract. They have not space — still less have radio and television — to examine local issues in detail. Local media are more able to devote space to local issues; and it is arguable that more people are ready to read about local issues in some detail than they are about remote national issues. However, there is a form of communication in politics which depends more on electors knowing their representatives who, in turn, have the time to get to know a proportion of their electors. Modern methods of participatory politics should make these easier. Mill admired the New England town meeting where ultimate local power rests in all adult inhabitants who meet together with equal opportunity to speak and vote on the decisions taken (Mill, 1910*b*). The town meeting still exists in much the same form as that in which Mill had heard of it, and is possibly the nearest modern equivalent to the Aristotelian ideal of the self-governing city-state. Mill accepted it would be impractical to introduce the town meeting into British local government, but in his argument for local authorities he stressed the advantage local administration had in local people being able to have 'under their eyes' those they themselves elected and could oust.

Even without the whole community participating, the closeness of local representation to the grass-roots should increase their understanding of what their electors want. The increase in size of local government from the old boroughs, urban and rural district councils has reduced the knowledge elected and electors have had of each other. Indeed, the current movement back towards parish politics in the form of neighbourhood councils reflects a widespread belief that local government has got too far away from its grass-roots. Though the belief that these should be consultative, not executive, reflects a belief that there are economies of scale in executive local government, it would probably be widely agreed that this feature of local government would be best expressed in a unit about as small as the ancient parish.

These diseconomies which, it is argued, increase with local government size are examples of what are called control-loss diseconomies of scale. In the theory of the firm, this refers to the greater difficulty management have in controlling a firm as it increases in size. Since the rationale of local democracy is that the elector should exercise control, it is the loss of control by the electorate because of increasing costs in gaining relevant information that is postulated to be a disadvantage of larger local authorities and will result in a less desired bundle of goods and services being provided. But, like all arguments involving particular economies of scale, they have to be weighed against other scale economies and diseconomies before any conclusion can be reached.

(2) CLOSER CONNECTION BETWEEN DECISIONS ON EXPENDITURE AND REVENUE

While this advantage of small government is often mentioned in the literature, it is only one of a large species of control-loss diseconomies caused by increased size. As government size increases, so congestion of business forces division of labour so that the unit of government is less able to pursue a coherent policy on all issues or have it discussed coherently by the legislative assembly. Thus matters on which policy would be better formulated and discussed in a connected fashion are dealt with separately at different times and often by different people. As the pressure of business grows, so executive and legislative and even judiciary find co-ordination of policy increasingly difficult. One example of this loss of control is a separation of decisions on expenditure from those on revenue. Rational politics requires that one should not decide to adopt a policy without considering simultaneously both its tax cost and its opportunity cost.[8] The protagonists of small government argue it should be possible to bring these decisions together better at lower levels of government and *a fortiori* the smaller is the jurisdiction. But to generalise the point away from this particular aspect of co-ordination, the movement towards corporate planning in local government reflects a recognition of the relationship between control-loss and size.[9] Whitehall has almost given up the attempt to relate the policy planning of its major sectors. It is difficult to co-ordinate issues within large departments − witness, for example, the problem there has been in Britain in co-ordinating road and rail policy, or even more, transport with environmental policy, or in working out a coherent policy towards the poor or the regions. Many administrative devices have been adopted to try to improve co-ordination − from the creation of large or new departments to the strengthening of the Cabinet Office with the Cabinet Policy Review Staff. They have co-ordinated policy in certain areas, for example on a few major issues, such as the management of the economy, the cutting of public expenditure (at a rather superficial level), and incomes policy. But they have not succeeded in producing co-ordination across Whitehall.

Corporate planning has been the major response of local government to the difficulty of co-ordination that increased as the volume of local expenditure grew in the 1960s. As so much of this was in redistributive or paternalistic public goods, the interactions with central government multiplied. Social services were a major component of this increase. As they were diverse in nature, the problems of co-ordinating the social services themselves created problems. The co-ordination of housing and social services, housing and transport, education and social services became harder and there were many demands, both inside and outside local government, that local government planning should be made more comprehensive (Drake *et al.*, 1975). Corporate planning was one attempt to deal with both this and the related financing problems caused by this increased expenditure. But this has also run into difficulties (Cockburn, 1977, ch. 3). It has been argued that corporate planning has increased the power of the paid officials of local government because, as full-timers and because of their training, they are better able to co-ordinate their thoughts and actions than they are those of unwieldy committees of part-time elected members. It may also have increased the influence of Whitehall because corporate, and indeed other plans, make it easier for it to exert its influence through being able to acquire more easily a better understanding of the local issues that interest it.

If co-ordination — whether of expenditure and revenue decisions, or of different sector policies — remains important, there will be a powerful argument for reducing the size of local government until it operates at a small-enough scale to make such co-ordination possible. This control-loss diseconomy of scale must be an undoubted disadvantage of larger governments. While something may be done by administrative measures to improve co-ordination, local government is always likely to be at a clear disadvantage compared with business in this respect for two reasons:

(a) Its elected members are part-time, liable to change at elections, and to rotate jobs between elections. They have to work through committees, of which few, if any, of the members are experienced administrators. Thus the effective management span of local members is likely to be less than that of professional management in industry.

(b) Moreover, the constraints on them and their criteria are vaguer, more complicated and more rapidly changing than in industry, so that corporate planning itself becomes a more complicated exercise, not able to rely on such relatively simple management tools as accounts, estimates, rates of return on investment, and rolling net revenue forecasts.

(3) LOCAL GOVERNMENT AS A POLITICAL NURSERY

Mill wrote that 'hardly any language is strong enough to express the strength of my conviction on the importance of that portion of the operation of free institutions which may be called the public education of the citizen. Now of this operation the local administrative institutions are the chief instrument' (1910*b*, p. 352). This political education serves two purposes. It encourages responsibility — the combination of thought and action — among those who take part in it. This is itself an advantage of small government, since those with such an education will be more numerous. Secondly, it is a training ground for national politicians. There are two aspects of this. First, as all have agreed, the art of the statesman or politician is difficult to acquire and matures with very general experience so that the most successful statesmen acquire their skills gradually and often retain that capacity to a great age. It is a shortcoming of the current British Cabinet system that departmental ministers have had little opportunity to train in executive skills. Most of them are heads of departments of state for a very few years, for which in most cases they have had little relevant preparation. Being the head of a business or a general — and few have been either or have held any comparable position of non-governmental responsibility — experience suggests might help, but it is no preparation for many important aspects of public life. A backbencher can develop certain skills of presentation but it is no training in responsibility and decision-making. Even a junior minister under the British system tends to have comparatively little responsibility delegated to him, and is more likely to acquire formal skills than judgement or the ability to prepare and take decisions. It is because, in microcosm, local government is much like national government that it is such a good nursery. Many of the politicians who are most constructive in home affairs have served an apprenticeship in local government — Joseph and Neville Chamberlain, Lloyd George, the Webbs, Herbert Morrison, Clement Attlee. This is not in itself an argument for small local governments, but there is a second aspect that is. If it is not, in effect, to be an oligarchy, democracy has a great problem in being representative of all types and conditions of people. Some of the most-valued people on both sides of the House of Commons are those whose abilities and judgement have been matured in very different occupations. This problem is easier in Parliament than in government where it is often very hard to find a trade unionist, indeed anyone with a working background, or a small tradesman or small manufacturer who is able to adapt his proven ability elsewhere in the inevitably more abstract activity of national government. Small local governments can encourage people of very different backgrounds and aptitudes to overcome shyness and develop those aptitudes which may lead them towards Westminster and Whitehall. Even today, there are many people who would once have felt that a parish council or even a borough council was within their reach, despite lack of formal education or paper knowledge of politics, but who would now not have the temerity to stand for anything as remote as a district council.

Formally this property of small local government is an externality benefiting central government.

(4) REFLECTION OF LOCAL PREFERENCES

When an individual or household buys a good or service, he will increase the quantity he obtains until the marginal satisfaction or utility he derives equals the price. If he buys less, he deprives himself of a net satisfaction. If he buys more, he is behaving irrationally since he is paying more at the margin than, by definition, the marginal unit of the commodity is worth. This is a standard finding of elementary books on economics.

The problem arises for public goods and services because government buys for its citizens. As we have argued before, the common assumption made is that the government acts as if it were the median voter. (We do not have to make that assumption. A similar problem arises provided it takes any of its voters, or any compromise between them, as its guide.) It then raises rates and buys commodities until the marginal satisfaction to that median voter equals the price (rates) paid by that voter in respect of all public goods bought. Therefore, all other voters are in a suboptimal position because they have different preferences from those of the median voter, or the influential voter. They will either be net gainers, gaining more in satisfaction than they pay in rates, or losers paying more in rates than they gain in satisfaction. Further, their preferences for different commodities will vary so that the marginal conditions will not obtain for them. Their utility is the less because they would have liked more of some services and less of others. These problems arise because of the nature of the goods local government provides. As has been commented on earlier, various authors have shown that to achieve economic efficiency, tax prices must vary between consumers of a public good (Lindahl, 1919; Head, 1962). Individual consumers will differ in their marginal valuations of a public good, though they have the same quantum available for consumption. For every consumer to be in equilibrium, defined as being in receipt of the quantum or package of public goods preferred, efficient tax prices would have to vary to reflect differences in marginal valuations. But, as has already been argued, there is a powerful reason why such price discrimination is not possible for public goods, since it requires knowledge of consumers' preferences. If there is uniformity of provision within an authority then all citizens whose preferences deviate from those of the median (or influential) voter will have a positive or negative fiscal wedge.

What remains is to show how these fiscal wedges will be affected by the size and number of local governments. If one considers not a pre-determined set of alternatives, but more realistically allows local areas to invent their own packages according to the preferences of their majority voters, one will find an increase in satisfaction or utility (Pennock, 1959).

It is important to note that this increase in satisfaction is simply the effect of subdividing a population into smaller and smaller local authority areas, and holds whenever decisions are made by majority vote.

Let us assume an area chooses a package, A. If the total area is divided in two, each of which is assumed to have a randomly selected population, then if the samples are large, the medians of their distributions — and thus the packages they will choose — will be similar and close to A. But as the number of samples increases and their size diminishes as further spatial subdivision takes place, there would be more variance between areas but less variance within areas, and on the lines set out above, more satisfaction since the 'distance' of each population from the median point would decline. The ultimate subdivision, of course, would be one person or a household in each area, when each would get the package voted for and no fiscal wedge would remain (Barzel, 1969; Tullock, 1970*a*).

(5) TIEBOUT EQUILIBRIUM

What was original about the Tiebout hypothesis was not its notion of fiscal wedges inducing migration. As we have seen, Cannan anticipated it as long ago as 1898. It was that a public-goods equilibrium could be achieved by a large number of local governments (Tiebout, 1956; Cannan, 1927). Previously, Samuelson had argued the inevitable inefficiency that must attach to the provision of public goods because government cannot estimate the potential valuation of each consumer, if there is no price mechanism (Samuelson, 1954). This is because of the advantage consumers get from not revealing their preferences. Tiebout showed that there was another equilibrating mechanism in intergovernmental migration. As we have seen there are many problems that arise in trying to formulate a satisfactory version of the equilibrating mechanism. However, these difficulties do not affect the relevance of the Tiebout argument to size in local government.

(a)   The cost of migration will be less the smaller local authorities are, so that the equilibrating mechanism will be more efficient. Households need to move a smaller distance to find an area better fitting their preferences.

(b)   Smaller governments mean more governments and therefore greater variety in the goods and services provided. This will also encourage migration because the gain in terms of reducing the fiscal wedge is likely to increase as households have more alternatives to choose from.

(c)   Because migration is likely to bring a greater net benefit to a household in non-optimal location, local authorities will have to become more competitive. If they are not to run into fiscal problems caused by out-migration or in-migration of costly newcomers, they must take what steps they can to produce the public goods their citizens want and keep the fiscal wedges down to a level which will prevent unwanted migration.

THE CASE FOR SMALLNESS IN GOVERNMENT: CONCLUSION

These amount to powerful arguments for small local governments. The first two – the Aristotelian and the various aspects of co-ordination – were variations on the proposition that there are control-loss scale diseconomies with increasing size. The second, the nursery argument, was an externality. The last pair – the Pennock and the Tiebout theses – were arguments that there would be a loss of consumer satisfaction – an increase in the magnitude of fiscal wedges – as local government size increased.

These arguments (or at least 1, 2, 4 and 5) may be combined in what Oates has called the 'Decentralisation Theorem' (1972, ch. 2). In an efficient world with no intergovernmental externalities:

> For a public good – the consumption of which is defined over geographical subsets of the population, and for which the costs of providing each level of output of the good in each jurisdiction are the same for the central or the respective local government – it will always be more efficient (or at least as efficient) for local government to provide the Pareto-efficient level of output for their respective jurisdictions than for central government to provide any specified and uniform level of output across all jurisdictions. (Ibid., p. 35)

Crucial to the truth of this theorem are what it assumes about the absence of economies of scale and intergovernmental externalities, as well as what is implied by presuming uniformity of central government output for all jurisdictions. Oates illustrates his general proposition with Figure 4.6.1. The curve *OC* measures vertically what Oates calls the hypothetical increase in welfare (increase in consumers' surplus) associated with an increase in the size of a local area. These are presumed to be caused by economies of scale or the internalisation of intergovernmental externalities. *OL* represents an expectation that 'the

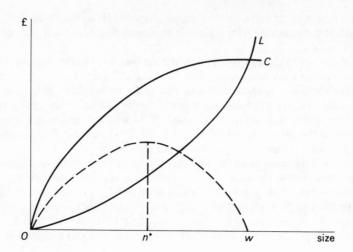

Figure 4.6.1   *Optimal size*

aggregate welfare loss from the differences between the actual and desired levels of consumption will tend to increase with size' (ibid., p. 41). In other words, consumers' satisfaction or surplus as measured in fiscal wedges will decline with size.

$$OW = OC - OL$$

where *OW* is a curve representing the net advantages of size. *n** represents a notional optimum size of local government jurisdiction.

In the first part of this section, we examined factors affecting *OL*. Now it is the turn of *OC*, but before that there is one matter to be cleared up. Otherwise local government might seem to be able to disappear altogether.

A DIGRESSION ON MINIMUM SIZE

The logic of four of the arguments for smallness suggests that the optimum might be reached if local government dwindled to vanishing point, so that one had a local anarchy of households. What are the facts that make it likely that one will want to have a local government unit larger than the household?

The basic reason why it makes economic sense for local authorities to have a contiguous spatial identity and a minimum size, lies in the technological characteristics of many of the beneficial monopolistic public goods it customarily provides. For example, street lighting, police and the repair and cleaning of roads. One other category is worth separate mention. There are those services where there are very substantial economies of scale in there being contiguity in the local distribution network. Many such services – electricity, gas, water and sewerage – have already been taken away from British local government for reasons we have already questioned. They are characterised by the high capital or labour costs of having competing supplies able to serve the same dwellings.

There are generally very great cost advantages in monopoly provision within a small area. In these cases, the argument rests on the use of local authorities to control local monopoly.

ARGUMENTS AGAINST SMALLNESS

(6) THE IRRELEVANCE OF ECONOMIES OF SCALE IN PRODUCTION

There have been many studies to estimate production functions in local government services so as to decide the optimal scale of provision and from that the general shape of the OC curve in Figure 4.6.1.

Broadly the conclusion is that there is very little satisfactory evidence on economies of scale in local government.[10] This follows the findings of others who have also examined the question. Even if one could establish sizes of government at which increasing costs set in, there is a rooted objection to accepting what local authorities do now as an indication of what is possible for them to do when they are most efficiently organised.

However, one can sidestep these problems of estimation and of deciding what is efficient, by the argument that economies of scale in production are irrelevant to the optimal size of local government. This is done by separating the provision of local services from their production. One method is through joint action or contracting from other local authorities. But production may also be private. In the USA this possibility is well known as the Lakewood Plan.

With the incorporation of the City of Lakewood in 1954, Los Angeles County, for example, expanded its system of contracting for the production of municipal services to a point approaching quasi-market conditions. Newly incorporated cities, operating under the so-called Lakewood Plan, contract with the county or other appropriate agencies to produce the general range of municipal services need in the local community. Each city contracts for municipal services for the city as a whole. Services beyond the general level of performance by county administration in unincorporated areas are subject to negotiation for most service functions. Each city also has the option of producing municipal services for itself. Private contractors too have undertaken such services as street sweeping, engineering, street maintenance and repair, and related public works. Some contracts have been negotiated with neighbouring cities. As the number of vendors increases, competition brings pressures towards greater responsiveness and efficiency. By separating the production from the provision of public goods it may be posssible to differentiate, unitise and measure the production while continuing to supply undifferentiated public goods to the citizen-consumer. Thus Los Angeles County has, under the Lakewood Plan, unitised the production of police services into packages, each consisting of a police-car-on-continuous-patrol with associated auxiliary services, and a municipality may contract for police service on that basis. Within the local community, police service is still provided as a public good for the community as a whole. Problems of scale arising from possible conflicts between criteria of production and criteria of political representation may be effectively resolved in this way. (Ostrom *et al.*, 1961, p. 839)

Thus any economies of scale can be realised on the production side. The local authority becomes a procurement agency buying services from others, except where it decides on efficiency grounds to produce its own either for itself alone, or for itself and others on a contractual basis. It may buy from other local authorities, private enterprise, central government of public corporations.

Of greatest importance to our argument at this point, this shows the irrelevance of economies of scale in the production of local goods and services to optimum government size. This conclusion would seem to be perfectly general. Economies of scale of this kind need never in themselves be an argument for larger size in local government. Even police service, it would seem, can be bought in or provided by joint arrangements. Indeed, there are many local authorities in the USA who now buy police services from private security organisations. There is, however, no need for such an ultimate intrusion of private enterprise which many in Britain would feel bizarre. To give more realism to the picture, one could imagine single-tier authorities no larger than pre-1974 boroughs, urban district or rural district councils, or pre-1964 London boroughs, or possibly current district or London bouroughs. These would realise many of the advantages of smallness that have been advanced (without going down to authorities as small as the ancient parish or current neighbourhood councils). These might be expected to be of large-enough size to provide most of the more important social services; though they might run some homes and other services on a joint basis with other local authorities or subcontract with voluntary societies or even with private enterprise. Similarly, in transport they might be expected to supply some road-repair and maintenance and construction services themselves, while buying in others from private enterprise or public enterprise road construction units, as they would bus services from the National Bus Company. While one might expect them to supply some police services, there is no need for this since they could engage in more joint action with other local authorities as many now do, even if they did not buy in services on the American model. If it were possible or desirable to turn the clock back, one can imagine such local authorities acting as intermediate procurement agencies for water and sewage, and even electricity and gas, negotiating with producer public corporations and possibly controlling the local distribution networks. There is no need to go through the other local services. In all cases, it would seem possible to devise joint or other contractual arrangements which would make it unnecessary to be influenced by production economies of scale in deciding on the optimal size of local government. Many of the arguments by Ostrom and others for the Lakewood Plan approach are more general, in that they postulate that the efficiency of local services will be improved if:

(a)   There is a separation between the procurement and production functions, the local authority retaining only the former and being able to use what

J. K. Galbraith called countervailing power to negotiate more efficient and possibly cheaper arrangements with the public or private contractors. Moreover, such a separation will reduce the tendency to inefficiency in local authority direct labour departments.

(b)   Local authorities are able to choose and change their suppliers on the basis of competitive tenders.

With such arguments, if true, a very general efficiency case can be produced for Lakewood forms of arrangement. Indeed, it is not necessary to demonstrate that contractual arrangements are always to be preferred. However, whenever a particular scale economy is alleged as a reason for increasing the size of local government, one should recognise that there is an alternative which if adopted would preserve both the benefits of small local governments and of the economies of scale.

So powerful this argument seems, that it immediately raises the question why, in Britain we seem to have paid little attention to it, particularly in recent arguments on local government reform. Interestingly, Ostrom and his co-authors cite Sidney and Beatrice Webb as authorities for their view of local authorities as procurement agencies (Ostrom *et al.*, 1961, p. 839).

In the Webbs's essay on *The Development of English Local Government* they made much of the historical transformation of local authorities into 'Associations of Consumers'. Their interest here was the same as Ostrom's. The Webbs noted:

When each inhabitant was under obligation to supply and light the lantern at his door, to pave and sweep the street in front of his own house or workshop, to supply his own horses or his own labour for the mending of the roads he used; to maintain at his cost the bit of primitive embankment that protected his holding from the flood, or even to perform in his turn the duties of the various Parish offices, it was of his own pains and costs, his own efforts and sacrifices in the process of production that he was most vividly conscious. (1963, pp. 130–1)

The ambivalence of the Webbs can, however, be seen in the contrast they make between this and the next stage of local authorities as consumers' associations:

But the minutes of the Manchester Police Commissioners or the Westminster Paving Commissioners exhibit these representatives of the consumers organising their growing services, and giving out their extensive contracts, on the basis of buying labour as a commodity, just like lamp irons or paving stones . . . All that they were concerned with – and this in their inexperience of public administration, they lamentably failed to secure – was 'buying in the cheapest market and getting the work done at the lowest possible monetary cost to the constituency they taxed'. (ibid.)

The Webbs go on to point out that under the influence of Jeremy Bentham and the Utilitarians, the nineteenth-century local authority developed a strong tendency to adopt contracting out, and the use of competitive tenders. One may speculate (1) that the motives and efficiency arguments were almost precisely the same as those of the American protagonists of the Lakewood scheme and (2) that such arrangements were quite as widespread in Britain in the nineteenth century as they are now in the USA.

There are still examples of joint action and of contracting out to private enterprise in British local government.[11] Local authorities do combine for certain police purposes, to provide certain forms of higher education, and various types of residential institution. There are local authorities which employ private builders, as there are those that use their own direct labour. But, in general, contracting out has declined enormously.

The Webbs suggest some of the reasons. Under the influence of Benthamite notions and the score of tradesmen and others that were often elected to Victorian local councils, very many developed as harsh a reputation as employers as had the Bounderbys and Gradgrinds of industry. Because so much of their labour was unskilled, municipal employees were slow to unionise. Very often the councils were very inefficient at procurement and quite often the private pecuniary interests of councillors clashed with their responsibilities to the ratepayers, so that there was corruption. As a result, many reforming local authorities began to hire their own labour with the not neccessarily consistent aims of becoming known as good employers and of being more efficient than the use of contract labour had often become in practice.

While one may understand why British local authorities turned away from the Lakewood Plan style, the question is whether the reasons are still relevant One may note:

(a)   that local authority workers are now protected by unions,
(b)   that the powers and competence of the District Auditor have been greatly strengthened and could be further strengthened so as to audit contracts and competitive tenders to reduce the possibility of corruption,
(c)   that the preservation of smallness was not then so much at risk because it is only in recent years that economies of scale in production have grown to jeopardise it; and
(d)   that direct provision does not eliminate opportunities for corruption.

As in any new arrangements, there are costs to be set against the benefits. If local authorities are to become buyers-in or joint providers with others, they will need to develop some of the skills of the procurement and contract branches of comparably sized firms; and there will be a cost to that.

(7)   ECONOMIES OF SCALE IN MANAGEMENT: THE CALIBRE OF MEMBERS AND OFFICIALS

We have discussed economics of scale, or contiguity, in local distribution and economies of scale in production. There are also economies of scale in management or control. As we have seen, diseconomies associated with control-loss are generally characteristic of increased size. Against this may be put the proposition that there is a counteracting gain from size in that local authorities are able to attract better-quality members and employ better officials. This was a proposition made much of by the 1969 Royal Commission on Local Government (Cmnd 4040). The roots of this attitude can be found yet again in Mill's seminal chapter, where he was brutal on this shortcoming of local government.

> The greatest imperfection of popular local institutions, and the chief cause of the failure which so often attends them, is the low calibre of the men by whom they are almost always carried on . . . Now it is quite hopeless to induce persons of a high class, either socially or intellectually, to take a share of local administration in a corner piecemeal, as members of a Paving Board or a Drainage Commission. The entire local business of a town is not more than a sufficient object to induce men whose tastes incline them for national affairs to become members of a mere local body and devote to it the time and study which are necessary to render their persons anything more than a screen for the jobbing of inferior persons under the shelter of their responsibility . . . the local representatives and their offices are almost certain to be of a much lower grade of intelligence and knowledge than Parliament and the national executive. (1910*b*, ch. XV)

Expressed with less blatant arrogance and moved upwards from the paving board or 'mere village' that were too piecemeal or small in Mill's belief to attract members and officials of sufficient calibre to the level of districts and counties, the same sentiments are found both in the Report of the 1969 Royal Commission and more widely held (Cmnd 4040; also the Herbert Commission, 1957–60). Such matters are so much a question of subjective impressions that one cannot easily come to a firm conclusion. But it may be worth speculating on the following:

(a) There is a vastly larger educated class in Britain than in Mill's day.
(b) Britain was able to provide a ruling class to govern an empire and lead in all sorts of other activities which have much diminished in recent years.
(c) Mill himself felt that something as small as a town should be able to find a sufficient number of able persons, though not a 'mere village'.
(d) What discourages able people both as members and officials, as it does people in every walk of life, may be the constraints and regulations which make the job narrow and in important respects less responsible, even the interference of central government, rather than the intrinsic interest of local government.

(8) CENTRAL GOVERNMENT'S SPAN OF CONTROL

As the essential issues have already been discussed in Part One, Chapter 2, only the ones that are relevant in the present context need to be rehearsed.

There can be no doubt that it is easier for central government to influence the 400 English and Welsh authorities that there have been since 1974 than the 1,400 there were before then, especially given the growing volume and complexity of local authority activity. Four hundred is a very large span of control. Central government's task would be made simpler if districts were strictly subordinated to counties which then became the units with which central government would have dealings on all matters. Since this was bitterly opposed by the local authorities and widespread political and public opinion – in general because of arguments for smallness of the kind we have already examined – central government has tended to develop another administrative device: the region. If elected and given clearly delegated powers and sources of taxation, the region could be a new form of local government. Regional government so far has not had this inspiration. Rather it has had the purpose of introducing a geographical tier within central government so that officials, in effect, could exercise better control by reducing the span of control to a more manageable number of authorities. In short, if one looks at the problem in this way – and it appears a strong influence on the thinking of the 1969 Royal Commission – there can be no doubt that ordinary management thinking about spans of control suggests either larger local authorities or more tiers, not necessarily, however, the former.

The relevance of the argument is doubtful for beneficial public goods, as has been argued earlier. It follows from three assumptions which we have already questioned:

(a)   The first is that the old Benthamite principle of Inspectability is really the best method of stimulating efficiency on local government.
(b)   The second is that even if inspection stimulates efficiency, the extent of intervention and inspection is not much greater than can be justified on efficiency grounds, being rather a method of introducing redistributive or paternalistic criteria into the provision of ostensibly beneficial public goods.
(c)   The third is that inspection of beneficial public goods, whatever its merits, is best practised directly by central government rather than by a more independent body on the lines of the corps of district auditors.

(9)   THE LIMITED RELEVANCE OF INTERGOVERNMENTAL EXTERNALITIES

This is the argument against smallness that Tullock (1969a) for example, as a protagonist of smallness, feels has the most weight.[12] Yet it is arguable that it is also almost or quite irrelevant.

Tullock illustrates his point with Figure 4.6.2. The internal or other costs of providing government services slope down to a least-cost point with size and then increase, so that on this criterion the least-cost size would be B. If one were to take an arbitrary criterion – say the internalisation of 90 per cent of externalities – then A would be the optimum size. But if one were to take both costs into account – total costs – then one would choose C. Because externality costs always fall with size, and economies of scale are postulated to be U-shaped, the size that takes into account externalities is always larger than that which does not. However, because Tullock argues that economies of scale as such are irrelevant to government size, the externality argument alone would lead to a

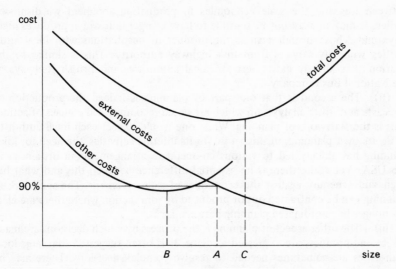

Figure 4.6.2   *External costs and optimal size*

demand for the abolition of all local government in favour of a single unitary national government. Rather unsatisfactorily he argues the need for an *ad hoc* assumption that 'we only try to internalise something like 95% of the externalities from each activity' (1969*a*, p. 21). 'Clearly continental or even world governmental agencies for street cleaning or fire protection are not desirable' (ibid.) just because there were external effects felt by an Afghan visitor to New York's dirty streets or because a foreign tourist's luggage is burnt in a London fire. But why 95 per cent? Why not some lower percentage? To this there is no easily quantifiable answer.

It is worth recalling what these governmental externalities are. As our previous analysis showed they tend to be of two kinds.

(a)   The literature is full of lakes breeding mosquitoes bordered by more than one local authority; smoke or other forms of pollution being blown by the wind from one community to another; or unsightly tall buildings blighting the sky-line of another neighbourhood; or rivers into which several neighbourhoods discharge their effluents. While theoretically interesting, most of these are of limited practical importance; and in so far as they are, internalising them by increasing the size of government so that all parts of the same lake or river are in the same authority is one of several possible courses of action. Our earlier analysis examined various alternatives of which the more important were bi-lateral negotiation, joint action or the intervention of central government to improve the situation.

(b)   The second category were externalities to be realised by planning – for example, the advantages of planning a transport system or land use on a large rather than a small scale. Three points are perhaps worth mentioning:

(i)   The first is that in many cases there is no real difference in principle between this and the scale economies in production argument we dismissed earlier. It may or may not be sensible to have a larger unit which produces highways and whose overall plan is the product of negotiations with local authotrities who buy services from that highway authority. This is similar to the relation that already exists between local authorities and British Railways or the National Bus Company.

(ii)   The second is that one part of planning is indeed the production of forecasts and other analyses on which are based recommended courses of action. This is the staffwork of planning. While one would expect each local authority to do its own planning, in this sense, for its internal activities, the need for joint planning has already led to various co-operative arrangements in Britain, as in the USA. Yet again, there is no essential difference between this and what has been said generally against the economies-of-scale argument. The staffwork of planning can be contracted out or produced by joint action where there are clear advantages in co-ordinated planning between areas.

(iii)   The other aspect of planning is the process by which decisions are made whose end-products are expressed as plans. It is often suggested that large local authorities are sometimes needed to resolve complex decisions. There may be force to this but it should be pointed out that this is to replace external by internal negotiations. This planning is the process of negotiation by which a final, even if ephemeral, plan or set of plans is produced. The control-loss diseconomy of planning that attempts to be too comprehensive functionally or geographically has already been mentioned.

Therefore, it would seem that the intergovernmental externality argument against smallness has as little force as the economies-of-scale argument, and for the same reasons.

THE EFFECT OF ASSUMING UNIFORM PROVISION WITHIN LOCAL GOVERNMENT AREAS

In his decentralisation theorem, Oates stated that with various reservations we have discussed it is 'more efficient or at least as efficient for local governments to provide Pareto-efficient levels of output . . . than for central government to provide any specified and uniform level of output across all jurisdictions' (1972, p. 35).

Implicit in his use of the word 'uniform' is the assumption that central provision or larger local government implies the provision of more uniform public goods.[13] If it did, there would be a welfare loss — an increase in fiscal wedges — but Oates gives no reason why central or larger local government should not take into account local differences in preferences as much as local jurisdictions might. One reason for presuming that there would be uniformity is that it might be thought to follow from a voting rule — such as majority voting. But this is incorrect. Properly interpreted, such a rule or similar rules imply securing a majority and establishing provision of public goods close to that of the median voter's preference. However, if one allows coalition and indeed ordinary prudent politics, part of the art of securing a majority is to provide services which please a majority of voters who are not identical in their tastes. No government secures a majority most efficiently by providing exactly the same services for everyone where differentiation is possible. Therefore, it has to be argued that central or larger local government is less able to differentiate between individual preferences than is local government where it is in the advantage of any government level to do this. Oates's decentralisation theorem requires more justification to achieve his result than he has given it. If it were not for control-loss diseconomies in scale which make differentiation harder, one could not suppose that an increase in scale, as such, need lead to greater uniformity in the provision of beneficial public goods.

One might not unreasonably rewrite Oates's decentralisation theorem as follows:

Because of control-loss diseconomies it will be always more efficient (or at least as efficient) for smaller local governments to provide Pareto-efficient levels of output for their respective jurisdictions than for central or larger local government. While quantification is not possible, the empirical presumption we have come to is that one can argue that such net economies are likely to be exhausted at the level of quite small local governments — at least in the provision of beneficial public goods.

Virtually all the writers we have quoted on optimum size have written about the question specifically in the context of a federal or quasi-federal system. However, all the arguments we have discussed are as applicable to a unitary system of government in which local authorities are considered as agents of the central government. As we have argued in the context of Oates's decentralisation theorem, it is the possibility of control-loss diseconomies which may make it inefficient for the central government to provide beneficial goods efficiently. Even if local governments politically are considered as agents of the central government such control-loss diseconomies would argue against all power being at the centre. In a unitary state the optimum degree of decentralisation is capable of determination on similar principles to those adduced for the determination of optimum size in a federal system.

REDISTRIBUTIVE PUBLIC GOODS

As was shown earlier in the discussion of the 'fiscal wedge', there is a limited and not very useful sense in which any production of public goods will result in redistribution. Since efficient marginal cost pricing is impossible by definition, the taxes public producers raise will not be such that the marginal benefit to the consumer equals the marginal cost; and the incidence of the taxes or tax prices will have a different distributive effect on the consumers of public goods by comparison with other tax policies which would have been feasible. We have defined beneficial public goods, however, to reflect an intention to set tax prices which reflect willingness to pay as far as possible and correspondingly no intention to use tax prices to pursue any particular redistributive policy. Any redistribution that occurs on these assumptions is unintended, whereas that which we are now interested in is intentional. The last pair of arguments on size (see p. 560

above) are only relevant where local authorities produce onerous public goods and their actions are intentionally redistributive or paternalistic or both. The two propositions were: (10) that local authorities are inappropriate, indeed economically inefficient, agents of redistribution by comparison with central government; and (11) that the larger their population, the easier it was for local authorities to redistribute or act paternalistically.

The relationship between redistribution and size is clear. Redistribution involves the intentional creation of fiscal wedges. Some people are forced to pay more in taxes than they receive in benefits. They have an incentive to avoid this burden, if they can, by migrating to other areas.

As the Tiebout argument showed, the smaller the authority the less costly will be migration for any household whose fiscal wedge is negative, in terms of movement, information and psychic costs; and the greater the attracting power of an authority to any household whose fiscal wedge would become positive when it moves to that local authority. Thus small local authorities are less likely to engage in redistributive or paternalistic policies which create or expand fiscal wedges because of their adverse effects on migration. Moreover, the smaller the population of a local authority, and therefore the more local authorities there are for a given population, the more socially and economically homogeneous will the population of each authority become as a result of migration. As long as communities do not become completely homogeneous in the relevant respects, redistribution and paternalism can still continue, but with greater homogeneity there will be diminishing returns to both within the local authority. Not that one would ever expect a complete absence of redistribution or complete household homogeneity.

Some citizens might be ready to pay rates, in part not to enjoy benefits themselves but to pay for others' benefits. For example, elderly couples who had children who lived in the area but have grown up, or indeed who never had children, may identify with the families with children around them sufficiently to want to contribute to their schooling or recreation.

Even so, it remains true that the smaller the population or area, the more likely it is that involuntary local redistribution and paternalism will not be feasible. Neither will it be much desired.

Conversely, the larger the population or area, the more possible and desired both redistribution and paternalism will be. The population will be more heterogeneous, socially and in terms of income distribution. The preferences of the voters will be more dispersed. Migration costs will be greater. The extreme, of course, is a local government so large that it is coterminous and identical with central government.

The arguments which were used to define in principle the optimum size of local government are not applicable when local governments provide onerous public goods and engage in redistribution. Moreover, the provision of such goods by local governments raises a major problem for a federal structure of government if the central government has its own distributive goals. If local governments have the freedom to determine the redistribution within their areas, they can offset the distributive policies desired by the central government.

The Wheare definition of federation was that each level was co-ordinate and independent in its sphere of influence (Part One, Chapter 2). A constitution was required, in some sense 'above' government, to define these spheres so that they might be clearly delimited.

The natural interpretation of the Wheare definition is that if the functions are divided between central and local government, so that it is clearly set out what subjects each has authority over and where residual authority lies, this is a sufficient definition of the 'spheres' of each. But such a definition in terms of legislative or executive powers cannot rule out the possibility of conflict, particularly in relation to policies which transcend subject areas. Earlier we were at some pains to consider how central government instruments for macroeconomic policy could be improved while interfering less with the actual subject-matter of local expenditure. The distribution of income is another policy on which central government has views which transcend the interests of particular subject areas. A problem, therefore, is that local government can alter the national income distribution deliberately or inadvertently as a consequence of what it does within its sphere of influence unless the 'constitution' is written so as to make clear the redistributive criteria it is to use, or alternatively whether any level of government is to be regarded as sovereign in relation to distribution, and if so, how it executes such a power. In no known case does a constitution specify 'spheres' in such terms. The federal constitutions of the USA, Canada and Australia are all under strain because of conflict between levels of government over what are either directly or indirectly questions of redistribution.

A possibility which may seem to avoid the problem is illusory. It follows from what was said earlier that a small local authority cannot pursue active redistributive or paternalistic policies. Thus a federal system might be set up with a single central government but a very large number of small local governments. Then, whatever freedom local governments were given to produce onerous public goods, because of easy migration practically redistributive and paternalistic policies would lie in the determination of central government. If it could be established, the effective political power of the centre would be so great that one doubts whether the situation could be called strictly federal. While it might work, central government would have to have very great power over the making of the constitution to achieve an outcome which so confined the political power of the lower tier – a power more to be expected within a unitary system. The avoidance of the problem is illusory, of course, because no federal or quasi-federal system remotely resembles such a confederation of numerous small units.

If it could be imagined that central and all the local governments had the same social-welfare function so that their redistributive and paternalistic objectives were the same, then there would be no conflict in this respect, but agreement. This is so unlikely, given the different population of which any geographically separated unit will be composed, as to be ruled out. An equally unlikely reason for absence of conflict would be if either level were simply not interested in redistributive or paternalistic impacts. Such political apathy is unimaginable.

Logically, therefore, the problem of optimum size in local government when it provides onerous public goods cannot be defined from the standpoints of all the governments concerned, central and local. Since all may be expected to have different social-welfare functions there is no unique solution even in principle.

Whether one defines an optimum from the standpoint of central or any individual local government, the outcome will be different. It will depend on the amount and type of redistribution each desires. The irony of so much discussion on optimum size in the context of fiscal federalism is that such an optimum can only be defined where it can be presumed that all government levels will use the same social-welfare function.

Yet, as we have said before, federalism is only a set of assumptions which are as unrealistic as those of the omnipotent unitary state. Power is diffused. The objectives of different governments are likely to conflict in all governmental systems. Both in a unitary and a federal system, signs of conflict over redistribution and paternalism are likely to be visible.

Those who are conservative in relation to income distribution often argue for small, powerful local governments. The more functions local government performs, the more central government will have to rely on cash distribution as it will have fewer activities through which to perform redistribution in kind. If these local governments are also small, the less they will be able to act redistributively. This would seem to be the position of many American fiscal conservatives, but a central government with a marked wish to redistribute might come to the same conclusion. It could choose small governments to minimise how far they can interfere with what central government is doing in redistribution.

When might central government prefer large local governments with redistribution in mind? It might prefer large local authorities where it was using local authorities as agents to pursue its own redistributive and paternalistic ends. This, in part, would seem to be the position of British government. However, it is a different situation from one in which central government deliberately prefers large local authorities which are free to pursue their own redistributive and paternalistic policies. The histories of federations give one a clue to a second major possibility. Where, in general, a conservative and anti-redistributive central government recognises that to preserve the state there must be some help given to the poor in some areas, and yet does not wish to impose national policies, possibly feeling it cannot get the required assent to them, it may encourage the formation of some areas large enough to practise some internal redistribution. Obvious candidates are large metropolitan areas in the centre of which congregate large numbers of urban poor. Despite resistance from its suburbs, one can see why a large New York able to practise some redistribution from rich to poor might be more attractive to the nation as a whole than a federal redistributive programme, though the per capita burden of that would be proportionately less on the rich, and more poor would benefit.

In British history, the reasons for enlarging jurisdictions to achieve redistributive ends have probably been its great convenience, in producing fewer but larger agents for central government to deal with. The ancient use of the parish for poor relief was a recognition that the state, even if it had wanted to, could not have administered poor relief nationally. The administration was beyond it. It could not have raised and disbursed the necessary taxation. Yet, as Cannan (1927, *passim*) shows, central government had constant difficulty in goading all parishes into achieving a minimum standard. The 1832 Act combined parishes into unions with boards of guardians primarily to spread the onerous load over a larger area with more internal capability for redistribution. That was the motive for abolishing the boards of guardians in 1929 and merging their functions into those of the counties. In 1934, when the counties lost most of their poor relief function to the Unemployment Assistance Board, this again was one reason, though another was an objection to different counties and county boroughs pursuing different redistributive policies.

In most federal, quasi-federal, and indeed unitary systems, one should recognise that the *status quo* on redistribution and paternalism will be some untidy compromise. As Scott has said, 'in a federation the object is to provide local autonomy. Each province may have its own ideas about the vertical redistributive effects of public finance and in a thorough-going federation is free to put them to work. Such differentiation of vertical policies may have an unfortunate effect on national economic efficiency, but this is a characteristic of federation (1964, p. 250). He might have added, 'unfortunate effect on national policies for redistribution which is also a characteristic of federation'. It was in this sense, even in a unitary system, that in the early 1930s local policies on relief to the unemployed were held to be inconsistent with national policies to the point that the powers of local government were diminished. It is not possible simultaneously to have a system in which the distributional impacts on persons are the same wherever they are, and leave significant autonomy to local jurisdictions in the provision of onerous public goods.

In Britain, this particular dilemma arose over the question of devolution. When the Royal Commission on the Constitution discussed devolution it noted that

> one of the main purposes of any system of devolution would be to allow free local choice which implies variety; and if the public at large did not really want variety there would be much less point in devolution . . . The evidence on this issue is conflicitng. Government departments told us that nearly all the pressures they get are for uniformity . . . There is a general underlying assumption that everyone in the country is entitled to the best that is going; and that it seems that if variety means less for some than for others it is not wanted . . . When respondents [to an attitude survey] were asked whether they thought that the standards of the various social services should be the same in every part of Great Britain or that each region should be allowed to set its own standards, 53% favoured uniformity and 44% regional discretion. (1973, Cmnd 5460)

Even this conceals an ambiguity because, as we have seen, through an equalisation grant different localities can have the same resources but provide different services. The real issue is not between diversity and uniform standard, but between locally determined and uniform services. Moreover, the issue is further obscured. In as much as failure to distinguish between beneficial and onerous services clouds it, even beneficial services may be provided uniformly, though this is neither justified in equity nor in efficiency.

The situation is never likely to be stable. The redistributive and paternalistic policies of central and local government will change — after elections and for other reasons. Indeed, it is possible that either central or local government could try to turn this into a gaming situation in which at the limit one might try to negate the redistributive or paternalistic policies of the other. Buchanan (1950) has suggested that a possible aim for central government would be to levy whatever discriminating taxes and subsidies are needed to return the locally affected distributions of income to those which are desired by national government. This would be very demanding in its data requirements and would indeed require central government to levy different tax rates in different places to offset local differences in fiscal wedges – a procedure which would be widely held to be inequitable and which Buchanan argued was, incidentally, unconstitutional in the USA. Presumably one could then imagine local authorities taking counter-corrective action so far as they were able. In which case, the outcome would be indeterminate as in any similar 'game' situation. But one does not have to go to the extreme of the model to realise that redistribution is an area where such interaction is likely. Both the drawing up of a federal constitution and of the relevant laws in a unitary state and the actions of government at the different levels within such a framework will reflect the different and changing interests and power of the levels concerned.

CONCLUSIONS

In conclusion on the problems of optimum size, it would seem as if all the best arguments were for smallness in elective local authorities, though all movement almost everywhere has been inexorably towards larger local authorities. In Britain and probably in may other countries one can explain it:

(1)   By the administrative convenience to central government of dealing with a smaller number of large authorities which pre-supposes the general wish of central government to use local authorities as agents for its own (not their) onerous policies.[14]

(2)   By the habit, and therefore administrative convenience, of using established elective bodies for performing onerous duties rather than invent new local organs of central government.

(3)   By a general disregard of the possibilities of joint action and the buying in of local services, and therefore the undue weight given to scale economies in production.

(4)   And by the argument that large size is better able 'to secure a structure of local authorities with units of sufficient size to allow efficient management and to command the skills needed for efficient and economical control of the services and resources for which they are responsible' (1969 Royal Commission on Local Government, Cmnd 4040, *Written Evidence of the Treasury*, p. 1).

To this one might add another argument (5) which has not so far been mentioned because it reflects the internal interests of bureaucracy rather than those of the electors of either central or local government. As the public sector grows it seems likely that the producer interest will carry greater weight in the political process (Beer, 1977). As in private firms the interest of management is in growth – requiring a higher more broadly based pyramid of power necessitating more administration and more highly paid administrators at the top – a process more than amply borne out by the 1974 reorganisation in England and Wales. The pressure is not only from local administrators. It is also from central administrators who may see that fewer large local governments will not only make intervention by central government more effective, but will in itself stimulate more growth in central government to take advantage of this opportunity. All this suggests that it would take a major political initiative to reverse the trend towards larger local governments and that because of the strength of the forces who gain from size it would be realistic to think that this may be impossible, without a major and very determined political initiative.

NOTES

1   Tiebout (1956), Ostrom, Tiebout and Warren (1961), Tullock (1969*a*), Rothenberg (1970), Oates (1972).
2   Simon (1948), Tiebout (1956 and 1961), Ostrom, Tiebout and Warren (1961), Tullock (1969*a*), Oates (1972).
3   Musgrave (1959, p. 181), Breton (1965), Rothenberg (1970), Royal Commission on Local Government, 1969, Cmnd 4040, Tullock (1970). There is a large literature on economies of scale to be discussed later in this chapter.
4   Breton (1965), Ostrom, Tiebout and Warren (1961), Tullock (1969*a*), Rothenberg (1970), Oates (1972).
5   The first half of the proposition is Musgrave's (1959, ch. 1) echoed by Oates (1972). The consequence drawn is our own.
6   Directly, because, as will be argued at the end of this section, all these arguments – for and against smallness – can be represented most clearly as different facets of economies or diseconomies of scale.
7   See Tullock (1969*a*, p. 21) for an Aristotelian echo.
8   Possibly this example of control-loss is commonly cited in the USA because legislatures at all levels do attempt to consider the financing of particular measures, as well as alternative means and levels of financing. How far, in practice, this leads to rational politics as defined above is questionable (cf. Wildavsky, 1964). In Britain, the Westminster rules, so-called, prevent Parliament from altering the costs of any particular measure either by voting a different level of expenditure from that proposed by the government or voting a different revenue source. Thus there is a self-imposed and damaging divorce between expenditure and revenue decisions at the national level which is already commonly reflected in local government.
9   The Royal Commission on Local Taxation (1901, Cd 638) argued that central government would break down without such decentralisation.
10 For a summary of such studies in the UK see Part Two, Chapter 4.
11 Robson (1954, pp. 155 ff.) discusses the various opportunities there have been for joint action. Sir James Hinchliffe once chairman of West Riding County Council seems to have seen as great advantages as Ostrom and others were to see in arrangements almost identical with those of the Lakewood Plan.
12 He uses the Pennock (1959) argument to reject the economies of scale argument. Rothenberg (1970) and Oates (1972) also give great weight to it.
13 It is formally similar to the mistake implied in assuming that the nature of public goods implies that the same amount of output will be consumed by everyone. On this see Part One Appendix 1.3.A1 above.
14 'The main point [of any increase in size] is the need for an effective dialogue between local authorities who have real responsibilities and the central government . . . At the present time the Ministry of Housing undertakes to allocate housebuilding authorisations amongst some 1400 bodies . . . [This] cannot be done with all the knowledge that is needed, over such a wide spread' (1969 Royal Commission on Local Government, Cmnd 4040, *Minutes of Evidence No 7*, Ministry of Housing and Local Government pp. 740–2).

7 Observations on Local Government Finance and some other Changes in Government Structure

This chapter analyses what may at first appear to be three very different questions: the case for special-purpose authorities, the problem of determining the right number of tiers of local government, and the transfer of functions between central and local, and between tiers of local government. But each issue is connected with the other two and all draw on the arguments of the last chapter as well as earlier parts of the book. They all relate to different forms of devolution. Each discussion is brief. In each case, a careful study — as might be undertaken by an expert in public administration or political science — could easily fill a book as the relevant permutations were considered and the many possibilities gone through. But we are not such experts. Instead we attempt a discussion of principles and major issues of application as they flow from our earlier arguments.

SPECIAL-PURPOSE AUTHORITIES

The key arguments are almost identical with those of the last chapter. The choice there was between authorities of different size, but on the tacit assumption that each authority would perform all local authority functions within its area. But existing general-purpose authorities could instead be split vertically so that different authorities performed distinct functions within the same area. So separate authorities could be created, for example for education, social services, housing and transport, all of them democratically elected.

As in the last chapter and generally for the same reasons, the balance of argument would again seem to be in favour of smaller rather than larger authorities — smallness here being achieved through vertical splitting instead of devolving duties to smaller geographical areas.

To adapt the conclusions of the last chapter:
(1) If there are economies of scale which transcend a special-purpose authority, then they could be achieved by joint action with other special-purpose authorities in the same area, or by contracting out those functions to some other body which could realise the scale economies. Intuitively, such scale economies are less likely between different functions than between the same services over neighbouring areas.

(2)   Vertical separation of functions should improve management and political control by reducing control-loss. A political leadership and an executive which is attempting to run many functions simultaneously will require more information and will have more difficulty in digesting it than will an authority – even one of larger area in many cases – which concentrates on a particular subject. Against this, however, such a local authority would only see its citizens in a particular aspect of their lives – as parents, or schoolchildren, or whatever. They would not see them in the round as arguably the councillor of a general-purpose authority can.

(3)   Public accountability should be improved. A voter would more easily relate a vote for a candidate for a particular authority to the issues raised in its policy area. He would not have to choose a candidate whom he may approve of on some issues but not on others. Moreover, he would need to have less information on the candidate's promises or performance since they also could be confined to the relevant subject area.

Against this must be set the confusion and often apathy caused by the multiplication of special-purpose authorities. In some parts of the USA voters are asked to vote for scores of candidates for numerous authorities at the same time. Experience suggests that so much choice can baffle the voter.

(4)   Public accountability can also be improved in another way from the standpoint of both voter and local politician. In special-purpose authorities it should be easier to relate revenue raising and expenditure so that the cost of expenditure proposals for the voter may be more clearly seen. This is easier if the authority has its own distinct revenue source than if it has to precept.

(5)   A special-purpose authority could also be a political nursery though it would, of course, encourage more specialisation.

(6)   Because the preferences of the median voter would be better expressed in relation to each purpose there should be a more efficient reflection of local preferences. Thus there should be a nearer approximation to a Tiebout equilibrium because of the better matching of tastes and local services in each area.

Therefore, it would seem as if the arguments for smaller rather than larger authorities are at least as strong and, in some cases, possibly stronger where smallness is achieved through vertical separtion of functions rather than through smaller size. Turning to the arguments against smallness mentioned in the last chapter:

(7)   Special-purpose authorities should find it less difficult to find politicians or officers of calibre. If for the sake of argument one assumes for the moment that a county-sized, special-purpose authority is roughly the same size as a district-sized general authority, then *ex hypothesi* there will be greater specialisation in the former.

(8)   Span of control by central government should be less of a problem in special-purpose authorities, since if again one were to imagine them the size of counties, each central department would have fewer to contend with than if devolution were to general purpose authorities the size of districts. Indeed, if each special-purpose authority were to relate to one central department only, central control would be easier – so far as that is desired.

(9)   Most difficult for special authorities is the disadvantage that arises directly

from their form and is inescapable. Even if we assume that special-purpose authorities all keep the same geographical areas — for example, the fission all takes place at the county (or district) level — there will be less political and administrative co-ordination. Recently one has heard much of the congestion caused by the attempt to plan local services in a co-ordinated manner, as well as the perceived danger in some areas that it has shifted the balance of power from the politicians who are not there all the time to the chief officers, and in particular the chief executive, who are.

That aside, the arguments for special-purpose authorities would seem to be stronger than for smaller general-purpose authorities if considered separately, as means of achieving smallness in local government. Of course, one could attempt both together by not only devolving functions to the district level but also separating them there between special-purpose authorities. However, as in the earlier discussion of optimal size, the distinctions made between beneficial and redistributive services remain relevant. The case for smallness is greater for beneficial than for onerous services.

That reflection suggests a basis for distinguishing between the functions of county (specialist) authorities and districts discussed below in the second section of this chapter.

But before recommending reform on such lines or exploring its implications for finance, such a move would be so counter to the tendency of local government in modern Britain as to warrant very careful consideration. Between 1748 and 1835 special-purpose authorities became the dominant form of British local government in number and effectiveness — each set up by its own Act of Parliament (Webbs, 1963, p. 130). They multiplied, but were increasingly criticised in the nineteenth century. The 1835 Royal Commission reported on the confusion they caused:

> Much confusion results from this divided authority. The powers of local taxation, and the superintendence of matters so closely connected with the comfort and wellbeing of the inhabitants which are now exercised by these bodies, appear to belong precisely to that class of objects for which corporate authority was originally conferred; but great dissatisfaction would prevail among the inhabitants if these powers were entrusted to the municipal corporations as at present constituted . . .
>
> Great jealousy often exists between the officers of police acting under the Corporation and those under the Commissioners of these local Acts, and the corporate body seldom takes any active share in the duties of the Board of which its members form a part. At Bristol a notoriously ineffective police cannot be improved, chiefly in consequence of the jealousy with which the Corporation is regarded by the inhabitants. At Hull, in consequence of the disunion between the governing body and the inhabitants, chiefly arising out of a dispute about the tolls and duties, only seven persons attended to suppress a riot out of 1000 who had been sworn in as special constables, and on another similar occasion none attended. At Coventry serious riots and disturbances frequently occur, and the officers of police, being usually selected from one political party, are often active in fomenting them. In some instances

the separate and conflicting authority of the Commissioners is avowedly used as a check and counterbalance to the political influence of the Corporation. At Leeds no persons are elected Commissioners of police whose political principles are not opposed to those of the Corporations.

An effectual attempt to obviate the evils resulting from the want of a well-organised system is made in some towns by subscriptions for private watch-men. At Winchester, after a local Act had been obtained, its powers were found to be insufficient, and the town is now watched by private subscrip-tion, to which the Commissioners contribute £100 from the rate.

The superintendence of the paving and lighting, etc., of the various towns is in the same unsatisfactory state, but in this branch of police the want of a single authority leads perhaps to less evil and inconvenience. (Quoted by Redlich and Hirst, 1970, p. 126)

In similar vein, Mill argues against the multiplication of authorities using London as his prime example (where the number of authorities was greatest), 'it prevents the possibility of consecutive or well-regulated cooperation for com-mon objects, precludes any uniform principle for the discharge of local duties, compels the general government to take on things on itself which would be best left to local authorities, if there was any whose authority extended to the whole metropolis' (1910*b*, ch. 15). Goschen fulminated against it in 1872 (pp. 190–1), and such arguments led Ritchie to transfer the powers of many special-purpose authorities to the counties in 1888. An argument for abolishing the school boards in 1902 was a confusion of responsibilities between them and the county councils (Curtis, 1952, p. 12). Thereafter, the boards of guardians administering poor relief were the most important surviving examples of special-purpose authorities. They were condemned by both the Majority and Minority Reports of the 1905–9 Royal Commission on the Poor Laws and the Relief of Distress which recommended the transfer of their functions to the county councils and county boroughs. Professor Robson has said that:

The case for abolishing the Boards of Guardians, formulated for the first time by the Minority Report of the Poor Law Commission of 1905–9, rested essentially on the irrefragable doctrine that it is wasteful and not conducive to good government to employ more than one local authority in one place to accomplish what is in effect a single task. It was because the Guardians of the poor were providing services for the destitute similar to those which were being provided for self-supporting members of the community by the general local authorities, with consequent waste and inefficiency, that irresistible force was given to the demand for the abolition of the Guardians. (1954, pp. 133–4)

This was an echo of the Mill dictum 'that in each local circumscription there should be but one elected body for all local business, not different bodies for different parts of it' (1910*b*, p. 351). This has been an accepted principle ever since, except in so far as the existence of more than one tier of local government violates that principle.

To question that principle may seem to attempt to reverse the experience and wisdom of a century and a half. Yet the conclusion that there should be only one all-purpose local authority is a *non sequitur* from the evidence. What was criticised by observers from the 1835 Royal Commission was a situation where:

(1)   Numerous authorities had been set up to do similar or overlapping activities in the same areas, not seldom because the first had failed and a second or third try was made with a second or third body.

(2)   Until the second half of the century virtually all these bodies had been set up by private Acts of Parliament. Little attempt had been made to define precisely the power and the duties of any one authority in relation to others operating in the same area so that there were endless opportunities for obstruction and litigation.

(3)   As Goschen observed, every kind of voting principle and co-option was used to select these bodies, so their representative nature varied and in many cases they were self-perpetuating cliques lining their own pockets at the expense of the ratepayer they raised money from (Goschen, 1872, pp. 190–1; Webbs, 1922, p. 135).

(4)   Their boundaries were overlapping so that it was not uncommon to find districts or municipal boroughs in more than one county, counties arbitrarily fragmented into non-contiguous areas and the greatest possible diversity of size even for authorities with similar functions.

While the Mill principle may be a natural reaction to such confusion, it remains a *non sequitur*. As the Webbs — no friends to special-purpose authorities — state:

When the special purpose authority was in its heyday, local government was in its infancy. To guide the new Local Authorities there was no administrative science . . . Not until the last quarter of the nineteenth century, and then only imperfectly, can even the educated public be said to have realized the necessity for the legal limitation and regulation of capitalist enterprise; . . . To replace the ordinary citizen temporarily conscripted to unpaid public service, there was . . . no body of trustworthy, trained, professional officials. The specially characteristic modern vocations, whether of engineers, architects, surveyors, accountants, and auditors; or of teachers, nurses, sanitary inspectors and medical officers of health; or even of draughtsmen, book-keepers, clerks and policemen, were as yet only beginning to be developed. Without effective vocational organization they were still without either tradition or training, and wholly unprovided with the code of professional ethics on which, as we now know, the highest administrative efficiency so much depends. (1922, pp. 186–7)

While the special-purpose authority failed in the nineteenth century, one cannot deduce that it would fail now, if recreated. Special-purpose authorities remain common in the USA, where they account for a high proportion of the 80,000 local authorities existing there (Committee for Economic Development,

1966, p. 17). School boards are the most widespread. While there are many in the USA who would argue that they have too many local authorities, there is no strong inclination to eliminate the more important special-purpose authorities. If they were to be resurrected in Britain, one could surely assume that the major faults of their eighteenth- and nineteenth-century predecessors could be avoided by:

(1) having a common voting principle – indeed One Person, One Vote;
(2) having non-overlapping boundaries so that their areas corresponded to those of other local authorities;
(3) having clear areas of authority and power so that they would not be duplicating each other's tasks.

If one feels able to set aside the incubus of past British experience, let us return to consider the drawbacks of establishing special-purpose authorities now. The arguments are different for beneficial and onerous public goods.

As an extreme, it can be postulated that every beneficial local government activity might have its own elected local government with its own electorate. The arguments against going so far would appear to be as follows:

(1) There are genuine economies of management in co-ordination – for example, that it is more efficient to run a diversity of social services together; or for these to have a common management with housing. Those are not at present considered beneficial public goods in Britain, but we have discussed elsewhere how the use of vouchers could mean their reclassification from onerous to beneficial. It is obvious that there are economies of co-ordination in the provision of most services which are now plainly beneficial; but there could be economies in running burial grounds, parks and recreation facilities together. These are empirical questions which require investigation. A common impression, however, is that there is not always much co-ordination within all-purpose authorities; and that committees are often anxious to keep distinct their own spheres of responsibility.
(2) Economies of contiguity or density can also be an argument for joining services within a single spatial authority. One of the commonest nineteenth-century complaints against the multiplication of special-purpose authorities was that the various paving, improvement, drainage and sewerage, gas and water authorities were so unco-ordinated that no sooner had one disembowelled and then replaced a street for its purpose when along came another and had the road up again. There are now fewer authorities that have this right, but most of those surviving are still separate though their activities seem somewhat better co-ordinated than a century ago. Again it is an empirical question as to how strong this argument is.
(3) The more difficult question is the likely effect on voting habits of dividing all-purpose into special-purpose authorities. Both Mill and the Webbs argued against the proliferation of special-purpose authorities characteristic of the nineteenth century by maintaining that there were too many to

capture the attention of the electorate. The electors were, in general, apathetic so that many of the authorities were self-governing and because of this often fell into the hands of vested interests who used their power for jobbery. We have already argued that the worst excesses of the nineteenth century are avoidable if special-purpose authorities were to have the same electoral system as do all-purpose local authorities and the national Parliament. The rather separate question is how far voters remain apathetic by being asked to vote too often for too many bodies. It is easy to assume that since the turnout at local elections is low for all-purpose authorities, it would be even lower if there were more authorities, but this is doubtful. No one would probably consider more than a small number of special-purpose authorities to vote for, say, six authorities at different times of the year or on the same occasion. That would surely be no greater burden than now. Much would depend on how interesting the electorate found the subject-matter.

It may be argued that local electors would become apathetic or confused if they felt that they had to acquire the information to make up their minds to elect the several authorities. But this is to mistake the nature of the information that is involved. Present electors have to vote for the entire policy of a local authority which includes its record on a widely divergent number of activities. Both common sense and a substantial theoretical literature suggest that voters would find it easier to make up their minds in relation to specific subject-matter than in relation to such a total package. Thus electors might react more positively and in a more informed manner when it came to voting on the policies and record of special-purpose authorities for different activities. One would expect vote-splitting as an electorate changed sides on different issues. This is itself a sign of more rational decision making. One advantage of the creation of special-purpose authorities might be the ending of local elections being decided on national issues. It is arguable that the main reason why local authorities are currently not judged on their policies or their records so that their fortunes follow those of the national parties they mirror, is that party allegiance is an oversimplification that the electorate resorts to because the all-purpose authority jumbles together so many issues that electors find it difficult to take a decision in any more rational manner. United States experience can again be used against the argument that the creation of special-purpose authorities would result in apathy in local government which reflected the local preferences less well than at present. As explained in Part Two, Chapter 7 there seems to be prima facie evidence that individual local preferences are to some extent being reflected in services where it would be least expected because of central intervention. In the USA there is not apathy for the more important functions when they are hived off. This is especially true of school boards.

If special-purpose authorities were created, financial problems would have to be faced. The financial problem is easier for beneficial services where charging can be adopted, since that would raise no problem for grant distribution. Where taxes had to be raised for such services either because of public-good characteristics of services or because of a reluctance to introduce charging, problems

of horizontal efficiency would have to be met. If there were more than one beneficial authority this would create the difficulty already referred to, unless
they either shared the same tax base or different types of authorities performing
distinct functions had distinct tax bases. In practice, as most beneficial services
could be charged for, and the rest could be financed from rates or any other
single local tax, there should be no financing restrictions on the multiplication of
beneficial authorities.

In general, the argument for some special-purpose authorities to provide
beneficial public goods would be stronger, the more the duties of local authorities are increased. If there were a rise in the watchdog functions of local
authorities so that their role as an Association of Consumers was increased, then
it is possible that control-loss diseconomies of scale might set in even within a
small geographical area. Rather than reduce the area to a still smaller size, an
alternative would be some division into special-purpose authorities.

Where local authorities provide redistributive goods, the considerations are
again similar to those raised in the discussion on optimum size. Except in the
most unlikely special circumstances, it is no longer possible to talk of a unique
optimum; but an old problem arises in a new form. The preferences of an area
will vary with its population, so that one cannot talk of the social-welfare function of an authority independent of its population. Who controls the division of
population into government jurisdictions constrains the social-welfare functions
that will emerge. Since no one level of government, even in a unitary state, can
be dictatorial about this, the boundaries that exist and the social-welfare functions that are reflected, are based on a balance of power. The creation of special-
purpose authorities will alter that balance of power. A new special electorate
will be formed which, though composed of voters who had voted before, will
reach a different conclusion because they are now part of a different constituency with different interests (even if geographical areas remain the same).
Recently legislation on health and water has taken away powers from elective
local authorities and placed them with non-elective special authorities. This is a
special case of this proposition. The effect must have been to increase the weight
given to central government wishes; but, in principle, a similar change in emphasis would have resulted if, say, services taken from a general-purpose district
authority were given to a special-purpose but elective county authority.

A number of arguments can be advanced for special-purpose authorities for
redistributive public goods. First, several — for example, education, housing and
health services — are probably of sufficient general interest to interest an electorate and to attract good representatives and officials. Second, they can be used
to help solve a particular problem of co-ordination. Relations between central
government and local authorities are confused. A number of suggestions have
been made earlier for making them more orderly and efficient. One possibility is
that each major central department should confront local special-purpose authorities across its interests. Organisationally this would seem to go well with the
notion of departmental block grants or specific grants for onerous services. Thus
there would be education authorities (covering a number of pertinent minor
services) set up in relation to the Department of Education; and so on for health
and social services, police and housing. This would be a recognition that these

are largely agency services, though with some discretion and some advantage in an elective element. Within the discretion given by statute and administrative arrangement, the advantage of an elective arrangement would be that local interests would better be able to reflect local preferences and so forewarn central government of any great opposition that might arise from too blind a central *dirigisme*.

One would expect such authorities to be larger because of the 1969 Royal Commission on Local Government (Cmnd 4040) argument that central government will be more efficient in its dealings with local authorities if they are relatively few in number. Tradition might suggest that any such special-purpose authorities might be on a county scale.

In conclusion on special-purpose authorities, the two strongest arguments against the vertical splitting of local government are very different in kind. The first is that too great a multiplication of local authorities will confuse and even bore the elector, so reducing democratic control. It is not merely a matter of the number of authorities but of their functions. Separating out some of the more humdrum functions might lead to a greater loss of public interest and control than the creation of separate authorities for functions which create greater public interest like education and social services. It is worth considering also services that might be transferred from central government or from public corporations. It is probably unlikely that separate locally elected bodies for handling the distribution of electricity, gas and water, and for negotiating with the suppliers of these services would command much public interest. On the other hand, separately elected local health authorities almost certainly would become of democratic interest. One could also imagine some recombination of functions. There might be, for example, a local authority for young persons' services covering education as well as social, welfare and corrective services for the young, so that all the problems of the young could be dealt with in a planned co-ordinated manner. Similarly, another authority could deal comprehensively with all the services available for the elderly. But, in any case, undue fragmentation should be avoided.

The second objection to vertical splitting is that it would destroy the possibility of planning certain services together, and that it would destroy the influence for restraint that a council as a whole exercises upon the enthusiasms of particular committees. One has to consider how necessary co-ordination is. It is questionable whether there really is, or need be, much co-ordination between a county education authority, or a social services, or health authority and other 'county' activities. Similar problems now arise between local authorities and undemocratic local boards. If there were one democratically elected body covering related services now divided, then co-ordination should be less of a problem. Similarly, it is arguable that the provision of housing, recreational facilities and libraries among others are mostly self-contained in the issues they generate. On the other hand, land-use planning and transport planning are closely connected, as also is the provision of infrastructure.

One way of meeting the problem might be to restrict special-purpose authorities to the few which are both likely to attract sufficient public interest for democratic control to be effective, and which are reasonably self-contained;

while retaining general-purpose authorities for other local services and activities. On the assumption that the latter would remain the land-use planning authorities, they would be able to use development control to influence the location and development of the special-purpose authorities' activities, who could be as liable to the need to seek planning permission as any private interest.

A rather different possibility would be to create a vertically federal structure at the local level in which the different special-purpose authorities, though separately elected, were in a sense 'committees' of the overall authority. The division of powers between such committees and the council could be various. (Moreover, some committees need not be separately elected for the reason given above that their operations were unlikely to excite enough democratic interest.) Without exploring all the possibilities, let us consider two. In the first, the budgets of each committee, whether or not democratically elected, would have to be approved by the whole council after considerations by its finance committee. Thus the freedom of a 'democratically' elected committee would be to formulate a budget which it would spend, once approved. What would be novel, of course, is that the policies, or indeed the politics, of a committee might differ from that of the council as a whole. How far a council could use its financial power to influence the policies of a committee is problematic; but one must remember that the electors are the same people voting in different capacities.

A second possibility would be to restrict council control over the 'democratic' committees of constituent authorities to the rate-fund contribution (with, of course, development control in the background). On this basis, each committee would have its own income from fees or charges and specific or department block grants, where appropriate. This would be at its disposal, subject to the law and central government regulations. But any rate-fund contributions would be voted by the whole council. Clearly the greater the rate-fund contribution, the greater the influence of the whole council. A democratic housing authority on this basis would have much greater independence of the full council if its income came from rents and central grants alone, than if it also relied on a rate-fund contribution. This is to relate discussion on structure to our earlier discussion on more radical uses of grant. The greater the extent that local services are dependent on charges or hypothecated local tax sources of central grants, the more one can take further the accountability implied by establishing a matching form of accountable democratic 'committee' organisation on the basis of a clear financial and functional differentiation. One should remember also the two main purposes of rate-fund contribution. The first is as a subsidy from the council as a whole to a service where, as an act of policy, the council wishes to spend its income helping a service after considering alternative expenditure patterns. Thus the more a financial regime reduced the proportion of a 'committee's' income derived from general rates granted to the whole authority and increased that derived from its own identifiable rate levy or other tax or charge, or from hypothecated grants, the more any local subsidy via the rate fund contribution would approximate to the subsidies central government makes, for example to nationalised industries, for the performance of unremunerative services in the public interest.

The second use of rate-fund contributions is to meet deficits. Thus just as nationalised industry or other public corporations go to central government when they run into deficit, so a local democratic committee could be forced to go to the whole council, which in such circumstances would have the right to demand some reduction in expenditure or increase in charges or specific taxes. Since the special-purpose authorities or committees would have tax-raising powers, this would be a less effective power than it is for central government (except, of course, that some nationalised industries have enough monopoly power for it to be possible for them to raise whatever is necessary in revenue to cover their expenditure, untroubled by competition).

HORIZONTAL SEPARATION OF AUTHORITIES

Far too much attention has been paid to the number of tiers there should be in government, mainly because of the belief in economies of scale we have argued to be irrelevant. If one believes that economies of scale should dominate local government size and that there is a different optimum level of provision and therefore optimal size for each local authority, then it would seem to follow that the ideal arrangement would be a patchwork quilt of authorities of different sizes and possibly also shapes — nothing regular enough to be called tiers of government. Not only are the problems of co-ordination likely to be formidable — even if the more egregious errors of the eighteenth and nineteenth centuries be avoided — but changes in demand and in technology should imply changes in boundaries to reflect changes in optimum service size. There could be incessant alterations. More recently, the practical alternatives considered have been variants of five or fewer tiers. The full five are central, regional, county, district and parochial or neighbourhood government.

It follows from the last chapter and the first part of this one, that we are unpersuaded that economies of scale are a sensible basis for splitting functions between the local, that is non-central, tiers. We have argued the probability that there are diseconomies of scale in very small government; and we do not propose to attempt to argue what could be devolved to neighbourhood councils or parishes, feeling that might be the subject of a special study which would have comparatively little to do with local government finance as such and more to do with policy on public participation. While we are unclear that the 1974 reorganisation of municipal boroughs, county boroughs, urban and rural districts into districts has brought about any great advantage, it seems clearer that the upheaval involved in reversing that change would not be worth it. Practically, it seems to us that the main choice is between counties and districts in terms of local services. To follow the arguments of the last section, they suggest some advantage in the district tier providing the beneficial services while the counties concentrated on the redistributive services. Thus districts might concentrate on waste collection and disposal, street cleaning and lighting, arts and recreation, cemeteries and crematoria, consumer protection, other aspects of environmental health, the fire service, footpaths and bridleways, markets and fairs, development control and most other aspects of planning. Counties on this basis would concentrate on education, social services and housing, which are the areas most affected by the paternalistic and redistributive interests of central government. Only one beneficial service might be dealt with best at county level. This is transport where the importance of intergovernmental externalities is such — with roads and bus routes crossing district boundaries — that there is probably an efficiency case for attention at the county level. Planning is always a difficulty since co-ordination is of its essence. The function which most needs pursuing at the county or possibly national level is whatever bears on the distribution of population and employment between districts, leaving development control a district function. Another function for the county could be to act as a half-way court of appeal on the way to the courts or the Secretary of State for the Environment.

Though such a division would mean that most of the functions were at district level, by far the higher proportion of expenditure would be with the counties. As we have observed earlier, most local expenditure is currently redistributive. However, the use of vouchers or other forms of grant could facilitate devolution of some or all these redistributive expenditures to the district level. The one redistributive service which (if one excludes the GLC) is almost invariably at district level is housing. The proposals for housing in the 1977 Housing Policy Green Paper imply that central government will have to scrutinise and approve the plans of 400 district housing authorities. If this scrutiny becomes detailed, precedent would suggest that the service should be raised to the county level. But one main reason for central provision — the need for uniformity of provision in distributive terms — is avoided by the method of operation of housing grant which (with some local variation because of imperfections and historical accidents in the way in which grant is provided) takes care of the price at which housing is to be offered to tenants. As we have argued earlier, such specific grants to authorities or vouchers to persons could be used to convert local authorities providing such services from the redistributive to the beneficial category. Therefore one could conceivably, on that basis, provide every service except transport at the district level provided, of course, that central intervention was practically limited to what could be achieved through vouchers and through inspection so that span of control problems for central government did not arise.

TRANSFER OF FUNCTIONS

Over a wide range of transfer of functions from one level of government to another, financing problems should not arise as such. If the objectives of horizontal efficiency and equity are disregarded there is no problem at all, whatever the division of functions between forms of government since the allocation of revenue sources can be pragmatic. So, for example, one might imagine regions financing their services through local sales taxes, counties through local income taxes, districts through rates, public corporations — to bring in another form of government — through charges, while central government relied on other taxes. But any division of revenue sources could work, provided central government retained enough variable taxation to exercise macroeconomic control and each authority could raise enough revenue to support its activities. Even so the multiplication of authorities without regard to horizontal efficiency and equity would accentuate the inefficiency and inequity of such a system – another factor which may have discredited the local authority patchwork of the mid-nineteenth century.

If horizontal efficiency and equity are retained as objectives, the transfer of functions to central government from other tiers of government present no financing difficulty since it is within the power of central government to get as much consistency, efficiency and equity within the tax structure as it pleases.

Difficulties arise when central government wishes to retain horizontal efficiency and equity and yet devolve functions to lower tiers of government. If rates were to remain the local tax base, it would be hard to devolve further functions to local authorities because it would mean either an appreciable rise in the effective rate poundage paid by the ratepayer or a sufficient rise in the grant proportion to keep the rate burden constant. Any such increase in rate poundage would be balanced by a reduction in the national taxes used previously to finance the service. The difficulty, of course, is that throwing a greater weight on rates by comparison with other taxes would emphasise the inefficient and inequitable aspects of rating.

The inequities of the rating system would stand out more clearly. Indeed one reason for the centralisation of government under the Attlee government was a feeling that any extension of functions to local government would need to have been preceded by a reform of local government finance which as Aneurin Bevan, the minister responsible at the time, said should ideally have preceded the setting up of the National Health Service. This was not done partly because political priority was given to what was considered the more practical reform, but also because there was no consensus even within the Labour Party on the direction that the reform of local government finance should take. In particular, what would have been needed, as seen at the time, were additional sources of local finance.

If substantial central functions of a redistributive kind were to be devolved to lower tiers of elected government, whether regional or local, some new financial source would have to be found on the assumption that increasing the grant proportion to avoid the need for this would not be seen as real devolution. One possibility would be to replace rates by local income tax, a tax base which could be shared by all tiers of government with the appropriate grants to achieve equalisation. Central government would have to retain enough of the yield of income tax in order to be able to vary income tax rates sufficiently in the interests of macroeconomic control and income distribution.

We would venture that central government retaining a 10p basic tax rate should be more than sufficient. If one then imagines rates being transferred to central government as a national tax, local and regional authorities' tax base would be sufficient to finance up to a 200 per cent expansion in existing local authorities' current expenditure, without any increase in income-tax yield. But that is no maximum since it would square with principles already laid down that, provided their functions are clearly defined, different tiers of local authorities might have different tax bases devolved to them. The constraints on this are the considerations on efficiency and equity which have run as a theme through our earlier discussions of the principles of the rationale of local taxes and the principles of grant distribution. To give any local authorities a tax base which implies a very substantial increase in tax rates over the present national average to support the functions allotted to them will increase any distortions in the allocation of resources already resulting from the tax as well as accentuating any inequities.

A second method of overcoming present constraints on devolution would be through the widespread adoption of charging, coupled with appropriate voucher systems to achieve the intended distributional impacts. Although there would have to be inventiveness in the design of the voucher systems, the same national tax structure as at present could be used to finance them.

The other main financial or economic constraint on devolution is held to be the effect that it will have in eroding economies of scale; but we have suggested that this in itself is a false argument if taken as a reason for transferring entire services to national government or nation-wide public corporations. Similarly, one can analyse candidates for devolution and consider particular parts of them where there may be appreciable economies of scale extending beyond local geographical areas. Where they exist, there is probably a strong argument for retaining that part of the service at a higher – as circumstances dictate, a national or regional – level. But one must try to distinguish genuine scale economy arguments from political or administrative convenience arguments. Experience and common sense both suggest that central politicians and officials are human enough to want to increase their power, which can be done through centralisation. Whether this is in the public interest is a wider question to be determined by Parliament rather than by those with a more direct self-interest.

Two broad models emerge from our discussion, their pattern set by different financial arrangements. The first would assume that local authorities, including regional authorities, would be financed by their own taxation, charges and central grants. The second would replace grants to authorities by grants to persons.

The first would generally suggest that beneficial services would be concentrated at the district level. A number of central government services might be candidates for such devolution. Among them are services now provided by some of the executive offshoots of central government: for example, the employment exchanges – now called job centres – and other services of the Manpower Services Commission, the local inspectorates and other offices of the Health and Safety Executive, and possibly also the design and contracting functions of the Property Services Executive. The first of them is centrally provided as we saw in Part One, Chapter 3 because Sir William Beveridge persuaded Winston Churchill that there was a unity in the labour market when their forerunners were set up. In general terms, the sudden and massive awakening of local authority interest in local economic matters suggests a reconsideration of what instruments of national industrial and employment policy could be devolved to local authorities, on the grounds that they have an interest in these matters quite as strong as the interests of central government. At the same time, it might be possible to return some of the activities of the gas, electricity and water authorities to the district level in order to set up a pattern of countervailing power. The same principle could be extended to the Post Office which has never been part of local government on the postal side, though there used to be municipal telephone systems of which one survives at Hull. In all these cases, complex organisational problems would have to be solved before devolution could be shown to be possible, let alone desirable. Yet the general notion that in the case of state monopoly services, a local authority in close touch with consumers could watch and negotiate with monopoly providers, is an attractive one. Local authorities could be responsible for that part of distribution that consisted in taking trunked services from the main network and supplying them to individual customers. In some cases, they might even be able to have some choice in their procurement policy, choosing between alternative suppliers.

With this set of financial arrangements, precedent would suggest that the major redistributive service now at the district level, housing, would move up to the county. The advantage of the county for redistributive services centrally determined or strongly influenced by central departments is that central government has fewer authorities to deal with. The strongest candidates for devolution to the county level must be health services, both hospitals and general practitioner services, where there is now widespread complaint that the present health authorities are too removed from local influence. On the other hand, if the separation can be made, many traffic and minor highway matters could be devolved to districts, as many counties do now under agency arrangements. Whether there is a single county or separate democratically elected county authorities for the more important and publicly interesting functions is another matter.

As experienced in Britain, regional devolution has mostly been a matter of administrative convenience for central government rather than any genuine devolution of power to the local level. That would require more than a democratically elected advisory assembly. It would need the equivalent of regional ministers or councillors presiding over the comparable departments or committees. The practical difficulty is that of converting what has historically been an instrument of central government into a democratic institution. There is no regional tradition to build on, and even in Scotland and Wales where there is, in modern times their governments have quite firmly remained outposts of Whitehall whose main functions have been to act as intermediaries between Westminster and Whitehall on the one hand and local authorities and other interests on the other. The other problem, more theoretical and empirical, is to find examples of services where it really can be shown that it would be better to devolve to regions which have no relevant tradition than to counties.

If the second financial framework based on vouchers is adopted, then still more flexibility is possible and even redistributive functions could be more easily devolved downwards to districts. Evidence for this is to be found in housing where the grant arrangements have approximated more closely than elsewhere in local government to one appropriate to a charged service. It has affinities with a combination of charges and vouchers, as we have seen.

No one can expect a return to the division of labour between central and local government that existed before the First World War, simply because the main domestic function of central government was policy making for which the main instruments were grants and inspection. Moreover, redistributive services were then devolved to local government in a way which created substantial horizontal inefficiency and inequity. But one could imagine a movement back to something more like the position before the transfer of public utilities and the health service from local government in the 1940s. The leading ideas could be that the policy for redistributive services could be set in Whitehall, working through county authorities who would act primarily as agents to get the knowledge and adaptability to local conditions that almost everyone since Mill has thought important. Or the same end could be achieved more ambitiously by central government concentrating on the use of personal vouchers, preferably in the context of a system of negative income tax or tax credits, to achieve their redistributive ends while leaving local authorities the discretion to provide the services according to local preferences. On both models, many beneficial activities now performed by central government could be devolved, even to district level where they would benefit from greater responsiveness to local wishes.

8 Findings and Recommendations on the Future of Local Finance with Some Observations on that of Local Government

Some readers, particularly those who read this chapter first, may find it speculative. This is inevitable. History does not stand still, and it requires as much science and imagination to forecast what will happen to local government finance without explicit policy change, as it does to predict the consequences of specific reforms.

Radical changes in local government finance might be forced by events or be freely chosen. The recurrent crises, so called, in local finance which have been a feature of the last hundred years have sometimes led to modification of the system. But though very often there has been much talk about more fundamental changes, the ending of the crisis has usually meant the shelving of the talk. In 1974, the Labour government promised a major reform of the system of local government finance in response to the crisis of that year, yet by 1977 its Green Paper in response to Layfield proposed to maintain all the main features of the present system virtually unchanged.

The Conservatives had been pledged to the abolition of domestic rates, but this pledge was dropped from their election manifesto in 1979. They are, however, pledged to a substantial reduction in public expenditure, including local government expenditure. Whatever the intentions of central governments, our historical analysis in Part One (Chapter 4) suggests that local authority expenditure tends to rise more rapidly than GDP. From 1870 to 1975 the relationship had been remarkably stable with each 1 per cent growth in income associated with a growth of between 2 per cent and 3 per cent in local government spending. We think it likely that within a period of a few years local government spending will start to grow again, albeit perhaps from a lower base.

Underlying this relationship is a trend common to most relatively affluent societies. As incomes rise, communities tend to spend a high proportion of the increase on services such as education, health, housing, welfare and environmental services. In Britain, most of these services are the responsibility of local government so that as long as these trends continue local government spending will rise faster than GDP.

While the growth in local current expenditure has been halted, the level of local capital spending has been severely cut back, falling by almost 40 per cent between 1975/6 and 1977/8. Some growth in capital spending is unavoidable if the capital stock is to be maintained. Historically, as we have shown, Conservative governments tend to favour capital expenditure while Labour have preferred current spending.

Further factors likely to lead to an increase in expenditure are changes in the age composition and geographical mobility of population. The total school population will be falling for many years as a result of the sharp drop in the birth rate since 1970, while the number of old people, and particularly people over the age of 85, is expected to increase substantially. With changes in composition, as with the consequences of geographical mobility, expenditure is not reduced when numbers fall as fast as it increases where numbers rise.

Of major significance is the increase in the power of producer interests, that is to say the public-sector unions and professional associations. Such groups have been effective not only in 'conventional' union activities (improving pay and conditions of work, resisting redundancies, etc.) but also have been an important influence in improving standards, often working through central government departments. Teachers, for example, have been a major influence behind the move towards smaller class sizes in schools. We would expect pressures from producer interests for the further improvement of services to be effective, and also for resistance to be successful to running down services where numbers have fallen (such as in education).

Historically, politicians have wished to satisfy demands for better public services while avoiding facing up to the costs involved. Just because rates are a more noticeable form of taxation, rate increases will be less popular with politicians than increased grants. As shown in Part One, domestic rates have been kept to an approximately constant proportion of personal after-tax incomes.

It is this gap between the desired growth of expenditure and the desired growth of rate income which has led to many of the crises in local government finance which have occurred every ten years or so over the last century. Such crises have often been marked by strong political pressures for new sources of local income. But new local taxes have not been found and instead, typically, the crises have been resolved by new grant arrangements allowing the grant proportion to increase. But with the present block grant system, the grant proportion can be increased by simple decision of central government requiring neither legislation nor new administrative arrangements. While, at the time of writing, the grant proportion seems likely to be cut in the short run, if expenditure starts to grow again, as we predict, more rapidly than income, we would expect the first reaction of central government to be to increase the grant proportion. The grant proportion might well increase from 61 per cent in 1978/9 to around 70 per cent by the late 1980s, but this increase of itself would not need any radical changes in the financial system.

In Part Three it seemed to us that the most probable changes would recognise more directly than at present central government's interest in how local authorities spend their money; but we did not see how any real change could be achieved in the grant system without altering central–local relationships. Still we were sceptical as to whether the present methods of grant distribution could continue for long; and believe that any change in the system would almost certainly be one which would increase central influence.

The most likely development, rather than solution, is a move towards departmental grants. There could be separate grants for education, social services, and so on, each administered by the appropriate central government department. Even if each of the departments were still to use regression analysis to determine the distribution of their grants, the outcome would not simply replicate the existing block grant. There would be a prior decision as to how large the various departments' grants would be, and in this way the payment of grant would be more closely related to the provision of particular services. But, equally, it would be possible for different departments to adopt different principles of grant distribution.

Departmental grants would undoubtedly entail greater central control, as departments could tailor their grants more closely to their own views of what services should be provided. An alternative, less centralist, reform would be to institute an independent commission for needs assessment, on the Australian model. But in Britain a move to 'take grant out of politics' would scarcely be feasible given the highly political nature of the issues involved. In our view, the increasing tension over methods of grant distribution could become such a disruptive force in the present system as to necessitate more radical reform.

But there are other, and more serious, threats to the system. The decision to cancel the revaluation due in 1982 means that the arbitrariness of domestic rating as a property tax will get progressively worse, and that the overassessment of poorer-quality housing will continue. And the inequity of rating a household with several earners the same as a pensioner household could be a major cause of concern with the increasing number of old people. While these problems could be offset by a greater use of rate rebates and rate reliefs, the political attractions of abolishing domestic rates will remain strong.

While unemployment remains high, governments are reluctant to burden industry and commerce with heavier taxes. But a resumption of economic growth and a revival of business prosperity could well lead to a resumption of the upward march of the domestic element, increasing the share of the non-domestic ratepayer in paying for services enjoyed in large measure by the domestic ratepayer. Industrial and commercial interests may complain against the burden of the tax relative to benefits received, but governments will continue to see advantages in a tax whose burden is largely hidden from the voter, tinkering as they have done in 1979 by helping the smallest commercial premises only on a basis which is not easily capable of national justification.

The share of local expenditure borne by the domestic ratepayer is thus likely to fall, which will, in turn, increase the upward pressure on local spending. Our findings in Part Two, Chapter 5 suggest that both grant and non-domestic rate payments have a positive expenditure elasticity. Local pressures may again lead to a faster growth of spending than central government would wish, and this, in turn, is likely to lead to an increase in central government invervention and control.

With increasing centralisation and the proportion of local expenditure financed by domestic rates falling to around 10 per cent or less, the argument for doing away with domestic rates altogether could become stronger. The idea might be that each local authority would receive a block grant but be accountable to its electorates as to how it spends it. In our view, local autonomy cannot survive unless local government has an independent source of finance. In the Republic of Ireland, where domestic rates have been abolished recently, local authorities already had few discretionary powers. We do not believe the 'Irish solution' can be imposed in Britain against local authority interests. Nor do we believe that the Conservatives can implement their proposal to abolish domestic rates unless they can offer local authorities a new source of tax revenue in its place. We expect the rating system to survive despite the criticisms that will continue to be levelled against it.

There seem to us three areas where the system is at more immediate risk. First, there is the possibility of another macroeconomic crisis comparable to that of 1974/5 with a combination of inflation, high interest rates and falling real incomes. If local authorities are as slow to respond to such a crisis as they were in 1974/5, their spending would almost inevitably come under much tighter central control.

Second, there is the conflict over the methods used to distribute grant. The consultations of the Consultative Council and its working parties will exacerbate this conflict without it being possible to find objective measures of need, because in many services the perception of need is a matter of political judgement. Grant distribution has become a political football with the regression method – whatever its merits in principle – being seen as favouring the higher-spending urban Labour authorities at the expense of the rural shire counties. This shift of grant had, under the Labour government of 1974–9, accorded with the political preferences of central government. But should the political preferences of central government change, the regresssion analysis cannot itself be doctored so as to reverse this shift. A new method of grant distribution would be required.

Another feature of the regression method is that grant is distributed on criteria quite different from central government's own definition of spending need. If central government wishes local authorities to spend more on one service and less on another, it cannot adjust the grant distribution to reflect that change. If local authorities do adjust their spending patterns to reflect the new policy, there may be a consequent change in the regression equation. But from the viewpoint of an individual local authority, there is no connection between the change in the pattern of its spending and its grant receipt. At present, there is a feeling that, while the total size of the grant is justified to a large extent by the costs of the education service, its method of distribution is such that it meets mainly the costs of higher spending on social services and housing subsidies in the cities.

The third factor that could force radical change would be a continuation, or even intensification, of the 'taxpayer revolt' which was one of the factors contributing to the Conservative election victory of 1979. If people demand a higher standard of local government services, but are not prepared to accept corresponding increases in tax bills, present arrangements could not survive. Greater use of charges, or the transfer of the local government services to the private sector are likely developments in these circumstances.

Therefore not only is it probable that events will force a change in local finance, but our judgement was that if this were to happen the outcome would be greater centralisation. However, changes need not be forced. They could be voluntary, the outcome of carefully prepared and debated initiatives. The important objectives of such reform will be: greater efficiency in the provision of local services; greater equity in the financing; and a better definition of the areas in which central control should be increased and those in which local autonomy should be revived.

We believe that the underlying causes of many of the crises in the past have been persistent failures to achieve these objectives in the mechanisms used to raise local revenue, distribute grants, and establish central–local relationships.

Part Four has considered a number of possible changes more radical than the amelioration discussed in Part Three. Of course, an infinite number of changes is conceivable. Those discussed have been chosen because they were felt to have merit in relation to one or more of the objectives for a local government system.

The basic argument for replacing rates by site value rating (Chapter 2) was greater economic efficiency. Because it freed buildings from a local tax it would remove the deterrent effect of rates on the construction and improvement of buildings. More than this, however, site value rating has the property that any fiscal wedges – differences between benefits received and taxes paid – tend to be capitalised, so avoiding vertical and horizontal inefficiency. Our main objection to site value rating is our belief that if it were introduced it would be introduced in such a way that all its properties of efficiency would be eliminated while administrative costs would be increased. The hold of the valuation and planning process is such that it seems most unlikely that site values would be allowed to reflect market values. It is probable that in practice they would reflect planners' overoptimistic valuations rather than the truth, thus weakening the efficiency arguments for site value rating.

Other new local taxes (Chapter 3) are mostly discussed in the literature as supplements to rates rather than as substitutes for them. However, resource equalisation on grounds of both equity and efficiency is an objective of local finance and has long been an integral part of the British system. We show the difficulties of achieving such equalisation with the multiplication of local taxes. Another argument against the multiplication of taxes is that it helps the public to deceive itself. The only new tax worthy of consideration as an alternative to rates is a local income tax. Because the income-tax base is much more equal between localities than are rateable values, and because the tax bill on households would be much more clearly related to ability to pay and would therefore be considered more equitable, there could be a drastic reduction in the amount of grants going to local authorities. This would result in a closer connection between the services provided and the cost. The greatest drawback of introducing an LIT at the moment is that it would be very costly to implement satisfactorily without a reform in general tax-assessment procedure. Moreover, without such reform many of the advantages claimed for an LIT disappear.

Other taxes – principally on sales or businesses – would introduce very great inefficiencies even if they could be imagined as a replacement for rates. If a satisfactory separation of accounts could be achieved, local services for non-domestic ratepayers might be financed through some form of business taxation.

We would argue it would be preferable, however, to continue with a form of non-domestic rates but with rate poundages set to cover only expenditure occasioned by such ratepayers. We believe, however, that charges for such services would be preferable to either.

Charging (Chapter 4) is the most efficient method of financing services. Charging can be proposed as a means of encouraging greater financial responsibility in the provision of particular services. But, perhaps more importantly, charging can be a way out of the dilemma of people demanding services but refusing to support their finance through taxation. The protagonists of charging usually hope that its introduction would be associated with a reduction in the amount of redistribution carried out by the combination of central and local government activity. But that is not essential. If charging is introduced, redistribution can be carried out by the central government either through a negative income tax system or through a system of grants to persons via a voucher system.

Chapter 5 considers some reforms of the grant system that might accompany more radical change. We examined how equity and efficiency might be maintained and the grant proportion reduced, if other taxes were introduced in place of, or in addition to, rates. We then examined the implications of relaxing the traditional emphasis on equalisation in favour of a grant system that would encourage local development.

The assessment of 'needs' has been the stumbling block of the grant system. We discuss the consequences of different systems of central–local relationships on methods of needs assessment. We argue that under a more centralised system a more detailed approach to need measurement, based, for example, on the client-group approach, would be appropriate. But such methods depend on greater central control of local services. We then examined whether shifting grants from local authorities to persons (vouchers) would be more consistent with a localist approach.

Chapter 5 ends the discussion of local government finance as such. The remaining chapters are concerned with different but related matters. Economists have argued for some time over the virtues of small and large local government. It is argued that the validity of the conclusion is different for redistributive and for beneficial services. For beneficial services a very strong argument indeed can be made for concluding that small government is efficient, though it depends crucially on assuming that local authorities are able to buy in services where economies of scale are important and also making what are argued to be plausible assumptions about the relative importance and the best methods of dealing with intergovernmental externalities or 'spillovers' from one authority to another.

The second half of Chapter 6 analyses optimum size where the services being provided are redistributive and centrally determined. It argues that no unique solution can be reached in principle.

A related problem is that of deciding (Chapter 7) the pros and cons of separating local government functions vertically – for example, having separately elected educational, housing and other authorities. It is argued that many of the reasons for abandoning such vertical separation which used to be common in the past are no longer valid. Such separation would make it possible to multiply tax instruments (one per authority type) while continuing to achieve resource equalisation. The factors determining the efficiency of such separation are considered. Finally, there is some discussion of the complications introduced by there being more than one tier of government.

Throughout the book and, in particular, in our discussions in this part of the radical solutions, we have used the distinction between beneficial and onerous or redistributive goods. It should be clear that these categories are blurred. Where the line is drawn depends on the views one has about society and government and the relationship between them. The importance of these categories, however, is in what each implies for the relationship between the structure of local government, its financing and the degree of control that should be imposed by the central government. In 1901 the Royal Commission on Local Taxation said

> we believe that the only method that can secure fair play all round is consistent adherence to a principle which has often been put forward in discussion but to which insufficient regard has frequently been paid in practice. That principle is the distinction between services which are preponderantly National in character and generally onerous to the ratepayers, and services which . . . confer upon ratepayers a direct and peculiar benefit more or less commensurate with the burden. (Cd 683, p. 12)

Though agreeing that it was contentious they tried to divide the then existing local services into these categories. Seventy-five years later the Layfield Committee saw the main problem with the present system of local government finance as one of 'a lack of clear accountability for local government expenditure which results from the confusion of responsibilities between the [central] government and local authorities' (Layfield, 1976, p. xxv.). But the solution the committee proposed for increasing local power did not in fact provide a clearer definition of responsibilities. Instead, they stated what would have to be done:

> The fields in which decisions are to be reserved to the [central] government would need to be defined for most services. In defining these fields, it is important that the matters which the [central] government reserves for decisions should be confined to essential issues of national policy and should exclude the wider range of provisions where its intervention is not required to secure the achievement of acceptable standards. (ibid., p. 78)

Even as a statement of what needs to be done, it is not as non-interventionist as one might have expected. Apparently central government is not to give local government freedom where the former does not mind the latter setting its standards in a manner which may be expected to vary from place to place, but only where the standards local government may be expected to set are 'acceptable' – presumably to central government. But supposing that it were a clearer call for a division of responsibilities it leaves begging who or what is to decide what are 'essential' issues of national policy, as well as what are acceptable standards. The Report itself did nothing to clarify what, in its view, should be the dividing line.

A more logical solution is that suggested by Professor Alan Day in his 'Note of Reservation' (Layfield, 1976, pp. 302–15). It entails defining central and local responsibilities for the various services on the basis, first, of identifying the requirements or standards of national policy in each. Central government might, therefore, lay down, for example, basic minimum standards in education, the social services and other services while allowing local authorities to decide and finance any additional provision. On the assumption that national government had requirements in relation to all or certainly most services this indeed is the only way in which a clear division of responsibility can be specified. The Layfield Committee majority came down against it, first, because they doubted if it were feasible in practice to chop services up in such a manner and, second, because they doubted if in itself it would stop central government interfering in areas of local responsibility using whatever powers or channels of influence were at its disposal, as we have discussed them in Chapter 7 of Part Two. It was following this line of argument that the Committee made what we have earlier held to be a *non sequitur*. They believed that if local authorities raised all their own revenue it would be much more difficult for central government to influence their behaviour except by means of legislation, and such legislation would clarify the division of responsibility. But in so arguing, they did not escape the horns of the dilemma. First, the localist solution they advocated did not entail complete financial autonomy but instead a relatively modest reduction in the grant proportion from about 60 per cent to 40 per cent. It is not obvious that a reduction of this size would bring about a significant shift in the balance of power. The non-financial instruments would remain. Moreover, unless central government gave up all interest in the services now mainly financed by local resources the same problem of relating financial responsibility to power of decision would survive. As long as central government retains – as we must assume it will – an interest in most local services, even if only to ensure some minimum standards it determines, it is not easy to see how a reduction in block grant proportion, as the Committee advocated, will clarify responsibilities.

Our own suggestions for increasing local autonomy are more various and arguably more radical than those of the Layfield Committee but they too lack force in the absence of a clear understanding on the division of responsibility between the tiers.

For example, we have suggested charging for many local government services. The presumption here is that central government would cease to be interested in the provision of such services, except perhaps in a well-defined context such as that of prices and incomes policy, and that local government would charge on marginal cost or cost-covering principles, or possibly modify this by some locally determined redistributive policy involving either cross-subsidisation or a rate-fund contribution. Whether that presumption would need to have the force of law to be effective is another question. In so far as it provided such services, a local authority's relationship with central government might be more like that of a nationalised industry which also tends to complain of interference by central government, not necessarily less than do local authorities.

A related suggestion was that charging should be adopted by local authorities for many services but that central government should modify consumers' ability to pay either by negative income tax or vouchers or grants to local authorities. If any of these are to make a major difference to local autonomy, the presumption similarly must be that — except for matters such as prices and incomes policy — central government confines its interest to settling the amount and distributional impact of the NIT, the vouchers or the grants and does not interfere with the way in which the services are provided or influence the choice made by consumers.

Another proposal was that rates might be replaced by LIT to finance many or even all services. Because the income tax base is more equal between authorities than are rateable values and because the tax bills on households would be more related to ability to pay, a system based on LIT without any central grants would be conceivable.

All the changes we have considered so far at least notionally have been comparatively easy to reflect in a division of responsibility between tiers of government, for the one reason that it has been implicit throughout that central government would consent to withdraw from influencing the provision of 'local' services or indeed their consumption. Either it would get out altogether or its paternalism would be limited to enabling individuals to consume or local authorities to provide more services of their own choosing than either could or would out of its own income. But that is to over-rule the major point made by Professor Day into a mainstay of his 'Note of Reservation' (Layfield, 1976, pp. 302—15): that as a matter of fact central government and its officials want to have some say in what is provided by local authorities in all or almost all their services and are unlikely to reduce their influence. None of the solutions above face up to the problem of how a reduction in intervention is to be gained.

It is to solve this problem that many American writers — especially those of the Virginia school — have called for a constitution. Returning to the federalism discussed in Chapter 1 of Part One, a constitution was then stated by writers on federalism to be necessary to secure a division of powers between tiers of government. That a distinction between statute and constitutional law is foreign to Britain is perhaps among the least of the difficulties. Even then we noted a number of difficulties that seemed fatal to basing a division of labour between central and local government upon a pure federal constitution. One of these can now be seen very clearly. Such a constitution would have to specify the sphere of central and local government not only in relation to those services which were the province of the one or the other, but for the great majority of services where both had an interest. The drafting of laws to state such a division of responsibilities would be exceptionally complicated, even with the advantage of a common principle such as that central government sets minimum standards in relation to each, while local authorities provide services above those standards. Not only would the constitution have to be extremely detailed; but it is virtually certain that some form of constitutional court would be needed to settle disputed cases often of great complexity.

If that were not difficult enough, constitutions are intended to be seldom altered. But something which went into sufficient detail to delimit the spheres of central and local government in respect of each local service would have to be altered fairly frequently because of changing circumstances and policies. Indeed, the kind of detail required – if specified at all – is now set down in regulations, that is in secondary legislation, just because it is often necessary to change them without revising statute law, let alone constitutional law. Furthermore, such details are likely to inspire different political views so that there will also be frequent political presssures for change. Therefore, it is really unimaginable that the detail required to specify a clear division of labour between central and local government could be set down in a constitution. In practical terms, it is not even easy to imagine it being set down in statute law – what was held in Chapter 1 of Part One to be the defining characteristic of quasi-federalism. Parliament tends to be so congested with legislation as it is – and the same is true of most legislatures – that it would not be easy to find the time for the enormous burden of such legislation in the first place, or possibly even for amending it later, without very substantial reforms in parliamentary procedures; and indeed one might wonder if it would be at all possible given the preoccupations of a democratic Parliament.

If it should prove impossible to achieve such a division in the way in which law is written, is there any other possibility? The root difficulty at present is that central government not only controls the central departments, but also finds it generally easy to alter the regulations which have some influence over the division of responsibilities, and furthermore legislates for local authorities in a Parliament where Members on both sides of both Houses tend to identify more with central than with local interests. The principal meeting place between central government and local authorities is now the Consultative Committee and its attendant committees. As its name implies, ministers led by the Secretary of State for the Environment consult with the local authority associations, but as is inevitable when such machinery is itself part of central government machinery, local authority associations have influence and no power. The influence of the local authorities themselves is indirect. Moreover, the internal processes of central government are such as normally to achieve its unanimity at the Council while the local authority side is less likely to be in effective agreement on many issues.

Very different, as we have seen, was the legislative position of local authorities in the eighteenth century. Then there was no distinction between the representation of the people and of the territorial local authorities. Local legislation piloted through Parliament by local interests was the main domestic civil legislation. Under the press of foreign and imperial affairs and the growth of national legislation, local legislation was reduced to a trickle in the second half of the nineteenth century; and over the same period through parliamentary reform and boundary changes, constituencies came generally to be divorced from local authority areas. At the start of this book we observed that, as far as we knew, there was no move in 1832 or later in measures of parliamentary reform to make the House of Lords into a territorial representative body on the lines of the US Senate. Writing towards the end of the nineteenth century, Henry Sidgwick speculated that it was because local authorities were felt to lack sufficient dignity (1891, p. 451).

However, there is a precedent for such a legislature in which the upper chamber is a more effective representation of local authorities, or at least regional authorities, than occurs in the USA. As it is put by the English authority on German politics, Nevil Johnson (1973, p. 106, but *passim* ch. 5), West Germany, though not a pure federal state, as Wheare (1968) defined pure federalism, since its tiers do not have separate and co-ordinate powers — central government being supreme — yet 'the organ which guarantees Länder involvement in national legislation is the Bundesrat or Federal Council which acts as the second chamber in the federal legislature. It consists of forty-one members appointed by and from the Länder'. In it representation is roughly proportional to size, but there are only ten Länder. However, the effect of plural representation is to some extent offset since the members for each Land must cast their votes collectively. There are no elections to the Bundesrat. Its composition changes with the political changes of the Länder, death and retirement. As Johnson says

> its real authority derives from requirements scattered throughout the Basic Law and subsequent legislation that its consent must be given to a wide range of secondary proposals and to any administrative decrees which affect the interests and functions of the Länder. Indeed in the field of what in some countries is called delegated legislation the Bundesrat is more important than the Bundestag. (ibid., p. 106)

One method of increasing local influence in Parliament would be to have it represented there. The electoral basis of the House of Commons could hardly be altered from popular representation, but one might convert the House of Lords in that respect into an equivalent of the US Senate, but representing all levels of local authorities. One possibility would be to go to the extreme and replace the Lords as it is now known. The electoral principle of the Senate is democratic election of two senators by each state irrespective of size and population. Thus one could imagine a House of Lords with a representative from each county, Scottish region and district; and that would make more sense than making their representation proportional to their populations. Not only would it be difficult without making the House of Lords very large indeed, but its composition would be similar to that of the House of Commons which would be pointless. However, since the purpose of the plan would be to represent local authorities which are themselves democratically elected, it might make still more sense to go back to the earlier principle of the US Senate and have each local authority elect its representative in the Lords — which in each case would represent the political majority in its council. Each representative would be in the House of Lords no longer than the majority that elected him on the Council remained the majority; but it would seem not unreasonable that he or she should have tenure once elected unless the majority changed.

If each authority had the same one representative, then by normal criteria the less populous areas, mainly rural, would be over-represented. If the Lords were given the powers they had before the 1910 Parliament Act, this would matter more than if they stayed a revising chamber. What one would have would be a situation similar to that of the Federal German Republic where the Upper House also represents the local authorities which as we have seen, is one reason why local authorities — the Länder — have more influence in Germany than in Britain.

As in Germany, we would imagine that central government would have to take more notice of local government opinion in its legislative proposals — primary and secondary — and in its interpretations of its powers if:

(1) There were a Local Government Grand Committee of the second chamber through which all local government legislation had to pass.
(2) Local government representatives in that chamber were appointed to committees dealing with other legislation of major interest to local authorities.
(3) If all relevant regulations and orders affecting local authorities were debated in the Lords, or in one of its Committees at the request of a quorum of local government representatives.
(4) And if the House of Lords Committee were able to question ministers and officials on their relations with local government.

Such a Grand Committee could give an especially detailed scrutiny of government and other private legislation affecting local government from the standpoint of local government. While not appropriating the financial prerogative of the Commons, it could ask whether new duties imposed on authorities were matched by sufficient extra resources; whether there was a clear distinction between central guidelines and the discretion of local authorities. If it were so minded, it could play a major role in re-establishing what in Chapter 2 of Part One we called quasi-federalism — a clearer division of labour between central and local government which defined the responsibilities of each. Even if it were not, it could perform a useful revising and reforming role.

Such a Grand Committee could also give more time for debating secondary legislation affecting local authorities than either House now finds possible. Since central government exerts much of its power over local authorities through ministerial orders that are, in practice, rarely debated, such debate could be an effective check on the abuse of such powers.

Such local peers could also contribute to a process of reviewing central government policies and machinery affecting local authorities. Either with other peers or jointly with MPs representing national interests, they could thus form select committees to review matters from the functioning of the Consultative Council and RSG to the activities of the District Auditor and the Valuation Office of the Inland Revenue, so far as that affects local authorities.

Finally, special functions aside, there is sense when so many functions of government are performed by local authorities, who are as much elected as the House of Commons, in representation to the point where they have some influence on the course of legislation. It would be likely to have some effect in reversing the decline in local autonomy without giving local authorities an effective power of veto.

There are, however, costs to a truly localist system. Even if local councillors represent the majority view amongst their electorate, there are still minorities whose rights central government may wish to protect. Of course, local authorities operate within the framework of the law and the principle of *ultra vires* can protect citizens from the abuse of local government powers. Nor is it obvious whether, under a system of greater local autonomy, local councillors would represent the views of the majority, or whether, as is often the case now, they would continue to reflect national party political viewpoints. People can, of course, always move out of an authority but the costs of so doing can be high. A powerful argument for centralism is that it can protect the individual from the arbitrary exercise of local political power. The great involvement of central government in local affairs in the middle of the nineteenth century arose to protect people from their local leaders' failure to provide local public services. We may now have turned full circle. The great involvement of central government in local affairs in the remaining years of the twentieth century could well arise to protect people from the provision of public services to excess. But whether central government should be called in to redress local government, or local government be called into Parliament to redress central government, is perhaps the most crucial issue upon which the reader must form his own judgement.

Postscript

Since this book was written some uncertainty over the future of local government finance in Britain has been ended by the publication of the Local Government and Planning (No. 2) Bill in January 1980. But while it proposes changes, they are not part of any consistent overall policy for local finance, either one of those suggested by the Layfield Inquiry or from another source. The Bill neither abolishes rates nor takes measures of the kind set out in Part Three which we argue to be necessary if rates are to survive. Indeed, we argue in Part Three, Chapter 2, for a move to capital valuation for rating purposes and other changes in the processes of valuation which, in our judgement, are vital if rates are to be efficient, equitable and politically acceptable. By contrast, if the Bill's proposal to put an end to the statutory five-yearly revaluation of domestic properties became law, rates cannot but become an increasingly arbitrary tax which is inequitable and anomalous in both concept and practice. If domestic rates are not reformed on lines similar to those we propose, our prediction of their likely eventual demise seems to us to be fortified by the Bill. Another contention in the book is that the share of the rate burden borne by non-domestic ratepayers has increased over time. It is likely that the divorce proposed in the Bill between the methods of revaluation to be adopted for domestic and non-domestic ratepayers will make it possible for the non-domestic ratepayers' share to increase further, contrary to what is efficient and equitable. We believe this reinforces our argument in Part Two, Chapter 3, that explicit principles need to be chosen as a basis for taxing or charging non-domestic ratepayers, and then followed through in practice.

Neither does the Bill espouse any alternative to rates. It would seem as if plans for a local income tax have been shelved, though a strong case can be made for them as the prime source of local revenues (as is done here in Part Four, Chapter 3). Nor is there any shift towards other local taxes or any substantial move towards greater reliance on charging (as we argue there could be in Part Four, Chapter 4).

The most difficult issue raised by the Bill — and that which at the moment of writing is generating the most heat — is its proposals on grant. The new block grant it proposes is essentially the unitary grant examined by the Layfield Inquiry. What we have to say about that in Part Three, Chapter 4, applies with equal force to the new block grant. Central is a change in philosophy or emphasis by which assessed spending need, which would be called standard expenditure, would become a normative or prescriptive concept. It would be the government's notion of the 'right' level of local spending and no longer simply a stage in the process of calculating grant which has no normative implication as has been the case in the past. Though not indicated in the Bill, the government has said it would wish to replace or modify regression analysis as the basis for distributing grant and so change the method of measuring standard expenditure, otherwise known as local spending 'need'. The difficulty remains that of finding a satisfactory alternative. Many apparently new approaches have been generated but most run into the grave problems we have analysed in Part Three, Chapter 4. They tend to be meaningless, or a variant of what is done already, or to be likely to tend towards even greater central government control. We ourselves discuss some of the directions in which grant distribution might go in Part Four, Chapter 5.

We argue (in Part Three, Chapter 4) that there is a case for making the block grant no longer a matching grant. Local authorities would be free to spend as much as they please, but their contribution from grant would be limited to a maximum amount, itself based on an explicit division of responsibilities between central and local government. We also consider the merits of a variant that would taper grant above that level, which is rather like what the government has proposed. Not only has it, in our proposal, the advantage of being a more rational basis on which to distribute grant, but it will also have some effect in restraining expenditure. What seems unfortunate is that much public discussion has argued as if a tapering grant of itself amounted to centralist control over expenditure which has indeed been strengthened by the government talking as if standard expenditure, however arbitrarily determined, were the 'right' level of expenditure rather than the level up to which it was ready to pay grant at an unchanged percentage rate. Therefore one cannot be surprised that the new transitional and permanent arrangements for tapering grant have been widely attacked as a major erosion of local autonomy. One can nevertheless understand central government's concern. When, at the margin, so large a part of local authorities' revenue expenditure is no longer financed by local residents who have a vote and to whom councils are democratically accountable, but by the taxpayer and by non-voting industry and commerce, they can no longer expect to be allowed to spend as much as they choose. The democratic constraints on them are too light. Indeed, the new controls can be seen in two ways: as a further infringement of local autonomy or, as we have predicted in the book, as the logical consequence of growing dependence on grant. Local authorities can surely not have it both ways — freedom to spend, and massive and generally increasing grant income in both relative and absolute terms. If they want more autonomy, as we argue in Part Four, Chapter 5, they should accept less grant, but they have become so addicted to grant they would seem to value it more than freedom.

The Bill also proposes more stringent controls on capital expenditure which have already been altered to a simple overall control for each authority on what it can borrow in a year. Except in a few places, there is little discussion of local government capital expenditure in the book. In Part Two, Chapter 8, we argue our own position against the view that central government should exercise a greater control over capital expenditure in the interest of macroeconomic policy; and suggest reasons for thinking that the capital controls practised may be difficult to justify on control of expenditure grounds but only as instruments of central intervention in local policy.

We had predicted in the book that the system of using cash limits to control local pay increases would collapse, as it did in the winter of 1978/9, after the final version of our typescript had been completed. That did not take remarkable prescience. The proposals made here, however (Part Two, Chapter 8), for other methods of dealing with inflation in local expenditure still seem to us to be correct. Indeed, the case for a more realistic system of price adjustment has increased with a new grant system. If local authorities are to be penalised for spending above a certain sum, that sum must be realistic in appreciating factors that are and are not under the authorities' control, separately or together; and not a gross underestimate occasioned by wishful thinking about inflation.

While no major decisions have been taken on devolution or centralisation of functions, we believe that what we have to say on this in Part Four, Chapters 6 and 7, is still pertinent to such issues as the future of ILEA, many QUANGOS, the health and water authorities, where often in the past too little thought has been given to financial considerations and to democratic accountability. There is an intention to reduce local expenditure and therefore the size of the local sector. If such a change were to materialise after a hundred years of expansion it could be traumatic. But as it stands, the 1980 Bill (like the 1978 Green Paper) is very like the 1928 Bill. Their local finance provisions reflected the policies of the Treasury most of all. In 1928 the main objective was to cut the central government deficit and there was no reluctance to pass the burden on to rate-payers — at least on grounds of economic policy. Now the scope has been widened to cut the burden on local as well as on central government expenditure. But the two measures are similar in that, as measures principally embodying a Treasury standpoint, they are not informed by any strong conception of the role of local government, its democratic status or the most appropriate division of labour between it and central government. And even as an exercise in pragmatism this Bill has many discordant parts. It will help the system survive the current economic crisis, as we have shown has been done often enough in the past. However, if we are right in our forecasts the job will have to be done again. It is a measure almost wholly directed to containing local expenditure in a slump. But the present recession will be over and, for reasons we analyse in Part One, Chapter 4, local expenditure will almost certainly rise again. To avoid running into another crisis the rating system will need to be reformed or replaced; if not, the grant proportion will start rising again. Or — to put the same point the other way round — more fundamental reforms are required if retaining, let alone increasing, what remains of the autonomy of local government is a worthwhile objective.

Bibliography

Aaron, H. J. (1975). *Who Pays the Property Tax?* (Washington, DC: Brookings Institution).

Abel-Smith, B. (1964). *The Hospitals* (London: Heinemann).

Alonso, W. (1964). *Location and Land Use: Towards a General Theory of Land Rent* (Cambridge, Mass.: Harvard University Press).

Alt, J. E. (1971). 'Some social and political correlates of county borough expenditures', *British Journal of Political Science*, vol. 1, part 1.

Aristotle (1934 edn). *Nicomachaean Ethics* (London: Heinemann).

Aristotle (1948). *Politics*, ed. E. Barker (Oxford: Oxford University Press).

Aronsen, J. R., and Schwartz, E. (1973). 'Financing public goods and the distribution of population in a system of local governments' *National Tax Journal*, vol. 26 no. 2.

Arrow, K. J., and Scitovsky, T. (1969). *Readings in Welfare Economics* (London: Allen & Unwin).

Ashford, D. E. (1974). 'The effects of central finance on the British local government system', *British Journal of Political Science*, vol. 4, part 3.

Ashford, D. E., Berne, R., and Schramm, R. (1976). 'The expenditure–financing decision in British local government', *Policy and Politics*, vol. 5, no. 1.

Barr, J., and Davis, O. (1966). 'An elementary political and economic theory of the expenditure of local government', *Southern Economic Journal*, vol. 33, no. 2.

Barr, N., James, S., and Prest, A. R. (1977). *Self-Assessment for Income Tax* (London: Institute for Fiscal Studies).

Barrett, W., and Aiken, H. D. (1962). *Philosophy in the Twentieth Century* (New York: Random House).

Barry, B. (1965). *Political Argument* (London: Routledge & Kegan Paul).

Barzel, Y. (1969). 'Two propositions of the optimum level of producing collective goods', *Public Choice*, vol. 6 (Summer).

Baumol, W. J. (1967). 'Macroeconomics of unbalanced growth: anatomy of urban crisis', *American Economic Review*, vol. 57, no. 3.

Baumol, W. J., and Oates, W. E. (1975). *Theory of Environmental Policy* (Englewood Cliffs, N.J.: Prentice-Hall).

Beer, S. H. (1977). 'A political scientist's view of fiscal federalism', in W. E. Oates (ed.), *The Political Economy of Fiscal Federalism* (Lexington, Mass.: D. C. Heath).

Beesley, M. E. (1973). *Urban Transport: Studies in Economic Policy* (London: Butterworth).

Bentham, J. (1948). *A Fragment on Government* (Oxford: Blackwell).

Bergstrom, T. C., and Goodman, R. P. (1973). 'Private demands for public goods', *American Economic Review*, vol. 63, no. 3.

Beveridge, W. H. (1931). *Unemployment* (London: Longmans, Green).

Bird, R. M. (1976). *Charging for Public Services: A New Look at an Old Problem*, Canadian Tax Papers No. 59 (Toronto: Canadian Tax Foundation).

Black, D. (1948). 'On the rationality of group decision making', *Journal of Political Economy*, vol. 56, no. 1.

Blackstone, Sir Wm. (1773). *Commentaries on the Laws of England* (London).

Blake, R. (1966). *Disraeli* (London: Eyre & Spottiswoode).

Boaden, N. (1971). *Urban Policy-Making: Influences on County Boroughs in England and Wales* (Cambridge: Cambridge University Press).

Boaden, N., and Alford, R. (1969). 'Sources of diversity in English local government decision', *Public Administration*, vol. 47 (Summer).

Borcheding, T. E., and Deacon, R. T. (1972). 'The demand for the services of non-federal governments', *American Economic Review*, vol. 62, no. 4.

Boyle, L. (1966). *Equalization and the Future of Local Government Finance* (Edinburgh: Oliver & Boyd).

Brainard, W., and Dolbear, F. T. (1967). 'The possibility of oversupply of local 'public' goods: a critical note', *Journal of Political Economy*, vol. 75, no. 1.

Breton, A. (1965). 'A theory of government grants', *Canadian Journal of Economics and Political Science*, vol. 31, no. 2.

Briggs, A. (1963). *Victorian Cities* (London: Odhams).

Briggs, E., and Deacon, A. (1973). 'Creation of the unemployment assistance board', *Policy and Politics*, vol. 2, no. 1.

Brittan, S. (1964). *The Treasury under the Tories* (Harmondsworth: Penguin).

Brock, M. (1973). *The Great Reform Act* (London: Hutchinson).

Buchanan, J. M. (1949). 'The pure theory of government finance: a suggested approach', *Journal of Political Economy*, vol. 57, no. 6.

Buchanan, J. M. (1950). 'Federalism and fiscal equity', *American Economic Review*, vol. 40, no. 4.

Buchanan, J. M. (1952). 'Federal grants and resources allocation', *Journal of Political Economy*, vol. 60, no. 3.

Buchanan, J. M. (1966). 'Peak load and efficient pricing comment', *Quarterly Journal of Economics*, vol. 80, no. 3.

Buchanan, J. M. (1967). *Public Finance in Democratic Process* (Chapell Hill, N.C.: University of North Carolina Press).

Buchanan, J. M. (1968). *Demand and Supply of Public Goods* (Chicago, Ill.: Rand McNally).

Buchanan, J. M., and Wagner, R. E. (1970). 'An efficiency basis for federal fiscal equalisation', in J. Margolis (ed.), *Analysis of Public Output*, National Bureau of Economic Research (New York: Columbia University Press).

Bulpitt, J. G. (1967). *Party Politics in English Local Government* (London: Longman).

Burke, Edmund (1780). 'A speech at the Guildhall in Bristol', published in *Works and Correspondence of Edmund Burke* (London: Francis and John Rivington, 1852).

Cannan, E. (1907). 'The proposed relief of buildings from land rates', *Economic Journal*, vol. 17, no. 65.

Cannan, E. (1927). *History of Local Rates in England* (London: King).

Carter, R. L. (1967). 'Pricing and the risk of fire', in *Essays in the Theory and Practice of Pricing* (London: Institute of Economic Affairs).

Caves, R., and Associates (1968). *Britain's Economic Prospect* (London: Allen & Unwin).

Central Statistical Office. *Annual Abstract of Statistics* (London: HMSO).

Chartered Institute of Public Finance and Accountancy (annual). *Education Statistics* (London: CIPFA).

Chartered Institute of Public Finance and Accountancy (annual). *Return of Rates and Rates Levied Per Head of Population* (England–Wales) (London: CIPFA).

Chester, D. N. (1951). *Central and Local Government* (London: Macmillan).
Chester, D. N. (1975). *Peacetime History: Nationalisation of British Industry 1945–51* (London: UK Cabinet Office).
Clapham, J. H. (1949). *A Concise Economic History of Britain from Earliest Times to 1750* (Cambridge: Cambridge University Press).
Clark, C. (1968). *Population Growth and Land Use* (London: Macmillan).
Clark, G. S. R. Kitson (1962). *The Making of Victorian England* (London: Methuen).
Clegg, H. A., and Chester, T. E. (1953). *Future of Nationalisation* (Oxford: Blackwell).
Coase, R. (1960). 'The problem of social cost', *Journal of Law and Economics*, vol. 3, no. 1.
Cockburn, C. (1977). *The Local State: The Management of Cities and People* (London: Pluto Press).
Cole, G. D. H. (1921). *Future of Local Government* (London: Cassell).
Committee for Economic Development (1966). *Managing Local Government* (New York: Committee for Economic Development).
Counter Inflation (Private Sector Residential Rents) England and Wales Order (London: HMSO).
Cripps, F., and Godley, W. (1976). *Local Government Finance and Its Reform: A Critique of the Layfield Committee's Report* (Department of Applied Economics, Cambridge: Cambridge University Press).
Crossman, R. H. S. (1975). *Diaries of a Cabinet Minister*, Vol. 1 (London: Hamish Hamilton and Cape).
Curtis, S. J. (1952). *Education in Britain since 1900* (London: Dakers).
Dahl, R. A. (1961). *Who Governs?* (New Haven, Conn.: Yale University Press).
Davenport, H. J. (1917). 'Theoretical issues in the single tax', *American Economic Review*, vol. 7, no. 1.
Davies, B. P. (1968). *Social Needs and Resources in Local Services* (London: Michael Joseph).
Davies, B. P., Barton, A. J., McMillan, I. S., and Williamson, V. K. (1971). *Variations in Services for the Aged* (London: Bell).
Davies, B. P., Barton, A. J., and McMillan, I. S. (1972). *Variations in Children's Services among British Urban Authorities* (London: Bell).
Davis, O. A., and Whinston, A. (1962). 'Externalities, welfare and the theory of games', *Journal of Political Economy*, vol. 70, no. 3.
Dawson, D. (1976). 'Determinants of local authority expenditure', in *Report of the Committee of Inquiry into Local Government Finance* (Layfield Report), app. 7 (London: HMSO).
Dearlove, J. (1973). *Politics of Policy in Local Government* (Cambridge: Cambridge University Press).
Department of Education and Science (1967). *Prices and Incomes Standstill: Period of Severe Restraint: Incentive Bonus Schemes*, Circular no. 11/67 (London: DES).
Department of Education and Science (10 January 1967). *School-building in Educational Priority Areas*, Circular no. 10/67 (London: DES).
Department of Employment (annual). *Family Expenditure Survey*.
Department of the Environment (1971a). *Future Shape of Local Government Finance*, Cmnd 4741 (London: HMSO).
Department of the Environment (1971b). *Local Government in England: Government Proposals for Reorganisation*, Cmnd 4584 (London: HMSO).

Department of the Environment (1971*c*). *Reorganisation of Water and Sewage Services*, Circular no. 92/71 (London: DoE).

Department of the Environment (1976*a*). *Local Government Expenditure for 1976/8*, Circular no. 84 (London DoE).

Department of the Environment (1976*b*). *Transport Policy: A Consultation Document* (London: DoE).

Department of the Environment (1977*a*). *Housing Policy Review Report. Technical Volume* (Parts 1, 2 and 3) (London: HMSO).

Department of the Environment (1977*b*). *Local Government Finance*, Cmnd 6813 (London: HMSO).

Department of the Environment (annual). *Rates and Rateable Values* (London: HMSO).

Dicey, A. V. (1905). *Law of the Constitution* (London: Macmillan).

Dodd, A. H. (1956). *The Growth of Responsible Government* (London: Routledge & Kegan Paul).

Donoghue, B., and Jones, G. W. (1973). *Herbert Morrison* (London: Weidenfeld).

Downs, A. (1957). *An Economic Theory of Democracy* (London: Harper).

Drake, M., McLoughlin, B., Thompson, R., and Thornley, J. (1975). *Aspects of Structure Planning in Britain*, Research paper 20 (London: Centre for Environmental Studies).

Due, J. F. (1961). 'Studies of State–local tax influences on location of industry', *National Tax Journal*, vol. 14, no. 2.

Dupuit, J. (1844). 'On the measurement of the utility of public works', reprinted in K. J. Arrow and T. Scitovsky, *Readings in Welfare Economics* (London: Allen & Unwin).

Eaglesham, E. J. R. (1956). *From School Board to Local Authority* (London: Routledge & Kegan Paul).

Economist, The (20 May 1848). 'The Health of Towns Bill'.

Economist, The (8 December 1928). 'The block grant and the formula'.

Edgeworth, F. (1906). 'Recent schemes for rating urban land values', *Economic Journal*, vol. 16, no. 61.

Education Act (1944). 748 Geo. 6, Ch. 31 (London: HMSO).

Else-Mitchell, R. (Chairman) (1976). *Commission of Inquiry into Land Tenure. Final Report* (Canberra: Australian Government Publishing Service).

Elton, G. R. (1953). *Tudor Revolution in Government* (Cambridge: Cambridge University Press).

Ensor, R. C. K. (1936). *England 1870–1914* (Oxford: Oxford University Press).

Finer, H. (1941). *Municipal Trading* (London: Allen & Unwin).

Finer, H. (1950). *English Local Government* (London: Methuen).

Fisher, G. W. (1964). 'Interstate variation in state and local government expenditure', *National Tax Journal*, vol. 17, no. 1.

Fishlow, A., and David, P. A. (1961). 'Optimal resource allocation in an imperfect market setting', *Journal of Political Economy*, vol. 69, no. 6.

Foot, M. (1962). *Aneurin Bevan* (London: Macgibbon & Kee).

Foster, C. D. (1973). 'The reform of local government finance', *Proceedings of a Conference on Local Government Finance* (London: Institute for Fiscal Studies).

Foster, C. D. (1975). *The Transport Problem* (London: Croom Helm, 1975).

Foster, C. D. (1976*a*). *Politics Finance and the Role of Economics* (London: Allen & Unwin).

Foster, C. D. (1976*b*). *Local Government Resources and Finance* (Centre for Environmental Studies).

Foster, C. D., and Beesley, M. E. (1963). 'Estimating the social benefit of constructing an underground railway in London', *Journal of the Royal Statistical Society*, series A, vol. 126.

Foster, C. D., and Glaister, S. (1975). 'Anatomy of a development land tax', *Urban Studies*, vol. 12, no. 2.

Foster, C. D., and Lynch, B. (1978). 'Capital valuation: a way forward' *Centre for Environmental Studies Review*, no. 4.

Frazer, D. (1973). *Evolution of the British Welfare State* (London: Macmillan).

Friedrich, C. J. (1937). *Constitutional Government and Politics* (New York: Harper).

Froude, J. A. (1877). 'On the uses of a landed gentry', in *Short Studies in Great Subjects* (Longmans).

Gaffney, M. (1972a). 'What is property tax reform?' *American Journal of Economics and Sociology*, vol. 31, no. 3.

Gaffney, M. (1972b). 'Land rent, taxation and public policy', *American Journal of Economics and Sociology*, vol. 31, no. 1.

Gaffney, M. (1973). 'Land rent, taxation and public policy: taxation and the function of urban land rent', *American Journal of Economics and Sociology*, vol. 32, no. 1 (January).

Garvin, J. L. (1932). *Life of Joseph Chamberlain* (London: Macmillan).

General Rate Act (1967). Eliz. 2, 1967, Ch. 9. (London: HMSO).

George, H. (1886). *Progress and Poverty* (London: Kegan Paul).

Gilbert, B. B. (1970). *British Social Policy 1914–1939* (London: Batsford).

Godley, W., and Rhodes, J. (1973). 'The rate support grant system', *Proceedings of a Conference on Local Government Finance*, (London: Institute of Fiscal Studies).

Gomme, G. L. (1897). *Lectures on the Principles of Local Government* (Westminster: Archibald Constable & Co.).

Goschen, G. J., Viscount (1872). *Reports and Speeches on Local Taxation* (London: Macmillan).

Goschen, G. J. Viscount (1905). 'The prospects of trade', in *Essays and Addresses on Economic Questions 1865–1893* (London: Edward Arnold).

Gramlich, E., and Galper, H. (1973). 'State and local fiscal behaviour and federal grant policy', *Brookings Papers on Economic Activity* (Washington, DC: Brookings Institution).

Greater London Council, *Annual Abstract of Greater London Statistics*.

Green, C. (1967). *Negative Taxes and the Poverty Problem* (Washington, DC: Brookings Institution).

Green, L. P. (1959). *Provincial Metropolis* (London: Allen & Unwin).

Green, T. H. (1889). 'Liberal legislation and freedom of contract', *Works*, Vol. 3. (London: Longmans, Green).

Gregory, R. (1969). 'Local elections and the rule of anticipated reactions', *Political Studies*, vol. 17, no. 1.

Gretton, R. H. (1922). *A Modern History of the English People 1880–1922* (London: Secker).

Griffith, J. A. G. (1966). *Central Departments and Local Authorities* (London: Allen & Unwin).

Gulick, L. (1937). 'Notes on the theory of organisation', in L. Gulick and L. Urwick (eds), *Papers on the Science of Administration* (New York: Institute of Public Administration).

Gupta, S. P., and Hutton, J. P. *'Economics of scale in local government services'* research report commissioned by the Royal Commission on Local Government in England, 1969 (York: Institute of Social and Economic Research, University of York).

Haavelmo, T. (1945). 'Multiplier effects of a balanced budget', *Econometrica*, vol. 13, no. 4.

Halévy, E. (1972). *Growth of Philosophic Radicalism* (London: Faber).

Hamilton, B. W. (1975). 'Zoning and property taxation in a system of local governments', *Urban Studies*, vol. 12, no. 2.

Hampshire, S. (1959). *Thought and Action* (London: Chatto).

Hansen, A., and Perloff, H. (1944). *State and Local Finance in the National Economy* (New York: Norton).

Harberger, A. C. (1962). 'The incidence of the corporate income tax', *Journal of Political Economy*, vol. 70, no. 3.

Harris, R., and Seldon, A. (1976). *Pricing or Taxing?* IEA Hobart Paper no. 71 (London: Institute of Economic Affairs).

Harrison, A. J., and Webber R. (1977). 'Capital spending on housing: control and distribution', *Centre for Environmental Studies Review*, no. 1.

Harrison, W. M. (1876). *Elizabethan England*, ed. L. Withington (London: Walter Scott).

Head, J. (1962). 'Public goods and public policy', *Public Finance*, vol. 17, no. 3.

Head, J. (1974). *Public Goods and Public Welfare* (Durham, N.C.: Duke University Press).

Heller, W. (1961). *New Dimensions of Political Economy* (Cambridge, Mass.: Harvard University Press).

Henry, S. G. B., Sawyer, M. C., and Smith, P. (1976). 'Models of inflation in the U.K.', *National Institute Economic Review*, no. 77.

Hepworth, N. P. (1976). *The Finance of Local Government*. (London: Allen & Unwin).

Hicks, J. R. (1956). *Revision of Demand Theory* (Oxford: Oxford University Press).

Hicks, J. R., and Hicks, U.K. (1944). *The Incidence of Local Rates in Great Britain* (London: National Institute of Economic and Social Research).

Hicks, U. K. (1938). *Finance of British Government, 1920–36* (Oxford: Oxford University Press).

Hicks, U.K. (1954). *British Public Finances: Their Structure and Development 1880–1952* (Oxford: Oxford University Press).

Hildersley, S. H. H., and Nottage, R. (1968). *Sources of Local Revenue* (London: Royal Institute of Public Administration).

Hirsch, W. (1960). 'Determinants of public education expenditure', *National Tax Journal*, vol. 13, no. 1.

Hirsch, W. (1970). *Economics of State and Local Government* (New York: McGraw-Hill).

Hochman, H. M., and Rodgers, J. D. (1969). 'Pareto Optimal Redistribution', *American Economic Review*, vol. 59, no. 3.

Holland, D. (ed.) (1970). *Assessment of Land Value* (Madison, Wis.: University of Wisconsin Press).

Housing Finance Act (1972). Eliz. II, 1972, Ch. 47 (London: HMSO).

Howard, D. L. (1960). *The English Prisons: Their Past and Their Future* (London: Methuen).

Ilersic, A. R. (1965). *Allen and After: A Review of the Report on the Committee of Inquiry into the Impact of Rates on Households* (London: Rating and Valuation Association).

Inland Revenue Board (annual). *Survey of Personal Incomes* (London: HMSO).

Institute of Municipal Treasurers and Accountants (1968). *Motor Tax as a Source of Local Finance* (London: IMTA).

International Bank for Reconstruction and Development (1976). *World Tables* (Baltimore, Md., and London: IBRD and Johns Hopkins University Press).

Jackman, R. A. (1979). 'London's Needs Grant', *Centre for Environmental Studies Review*, no. 5.

Jackman, R. A., and Klappholz, K. (1975). *Taming the Tiger*, IEA Hobart Paper no. 63. (London: Institute of Economic Affairs).

Jackman, R. A., and Sellars, M. (1977*a*). 'The distribution of RSG: the hows and whys of the new needs formula', *Centre for Environmental Studies Review*, no. 1.

Jackman, R. A., and Sellars, M. (1977*b*). 'Why rate poundages differ: the case of the metropolitan districts', *Centre for Environmental Studies Review*, no. 2.

Jackman, R. A., and Sellars, M. (1978). 'Local expenditure and local discretion', *Centre for Environmental Studies Review*, no. 3.

Jackson, R. M. (1965). *Machinery of Local Government*, 2nd edn (London: Macmillan).

Jenkins, R. H. (1954). *Mr. Balfour's Poodle* (London: Heinemann).

Jennings, W. I. (1947). *Principles of Local Government Law*, 3rd edn (London: University of London Press).

Jewell, H. M. (1972). *English Local Administration in the Middle Ages* (Newton Abbott: David & Charles).

Johnson, Nevil (1973). *Government in the Federal Republic of Germany: The Executive at Work* (Oxford: Pergamon).

Johnston, J., and Timbrell, M. (1973). 'Empirical tests of a bargaining theory of wage rate determination', *Manchester School*, vol. 41, no. 2.

Jones, A. (1968). *Local Governors at Work* (London: Conservative Political Centre).

Jones, G. W. (1969). *Borough Politics: A Study of Wolverhampton Town Council 1868–1964* (London: Macmillan).

Jones, G. W. (1977). *Responsibility and Government*, Inaugural Lecture, London School of Economics (London: LSE).

Keir, Sir David (1948). *Constitutional History of Modern Britain* (London: A. & C. Black).

Keith-Lucas, B. (1952). *The English Local Government Franchise: A Short History* (Oxford: Blackwell).

Kempe Committee (1914). *Report of Departmental Committee on Local Taxation*, Cd 7315 (London: HMSO).

Keynes, J. M. (1936). *General Theory of Employment, Interest and Money* (London: Macmillan).

Keynes, J. M. (1940). *How To Pay for the War* (London: Macmillan).

King, D. N. (1973). 'Why do local authority rate poundages differ?', *Public Administration*, vol. 51 (Summer).

Knight, F. H. (1924). 'Some fallacies in the interpretation of social cost', *Quarterly Journal of Economics*, vol. 38, no. 4.

Layfield Committee (1976). *Report of the Committee of Inquiry into Local Government Finance*. Cmnd 6453 (London: HMSO).

Lees, D. S., *et al.* (1956). *Local Expenditure and Exchequer Grants* (London: Institute of Municipal Treasurers and Accountants).

Lindahl, E. (1919). *Die Gerechtigkeit der Besteuerung* (Lund). An English translation of part of this work appears in R. A. Musgrave and A. T. Peacock (eds), *Classics in the Theory of Public Finance* (London: Macmillan), pp. 168–76.

Lipset, S. M. (1960). *Political Man* (New York: Doubleday).

Little, I. M. D. (1957). *A Critique of Welfare Economics*, 2nd edn (Oxford: Oxford University Press).

Local Government Act (1948). 11 & 12 Geo. 6, Ch. 26 (London: HMSO).

Long, E. (ed.) (1939). *The Taxation of Land Values* (London).

Lubenow, W. C. (1971). *Politics of Government Growth: Early Victorian Attitudes towards State Intervention* (Newton Abbott: David & Charles).

Lynch, B. (1977). 'RSG resources element: its uses and misuses', *Centre for Environmental Studies Review*, no. 2.

McKenzie, R. T. (1955). *British Political Parties* (London: Heinemann).

McLure, C. E. (1967). 'The interstate exporting of state and local taxes: estimates for 1962', *National Tax Journal*, vol. 20, no. 1.

McLure, C. E. (1969). 'Inter-regional incidence of general regional taxes', *Public Finance*, vol. 24, no. 3.

McLure, C. E. (1977). 'Taxation of multijurisdictional corporate income – lessons from US experience', in W. E. Oates (ed.), *The Political Economy of Fiscal Federalism* (Lexington, Mass.: D. C. Heath).

Maine, Sir Henry (1871). *Village Communities in the East and West* (London: John Murray).

Mair, D. (1975). 'Differentials Incidence of Industrial Rates', Heriot-Watt University, Dept. of Economics Working Paper, unpublished.

Mair, D. (1978). 'The incidence of non-domestic rates', in R. Jackman (ed.), *The Impact of Rates on Industry and Commerce*, CES Policy Series no. 5 (London: Centre of Environmental Studies).

Manvel, A. (1968). *Trends in the Value of Real Estate and Land*. US National Commission on Urban Problems, Research Report no. 12 (Washington, DC).

Marris, R. (1964). *The Economic Theory of 'Managerial' Capitalism* (London: Macmillan).

Marshall, A. (1899). *Classification and Incidence of Imperial and Local Taxes*, report issued by Royal Commission on Local Taxation, C. 9528 (London: HMSO).

Marshall, A. (1926). *Official Papers* (London: Macmillan).

Marshall, A. H. (1960). *Financial Administration in Local Government* (London: Allen & Unwin).

Maynard, A. K. (1975). *Experiment with Choice in Education*, IEA Hobart Paper no. 64 (London: Institute of Economic Affairs).

Maynard, A. K., and King, D. N. (1972). *Rates or Prices*, IEA Hobart Paper no. 54 (London: Institute of Economic Affairs).

Miezkowski, P. (1972). 'The property tax: an excise tax or a profits tax', *Journal of Public Economics*, vol. 1, no. 1.

Mill, J. S. (1848). *Principles of Political Economy* (London: Parker).

Mill, J. S. (1910*a*). 'On Liberty', in his *Utilitarianism Liberty and Representative Government*, Everyman Edition (London: Dent).

Mill, J. S. (1910*b*). 'Representative Government', in his *Utilitarianism, Liberty and Representative Government*, Everyman Edition (London: Dent).

Millett, J. D. (1940). *Unemployment Assistance Board* (London: Allen & Unwin).

Ministry of Health (1939). *Report on Valuation for Rates* (Fitzgerald Report) (London: HMSO, published 1944).

Ministry of Housing and Local Government (1928). *Proposals for Reform in Local Government and in the Financial Relations between the Exchequer and Local Authorities*, Cmnd 3134 (London: HMSO).

Ministry of Housing and Local Government (1952). *The Rating of Site Values: Report of the Committee of Enquiry* (Erskine Sime Report) (London: HMSO).

Ministry of Housing and Local Government (1956–7). *Local Government Finance – England and Wales*, Cmnd 209 (London: HMSO).

Ministry of Housing and Local Government (1965). *Report of the Committee of Inquiry into the Impact of Rates on Households* (Allen Report) Cmnd 2582 (London: HMSO).

Ministry of Housing and Local Government (1965–6). *Local Government Finance – England and Wales*, Cmnd 2923 (London: HMSO).

Ministry of Housing and Local Government (1970). *Reform of Local Government in England*, Cmnd 4276 (London: HMSO).

Ministry of Reconstruction (1944). *Employment Policy*, Cmnd 6527 (London: HMSO).

Mishan, E. J. (1960). 'A survey of welfare economics 1939–59', *Economic Journal*, vol. 70, no. 278.

Mishan, E. J. (1971). *Cost–Benefit Analysis* (London: Allen & Unwin).

Mitchell, B. R., and Deane, P. (1962). *Abstract of British Historical Statistics*, (Cambridge: Cambridge University Press).

Mitchell, B. R., and Jones, H. G. (1971). *Second Abstract of British Historical Statistics* (Cambridge: Cambridge University Press).

Money Payment (Justice Procedure) Act (1935). 25 & 26 Geo. 5, Ch. 46 (London: HMSO).

Moore, B., and Rhodes, J. (1976). 'The relative needs of local authorities', in *Report of the Committee of Inquiry into Local Government Finance* (Layfield Report), app. 7 (London: HMSO).

Moore, G. E. (1903). *Principia Ethica* (Cambridge: Cambridge University Press).

Morley, J. (1903). *The Life of Richard Cobden*, 2nd edn (London: T. Fisher Unwin).

Municipal Yearbook (London: published by *Municipal Journal*, annually).

Musgrave, R. (1959). *Theory of Public Finance* (New York: McGraw-Hill).

Musgrave, R. (1961). 'Approaches to fiscal theory of political federalism', in National Bureau of Economic Research, *Public Finances: Needs, Sources and Utilization* (Princeton, N.J.: Princeton University Press).

Musgrave, R. (1969). *Fiscal Systems* (New Haven and London: Yale University Press).

Muth, R. (1969). *Cities and Housing* (Chicago, Ill.: Chicago University Press).

Netzer, D. (1966). *Economics of the Property Tax* (Washington, DC: Brookings Institution).

Netzer, D. (1968). *Federal State and Local Finance in a Metropolitan Context*, in H. S. Perloff and L. Wingo (eds), *Issues in Urban Economics*. (Baltimore, Md.: Johns Hopkins Press).

Netzer, D. (1970). *Economics and Urban Problems* (New York: Basic Books).

Newcomer, Mabel (1937). *Central and Local Finance in Germany and England* (New York: Columbia University Press).

Nicholson, R. J., and Topham, N. (1971). 'The determinants of investment in housing by local authorities: an econometric approach', *Journal of the Royal Statistical Society*, series A, vol. 134, pt 3.

Oates, W. E. (1969). 'The effects of property taxes and local public spending on property values: an empirical study of tax capitalization and the Tiebout hypothesis', *Journal of Political Economy*, vol. 77, no. 6.

Oates, W. E. (1972). *Fiscal Federalism* (New York: Harcourt, Brace).

Oates, W. E. (1975). 'Automatic' increases in tax revenue – the effect on the size of the public budget', in W. E. Oates (ed.), *Financing the New Federalism* (Baltimore, Md.: Johns Hopkins Press).

Ohls, J. C., and Wales, T. J. (1972). 'Supply and demand for state and local services', *Review of Economics and Statistics*, vol. 54, no. 4.

Oliver, F. R., and Stanyer, J. (1969). 'Some aspects of the financial behaviour of county boroughs', *Public Administration*, vol. 47 (Spring).

Olson, M., and Zeckhauser, R. (1966). 'The economic theory of alliances', *Review of Economics and Statistics*, vol. 48, no. 3.

Osborne, M. (1975). 'Alternative methods of predicting local incomes', LSE Working Paper, unpublished.

Ostrogorski, M. (1902). *Democracy and the Organisation of Political Parties* (London: Macmillan).

Ostrom, V. (1973). *The Intellectual Crisis in American Public Administration* (Alabama: University of Alabama).

Ostrom, V., Tiebout, C. M., and Warren, R. (1961). 'The organisation of government in metropolitan areas', *American Political Science Review*, vol. 55, no. 4.

Parkin, M., Sumner, M., and Ward R. (1975). 'The effects of excess demand, generalised expectations and wage-price controls on wage inflation in the UK', in K. Brunner and A. Meltzer (eds), *The Economics of Price and Wage Controls* (Amsterdam: North-Holland Publishing Co.).

Pauly, M. V. (1973). 'Income redistribution as a local public good', *Journal of Public Economics*, vol. 2, no. 1.

Peacock, A., and Wiseman, J. (1961). *The Growth of Public Expenditure in the United Kingdom* (Princeton, N.J.: National Bureau of Economic Research).

Pennock, J. R. (1959). 'Federal and unitary government: disharmony and frustration', *Behavioural Science*, vol. 4. no. 2.

Perkin, H. J. (1969). *Origins of Modern English Society 1780–1880* (London: Routledge & Kegan Paul).

Perlman, M., and Lynch, B. (1977). 'Forecasting, control and inflation', *Centre for Environmental Studies Review*, no. 1.

Peterson, G. E. (1975). 'Voter demand for public school expenditures', in J. E. Jackson (ed.), *Public Needs and Private Behaviour in Metropolitan Areas* (Cambridge, Mass.: Bellinger).

Plowden Committee (1961). *The Control of Public Expenditure. Report*, Cmnd 1432 (London: HMSO).

Plumb, J. H. (1950). *England in the Eighteenth Century* (Harmondsworth: Penguin).

Political and Economic Planning (1960). *Growth in the British Economy: A Study of Economic Problems and Policies in Contemporary Britain* (London: PEP).

Popper, K. (1957). *The Poverty of Historicism* (London: Routledge & Kegan Paul).

Popper, K. (1966). *The Open Society and Its Enemies*, Vol. I: Plato (London: Routledge & Kegan Paul).

Prest, A. R. (1958). *Public Finance in Theory and Practice* (London: Weidenfeld).

Rabinowitz, A. (1977). 'Rates, Capital Valuation, Market and Planning' unpublished.

Rating and Valuation Act (1925). 15 & 16 Geo. 5, Ch. 90 (London: HMSO).

Redfern, P. (1955). 'Net investment in fixed assets in the United Kingdom 1938–1953', *Journal of the Royal Statistical Society*, series A, vol. 118.

Redlich, J., and Hirst, F. W. (1970). *History of Local Government in England*, 2nd abridged edn, ed. B. Keith-Lucas (London: Macmillan).

Rent Act (1965). Eliz. 2, 1965, Ch. 75 (London: HMSO).

Rent Act (1968). Eliz. 2, 1968, Ch. 23 (London: HMSO).

Rent Act (1974). Eliz. 2, 1974, Ch. 51 (London: HMSO).

Reports of Royal Commission:

Royal Commission on Local Taxation (Chairman: Lord Balfour of Burleigh) (1901). *Final Report*, Cd 638 (London: HMSO).

Royal Commission of the Poor Laws and Relief of Distress (1905/9). *Reports* issued 1909–10 (London: HMSO).

Royal Commission on Local Government in England (Redcliffe–Maud Report) (1969). *Report*, Cmnd 4040 (London: HMSO).

Royal Commission on Local Government in Greater London (Herbert Report). (1957–60). *Report*, Cmnd 1164 (London: HMSO).

Royal Commission on the Constitution (Kilbrandon Report) (1973). *Report*, Cmnd 5460 (London: HMSO).

Rhodes, R. A. W. (1975). 'Lost world of British local politics', *Local Government Studies*, new series, vol. 1, no. 3.

Rhodes, R. A. W. (1976). 'Central-local relations', in *Report of the Committee of Inquiry into Local Government Finance* (Layfield Report), app. 6 (London: HMSO).

Ricardo, D. (1962). *Principles of Political Economy* (Cambridge: Cambridge University Press).

Roberts, D. (1960). *Victorian Origins of the Welfare State* (New Haven, Conn.: Yale University Press).

Robson, W. A. (1933). 'The central domination of local government', *Political Quarterly*, vol. 4, no. 1.

Robson, W. A. (1952). *Problems of Nationalised Industry* (London: Allen & Unwin).

Robson, W. A. (1954). *Development of Local Government* (London: Allen & Unwin).

Robson, W. A. (1966). *Local Government in Crisis*, rev. edn (London: Allen & Unwin).

Rose, R., and Mossawir, H. (1967). 'Voting and elections: a functional analysis', *Political Studies*, vol. 15, no. 2.

Rostow, W. W. (1948). *British Economy of the Nineteenth Century: Essays* (Oxford: Clarendon Press).

Rothenberg, J. (1967). *Economic Evaluation of Urban Renewal* (Washington, DC: Brookings Institute).

Rothenberg, J. (1970). 'Local decentralisation and the theory of optimal government', in J. Margolis (ed.), *Analysis of Public Output*, National Bureau of Economic Research (New York: Columbia University Press).

Rothenberg, J., and Heggie, I. G. (eds) (1974). *Transport and the Urban Environment* (London: Macmillan).

Royal Institute of Chartered Surveyors (1964). *Rating of Site Values* (London: RICS).

Royal Institute of Public Administration (1968). *Performance and Size of Local Education Authorities*, Royal Commission on Local Government Research Study no. 4 (London: HMSO).

Rozental, A. A. (1960). 'Census of governments – footnotes on a shoehorn', *National Tax Journal*, vol. 13, no. 2.

Ryle, G. (1950). 'The Physical Basis of Mind: A Philosophers' Symposium', in P. Laslett (ed.), *Physical Basis of Mind* (Oxford: Blackwell).

Samuelson, P. A. (1954). 'Pure theory of public expenditures', *Review of Economics and Statistics*, vol. 36, no. 4.

Samuelson, P. A. (1955). 'Diagrammatic exposition of a theory of public expenditure', *Review of Economics and Statistics*, vol. 37, no. 4.

Sargan, J. D. (1964). 'Wages and prices in the UK', in P. E. Hart *et al.* (ed.), *Econometric Analysis for National Economic Planning* (London: Butterworth).

Scott, A. D. (1950). 'Evaluation of federal grants', *Economica*, vol. 17, no. 68.

Scott, A. D. (1964). 'The economic goals of federal finance', *Public Finance*, vol. 19, no. 3.

Seldon, A. (1977). *Charge* (London: Temple Smith).

Sharpe, L. J. (1960). 'The politics of local government in Greater London', *Public Administration*, vol. 38 (Summer).

Shoup, C. S. (1969). *Public Finance* (London: Weidenfeld).

Sidgwick, H. (1887). *Principles of Political Economy*, 2nd edn (London: Macmillan).

Sidgwick, H. (1891). *Elements of Politics* (London: Macmillan).

Simon, H. A. (1943). 'Incidence of a tax on urban real property', *Quarterly Journal of Economics*, vol. 57, no. 3.

Simons, H. C. (1938). *Personal Income Taxation* (Chicago, Ill.: University Press).

Simons, H. C. (1948). *Economic Policy for a Free Society* (Chicago, Ill.: University of Chicago Press).

Skidelsky, R. J. (1976). *Politicians and the Slump* (London: Macmillan).

Smellie, K. B. (1968). *History of Local Government*, 4th edn (London: Allen & Unwin).

Smith, A. (1776). *The Wealth of Nations* (London).

Smith, J. Toulmin (1851). *Local Self-Government and Centralisation* (London: John Chapman).

Storey, D. J. (1975). 'Statistical analysis of educational expenditure in county councils', *Local Government Studies*, new series, vol. 1, no. 4.

Stubbs, W. (1896). *Selected Charters* (Oxford: Oxford University Press).

Taylor, A. J. P. (1965). *English History 1914–45* (Oxford: Oxford University Press).

Thompson, E. P. (1968). *Making of the English Working Class* (Harmondsworth: Penguin).

Thornhill, W. (1971). *The Growth and Reform of English Local Government* (London: Weidenfeld).

Thurow, L. C. (1971). 'The income distribution as a pure public good', *Quarterly Journal of Economics*, vol. 85, no. 2.

Tiebout, C. (1956). 'A pure theory of local expenditure', *Journal of Political Economy*, vol. 64, no. 5.

Tiebout, C. (1961). 'An economic theory of fiscal decentralization', in *Public Finance: Needs, Sources and Utilization*, National Bureau of Economic Research (Princeton, N.J.: Princeton University Press).

Treasury, The (1977). *Public Expenditure*, Cmnd 6721 (London: HMSO).

Tullock, G. (1969a). 'Federalism: problems of scale' *Public Choice*, vol. 6 (Summer).

Tullock, G. (1969b). 'Social cost and government action', *American Economic Review*, vol. 59, no. 1.

Tullock, G. (1970a). *Private Wants: Public Means* (New York: Basic Books).

Tullock, G. (1970*b*). 'Comment on J. Rothenberg's "Local Decentralisation and the Theory of Optimal Government"', in J. Margolis (ed.), *Analysis of Public Output*, National Bureau of Economic Research (New York: Columbia University Press).

US Department of Commerce (1972). *Local Government Finances in Selected Metropolitan Areas and Larger Counties*: 1970 – (Washington: Bureau of the Census, US Govt. Printing Office).

Valuation for Rating Act (1953). 1 & 2 Eliz. 2. Ch 42 (London: HMSO).

Valuation (Statutory Deduction Order (1973)). SI 1973/2139 (London: HMSO).

Veverka, J. (1963). 'Growth of government expenditure in the United Kingdom since 1790', in A. T. Peacock and D. J. Robertson (eds), *Public Expenditure: Appraisal and Control* (Edinburgh: Oliver & Boyd).

Wald, H. P. (1959). *Taxation of Agricultural Land in Underdeveloped Countries* (Cambridge, Mass.: Harvard University Press).

Wallas, G. (1908). *Human Nature in Politics* (London: Constable).

Walters, A. A. (1961). 'The theory and measurement of private and social cost of highway congestion', *Econometrica*, vol. 29, no. 4.

Walters, A. A. (1968). *Economics of Road User Charges*, IBRD Staff Occasional Papers, No. 5. (Washington, DC: IBRD).

Webb, B. (1948). *Our Partnership* (London: Longmans).

Webb, S. (1920). *Grants in Aid* (London: Longmans, Green).

Webb, S., and Webb, B. (1922). *English Local Government: Statutory Authorities for Special Purposes* (London: Longmans, Green).

Webb, S., and Webb, B. (1963). *The Development of English Local Government* (Oxford: Oxford University Press).

West, E. G. (1970). *Education and the State: A Study in Political Economy*, 2nd edn (London: Institute of Economic Affairs).

West Midland Study Group (1956). *Local Government and Central Control* (London: Routledge & Kegan Paul).

Whalley, J. E. (1975). 'Distortionary factor taxation in a calculation of effective tax rates in the UK, 1968–1970', *Manchester School*, vol. 43, no. 1.

Wheare, K. C. (1968). *Federal Government*, 4th edn (Oxford: Oxford University Press).

Wheaton, W. C. (1975). 'Consumer mobility and community tax bases: the financing of local public goods', *Journal of Public Economics*, vol. 4, no. 4.

White, R. J. (1957). *Waterloo to Peterloo* (London: Heinemann).

Wildavsky, A. B. (1964). *Politics of the Budgetary Process* (Boston, Mass.: Little).

Wilde, J. A. (June 1971). 'Grants-in-aid: the analytics of design and response', *National Tax Journal*, vol. 24, no. 2.

Wilkinson, F., and Turner, H. A. (1972). 'The wage-tax spiral and labour militancy', in D. Jackson, H. A. Turner and F. Wilkinson (eds), *Do Trade Unions Cause Inflation?* (Cambridge).

Wilks, H. M. (1964). *Rating of Site Values: Report of a Pilot Survey at Whitstable* (London: Rating and Valuation Association).

Wilks, H. M. (1974). *Site Value Rating: Report on a Research Exercise Carried Out in the Town of Whitstable to Throw Further Light on the Rating of Site Values as a Suitable Source of Public Revenue* (London: Land Insititute).

Williams, A. (1966). 'The optimal provision of public goods in a system of local government', *Journal of Political Economy*, vol. 74, no. 1.

Williamson, O. E. (April 1967). 'Hierarchical control and optimum firm size', *Journal of Political Economy*, vol. 75, no. 2.

Wolf, M. (1968). *Local Authority Services and the Characteristics of Administrative Areas*. Royal Commission on Local Government Research Study no. 5 (London: HMSO).

Wright, H. J. *et al.* (1974). *Rating Law and Practice* (London: Rating and Valuation Association).

Young, G. M. (1950). 'Government', in *Last Essays* (London: Hart-Davis).

Young, G. M. (1953). *Portrait of an Age* (Oxford: University Press).

Index